Baedeker
Belgium

D1407953

Baedeker's
BELGIUM

Imprint

189 illustrations, 52 maps and plans, 10 drawings, 1 large map at end of book

Original German text: Vera Beck, Rainer Eisenschmid, Prof. Dr Hans-Dieter Haas, Prof. Dr Wolfgang Hassenpflug, Dr Udo Moll, Reinhard Struber
Editorial work: Baedeker, Stuttgart
English language edition: Alec Court
General direction: Dr Peter Baumgarten, Baedeker Stuttgart

Cartography: Gert Oberländer, München; Mairs Geographischer Verlag, Oostfildern 4 (large map)
English translation: Wendy Bell, Julie Bullock, David Cocking, Alec Court, Julie Waller

Following the tradition established by Karl Baedeker in 1844, sights of particular interest and hotels and restaurants of particular quality are distinguished by either one or two asterisks.
To make it easier to locate the various places listed in the "A to Z" section of the Guide, their co-ordinates on the large city map are shown in red at the head of each entry.
Only a selection of hotels and restaurants can be given: no reflection is implied, therefore, on establishments not included.

In a time of rapid change it is difficult to ensure that all the information given is entirely accurate and up-to-date, and the possibility of error can never be completely eliminated. Although the publishers can accept no responsibility for inaccuracies and omissions, they are always grateful for corrections and suggestions for improvement.

1st English edition 1993

© Baedeker Stuttgart
Original German edition

© 1993 Jarrold and Sons Limited
English language edition worldwide

© 1993 The Automobile Association
United Kingdom and Ireland

Prentice Hall General Reference
US and Canadian edition

PRENTICE HALL and colophon are registered trademarks of Simon & Schuster, Inc.

Distributed in the United Kingdom by the Publishing Division of the Automobile Association, Fanum House, Basingstoke, Hampshire RG21 2EA

All rights reserved. No part of this publication may be reproduced, stored in a retrieval system or transmitted in any form by any means – electronic, photocopying, recording or otherwise – unless the written permission of the publisher has been obtained.

Licensed user:
Mairs Geographischer Verlag GmbH & Co., Ostfildern-Kemnat bei Stuttgart

The name *Baedeker* is a registered trade mark
A CIP catalogue record of this book is available from the British Library

Printed in Italy by G. Canale & C.S.p.A – Borgaro T.se –Turin

ISBN UK 0 7495 0674 1
      US and Canada 0–671–87155–2

Library of Congress Catalog Card Number: 92–083090

Contents

Note: A few Belgian towns and two rivers are more familiar to English readers either in a
distinct English spelling or in their French form. The following have been used in the text of
this book: Bruges, Brussels, Ghent, Ostend, Ypres, and the Rivers Meuse and Scheldt. In all
cases in the "A to Z" section both the Flemish and French names appear wherever relevant.
The adjective Mosan applies to the River Meuse. The French word Béguinage is preferred as
probably more familiar to English readers than the Flemish Beguijnhof.

The Principal Tourist Destinations in Belgium

Note: The above list includes only the more important places of touristic interest in Belgium which are worth seeing either for themselves or for other attractions in the vicinity. In addition there are many other notable sights which are designated by one or two asterisks within the text of each entry.

Preface

This guide to Belgium is one of the new generation of Baedeker guides.

These guides, illustrated throughout in colour, are designed to meet the needs of the modern traveller. They are quick and easy to consult, with the principal places of interest described in alphabetical order, and the information is presented in a format that is both attractive and easy to follow.

The subject of this guide is the west European Kingdom of Belgium – from the Ardennes to the North Sea.

The guide is in three parts. The first part gives a general account of the country, its political and geographical divisions, its landscape, climate, flora and fauna, population, educational systems, government and administration, economy, history, famous people, art and culture, and in particular the rich folkloristic life of Belgium. A brief selection of quotations and a number of suggested itineraries provide a transition to the second part, in which the country's places and features of tourist interest – towns, provinces, scenery – are described. The third part contains a variety of practical information. Both the sights and the practical information are listed in alphabetical order.

The new Baedeker guides are noted for their concentration on essentials and their convenience of use. They contain numerous specially drawn plans and colour illustrations; and at the end of the book is a large map making it easy to locate the various places described in the "A to Z" section of the guide with the help of the co-ordinates given at the head of each entry.

Facts and Figures

The Kingdom of Belgium ("Koninkrijk België" in Flemish, "Royaume de Belgique" in French) is perhaps one of the less popular European destinations. Many people merely pass through it on their way to the Netherlands or to Germany. In fact Belgium today is rich in places of interest to the tourist, largely because it was here that two European cultural groups once met and overlapped. The interesting countryside and many cultural attractions make it well worth a visit at any time of the year.

The summer holidaymaker will find extensive beaches and picturesque dunes in the resorts along the Belgian North Sea coast. Those interested in art will enthuse over the superb museums and collections as well as the historical town centres, many with rivers and other waterways and impressive secular and religious buildings, such as those in Ghent and Bruges. Anyone keen on technical achievements will be fascinated by the harbour installations in Antwerp and the bridges, sluices, canals or ship-lifting gear, such as that found at La Louvière or Ronquières. Walkers and nature-lovers will be attracted by the woodland regions of the Ardennes, where they will find the largest dripstone cave in Europe and Spa, a spa town (hence the word) of high quality. Belgium is also famous for its gastronomic delights – per head of population, no other European country can boast as many restaurants awarded stars or medals by international gourmets as can Belgium.

General

The Kingdom of Belgium lies in the north-west of Central Europe, between 49° 30' and 51° 30' north and 2° 33' and 6° 24' east. In the north and east it has borders with the Netherlands, and further east with Germany and Luxembourg, as well as with France to the south and the North Sea to the west, but only for a length of some 67km/42 miles. The total extent of its borders with Germany, Luxembourg and France amounts to 1445km/898 miles. To the north of Turnhout lies Baarle-Hertog, a small Dutch enclave within which curiously will be found the two even smaller Dutch enclaves of Baarle-Nassau.

Location

Belgium covers an area of only 30,519sq.km/11,783sq.miles, making it one of the smallest of the European states. Its maximum length is 290km/180 miles, from Ostend to Arlon. From the capital Brussels all parts of the country can be reached by car in two hours at the most and by train in two and a half, so Belgium can genuinely be called a "country of short roads".

Area

Topography

From its narrow coastal border Belgium extends well inland to the south-east and then by way of the River Meuse as far as the western foothills of

Geographical divisions

◄ *The Meuse Valley near Dinant*

the German low mountain range. Its varied landscape is divided into sections running from east to west. In the north the North Sea coast, marshland and coastal moorlands (or "geest") form a natural continuation of the Netherlands. Taken together these areas comprise what is known as Lower Belgium. Central Belgium is a hilly region of sandy, clay and limestone strata of the Tertiary and Cretaceous periods. The plateaux to the south are covered with loess, a fine fertile soil, making them rich agricultural land akin to that found in the neighbouring Rhineland and northern France. The Meuse and Sambre valley is the beginning of Upper Belgium, the Ardennes, divided into the Lower and Upper Ardennes. This ancient mountain massif of slate, boulders and limestone forms the western wing of the Rhine slate mountains. To the south Upper Belgium extends to the terraced Lorraine countryside, the north-eastern edge of the Paris Basin. The latter consists of flat stone layers of varying hardness, lying in terraces one above the other.

Lower Belgium

Coastal
region

In Lower Belgium the coastal strip, only 67km/42 miles in length and with fine sandy beaches and dunes, has but few openings leading down to the sea, among these being the mouth of the Yser near Nieuwpoort. Of varying width, the lines of sand dunes are as high as 30m/100ft in the great De Panne field. This dune region is one of best-known and most popular beaches in Europe and extends on both sides of the ferry port of Oostende (Ostend). Behind the dunes and along the Westerschelde (the southern bank of which, the Zeeuws Vlaanderen, or Zeeland Flanders, forms part of the Netherlands) lies marshland enclosed with polders, narrower than those in Holland, being only 12km/7½ miles wide near Blankenberge. In the main these marshes are safe, well-cultivated land. The old inlets, which once extended far inland, are now silted up; an example of this is Het Zwin, which at one time led from the mouth of the Scheldt to Bruges, the great Flemish seaside town of the Middle Ages. The silting-up of the river led to the decline of Bruges. The building of Zeebrugge around 1900 in the dunes and the channel leading to it failed to restore the old metropolis to its

Natural Regions and Waterways

former importance. Bruges, although pierced by canals, rests on the flat and sandy coastal moorland, in the same way as Ghent and Antwerp. The famous Flanders seaports are therefore not marshland towns like those of the neighbouring Netherlands.

Geest, a sandy fluvial deposit, refers strictly speaking to that area known as Kempen (Campine) east of the Scheldt and Dijle and north of the Demer, the northern part of which forms part of the Netherlands. It is the most thinly populated region of Belgium, with heathland and areas of fluvial sand, patches of pine woods here and there, scattered villages on barren land and just a few small towns. In the Middle Ages monasteries were built in this wilderness, such as those at Westmalle and Tongerlo; one of Belgium's largest military training grounds, Leopoldsburg, was established here in 1850. In recent years environmentally hazardous industries such as lead and zinc foundries or nuclear plants such as the atomic research centre and recycling plant at Mol have been built. Large coal deposits are mined between Maastricht and Antwerp. This area of Kempen and Limburg, not yet fully developed, with Genk as its centre, is the northern arm of the great European coal seam which divides at Aachen. As this seam runs under a massive mountain the mining has to be carried out by large concerns.

"Geest" in the Kempen region

To the west, in Flanders, the geest is partly a plain formed from comparatively recent deposits and partly hilly land of sand and clay, not very high, between the Scheldt, Leie and the marshland region. Whereas Kempen along the Demer finishes sharply where it meets Central Belgium, to the west, in Brabant and Flanders, roughly on a line from Leuven to Brussels and Kortrijk, there is a more gradual transition to the higher and more fertile land of Central Belgium. Although woodland by nature, and in many places covered in heathland on sandy soil, this area of Flanders has nevertheless been thickly populated and carefully cultivated since medieval times, and is typified by small individual farms in groups and rows, each

"Geest" in Flanders

A quiet canal in Flanders

separated from its neighbour by hedges or poplar trees. In spite of the barren soil the land is cultivated very intensively, some on smallholdings, as in the Waas region around Sint Niklaas, where many vegetables are grown. In addition to agriculture and horticulture, however, homeworkers have always produced traditional cloth goods and the famous pillow lace which was then sold in the streets of Lokeren and Tielt, for example. The banks of the Leie are lined with fields of flax. The larger towns, especially Ghent, are now modern textile centres.

Antwerp

Towards the end of the Middle Ages Antwerp assumed the mantle of Bruges and developed into the most prosperous town in northern Europe, before the damming of the Scheldt by the newly independent Netherlands in 1648 robbed it of its lifeblood for two hundred years. Situated on the higher bank of a meander of the Scheldt, which is some 500m/550yds wide at this point and affected by strong tides and a rise and fall of 4m/13ft, the old trading harbour faces the open river. In the first half of the 20th c. Antwerp once again became an international port. Large harbour basins equipped with locks were built in the river marshes downstream.

Human geographical development

From a communications point of view the country is ideally situated as far as the famous medieval ports and trading towns of Flanders are concerned. Trading ships sail to other countries by sea and river. To the south roads lead through flat open country to Picardy and Champagne, and by way of Burgundy to the Alpine passes and the Mediterranean. Flanders provided the link between North Sea and Baltic countries to the far Baltic and southern Europe, until historical events blocked all land and sea routes and caused the country to stagnate. The centre of the town of Ghent, situated at the confluence of the Scheldt and the Leie and just above the tidal limit, has retained its old splendour. Modern Ghent is a modest textile centre and even a sea port, being linked by canal to Terneuzen on the Westerschelde.

The silhouette of Antwerp

Central Belgium

If the Meuse-Sambre valley between Liège (Luik) and Charleroi is included, Central Belgium with its varied geographical features can be regarded as the very heartland of the country. A Tertiary and Cretaceous plateau, it is scarcely 100m/330ft above sea-level in the north, rising gradually to some 200m/660ft in the south. The northern part, although lower, is very hilly and dissected by the rivers Dijle, Senne, Dender and Scheldt, and its border with Flanders is somewhat ill-defined owing to the existence of numerous secondary plateaux which have become separated by erosion from the parent plateau. The more recent, upper strata in the hilly region is formed from conglomerates from the Late Tertiary period and protects the individual hills from being eroded. These include Pellenberg near Leuven, Kemmelberg south of Ypres (Ieper), scene of a famous battle in the First World War, and Mont St Aubert overlooking the countryside of Tournai.

The Tertiary layer is not very deep, and the valleys which are scarcely 100m/330ft in depth cut their way into the very old Brabant Massif below. The latter is formed partly from crystalline stone which is mined in large quarries at Lessines and Tournai. Layers of clay and sand have formed above the Tertiary stone and these are somewhat more productive than the geest-like sandy soil of northern Flanders. In addition deposits of fertile loess are to be found here and there on the slopes and hills. Small farmsteads on undulating and intensively cultivated land and green stretches dotted with trees give central Brabant its character. In between lie remains of the former vast forests, such as that of Soignes south of Brussels.

To the south it is a slow climb over broad, open plateaux covered in loess, Hesbaye (Haspengouw) in the east and Hainaut in the south. Large self-contained villages nestle in the valleys. Vast fields of corn and sugar-beet cover the plateaux, rich farmland like that found in the Rhineland or in Picardy.

Fertile rolling countryside in Brabant

There are, however, regional differences: if Tertiary clay lies under the loess the land is better irrigated and grass grows in abundance, for example in the damp Hesbaye region north of Sint Truiden and also in parts of Hainaut. If the subsoil is chalk and limestone, however, the character of the land matches that of fertile plains. That is particularly true of the dry Hesbaye region around Tongeren and Waremme.

Brussels

Situated between fertile plains and Lower Belgium, Brussels grew in strength to become the political capital of the Kingdom when Belgium declared its independence in 1830. It is accessible from the sea along the River Senne and is also linked to the naturally richer south. Following the decline of the Flemish towns when they found themselves shut off from the sea as a result of the rivers silting up, Brussels became a Brabant royal seat and the country's chief city. Although situated in the Flemish-speaking region of Brabant Brussels was strongly influenced by the French language, from the royal court down to the man in the street. Large open spaces and boulevards built in the 19th c. gave it something of the appearance of a second Paris, but without entirely losing its Flemish character. Linked to the Scheldt by a maritime canal Brussels has now grown into a community of almost a million inhabitants.

Meuse-Sambre Valley (Vallée de la Meuse)

Forming a natural part of the Ardennes, the Meuse-Sambre valley stretches along the border of Upper Belgium. Along its flanks lie layers of soft coal and it links up with a number of coalfields. In between, layers of limestone under the carboniferous strata produce rocky and narrow stretches of valley, such as that below Namur. West of Charleroi the carboniferous zone merges into the fertile plains of Hainaut. Prior to industrialisation the valley lay in charming countryside, with palaces nesting in parkland, vineyards, hop and fruit fields along its flanks and castles on the spurs of the hills. Although the hard coal was in fact mined many years ago, as it was in the Ruhr valley, there was in fact little demand for it, as the iron industry established itself by the small streams running from the Ardennes rather

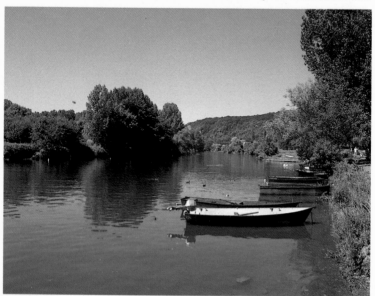

On the Meuse

than near the capital itself. Hard coal forms part of the main carboniferous seam stretching from the Ruhr to England by way of Aachen, Belgium, Northern France. In Belgium it skirts the southern side of the Brabant Massif, which separates it from the coalfields of Kempen. In the tectonic boundary zone of the Brabant and Ardennes Massifs the coal is in marked folds and in part covered by older layers of stone. This results in high mining costs, although these are partially offset by lower wastage. There is a preponderence of lower-quality coal rather than that which can be made into charcoal or coke. Going from east to west, the coalfields are those of Liège, Charleroi, Bassin du Centre and Borinage near Mons, where the coal comes to the surface between chalk hills.

Industrialisation began in the first half of the 19th c. when for the first time on the mainland of Europe the Cockerill works in Seraing developed the system whereby collieries, iron foundries and rolling mills worked in conjunction with one another. This had important technical and economic repercussions on industry throughout the whole of continental Europe. The highly-industrialised Walloon region is very interesting. In the early days of its "industrial revolution" it had to face many problems connected with the living and social conditions of the workers, but on the other hand it has shown itself to be a pioneer in the fields of working conditions and housing for more than a century.

However, the coal-mining industry appears to be under threat in the foreseeable future, as the worldwide steel crisis is affecting the Walloon and the neighbouring Lorraine regions too, bringing closures and unemployment in its wake. However, this is compensated to some degree by glassworks, non-ferrous metal factories, large chemical works and a highly-specialised finished product industry, and the unemployment rate has fallen in recent years. The region's position is safeguarded by means of the Albert Canal between Liège and Antwerp, which will take large ships, as well as the Meuse and Sambre canals, while the important Canal du Centre from Brussels to Charleroi is due for extension. The iron ore comes mainly from Minette in Lorraine. Liège, whose old churches date back to Carolingian and Early Romanesque times, and the fortified town of Charleroi, named after Charles II of Spain, have grown during the last century into conurbations of some half a million inhabitants each, although there are no actual statistics to show this, as in Belgium all such surrounding communities have remained independent.

The importance of the Central Belgian regions in the context of human geographical development has changed many times. From earliest prehistory up to Roman times the fertile plains were centres of settlement, closely linked to the cultures of central Europe. There were barely any links with the country to the north. The great Roman road from Cologne to Rheims stretched from east to west across the fertile plains, from Maastricht via Tongeren-Gembloux to Bavay in France. Tongeren, the Roman civitas of Tongres, is the oldest town in the country.

Human geographical development

Towards the end of the period of antiquity the Meuse valley gained in importance. First Maastricht and then the as yet unknown town of Liège succeeded Tongeren as diocesan towns and ruling centres. Although the fertile plains did not deteriorate to any great extent, traffic nevertheless tended to move from the main road to the waterways of the Meuse and Sambre. In the west Tournai, situated on the Scheldt, the civitas of Nervier and the first capital city of the Franks, increased in importance. On the Meuse Huy and Dinant developed into major towns. It was not until the early Middle Ages that the Flemish wastes along the waterways were opened up and the coastal regions developed into important economic centres, and have remained so to this day.

Upper Belgium

The Ardennes form Upper Belgium. They are part of the west side of the Rhine range of slate mountains and a continuation of the Eifel. The Signal

Ardennes

In the Lower Ardennes

de Botrange, 694m/2278ft high, is the highest point in Belgium. The Ardennes are an old stretch of mountains the surface of which intersects the folded strata, but are recognisable as mountains only in the deeply slashed valleys.

The Upper Ardennes are to be distinguished from the Lower Ardennes. At one time rather isolated and with few roads, they are now fully developed and a favourite "villégiature", or holiday region, for the towns in the north.

Lower Ardennes

The Lower Ardennes reach heights of only 200–500m/660–1640ft, and extend south of the Meuse; they are characterised by forest-covered plateaux divided by areas of meadowland, without any heights worthy of mention. The regions of Condroz, Entre-Sambre-et-Meuse, Fagne and Famenne all form part of the Lower Ardennes. The Meuse tributaries of Ourthe and Lesse have dug out giant caves with magnificent limestone stalactite formations (Han-sur-Lesse, Rochefort).

Upper Ardennes

The Upper Ardennes, which go up to more than 500m/1640ft, boast some scenery which is unique in central Europe. There are the high moors known as the High Fenns (Hohe Venn or Hautes Fagnes), where the geomorphological and climatic conditions – an impermeable layer of clay and slate and high rainfall – are ideal for the formation of moorland. The amount of rainfall exceeds that of the water which flows away, producing the characteristic "hour-glass" moor, with sections filled or saturated with water. The High Fenns today form part of the Belgo-German natural park.

Climate

Climatic zones

The climate in Belgium is generally temperate and humid, the result of its position in the temperate latitudes. It is quite strongly influenced by the sea, as it lies very close to the coast and the predominant westerly winds come in off the sea. In more detail, the country can be divided into three climatic zones, i.e. that immediately adjoining the coast, the interior lowlands and the Ardennes range of low mountains.

The climates experienced in the various regions are illustrated in the climatic diagrams of various places showing the annual range of temperature and precipitation. The letters represent the individual months. Temperatures are shown as an orange-red band. The upper edge corresponds to the average maximum day temperature, the lower to the average minimum night temperature. The corresponding temperature figures can be read off the scale at the side. The blue rain/snowfall columns show the average precipitation (in mm) in the month concerned.

Climatic stations (see map and diagrams)

Working from these diagrams, it is possible to estimate the climatic conditions in the intervening areas, while bearing the following rules in mind. Moving inland, the influence of the sea obviously becomes weaker, and variations in temperature between day and night and winter and summer increase; periods of sunshine, precipitation and other climatic features change accordingly.

The higher above sea-level the more temperatures decrease, roughly at a rate of 0·5°C/1°F per hundred metres/330 feet. For example, the average annual temperature in Brussels, which is 100m/330ft above sea-level, is 9·9°C/49°F, while that on the Botrange, at 694m/2278ft, is 5·7°C/42°F. The number of frosty days and the amount of rainfall also increase accordingly.

The ribbon of land running immediately along the coast differs climatically in some important respects from the coastal hinterland.

In the summer months in particular the periods of sunshine are greater and cloud amounts less than those found just a few miles inland. The reason is

The strip of land along the coast (Ostend diagram)

Five typical regional climatic stations

Oostende

Gedingen

Bruxelles / Brussel

© Baedeker

Denée

Botrange

Explanation in text

Sketch: Prof. Dr. Wolfgang Hassenpflug

as follows: as moisture-laden air masses from the North Sea pass over the land on the prevailing westerly air currents they are interrupted by the relatively rough land surface, pile up, climb and produce condensation and cloud-formations. In the coastal hinterland, to where the wind takes the clouds, the tendency towards cloud build-up and rain is much greater, while along the beach it remains sunny with very little cloud. Close to the sea there are more than 1750 hours of sunshine in the course of a year, e.g. Ostend has 1760 hours, the maximum being 230 hours in June. The strong sunshine – aided by the clean air – never becomes unpleasantly hot because of the fresh winds which always blow, mainly from the west, making the days cooler and avoiding risks of sunburn. Inhaling the ozone is also very beneficial to health.

Even in January minimum temperatures lie just above freezing point, and the average maxima are about 5°C/40°F. The highest temperatures are not reached until August, when the average minimum is at least 13°C/55°F and the maximum just under 20°C/68°F.

The wind always blows on to the coast, being at its strongest during the winter months; the average wind force over the year in Ostend, for example, is 6·5m per second/14½mph, increasing to 7·1m per second/16mph in January. Because of the considerable differences in air pressure wind strengths in winter are about 2¼ to 3mph more than those in summer. Westerlies predominate, with southerlies quite often from October to January and north-easterlies in spring. The annual rainfall in southern Flanders as far as the Lille region remains below 600mm/24in, while in the north-west of Ghent more than 600mm/24in. fall; Ostend has 579mm/23in. The number of days on which rain falls is less than 150 (Ostend 143). From March to June about 30mm/1¼in. falls in a month; from July to November this increases to 60mm/2½in., the most – 70mm/2¾in. – falling in October. During the first of the above periods there are ten days in each month on which it rains, and in the second period this increases to fourteen. Generally speaking, in summer the rain is often in the form of heavy showers.

Water temperatures are highest in July and August, when they reach 16°C/60°F. In the month of February the effects of the Gulf Stream keeps them above 6°C/43°F. The balancing effect of the sea means that land temperatures are not excessively high in summer and are seldom very low in winter; the number of days of frost in winter is 40. Accordingly the temperature band shown in the diagrams is narrow and fairly straight, and generally above freezing point.

Lowlands of the interior (see climatic diagrams for Brussels and Gerdingen)

There are regular and marked differences in climate between the coastal strip and the interior of the country, while variations within the interior are minor.

The daily and annual variations in temperature increase. If the climatic diagrams for Brussels and Gerdingen are compared with those for Ostend, the wider and more curved temperature bands will indicate this. In summer it is considerably warmer during the day than on the coast. The average minima in January lie below freezing point (Brussels minus 1·2°C/30°F), the average maxima between 4° and 5°C/39° and 41°F (Brussels 4·3°C/39·7°F). The highest temperatures are reached in July, with maxima well above 20°C/68°F (Brussels 22·7°C/73°F) and minima 12°C/53·6°F (Brussels 12·1°C/53.8°F) or lower. Thus the daily variation of more than 10°C/18°F clearly exceeds the figures at the coastal situations (e.g., in August the daily variation in Ostend is only 6·3°C/11·3°F).

Away from the coast the length of the period of the year which is free from frost is shorter, and the number of frosty days increases from about 40 to 60.

Also, away from the coast the number of hours of sunshine each year reduces by more than 100 (Brussels 1585 hours, compared with 1760 in Ostend). Equally, this means an increase in cloud amounts inland; while on the coast 140 to 160 days have a cloud amount of 80%, there are 170 to 180 such days in the eastern inland regions. Cloud amounts are particularly small in September in those areas away from the coast.

As the land rises towards the Ardennes region, so the annual rainfall increases from 700mm/28in. to more than 800mm/32in. Even small hills can result in localised increases in rainfall, in the same way that air, condensation and cloud formation produces precipitation on the coast. From September to November it can usually be assumed that rainfall amounts inland will be less than on the coast. As the relative atmospheric humidity is greatest in the winter months (monthly average just under 90%), this is when most foggy days occur (about 30 to 50 in the course of a year).

Wind strengths slacken noticeably as one moves inland; the average wind strength in Brussels is 3·8m per second/8½mph compared with 6·5/14½ in Ostend. In winter they are without exception about 0·5 to 1m per second/ 1 to 2mph stronger than in summer. South-westerly winds predominate. They influence the nature of the countryside in several ways: they blow away clouds, drive old and new windmills or deform trees by their force and as a result of the salt they contain render it necessary for farmers and others to erect hedgerows as protection.

Because they are higher the Ardennes have their own climate, particularly noticeable at the high point of the Botrange (694m/2278ft), and progressively less so where the ground is lower.

On the Botrange the average annual temperature is 5·7°C/42°F. On the high ground too the daily maxima in January lie below freezing point, while the night minima sink to below minus 4°C/25°F. In July the daily maxima rise to 17°C/63°F, while the minima remain below the 10°C/50°F mark (Botrange 9·3°C/48·7°F). Thus there are only a few months when the night minima are well above freezing; only the period from the middle of May to early October is frost-free; 120 frosty days are recorded.

As the height above sea-level increases, so does the amount of rainfall. Annual precipitation often exceeds 1500mm/60in. (Botrange 1510mm/ 60½in.); it increases yet further on the lee side of the mountain. The number of days with rain is not much more than that on the plains (Botrange 213, Brussels 206 per annum), but they are heavier. Thus in autumn it is possible to have 100mm/4in. in a day.

As a result of the lower temperatures a large proportion of the precipitation falls as snow, on 140 to 160 days. The nature of the climate, however, means that it seldom lies for more then 25 days.

Ardennes (see climatic diagrams for Botrange and Denée-Maredsous)

Flora and Fauna

Flora

Large areas of Belgium have been put to the plough or subjected to planned afforestation, with the result that comparatively little of its native vegetation remains.

Cultivated and arable land

Originally there were extensive forests of birch, oak and other trees to be found in the sandy "geest" region, but over the years cultivation reduced these to vast tracts of heathland which in recent centuries have been planted with pine trees. The natural deciduous forests of the loess and loamy soils of Belgium, comprising mainly oak, hornbeam and beech in the Ardennes, have largely been replaced with coniferous forests of pine and fir, because the latter grow faster and are more profitable. The natural vegetation of the south-eastern parts of the Ardennes, protected from the winds, includes forests of oak and beech. Stands of oak and hornbeam are characteristic of the Pays Gaumais in the south of Belgium, where vineyards are also to be found. Forests of oak and birch are also native to the barren sandstone soil where Belgium borders on Luxembourg, like those in the sandy "geest" region.

The dunes and polders along the North Sea coast and the few remaining moorland regions have some particularly interesting species of plant life.

Dunes and polders

Flora and Fauna

Typical beach plants include halophytes, which need salt to survive and so are found only where the soil contains salt. The best known examples of this genus are samphire and saltwort, which are found growing on strips of the coast which are flooded by the sea as well as on newly reclaimed polderland. To protect them against erosion the dunes are planted with varieties of mat-grass, marram grass and small fir trees. As well as these halophilic plants sea-violets are also found in the dunes. An extensive programme to neutralise the marshland soil has meant that meadows and lush grass have replaced the halophytes to a large degree.

Moors

Very characteristic are the moors to be found in parts of Peel, with cotton grass, other acid-loving grasses, cranberries and wild rosemary or marsh tea. Heathers and trees such as alder, pine and birch are gradually being added.

Fauna

Wild animals

The original fauna, never very varied at the best of times, has been further decimated as the result of man seeking to cultivate every available corner of the countryside. Apart from in the Ardennes there is scarcely any natural habitat left for the larger species of animal. Roe deer are to be found in the Sambre–Meuse valley. Red deer are seen only in the Ardennes, together with wild boar. The very rare wild cat is occasionally seen in the southern Ardennes; they hide by day in deserted foxholes. The tree marten is more common. Among the interesting birds seen here are the hoopoe and the tree-creeper, which frequent only the meadows and arable land to the north of the Sambre–Meuse valley or the dense forests to the south of it. As a result of the increasing pollution the number of fish found in rivers and canals has reduced drastically.

Belgian carthorses

If there is an animal typical of Belgium – apart from the species of rabbit known as the "Belgian Giant" – then it must be the Belgian carthorse.

Carthorses – the working animals of the Ardennes

20

These powerful horses were used in agriculture and forestry as draught animals, but rendered obsolete with the arrival of the tractor. However, they are still traditionally reared in the Ardennes and win many prizes at various annual horse-shows. In the Musée de la Vie Rurale en Wallonie near Saint-Hubert (see A to Z) an exhibition is devoted to the Belgian carthouse.

Population

A 1990 estimate indicates that some 9,950,000 people live in Belgium, equivalent to 326 inhabitants per sq.km/844 per sq. mile, a figure exceeded in Europe only by Monaco and the Netherlands (U.K. 609 per sq. mile). However, it must be borne in mind that there are marked regional variations in this average figure. At one extreme lie the six most densely populated regions, those of Brussels, Antwerp, Liège, Ghent, Charleroi and Mons. These account for more than one-third of the total population of Belgium, with a density of more than 1000 inhabitants per sq.km/2590 per sq. mile. The provinces of Antwerp and East and West Flanders are also above average in density, with some 500 per sq.km/1300 per sq. mile. In contrast, the central mountainous region of the Ardennes can boast only 50 folk per sq.km/130 per sq. mile, and even fewer in some parts.
57.6% of the total population live in Flanders, 32.5% in Wallonia and 10% in Brussels. The German-speaking minority accounts for about 0.6%.

Population density

Belgium's dense population is an indication of the extensive degree of urbanisation which has taken place. Almost one-half of the people live in towns and cities, with a further 38% in urbanised communities. Only about 13% are to be found in rural districts.

Urbanisation

After the Second World War the rate of population increase reduced markedly. The birth rate is the lowest in Europe, having remained relatively static overall in the 1980s, while the death rate, at 1.2%, is relatively high as a result of the increase in the percentage of old people. However, the birth rate in the Flemish regions is above the average for the country.

Population changes

Nearly 90% of Belgians are adherents of the Roman Catholic faith, only 0.9% being Protestants. Moslems account for 1.1%, and 7.6% belong to other religious groups or are atheists or agnostics. Finally, 35,000 Jews (0.4%) live in Belgium, mainly in Antwerp, the largest Jewish community in Europe.

Religion

The employment structure of the Belgian people reflects the high degree of industrialisation and urbanisation. Agriculture, the most important branch of the economy prior to industrialisation, now employs only three per cent of the work force. The percentage of those engaged in industry, on the other hand, is now over 33%. Even higher, however, is the number of people working in the service sector – currently 64% and still growing. After having reached an all-time high of some 15% of the work force in the 1980s, the unemployment rate sank to 10% by the beginning of the 1990s. It is expected to continue to fall.

Employment structure

About 850,000 foreigners live in Belgium, of which some 520,000 are from other EC countries. The remainder are guest workers from North Africa and Turkey.

Foreigners

Ethnic Groups and Language Areas

Belgium is divided into areas where either Germanic or Romance ethnic backgrounds and languages predominate. The Walloons live in the southern part and speak French, while Walloon, a French dialect differing from

Flemings, Walloons and Germans

the Parisian dialect mainly in being less nasal, now lives on only in certain idiomatic expressions. The Flemings, speaking a Dutch dialect, live in the northern regions of the country. Strictly speaking, there are three dialects – the Zeeland dialect spoken at the mouth of the Scheldt and in West Flanders, the Brabant and the Limburg. The dividing line between the two ethnic groups, which has remained almost unchanged since the Middle Ages, is the Flemish–Walloon language border, running roughly from Visé on the Meuse in an east–west direction by way of Waremme, Halle and Ronse to Menen on the French border.

In addition to Flemings and Walloons, Germans form a third ethnic and linguistic group around Eupen St.-Vith and Arlon.

Brussels, a Walloon enclave in the Flemish region, is officially bilingual, although it cannot be denied that it is fundamentally French-speaking. Over the years "Brusselese", a dialect which is a mixture of French and Dutch, has developed.

Linguistic divisions

For many years conflicts have existed between Flemings and Walloons which the phrase "linguistic differences" does not really explain adequately. Disputes on the matter of language are but one way of expressing far-reaching cultural and economic contrasts.

It could be argued that past attempts to link Belgium with France were a basic error. French became the official language as the upper classes spoke, dressed and acted like the French, while Flemish was considered good enough only for the lower and middle classes. As a result industry flourished in and the resultant prosperity benefited the coal region of Wallonia, while Flanders remained largely rural. This situation produced a breeding-ground for the Flemish Movement in its fight for equality for the Flemish people. In 1898 it succeeded in forcing through the Equality Act, which decreed that official texts in French and Flemish were equally valid. However, by 1936 French had again become the only language accepted in Parliament, and it was not until 1962 that a Dutch translation of the criminal code was produced.

Detrimental to the Flemish cause was the fact that, during the German occupation in the Second World War, the Flemish Movement to a large

Linguistic Regions

──── Linguistic boundary
▢ German
▢ Dutch (Flemish)
▢ French
▢ Bilingualism (French and Flemish)

degree co-operated with the occupying forces because they hoped to achieve Flemish autonomy from the Germans, who in fact did their best to enforce it. This background helps the foreigner to understand the disputes in the 1930s over the language laws and making Flemish the compulsory language in Ghent University; this latter change did much to further the Flemish cause.

After the Second World War these disputes became even fiercer. The marked recession in the Wallonian steel industry from the early 1970s onwards and the simultaneous growth of new industries in Flanders shook the Walloons' self-confidence; at the same time the Flemings fought against the non-observance of the language laws. When the language border was fixed in 1962 it had been hoped that this would produce a peaceful solution to the problem, but in fact right up to the present day there are still violent disputes between Flemings and Walloons. Thus in October 1991 the last government of Wilfried Martens foundered on a typical Belgian dispute: the Flemish minister refused to support the idea put forward by Walloon armaments firms to export to the Near East; as a countermove, the Walloons tried to prevent Flemish telephone companies from acquiring a large block of business and also called for payment of the national radio and television fees to be apportioned by regions. The dispute ended with the withdrawal of the Flemish People's Union from the government coalition resulting in new elections, which produced large gains for the radical Flemish Nationalists.

There are hopes that converting Belgium into a federal state will bring about a solution, but already there are complications and doubts as to whether it will be possible to obtain a responsible reaction from the various local governments and councils, cultural bodies and regions as well as signs of an increasingly strained atmosphere in dealings between the various factions. The situation now reflects more than anything else the contrast which exists between the "rich" Flemish north and the "poor" Wallonian south, such as is indicated by the resistance shown by the Flemings to a suggestion that there should be a redistribution of taxes to aid the Walloons. The Walloons fear a Flemish "takeover", as their economic decline is exacerbated by the fact that a low birth-rate means that the number of French-speaking Belgians is continually on the decline.

Federal state as a solution?

The tourist will probably be little affected by these problems; the only times he is likely to notice them is when crossing the language border or in talks given by bi-lingual guides and couriers. Examples of a rather more radical attitude may however be found in the German-speaking part of Belgium which actually forms part of Wallonia; many traffic signs have had the French place-names painted out and replaced with the German equivalent.

State and Society

The flag of the Kingdom of Belgium is in the form of three vertical stripes of black, yellow and red. They are the Brabant colours, which first appeared in this form in 1797 during an unsuccessful uprising against its Austrian overlords.

Flag and Coat of Arms

The Belgian coat-of-arms depicts the Lion of Brabant, with the larger versions also containing the motto "L'Union fait la force" (Unity is Strength) and the banners of the nine Belgian provinces.

Under the Constitution of 1831 the Kingdom of Belgium is a constitutional monarchy. King Baudouin I (Boudewijn, Baldwin) has been on the throne since 1951. Since 1991 succession to the throne has no longer been linked to the male line. Under the constitution the King does possess executive powers, but in practice his sole function is that of an official figurehead.

Constitutional monarchy

The Belgian royal couple, Baudouin and Fabiola

Parliament

The Belgian Parliament is composed of two Houses. The House of Representatives (Chambre des Représentants, Kamer van Volksvertegenwoordigers), the Lower House, has 212 members who are elected directly by the people. Voting is obligatory. At the request of the government the King can dissolve the House of Representatives. In addition to sitting on different party benches the members of the House are also split into separate linguistic groups.

The number of members in the Upper House, the Senate (Sénat, Senaat) fluctuates around the 180 mark. Half its members are directly elected, a further part by provincial councils according to the size of the province, and a third part (equal to one-half of those elected by the provinces) is co-opted by the Senate itself. Finally, all those members of the royal family who are in line to the throne are also members of the Senate.

Both houses have the right to put forward bills, but the Lower House plays a considerably more important role in this respect. An opposing vote by three-quarters of one of the "language groups" can prevent a bill from going through.

Government

The Belgian government is nominated by the King, but must be confirmed by both Houses of Parliament. The head of government is the prime minister, but he has no powers to lay down guidelines. The government must comprise an equal number of French and Dutch-speaking ministers, apart from the prime minister.

Regionalism and federalism

Belgium's regional and federal structure is extremely confusing. It is mainly the result of disputes between Flemings and Walloons and subsequent concessions made to the popular groups. Since 1971 Belgium has been divided into four linguistic areas, three cultural communes and three regions. Added to this there is the historical sub-division into provinces. The division of Belgium into nine provinces is quite simple to explain. Each is administered by a directly elected provincial council with a governor at

Belgium

Koninkrijk België
Royaume de Belgique
Kingdom of Belgium

—— Provincial
Boundaries

its head. The council of state was designed back in 1946 to negotiate between communes and provinces. However, in the context of the conversion of Belgium to a federal state the future importance of the provinces becomes unclear.

The four linguistic areas referred to above are the Flemish-speaking, the French-speaking and the German-speaking areas plus the (officially) bilingual city of Brussels.

The communes are the Flemish, French and German-speaking ones. In all three there is an elected community council, some with an executive arm, which deals with cultural matters and subjects affecting the individual such as health and social politics.

The three regions are the Flemish, the Walloon and the Brussels regions. Each has a regional council with an executive arm which inter alia is responsible for environmental matters, nature conservation, administration and regional economic, financial and social policies. In the Flemish council, however, the community council and regional council are combined, but in matters affecting the Flemish region Brussels members may not vote, although they can do so on community matters.

The latest development is a move towards a federal state. Since early 1989 Flanders and Wallonia have been largely autonomous in matters involving economic, financial, commercial, labour, environmental and energy policies. The third federal state, the Brussels region, enjoys special status.

No less confused is the picture relating to the Belgian political parties, for they too are shaped both by ideological and cultural differences. The language barrier also runs through the main parties. **Parties**

The strongest is the Christian Democratic Party (CVP = Christelijke Volkspartei or PSC = Parti Social Chrétien), with its major stronghold in Flanders, followed by the Socialist Party (PS = Parti Socialiste or SP = Socialistische Partij), which leads in Wallonia. The third country-wide party is the Liberal Party (PVV = Partij voor Vrijheid en Vooruitgang or PRL = Parti Réformateur Libéral). Following the latest elections the minority regional and language parties in parliament made their presence felt. For example, the right-wing radical and xenophobic Vlaams Blok, which campaigns for the dissolution

Province Town	Area in km²	Population	Chief town
1 Antwerpen	2 867	1 587 500	Antwerpen
Antwerpen	1 001	919 000	Antwerpen
Mechelen	510	293 000	Mechelen
Turnhout	1 365	375 000	Turnhout
2 Brabant	3 358	2 222 000	Bruxelles/Brussel
Bruxelles/Brussel	162	970 000	Bruxelles/Brussel
Halle-Vilvoorde	943	525 000	Halle/Vilvoorde
Leuven	1 163	423 000	Leuven
Nivelles	1 090	303 000	Nivelles
3 Hainaut	3 788	1 272 000	Mons
Ath	487	76 000	Ath
Charleroi	555	429 000	Charleroi
Mons	585	250 000	Mons
Mouscron	101	71 000	Mouscron
Soignies	518	166 000	Soignies
Thuin	934	141 000	Thuin
Tournai	608	140 000	Tournai
4 Liège	3 863	992 000	Liège
Huy	659	91 000	Huy
Liège	798	591 000	Liège
Verviers	2 016	249 000	Verviers
Waremme	390	61 000	Waremme
5 Limburg	2 422	737 000	Hasselt
Hasselt	907	361 000	Hasselt
Maaseik	884	197 000	Maaseik
Tongeren	631	179 000	Tongeren
6 Luxembourg	3 755	226 000	Arlon
Arlon	317	47 000	Arlon
Bastogne	1 043	37 000	Bastogne
Marche-en-Famenne	955	45 000	Marche-en-Famenne
Neufchâteau	1 353	52 000	Neufchâteau
Virton	77	45 000	Virton
7 Namur	3 666	415 000	Namur
Dinant	1 592	92 000	Dinant
Namur	1 152	266 000	Namur
Philippeville	909	58 000	Philippeville
8 Oost-Vlaanderen	2 982	1 329 000	Gent
Aalst	469	258 000	Aalst
Dendermonde	343	181 000	Dendermonde
Eeklo	334	79 000	Eeklo
Gent	943	485 000	Gent
Oudenaarde	418	112 000	Oudenaarde
Sint-Niklaas	475	213 000	Sint-Niklaas
9 West-Vlaanderen	3 134	1 095 000	Brugge
Brugge	651	261 000	Brugge
Diksmuide	362	47 000	Diksmuide
Ieper	550	104 000	Ieper
Kortrijk	403	275 000	Kortrijk
Oostende	292	135 000	Oostende
Roeselaere	272	137 000	Roeselaere
Tielt	329	85 000	Tielt
Veurne	275	51 000	Veurne
Region Vlaanderen	13 511	5 696 000	Antwerpen
Region Wallonie	16 848	3 209 000	Namur
Region Bruxelles/Brussel	**162**	**970 000**	
Königreich Belgien	30 514	Estimate 1990: 9 920 000	Bruxelles/Brussel

of the Belgian state and for an independent Flanders, won a considerable number of votes. Its Walloon counterpart is the Rassemblement Wallon together with the Front Démocratique de Bruxellois Francophones. The Vlaams Blok outstripped what until then had been the strongest Flemish party, the Volksunie (VU). The "Greens", the Ecolo (Ecologistes) or Agalev (Anders gaan leven) also made gains, especially in Wallonia. The Communists are the only party not split by language; however, they play little part in Belgian political life. The PDB, the Partei der Deutschsprachigen Belger (Party of German-speaking Belgians), is of importance only in East Belgium where German is spoken.

The trade unions have avoided being divided into culturally different branches. There are three ideologically different employees' organisations: the Socialist Federation of Trade Unions (FGTB or ABVV), with 1,100,000 members, the Christian Federation of Trade Unions (CSC or ACV), with 1,400,000 members, and the Federation of Liberal Trade Unions (CGLSB or ACLVB), with 210,000 members.

Trade unions

Belgium is a member of the EC and of NATO, and linked to both organisations in a special way, Brussels being the seat of the European Council of Ministers and, together with Strasbourg, the seat of the European parliament and thus the effective political capital of Europe. NATO also has its most important divisions in Belgium, namely, the NATO Council in Brussels and its military headquarters in Casteau near Mons.

Foreign policy

Education and Science

School attendance is obligatory for all children and young people aged between six and eighteen. This can be at a state school (Athenée, Atheneum) or private school (Collège, College), which may concentrate on providing a general education or technical, artistic or professional qualifications. The private schools are mostly Catholic, as generally speaking the Catholic Church has had a considerable influence on education. The schooling system is divided into voluntary nursery and pre-school instruction for three to six-year-olds, followed by six years in primary school and then six years of secondary education, split into three two-year cycles each with its own final examination.

School system

Belgium's universities are under either state, church or private control. Differences between Flemings and Walloons have led to the universities of Brussels and Leuven (Louvain) each being divided into two independent Flemish and French colleges. In Leuven, founded in 1425 and the Belgian university which is most steeped in tradition, this division has been taken to the point where the French-speaking tutors and students have founded a new model university at Louvain-la-Neuve 30km/20 miles south of Brussels. The way in which the library of Leuven university, so rich in tradition, is split up is really quite incomprehensible: one part contains all the odd shelf-numbers, the other the even ones! There are other full universities in Ghent, Liège and Mons. In addition there are university centres in Antwerp and Limburg as well as nine part-universities, fifteen institutes and technical colleges, five music colleges and five art colleges.

Universities

Economy

Because of its lack of raw materials and small indigenous market the country is very export-orientated, and more than 70% of its products go abroad. Belgium, which forms one economic, customs and currency union with Luxembourg, is in tenth position among the world's trading nations. In 1989 goods valued at 98·1 billion US dollars were imported, mainly machinery, vehicles and foodstuffs. Exports in the same year were 99·3 billion dollars, mainly machinery and vehicles, chemical products and foodstuffs. Its major trading partners in the import field are Germany and the Netherlands, and France and Germany export-wise.

The gross national product (GNP) in 1989 amounted to 162 billion dollars, which statistically speaking means that each Belgian citizen contributed 16,390 dollars. On the other side of the coin, there is an immense national debt equivalent to 113% of the GNP, the highest of any EC country, as well as a high foreign debt of 10·5 billion dollars, or 6·6% of the GNP. However, compared to figures for earlier years, these do begin to show signs of the success of the government's stabilisation measures and of an economic upswing, which is reflected in increased investment activity and a noticeable fall in the rate of unemployment. However, this did not prevent a rise in the inflation rate to 3·1% in 1989.

Industry

Decline of
heavy industry

The Belgian economy is supported in the main by the country's highly-developed industry. The industrialisation process started in the early 19th century, thanks to the hard coal and iron-ore deposits found in Wallonia, and then spread from there to the rest of mainland Europe. However, it was this very advantage which proved to be its downfall after the Second World War. Industrial plant quickly became obsolete as the result of lack of investment. This, and the loss of the Belgian Congo from whence much of the raw materials had come, led to an economic crisis which the government tried to meet by means of tax reliefs on investment, but which was made worse by the economic situation within the European Community. With this government aid the Wallonian heavy industry was able to expand until the mid-1970s, but then the worldwide steel crisis hit Belgium harder than most, with the result that Wallonia's once flourishing industries are

Natural gas liquefaction plant in the port of Antwerp

now in a state of depression, as assembly and production plants have not been modernised and in consequence the Belgian coal and steel industry is no longer competitive and relies on support from the state and the EC.

After the Second World War there was a noticeable relocation of the main centres of industry in Belgium, combined with structural changes some of which were far-reaching. Expansion moved away from iron and steel in favour of the petro-chemical and chemical industries. As a result Belgium's two largest companies are now Petrofina (oil) and Solvay S.A. (chemicals); the steel industry can manage only third place, in the shape of the Cockerill-Sambre Works, which can claim only a third of the turnover of Petrofina. In fourth place lies Agfa-Gevaert, another chemical company, with Ford in fifth place.

Increasing imports of raw materials have shown that the favourable situations of the ports make them very cost-effective. Antwerp in particular has profited from this fact, so that it and the surrounding countryside have developed into a giant industrial conglomerate, composed predominantly of huge chemical and petro-chemical plants. In contrast, the capital Brussels is home to much smaller firms, and its share of the country's total industrial production is about one-fifth.

As the Flemish north grew in economic power so the Walloon south declined. Promising new industries such as the chemical, metal-working and service sectors set up mainly in Flanders because of the locational advantages; 60% of Belgium's gross national product now comes from there. This fact also served to exacerbate the long-standing animosity between Flemings and Walloons – the one side has no wish to be the nation's paymaster, while the other resents being its poorhouse.

Belgium's major branch of industry continues to be its export-orientated metalworking industry. The most important locations are at Namur, Liège and Antwerp. The products range from investment plant, machinery, industrial equipment and consumer goods to enamelware and the manufacture of railway coaches, locomotives, textile machinery and sea-going ships. Belgium also manufactures more than one million cars a year, 90% of which are exported, making it one of Europe's major producers. One of the most stable branches of the metal industry is arms production, mainly firearms and munitions made in the Fabriques Nationales (FN), which also has considerable exports.

The future appears rosy for the chemical and petro-chemical industry centred in Antwerp. Mile upon mile of tanks and plant belonging to mineral oil and chemical companies lie along the banks of the Scheldt. The major products are paints, dyes, fertilisers, medicines and photo-chemical materials. However, the growth of the chemical industry has meant that a high price has had to be paid in the shape of contamination of rivers and the atmosphere.

The textile industry is traditionally located in Flanders and Brabant. The once-important linen industry is now in a state of stagnation and has been almost completely overshadowed by the cotton and man-made fibre industries. Flax is grown around Ghent, Kortrijk and Aalst, while Antwerp leads in the field of wool-processing.

Just as important is the Belgian glass industry in Flanders, Hainaut, Liège and Namur. The main products are mirror and window glass. About 25% of world requirements are manufactured in the export-orientated factories in these provinces.

Mining and Energy

Hard coal is the only important raw material mined in Belgium today. The area along the Sambre–Meuse valley, with the old Wallonian districts of

Borinage, Centre, Charleroi and Liège was where the industrialisation of Belgium first began. The stocks of coal and those of iron-ore, now exhausted, were important factors which led the iron and steel industries to establish themselves here as long ago as the early 19th century. However, it was not long before demand for raw materials exceeded local supplies, so that coal and iron-ore had to be imported even in the last century. Competition from cheaper imported coal, mainly from the USA, led in the 1960s to the closure of many large mines, just as it did in other places in Europe, reaching its peak with the final closing of mines in the South Basin in 1984. Today indigenous coal supplies are mined in the Kempen region, where the less complex nature and position of the seams means that considerably less expensive mining methods can be employed than those used in the heavily-folded seams along the Sambre–Meuse valley; in addition, the quality of the Kempen coal is better. However, the amount of foreign coal used continues to increase.

Energy

An annual consumption of 4·85 thousand oil units per head of population puts Belgium at the head of all EC countries. The Belgian government continues to back nuclear energy as the main energy-producer. Seven nuclear power stations, the most productive being that at Mol near the Dutch border, produced 65·5% of Belgium's energy needs in 1988, while conventional power stations using fossil fuels accounted for 32·7%. Water-power provided 1·1% and solar power 1·8%. The bias towards atomic energy is being criticised more and more, particularly because in a thickly-populated country like Belgium there is no location where the safety of the population can be assured – for example, the Tihange and Doel reactors are on the edges of the Liège and Antwerp conurbations respectively. Also in recent years the atomic research centre at Mol has suffered much adverse press because of its out-dated plant, lax use of hazardous materials and questionable business ethics in connection inter alia with the German atomic waste episode.

Agriculture and Fishing

Minor importance

Belgian agriculture, working to high technical standards, produces mainly for the home market. Amounts produced per hectare are considerably above the EC average, but this is achieved only by over-fertilisation of the soil. However, demand still cannot be fully met, so 40% of the country's needs have to be imported. The fact that agriculture contributes only two per cent of the GNP shows that it, adds little to the total economy. The 1·4 million ha/3·5 million acres of agricultural land are worked mainly by small farmers owning at the most 50ha/125 acres each, for a third of whom it is only a second occupation. As in the rest of Europe, many farmers have been obliged to give up their farms in recent years.

Cattle industry

About 60% of the value of agricultural production comes from cattle and dairy farming, the centres of which are found in the Ardennes, the Famenne, Kempen and the polder regions. The breeding of Belgian cart-horses in the Ardennes is nowadays carried on mainly for sporting and traditional reasons.

Arable farming and horticulture

The main crops grown in Belgium are wheat, barley, sugar-beet and pota-toes, together with fruit and vegetables of all kinds, including chicory used in salads or as a vegetable, which is a Belgian speciality. Around Ghent flowers are grown together with industrial crops such as flax and tobacco. The main centres of agricultural production are determined mainly by the natural conditions prevailing. In addition, however, the proximity of local markets is often a decisive factor, especially when culture is specialised or intensive. They are concentrated mainly in the triangle formed by Meche-len, Leuven and Brussels with its light soil, where vegetables are grown in huge glasshouses. Fruit is extensively grown south-east and south-west of

Antwerp in the Kempen and Waas regions as well as near Sint-Truiden, Namur, Liège, Mons and Charleroi. The fertile plains of Hainaut and Hesbaye (Haspengouw) are also extensively cultivated, where wheat and sugar-beet predominate, as well as being grown in the marshy areas. The "geest" soil of Flanders and of the Kempen region is best suited to growing potatoes, wheat and barley. Grassland is found mainly in the Ardennes, in Herver and in Famenne, followed by parts of Kempen, Sietland and the marshes.

Belgian fishing is suffering as a result of the EC fishing-quota rules as well as from the trend towards high-tech trawlers and factory ships, which local fishermen seem unable to come to terms with. As a result traditional coastal fishing from the ports of Nieuwpoort and Ostend now plays only a minor role.

Fishing

Service Sector

In recent years the Belgian service sector has continually increased in importance, and the number of people employed in this sphere now far exceeds that of those in industry. Naturally, it is concentrated in the larger towns, especially Brussels, it being the seat of many EC bodies and institutions as well as of NATO. Being so favourably situated from a communications point of view Belgium is very important to commerce and the transport industry. There is little doubt when the Common Market becomes a total reality the services sector will become even more important.

Tourism

To the regret of the Belgian tourist authorities, tourism plays only a minor role in the country's economy. In the main Belgium is just a country which

"Strongholds for Tourists" along Ostend beach

31

travellers pass through, with merely a fleeting glance at any sights they may see along the way. The majority of visitors to Belgium come from the Netherlands, followed by Germany, Great Britain, France and the USA.

The bulk of holidaymakers are concentrated at the seaside resorts along Belgium's coastal strip, especially at Ostend, but in fact it is predominantly native visitors who come to the coast, almost the entire length of which is lined with hotels and which is not really very attractive. Far behind it lies the Ardennes holiday region, which is particularly favoured by the Dutch, with its charming river valleys (Semois, Meuse, Ourthe and Lesse) and extensive forests. However, in recent years the spas here, such as that at Spa itself, have shown smaller increases in the number of visitors than the resorts on the North Sea coast have experienced. Historically important towns, such as Brussels, Ghent and Bruges, have become increasingly popular for short-stay breaks.

Communications

As the result of its high concentration of industry and population and its position between the North Sea coast and central Europe, communications within Belgium have been excellent ever since the nineteenth century.

Railways — First mention must go to the rail network. It was in 1835 that the first train on the mainland of Europe ran between Mechelen and Brussels; now Belgium can boast some 4000km/2500 miles of railway, making it one of the densest networks in the world, even though parts of it are now rather old. Transit traffic acounts for about one-fifth of the total transport capacity.

Road network — The road network is first-class. The motorways, most of which are lit, are justifiably famous.

Waterways — The waterways, which form a self-contained transport system in themselves, cover a total length of 1569km/975 miles. The volume of goods conveyed on inland waterways far exceeds that carried by rail. The major natural waterways are the Meuse and the Scheldt. Of the artificial canals the Albert Canal from Maastricht to Antwerp, the Ghent–Bruges–Ostend Canal, the Canal du Centre and that running from Charleroi to Brussels are of great importance; the latter two canals link the Belgian waterway network with that of France. Of the larger ports particular mention must be made of Antwerp, Brussels, Bruges and Ghent, which are also accessible to sea-going ships. Ostend is one of the major ports linking the continent of Europe with Great Britain.

Air traffic — Air traffic plays little part within Belgium itself. From Brussels-Zaventem airport the state airline Sabena provides good connections to Africa in particular.

History

Strictly speaking, the history of Belgium as such did not commence until 1830, the year in which the State of Belgium was founded. However, the country's name does in fact perpetuate the name of the ancient tribe, the "Belgae", mentioned by Caesar in his "Gallic Wars". Until the Kingdom of Belgium was formed the history of this country was generally speaking merged with that of the Netherlands, with the result that historians often spoke of the Netherlands when they really meant the whole region of Belgium, the Netherlands and Luxembourg. The year 1568 is of decisive importance, for it was then that in the Netherlands as we know them today the War of Independence against Spain began, but those provinces which now comprise Belgium supported Spain.

From Pre-history to the Division of the Carolingian Empire

In the Neolithic Age the loess regions of present-day Belgium are inhabited by Celts. Germanic tribes first emerge from the marshlands c. 1500 B.C.
c. 4000–1500 B.C.

Julius Caesar conquers the whole of Gaul, the northern part of which is inhabited by the Celtic Belgae. These include the Aduatukes, Menapi, Eburons, Trevers, Nervi and Morins.
58–51 B.C.

The Eburon Prince Ambiorix rises up against the Romans but is decisively defeated.
54–53 B.C.

The Romans attempt in vain to conquer the Germanic regions on the right bank of the Rhine.
12–9 B.C.

Until the early 5th c. the area which now forms Belgium, the "Provincia Gallia Belgica", forms part of the Roman Empire. From the 1st to the 3rd c. present-day Tongeren, then known as "Aduatuca Tungrorum", is the most important city in the province.
to 400 B.C.

Salian Franks occupy the region between the Meuse, Scheldt and Lower Rhine. Servatius founds the diocese of Tongeren and commences to convert the region to Christianity with the aid of Irish and Scottish missionaries.
4th and 5th centuries A.D.

Chlodio, progenitor of the Merovingians, makes Tournai his capital.
c. 440

From Tournai Childerich reigns over the whole region between the Scheldt and the Somme.
476

Chlodwig extends the rule of the Franks to the whole of Gaul.
482–511

In the course of a second wave of Christianity large monasteries are built.
7th century

St Hubert moves the seat of his diocese from Maastricht to Liège.
721

Charlemagne is born near Liège.
742

Under the Treaty of Verdun the Carolingian Empire is divided up. The area west of the Scheldt is ceded to France, ruled by Charles the Bald, while that east of the Scheldt passes to Lother I (hence Lothringia = Lorraine). The region of present-day Belgium is thus divided into two.
843

Emergence of Earldoms and Dukedoms

Between the 10th and 14th c., following the fall of the Carolingian Empire, large numbers of individual rulers ally themselves with others in various ways in an attempt to increase their power and to weaken the feudal power of the great neighbouring states. In the 11th c. the name "Netherlands" is applied for the first time to this collection of regions; by the end of the 18th c. it also embraces what is now known as Belgium.

Brabant

In 1006 Count Lambrecht of Leuven raises the region to the status of dukedom, and originally names it Lower Lothringia. In 1248 Brabant becomes the first European state to abolish bondage. Brabant is joined with Limburg in 1288, Luxembourg in 1355 and Burgundy in 1430. The Golden Bull issued by Emperor Charles IV in 1349 grants freedom from any foreign jurisdiction. In the 15th c. Brabant is a major centre of commerce, trade and culture in the Netherlands. In 1648 it is divided into North and South Brabant.

Bourgogne
(Burgundy)

Established in 884, during the 14th and 15th c. this dukedom becomes the most powerful state between France and Germany. Between 1384 and 1473 the dukes gain power over almost all the temporal domains in the Netherlands – Flanders, Namur, Brabant, Limburg, Hainaut, Luxembourg, Holland, Zeeland and Picardy. Brussels becomes the glittering centre of the dukedom. After the death of the last duke Charles the Bold, who is slain in 1477, the Burgundian Netherlands pass to the Habsburgs.

Hainaut

In the mid-9th c. an earldom is formed to fight the Normans. In the 11th to 13th c. it is several times linked with Flanders, and in 1299 passes to Holland, 1345 to Wittelsbach and 1433 to Burgundy.

Limburg

Formed as an earldom *c.* 1060, it becomes a dukedom in the early 12th c. and forms a part of Lower Lorraine (Lothringia). From 1221 to 1226 it is united with Luxembourg, with Brabant from 1288 and then divided up in 1648.

Liège

In 721 the town becomes a diocese, its land belonging to Germany as a religious principality. During the 15th and 17th c. the citizens fight several times for their freedom. After the town is stormed by Charles the Bold in 1477 the region shares the same fate as Burgundy.

Luxembourg

Having been formed in the 10th c., Luxembourg has links with Namur, Limburg and Brabant until the 13th c. In 1354 it becomes a dukedom, and in 1443 it passes to Burgundy and in 1477 to the Habsburgs.

Namur

Formed in the 10th c., this dukedom passes to Hainaut *c.* 1200, to Flanders in 1262 and to Burgundy in 1420.

Vlaanderen
(Flanders)

As a result of continuing Norman attacks the earldom of Flanders is formed in 864. The first Count of Flanders is Baldwin Iron-Arm. His successors extend their sphere of influence north and south. As, following the Treaty of Verdun, the Scheldt divides the area of authority, the Flemish counts are feudal lords of the French king ("Crown Flanders" west of the Scheldt) as well as of the German emperor ("Imperial Flanders" east of the Scheldt). Under Theodoric and Philip of Alsace the rule of the Counts reaches its zenith. In the Crusades Counts of Flanders become "Latin" emperors of Constantinople in the years 1204–61.

The growth of the towns results in serious opposition to the Counts. The citizens of the Flemish towns, particulary Ghent, Ypres (Ieper), Kortrijk and Bruges, acquire considerable economic and political power through trade and the textile industry. In the mid-14th c. Bruges and Ghent, together with Paris, are the largest towns north of the Alps. The towns repulse attacks by the French King Philip the Fair (and with him the Count of Flanders), who had annexed Flanders to France. On May 18th 1302 rebel citizens of Bruges who had been expelled and had now returned, led by Pieter de Coninck and Jan Breydel, butchered the men of France at the "Matines of Bruges"; on July 11th of the same year the Flemish army routed the might of French chivalry at the Battle of the Golden Spurs. This battle is of worldwide significance; the defeat of France means that England now has landing places on the continent which are available to it during the Hundred Years' War. In 1337, with support from England, Ghent under Jacob van Artevelde rises up against the French. However, after Artevelde is murdered the Flemish towns lose their influence, and 45 years later his son is also killed in the Battle of Roosebecke. In 1384 Flanders becomes part of Burgundy.

From the Merger of the Netherlands to the Spanish Conquest

The separation of the Netherlands by the Holy Roman Empire is initiated by the Burgundian Duke Philip the Good, who gains possession of several duchies. A little later the Netherlands fall to the Austrian Habsburgs, who annex other territories. Spain gains power by inheritance.

After the death of Louis, Count of Flanders, the Burgundian Duke Philip the Bold, having married Louis' daughter Margaret in 1369, inherits Flanders together with Antwerp and Mechelen.	1384
Philip the Good enlarges his possessions still further. Brussels and Leuven become the centres of the Burgundian dukedom. Under Philip's regency the Netherlands experience their first period of economic prosperity and enjoy wealth and luxury. Painting, architecture and tapestry-making flourish, and the Netherlands are regarded as the "treasure-house of Europe".	1419–67
The Burgundian General Assemblies meet in Bruges.	1464
Duke Charles the Bold, the richest and most ambitious prince of his time, oppresses the nobles and towns (Liège). He dies at the siege of Nancy in 1477.	1467–77
Mary, the first daughter of Charles the Bold, marries Maximilian, son of Frederick III of Austria and later to be Emperor Maximilian I.	1477
Mary of Burgundy dies. The Netherlands fall to Maximilian and thus to the Habsburgs.	1482
Maximilian is held prisoner in Bruges for eleven weeks.	1488
Philip the Fair, son of Maximilian and Mary, marries in Lier Juana, the daughter of Ferdinand and Isabella, joint sovereigns of Spain. Charles, later Charles V, is born to them in 1500 in Ghent.	1496
Margaret of Austria, daughter of Maximilian, reigns over the Netherlands following the death of Philip.	1507–17
Charles, King of Spain since 1516, following the death of Maximilian in 1519 in Brussels is made Emperor of the Holy Roman Empire. He brings Utrecht (1528) and Geldern (1538), among others, under Habsburg rule. His aim is to combine the whole region into one strong state and to limit the old freedoms, which restrict the power of the crown. After 1520 Luther's teachings gain popularity, but after 1550 Calvinism becomes the prevailing religious belief in the northern provinces. Charles fiercely resists the new teachings and sets up Courts of Inquisition after 1552.	1519–56
The Netherlands come under Spanish rule when the empire of Charles V is broken up following his abdication. The new ruler is Philip II.	1556

The Partitioning of the Southern Netherlands and the End of Spanish Rule

With the help of political, economic and religious repression Spain tries to enforce its rule upon the Netherlands. This leads to uprisings by the nobles and the estates and finally to war. The Seven Provinces of the northern Netherlands are able to free themselves from Spanish domination and form the Republic of the United Netherlands, while the Catholic Wallonian and Flemish southern provinces swear allegiance to Spain under the Union of Arras. This completes the separation between the two sections of the country and the territorial limits of Belgium and the Netherlands as they are known today are largely laid down.

Philip II of Spain, son of Charles V and the dominant force behind the Counter-Reformation, wants to prevent any break with Catholicism in the Netherlands or any attempts to obtain independence. He sends Spanish troops into the country, disregards the rights of the estates and the nobility and displays fantastic intolerance in seeking to stamp out Protestantism. As a result of the struggle which lasts for decades the Netherlands are financially ruined; more than 100,000 people flee to the northern provinces.

1559–67	Under the governorship of Margaret of Parma, daughter of Charles V, riots and resistance grow. Cardinal Granvelle, advisor to the throne, is recalled at the insistence of the Prince of Orange.
1566	The Dutch nobles form an alliance in Breda and call themselves "geusen", or beggars, a name derived from a derisive nickname given to them when they hand a petition to the governess – "Comment, Madame, peur de ces gueux?" or "What, madam, are you afraid of these beggars?". Later this term is used to describe their armed resistance, particularly at sea ("sea-beggars"). They are led by William of Orange, Egmont and Hoorn. In the "Iconoclasm" Catholic churches are laid waste.
1567	Philip II sends the Count of Alba with new troops to quell the uprising.
1568	The struggle for liberation begins in the north of the Low Countries. The Seven Provinces rise up under the leadership of William I, the Silent One. Alba's troops cause havoc; tens of thousands are killed. William flees to Germany. The Counts Egmont and Hoorn are taken prisoner and executed in Brussels.
1579	The unity of the Low Countries falls apart. In the Union of Utrecht the Protestant northern provinces form a protective alliance against Spain which proves to be the forerunner of the Republic of the United Netherlands. In the Union of Arras the pro-Spain provinces in the south unite.
1579–1604	In these years of struggle the Spaniards take one south Netherlands town after another. In 1604, after a three-year siege, they succeed in taking the fortress of Ostend, the last surviving Dutch stronghold in the southern provinces. Apart from a brief interlude (1792–1830) this determines the division of the Low Countries into northern and southern parts.
1598–1621	There is an economic recovery under the reign of Archduke Albert of Austria, married to Isabella, daughter of Philip II. Baroque art is at its peak – Rubens, van Dyck, Jordaens, Brouwer.
1648	The Treaty of Westphalia sees the end of the Eighty Years' War in the Low Countries and the Thirty Years' War in Germany. The southern provinces – later to become Belgium – remain under Spanish rule; s'Hertogenbosch, Maastricht, Venlo, Roermond, Breda and Zeeland-Flanders pass to Holland, while France receives Artois, French Flanders, Franche-Comté and French Hainaut.
1667–97	During the wars of conquest waged by Louis XIV French armies fight on several occasions in the Spanish Netherlands.
1695	The French bombard Brussels and destroy over 4000 buildings.

The execution of Egmont and Hoorn

In the Wars of the Spanish Succession the French are defeated by the English under Marlborough and the Austrians under Prince Eugen. In the Spanish Low Countries they are defeated at Ramillies (1706), Oudenaarde (1708) and Malplaquet (1709). 1701–14

Under the Peace of Utrecht the southern Low Countries are promised to Austria. This sees the end of Spanish rule. 1713

Austrian Rule and the Union of Belgium and the Netherlands

In the War of the Austrian Succession the French conquer almost the whole of the Austrian Netherlands (Battle of Fontenoy 1745), but these are returned to Austria under the terms of the peace treaty. 1745–48

Emperor Joseph II rules in an enlightened fashion. His well-meaning but over-zealous reforms offend the traditional religious order of the people. 1780–89

Against the backdrop of the French Revolution the people rise up and the Austrian Netherlands declare themselves to be "The United States of Belgium" (this is the first time the name "Belgium" has been used since Roman times), an independent republic, and they defeat the Austrians in the Battle of Turnhout. The revolutionaries carry the Brabant colours of black, yellow and red.
The Austrians are able to regain control of the territory by the end of 1790, however, and Leopold II is restored to power. 1789–90

Belgium and the Low Countries are taken by the French. In the First Coalition War the Austrians are defeated at Jemappes (1792) and Fleurus (1794) by a French revolutionary army, but the latter is held up by the Netherlanders. 1792–94

History

1795–1813	After the conquest of the Low Countries both countries are united in the Batavian Republic. The territory now known as Belgium is divided into nine départements, which remain the provincial borders to this day. During almost twenty years of French occupation the Belgian territory becomes the most industrially-rich region in Europe, as there is no competition from England as a result of Napoleon's economic war against that country and the retaliatory English sea blockade.
1815	In the Battle of Waterloo (south of Brussels) Napoleon is decisively beaten by the combined British, Prussian and Dutch armies.
1814–15	The Congress of Vienna establishes the Kingdom of the United Netherlands under William I of Orange. The Kingdom embraces the northern Netherlands, Belgium and the former diocese of Liège. Eupen and Malmedy are ceded to Prussia. Luxembourg becomes a Grand Duchy and a German federal state; the Kings of the Netherlands are at the same time Grand Dukes of Luxembourg.
1816–17	Universities are founded in Ghent in 1816 and in Liège in 1817.

The Kingdom of Belgium until the Second World War

The economic, religious and linguistic differences between the northern and southern parts of the United Netherlands lead to a popular uprising in Belgium; in the struggle against the Dutch troops Belgium gains the upper hand and becomes independent. After overcoming some teething troubles Belgium becomes one of the leading industrial countries on the European mainland and builds a considerable colonial empire (Belgian Congo). In the First World War almost the whole of Belgium is occupied by German troops. In the period between the wars the dispute between Flemings and Walloons intensifies.

1830	Influenced by the July revolution in Paris, the revolution which is to lead to the Kingdom of Belgium begins in Brussels on August 25th. On October 4th Belgium declares its independence from the United Netherlands.
1831	A Dutch army defeats the Belgians at Leuven, but retreats before the advancing French. Leopold of Saxe-Coburg-Gotha (an uncle of Queen Victoria) is crowned King of Belgium on July 21st. He reigned until 1865.
1834	Founding of Brussels University.
1835	Opening of the first railway line on the European mainland, between Mechelen and Brussels.
1839	Belgium's neutrality is guaranteed by the major powers. Belgium is given the western part of Limburg and Luxembourg and the southern part of Brabant.
from 1840	The "Flemish Movement", which seeks to promote the equal status of Flemings with Walloons in political and cultural life, attracts more and more adherents.
1863	Abolition of the Scheldt customs duty; the Netherlands receive compensation.
1865–1909	During the reign of Leopold II Belgium becomes the fifth largest industrial state in Europe. Internal development is governed by differences between liberal and clerical forces as well as the ever more urgent social problems. Since the Workers' Congress in Brussels in 1886 socialism gains in impor-

tance. At the end of the 19th c., after bloody strikes and riots by workers agreements are formulated on workers' rights and social matters.

For 30 years the Congo, now Zaire, is privately owned by King Leopold II, 1878–1908
who exploits it mercilessly, causing thousands of deaths. In 1908, following intervention by an international commission, the Congo becomes a Belgian colony, the Congo Belge.

All adult males have the vote.   1893

After a German ultimatum demanding the right of the German army to   1914–18
march through Belgium is rejected, German troops invade Belgium on August 3rd 1914 and occupy the whole country, with much devastation. The government flees to Le Havre in France. Initially the German advance is halted at the Ijzer Canal in Flanders by detonating the dykes near Nieuwpoort and flooding the countryside. The Belgian army, under the command of King Albert I, with its French and British allies, fights a bitter trench war against the Germans and Austrians which lasts four years. During this time Flanders suffers terrible damage; among other places, Ypres and Diksmuide are completely destroyed. In April 1915 poison gas is used for the first time by the German troops at Ypres.

Under the Treaty of Versailles Belgium is granted Eupen-Malmedy, St Vith   1919
and Moresnet, as well as the right to reparations.

Equal franchise for male adults.   1921

Creation of the Belgian-Luxembourg Economic Community.   1922

Belgian troops participate in the occupation of the Ruhr.   1923

Ghent University is made Flemish.   1930

The centre of Ypres at the end of the First World War

1932–38	Language legislation: all central administrative offices will be bi-lingual; administration, lower courts, the law and the army will be monolingual according to which section of the country they apply to. Brussels is officially bi-lingual.
1934	On February 17th King Albert has a fatal accident. He will be succeeded by Leopold III.
1935	Queen Astrid, wife of Leopold III, dies in a motor accident in Switzerland.
1940–44	In the Second World War German troops occupy Belgium in May 1940, in spite of its neutrality. The Cabinet escapes to England, but King Leopold III stays in Belgium, signs the Capitulation Document and is interned. During the period of occupation the Gestapo and SS terrorise the country. Breendonk concentration camp is set up. Flemish Nationalists and the Fascist Rexists of Léon Degrelle collaborate with the Germans. The Resistance succeeds in helping half the Jews in Belgium to escape abroad. Following the Allied landings in Normandy in June 1944 most of Belgium is liberated by September 1944. A final attempt by the Germans to regain the upper hand fails in the Ardennes offensive 1944–45. This failure signifies the final end of the German occupation. In the years following the liberation over 55,000 trials are held of war criminals and collaborators.

Belgium after 1945

After the Second World War Belgium gives up its ineffective neutrality and joins NATO and the European Economic Community (EEC). Since the 1960s there have been marked disputes between Flemings and Walloons, mainly in the linguistic sphere but also on social and cultural grounds.

1944	Founding of the Benelux Customs Union between Belgium, the Netherlands and Luxembourg, to come into force in stages by 1948.
1948	Franchise for women.
1949	Belgium joins NATO.
1950	After fierce political disputes Leopold III gives up the throne. In 1951 his son Baudouin, born 1930, becomes King.
1957	Belgium is a founder-member of the EEC, and Brussels becomes the headquarters of the EEC bodies.
1958	Under the Treaty of Hague the Customs and Economic Union between the Benelux States is ratified initially for 50 years. The Economic Union comes into force on January 1st 1960.
1960	Congo crisis. On June 29th the Belgian Congo becomes independent. A few days later there is a military uprising leading to the arrival of UN troops. When the rich mining province of Katanga under Moise Tshombe declares itself independent of the new Congo state UN troops act as an emergency government. Following the murder of the prime minister Lumumba open war breaks out between Congolese and UN troops on the one hand and Katanga troops on the other. Tshombe is supported by the Belgian Union Minière which supports him with arms and (mainly Belgian) mercenaries. It is 1964 before the last UN soldiers leave the Congo Republic (known as Zaire after 1971). In the same year King Baudouin I marries the Spanish aristocrat Fabiola de Mora y Aragón. After 1960 the dispute between the Flemish-speaking Flemings and the French-speaking Walloons intensifies.

The Flemish-Walloon language border is laid down.   1963

After France withdraws from the NATO defence organisation the latter   1967
moves its headquarters from Paris to Brussels. The military headquarters
are set up in Casteau near Mons.

Creation of four language regions: one Flemish, one French, one German   1970
and the capital Brussels, which is officially to be bi-lingual (Flemish and
French). The Universities of Leuven and Brussels are divided into two
independent colleges, one Flemish and one French.

In addition to the Christian churches and Jewish communities, Islam is also   1974
given equal religious rights.

The setting up of three regional parliaments in Brussels, Mechelen (for   1975
Flanders) and Namur (for Wallonia and the German-speaking regions in
east Belgium). Dispute about Brussels.

Agreement in principle on state reform – the Egmont Constitutional   1978
Reform – for the regionalisation of the country.
French and Belgian paratroopers intervene in Zaire in support of the au-
thoritarian regime of General Mobutu.

Parliament gives the green light to regionalisation. Two regions – Flanders   1980
and Wallonia – are formed with extensive degrees of autonomy. Brussels
receives special status and is to become a region in its own right at a later
date.

Government crises and strikes are the result of serious economic and   1981–83
financial problems. High rate of unemployment.

The German-speaking minority in eastern Belgium is given its own parlia-   1984
ment and local government in Eupen, making it equal in status to the
Walloons and Flemings.

Programme of action to improve the economy and public finances.   1985
In May there is a disaster in the Heysel football stadium before the start of
the European Cup match between Liverpool and Juventus of Turin. British
"fans" provoke bloody riots with the Italian supporters, and 39 people are
crushed fleeing from the rioting.

On March 6th, shortly after leaving Zeebrugge harbour, the British car-ferry   1987
"Herald of Free Enterprise" capsizes. 209 people die.

The death takes place on January 3rd of Gaston Eyskens, Belgian prime   1988
minister in the years 1949, 1958–61 and 1968–72.
On July 31st the Belgian parliament passes a bill making Belgium a Federal
State, with Flanders and Wallonia as autonomous regions and Brussels as
a region with special status.

On January 9th the Belgian parliament passes the Finance Bill for the   1989
regions of Flanders and Wallonia and the statute for the city of Brussels and
its environs. This completes the transition to a Federal State.
On April 28th the courts announce their findings on the Heysel Stadium
disaster of May 1985. Fourteen Britons are imprisoned and fined; the
president of the Belgian football association and the police officer responsible are also convicted.

On April 4th and 5th King Baudouin declares that he is no longer able to   1990
perform his royal duties. He does this in order not to have to sign an
Abortion Bill which he disagrees with, and also to enable the government
to make the bill law, as in such cases the Belgian constitution provides for
the government to take over the authority of the king.

History

1991   In March parliament passes a law which enables female members of the royal line to accede to the throne.

In October the ninth coalition government led by Wilfried Martens breaks down. The elections held in November are described as a "landfall", as the established parties lose many seats and the right-wing radical party "Vlaams Blok" makes considerable gains, as do the "Greens".

1992   At the end of February the ruling Christian Democrats, Socialists and People's Union combine to form a new coalition. The Flemish Christian Democrat Jean-Luc Dehaene is made prime minister. However, this does not prevent the Belgian state from finding itself in the middle of a serious crisis nor hide the fact that many consider Belgium to be increasingly incapable of government as a result of the continual attempts at compromise between the individual popular factions.

In March the physicist Dirk Frimout goes up in an American space-shuttle, making him the first Belgian to enter space.

Famous People

The following lists in alphabetical order people who are associated with Belgium through birth, residence or death and have gained national, even international recognition.

Albert I was the son of Count Philip of Flanders and Mary of Hohenzollern-Sigmarinen. On December 23rd 1909 he succeeded his uncle Leopold II to the throne, the latter's son having died young. In 1900 he married the Bavarian duchess Elisabeth von Wittelsbach. After German troops invaded Belgium in 1914 Albert I set himself at the head of the Belgian army and for four years defended the only unoccupied region in Flanders west of the Ijzer. As Belgian commander he played an important part in the decisive battles after September 1918, when he earned the nickname "Koning-Ridder", or "King Knight". After the First World War he applied himself to rebuilding his country and to introducing various reforms, such as overall male franchise (women had to wait until 1948), equality of the two languages and improving the infrastructure. He was killed while climbing in the Meuse valley in 1934.

Albert I (1875–1934)

Jacob van Artevelde, a memorial to whom stands on the Vrijdagsmarkt in Ghent, was a forerunner of Flemish self-awareness. The son of a merchant family, he first of all went about his business without showing any interest in politics, but political events forced him to change his ideas. When Louis of Nevers Count of Flanders, in the conflict leading up to the Hundred Years' War, took the side of the French, England promptly stopped the export of wool to the Flemish towns, which caused much loss of income and distress to the local weavers, clothmakers and traders. This led to uprisings by the trade guilds in which Jacob van Artevelde was elected a leading figure and finally in 1338 made leader of the town of Ghent. He was successful in forming the powerful towns of Bruges, Ghent and Ypres (Ieper) into an alliance and in wringing considerable concessions out of the Count of Flanders, including his agreement to accept only Flemings as advisors. He ensured that the Flemish language, as well as Latin and French, was accepted in legal circles. In the dispute between England and France he remained neutral at first, but after the start of the Hundred Years' War he sided with England, from whom he hoped to obtain guarantees of Flanders' independence. On January 26th 1340 King Edward III of England came to Ghent and was proclaimed King of France. Jacob van Artevelde, who was becoming increasingly high-handed in his official dealings, even thought of disinheriting Louis of Nevers in favour of the Prince of Wales, but before he could put this plan into operation he was murdered by members of the weavers' guild.

Jacob van Artevelde (1290–1345)

Jacques Brel, who became famous in Paris as a poet, a singer of satirical songs and an actor, was a native of Brussels. He had made a name for himself with his songs satirising society and sung in his distinctive voice. His songs "Les Flamandes", "Marieke" and "Ne me quitte pas" are very well-known. As the result of a serious illness he retired to the South Pacific in 1975, returning home only occasionally. He died in Paris in 1978. A cultural centre and youth hostel in Brussels has been named in his honour.

Jacques Brel (1929–78)

Peter Bruegel the Elder, also known as "Peasant Bruegel", was born about 1525 in Brogel (Kempen) or near Breda. He is one of the most important painters of the 16th c. His extensive works include about 45 paintings as well as drawings and engravings. He is particularly well-known for his paintings of peasant life and his landscapes, scenes which accurately portray his Flemish homeland. What is known of Bruegel's life is based on

Peter Bruegel the Elder (c. 1525–69)

Famous People

Albert I

Jacques Brel

Lamoral, Count of Egmont

only a few definite dates and other documentary evidence. In 1551 at the latest he was a member of the Antwerp Guild, and as a Master of that guild he undertook a journey to Italy about 1552–54 which is partly chronicled by drawings and engravings. After his marriage to Mayken Coeke, the daughter of his teacher Pieter Coeke of Aelst, he moved to Brussels in 1561. This marriage produced both sons, Pieter Bruegel the Younger ("Inferno" Bruegel, 1564–1638) and Jan the Elder ("Flower" Bruegel or "Velvet" Bruegel, 1568–1625).

His most famous works include two engravings, "Seven Virtues" and "Seven Vices", his crowd scenes such as "Children's Games" and "The Battle between Carnival and Lent", as well as "Peasant Wedding", "Peasant Dance", "Land of Milk and Honey", "Hunters in the Snow", "Massacre of the Innocents" and "The Building of the Tower of Babel".

Charles de Coster (1827–89)

Fame came only posthumously to Charles de Coster, who was born in Munich but lived in Brussels from early childhood. In his lifetime he had many money worries, and it was 1870 before he obtained a post as German teacher at the Brussels Military Academy and was assured of a regular income. In "La légende d'Ulenspiegel", which took him ten years to write, he created in strong and vivid language a literary memorial to the struggle for freedom in the Spanish Netherlands. The central characters of the book are the satirist and enemy of tyranny Ulenspiegel from the Flemish dykes and his friend Lamme Goedzak.

Lamoral Count of Egmont (1522–68)

Lamoraal Count of Egmont (Egmond) was the second son of Jan van Egmond, ruler of Egmond op de Hoef near Alkmaar, and Francisca of Luxembourg. He was born in La Hamaide near Ath. At a very young age he came to the court of Emperor Charles V, where he entered on an outstanding military career and carried out several important diplomatic missions. When only 24 he was made a Knight of the Golden Fleece, and in 1554 was entrusted with the arrangements for the marriage by proxy of Philip II and Mary Tudor. In 1555 he was present at the abdication of Charles V, and he defeated the French army at Saint-Quentin in 1557 and at Gravelines in 1558.

The accession to the throne of Philip II was the beginning of a new period for the Count. In 1559 he became a member of the town council and governor of Flanders and Artois. When the Dutch nobles, with William of Orange at their head, demanded from the general governess Margaret of Parma tolerance towards those of different religions and more rights for their own representatives in the state assemblies, Egmont originally hesitated but then conveyed these requests when he went on a mission to the Court of Madrid in 1565. However, he was refused an audience by Philip II who adopted a hard line. After the iconoclasm of 1567 Philip sent the Duke of Alba to the Netherlands, where he crushed any resistance in the most cruel fashion. He had Egmont, who had meanwhile sided with the "geusen" party (see History – 1566), and Count Hoorn imprisoned and charged in Brussels with high treason. The trial ended with a sentence of death, which was immediately carried out on the Grand' Place. After some time Egmont's remains were taken to his house at Zottegem and buried in the crypt there. The grave was only re-discovered during restoration work in 1804.

Egmont is remembered in Goethe's drama (although this does not keep to the historical facts) and in Beethoven's "Egmont Overture".

Born in Maaseik, Jan van Eyck had a very marked influence on the development of Western painting. His realistic portrayals of people and landscapes. with freely-expressed religiously symbolic themes harmoniously set out, exemplify the new way of looking at the world which was coming to the fore at the end of the Middle Ages and which attempted to give a deeper meaning to the realities of the universe.

Van Eyck, initially court painter to John of Bavaria in Den Haag, entered the service of Philip of Burgundy in 1425. After 1430 he lived in Bruges, where he died in 1441. Far and away his best-known work is the "Altar of Ghent" in the cathedral of Sint-Baaf, on which he worked with his brother Hubert.

Jan van Eyck (c. 1390–1441)

César Franck was born in Liège but when quite young moved to Paris where from 1843 he worked as organist, and in 1872 became a teacher of the organ in the Paris Conservatory. Franck pioneered the Impressionist movement in France and introduced the cyclical form, the return of a theme in almost all parts of a piece of music. His works embrace both instrumental and vocal music, including opera and oratorios. He made a major contribution to organ music, not only as a composer but also as an improviser.

César Franck (1822–90)

Legend has presented Godfrey of Bouillon as the very ideal of Christian chivalry. In 1089, as the feudal servant of the Duke of Lorraine, he was the first imperial knight to answer the call by Pope Urban II to follow the crusades to the Holy Land. In 1096, together with his brothers Baldwin and Eustace, he travelled at the head of an army of 20,000 men down the Danube to Constantinople, where they met the armies of other princes and then marched on into Palestine. In 1098 the armies conquered Antiocheia, and in 1099 Godfrey took part in the storming of Jerusalem after a five-week siege, following which he was granted the title of "Steward and Protector of the Holy Sepulchre". In the same year he defeated the Sultan of Egypt at Askalon; shortly after he died in Jerusalem and was buried in the church there. However, his remains were destroyed in the 13th c. and in 1808 fanatical Greek monks desecrated his grave.

Godfrey of Bouillon (c. 1060–1100)

Born in Ghent, Victor Horta was one of the Belgian architects who pointed the way forward at the end of the 19th c. and during the first half of the 20th c. In particular he was an advocate of the Art Nouveau style, as witnessed by such buildings as the Hôtel Tassel, Hôtel Solvay and the Maison du People in Brussels. After living in the United States of America from 1916 to 1919 his designs again showed Classical influences; this is clearly shown in the Palais des Beaux-Arts in Brussels which was built to Horta's design in the 1920s.

Victor Horta (1861–1947)

Charles V, grandson of Emperor Maximilian I and son of Philip the Fair and Joanna of Castille, was born in Ghent. In 1506 he inherited from his father the estate of Burgundy and in 1516 was crowned King of Spain in Brussels cathedral. With strong support from Brussels and Brabant Charles V was made German emperor in opposition to Francis I of France. This latter event is widely celebrated in Brussels in the form of the "Ommegang" on the first Thursday in July every year. The foundations of the Spanish colonial empire were laid during the reign of Charles V, and it was during this time, too, that the Reformation took place and with it the beginning of

Charles V (1500–58)

Famous People

César Franck

Leopold I

Margaret of Parma

the clashes between Catholicism and Protestantism which were to prove so momentous in the history of Europe. In 1556 Charles V abdicated; the Spanish throne passed to his son Philip II and the German emperorship to his brother Ferdinand I. Charles then entered a monastery in Spain.

Leopold I
(1790–1865)

As the result of his marriage to Charlotte, the heir to the English throne, Leopold, son of Duke Francis of Saxe-Coburg, seemed about to enter on a glittering career. However, Charlotte's early death in 1817 put an end to that. In 1830 Leopold was offered the Greek throne, but withdrew his acceptance. A year later he was chosen as the first King of the Belgians and was crowned on July 21st 1831. As a constitutional monarch he removed himself as far as possible from politics and thus enjoyed the esteem of his people. Under his reign Brussels developed markedly. At times Leopold played a leading role in Europe and frequently acted in an advisory capacity to Queen Victoria. In 1832 he married Louise-Marie, daughter of King Louis Philippe of France.

Leopold II
(1835–1909)

As Crown Prince, Leopold II, son of King Leopold I, bore the title of Duke of Brabant, and on December 10th 1865 he was made king. He proved to be skilled in financial matters, and during his reign Belgium enjoyed an unprecedented economic boom. Markets for Belgian products sprang up in Russia, Asia and Egypt. However, Leopold II proved unpopular, even hated, because of his colonial policies. When in 1878 Henry Morton Stanley offered him his discoveries in the Congo Leopold promptly seized them and in 1885 declared himself sovereign and sole owner of the Congo State which became recognised in that year. By 1908, when an international commission intervened, the Congo – eighty times larger then its Belgian motherland – had been mercilessly and bloodily plundered for Leopold's personal gain, which led to his being described by Mark Twain as "the king with ten million dead on his conscience". On the credit side, however, it must be pointed out that through his policy of strict neutrality he was able to keep Belgium out of the Franco-Prussian War of 1870–71.

Leopold III
(1901–83)

In 1934 Leopold III succeeded his father Albert I to the throne. He had married the Swedish Princess Astrid in 1926, but she was killed in an accident in 1935. Under Leopold's reign Belgium cut its ties with the Western Powers and became universally neutral. In spite of that German troops invaded in May 1940. After a war lasting eighteen days the King and his army capitulated but – unlike his government, which fled to London – he remained in Belgium. Until June 1944 he was held prisoner in his palace in Laeken, but then he and his family were transported by the SS to Germany and Austria, where he was freed by American troops in 1945. When Belgium was liberated his brother Charles, Count of Flanders, was made regent. After the end of the war Leopold became the subject of fierce controversy, as it was, and remains to this day, not clear whether and to what extent he had tried to collaborate with Hitler, with whom he had a private conversation. Right up to 1950 he was prevented from returning to Belgium and resuming his position as King, even though a referendum showed that only 58% of the people were in favour. When he did in fact return there was a general strike in Wallonia (which had voted against him) resulting in martial law being imposed. In August 1950 he abdicated and assigned his rights to his son Baudouin. Baudouin adopted the title of Royal Prince until he became the fifth King of the Belgians on July 17th 1951. Leopold retained the title of "king" right up to the time of his death.

Maurice Maeterlink, born in Ghent, a pioneer of the Surrealist movement in literature, studied law initially but then changed over to writing. When staying in Paris in 1887 he first made contact with the Symbolists, and in 1896 he finally moved to Paris, but was obliged to leave it in 1940. His dramatic piece "La Princesse Maleine" (1889) brought him instant success; his other dramatic writings are some of the major Symbolic works. He became world-famous, however, through his essays in which he set out to explain how human existence is threatened by the Powers of Darkness. His lyric verse is based on associations and fantastic sequences. In 1911 Maeterlink received the Nobel Prize for Literature; in 1947 he became President of the International PEN Club.

Maurice Maeterlink (1862–1949)

The artist Magritte, born in Lessines, was the chief initiator of Surrealism in Belgium. After completing his training at the Academy of Art in Brussels he first obtained employment as a commercial artist. He was strongly influenced by the work of Giorgio de Chiricos. After a stay in Paris from 1927 to 1930 he settled in Brussels and founded his own school where the emphasis was on Surrealism. His pictures are detailed paintings of commonplace objects in novel contexts. In addition to large panels he also painted impressive murals, such as those in the Knokke Casino (1953) and in the Palais des Congrès in Brussels (1961).

René Magritte (1898–1967)

Margaret of Parma was born in Oudenaarde, the illegitimate daughter of Johanna van der Gheynst. She was taken to Brussels, where she was educated by Margaret of Austria and Mary of Hungary. After a short marriage to the nephew of Pope Clemens VII, Alessandro de Medici, who was murdered, she was married in 1538 for political reasons to Ottavio Farnese, grandson of Pope Paul III, following which she moved first to Rome and then to Parma. In 1559 the Spanish King Philip II appointed her governess of the Spanish Netherlands. Under her rule the attempts by the Netherlands – led by the nobles with whom she initially tried to negotiate – to obtain independence became even stronger. After the iconoclasm of 1567 and the uprising by the "beggar nobles", however, she resorted to force which culminated in her attempting to exile the Duke of Alba who promptly relieved her of her position. She returned to Italy, but was sent back again by Philip II in 1580 with orders to pacify the provinces in the Netherlands, but this she failed to do. She died in Ortona in Italy.

Margaret of Parma (1522–86)

The famous cartographer and geographer Gerhard Mercator was born in Rupelmonde, south of Brussels. He studied in Leuven and in 1537 produced a map of the Holy Land, followed by his first map of the world in 1538 and a terrestrial and celestial globe in 1541. After moving to Duisburg in Germany he engraved his fifteen-page map of Europe and finally his famous world map which was to prove invaluable to seafarers. Not until after his death did all his work appear together in the form of an atlas.

Gerhard Mercator (1512–94)

Between 1966 and 1973 Eddy Merckx, from the Meenzel-Kiesegem district of Brabant, dominated the world's cycling-tracks. He was the winner in the major cycling classics several times in succession; for example, he won the Milan–San Remo race five times, the Paris–Roubaix three times, the Flèche

Eddy Merckx (b. 1945)

Antoine-Joseph Sax

Georges Simenon

Paul-Henri Spaak

Wallone three times, the Italian circuit three times and the Tour de France on four consecutive occasions. In 1967 and 1971 he was world champion road-racer, and in 1972 he produced a world speed record. Together with his fellow-countryman Patrick Sercu, Eddy Merckx was also successful in indoor six-day races. He still ranks as one of the best racing cyclists of all time.

Peter Paul Rubens (1577–1640)

Peter Paul Rubens was born in Siegen in Westphalia, the son of an Antwerp lawyer who, being a Protestant, had fled to Germany; however, Rubens and his mother returned to Antwerp, where he attended the Latin School and was educated in the humanities and the classics. In 1598 he was made a Master in the Lucas Guild. In 1600 he travelled to Italy, where he lived in Venice, Florence and Mantua as court painter to Duke Vincenzo Gonzaga. Rome, Spain, back to Mantua and Rome and finally Genoa were his other stops on this "Grand Tour". In 1608 he returned to Antwerp, where he married Isabella Brant in 1609; she died in 1626. He became court painter to Archduke Albert and founded his own workshop in which he employed large numbers of artists. As a diplomat, Rubens also attended the French, English and Spanish courts on several occasions. In 1630 he married the sixteen-year-old Helene Fourment. After 1635 he lived in his country mansion at Steen near Antwerp. His tomb can be seen in St Jacob's Church in Antwerp.

Of the 2000 to 3000 paintings which came out of his studio some 600 are ascribed to him. In addition there are the items he produced when abroad. His works include portraits, nudes, animals, still-lifes and landscapes, battle and hunting scenes and religious and historical subjects. His second wife was often his model for nude drawings and portraits.

Antoine-Joseph (Adolphe) Sax (1814–94)

Antoine-Joseph Sax, also known as Adolphe, was born in Dinant, the son of a musical instrument maker. He was apprenticed in the same profession, and initially worked in his father's workshop. In 1842 he moved to Paris, where he developed a new instrument, based on the clarinet, which was capable of producing notes beyond the octave; it was the saxophone, which he patented in 1846, and followed it up with the saxhorn, saxtromba and saxtuba. Sax's instruments quickly found acceptance in French military music and later in orchestral music; Sax himself taught the saxophone and his other instruments at the Paris Conservatory, but failed to make his inventions commercially successful. In fact he became so poor that prominent supporters had to ask the Minister of Arts to make maintenance payments to him.

Georges Simenon (1903–89)

Born in Liège, Georges Simenon created one of the most famous police characters in criminal literature; this was Commissioner Maigret of the

Paris police, who was able to put himself in the place of the criminals and to bring them to justice more by instinct than through tough investigation work. For seventeen years Simenon worked on the "Gazette de Liège". In 1923 he went to Paris, where he wrote his first Maigret novel in 1930, which was to be followed by over a hundred more, bringing their author world-wide fame. Georges Simenon was an extremely productive writer; in addition to the Maigret books he produced psychological novels and over 100 short stories and poems, 21 volumes of his "Dictées" and further novels under the pseudonym "G. Sim". About 60 of his books were made into films, and most have been translated into all the world languages.

The Socialist Paul-Henri Spaak was the most important Belgian politician of the post-war era. With a few intermissions he served his country as Foreign Minister from 1936 to 1966, including the years 1940–44 spent in exile in London, and was Prime Minister in 1938–39, 1946 and 1947–49. During the period spent in London he began to work with others in creating the Benelux Customs Union. In 1945 he helped to formulate the UN Charter and was President of the first full UN Assembly in 1946. Spaak was a decisive influence in the abdication of King Leopold III. In the 1950s he was one of the prime movers in seeking European integration.
Montanunion and the founding of the EEC and EURATOM bear the signature of Paul-Henri Spaak who, after having been General Secretary of NATO from 1957–61, finally held office as Foreign Minister in a coalition government until 1966.

Paul-Henri
Spaak
(1899–1972)

The Antwerp-born Henry van der Velde was one of the major architects to pioneer the Art Nouveau style; he was also influential in the field of arts and crafts. First he studied painting, but then changed over to architecture. He built his first house for his family in Uccle near Brussels in 1892–95; everything, right down to the furniture and the cutlery, was designed by himself. The products of his workshops, the "Ateliers d'Art Industriels", proved very successful in Germany, to where he moved in 1899 and where he did most of his work. Among other things, he fitted out the Folkwang Museum in Hagen and built the School of Applied Art in Weimar and became its principal in 1902. During the First World War he left Germany and went via Switzerland to Holland, where the Kröller-Müller family engaged him to build a new museum in Otterlo which did not finally come to fruition until 1937–54. He returned to Belgium in 1925, where he founded the Institut des Arts Décoratifs in Brussels and became its principal. He also taught architecture at Ghent University, the library of which he designed (1935–40). In 1947 van der Velde returned to Switzerland where he lived until his death in 1957.

Henry van
de Velde
(1863–1957)

Together with Stijn Streuvels, Felix Timmermans, born in Lier, was one of the major exponents of Belgian regional art and one of the best-known Flemish writers. In his books he idealised life in the countryside and in small towns, and painted a picture of a love of nature and simple piety. In 1916 his novel "Pallieter", whose hero was the archetypal Belgian peasant farmer with a love of life, made him famous almost overnight. His best-known work, "Het kindeken Jezus in Vlaanderen" (The Infant Jesus in Flanders) came out in 1917 and again describes idyllic rural life. Perhaps his best book is "Boerenspsalm" (Peasants' Psalm, 1935), a more thought-provoking work. Timmermans does have his critics. The underlying tone of his books comes near to "blood and soil literature" (the idea that political stability and power depend on unification of race and territory), and after the invasion by German troops in the Second World War he was not afraid to arrange pan-Germanic propaganda events.

Felix Timmermans
(1886–1947)

Rogier van der Weyden was the major Flemish artist of the Renaissance whose first recorded date is 1427, when he completed his apprenticeship in Tournai to Robert Campin, the Master of Flémalle and former pupil of Jan van Eyck. In 1435 van der Weyden became the city artist in Brussels where

Rogier van
der Weyden
(probably
1400–64)

he achieved a great reputation and solid fortune. He visited Rome, Florence, Ferrara and Venice about 1450 at the invitation of their princes, journeyed to Cologne some ten years later to paint the "Altar of the Magi" (now in Munich) for St Columba, always returning to Brussels, where he died.

Since none of his works was signed, and there are no contemporary sources as to their authorship, it is often difficult to attribute them with absolute certainty. What was new about this artist was above all the dramatic nature of his compositions, compared with the almost wholly static nature of the figures painted by his contemporaries. His most important work is the "Descent from the Cross" (1435–40) in the Escorial in Spain.

Marguerite
Yourcenar
(1903–87)

Born in Brussels, this writer of psychological novels and short stories, whose real name was Marguerite de Crayencour, was the first woman to be elected to the Académie Française in 1980. Her best-known work is the imaginary "Mémoires d'Hadrien".

Art and Culture

Art History

Strictly speaking, it would only be correct to speak of Belgian art as applying to the period after the founding of the Kingdom of Belgium in 1830.
However, in order to obtain a clearer picture of the varied cultural history of
this country situated between the North Sea, the Meuse, Scheldt and the
Ardennes, it makes more sense to give a resumée of the earlier periods of
art in the whole of the area which is now known as Belgium.

Although only covering a small area, divided into regions speaking Flemish
and French respectively, Belgian art does in fact reflect the whole history of
the subject through all the major European epochs and supplements it with
the individual artistic achievements of the Flemish-Walloon region itself.

Early History

Information about the hunters and gatherers of the Neolithic and Meso-
lithic Ages is provided by the few tools and everyday objects made from
animal bones and stone which are exhibited in the prehistoric departments
of the provincial museums (such as that at Tongeren) and in the Museum of
Art and History in Brussels.

Since about 4000 B.C., the beginning of the Neolithic Age, arable farming
and cattle-raising developed in the fertile hilly regions. At the same time
more refined articles were made, especially pottery vessels showing the
influence of those successive civilisations which spread through the whole
of Europe, known as the beaker, ribbon-decorated and braid-decorated
cultures. After about 1700 B.C. the use of copper and bronze enabled
decorated weapons and jewellery to be made.

The death-cult found expression in a large number of burial-mounds or
barrows containing artistically worked burial objects such as bronze weapons and bejewelled pendants. After about 1300 B.C. cremation came more
into vogue; the dead were burned on pyres and their ashes buried in urns in
large burial grounds. During the Iron Age, from about 800 B.C. onwards, the
Meuse–Scheldt region came under the influence of the Hallstatt culture.
Long iron swords and elaborate clasps were either obtained by trading or
made locally, as well as beautifully-shaped vessels of precious metal or
pottery, stamped or engraved, filigree gold jewellery and lavish
ornaments.

In the centuries which followed and up to the time of the Roman Conquest,
that region which was later to become known as Belgium was dominated
by Celtic and Germanic cultures. The use of the potter's wheel often led to
the mass production of pots of more uniform shape and decoration.

Roman Period

When seeking to extend the Roman Empire north-westward Caesar conquered the Belgae, those North Gallic tribes who had settled between the
Seine and the Rhine and who were mostly of Celtic but some of Teutonic
descent, such as the Bellovaks, Nervi, Manapi, Eburons, Ambians and
others. The regions they inhabited were combined to form the Roman

province of Gallia Belgica, ruled by Augustus and administered from the capital Durocortororum (Rheims). The Rhine formed the frontier of the Roman Empire and also the cultural border with the Teutons. Roman rule brought with it a fresh cultural impetus arising out of the new style of living. In Arlon, the Roman Orolaunum, a row of stone reliefs have been found which superbly illustrate Roman everyday life in the province. In Tongeren, which was probably Aduatuca Tungrorum in Roman Gaul and an important centre and junction of the Roman roads leading from Bavay to Cologne, remains of the Roman town fortifications have been found. In the Gallo-Roman Museum visitors can see various archaeological finds dating from Roman times which provide detailed information about handicrafts and engineering achievements as well as of the cult of the dead and worship of the gods in the oldest Roman town in Belgium.

The top of a Roman standard

Early Middle Ages

Conversion to Christianity

From the early 4th. c. B.C., in the course of the mass migration which took place throughout the whole of Europe, the warlike Germanic tribes from the east of the Rhine suppressed the cultures and way of life left behind by the Romans. Franks settled between the Meuse and the Scheldt basin. Around A.D. 500 the Merovingian king Chlodwig ruled this region from his capital city Tournai. Conversion to Christianity began with the missionary work of St Servatius, who founded the diocese of Tongeren as early as the 4th c. Other Christian centres were Tournai and Arlon, where Early Christian basilicas were built. As Christianity spread through Franconia a large number of churches and monasteries sprang up. In the 7th c. in particular monasticism, in close alliance with the Frankish imperial nobility, was able to carry out a wide programme of instilling the Christian religion into the people. St Amandus (594–684), known as the Apostle of the Belgians, and his pupil, St Bavo (or Baaf; d. 654), patron saint of Ghent, were both of noble descent and typical representatives of this period. The Benedictine abbeys of Sint-Baaf in Ghent (founded 647), Saint-Hubert (687), Stavelot-Malmédy and Nivelles (both c. 650) were centres of teaching and education. The priesthood also remained an important pillar of Carolingian society. Around the year 800, with the help of the clergy, Charlemagne was able to effect the Carolingian cultural renaissance, nurtured on a mixture of ancient bodies of thought and Roman appreciation of art leavened with Christian ideals. The small Carolingian cursive script became the favoured form of writing. Book illumination and work in ivory and gold flourished. Church architecture was based on the T-shaped plan with a nave and transept, somewhat reminiscent of the Roman basilica. The octagonal Palace Chapel in Aachen, the model for similar chapels at Nijmegen and Sint-Donatus in the Meuse region, was a revival of ancient ideas of building round a central hall.

Evidence of Early Christian artistic skills

Unfortunately, few buildings and works of art from this early medieval period have survived. All the original wooden churches have been destroyed, and only fragments of the first stone churches and monastic cells remain to provide any sort of archaeological and documentary evidence, such as the remnants of the 4th c. precursor of the present churches at

Tongeren, Tournai and Arlon and the above-mentioned 7th c. abbeys. Only the treasuries of the Church of the Holy Virgin in Tongeren and of Tournai cathedral contain impressive works of art from the early Middle Ages, such as a 6th c. ivory plate with a carving of St Paul the Apostle and a Mero-vingian gold clasp at Tongeren, a valuable Byzantine reliquary crucifix decorated with ivory (6th–7th c.) and a 9th c. ivory carving of St Nicolas at Tournai. The famous 7th c. ivory diptych from Genoels-Elderen, showing Christ and two angels standing in triumph on the Devil disguised as an animal, is now on display in the Brussels Museum of Art and History.

Romanesque

None of the wall-paintings in churches and abbeys has been preserved, apart from the remains of some 12th c. frescoes depicting St Margaret in the transept of Tournai cathedral. It is only the sheer quality of the book illuminations that leads experts to think that wall-paintings and the like must have been of an equally high standard. Sumptuously decorated Bibles and Gospels from the Benedictine abbey at Stavelot, the Premon-stratensian abbeys at Floreffe and Park near Leuven as well as from Ech-ternach near Luxembourg (codex aureus, 11th c.) have been saved for posterity.

Wall painting and book illumination

In the Ottonian and Early Salian period (10th–11th c.) Byzantine ivory carvings continued to predominate. One outstanding example is the book-cover of the Notker Gospels (c. 980–1000) in the Maison Curtius in Liège. Few stone sculptures remain. The total range of such artistic development is now limited to an archaically abstract 12th c. tympanum showing the Baptism of St Basil in the undercroft of the Church of the Blood of Christ in Bruges and an emotive and moving relief of the Virgin Mary (c. 1149–58) which is also to be seen in the Maison Curtius in Liège.
There are two fine examples of 11th c. wood-sculpture – the large crucifix in the chapel at Tancrémont with an usual depiction of the crucified Christ in a long, folded robe gazing rapturously up to heaven, as well as the dignified head of Christ in the treasury of the Church of the Holy Virgin at Tongeren.

Sculpture

Skills displayed in metal-working in the Meuse region during the 12th c. made it famous throughout Europe. In addition to bronze-casting and relief engraving, enamelling and artistic work in gold were also carried out. In competition with more ancient sculpture, the art of metal-working first reached its zenith under Renier de Huy with the font (1107–18) ascribed to him and made for the church of Notre-Dame-aux-Fonts in Liège; it is now in the church of Saint-Barthélemy. This brass font is supported by twelve cows (only ten are still the originals) – symbolising the Twelve Apostles and the Twelve Tribes of Israel. Five baptismal scenes in high-relief on the wall of the font illustrate the First Sacrament – the Baptism of Christ in Jordan, the Sermons of John the Baptist, the Baptism of the Newly Converted, the Baptism of the Roman Centurio Cornelius and of the Greek philosopher Crato, so that in the baptismal and salvation ceremonies conversion to Christianity was shown as extending from the Jewish world by way of that of the Greeks and Romans and thus into the present. Finely-modelled figures with restrained gestures and arranged in groups to provide the fullest effect, combined with the way in which trees encompass and pro-vide a frame to the christening scenes, all bear witness to the maker's detailed knowledge of ancient Roman sculpture and to his keen and mature feeling for and understanding of form and composition. Other major works from the Meuse workshops working in gold and brass are in the form of reliquaries, small altars and shrines. Examples are the bust of Pope Alexan-der, dating from pre-1145 and to be seen in the Royal Museum of Art and History in Brussels, probably by Godfrey de Huy; the gleaming gold relic of the true Cross from c. 1160 in the church of Saint-Croix in Liège, in the form of a small triptych with relief figures of the Apostles around a central cross

Metallurgy in the Meuse region

The font by Renier de Huy in Liège

held by one of two angels; the altar by Stablo, *c.* 1150–60, also in the Royal Museum of Art and History in Brussels, made from enamel sheets with carvings showing public assemblies and synagogues as well as Jonah and Samson around a central panel of rock-crystal; and the Processional Cross (*c.* 1160–75, also in the above museum) set with precious stones and with dimpled enamelled panels portraying scenes from the Old and New Testaments showing Christ's Passion.

One of the oldest reliquary shrines to survive in the Meuse region is the house-shaped Shrine to St Hadelinus (in Saint-Martin's, Visé), the 11th c. gable-ends of which show a figure of Christ and the crowning of SS Hadelinus and Remaklus, while the eight clearly defined relief panels along the sides probably date from *c.* 1140 and show the influence of Renier de Huy. The shrine to SS Oda and George was built one hundred years later (1230–40, parish church of Amay), as was the shrine to St Remaklus (*c.* 1240–68, church of Saint-Sebastian, Stavelot), and these display a distinctively different and more realistic and captivating portrayal of the human form. Somewhat similar are the works by Hugo of Oignies, dating from around 1230–35 and found in the treasury of the Sœurs de Notre Dame in Namur, the phylactery of St Martin, the two book covers with the Crucifixion and majestas domini, as well as the chalice by Gilles de Walcourt worked in the niello technique of chasing out lines and forms and inlaying a black composition.

Nicolas
of Verdun

However, the supreme master of gold and silver work in the 13th c. was undoubtedly Nicolas of Verdun, whose major work, the Shrine to Our Lady of 1205, together with the 1247 Shrine to St Eleutherius which also shows his influence, is housed in the treasury of Tournai cathedral. In spite of numerous restorations, especially in the 19th c., the sculpted figures, spacious areas of relief, enamelled panels and fine engraving on the Shrine to Our Lady reflect an awakened interest in the human form and in nature. Purity of form and freedom of movement are also the hallmarks of this shrine.

In church architecture the Romanesque basilica style predominated, as exemplified by the schools of architecture on the Lower Rhine, especially in Cologne. The Romanesque church is recognised by the rectangular shape of the main building, together with twin towers on the west front and a group of towers above the crossing. The choir may be stepped, semi-circular with a triple-domed roof or end in a straight line. Inside, those sections which branch out from the crossing serve to unify the whole structure. The arcades of rounded arches, blind arcades and triforium galleries added a degree of subtle refinement. Barrel-vaulting and groin-vaulting replaced flat roofs.

Religious
building

The 11th c. church of St Gertrude at Nivelles still has the Early Romanesque flat-roof, and so has the church of St Vincent in Soignies, while in Liège the west side of the church of the Holy Cross and the fortified twin towers of the west front of Saint-Barthélemy are examples of a different stage in the development of Romanesque architecture. The most impressive of all is the group of five towers to be seen above the transept of the Cathedral of Notre Dame in Tournai with its 12th c. Late Romanesque nave, providing a better example of a medieval house of worship than any other church anywhere in Belgium. .

Two imposing 12th c. castles have survived. On a rock above Bouillon towers the castle of Godfrey of Bouillon, dating from c. 1100. Even more massive is the Château des Comtes in Ghent, built between 1180 and 1200 on 9th c. foundations. It is a splendid example of medieval fortification techniques, with an encircling wall and battlement-walk and flanked by a number of defensive towers and with a massive keep. The Château de Namur, built c. 1230, has slender towers which give it a less fortified look. On the other hand, the 14th c. brick-built castle built in the water at Beersel near Brussels has two massive keeps which dominate the surrounding countryside.

Secular
building

St Gertrude in Nivelles

The keep of the Gravensteen in Ghent

The greatest Gothic achievements are to be found in the religious and secular architecture of the 14th c. It was not until the 15th c. that panel painting came to the fore, while sculpture remained somewhat mundane and was also seriously decimated by the 16th c. iconoclasts.

The re-building of the choir of the Cathedral of Notre Dame in Tournai, which began in 1242 and was influenced by the style of French cathedrals, marked the beginning of Gothic architecture in Belgium. It took until 1325 to complete and is a masterpiece of the Gothic filigree building principle, with load-bearing buttresses supporting the tall and finely-proportioned walls and the groin-vaulted roofs which rest upon them. Brussels Cathedral, too, began in 1220 as the church of Saint-Gudule, with its massive 15th c. twin-towered front and rich tracery, is reminiscent of Notre-Dame in Paris. The building of the seven-aisled Antwerp Cathedral in 1352–56 was the crowning glory of Gothic architecture in the region now known as Belgium. In addition a considerable number of impressive single-towered churches sprang up in the prosperous Flemish textile towns, such as that of Notre Dame in Bruges, the tower of which was finally completed in 1297, and that of St Salvatore in the same town, an Early Gothic brick building with a massive west tower built in various phases during the 12th, 14th and 19th c. Also worthy of mention are the Ghent churches of Sint-Niklaas (13th c.) and Sint-Baafs, a plain granite building. St Peter's in Leuven, with its uncompleted front, its light and high interior and hall-like choir ambulatory, is one of the more important Late Gothic edifices. The richly-traceried walls and magnificent fan-vaulted roof of the church of Saint-Jacques in Liège also belong to this era. The cathedral of St-Rombout (Sint-Romuald) in Mechelen, built in 1342–1487) was originally to have the highest tower of any Christian church, namely 168m/550ft, but when finally completed in 1578 it measured only 97m/318ft. Nevertheless it is an important landmark in the town, a symbol both of fear of God and of civic pride.

Little Gothic architectural sculpture has survived the ravages of time. In the church of Saint-Jacques in Liège there is a Coronation of the Virgin Mary from *c.* 1380–90 in the north porch, showing Mary and Christ seated and wearing artistically-draped robes. The tympanum of the late 14th c. Door of Bethlehem in the Collegiate Church of Notre Dame in Huy depicts in carved stone the Birth of Christ, with Mary lying-in after the birth, above the Adoration of the Shepherds and the Magi and the Massacre of the Innocents. In the three pediments above the doors in the portico of Notre-Dame in Tournai sculpture cycles from *c.* 1400 have been preserved; these show prophets, fathers of the church and a portrayal of the Fall of Man and the Expulsion of the Jews.

Sculpture: City Hall, Leuven

Only the Basilica of Our Lady (St Martinus Basiliek) in Halle and that of St Leonard in Zoutleeuw have retained almost in their entirety their Late Gothic (15th–16th c.) interiors, making them treasure-chambers of sculpture in stone, wood and brass. The figure of the Virgin Mary above the west door and the 14th c. Coronation of the Virgin Mary on the south door of the Halle church, like the apostolic events depicted in the choir (*c.* 1400), are all evidence of the high-quality stonemasons' skills displayed in a period when Claus Sluter in Dijon was producing his greatest sculptures for the Dukes of Burgundy. In St Leonard's in Zoutleeuw there are a number of altar-carvings describing the legend of St Leonard, abbot of Nibliac, the childhood and sufferings of Jesus and the life of Mary. In the vaulted roof of the nave hangs a double-sided Madonna, known as a Marianum, as well as a magnificent triumphal cross. To the right and left of the altar are some valuable dinanderies, yellowish-gold brass work from Dinant, a six-armed Easter lantern dated 1483, several hanging lanterns and a superb 1469 lectern. The treasure-chamber of the cathedral of St Paul in Liège houses two further outstanding Late Gothic sculptures in metal – the group of figures carved by Gerard Loyet in 1470, showing Charles the Bald, Duke of Burgundy kneeling with St George before the Virgin Mary, and the silver bust of St Lambert, the patron saint of the town, by the Aachen goldsmith Hans von Reutlingen (c. 1505).

In competition with the church-building, a unique form of secular architecture came to the fore in Flanders from about 1300 onwards – town gates, cloth halls, guild buildings, urban residences and town-halls. Public buildings in particular, with their belfries visible from afar, bore witness to the prevailing sense of civic pride and commercial enterprise. Their façades were prime examples of the Late Gothic love of flamboyant decoration. Good instances of this are the town-halls of Bruges (1376–1420), Leuven (1448–63), Brussels (east wing, 15th c.), Ghent (north front, 1518–35) and Oudenarde (1526–30). The cloth halls, some of which were huge – the one in Ypres is 132m/433ft long – still serve as a reminder of the economic power wielded by the Flemish towns. The same was true of the multi-gabled market halls, such as the meat hall in Ghent (c. 1400) or the corn hall in the same town, a trading centre dating from the early 13th c., making it one of the earliest public buildings. Among the many beautiful palaces and castles are those of Gaasbeek south-west of Brussels and that at Spontin near Dinant, which is surrounded by water.

Secular architecture

The rooms of noblemen's houses, guild and court-buildings, town halls and some private houses were bedecked with paintings of all kinds. These included historical pictures, hunting scenes, those portraying rectitude and incorruptibility, and also landscapes. Apart from some portraits most of this rich store of secular paintings have been lost to posterity, although details of their provenance are preserved in the form of documentary evidence. Only the Late Gothic religious paintings from 1400 to 1500 still to be seen on church panels remain as witness to the prodigious output of the Old Dutch and Flemish painters. It originated in the painting of miniatures, colourful illustrations in the "books of hours", intended to assist the nobility in carrying out their devotions. Such miniatures were ordered, for example, by the Dukes of Burgundy, who also ruled over Flanders after 1384. There is evidence to show that Melchior Broederlam from Ypres (Ieper) worked on such miniatures in Dijon from 1381 to 1409 for Duke Philip the Bald, and that the brothers Paul, Jan and Hermann of Limburg did the same. Their paintings which embellished the "Très Riches Heures" (1413–16) for the Duke of Berry show a high degree of realism in the way they depict the lives of the nobility, citizens and peasants as the seasons change in town and countryside.

Painting

The van Eyck brothers worked for a short time as painters of miniatures, for example, on the Turin-Milan "book of hours", but it was in the field of panel-painting that their epoch-making work was done and through which they, together with Italian Renaissance painters, helped to make this form of art finally take precedence over sculpture. Jan van Eyck (c. 1390–1441) in particular was the most notable artist to learn from studying the old pictures which had been painted in Dijon and Paris and then – with the aid of the new techniques using oils – to succeed in producing paintings with an unprecedented degree of realism. The principal work by the van Eyck brothers is the "Altar of Ghent", completed in 1432; nobody can now tell which parts are the work of Hubert, who died in 1426, and which are by Jan van Eyck. This magnificent polyptych of ten sections was donated by the well-to-do patrician and Lord Mayor Joos Vijd and his wife Isabella Boorluut to their chapel in Sint-Baafs (St Bavon) in Ghent. Although researchers differ as to the origin and interpretation of this altar-piece – variations in the manner in which the large figures at the top and the smaller ones engaged

Hubert and Jan van Eyck

Van Eyck 1432

in the Adoration of the Lamb of God are painted seem to suggest a "marriage" of the various panels – the Ghent Altar is nevertheless generally regarded as representing the Blessed Sacrament, with the celebration of Holy Communion (symbolised by the Lamb and the Goblet) in the presence of all the major Christian saints, and as having been painted in a more realistically faithful and colourful manner than had ever been achieved before. Another major work by Jan van Eyck, the Madonna of Canon van der Paele, hangs in the Groeninge Museum in Bruges. In a unique manner he succeeded in combining an icon – showing the Enthroned Virgin Mary in the centre flanked by St Donatius and St George on horseback – with a picture of an interior scene, thus merging the worlds of Heaven and Earth in a most magical manner. On the tiled floor a soft, patterned carpet is spread before the Virgin's throne. The bishop's robe is bedecked with precious stones; the surrounding objects and figures are colourfully reflected in the armour worn by St George and his horse. Plagued by gout, the venerable old canon, holding an open book and spectacles, kneels before the Virgin Mary and the child Jesus. When closed the doors reveal a portrait of the donor and his wife, a masterpiece of naturalistic painting portraying age in an uncomprising fashion.

As well as Jan van Eyck there were a number of other excellent painters working in Flanders between 1400 and 1500. The interiors painted by the elder Master of Flémalle, who was probably Robert Campin (d. 1444 in Tournai), show that religious themes were becoming more bourgeois. The realism, vividness and strength of composition shown in his painting contrast with the softer and more delicate style of van Eyck. Master of Flémalle

Roger van der Weyden (c. 1400–64) was a product of the studio of Robert Campin. He concentrated on painting portraits, often three-quarter face, which is how he painted the dukes of Burgundy as well as members of the nobility and the middle classes. Hung in the Art Museums of Brussels and Antwerp are portraits of Laurant Forimont and Philipp de Croy, as well as panels from two diptychs showing the Adoration of the Magi. His major religious paintings, the "Descent from the Cross" which was originally intended for the church of Notre Dame in Leuven and today hangs in the Prado in Madrid, as well as the Last Judgment altar-piece painted between 1443 and 1450 for the Burgundian Chancellor Rolin and now in the Hôtel de Dieu in Beaune, both display perfect line, natural-looking figures and exude a sense of dramatic tension. Rogier van der Weyden

The painter Dirk Bouts (c. 1415–75) made a great impression through the dignity and solemnity he portrayed together with his effective use of depth of perspective. The vertical pictures he painted c. 1468 depicting justice, which were intended to act as an example to the guardians of the law in the court-room of the Leuven town hall and which now hang in the Musées Royaux des Beaux-Arts in Brussels, are good examples of his skill, as is the altar-piece showing the Last Supper in the church of St Peter in Leuven. The lines and perspective of the room in which the Last Supper took place are so precisely drawn that all the rays emanating from the head of Christ converge in front of the cruciform panelling above the fire-place in such a way that not only is Christ the centre of the composition but also appears as the radiant centre of the universe, as indicated by the Old Testament precursors of the Holy Communion which are depicted on the side-panels. Dirk Bouts

The panels painted by Petrus Christus (1410–73), a pupil of Van Eyck and the head of his studio from 1441, initially showed his teacher's influence. Subsequently, however, he progressively simplified the latter's somewhat effusive and gushing style to produce a more unified spatial effect which in turn gave a sense of cohesion to his previously isolated figures. The "Mourning of Christ" in the Musées Royaux des Beaux-Arts in Brussels is a good example of this. Petrus Christus

One of the more important members of the Old Dutch school of painting in the second half of the 15th c. was Hugo van der Goes (1440–82). Between Hugo van der Goes

◀ *The central panel of the altar of Ghent*

Hans Memling: "Christ and Angels"

Hans Memling

1476 and 1478 he produced his major work, the Portinari Altar, depicting the "Adoration of the Shepherds", which is now housed in the Uffizi in Florence. It was donated by Tommaso Portinari, the manager of the Bruges branch of the Medici Bank. Something of the splendour of this altar-piece can also be found in his "Anna Selbdritt" in the Musées des Beaux-Arts in Brussels. His later work – such as the "Death of the Virgin Mary" in the Groeninge Museum in Bruges – shows signs of the onset of insanity, as reflected in the restless composition and the pain-racked faces of the Apostles painted in flickering and coldly iridescent colours.

A contemporary of van der Goes was Hans Memling (1430–95), who was actually born in Germany but worked in Bruges after 1465. Some of his major works can be seen in the Hopital St-Jean in Bruges; these include a painted shrine of St Ursula with contemporary views of Cologne, a triptych showing the Adoration of the Magi and a superb two-part picture donated by Martin Niewenhove in 1487. The most outstanding work, however, is the 1479 St-Jean Altar dedicated to the patron saints of the hospital, John the Baptist and John the Evangelist, with the Beheading and Revelation of the latter on the side panels. The centre panel of this triptych shows the mystic marriage of St Catharine in the presence of the two patron saints. In an open columned chancel – with a view of the town of Bruges and a large crane in the distance – the Christ child is shown handing over the ring while to the far right of the Virgin Mary St Barbara appears engrossed in a book. The enchanting figures of St Catharine and St Barbara are also portraits of Mary of Burgundy, later to be the wife of Emperor Maximilian, and of her stepmother Margaret of York; in this way, idealism and mortality are combined. The world of Memling's pictures typically portrayed contemplative peace, with little in the way of dramatic presentation; he created pictures of situations in which the individual form was of more importance than ingenious groups or complex composition. His works are timeless pictures of devotion and meditation, showing a medieval conservative approach with few signs of a Renaissance awareness.

After Memling's death Gerard David (*c.* 1460–1523) became head of the   Gerard David
Bruges school of painting. A selection of his work can be seen in the
Groeninge Museum there. David's art was in the tradition of van Eyck and
Memling, but with a truer grasp of perspective he achieved greater spatial
clarity in his composition with the naturally-painted figures grouped in
such a way as to give a more realistic impression overall.

Quentin Massys (1466–1530), a contemporary of David, lived and worked   Quentin Massys
in Antwerp. His works included the Altar of St Anne in 1509 (now in the
Musées Royaux des Beaux-Arts in Brussels) for the St Anne Brotherhood,
and the Altar of St John for the Guild of Carpenters; this is now to be seen in
the Musée Royale des Beaux-Arts in Antwerp. The winged Altar of St Anne
shows strong Renaissance influences; the overall impression is one of size,
harmony and clarity of composition. While the architectural background to
the centre panel emphasises the sense of peace and the balanced placing
of the figures, the lines of the composition as they fall on the left side-panel
and rise on the right dictate the formal content – the Annunciation and the
Death of St Anne.

Renaissance

The transition from the medieval iconic concept of imagery to the authentic   **Painting**
Renaissance generic form of portraiture, group portraits, landscapes, still-
life and genre pictures took a long time to come to fruition, namely, from
the 15th to the 16th c.

Joachim Patinir (*c.* 1485–1524) may be regarded as the founder of the   Joachim Patinir
Flemish-Dutch school of landscape painting. He worked in Antwerp at the
same time as Massys and was a personal friend of Dürer. However, Patinir
still did not paint pure natural scenes; his idealistic landscapes, mainly
painted as if viewed from the air, were somewhat heavy in comparison to
the small, often biblical figures they contained. Only a few of his works
were signed; those definitely attributed to him include the "Flight into
Egypt", which is in the Musée des Beaux-Arts in Antwerp, and the "Preach-
ings of John the Baptist", in the museum of the same name in Brussels.

Influenced by the Roman High Renaissance and Italian painting, a group of   Romanists
painters calling themselves the Romanists introduced into Flanders – albeit
in a rather different manner – the style of composition and feeling for
colour shown by the somewhat affected Italian painters, particularly in the
field of nude painting. This is reflected very strongly in the work of Jan
Gossaert, known as Mabuse (1478–1533), who showed the extent to which
he had been influenced during his trip to Rome as a student in 1508–09 by
the powerful way in which he drew figures and in his work in the field of
Renaissance architecture. Another artist working at about this same time
was Bernaert van Orley (*c.* 1488–1541), who had been influenced by
Raphael. He was employed as court painter in Brussels for the Stadholder
Margaret of Austria and for Mary of Hungary. His monumental style is
expressed in the Altar of the Last Judgment of the Givers of Alms, dated
1525 and now housed in the Musée Royale des Beaux-Arts in Antwerp, and
especially in his wall-hanging drawings showing scenes from the lives of
Abraham and Jacob, as well as in the large stained-glass windows of
Brussels Cathedral. Also worthy of mention is Frans Floris (1516–70), who
ran a studio of four in Antwerp which produced large compositions containing many human figures.

The most significant opponent of the Romanists was Pieter Breugel the   Pieter Bruegel
Elder (1525–69), even though he learned something from them. His major   the Elder
creation was the "peasant picture", and he elevated the art of the rustic   (Brueghel,
landscape so as to make it universally popular as a genre in its own right.   Breughel)
Bruegel depicted the comedy and tragedy reflected in the lives of the
simple peasant folk as they pursued their labours through the changing
seasons or followed their customs and traditions. His "Census at Bethlehem" (1566, Musées Royaux des Beaux-Arts, Brussels) is a splendid

Peter Bruegal the Elder: "Census in Bethlehem"

panorama of Dutch village life in winter-time. Children are shown playing on the frozen lakes, peasants pulling sleds piled with stores for the winter, men are gathered in front of the inn, a pig is being slaughtered, in the twilight figures are grouped around a hollow tree-stump, and in the middle of all this can be seen the unobtrusive forms of Jesus and Mary. Bruegel was able successfully to find a synthesis with the event in Christ's life set in a traditional rustic scene; in the middle of winter, in front of a ruined castle, a new house is being built, symbolising the House of God being newly built on Earth through the Birth of Christ. Mythologial subjects, such as the "Fall of Icarus", painted in 1558 and also housed in the Brussels museum, are shown by Bruegel against the background of a quiet rustic world. The death of Icarus – who considers himself to be godlike, with the result that pride inevitably comes before a fall! – goes almost unnoticed, in the same way that the death of any individual does not shake the world, which still revolves in much the same way as the peasant continues to plough his field, the shepherd still watches his flock and the fisherman and the crew of the ship in the distance still sail the deep. As Bruegel saw it, it is not the ordinary, genial and imaginative individual who changes the world, but rather the constant work done to please God by so many anonymous people. However, it was not just the vitality of the peasant which intrigued Bruegel – he was equally fascinated by the world of evil. The "Fall of the Angels", in the Brussels museum and "Dulle Griet" (Mean Maggie) in the Museum van den Bergh, Antwerp, both dating from 1562, come close to the demon-world of Hieronymus Bosch. Numerous grotesque and cruel beings, part man, part beast, populate an inferno with renegade angels and "Mean Maggie", the very personification of greed in a devastating world of lust and Satanism. In an enigmatic and sinister way Bruegel mirrors the conflict man faces between good and evil, reason and physical desire, at a time when religious struggles were rife between Protestants and Catholics. The sons of Pieter Bruegel were also artists, especially Jan Bruegel (1568–1625), who made such a name for himself with his still-lifes of flowers and small thematic landscapes that even Rubens took him under his wing. Pieter Bruegel the Younger imitated his father, with his ghostly scenes and religious pictures.

Architecturally speaking, the Renaissance primarily affected the interior decoration of buildings. Examples are the alabaster, black marble and oak fire-place in the court buildings in Bruges, designed by L. Blondeel and G. de Beaugrant in 1529–31, as well as the huge alabaster altar made in 1533 by Jean Mone for the church of Notre Dame in Halle. Few castles and palaces, the hallmark of Renaissance secular building elsewhere, were built at this time in the Netherlands.

The only exceptions to this are the residence of the royal bishops of Liège (1526–40) and the palace of the Stadholder Margaret of Austria in Mechelen. The architects Guyot de Beaugrant and Rombout Keldermans were responsible for the Mechelen building (1507–25), with its mélange of flamboyantly Gothic and more balanced Renaissance ornamentation. The latter architect, together with Dominicus de Waghemaker, designed the somewhat similar north front of Ghent Town Hall (1516–38). Cornelius Floris de Vriendt (1514–75), an architect, sculptor and artist all in one, made his mark when he built Antwerp Town Hall between 1561 and 1565. Schooled in designing façades for Italian palaces, he combined this skill with the North European preference for gables and oriel windows to which he added lavish ornamentation and scroll-work. This produced the Floris Style, named after him and which pointed the way ahead for the future. The elegant guild-houses in the Antwerp market-place were built in this elegant style, as were the house built for the mayor and patron of Rubens Nicolas Rockox and the palace belonging to Plantin-Moretus, a famous printer and publisher.

The richly-carved choir-screen of 1570–73 in Tournai Cathedral and the figured, tower-like tabernacle of Sint-Leonardus in Zoutleeuw (1549) are highlights in the sculptural career of Cornelius Floris. The major Renais-

Antwerp City Hall

sance sculptors of the second half of the 16th c., however, worked abroad; these included Jean de Boulogne, known as Giambologna, a pupil of Jacques Dubroeuq from Mons, in Italy, and Adrian de Vries in Germany.

Baroque

Painting

When the political and religious split between the northern and southern provinces took place at the end of the 16th c. this resulted in a simultaneous divorce between Dutch art in the north and Flemish in the south. Any common factors remaining in the field of painting finally disappeared in the 17th c. when the two major artists from the two regions, Rembrandt and Rubens respectively, went their separate ways with their different interpretations of both form and colour.

Peter Paul Rubens

Peter Paul Rubens (1577–1640) set new horizons in Flemish and European painting. Displaying a marked degree of sensuousness together with a Classical and Humanist attitude and an inexhaustible imagination Rubens produced paintings covering many religious and secular subjects, from altar-pieces to allegory, from historical scenes to portraits and landscapes. He soon became rich and famous and in the grand house and studio in Antwerp where he lived and worked in style, assisted by such specialists as F. Snyders, J. Bruegel the Younger, van Dyck and others, more than 3000 paintings were produced, of which some 500 to 600 were definitely by him or are attributed to him. Rubens lived in Italy between 1600 and 1608, visiting Mantua, Genoa and Rome, and this had a great bearing on his artistic development. He was particularly influenced by the Early Baroque work of Caravaggio and Caracci and the Renaissance skills of Leonardo da Vinci and Titian, as well as by older paintings. Soon after returning to Antwerp he produced his monumental masterpiece, the triptych in Antwerp Cathedral in 1610. The powerful and muscular figures in the "Raising

Peter Paul Rubens: "The Crucifixion" . . .

of the Cross" are reminiscent of the ceiling frescoes in the Sistine Chapel, the use of light and shade being modelled on the style of Carvaggio. The dramatic composition, aided by the diagonal line and colouring used in the centre panel, is typically Romo-Baroque, while the precise and detailed brushwork conforms to traditional Flemish realism. The "Descent from the Cross" (1612) is more restful and formal; the diagonal line is less dynamic and broken, and the contrast between light and dark successfully gives the impression of the body of Christ being raised, while in death it appears as a source of radiant light. The overall coloration differs; in particular, the red of John's robe in the centre panel, that of the priest in the temple in the right-hand panel and of Mary's cloak in the left-hand panel depicting the Visitation all serve to compose the individual panels into one large compositional unit.

Subsequently Rubens concentrated on nudes and figures, dramatic hunting and fighting scenes, pictures illustrating historical tales, and large altar-pieces in a multiplicity of forms – see the Museums of Art in Brussels and Antwerp. The painting above the high altar in the Cathedral of Notre-Dame in Antwerp, the "Assumption of the Virgin Mary" completed in 1626, showed early signs of the lyrical and delicate later style of Rubens as inspired by Titian. During the final decade of his work he produced some idyllic landscapes and portraits.

Rubens' most distinguished pupil was Anthonis van Dyck (1599–1641). He too travelled to Italy, primarily in order to study the painting of Titian. After being employed for a short time as court painter to the Archduchess Isabella in Antwerp he went to London in 1632 where he became court painter to King Charles I. His altar-pieces – such as those in Sint-Paul and Sint-Augustinus in Antwerp, the church of Notre-Dame in Kortrijk and Sint-Romuald in Mechelen – give an impression of muted pathos and religious sensitivity. He achieved fame mainly for his portraits, some of which hang in the Art Museums in Antwerp and Brussels. His portrayals of

Anthonis van Dyck

... and "Descent from the Cross"

figures are distinguished by keen individual observance, a noble style of composition and balanced use of colour.

Jacob Jordaens

His contemporary Jacob Jordaens (1593–1678) was a master of genre painting, portraying the earthier pleasures of life, such as carousing, eating and so on. His vigorous and muscular characters and sensuous female nudes reflect the influence of Italian Baroque, which he must have received from Rubens, as he never actually visited Italy himself.

Adriaen Brouwer

Adriaen Brouwer (c. 1606–38), actually a Dutchman by birth who lived in Antwerp, painted folksy and graphic everyday scenes – the peasant in the ale-house, at play or involved in a rough and tumble, as well as festivities of all kinds.

David Teniers
the Younger

David Teniers the Younger (1610–90) is another 17th c. Antwerp genre painter, who was employed after 1651 as court painter in Brussels and curator of the archduke's art collections. He was a humorous painter of Flemish rustic life and also provides an interesting insight into contemporary art-galleries and collections.

Sculpture

Duquesnoy

Although Baroque sculpture was overshadowed by painting, it nevertheless produced some noteworthy works and artists, such as the Duquesnoy family of Jerôme the Elder and his sons Jerôme the Younger and François. In 1619 the father sculpted the famous bronze fountain-statue of the Manneken-Pis in Brussels as well as the tabernacle of the collegiate church in Aalst in black and white marble. François worked mainly in Rome in a somewhat Neo-Classical variation on the Baroque. The works of his brother Jerôme, who lived from 1602 to 1654, included the monument for Bishop Anton Triest in the Cathédrale St-Bavon in Ghent. The Baroque interior of the church of Notre-Dame-les-Victoires-au-Sablon in Brussels is also his work.

Quellin

The Quellin family of sculptors worked both in Holland and Flanders. Artus the Elder (1609–68) and his pupils were responsible between 1648 and 1655 for all the sculpture-work in Amsterdam City Hall. His nephew and pupil Artus the Younger (1625–1700) copied the Rubens' style of sculpting from his uncle and produced a large number of pulpits and monuments in Flemish churches. Also worthy of mention are the communion rail in Sint-Romuald in Mechelen and the impressive 1682 figure of God the Father on the rood-screen of Sint-Salvator in Bruges.

Verbruggen

Pieter Verbruggen the Elder (1615–86) made religious statues and altar-figures for churches in Antwerp, while his son Pieter the Younger (1640–91) was responsible for the marble altar in the church of St Dominic in Antwerp and his other son Hendrik (1654–1724) carved the Baroque pulpits in Leuven and Brussels.

Jean Delcour

Mention should be made of the 1673 monument to the Bishop of Allamont by the Liège sculptor Jean Delcour in the church of Sint-Baaf in Ghent, carved on the lines of Italian Baroque à la Bernini.

Architecture

One of the earliest examples of the Baroque style being used in religious buildings was the Carmelite church in Brussels, built between 1607 and 1671, but now destroyed. It was designed by the architect Wenceslas Coeberger. Lavish High Baroque design was used by Jacques Francart in the convent church in Mechelen (1629–47) and the church of St Augustus in Brussels. The church of St Carolus Borromeüs in Antwerp (1614–21) and that of St Peter in Ghent (1629–44) were built by F. Aguillon and P. Huyssens. Huyssens also designed the Église St-Loup in Namur between 1621 and 1645.

The field of secular architecture saw the building of town residences, palaces modelled on those of Italy and France, as well as the magnificent guildhalls on the Grand'Place in Brussels. After most of the buildings on the Grand'Place had been destroyed by the French during the siege of 1695 29 such guildhalls with slender multi-storey façades were built between 1695 and 1710, using a mélange of decorative styles ranging from the historical to the Renaissance and the Baroque. By thus imitating the feudal image the middle-classes tried to make their buildings the equal in style to the palaces of the nobility.

18th Century

The period between Rococo and Neo-Classicism had little impact on Belgian art. Painters turned again to the Rubens and French schools without being able seriously to compete with either. Towards the end of the 18th c. Jacques-Louis David from Paris hastened the reaction in favour of Neo-Classicism. In his paintings of the French Revolution and as court painter to Napoleon he portrayed the traumatic events of his time in programmatic pictures; the Brussels Museum of Art owns his oil-painting "The Murder of Marat" (1793).

In the field of sculpture church interiors continued to be vested with work of high quality. Particular mention should be made of the pulpit by Michiel van der Voort the Elder in the Cathedral of Notre-Dame in Antwerp, decorated with carvings of animals of all kinds, as well as of the Rococo pulpit of marble and oak (1741–45) by Laurent Delvaux which can be seen in Sint-Baaf's in Ghent. In 1740 Josef Couven from Aachen constructed the high-altar framed with clustered columns.

In architecture too ideas came from outside the country. In Namur Gaetono Pizzoni from Milan built the Cathedral between 1751 and 1767; the monumental pillars of the curved façade were early precursors of Neo-Classicism. In Liège the main façade of the 1737 Bishop's Residence is powerfully articulated with columns and pilasters, in the French style of the time. In the upper town of Brussels some splendid town-houses were built to the design of the French architect Guimard in the Rue Royale and the Place Royale and surrounded by a large park. Of the many noble mansions built in the countryside particular mention should be made of the Palace and Park of Belœil, seat of the Prince of Ligne.

Painting

Sculpture

Architecture

19th Century

Nineteenth century Belgian artists followed the styles then current in the rest of Europe. Many of their works are on dispaly in the Musées Royaux des Beaux-Arts in Antwerp and Brussels. Historical art originally followed the precedents set by the French painters Jacques-Louis David and Delacroix; their chief followers in Belgium were Gustav Wappers, L. Gallait and Nicaise de Keyser who, especially after Belgium became independent in 1830, painted national subjects in a romantic manner. Henri Leys – who did the frescoes in the Antwerp Town Hall – painted in a more objective and down-to-earth fashion. Antoine Wiertz concentrated on monumental painting with a moral or philosophical theme, sometimes using effective nightmarish scenes, such as those in the Musée Wiertz in Brussels. F. Courtens and A. Baertson made a name for themselves as landscape painters. Among the Realists mention must be made of François Lamorinière and Hippolyte Boulenger as well as of the socially-biased works of Willem Vogels and Jan Stobbaerts. The lives of the peasants and the underprivileged formed the theme of paintings by E. Laermans, a subject again used in Expressionist form by Charles de Grux towards the end of the century. Impressionism, which was rapidly spreading from France to the rest of Europe, was reflected in the Parisian boudoir themes and still-life of Albert Steven, in the idyllically luminous paintings of Henri de Braekelaar and in the charming society portraits and landscapes of Henri Evenepoel. Another Neo-Impressionist who should be mentioned was Theo van Rysselberghe, a member of the Cercle de Vingts (1884–93), to which Fernand Khnopff also belonged, albeit as an exponent of Symbolism as favoured by the Viennese Secessionists. The works of George Minne, Valerius de Saedeleer, Gustave van de Woestyne and Jakob Smits all reflect in different ways the mystical and religious variations of Symbolism. Mention should also be made of the graphic artist and engraver Félicien Rops, who was close to Gustave Moreau in the style of his Symbolistic paintings and

Painting

James Ensor

portrayed the darker side of life. His opposite was Rik Wouters, an advocate of Fauvism who painted vital compositions with a strong use of colour.
European recognition came late to James Ensor (1860–1949), but he was a strong influence on Expressionist and Surrealist painters. The stories of Edgar Allan Poe, together with the thousands of objects to be found in the souvenir shop run by his uncle and aunt in Ostend, impelled him to paint his colourful but grotesque, bizarre, even nightmare-impressionistic scenes of people in masks who are caricatures either of themselves or of society. For example, his huge oil-painting called "The Entry of Christ into Brussels" (1888–89) shows an endless, almost carnival-like mass of people surging through the streets, representing various walks of life such as soldiers, priests, judges and so on, with Christ standing on the sidelines and with the features of James Ensor himself. It was in this way that this eccentric artist wrestled with his fantasy world. His pictures "Strange Masks" (1892, Musées Royaux des Beaux-Arts, Brussels) and "The Intrigue" (1890, in the museum of the same name in Antwerp) also convey an eerie and ghostly atmosphere. Instead of a world of outward appearances and phenomena, which so fascinated the Impressionists, Ensor lived in one governed by experiences, emotions and psychological fantasies, and was in some ways well ahead of his time.

Sculpture

Constantin Meunier

In the early 19th c. Belgian sculpture was still modelled on that of France and showed a mixture of styles involving Realism and emotional Baroque pathos. Towards the end of the century the naturalistic style of Constantin Meunier (1831–1905) caught on, especially in the shape of monumental, sometimes heroised figures. Much of his work is to be found in the Meunier Museum in Brussels. George Minne (1866–1941) preferred the delicate lyricism of the Art Nouveau style in his figures, for example, in the Fountain of Youth in his home town of Ghent.

Architecture

Victor Horta

Henry van de Velde

In the early 19th c. the tradition of French Neo-Classicisim was perpetrated in Belgian architecture, together with an increased Baroque impact and perhaps an excessive regard for past styles. The master-builder Jean-Pierre Cluysenaer, for example, worked on the long covered passages in Brussels. In Ghent L. Roelandt built the University and the Palais de Justice, and in Antwerp P. Bourla was the city architect. Brussels, freshly chosen as capital of Belgium in 1831, was the scene of extensive building alterations. Wide boulevards were laid out and large prestigious buildings erected. The economic boom was reflected in the building of the Neo-Classical Stock Exchange (1830–73), the National Bank (1859–64), glass-covered passages such as the Galeries Saint-Hubert (1847) and the temple-like opera house, the Théâtre Royal de la Monnaie. The apotheosis of how the upper-classes now saw themselves and of the sovereignty of the rule of law were reflected in the building of the giant Palais de Justice (Law Courts) by J. Poelaert in 1883, with its giant dome which still dominates the city's skyline.
Towards the end of the 19th c. the Art Nouveau style took hold in Brussels; a prime example is the Hôtel Tassel, built in 1892–93 by Victor Horta (1861–1947). His own house and office were richly decorated and furnished in the Art Nouveau style. Paul Hankar, too, was an advocate of the new movement, an example being Klever House in Brussels (1898); so was Henryvan de Velde, but he left Brussels in 1902 to attend the school of art in Weimar, Germany.

Modern

Painting

Constant Permeke

Expressionism played a leading role in Belgian painting at the beginning of the 20th c. Constant Permeke (1886–1952) and Frans Masereel (1889–1972) were its leading lights. From time to time Permeke returned to traditional Flemish styles of painting. His "Winter Landscape" of 1912, now in the Musées des Beaux-Arts in Antwerp, is strongly reminiscent of Bruegel,

In the house of Victor Horta

while his later landscapes and seascapes are more on the lines of French Realism à la Gustave Courbet. In between these two extremes he produced many sensitive studies of the lives of ordinary folk, such as "The Sower" (1933) which, together with many others, now hangs in the Constant Permeke Provincial Museum in Jabbeke near Bruges.

Masereel, who was born in Ghent and trained there as a painter and graphic artist, lived in Paris from 1921, where his black-and-white wood-cuts denounced the exploitation of the Paris workers and the hedonism of the bourgeoisie. The powerful brush-strokes of his oils vividly portray simple folk, such as fishermen or barmaids. His landscapes are rather sombre, as if reflecting the destructive powers of two world wars.

Frans Masereel

Other Expressionists worthy of mention are Jean Brusselsmans, some of whose paintings are reminiscent of the early works of Paul Klee, for example, his landscape "In the Country of the Payotte", painted in 1928 and now in the Musées des Beaux-Arts in Antwerp, as well as Gust de Smet, who came close to Cubism, and Fritz van den Berghe, who felt himself to be in empathy with the German Expressionists.

The Belgian Surrealist painters René Magritte and Paul Delvaux (b. 1897) have gained international acclaim. In contrast to Salvador Dali or Max Ernst, Magritte represented the realistic form of Surrealism which, by means of a precise and accurate painting technique, manages to combine various levels of factuality in such a way as to reflect both reality and appearance, fact and fiction. Of one of his major works, "The Constitution of Man", painted in 1939 and now in the Claude Spaak Collection, Magritte himself explained "Before a window of a room through which one looked outside I had placed a picture. The picture was exactly that section of the landscape which it covered up; thus, the tree in the picture concealed the tree which was outside. To the observer, therefore, it (the tree) was both inside on the picture and also – in his imagination – outside, in the land-scape itself. This is how we see the world; we see it as something outside, even though we carry a picture of it within ourselves. In the same way we

René Magritte

René Magritte: "This is not a pipe"

transpose into the past many things which are happening in the present. Time and space thus lose their trivial meaning, the latter being of importance only as an everyday experience."

Also of significance are Magritte's "Talking Pictures", such as that of a pipe with the words underneath informing us that "This is not a pipe". In this way Magritte presents the observer with ambiguities and contradictions, arguing that words are not the things themselves, merely a symbol to represent them, and that pictures are not actuality, only an imaginary presentation of it, and that as they all depend on conventional ways of thinking and recognising they restrict freedom of thought. In addition to framed pictures Magritte also painted murals in public buildings, for example, in the Knokke Casino (1953), in the Palais des Beaux-Arts in Charleroi (1957) and in the Palais des Congrès in Brussels (1961).

Paul Delvaux

The pictures of Paul Delvaux explored much more deeply the Kingdom of the Unconscious, which began to fascinate artists in the early 20th c. as a result of the psychoanalytical theses published by Freud and Jung. These argued that the external world which we know and trust is being increasingly defamiliarised by the dream world or even replaced by it as a form of higher reality. Bringing to the fore this concept of the Forces of the Unconscious led coincidentally to pictures being painted which were psychically associated with and shaped by it. Using precise and realistic draughtsmanship and cold colours, Delvaux painted many female nudes against landscape backgrounds, in murky interiors, on railway stations or in the presence of skeletons reacting as human beings. His statuesque women emit an eerie atmosphere of cold eroticism. Some of the works produced by Delvaux during his long life hang in the Modern departments of the art museums in Brussels and Antwerp and also in the Paul Delvaux Foundation in Sint-Idesbald.

Constructivism

Abstract art in Belgium began with the Constructivist painters Jozef Peeters and Georges Vontangerloo. They were members of the Dutch De Stil-Bewegung, founded in 1917, during the 1920s, and of the Parisian group, the Abstraction-Création (founded 1931) during the 1930s. Constructivism, and Concrete Art which followed it, aimed at creating, by the use of geometrically abstract forms, an aesthetic discipline not dependent on nature and which was also intended to represent universal harmony. Other major exponents of Belgian Constructivism are Victor Servranckx and Félix de Boeck.

After the Second World War abstract art received a further impetus through the work of Corneille (actually Cornelis van Beverloo) and Pierre Alechinsky, members of the international group of artists known as COBRA, formed in 1948–50 from the first two letters of Copenhagen and Brussels and the "A" of Amsterdam. They practised a spontaneous and informal method of painting with naïvely happy elements of popular art combined with the archaically primitive sign language of earlier cultures.

COBRA

In the 1950s Zero Art, with such exponents as Heinz Mack, Otto Piene and Günther Uecker, received an enthusiastic reception in Antwerp, and an exhibition, Vision in Motion, was held in 1959. These artists reduced all figures in both painting and sculpture to mere suggestions of colour and light in space, something which was later to be used again and developed further in Op Art.

From 1958 to 1962 Maurice Wyckaert, an advocate of informal painting, was a member of the International Situationists formed in 1957 who – together with writers – aimed at changing through the medium of art the alienated world in which man found himself.

From the mid-1960s Conceptual Art in Belgium found an enthusiastic advocate in M. Broodthaers. The painter Panamarenko produced a style all of his own with his technically Utopian flying objects, but is better known perhaps, in company with such as Paul Thek and Michael Buthe, under the collective concept of individual mythology. Panamarenko's flying machines portray the dream of a modern-day Icarus setting off to discover the Universe.

In the field of contemporary sculpture mention must be made of Roel d'Haese and his abstractly bizarre metal sculptures, and of P. Bury, known for his kinetic objects. A good overall idea of international trends in modern sculpture can be obtained by visiting the Middelheim Sculpture Park in Antwerp.

Sculpture

Early 20th c. architecture was strongly influenced by the Art Nouveau style. After the First World War the architect V. Bourgeois designed the Cité Moderne in Berchem-Sainte-Agathe near Brussels between 1922 and 1925; this is a town quarter in the International style. L. Stijnen was an exponent of Functionalism, based on practical yet constructively aesthetic concepts.

Architecture

Of contemporary buildings, special mention should be made of the University Quarter in Woluwé-Saint-Lambert near Brussels, built under the guidance of L. Kroll, and the university town of Louvain-La-Neuve southeast of Brussels, planned after 1970 by Raymond Lemaire and some 80 other architects in individual building styles.

Flanders' Tapestries

Embroidery and tapestry work is an old art-form going back to pre-Christian times, as shown by finds from ancient Egypt and Greece. Pictures worked in wool are also known from Early Christian times. In Byzantium and in Moorish Spain silk hangings were made to decorate the walls. In the Middle Ages, especially in France, there were periods during which some famous tapestries were made, such as the Bayeux Tapestry in the 11th c. and that portraying the Apocalypse which was made in the workshop of Nicolas Bataille in Paris between 1376 and 1381 and placed in the Cathedral of Angers. Around 1400 first Arras – after which tapestries generally became known in Italy as "arazzi" – and then Tournai became further centres of tapestry-work. The word "tapestry" was derived from "tapis", the French word for carpet.

Brussels

The boom in Flemish wool and cloth production towards the end of the 15th c. led to further workshops being set up, mainly in Lille, Oudenaarde, Ghent, Bruges and Leuven. However, after the decline of Paris as a centre of tapestry-making it was Brussels which became the new centre of the industry; between 1500 and 1700 the most magnificent tapestries in Europe were produced here – see the collection displayed in the Musées Royaux d'Art et d'Histoire in Brussels. Being a sophisticated court centre under the Dukes of Burgundy and the Spanish and Habsburg rulers, Brussels was also a city of art and culture and closely involved in the fields of painting and tapestry. These wall-hangings were made from a sketch, usually a pen and wash drawing, known as a "petit patron", which was provided by the artist and then used by the pattern-maker – who was often better-paid than the artist – in the form of a mirror image to provide a full-sized pattern for the embroiderers to work from. After Raphael had painted with his own hand the original sketches for the famous series of tapestries depicting the Acts of the Apostles this became the accepted practice, and many famous artists right up to and including Peter Paul Rubens made their own sketches.

Method of production

The actual embroidering was usually shared out between a number of people employed in central workshops. The width of the loom was sufficient to allow five, sometimes as many as seven weavers to sit side by side. However, because it was necessary constantly to change over to threads of a different colour, it was possible for each worker to produce only a few square inches in the course of a ten-hour day, and it took at least six months to complete a large tapestry, which accounts for the high prices charged. A large number of linen warp-threads were stretched across the loom – between 3000 and 4000 on a 5m/16½ft wide loom. When they were

18th century tapestry: "The Life of Jacob"

stretched vertically it was known as hautelisse work, and as basselisse work when they were horizontal. Products made on the "basselisse" looms were cheaper, as the work went faster because by stepping on the pedals the weaver could raise and lower the warp, whereas when working with the "hautelisse" loom opening up the warp had to be done with one hand, leaving only the other hand to work with. Somewhat differently from normal weaving, where the weft thread passes through the warp from edge to edge of the loom, when embroidering tapestry differently coloured weft threads of wool or silk – later of gold and silver as well – are led over and under as many warp threads as is necessary to produce the required shape and area in that colour. Frequently changing the colours of the threads used results in vertical slits appearing where the different colours meet, and these then have to be sewn together.

Among the major Brussels workshops was that of Pierre van Aelst, where the famous tapestries now in the Vatican and portraying the Acts of the Apostles were woven between 1516 and 1519 on instructions from Pope Leo X and to the designs by Raphael. The many commissions by King Charles V were executed mainly by the Brussels factory of Pieter Panne-maker. The most outstanding designer of patterns for tapestries from this period was the Brussels court painter Bernaert van Orley, who lived from about 1488 to 1541. His designs, based somewhat on those of Raphael, were marked by strict draughtsmanship, monumental configuration and the effect of depth and space – see Scenes from the Life of Jacob in the Brussels Musées Royaux d'Art et d'Histoire. The decorative sparkle of his tapestries was intensified by the use of gold and silver threads. In addition to van Orley, Pieter Coecke van Aelst and Jan Vermeyen were also well-known designers of tapestries. The increasing reputation of the workshops soon led to the tapestries being signed with the workshop's own trade mark, to avoid imitations.

Workshops

The themes and motifs used in the tapestries were many and varied. They included tales from olden times, mythological scenes, stories from the Old and New Testaments, allegories, tales of chivalry and hunting and scenes from everyday life. In addition to these where the picture told a story there were also purely decorative "green tapestries" or "tapis de verdures", with leaves and plants and later often whole landscapes. The best quality "green" tapestries were produced in Oudenaarde, where they can be seen today in the local museum. In France in the 16th c. lavish flower patterns "à mille fleurs" were very popular. The decorative borders around the wall-hangings were also very artistically done but sometimes over-decorated to the extent that they tend to divert one's attention from the main centre section.

Motifs

Tapestry-making in Flanders reached its peak during the Baroque period in the 17th c., and the demands of palaces, mansions and churches could scarcely be met. In the first half of the 17th c. Peter Paul Rubens was the top designer and gave the tapestries their distinctive artistic quality. The Decius-Mus Series in Vienna, the Eucharistic Cycle and the "Vatican Tapestries" constitute the epoch-making products of the Brussels manu-facturers. Ruben's successor David Teniers was soon to feel the effects of French competition.

Baroque heyday

In 1662 King Louis XIV established the first Royal Manufactory in Paris, with the aim of supplying locally the wall-hangings needed for his many castles and palaces, As it was set up in the workshop of the Gobelin family its products were given the name of gobelins, and soon the term was applied generally to all tapestries. The true gobelins were hand-embroidered, while the machine-woven Jacquard tapestries, named after their inventor J. M. Jacquard (1752–1834) were frequently regarded as non-genuine "gobelins". The factories in Beauvais, Aubusson and Paris led in the field of tapestry-making in the 18th c. until the French Revolution caused its rapid demise.

Literature

The border between the Dutch and French-speaking regions runs across Belgium. One consequence of this has been that since the Middle Ages two distinct literary traditions have evolved; that written in the Dutch language is described as Flemish literature, while French-worded books from the Walloon region form a completely separate branch of writing. As a result it is not possible simply to talk of Belgian national literature as such. Flemish authors have always compiled their writings against a background of Dutch tradition, in spite of attempts to distance themselves from it, because they have followed the history and traditions of the Flemings, while many of the French-speaking writers regarded themselves as forming part of the literature of France and frequently chose to live there, especially in Paris.

Flemish Literature

Middle Ages

Henry of Veldeke

Flemish literature first flowered in the 12th–14th centuries. Henry of Veldeke (c. 1140/50–c. 1210) can be said to have been the founder of the courtly romance novel with his poem "Eneïde". His minnelieder (courtly love songs) governed the styles of many of his contemporaries and those that came after him.

Jacob van Maerlant (c. 1230–c. 1288) distinguished himself in many literary spheres. His works included the oldest romance about the quest for the Holy Grail written in the Dutch language, a rhyming Bible, a history book and poems. Hadewijch, one of the few renowned female figures of medieval literature, was a mystic who expressed her visions in poetry and letters.

It was at this time too that the most important work to come from the central Netherlands, the romance of chivalry known as "Karel ende Elegast", was written, together with that famous medieval animal epic "Van den vos Reinaerde" (Reynard the Fox), which has continued to inspire writers up to the present day. Other highlights of the times were the mystical works of Jan van Ruusbroec (1293–1381) and the dialect folk play "Elckerlyc" by Petrus Dorlandus (1454–1507). The "rederijkerkamers" at the end of the Middle Ages formed a movement similar to the "meistersingers" in Germany.

19th Century

From the 16th to 19th c. Flemish literature tended to play second fiddle to the French. It was not until 1815, when the northern and southern provinces were united, that it received a fresh impetus. It was only then that – very belatedly – the linguistic transition from Middle to High Dutch reached completion. Jan Frans Willems and the movement he started, the "Vlaamse Beweging" campaigned strongly for Dutch to be the language of the Flemings.

Hendrik Conscience

The prime mover in the new beginning to Flemish literature was the Romantic writer Hendrik Conscience (1812–83), whose novel "De leeuw van Vlaanderen" (The Lion of Flanders), which took the Battle of the Spurs of 1302 as its subject, became a Flemish national epic. August Snieders (1825–1904) was also one of the major writers of his time.

Guido Gezelle

The outstanding personality of the second half of the 19th c. was the priest and lyricist Guido Gezelle (1830–99), who used a variety of Flemish dialects in his deeply pious anthologies. His pupil Albrecht Rodenbach (1856–80) was one of the founders of the Flemish popular theatre.

20th Century

Towards the end of the 19th c. a group of young writers came to the fore and issued a periodical with the name "Van nu en straks" (Here and Now) which deprecated Romanticism and traditional historical awareness. Among those who remained outside this new trend were August Vermeylen (1872–1945), Karel van de Woestijne (1878–1929) and Hermann Teirlinck (1879–1967). Stijn Streuvels, or Frank Lateur (1871–1969), a nephew of Gezelle, described in objective and committed terms the hard lives led by the Flemish peasants. Cyriel Buysse (1859–1932), who initially expressed his support for this same group, later changed direction and became the founder of Flemish Naturalism.

"Van nu en straks"

The events of the First World War led to the emergence of the "homeland novel", of which Felix Timmermans was one of the principal exponents.

Felix Timmermans

At the same time Expressionism found its way into Flemish literature. However, authors such as Paul André van Ostaijen (1896–1928), Victor J. Brunclair (1899–1944) and Wies Moens (1898–1982) restricted themselves almost entirely to lyric writings, producing hardly any Expressionist novels or stories.

Expressionism

However, it was not until after the Second World War that Belgium entered the international rankings, beginning with Maurice Roelants (1895–1966) with his psychological novels. Flemish Realism flourished through the works of Marcel Matthijs (1899–1964) and Johan Daisne (b. 1912). The latter was inspired by the works of Prandello and E. T. A. Hoffman and was the first to develop a specifically Flemish literary trend. Equally important was Maurice Gilliams (1900–82), the creator of Flemish Individualism. In his novels and stories Louis Paul Boon (1912–1979) takes the side of the socially deprived.
Through his novels "The Book of Alpha" (1963) and "Orclies Militaris" (1968) Ivo Michiels (b. 1923) strives for international recognition of Flemish "nouveau réalisme".
In more recent years, however, Michiels has been somewhat overshadowed by Hugo Claus (b. 1929), the successful Flemish contemporary writer. He uses almost exclusively material gleaned from his Belgian homeland and is not afraid to tackle delicate subjects such as that of collaborating with the German occupying forces during the Second World War. Claus writes drama, poems and novels, such as "Het verdriet van Belgie" (The Sorrow of Belgium).

After 1945

Hugo Claus

Lyric verse calls to mind such names as Hubert van Herreweghen (b. 1920), Jan Veulemans (b. 1928), Paul Snoek (b. 1933) and Pieter Aerts (b. 1928). Their work re-awakens the traditions established in the first half of this century.

Lyric verse

Literature in the French Language

For hundreds of years before the Kingdom of Belgium was founded literature of that country written in the French language formed a part of French literature in the widest sense. Chroniclers of the Hundred Years' War who have been remembered include Jean Froissart (1337–1400) and Philippe de Commynes (1447–1511), whose preserved memoirs from 1464–98 entitle him to be considered as the originator of modern French historical narrative.

Medieval chroniclers

Between the medieval chroniclers and the time when Belgium could claim to have established its own independent literary forms there was a large

Charles Joseph de Ligne

gap, which even Prince Charles Joseph de Ligne (1735–1814) could fill only to a small degree. The Prince, a field-marshal in the Austrian army, wrote letters, essays and polished cameos of the rulers of the time.

19th Century

Even after this two-language country became independent little changed initially; Belgian authors tended to maintain close contacts with France, especially Paris, and at first there was no sign of the emergence of any original and independent literary trends. Even a number of Flemish authors wrote in French.

Charles de Coster

However it was one of those very writers, Charles de Coster (1827–79; see Famous People) who achieved a breakthrough in 1867 with his novel "La légende de Thyl Ulenspiegel". Coster told the tale of Thyl Ulenspiegel (or Till Eulenspiegel) in his Flemish home town during the War of Liberation against the Spaniards. In powerful language studded with vivid

Thyl Ulenspiegel by Franz Mansereel

descriptive passages he describes the cruelty and pitilessness of the struggle, in which Thyl and his friend Lamme Goedzak are the symbols of the Flemings' desire for freedom and love of their homeland.

A contemporary of Coster was Camille Lemonnier (1844–1913), whose realistic novels bring out his love of nature. In works such as "Happe-Chair" he also wrote about the lives of Walloon mineworkers and could see help for them only in a socialist society. In addition to his poems, Georges Rodenbach (1855–98) also produced one novel, "Bruges morte" (Dead Bruges).

"La jeune Belgique"

The efforts to bring about an original literary form in the French language in Belgium led in 1881 to the launching of the publication called "La jeune Belgique" by Max Waller (1860–89). The best-known members of his circle included Albert Giraud (1860–1929). a lyric poet who lived and worked in Paris, and Emile Verhaeren (1855–1916).

"L'Art Moderne"

In 1881 also, in competition to the above, the magazine "L'Art Moderne", whose allegiance was to France, was founded.

"La Wallonie"

A further publication which took up a position between "La jeune Belgique" and "L'Art Moderne" was "La Wallonie"; founded in 1886, it allowed writers of both leanings to express their views. Those who contributed articles included Emile Verhaeren, Charles van Leberghe (1861–1907), Grégoire Le Roy (1862–1941) and Max Elskamp (1862–1931).

20th Century

Maurice Maeterlinck

The Symbolist Maurice Maeterlinck (1862–1949; see Famous People) was one of the outstanding Belgian literary figures of the 20th century. His lyrical works – such as "Serres Chaudes" and "Douze Chansons" – and his drama and philosophical essays won him the Noble Prize for Literature in 1911.

The Surrealist Henri Michaux (1899–1984), who settled in Paris in the 1920s, will be remembered for his absurd poems, novels and descriptions of his travels to imaginary countries.

Henri Michaux

The "Belgian School of the Fantastic" has gained considerable recognition outside Belgium, at least with its afficionados. Writers who belong to it include Jean Ray, Frans Hellens and Mobique Wayyeau.

"School of the Fantastic"

Great stage success was gained by Fernand Crommelynck (1885–1970) and, above all, by Michel de Ghelderode (1898–1962), who deliberately included repulsive and violent themes in his plays in order to provoke criticism and discussion.

Drama

The most popular of all French-speaking Belgian writers must be Georges Simenon (1903–89), but few people will know that he was born in Liège. That is largely due to the fact that his "Inspector Maigret" stories, which have appeared since 1930 and centre around this intelligent and instinctive detective, were set in Paris, where Simenon actually lived. He has left behind a vast range of books and films which have been translated into many languages (see Famous People).

Georges Simenon

Other important contemporary writers include Marcel Moreau, the politically-involved professor of literature and novelist Pierre Mertens, and Marguerite Yourcenar (1903–87; see Famous People).

Music

Dutch Music

Evolution in the field of music can be said to have commenced with the merging of most of the individual Dutch domains under the Dukes of Burgundy, to have enjoyed its heyday under Charles the Bald and Charles V, and to have come to an end shortly after the northern provinces (now the Netherlands) finally became separated from those in the south which make up Belgium as we know it today. As the original Netherlands comprised roughly the whole region now known as the Benelux states the music of the period is usually described under the general heading of Dutch music; thus this term should not be taken to mean only the work of Dutch composers in the narrower sense, but rather that of Flemish and Walloon masters together with those from the north of France.

About the year 1400 Dutch music developed a highly-perfected style centred on a choir of four or five voices. A form of counterpoint was created in which the individual registers sang the same melody in harmony.

Characteristics

The earliest epoch of Netherlands' music was closely linked with the court of the 15th c. Dukes of Burgundy, Philip the Good and Charles the Bald. The major composers of that era were Johannes Ciconia (c. 1335–1411), who was employed at the courts of Venice and Padua, among others, and Guillaume Dufay (1400–74), who for a time also went to Italy and whose further elaboration of 14th c. motets and ballads led to the first apotheosis of Dutch music. Gilles Binchois (c. 1400–60), composer at the Burgundian court in Dijon, should also be mentioned.

Court music

Music

Towards the end of the 15th c. it was the famous Cambrai and Antwerp schools (the Franco-Flemish school) which set the tone. Under the latter's guidance the music of the Netherlands was able to hold its own against that of England and to compete on equal terms with that composed by almost all the European master musicians. It maintained this dominant role until the end of the 16th c. The motets, secular songs and masses sung in harmony, by such composers as Pierre de la Rue, Nicolas Gombert, Johannes Ockeghem, Josquin Desprez, Adriaan Willaert, Henri Isaak and Clemens non Papa became widely known, especially after the invention of printed music in the early 16th c. A famous theoretician of his age was Johannes Tinctoris (*c.* 1435–1511).

In the later periods of Dutch music names such as Philippe de Monte, Jacob der Kerle and, in particular, Orlando di Lasso from Mons all became known outside the Netherlands. Di Lasso (actually Roland de Lassus, b. *c.* 1532), together with Giovanni Palestrina, is the most respected composer of the 16th c. For a long time he worked in Germany and from 1560 until his death in 1594 was the leader of the court orchestra in Munich.

The work of Jan Pieter Sweelinck (1562–1622) clearly showed the gradual move that was taking place away from the principle of Dutch counterpoint. Although he also was a very important figure in the field of 17th c. organ music he was to prove the last of the great Dutch musicians, and towards the end of the 17th c. the Dutch school, which until then had been universal and European in concept, fell into decline. Various external trends and influences were imported, differing according to region; the composers of the Netherlands increasingly became imitators, after centuries spent improving and developing their own styles.

Walloon Composers

French classical music had a profound influence on the Walloon composers who moved to Paris in increasing numbers, while most of those in what are now the Flemish and Dutch regions stayed at home, with the result that they remained unaffected by the trends sweeping the rest of Europe and so became largely forgotten. It was not until the early 20th c. that the Flemings finally emerged from their long period of lethargy.

Among the Walloon composers from the present-day Belgium who were able to make their mark in Paris in the 18th c. were Jean-Noël Hamal (oratorio "In Exitu Israel"), Jean-Baptiste Lœillet, Jean-François Gossec ("Messe des Morts"), Pierre van Maldere and André Ernest Modeste Grétry (1742–1813), one of the founders of the French Opéra Comique, who wrote "Zemire et Azor", "Richard Cœur de Lion" and "Céphale et Procis".

In the 19th c. it was only César Franck, a native of Liège (1822–90; see Famous People), who gained international recognition. After adopting French citizenship and settling in Paris, where he became a celebrated organ teacher, he composed his extremely unconventional Symphony in D minor, a number of symphonic poems, an oratorio, a violin sonata and numerous pieces for the organ. Franck successfully strove to revise the French style to accord with German taste, which he taught to his pupils. Among the most talented of these were the Frenchman Vincent d'Indy and the Belgian Guillaume Lekeu, but the latter unfortunately died young before his talents could be developed to the full. He left behind a beautiful violin sonata and a fine adagio for strings.

Charles de Bériot (1802–70) and Henri Vieuxtemps (1820–81) founded the Belgian School of Violin Music which has remained famous to this day. Both composed several virtuoso violin concertos, of which the 4th and 5th by Vieuxtemps are still played quite often, especially in French-speaking and Anglo-Saxon countries. Eugène Ysaye (1858–1931), one of the greatest violin virtuosos of all time, continued this tradition into the 20th c. As a composer his six sonatas for solo violin were well received. An important music teacher of the time was Mathieu Crickboom, whose piano-teaching is still recognised as having been of the best.

20th Century

The Belgian Romantic Benoît (1834–1901) played an important part in his country's music in the years leading up to the 20th c., producing his own unique brand of Flemish music. His works – often popular and folksy, always full of effect and reflecting the national character – included "De Pacificatie van Gent" and "Rubenscantate". At the same time, some of his compositions anticipated new musical trends.

Peter Benoît

In the early 20th c. Paul Gilson (1865–1942) dominated the Belgian music scene. His many splendidly orchestrated symphonic works include a highly original suite entitled "La Mer". Gilson can be regarded as the founder of the Brabant-Flemish School, which numbered among its members Auguste de Boeck, Gaston Brenta and Marcel Poot (b. 1901). The latter is without doubt the most popular Belgian composer of the 20th c. His exclusively tonal music combines colour, rhythm and melody into a cavalcade which reflects the Belgian's predeliction for folk-lore, mass processions, festivals and religious celebrations. Poot's adherents were also known as "Synthesists".

Brabant-Flemish School

The New Antwerp School – much less subject to Latin influences than the Brabant-Flemish School and with strong Romantic characteristics – numbered among its members Marinus de Jong, Karel Candael, Lodewijk Mortelmans, Flor Alpaerts and the famous organist and composer Flor Peeters.

New Antwerp School

Examples of the Liège School are César Franck and Vincent D'Indy, as well as Gabriel Fauré and Gabriel Pierné. Joseph Jomgen, who wrote his sinfonia concertante for organ and orchestra in 1928, and his brother Léon Jongen are the most important adherents of this school. Scarcely known outside Belgium are such composers as Armand Marsick, Jean Rogister and Albert Dupuis.

Liège School

A composer who does not fit into any particular category is René Bernier (b. 1905) whose music displays Mediterranean spirit, elegance and clarity.

René Bernier

Belgium has produced a number of fine interpreters of classical music, one of the best-known being the violinist Arthur Grumiaux (1921–86). The Théâtre Royal de la Monnaie opera house in Brussels has an international reputation and is particulary famous for its "Ballet of the 20th Century" founded by Maurice Béjart.
The Flanders Festival, which is held mainly in Ghent and Bruges, is one of the major European music festivals. One of the most demanding competitions held anywhere in Europe is the "Concours Reine Elisabeth", which takes place every two years and alternates between violin and piano. Previous prizewinners include David Oistrach, Malcolm Frager, Vladimir Ashkenazy and Gidon Kremer.

The music scene today

Belgium has not had much to offer in the field of popular music. However, the singer of satirical songs Jacques Brel (1928–78; see Famous People) did make a considerable contribution. The Belgian Salvatore Adamo, who was born in Italy, and the female singer Tonia are also quite well-known abroad as pop-singers. In the world of jazz the guitarist and harmonica

Popular music Jacques Brel

virtuoso Jean "Toots" Thielemans (b. 1928) has made a name for himself as an interpreter of swing, a composer and arranger.

Folk music

Belgian folk music has no particularly distinctive style. In addition to the folk songs, most of which Belgium shares with France and the Netherlands, Wallonia especially has a number of dances which show a strong French influence both in their movements and in the music which accompanies them. The latter is usually characterised by drums and pipes as well as brass bands which play music that is somewhat shrill, loud and high-pitched. In Flanders folk-dancing is often accompanied by the Flemish spinet, fiddle, flute and accordion.

Films

"There is Belgian painting and Belgian literature which stays Belgian even though written in the French language. There are the varied forms of Belgian life embracing Antwerp as well as Charleroi, the fishermen of Ostend as well as the forests of the Ardennes; the country has its unique landscape and its own customs ... Surely there is enough there to form the basis of a good film?" complained Georges Simenon in 1940. In fact little has changed since then, and Belgium is still the poor man of Europe as far as films are concerned.

At best the pre-war Belgian film industry could boast a few notable documentaries produced by such directors as Henri Storck and Charles Dekeukerleire and which dealt mainly with historical and cultural subjects. The best-known film from that era was made by a Dutchman, Joris Ivens, in co-operation with Storck; it was "Misère au Borinage" (1934), which took as its theme the strikes and living conditions then prevailing in the coal-mining region of southern Belgium and was the prototype of the contentious documentary we know today. During the German occupation in the Second World War Storck again emerged as writer, director and cameraman in the film "Symphonie Paysanne", a study of peasant life over the years. The feature films of this period, mainly in Flemish, were undistinguished.

Little has emerged in the post-war years either. Worthy of mention are the directors André Delvaux, the only one to encourage Marguerite Yourcenar to make one of her works, "L'Œuvre au Noir", into a film, and also the younger Chantal Akerman and Marion Hänsel.

Jacques Feyder

While the Belgian film industry has developed very modestly indeed many native Belgian film-makers have tried their luck in France. Outstanding among these was Jacques Feyder, who before his death in 1948 made numerous films and had considerable success with "La Kermesse Héroïque" (1935). This film, for which the Belgian Charles Spaak wrote the script, is set in Flanders at the time of the War of Liberation against the Spaniards and in a congenial way transposes the metaphorical language of Flemish masters into the form of a film.

Comics

Belgium the
Land of Comics

In no other European country – with the possible exception of France – are comics (*bandes dessinées* in French) so popular nor is there such a variety of strip cartoons as in Belgium.

The reasons for this are many. For one thing, Belgium can look back on a long tradition of comic strips which are quite independent of those produced in the "classical" land of comics, the USA. In 1929 appeared the first "Adventures of Tin Tin", undoubtedly the most famous comic figure to come out of Belgium, which soon enjoyed great success and was able to pick up the threads after the war without any trouble. Back in 1946 Raymond Leblanc produced "Tin Tin", a magazine for young people which, under its revised title of "Hello B. D." has remained to this day Belgium's most successful comic publication. Not only does it include comic strips and serials but it also has an excellent editorial section and gives many young artists their first chance of getting something published. Another important factor is the close co-operation which has already developed between publishers of comics and the other media. As well as appearing in newspapers and cheap paperbacks comic strips have been published as "real" books in album form. Many of the adventures of Tin Tin have been produced as animated cartoons or feature films, and the stories centred around the "Schtroumpfs" (The Smurfs), "Lucky Luke" or "Spirou" have been seen in cinemas and on television. Comics have become an accepted feature of Belgian life.

Belgium's chief publishers of comics today are Casterman in Tournai ("Tin Tin"), Dupuis in Charleroi ("Les Schtroumpfs", "Spirou and Fantasio") and Lombard in Brussels ("Cubitus", "Ric Hochet"). — Publishers

"Tin Tin" is arguably the most successful of all European comic series. Its creator was Georges Remi, born in Brussels in 1907, who inverted his initials and used them phonetically to form his pseudonym "Hergé". The first Tin Tin story, "Tin Tin in the Land of the Soviets", appeared as a serial in 1929 in the children's supplement "Petit XXième" to the daily newspaper "Le Vingtième Siècle". The hero of the stories is the young and cool-thinking reporter Tin Tin with the unusual blond hair-style who, accompanied by his fox-terrier Milou and assisted by the grumpy Captain Haddock, has adventures all over the world and even on the moon. Apart from the tension and excitement the charm of the stories lies in the simple caricaturised portrayal of the main characters and the detailed background and surroundings, especially the technical equipment, vehicles and buildings. Tin Tin is incredibly popular; there are Tin Tin figures, records, T-shirts, two theatrical plays, feature films and animated cartoons. In 1985 the Belgian astronaut Patrick Boudry even took a replica of his hero with him into space on board an American space-craft and held it up in front of the camera. In addition to "Tin Tin" Hergé also drew the "Jo et Zette" and "Quick et Fluppke" comic strips. — "Tin Tin"

"Spirou" is the name of a hotel page boy or bellhop and was invented by "Bob Vel" (Robert Velter), although he has been drawn by André Franquin since 1946. Together with his friends, the reporter Fantasio and the scientist Comte de Champignac, Spirou enjoys numerous adventures with a humorous side to them. Our heroes are actively supported by Kokomiko, the legendary marsupial from the jungles of South America, an ape-like creature with the skin of a leopard and an incredibly long tail who possesses unbounded strength. As in the case of Tin Tin, Spirou has been the subject of a comic paper of the same name which is still published. In the series the figure of Gaston Lagaffe also comes to life after starting out as a doodle drawn by Franquin, the office junior in the newspaper office where Fantasio works. Gaston thinks of everything except work and causes havoc especially when Monsieur de Mesmaeker is trying to complete important business deals which Gaston inevitably, if unintentionally, sabotages. — "Spirou and Fantasio"

Since 1952 Pierre Culliford has been drawing for the "Spirou" magazine the adventures of the knight "Johan" and his squire "Pirlouit". In 1958 small blue dwarfs with bulbous noses, white tights and white pointed caps were also introduced; they lived in toadstool houses and spoke "Smurfish" – in the anglicised version the series was known as "The Smurfs". They soon became more popular than the knight and plastic replicas sold like hot cakes and held pride of place in most children's bedrooms. — "Les Schtroumpfs" (The Smurfs)

"Lucky Luke"

The Wild West comic strip about the cool cowboy "Lucky Luke", who was faster on the draw than his own shadow, also originated in Belgium. He was "born" in 1947, the brainchild of Maurice de Bevere ("Morris"). After 1959 René Goscinny (also the writer of "Asterix"), who died in 1977, wrote the stories about the cowboy who, accompanied by his faithful horse Jolly Jumper, tangled with such people as the Dalton Brothers and Calamity Jane, and even rode for the Belgian mail service.

Adventure comics

As well as the more or less funny comic strips there are a large number of adventure series of various kinds, all drawn in a most realistic way. Most were conceived in the 1950s and 1960s and have remained successful ever since. These "classics" include stories about such figures as the reporter and detective "Ric Hochet" by Gilbert Gascard, the racing-cyclist "Michel Vaillant" (Mike Valiant) by Jean Graton and the agent "Bruno Brazil" by "William Vance (William van Cutsem), as well as the science fiction series "Luc Orient" by Eddy Paape. One of the best artists in this field is "Hermann" (Hermann Huppen) with the series "Bernard Prince", "Jugurtha" and "Comanche". Edgar P. Jacobs ("Blake and Mortimer"), Jacques Martin ("L. Frank") and Bob de Moor ("Barelli"), together with Hergé, can be considered to be the founders of the Brussels comic tradition.

Younger artists

A new star in the Belgian comic firmament is François Walthéry with a series about a little boy called "Nickel" and his humorous adventure-strip about the stewardess "Natasha". Benoît Sokal ("Canardo"), Eric Warnauts and Guy Raives ("Lou Cale", "Congo 40") are also making a name for themselves.

Brussels Comic Museum

As comics are so many and so popular it will come as no surprise to learn that Brussels has the largest Comic Museum in the world. It is housed in a former department store designed by Victor Horta and owns 25,000 comics and numerous original printing plates of 650 Belgian artists (see Practical Information, Museums).

Béguinages (Begijnhofen)

Béguines

Béguinages, to give them their French form, or begijnhofen in Flemish, a form of medieval closed community, can still be found in some old Flemish towns. They represent a small "town within a town", in which pious women lived either as groups in large houses or alone in small ones. Many of the buildings were destroyed in the iconoclasm or during the struggles for liberation during the 16th c., but were rebuilt in the 17th c. Today a few still exist. The women do not take lifelong vows but do promise to obey the rules of the community; few feel obliged to leave. The "béguines" are allowed out alone by day but must return to the béguinage in the evening. Some béguinages are now occupied by nuns, usually of the Benedictine order.

History

These communities were started in the late 12th c. and flourished in the 13th and 14th c. in the Netherlands, France and Germany. They began as Catholic lay movements, free associations of female workers who met initially to discuss economic and religious matters, but who later decided that their purpose in life was to minister to the poor, sick and old. These communities became subjected to strict discipline through the church and were housed in closed complexes with a chapel or church, were later made into parishes and finally into "béguinages". Because of their allegiance to the church they escaped condemnation by Pope Clemens V in 1311,

In Dendermonde béguinage

whereas similar communities in, for example, Germany were affected by that punitive decree. The male equivalent of the béguines were the beghards, associations who looked after the sick.

The béguinage is headed by a Mother Superior nominated by the bishop; she is known as the "Grootjuffrouw" or "Grande Dame". The sisters live in convents at first and do communal work, such as lace-making and sewing. After six years they are allowed to move into little cottages containing two or four flatlets. Two or three times a day they all congregate for mass. While at work they wear their traditional greyish-brown habit, together with the black Flemish hooded cloak – the faille or falie – when they go out.

Daily life

Today very few béguines still live in Belgium; only the community of St-Amandsberg near Ghent is still of some importance. The sober and isolated life holds few attractions for young ladies today. The béguinages – perhaps rented to old people or to students as in Leuven – are now favourite tourist attractions. In a few, like that in Kortrijk (Courtrai), some of the houses have been made into museums illustrating the life of the béguines. The most attractive places are to be found in Kortrijk (Courtrai), Bruges, Ghent, Diest, Oudenaarde, Leuven, Lier and Dendermonde.

Béguinages today

Carillon

Everywhere in Belgium can be heard the sound of the carillon, often ringing out across the market-square every quarter of an hour. This custom originated from the clocks which sounded the hour from church towers or belfries and which first appeared in Belgium in 1370. At first it was just a simple bell rung by hand, but as time went by the number of bells was increased so that melodies could be played; with the introduction of the keyboard and pedals in the 16th c. these became more and more complicated and ended in the chimes of the bells being controlled by clockwork. The chimes (Flemish beiaard, French carillon) rung in Belgian towns usually have between 45 and 50 bells and can also be played by hand. Some beautiful chimes can be heard in Antwerp, Bruges, Mechelen, Brussels, Ghent, Hasselt, Hoogstraten, Leuven, Kortrijk (Courtrai), Oudenaarde, Ostend and Tournai.

Mechelen Carillon school

Bell-ringers learn their art in Mechelen in the province of Antwerp. There can be found the only "carillon school" in the world, founded in 1922 and named after the master bell-ringer from Mechelen, Jef Denyn. The school also has a museum.

Folklore

Living traditions

Belgium is steeped in living folklore which finds expression through an almost incredible list of public festivals, processions and fairs, some of them on a very large scale and nearly always boisterous and full of festive spirit. Giants are an important part of many processions and parades. These grand events, organised by various companies or clubs, are held mostly on religious feast-days or historical anniversaries spread throughout the year. In between these many towns hold smaller celebrations at, for instance, race-tracks or when the maypole is erected. Very popular indeed are the "Kermesses aux Boudins", at which many publicans invite their regulars to a huge meal of sausages with plenty of free beer.

Dates of events

The dates of the most important festivals will be found under "Events" in the Practical Information section of this book.

Carnival

The first big festival of the year is the Carnival (Carnaval), which is celebrated in the Walloon region in particular in a most original fashion. The earliest procession is held in January in Ronse south of Oudenaarde, when thousands of folk dressed in costume celebrate "Fools' Monday" on the first Monday after Epiphany.

Binche

The traditional home of carnival is Binche, between Charleroi and Mons, with its characteristic "gilles". This tradition, going back to the 14th c., literally takes over the town for four whole days and reaches its peak on "Mardi Gras" (Shrove Tuesday), when the "Gilles" make an appearance dressed in their gloriously colourful costumes decorated with twelve heraldic lions, bright ribbons, pointed toes and bells hanging from their belts. To the rhythm of drums and brass bands they dance all day and night, swing bundles of birch-twigs to frighten away evil spirits and throw oranges to (or at!) the onlookers. On their heads they wear eight giant white ostrich-plumes to the final dance held in the market-place. At the end of this dance, in which everybody joins, a huge fire is lit and the "Gilles" dance through the streets, where they are only allowed to drink champagne. As long as four weeks before the carnival processions and dancers can be seen practising for the big day, these rehearsals being known as the "répétitions de batteries".

Malmédy

The Malmédy Festival, known as "Cwarmê", is equally famous. On the Saturday the "Trouv'Lê" (ladle or scoop) takes over the town. On the Sunday the "bânes corantes" (roving bands) roam the streets and frolic with passers-by, on the Monday plays are performed based on events which occurred locally during the past year, and finally on the Tuesday the "haguètes", the symbolic carnival figures, are burned. The "haguètes" are the much-feared masks worn by the "bânes corantes", together with ostrich-plumes, horns on their heads, a cowl and the Austrian double eagle on their backs. They perform a huge "conga" through the streets and pull

The "Gilles" are abroad . . .   *. . . in Binche*

unwilling onlookers into the line with them. Other masks are the "sotê", a goblin with a big top-hat reaching down to the shoulders, the "vèheû" (skunk), which hits people on the head with an inflated pig's bladder, as well as the "sâvadje" (savage).

Eupen is also renowned for its carnival, with a Carnival Prince and a Council of Eleven.

Eupen

In the Flemish region of the country the Aalst Carnival attracts thousands of spectators every year. Carnival Sunday is the day of the Giants, the Monday sees the Throwing of the Onions, and on the Tuesday the "Vuil Jeannetten" ("dirty aunts") parade through the streets in their curious old costumes.

Aalst

Festivals during Lent

In Belgium Ash Wednesday is not the end of things by any means. During Lent a number of carnivals and events are held. For example, on the Saturday following Shrove Tuesday (Mardi Gras) the masked ball of the "Rat Mort" (dead rat) is held in Ostend. Mid-Lent processions take place in Hasselt, Tilff, Stavelot and Fosses.

Spectacular festivals

The traditional figure seen in Stavelot is the "Blanc Moussis", wearing a long-nosed mask and a white habit who gets up to all sorts of pranks.

Stavelot

In Fosses can be seen the "Chinels" (an abbreviation of Polichinelle or Pulcinella), who dance like living dolls.

Fosses

At the end of February Geraardsbergen holds its curious "Cracknel Festival" (Krakelingenworp). A procession of several hundred people climbs the Oudenberg and then throws down to the spectators some 8000 "cracknels" or rusks. Finally the town dignitaries have to drink down small live fish from a silver beaker. In the evening the "Tonnekenbrand" is lit in a barrel.

Geraardsbergen

Processions

Holy Week	Belgium being almost totally Roman Catholic, processions play an important role, especially in Holy Week, although not all of them need be taken too seriously. The best-known of the Easter processions take place in Rupelmonde near Antwerp on Maundy Thursday, in Hakendover on Easter Monday and in Veurne during the night of Maundy Thursday to Good Friday.
Processions worth seeing Veurne	Veurne offers two impressive processions – one on the Sunday preceding May 3rd, and the famous Procession of the Penitents on the last Sunday in July. Praying and hidden under dark hoods, the penitents walk carrying a Cross weighing 40kg/70lb. Reminiscent of Spain, this procession does in fact date from the time when Spain ruled the Netherlands.
Lessines	Also worth seeing is the Procession of the Penitents in Lessines on Good Friday. The disguised and cloaked figures carry torches in their hands, thus giving the whole a ghostly atmosphere.
Bruges	The Ascension Day Procession of the Holy Blood at Bruges is world-famous. Numerous pedestrians and cars pass through the festively decorated town, depicting the Biblical story from the Fall of Man to the Redemption. Members of the clergy bear a reliquary said to contain drops of the Blood of Christ thought to have been given to Theodoric of Alsace, Count of Flanders, by the patriarchy of Jerusalem in 1150.
Mons	On Trinity Sunday in Mons the reliquary of St Waltraud is carried through the streets in the "Procession of the Golden Carriage". It ends with St George killing the green dragon – a symbol of the victory of Good over Evil.
Military processions	Typical of the region between Sambre and Meuse are the Military Processions, a tradition dating back to the time when the valuable holy relics had to be defended against robbers. The marchers dress in uniform, some dating from the time of Napoleon, and parade through the town in strict order, firing their arms. Among the better-known military processions are those held in Gerpinnes near Charleroi on Whit Monday and in Jumet around July 20th.
Pilgrimages	Well-known places of pilgrimage include Halle, Hakendover, Scherpenheuvel, St-Hubert and Nivelles.
St Martin	Children in particular enjoy celebrating the Feast of St Martin in November, when they receive gifts. This tradition lives on in a number of places, including Eupen, Genk, Retie and Visé.

Secular Festivals

Brussels	The most famous non-religious celebration is undoubtedly the "Ommegang", the origin of which dates back to processions held in the Middle Ages seeking protection against plagues of all kinds. The present "Ommegang" copies that held on July 2nd 1549 in the presence of Charles V. On the first Thursday in July over 2000 people wearing costume and carrying some 300 flags, representatives of ancient trade guilds, drummers and numerous vehicles file past characters representing the imperial family on the Grand'Place.
Waterloo	Every year, on its anniversary, the Battle of Waterloo is re-enacted in historical costume on the actual battlefield. The "armies" are made up of groups from various countries.
Ath	At the end of August the "Kermis of the Giants" ("ducasse") is held in Ath. Figures up to 4m/13ft tall parade through the town; they represent Goliath, the four children of Haimon with the horse Bayard, Samson, Ambiorix and "Mam'selle Victoire", who personifies the town. The highlight is the fight

Cat festival in Ypres

between David and Goliath. The festival ends with the wedding of Goliath ("Monsieur et Madame Gouyasse").

The Bruges "Procession of the Golden Tree" is held only every five years; the next time will be in 1995. It commemorates the glittering times of Burgundian rule. **Bruges**

The Festival of the Cats in Ypres is unique. In the Middle Ages cats were often considered to be the Devil incarnate. Count Baudouin III decided to put a stop to this superstition and ordered that all existing cats were to be thrown down from the tower of the town hall in order to prove that they were merely mortal animals. This cruel game was still played right up to the early 19th c. Today only soft toys are thrown down. There is also a large procession portraying the role played by the cat in culture and folklore. **Ypres (Ieper)**

The Flemings remember their famous predecessors in many ways. As an example, the Beer Festival held in Oudenaarde in June is in memory of the painter Adriaan Brouwer (1605–38). **Oudenaarde**

Every two years in Wingene the good people of the town remember the artist Pieter Bruegel the Elder by acting out some of his paintings. **Wingene**

Autumn in Belgium is the time of thanksgiving for beer, hops and harvests. In the little town of Wieze near Aalst the "Wieze Oktoberfeesten" have become famous. In a giant marquee holding up to 10,000 people beer from the Wieze brewery flows like water. Entertainment is provided by three bands, usually Bavarian, with a Flemish compère. **Wieze**

Belgium in Quotations

Edmund Burke
(1729–97)

A country belonging to our Allies, and indeed a great deal more, which they who can speak no language but the new French, choose to call Belgium, but which neither by that name, nor with any certain bounds or limits is to be found in any Map . . . These new Appelations have been adopted in order to support the new System of giving to modern France the limits of ancient Gaul.
Letter to French Laurence, March 1st 1797

Lord Byron
(1788–1824)

Imagine to yourself a succession of avenues with a Dutch spire at the end of each – and you see the road; – an accompaniment of highly cultivated farms on each side intersected with small canals or ditches – and sprinkled with very neat and clean cottages – a village every two miles – and you see the country – not a rise from Ostend to Antwerp – a molehill would make the inhabitants think that the Alps had come here on a visit – it is a perpetuity of plain & an eternity of pavement (on the road) but it is a country of great apparent comfort – and a singular though tame beauty.
Letter to Augusta Leigh, May 1st 1816

Sydney Smith
(1771–1845)

Fine cities – admirable architects, far exceeding ours, both in their old and new buildings – good bakers – very ugly – stink of tobacco – horses all fat – soldiers little – inns dirty and very expensive; – better modern painters than we are . . .
I went to the Belgic Parliament. There was a pound short in the public accounts, and they were speaking about it . . .
All the great cities of Flanders are underpeopled.
Letter to Sir George Philips, May 20th 1837

Antwerp

James Howell
(1593–1666)

This goodly ancient City methinks looks like a disconsolate Widow, or rather some super-annuated Virgin, that hath lost her Lover, being almost quite bereft of that flourishing Commerce wherewith before the falling off the rest of the Provinces from Spain she abounded to the envy of all other Cities and Marts of Europe. There are few Places this side the Alps better built and so well streeted as this; and none at all so well girt with Bastions and Ramparts, which in some place are so spacious that they usually take the Air in Coaches upon the very Walls, which are beautified with divers rows of Trees and pleasant Walks. The Citadel here, tho' it be an addition to the stateliness and strength of the Town, yet it serves as a shrewd Curb unto her; which makes her chomp upon the Bit, and foam sometimes with anger, but she cannot help it.
Letter to Sir James Crofts, July 5th 1645

John Evelyn
(1620–1706)

View from the spire of the Vrou-Kirke
It is a very venerable fabrique, built after the Gotik manner, and especially the Tower, which is in truth of an excessive height: This I ascended, that I might the better take a view of the Country about it, which happning on a day when the sunn shone exceedingly hot, and darted the rayes without any interruption, afforded so bright a reflection to us who were above, and had a full prospect of both the Land and Water about it, that I was much confirm'd in my opinion of the Moones being of some such substance as this earthly Globe consists of; perceiving all the subjacent Country (at so smale an horizontal distance) to repercusse such a light as I could hardly looke against; save where the River and other large water within our View appeared of a more darke & uniforme Colour, resembling those spotts in

the Moone, attributed to the seas there &c according to our new Philosophy
& the Phaenomenas by optical Glasses.
Diary, October 4th 1641

Were any man to ask my advice upon the subject of retirement, I should tell
him: By all means repair to Antwerp. No village amongst the Alps, or
hermitage upon Mount Lebanon is less disturbed: you may pass your days
in this great city without being the least conscious of its sixty thousand
inhabitants, unless you visit the churches.
Dreams, Waking Thoughts and Incidents, 1783

William Beckford
(1760–1844)

Bruges (Brugge)

When you have seen what this town offers to the notice of a stranger, you
will be, as I was, glad to quit it, for the inhabitants (quite the reverse of their
neighbours the French) are all shut up within their houses, and a stranger is
apt at Bruges, to think himself in a city just depopulated by the plague.
A Journey through the Austrian Netherlands, 1786

Philip Thicknesse
(1720–92)

One might fancy that as the city had been built so it had remained. . . . The
general effect upon the mind can never be forgotten. The race of the Great
and Powerful by whom the noble public edifices were raised has passed
away, yet the attire, the staid motions and demeanour of the present
inhabitants are accordant with the stateliness of former ages; and the City
remains as if self-sustained – no new houses to be seen, no repairs going
on! you might fancy that the sound of the Builder's hammer was never
heard in these days!
Journal, July 14th 1820

Dorothy
Wordsworth
(1771–1855)

In Brugès town is many a street
Whence busy life hath fled;
Where, without hurry, noiseless feet
The grass-grown pavement tread
There heard we, halting in the shade
Flung from a Convent-tower,
A harp that tuneful prelude made
To a voice of thrilling power
Incident at Bruges, 1828

William
Wordsworth
(1770–1850)

In the market-place of Bruges stands the Belfry old and brown;
Thrice consumed and thrive rebuilt, still it watches o'er the town.

As the summer morn was breaking, on that lofty tower I stood,
And the world threw off the darkness, like the weeds of widowhood.

Thick with towns and hamlets studded, and with streams and vapors gray
Like a shield embossed with silver, round and vast the landscape lay.

At my feet the city slumbered. From its chimneys, here and there,
Wreaths of snow-white smoke ascending, vanished ghost-like into air.

Not a sound rose from the city at that early morning hour,
But I heard a heart of iron beating in that ancient tower. . . .

Visions of the day departed, snowy phantoms filled my brain;
They who live in history only seemed to walk the earth again.
The Belfry of Bruges, 1845

Henry Wadsworth
Longfellow
(1807–82)

Belgium in Quotations

Brussels

William Makepeace Thackeray (1811–63)

My impressions of this city are certainly anything but respectful. It has an absurd kind of Lilliput look with it. There are soldiers, just as in Paris, better dressed, and doing a vast deal of drumming and bustle; and yet, somehow, far from being frightened at them, I feel inclined to laugh in their faces. There are little Ministers, who work at their little bureaux; and to read the journals, how fierce they are! A great thundering Times could hardly talk more big . . . Think what a comfort it would be to belong to a little state like this; not to abuse their privilege, but philosophicaly to use it. If I were a Belgian I would not care one single fig about politics. I would not read thundering leading articles. I would not have an opinion. What is the use of an opinion here? Happy fellows! do not the French, the English and the Prussians spare them the trouble of thinking, and make all their opinions for them. Think of living in a country, free, easy, respectable, wealthy, and with the nuisance of talking politics removed from out of it. All this might the Belgians have, and a part do they enjoy, but not the best part: no, these people will be brawling and by the ears, and parties run as high here as at Stoke Pogis or Little Pedlington.

The Parc
Numbers of statues decorate the place, the very worst I ever saw. These Cupids must have been erected in the time of the Dutch dynasty, as I judge from the immense posterior developments.
From Richmond to Brussels, May 1844

Robert Louis Stevenson (1850–94)

If any person wants to be happy I should advise the Parc. You sit drinking iced drinks and smoking penny cigars under great old trees. The band place, covered walks, etc. are all lit up. And you can't fancy how beautiful was the contrast of the great masses of lamplit foliage and the dark sapphire night sky, with just one blue star set overhead in the middle of the largest patch. In the dark walks, too, there are crowds of people whose faces you cannot see, and here and there a colossal white statue at the corner of an alley that gives the place a nice artificial, eighteenth century sentiment. There was a good deal of summer lightning blinking overhead, and the black avenues and white statues lean out every minute into short-lived distinctness.
Letter to his Mother, July 25th 1872

Ghent

John Evelyn

Ghendt is an extravagant Citty of so vast a Circumference, that it is reported to be no lesse than 7 leagues in compasse; but there is not an halfe part of it now built; much of it remaining in the feilds and desolate pastures, even within the Wales, which had marvailous strong Gates towards the West, and two faire Churches in one of which I heard a Sermon . . . The Ley and Scheld, meeting in this vast Citty divide it into 26 Hands which are united together by many bridges somewhat resembling Venice.

William Beckford

To one so far gone in the poetic antiquity, Ghent is not the most likely place to recall his attention; and I know nothing more about it, than that it is a large, ill-paved dismal-looking city, with a decent proportion of convents and chapels stuffed with monuments, brazen gates, and glittering marbles.
Dreams, Waking Thoughts and Incidents, 1783

Dorothy Wordsworth

The buildings, streets and squares, all are picturesque; the houses green, blue, pink, yellow, with richest ornaments still varying. Strange it is that so many and such strongly contrasted colours should compose an undiscordant whole.
Journal, July 14th 1820

Ghent has, I believe, been called a vulgar Venice. It contains dirty canals and old houses that must satisfy the most eager antiquary, though the buildings are not in quite so good preservation as others that may be seen in the Netherlands. The commercial bustle of the place seems considerable, and it contains more beershops than any city I ever saw.
Little Travels and Roadside Sketches, October 1844

William
Makepeace
Thackeray

Liège

Near Liège, the gradient being steep, we are pulled up to Hautpré by a rope; and soon coming to the top, have a grand view of the Belgian Birmingham, nearly as well supplied with tall chimnies, but more countryfied and much prettier. Liège is quite an urbs in rure, – houses and manaufactories dotted about among trees and hills, and winding streams, with turreted and spired and cupola'd churches here and there, picturesque enough. Within, however, most of the streets are narrow wind-about and roughly trottoired – dirty withal and smelly; and the rapid Meuse, from thunder-showers I suppose, a river of mud.
Diary of Everybody's Tour, 1856

Martin Farquhar
Tupper
(1810–89)

Spa

The town of Spa is situated in a stoney, mountainous country, on the banks of what in Summer is a murmuring stream, but in Winter is sometimes a rapid river. The air is good, and the environs, in general are pleasant, though rude, and uncultivated, having much the appearance of a part of the globe which has been broken up by earthquakes, or some violent convulsions of Nature. . . .
Having mentioned that the Pohoun is the spring from which the bottled Spa-water is taken, it may be necessary to inform you that there are near Spa, several other mineral springs, viz. the Geronstere, and about two miles from Spa, the Sauveniere and the Tonnelet, somewhat nearer; and all these waters are used by those who are within the reach of them. I cannot pretend to tell you what the healing powers of the last mentioned springs are; but I suppose there must be some extraordinary virture in the Geronstere water, as it is exceedingly nauseous, and tastes and smells like rotten eggs, but it is perfectly clear.
A Journey through the Austrian Netherlands, 1786

Philip Thickness

Waterloo

The Plain at Waterloo is a fine one, but not much after Marathon & Troy – Cheronea – & Platea. Perhaps there is something of prejudice in this, but I detest the cause & the victors – & the victory including Blucher and the Bourbons.
Letter to John Cam Hobhouse, May 16th 1816

Lord Byron
(1788–1824)

We stood upon grass and cornfields where heaps of our countrymen lay buried beneath our feet. There was little to be seen; but much to be felt; sorrow and sadness, and even something like horror breathed out of the ground as we stood upon it! . . . The ruins of the severely contested château of Hougamont had been ridded away since the battle, and the injuries done to the farm-house repaired. Even these circumstances, natural and trivial as they were, suggested melancholy thoughts, by furnishing grounds for a charge of ingratitude against the course of things, that was thus hastily removing from the spot all vestiges of so momentous an event.
Journal, July 17th 1820

Dorothy
Wordsworth

I have seldom been more interested. One has read the account of the battle so often, the area is so limited, and the main points of the battle so simple, that one understands it the moment one sees the place with one's eyes.
Letter to Miss Arnold, October 9th 1860

Matthew Arnold
(1822–88)

Suggested Routes

Tips

The following two suggested routes through the eastern and western parts of Belgium should give those touring by car some ideas without depriving them of the freedom to make their own plans. In addition, the routes can be combined to form a "Grand Tour" of the whole of Belgium.

The roads to take have been chosen so as to pass close to all the main places of interest to visitors. Nevertheless, not all the places described elsewhere in this guide can be reached without making some detours; details can be found in the suggestions and recommendations for detours, excursions and surrounding places of interest which are given under the individual entries in the main A to Z section and which complement these main routes.

The routes can be followed on the map accompanying this book, thereby facilitating more detailed planning.

Places and regions listed in the A to Z section under a main heading are printed in **bold** type; where there is a French or Flemish alternative name this is added in brackets.

All the places of interest, towns, regions, rivers and archaeological sites mentioned are to be found in the index at the end of this guide.

The distances in brackets following the titles of the routes are approximate and refer to direct routes. Distances for the longer recommended diversions or detours are also given.

Tourist Routes

Many of the places mentioned in the following routes are on or form the setting-out point for "Tourist Routes". Most of the latter are along minor roads off the major link-roads, are marked by a distinctive sign and thread through the Belgian countryside for between 50 and 150km/30 and 90 miles.

These Tourist Routes, of which there are 63 in all in Belgium, are marked with a hexagonal, bright yellow sign with a blue inscription. Informative leaflets can be obtained from local tourist information offices (see Practical Information, Information).

Cycling tours

The Tourist Routes are particularly well-suited to cycling tours lasting one or several days.

First Circular Tour through Eastern Belgium (about 330km/205 miles)

The setting-out point of this journey, most of which passes through Wallonia, the French-speaking region of Belgium, is **Liège** (Luik). Liège, the capital of Wallonia, is predominantly a heavy-industrial town, but offers the visitor some excellent museums which house treasures from the time when it was an independent principality. The N2 leaves Liège and proceeds west along the right bank of the Meuse. The first stop is **Huy** (Hoei), whose collegiate church is the most important High Gothic church in Belgium. The N2 continues along the river to **Namur** (Namen), which stands at the confluence of the Mass and Sambre and is dominated by its massive citadel. From here take the N92 south and enjoy the picturesque and rocky Meuse Valley **(Vallée de la Meuse)** until you reach **Dinant**. This town too is dominated by a fortress high up on a rock, in the shadow of which stands the Collegiate Church.

From Dinant it is worth making a detour into the lovely Fagne countryside, with French territory on three sides of it. Take the N96 along the Meuse and, after passing through Herr-Agimont, continue via Doische and Viroinval through some lovely countryside to Couvin, a little to the north of which lie the caves known as the Grottes de Neptune. From Couvin the N99 leads to **Chimay**, seat of a Trappist monastery, and thence via Rance with its Marble Museum to **Beaumont**. Here turn east again along the N40, past the holiday region of the Barrages de l'Eau d'Heure near **Walcourt** and then finally, after passing through the fortified town of Philippeville, return to Dinant along the N97 (about 155km/97 miles)

Detour from Dinant

The original main route through eastern Belgium now continues southward on the N95 via Beauring and through forests and fields to **Bouillon**, the massive castle of which towers over the charming Semois Valley **(Vallée de la Semois)**. Bouillon is a good starting point for some beautiful walks in the surrounding forests or for an excursion to the very interesting Trappist monastery of **Orval** 45km/28 miles to the south-east. From Bouillon continue north – first on the N89, then on the N899 – deeper and deeper into the Ardennes, making the next stop in **Rochefort** near the Lesse et Lomme Nature Park. A little way from Rochefort lie the caves of **Han-sur-Lesse**, the largest accessible dripstone caves in Europe; a visit is followed by a drive through the forests with their abundance of game and wild-life to **Saint-Hubert**, the home of St Hubert. From this little town the N89 leads to La-Roche-en-Ardenne, the central point of the Ourthe Valley **(Vallée de l'Ourthe)**. Continuing now north-east from La-Roche, on the N89 via Vielsam and then on the N68 via **Stavelot** to **Malmédy**, the traveller will finally reach the Upper Ardennes and the Hohe Venn (Hautes Fagnes); the best way to get to know this region is by walking through the **Belgian-German Nature Park**. Finally spend a time in the famous health resort of **Spa** before returning to Liège by way of **Verviers**.

North of Liège lies the Province of Limburg, with a number of towns which are worth a visit. First take the N20 to **Tongeren** (Tongres), the town built by Ambiorix, the father of all Belgium's resistance movements and which claims to be the oldest town in the country. Continue westward via **Sint-Truiden** (Saint-Trond) to **Zoutleeuw** (Léau), where the church is a little gem; it is the only church in Belgium to have withstood the iconoclasm of the 16th c. completely unharmed. From Sint-Truiden the N80 continues to **Hasselt**, where the Bokrik open-air museum a little way to the north is worth a visit. From there return finally to Liège by way of Tongeren (about 100km/62 miles).

Detour from Liège

Second Circular Tour through Western Belgium (about 470km/292 miles)

This tour takes in the major and most beautiful towns in Flanders and Brabant. It begins in **Brussels**, whose magnificent buildings such as the City Hall on the Grand'Place or the Atomium, together with its world-famous museums make it worth staying there for several days if possible. The tour starts with a visit to the battlefield at **Waterloo**, scene of Napoleon's final defeat. In **Nivelles** (Nijvel) south of Waterloo the Collégiale Sainte-Gertrude is one of the most important Romanesque churches in Belgium. From Nivelles take the N27 south to **Binche**, the true home of Belgian carnival, as will be proved by a visit to the Carnival and Mask Museum (Musée International du Carnaval et du Masque). The technically-minded will benefit from a visit to the nearby old La Louvière shipyards and the new Strépy-Thieu ones. Proceed by way of **Mons** (Bergen) to the west of Binche and thence close to the French border on the N50 to **Tournai** (Doornik), where the cathedral is a masterpiece of Romanesque church architecture in the Scheldt region; even some Romanesque middle-class houses have been preserved. **Kortrijk** (Courtrai), the sister town of Tournai to the north,

Béguinage cottages in Kortrijk

possesses one of the country's most romantic "béguinages" (see entry) and is also a good starting point for an excursion to **Oudenaarde** (Audenarde) with its magnificent town hall (30km/19 miles to the east).

In Kortrijk the visitor will find himself in Flanders, in the Middle Ages one of the richest strips of land in Europe with numerous proud towns which had the cloth industry to thank for their prosperity. One of these towns is **Ypres** (Ieper), on the N8. Ypres lies in the centre of the First World War battlefields, by the end of which it had been completely destroyed. The large Cloth Hall and the Town Hall, which can be admired today, were built later. From Ypres the tour continues gradually to the Belgian North Sea coast. Passing through the polder countryside the N8 leads to **Veurne** (Furnes), where the traveller can rest in a café on the picturesque old market place before continuing to **De Panne** (La Panne), the first of the well-known seaside resorts. Then follow one upon the other along the coast road – with many a view of dreary hotel blocks – **Koksijde** (Coxyde), **Nieuwpoort and then Belgium's best-known resort, Ostend**, which is more or less exactly in the middle of the Belgian coastal strip, the total length of which is 67km/42 miles. Our route continues via **Blankenberge** and the important port of **Zeebrugge** to **Knokke-Heist**, the last of the seaside resorts, known for its casino. From here return inland, turn south near Westkapelle towards Bruges, and then – after crossing the Schipdonk Canal with its seemingly endless rows of poplars – proceed to the charming town of **Damme**, the home of Thyl Ulenspiegel (Till Eulenspiegel; see Literature, 19th Century – Charles de Coster). **Bruges** (Brugge), a few miles to the south, will probably leave a more lasting impression on the visitor than any other Belgian town. The medieval town centre, completely preserved and pierced with canals, is uniquely beautiful and when the visitor sees the Town Hall (stadhuis) and Cloth-Hall and the Belfry he will soon realise why in the Middle Ages Bruges was the richest and most magnificent town north of the Alps. Almost as splendid is **Ghent**, easily reached from Bruges by the A10/E40 motorway. Here, too, the visitor will be inspired by the great Belfry, the splendid guild-houses and noblemen's dwellings along the canals and the magnificent churches, the largest of which, Sint-Baafskathedraal, contains the "Altar of Ghent", a masterpiece of Late Gothic painting.

The next stop on the tour is also a city – **Antwerp**, best approached along the A14/E17. Antwerp is Belgium's second largest city, the second largest European port after Rotterdam and one of the major diamond-dealing centres on the Continent. Peter Paul Rubens and the famous printing family of Plantin both lived here; their houses and studios have today been converted into museums which are well worth a visit. Two of Rubens' masterpieces, the "Raising of the Cross" and the "Descent from the Cross" are in the Cathedral, the tall, slender tower of which dominates the skyline. This suggested route then passes through two more places in which to stop. South of Antwerp lies **Mechelen** (Malines), the centre of Belgian campanology, with its very fine Late Gothic Town Hall. To its south – on the N26 from Mechelen – will be found the old university town of **Leuven** (Louvain), with its proud Town Hall surpassed only by that of Brussels. From Leuven it is only 15km/9 miles back along the N2 to Brussels where the tour began.

Belgium from A to Z

N.B.

The first name in each heading of this section is normally the Flemish or
French name, depending on the linguistic area concerned. In a few cases
where there is a distinct English form of the name, or where the French
name is more familiar to English readers, this is given first (see List of
Contents, p. 5). In all cases the alternative place name follows.
References to "the Netherlands" are always to the present-day Low Countries as a whole, i.e. the kingdoms of Belgium and the Netherlands (Holland) together with the Grand Duchy of Luxembourg.

Aalst · Alost

D 5

Province: Oost-Vlaanderen
Altitude: 7–29m/23–95ft
Population: 77,300
Intercity and Inter-regional Station (bicycle rental at station)

Aalst (French Alost), once the capital of a largely autonomous Flanders,
straddles the banks of the river Dender. It is the administrative centre of the
arrondisement, with schools which serve a large rural catchment area.
Cotton processing, textile manufacture and mechanical engineering are
among Aalst's many well-established industries; hops are grown in the
surrounding countryside and marketed in the town. Flower-growing is now
a particularly important source of employment. Every morning whole-
salers gather to buy cut flowers at the modern flower market (Bloemen-
veilingshal) in Albrechtlaan. Since the Belgian capital with its wealth of job
opportunities lies only 28km/17 miles to the south-east, many of Aalst's
residents are commuters who work in the Brussels area.

Location

Aalst Castle is mentioned in documents dating from as early as 866. The
town itself received its charter in 1164 having previously been granted in
fief to the counts of Flanders. In the Middle Ages because of its location on
the navigable Dender and the trade route between Bruges and Cologne,
Aalst quickly developed into the major centre of the Flemish county of that
name. During the Netherlands' long struggle for independence the town
was the scene of repeated fighting in which many of its inhabitants were
killed and numerous of its buildings destroyed or damaged. The same fate
befell it at the time of Louis XIV's wars and again in the two World Wars. A
number of buildings of historic interest have nevertheless survived.
The printer Dirk Martens (1446–1534) and the priest Adolf Daens (1839–
1907) were both born in Aalst. The Flemish writer Louis Paul Boon also
lived there.

History

One of Aalst's major attractions is its carnival which opens on the Sunday
before Shrove Tuesday with a "Parade of the Giants", among them Aalst's
"own" giant Ross Bayard. The celebrations continue on the Monday with
onion throwing from the Belfry and end on Tuesday with the procession of
"Vuil Jeannetten" ("Dirty Jeanette").

Carnival

Sights

Begun in 1225 and now the oldest building of its kind in the Netherlands,
the Schepenhuis (the original town hall) dominates the Grote Markt. The

**Schepenhuis
and Belfry*

◀ *Schepenhuis and belfry in Aalst*

entire evolution of Gothic architecture over three centuries can be clearly traced in this ancient sandstone edifice. The rear façade and side facing onto Kattestraat both date from the first half of the 13th c. and are of particular interest. The other side and the main façade were built later, following a fire in 1407. The beautiful Belfry (1470) with its carillon of 52 bells juts out to the right of the main façade. Embellished with Flamboyant Gothic pinnacles (1543–44) the tower bears the town's motto "Nec spe nec metu" ("Neither hope nor fear").

D.A.V.S.

Opening times
Wed. and Sat.
9am–noon and
2–5pm

The Daensmuseum en Archief van de Vlaamse Sociale Strijd (D.A.V.S.) on the second floor of the Belfry is dedicated to the movement for social justice founded by the priest Adolf Daens. Expelled from the Catholic Church because of his political activities Daens established the social-democratic "Christian People's Party" which, after the First World War, was absorbed into the "Vlaamse Beweging".

Dirk Martens
Memorial

In front of the Schepenhuis a memorial (1856) by Jan Geef commemorates the south Netherland's most famous printer, Dirk Martens. A close friend of Erasmus of Rotterdam, Martens began printing in 1473. He developed his own lettering system and was the first person in the Netherlands to print Greek and Hebrew texts. After spending many years in Antwerp, Louvain and also Spain he eventually returned to his birth-place at Aalst. From his printing press came, for example the first editions of Thomas More's "Utopia", major works by Erasmus, and the first report of Columbus's journey of discovery, the latter appearing little more than a year after the navigator's return.

Borse van
Amsterdam

Built between 1630 and 1634 the brick and sandstone Flemish Late Renaissance Borse van Amsterdam (Amsterdam Bourse) on the west side of the Grote Markt was once the site of the Vrije Vleeshuis (Butchers' Hall) and then later the headquarters of the Barbaristes, a literary guild. Above its arcaded lower storey rise four round Baroque gables and a slender central tower (1908).

Stadhuis

The Stadhuis (Town Hall) on the opposite side of the market square was rebuilt in 1830, at which time it acquired its Rococo façade and Late Neo-Classical banqueting hall. The original building, the "Landhuis", constructed between 1643 and 1645, was the meeting place of the Aalst provincial assembly which represented not just Aalst itself but also Geraardsbergen (see entry) and 150 rural parishes.

**Sint-Martinus-
kerk**

A short distance east of the Grote Markt the road opens onto Priester Daensplein with Sint-Martinuskerk in the centre. The church was begun around 1480 under the direction of a little known masterbuilder Jan van der Wouwe. However, the choir and its ring of chapels, much the most interesting part of the building, are the work of more famous architects, in particular Herman and Dominic de Waghemakere who built Antwerp Cathedral, and the great Laurens Keldermans from Mechelen. The religious wars of the 16th c. prevented the church's completion.

Interior

*Rubens Painting

The church interior, plain in itself, contains some exceptionally fine works of art, outstanding among which is the painting "St Roch and the Plague Sufferers" attributed to Peter Paul Rubens. This hangs in the chapel of the brewers' guild located to the left of the right-hand aisle.

On the left of the altar can be seen a stone tabernacle by Jerome Duquesnoy the Elder (1604). Two of the chapels encircling the choir deserve particular mention: the first chapel on the right, in which hangs an especially fine painting by Ambroise Francken entitled "Shepherds Praying"; and the fourth chapel along, containing the tomb of Dirk Martens. Amongst the church's other treasures is a three-part monstrance by the Antwerp goldsmith Lestiens (1631).

Oud-Hospitaal

In 1224 Joanna of Constantinople, Countess of Flanders, made a gift to the town of a site for a hospital. The present building, situated on the Vismarkt behind Sint-Martinuskerk, dates from the 14th and 16th centuries. Having been restored between 1959 and 1965 it now houses the Academie voor Schone Kunsten (Academy of Fine Art) and the Stedelijk Oudheidkundig Museum. Items on display in the latter include chains of office belonging to the various guilds, mementoes of the Battle of the Golden Spurs, carnival costumes and furniture.

Opening times
Tues., Thur.
10am–noon and
2–5pm, Sat.,
Sun. 2–5pm

Of the once thriving béguinage in Pontstraat to the south-east of Sint-Martinuskerk only the Neo-Baroque Sint-Antoniuskapel and Neo-Classical Sint-Catherinekerk remain.

Begijnhof

Surroundings

The world famous "Oktoberfeesten", a Munich style beer festival, takes place every autumn in Wieze, 6km/4 miles north-east of Aalst.

Wieze

Gijzegem, 12km/7 miles north-east of Aalst, is noteworthy for a farm dating back to 1688. This originally belonged to Gijzegem Castle of which, with the exception of two pavilions, no trace now remains. Its name, however, lives on as that of the farm, known today as "Hof van Gijzegem" or "Neerhof". The parish church of Sint-Martinus (second half of the 18th c.) has a splendid high altar.

Gijzegem

3km/2 miles east lies the Abdij van Affligem, founded by Benedictine monks in 1083. The old abbey was largely destroyed in 1797 by French Revolutionary troops. Rebuilding began in 1869 and has continued in a variety of architectural styles. Parts of the original 12th and 13th c. nave can be seen in the garden. There is also a museum in which items of archaeological interest from the abbey grounds are displayed.

Abdij van
Affligem

Opening times
Sat. 2.30–8pm,
Sun. 11am–1pm
and 2.30–8pm

At Moorsel, 5km/3 miles east of Aalst, there is a moated castle (water-kasteel). This Renaissance château, constructed entirely in red brick, was built in 1520 as a summer residence by Charles de Croy, Abbot of Affligem and later Cardinal of Tournai.
According to tradition Moorsel's 13th–15th c. Sint-Martinuskerk grew out of a 7th c. communion chapel dedicated to St Gudula. The present church contains three Baroque altars by Jacob Ulner.

Moorsel

The original Sint-Margarethakerk in Baardegem (8km/5 miles), a three-aisle Late Romanesque church first constructed in 1260, was extensively damaged by fire in 1592. Restored in the 17th c. and partly rebuilt, further restoration work in 1969 revealed the choir to have been part of a 10th c. pre-Romanesque hall church. Above the high altar hangs a painting of "St Veronica" by Gaspar de Crayer (1650).
Baardegem's imposing Hof ter Linde dates from 1803 and is also well worth a visit.

Baardegem

Aarschot   F 5

Province: Brabant
Altitude: 15m/50ft
Population: 26,000
Inter-regional Station (bicycle rental at station)

The small Hageland town of Aarschot is situated on the river Demer on the border with Kempenland. It is the centre of an asparagus-growing area but also has some industry (batteries, textiles).

Location

First mentioned in 825 Aarschot became part of Brabant in 1172. In 1212 it joined the Hanseatic League, quickly developing into the principal centre of

History

the Flanders cloth industry. Its heyday period ended with Maximilian I's siege and sacking of the town in 1489, a fate it was to suffer again at the hands of the Spaniards in the 16th c. In 1782 Aarschot was captured by the Austrians and in the First World War it was the scene of a bloody Belgian rearguard action against the Germans. Between 1940 and 1944 the town was several times subject to heavy bombardment.

Aarschot was the birthplace of the artist Pieter Joseph Verhaghen (1728–1811) whose work – contrary to prevailing fashion – was greatly influenced by Rubens. He achieved success as a court painter in Vienna.

Sights

Onze Lieve Vrouwkerk

Begun in 1337 with construction of the choir by the French masterbuilder Jacques Piccart, the Onze Lieve Vrouwkerk was completed in 1400 when the 85m/279ft high tower was finished. The sandstone church is an outstanding example of Demer Gothic, a regional variation of Brabant High Gothic.

Interior

The interior furnishings of the church include a number of items of interest, chief among which is the 16th c. Flamboyant choir-screen surmounted by a Late Gothic crucifix. The choir stalls (also 16th c.) are decorated with satirical carvings, e.g. of "The Wolf and the Stork", attributed to Jan Borchman of Eindhoven. A painting "The Disciples of Emmaus" by Verhaghen (1788) hangs in a chapel to the right of the choir.

Begijnhof

Adjacent to the church stands the former béguinage, originally founded in 1251 but rebuilt in 1635. Nos. 15–19 are the only houses surviving from those early days, however. The Stedelijk Museum voor Heemkunde en Folklore in No. 25 offers an evocative insight into everyday life in the 18th and 19th c. (open: daily 10am–noon and 2–5pm).

s'Hertogenmolens

Still standing on the banks of the Demer these brick ducal mills were built between the 13th and 16th c., doubling as part of the town's fortifications.

Onze-Lieve-Vrouwkerk in Aarschot

Rising above the Grote Markt the 14th c. tower known as Sint-Rochustoren was originally part of the Weavers' Hall.

Sint-Rochustoren

The Orleanstoren (Aurelianus Tower) on the southern edge of the town offers splendid views over the surrounding countryside.

Orleanstoren

Surroundings

An outing to the Kasteel van Horst at Sint-Pieters-Rhode, 13km/8 miles south of Aarschot, is deservedly popular among local people. Set in delightful parkland, the moated château began life as a medieval castle of which only the magnificent tower escaped destruction at the hands of Maximilian I's troops. The existing brick building, polygonal in shape and with sandstone ornamentation, is largely the product of 16th and 17th c. rebuilding and conversion.

Kasteel van Horst

Amay

See Huy, Surroundings

Amblève valley

See Stavelot, Vallée de l'Amblève

Andenne

See Vallée de la Meuse

Antwerp · Antwerpen · Anvers

E 4

Province: Antwerpen
Altitude: 3–9m/10–30ft
Population: 475,000
Intercity and Inter-regional Station

artwerpen 93

European City
of Culture 1993

Antwerp (Flemish Antwerpen, French Anvers) is situated on the right bank of the river Scheldt (Flemish Schelde, French Escaut), 88km/55 miles from its mouth in the North Sea. The river at this point is some 500m/550yds wide and, despite the distance from the sea, still experiences a tidal range of over 4m/13ft. Antwerp is the capital of the province of Antwerpen and the second largest seaport in Europe.

Location

** Commercial and cultural metropolis

Thanks to its harbour Antwerp was an important centre of trade and commerce even before records began. In addition to its long established traditions in banking and insurance, the continual expansion and moderni-sation of the port has seen the emergence of a multitude of trades and industries processing imported raw materials on the spot. Today Greater Antwerp is the biggest industrial conurbation in Belgium with shipbuilding and ship repair, petro-chemicals, vehicle assembly and food manufacture among its principal activities. The city is also a major export outlet, not just for Belgium but for Europe as a whole. Five rail routes and several canals terminate at the Port of Antwerp.

International
port and centre of
industry

Antwerp · Antwerpen · Anvers

The diamond industry

Antwerp's international reputation is in part due to the diamond industry and the special role the city plays in the diamond trade worldwide. If Amsterdam (Holland) is the diamond cutting capital of the world – although Antwerp has more than 250 diamond cutting firms of its own – then Antwerp is the premier marketplace for industrial and ornamental cut diamonds. It accounts in fact for about 70% of the global trade. The centre of all this commerial activity lies in the district along the Pelikaanstraat, in the Jewish Quarter near the main railway station. There are several show-rooms and other diamond trade outlets catering for prospective buyers (Diamondland, Appelmansstraat 33, Mon.–Sat. 9am–6pm; Dilady, Lange Herentalstraat 29, Mon.–Fri. 8am–5pm). Further information is available from the Diamond Advisory Council at Hoveniersstraat 22.

Cultural centre

The city's remarkable reputation does not rest solely on its trade and industry, however; it is also the cultural capital of Flanders. Centuries of prosperity have bequeathed an inheritance which includes the magnificent cathedral, the town hall, many other outstanding historic buildings and, above all, the city's paintings, an incomparable collection of 15th to 17th c. masterpieces from a time when the work of artists of the South Nether-lands school attained extraordinary heights. Quentin Massys, the "Velvet" Bruegel, Rubens, van Dyck, Jordaens, Cornelis de Vos and many others all lived and worked in Antwerp. This rich cultural tradition is maintained today by the city's numerous museums, theatres, three universities and several academies and institutes, in recognition of which Antwerp was chosen European City of Culture 1993.

Among the groups contributing to Antwerp's cultural diversity are 20,000 members of the Jewish community, the largest in Europe.

"The City on the River"

The relocation of port facilities around a newly constructed basin to the north has opened the way for redevelopment of the old wharves close to the city centre. This dockland area is now the focus of Antwerp's most ambitious building project in recent times, known as "the City on the River". Architects invited to take part in a design competition submitted outline schemes, three of which have now been selected for further ap-praisal. Assuming plans come to fruition the old basin north of the Steen will become a residential area incorporating an open-air maritime museum. The embankments on either side will also be redeveloped and a multi-level square with a subterranean arts centre will be built on the site of the former south dock.

History

Origin of the name

Traditionally the name Antwerp originates with a giant, Druon Antigonus, whose castle stood on the site in Roman times. He reputedly cut off the hand of any passing seafarer who refused to pay a toll, throwing the severed hand into the Scheldt. Antigonus is supposed to have been slain by the Roman Silvius Brabo who, it is said, himself hacked off one of the giant's hands and tossed it ("handwerpen") into the river. More mundane is the suggestion that the name is derived from the word "aanworp" or "aanwerpen" (meaning "thrown up ground") – referring to a piece of land which jutted out into the river abreast of the Steen and where there was once a settlement.

Early period

Whatever the truth about its name, in the 2nd and 3rd centuries A.D. a Gallo-Roman settlement most certainly existed on a site now occupied by part of southern Antwerp. This was followed in the 4th and 5th centuries by a Frankish village. Christian missionaries established themselves in the area around Antwerp in the 7th and 8th centuries, during which time St Amand is believed to have founded the "Infra castrum Antwerpis",

Antwerp Cathedral viewed from the Scheldt quai ▶

destroyed by the Normans in 836. Under the Treaty of Verdun of 843 Antwerp became part of Lothringia, and in the 10th c. it was made a margravate of the Holy Roman Empire. The city's emergence as a port began in 1031, the Hansa establishing a presence there in 1313.

Heyday and decline

Having earlier, in 1106, passed to the dukes of Brabant, the city on the Scheldt was now transformed into the North Sea's leading trading port, its wealth founded on its wool warehouses. In addition to new fortifications the building of the cathedral reflected growing prosperity, and Antwerp was already thriving when, at the end of the 15th c., the Zwin silted up, bringing even more trade to the city at the expense of its great rival Bruges. Under the protection of the emperor Charles V, Antwerp swiftly developed into the busiest and richest commercial city in Christendom. By the year 1560 the population had risen to around 100,000 inhabitants, 100 ships entered or departed the port every day, and more than 1000 business-houses had become established.

From the 16th c. onwards Antwerp also enjoyed a reputation for high standards of craftsmanship, its products being in demand as far afield as Arabia, Persia and India. This economic success was marked by the building of the old Beurs, the commercial exchange, and numerous artists including the painters Massys, Venius and the Bruegels, the sculptors Coecke van Aelst and de Vriendt, the writers Marnix van Sint-Aldegonde and Anna Bijns and the musicians Ockegem, De Hertogen and Cornet worked in the city, as did scientists such as Mercator, Dodoens, Ortelius and Lipsius and the printer Plantin.

This heydey period was, however, doomed not to last, the seeds of destruction being sown during the reign of Philip II when the Inquisition caused thousands of Antwerp's citizens to flee the port. In 1576 the mutinous Spanish garrison went on the rampage, plundering the city and killing an estimated 7,000 of its inhabitants. Capture by Duke Alexander Farnese in 1585 further hastened its decline. Antwerp's commercial mantle was assumed by Amsterdam and Rotterdam, whence the persecuted Protestants had fled. By 1590 the city's population had more than halved to just 40,000 people.

Many masters

Antwerp suffered another mortal blow when, following unification of the seven provinces, control of shipping on the Scheldt fell into Dutch hands, eventually leading to the closure of the river under the terms of the 1648 Treaty of Westphalia. Even so Antwerp still retained its status as the cultural centre of the region. Painters including Rubens, van Dyck, Jordaens and Teniers, and sculptors such as Quellin, were among the artists living and working in the city where, in 1663, Philip IV of Spain founded an Academy of Art modelled on those of Rome and Paris.

It was not until the French conquests at the end of the 18th c. that Antwerp's fortunes revived. The Scheldt was reopened for navigation in 1795 and between 1800 and 1803 Napoleon I laid out the Scheldt quays and old dock. The port assumed a crucial role in the Emperor's blockade of England ("Antwerp is the pistol aimed at the heart of England").

The 1815 Congress of Vienna gave Antwerp to the Kingdom of the Netherlands, bringing a significant boost to the city's prosperity (population 73,500 in 1830). This was mainly the result of trade with the Dutch colonies, trade which Antwerp was soon to lose once more to Rotterdam and Amsterdam. Bombardment of the city during the sieges of 1830 and 1832 caused massive damage. In 1863 Belgium bought back from the Dutch the right to levy dues on shipping in the Scheldt, a right which the Dutch had exercised since 1839. This brought a revitalisation of trade and commerce in the second half of the 19th c., marked by the fact that both the world trade exhibitions of 1885 and 1894 were held in Antwerp. In parallel with its economic growth, after 1859 Antwerp was also transformed into one of Europe's most heavily fortified cities. When the inner defences were finally dismantled, the massive ramparts were replaced by wide boulevards.

In the First World War the Germans beseiged Antwerp in September and October 1914, eventually occupying the city. Between the two wars the tonnage of freight passing through the port increased steadily and Antwerp soon regained its former prominence, being the venue of the seventh modern Olympic Games held in 1920 and ten years later of another world trade exhibition. In the Second World War the city was again occupied by the Germans. It continued to suffer heavy bombing even after the Allied liberation, being the target of some 800 German V1 and V2 rockets.

First and Second World Wars

Following the Second World War the volume of freight traffic continued to expand. Antwerp's outer fortifications were demolished, the only remaining vestige now being the "Vestingwater", the former moat. An apparently endless series of new tunnels, docks and locks were constructed and in 1975 work commenced on the city's underground. Since 1989 Antwerp has boasted the largest sea-lock in the world, the Berendrechtsluis.

The present

Sightseeing

Visitors with only a day to spend in Antwerp probably do best to limit themselves to the major city centre sights, principally the Grote Markt with its town hall and numerous guild-houses and, only a short distance away, the cathedral. Both can be viewed without haste in a morning leaving the afternoon free for a visit to one, or perhaps two, of Antwerp's museums. Usually the choice can be narrowed down to either the Plantijn Moretus Museum and Rubens' House, for which an afternoon suffices, or the Museum voor Schone Kunsten, which really requires more time to do it justice. A trip on the Scheldt, or one of the longer tours of the harbour, provides a different kind of alternative to the museums.
Having two days available for sightseeing means the added options of a visit to the Maritime Museum in the Steen, or a walk through the Jewish Quarter calling in at the Diamond Museum and Antwerp's famous zoo. Also highly recommended are the Museum Mayer van den Bergh and the Sint-Jacobskerk where Peter Paul Rubens lies buried.

What to see

As well as organising coach tours the Antwerp Tourist Office (see Practical Information) publishes brochures detailing various signposted walks around the city. The Office will also arrange the services of a guide. On Saturdays, Sundays and public holidays between Easter and the end of October (but daily throughout July and August) horse-drawn carriages are available for hire in the Grote Markt.

Round and guided tours

The Flandria Shipping Co. runs boat trips on the Scheldt and tours of the docks, daily from April to September, departing at 10am. Tickets can be obtained from the Flandria office at Vlotbrug. Available excursions include:
Short trip on the Scheldt lasting 50 minutes, from Vlotbrug;
Longer trip on the Scheldt lasting 1 hour 20 minutes, also from Vlotbrug;
Harbour tour lasting 2 hours 20 minutes, from Quay 13 at Londenbrug (courtesy bus from Steenplein).

Scheldt and harbour trips

Antwerp's Metro links Groenplaats in the city centre via Centraal Station to the terminus at Plantin in the Jewish Quarter. Several tram routes make their way around the narrow streets of the inner city through which also pass all bus services bar one (No. 9 via the Minderbroederrui). Buses Nos. 6 and 34 run from the Scheldt embankment to the districts south of the city centre. Groenplaats is the main city centre tram stop. Most bus lines call at Franklin D. Rooseveltplein, not far from Centraal Station.
The inner city area can easily be explored on foot without the need for any form of transport. In what follows therefore, advice about getting to places is limited to sights further afield.

Public transport

Antwerp · Antwerpen · Anvers

••• Grenze des Judenviertels

Mechelen, Brussel, Middelheim

Inner Old City and the Scheldt Embankment

*Grote Markt

In the middle of the Grote Markt, the heart of old Antwerp, stands the large Brabo Fontein (Brabo Fountain) by Jef Lambeaux. Erected in 1887 it depicts the Roman soldier Silvius Brabo tossing the severed hand of the giant Antigonus into the Scheldt.

Brabo Fontein

The Stadhuis, the 78m/256ft-long façade of which forms the western side of the Grote Markt, was built by Cornelis Floris de Vriendt between 1561 and 1565. Beneath the statue of the Virgin which adorns the central gable can be seen, from left to right, the arms of the dukes of Brabant, Philip II and the margravate of Antwerp with, separating them, allegorical figures of Wisdom and Justice. Inside the town hall the rooms are hung with 19th c. paintings by H. Leys illustrating the history of Antwerp (open: Mon. 9am–noon, Tues.–Fri. 9am–3pm, Sat. noon–4pm).

Stadhuis

Apart from the Stadhuis most of the buildings bordering the Grote Markt are former "gildehuizen", originally the headquarters of the city's 16th and 17th c. guilds. Among those on the north side are the Gildehuis der Kuipers (Coopers' House; No. 5), the Huis van de Schutters (Archer's House; No. 7) and the Huis van de Kruideniers (Grocers' House; No. 11), while on the south-east side stand the Huis van de Kleermakers (Tailors' House; No. 38) and the Huis van de Timmerlieden (Carpenters' House; No. 40). The streets behind and to the north of the Stadhuis (Gildekamersstraat, Zilversmid-, Braderij- and Kuipersstraat) offer further glimpses of the beauty that was once old Antwerp.

Guild-houses

Immediately behind the town hall, in the Gildekamersstraat, two former guild-houses have been turned into a folk museum devoted to the many traditional arts and crafts found in the Antwerp area. The museum has collections of marionettes and costumes, etc. and a complete chemists shop and pharmacy (open: Tues.–Sun. 10am–5pm).

Folk museum

No. 19 Suikerrui – the street leading off from the southern corner of the Grote

Ethnographic museum

Brabo Fountain and guild-houses in the Grote Markt

Markt – is now the home of Antwerp's recently established and extremely interesting ethnographic museum (open: Tues.–Sun. 10am–5pm).

North of the Grote Markt

°Vleeshuis

The elegant rooms of the late Gothic Vleeshuis (Butchers' Hall) in the Vleeshouwerstraat include the former council chamber of the butchers' guild. The impressive brick building, built in 1501–04, was deliberately sited close to the Scheldt, allowing the blood of slaughtered animals to run off into the river.

The Vleeshuis is now a museum of applied art and archaeology with collections of pre-historic, Egyptian, Roman and Merovingian artefacts; weapons and armour; ceramics; furniture; sculpture and woodwork; and coins. Among its most prized possessions are a depiction of the conversion of Saul in 16th c. Antwerp tiles, the Averbode Retable by Pieter Coecke van Aelst, and an outstanding collection of musical instruments including the remarkable harpsichord from the workshop of Ruckers the instrument-makers (open: Tues.–Sun. 10am–5pm).

°Musical instruments

Poesjenellen-keller

In the Poesjenellenkeller in the little Repenstraat opposite the Vleeshuis puppet shows are perfomed in the Antwerp dialect, maintaining a tradition which goes back to the 18th c.

Sint-Pauluskerk

At its northern end Vleeshouwerstraat opens out into the Veemarkt, the former cattle market. The Late Gothic Sint-Pauluskerk in the north-east corner, begun in 1517, was not completed until 1639. The Baroque clock tower dates from 1680. A fire in 1968 badly damaged the church and only the spirited efforts of local people prevented the loss of valuable interior furnishings. These include the superb Baroque confessionals by Pieter

Verbruggen the Elder and three paintings by Rubens: "The Scourging of Christ" (1617) in the left aisle and the "Adoration of the Shepherds" and "Disputation on the Blessed Sacrament" in the left transept (open: May–Sept. daily 2–5pm; Oct.–Apr. 9am–noon).

**Onze Lieve Vrouwkathedraal

The Onze Lieve Vrouwkathedraal, Belgium's largest Gothic church and the largest of its kind in the Netherlands, stands a short distance south-east of the Grote Markt. Work was started on the cathedral in 1352, continuing until 1521. Jacob van Thienen, Pieter Appelmans, Jan Tac, Everaert Spoorwater, Hermann and Dominic de Waghemakere and Rombout Keldermans were among the architects and masterbuilders who contributed to its construction.

Onze Lieve Vrouwekathedraal

© *Baedeker*

A Baptistery
B Lady Chapel
C Chapel of the Sacrament
1 C. de Gheete: "St John" (wood; 1499)
2 C. de Gheete: "Maria" (wood; 1499)
3 H. van Balen: "Madonna with angels" (17th c.)
4 H. van Balen: "St John and Herod" (17th c.)
5 A. Quellin the Younger: "Immaculate Conception" (marble; 17th c.)
6 H. van Mildert: "St Paul" (alabaster; 16th c.)
7 M. Pepijn: "St Francis" (17th c.)
8 M. Pepijn: "Aaron" (17th c.)
9 F. Francken the Elder (?): "15 Blood Sacrifices (16th c.)
10 A. Quellin: "Gideon" (stone; 17th c.)
11 C. Schut: "The Assumption" (1647)
12 P. P. Rubens: "The Raising of the Cross" (1610)
13 M. de Vos: "The Wedding at Cana" (1597)
14 F. Francken: "Jesus in the Temple" (1587)
15 Unknown master: "Madonna of the Meuse" (alabaster; 14th c.)
16 Unknown master: "Our Lady of Antwerp" (wood; 16th c.)
17 St Mary's Altar (by A. Quellin the Younger)
18 O. van Veen: "The Last Supper" (17th c.)
19 A. Quellin the Younger: "Pieta" (wood; 17th c.)
20 P. P. Rubens: "The Assumption" (1626)
21 P. P. Rubens: "Descent from the Cross" (1612)
22 Unknown: "The Adoration of the Magi" (window, 1537)
23 H. van Olim: "Conversion of St Paul" (window 1537)
24 J. van Gérinnes (?): Tomb of Isabella of Bourbon (1478)
25 N. Rombouts "The Last Supper" (window 1503)
26 Unknown: "John the Baptist and John the Apostle (window; 1525)
27 Unknown master: "John the Baptist" (16th c.)
28 Unknown master: "St Peter" (wood; 17th c.)
29 Unknown master: "The Bearer of the Cross" (fresco; 15th c.)
30 A. Quellin the Younger: "Jonathan" (17th c.)
31 A. Quellin the Younger: Epitaph for Ambrosius Capello" (1676)
32 A. ven Noort (?): "The Miraculous Draught of Fishes" (1587)

Opening times
Mon.–Fri.
10am–5pm,
Sat. 10am–3pm,
Sun. and public
holidays 1–4pm,
(but 10am–3pm on
the eve of public
holidays)

The church has suffered serious damage on a number of occasions over the years, depriving it of many of its most precious works of art. First came a fire in 1533, then despoliation at the hands of dissident iconoclasts in 1566, Calvinists in 1581 and French Republican troops in 1794 and 1800. Sadly only a few of the lost treasures have since been recovered.

Restoration of the exterior was begun in the 19th c. and all the carved stonework on the outside of the building is therefore recent. Work on the interior began in 1965, starting with the nave where repairs were completed in 1983. Currently the choir and transepts are being restored and will not be fully accessible for quite some time. The finest of the remaining works of art are meanwhile displayed in the nave and aisles as well as in the cathedral treasury.

North Tower

The 123m/404ft North Tower, radiating lightness, can be seen from miles away along the Scheldt. No wonder that the tower with its carillon of 47 bells has become the emblem of Antwerp. A memorial plaque at its foot commemorates Quentin Massys. The south tower was never finished.

Interior

The interior of the cathedral, 117m/384ft long, 55m/180ft wide and 40m/131ft high, is notable for its spaciousness and the perspectival artistry of the nave and six aisles. The Baroque pulpit (1713) is the work of Michel van der Voort.

**Rubens

Famous throughout the world and outstanding even among the cathedral's many exceptional works of art are two masterpieces by Peter Paul Rubens: "The Elevation of the Cross" in the left aisle and "The Deposition" on the central panel of the choir screen. Considered among the finest of all Baroque paintings both were executed between 1610 and 1614, shortly after Rubens returned from Italy. While "The Deposition" was commissioned by the Antwerp Guild of Archers, "The Elevation of the Cross" was painted for the high altar of Sint-Walburgakerk. There are in addition two other major works by Rubens to admire: "The Assumption" (1626) – hung for the time being next to "The Deposition" but actually the cathedral altar-piece and perhaps the finest of the ten such works from the artist's brush – and "The Resurrection" (1612), originally painted for the Moretus family, the famous printers, but now hanging in the cathedral treasury (in the left aisle).

*Treasury

Also displayed in the treasury are priceless liturgical accoutrements, vestments and paintings, including a "Pietà" (1556) by Maarten de Vos, a 17th c. "St Francis" by Murillo, and "The Mourning of Christ" by Cornelis de Vos. The marble "Head of Christ" is a gem, possible by Leonardo da Vinci.

In the vicinity of the cathedral

Handschoenmarkt

The Put (well) on the Handschoenmarkt, the former glove market in front of the cathedral, has a 15th c. wrought-iron canopy adorned by a figure of Silvius Brabo attributed to Quentin Massys.

Vlaeykensgang

The Handschoenmarkt leads into a street known as the Oude Koornmarkt, off which (at the side of No. 16) runs the Vlaeykensgang, an alleyway of houses dating back to the 16th c. and altogether typical of old Antwerp.

Groenplaats

Immediately south of the cathedral lies the bustling Groenplaats, cafés on every side. The statue of Rubens was erected in 1840.

Sint-Carolus
Borromeuskerk

Two Jesuit priests named d'Aguillon and Huyssens were the architects of Sint-Carolus Borromeuskerk, built between 1614 and 1621 on Hendrik Conscienceplein, a couple of minute's walk north-east of the cathedral. A devastating fire in 1718 largely destroyed the church, after which it was rebuilt in a less opulent style. Among the decorations lost for ever were ceiling paintings, 39 in all, by artists from Rubens' workshop and also by van Dyck. The full Baroque splendour of the original church can now only be glimpsed, primarily in the magnificent, clearly articulated main façade the design of which is attributed to Rubens himself. The 58m/190ft bell tower is considered one of the loveliest in Belgium.

Specially noteworthy in the interior are the carved Baroque confessionals guarded by angels and, between them, the wood reliefs showing scenes from the lives of St Ignatius and St Francis Xavier. Rubens painted three pictures for the altar but these are now in the Kunsthistorisches Museum in Vienna. The gallery, crypt and sacristy have been turned into a museum displaying, among other things, some exquisite lace (open: weekdays except Tues. 7.30am–1pm; Sat. 7.30am–noon and 3–6.15pm).

✶✶ Plantin-Moretus Museum

In 1576 Christophe Plantin the printer, who hailed originally from France, moved into a house he christened "De gulden Passer" – the Golden Compasses – close by the Vrijdagmarkt (south of the Grote Markt). Thereafter Plantin and his heirs the Moretus family extended the house, ultimately bequeathing to posterity a supreme example of Flemish Renaissance architecture (though the façade facing the Vrijdagmarkt was an 18th c. addition). Today the building is a museum. It incorporates the Old Flemish patrician house, the quiet, vine-covered inner courtyard, and the commercial premises, the latter including an early print-works complete with office and typesetters' room, all in an unparalleled state of preservation. The original furnishings, the wide-ranging exhibits, some of which are unique, but above all the still tangible atmosphere arising from the proximity of home and workplace, enthral every visitor and make the Plantin-Moretus Museum one of Antwerp's premier attractions.

Address
Vrijdagmarkt 22

Opening times
10am–5pm

Having set up as a printer in 1549, Christophe Plantin (1520–89) transferred his print-works lock, stock and barrel to his new home when he moved to

Plantin's
printing-works

The Plantin printing works

the Vrijdagmarkt in 1576. After his death the business carried on more or less unchanged under his son-in-law and successor Jan Moerentorf/Moretus, and subsequently the latter's family. The print-works with its sixteen presses was by far the largest in the Europe of the day. Plantin's greatest masterpiece was the eight-volume "Biblia Regia", or "Biblia Polyglotta", in five languages, Latin, Greek, Hebrew, Syrian and Aramaic, over 1500 copies of which were produced in the workshop. The most distinguished member of the Plantin-Moretus family proved to be Jan's son Balthazar who, on many occasions between 1613 and 1637, employed Rubens as an illustrator. From the mid 17th c. onwards the printing-house concentrated almost exclusively on missals and prayer books, Philip II having earlier granted Plantin a monopoly in the printing of liturgical books throughout the Spanish empire. When in 1800 the Spanish government finally withdrew this privilege, printing operations ceased, resuming only intermittently thereafter.

Museum tour	The tour of the house covers 34 rooms. Videos in several different languages recounting the story of the Plantin-Moretus family and the history of printing are shown in one of the ground-floor rooms reached via the courtyard. Since a short guide to the museum is included in the price of entry, only the items of most interest receive mention below.
Room 3	Room 3 contains manuscripts from the 9th to the 16th c. including an edition of the Chronicle of Jean Froissart, written in the 15th c., and the Bohemian bible of 1401/02 belonging to King Wenceslas.
Room 7	This room is devoted to the history of books and the processes involved in their production, from the earliest forms of writing and development of the alphabet – exhibits include important archaeological finds and manuscripts – to Johannes Gutenberg and the invention of letterpress printing using movable type. Later developments in printing technology are also featured, culminating in the phototypesetting of today.
Room 9	The proof-readers' room. Original proof-correction sheets dating back to the 16th and 17th c. can be seen on the desks.
Room 11	The humanist scholar Justus Lipsius (1547–1606) was a close friend of the family, often working in this room. The walls are hung with rare gold 16th c. Spanish leather.
Room 14	The print-works, the core of the old family business, with a total of eight printing presses on display.
Room 16	The "Second Plantin Room". Among the exhibits is an edition of the famous "Biblia Regia".
Room 18	Room 18 is principally devoted to the Moretus family. One of the books on display contains the earliest known European illustration of a potato plant (1588).
Room 19	Peter Paul Rubens had a close association with the Moretus family. Here his work as an illustrator is recorded.
Room 24	This room is a celebration of the art of printing in Europe as a whole, the jewel in the crown being a 36-line Gutenberg Bible.
Room 30	The type foundry, originally set up in the 17th c. The various processes used in the manufacture of metal printing-types are displayed.
Room 33	A room to delight any bibliophile, housing the Max Horn Collection of rare books from the 16th to 18th c.
Prentenkabinett	Antwerp's civic collection of copperplate engravings (Prentenkabinett) is housed next door to the museum at Vrijdagmarkt 23. Access is for purposes of research only.

Scheldt embankment

Riverside terraces	To left and right respectively at the western end of Suikerrui, the Ernest van Dijckkaai and the Jordaenskaai separate the Old City from the Scheldt,

Vlotbrug, riverside terraces and the Steen

forming a no-man's-land ripe for redevelopment and a challenge for the architects and planners of the "City on the River" project. Antwerp's 100m/330ft-wide quays, built in the 19th c., extend along the river for 5.5km/3½ miles providing berthing for the largest sea-going ships. Considerable areas of the Old City were ruthlessly demolished to make way for them, including sections of the fortress. Running the length of the two quays, above the warehouses, are pedestrian terraces, complete with cafés, from where excellent views are obtained of the busy river, the Cathedral and the Steen. Mid way along is the Vlotbrug (floating bridge), also constructed in the last century, from which the River Scheldt excursion boats depart.

A tunnel 572m/625yds long and 31.5m/103ft below the river provides a pedestrian crossing to the west bank of the Scheldt. The entrance (escalator or lift) faces the south end of the southern riverside terrace at Sint-Jansvliet.

Pedestrian tunnel

A short distance north of the Vlotbrug the road opens out into Steenplein, named after Antwerp's ancient citadel the Steen. The fortress's various phases of construction span a period from the 10th to the 16th c. For much of the time up to 1823 it was used as a prison. Not far from the entrance stands a modern statue of the "Lange Wapper", a notorious figure in Antwerp folklore.

*Nationaal Scheepvaart-museum in the Steen

Having been restored in both the 19th and the present century, the Steen was converted in 1952 into the Nationaal Scheepvaartsmuseum (National Maritime Museum). The museum occupies twelve rooms, one of the highlights being a marvellous collection of model ships, among them a 15th c. Flemish warship as well as junks and other oriental craft. There are also ships-in-bottles, figure-heads and comprehensive displays of navigational instruments, tools, old maps and charts. One section is devoted to the

113

influence of the sea upon religion, mysticism and art. Temporary exhibitions are held aboard the "Lauranda", a ship which belongs to the museum and is berthed permanently in the river (open: daily 10am–5pm).

Maritim Openlucht Museum

More vessels are moored across on the left bank of the river, near the western entrance to the pedestrian tunnel. These make up the Maritim Openlucht Museum (Open-air Maritime Museum).

Old City – North-east

Along the Meir

Meir

The Meir is Antwerp's main shopping street. Meirbrug, in the centre of which stands a modern memorial to Anton Van Dyck, links the inner nucleus of the Old City with the eastern part. The Torengebouw, at the western end of the Meir, was Europe's first skyscraper.

Walking east along the Meir, the handsome Rococo facade of No. 50, the former Koninklijke Paleis (Royal Palace), is the first to catch the eye. Having begun life as a patrician mansion in 1745, the house was Napoleon's Antwerp residence during the French occupation. In its latter day role as an international culture centre (I.C.C.), it provides a venue for exhibitions of contemporary art.

Meir No. 85, Osterrieth Huis, another 18th c. Rococo former mansion, is now the headquarters of a bank.

At the eastern end of the Meir a pair of identical department stores in Art Nouveau style face each other across the street.

* **Rubenshuis**

Open
daily
10am–5pm

Immediately beyond the old Koninklijke Paleis the open Wappersstraat turns south off the Meir. Peter Paul Rubens acquired No. 9 in 1610 – a year after his marriage to Isabella Brant – living there until his death in 1640. He arranged the house to his own taste and requirements, making his home to the left of the entrance and turning the right wing into his studio. The two parts are joined by an elaborate and much admired portico. In the 18th c. the house was owned for a time by an English aristocrat. Following the French Revolution it was used as a prison, thereafter falling more and more into disrepair. Rubenshuis (Rubens' house) finally came into the possession of the City of Antwerp in 1937 and, between 1939 and 1946, was meticulously restored with the aid of old documents and drawings.

Furnishings

The ten rooms of the house are furnished in the style of the period and contain numerous original paintings. These include works by Rubens (self-portrait, c. 1625/28, in the dining room) as well as by Snyders, Jan Bruegel, Veronese, Jordaens and Otto Venius. The large studio contains several more works by Rubens ("Adam and Eve in Paradise") and others by his pupils.

Courtyard and garden

The Baroque façade of the studio overlooks the courtyard, from which three archways lead into the garden. Both portico and garden were designed by Rubens himself.

Bird market

The Wapper continues at its southern end into Maria Pijpelincxstraat and then Oude Vaartplaats where a Sunday bird market is held. Plants, clothing, food, antiques and junk are among the items sold, as well as birds.

Theaterplein

Both streets open out onto Theaterplein, a large amphitheatre-like square with, on its north side, the Theatre Centre and Stadsschouwburg (Civic Theatre).

North of the Meir

Handelsbeurs

Off to the left of the Meir coming from Meirbrug the Handelsbeurs (Commercial Exchange) in Twaalfmaandenstraat was erected in 1868–72 as a

Dwelling and studio of Peter Paul Rubens

replacement for Dominic de Waghemakere's original (1531) destroyed by fire in 1858. Jos Schadde's building features a huge glass-covered hall on which a great many other stock exchanges were subsequently modelled. The Exchange is a public thoroughfare with access on all four sides.

Set in a pleasant court at the western end of Lange Nieuwstraat, a few steps north of the Beurs, are the buildings of the former 15th c. Sint-Niklaashospitaal (Nos. 3–5), including a Late Gothic chapel.
Further along the street the Burgundian Chapel (No. 31) takes its name from the 15th c. heraldic wall-paintings which decorate it.

Lange
Nieuwstraat

The 15th to 17th c. Gothic Sint-Jacobskerk, its exterior at present under restoration, faces onto Sint-Jacobsstraat on the north side of Lange Nieuwstraat.
With its sumptuously ornate Baroque interior Sint-Jacobskerk is one of the richest ecclesiatical buildings in Antwerp, blessed with an exceptional endowment of art treasures. It was the church at which the city's patrician families worshipped, and they regularly commissioned leading artists to design their private chapels, altars and tombs. Each family had its own seats in the choir stalls, the twelfth along on the left being that of the Rubens family for instance, marked as are the others with the family arms. Inevitably the Rubens Chapel provides the chief focus of interest for visitors.
Situated behind the high altar it contains the tomb of the artist (1640) and those of other members of his family. The altar-piece, "The Virgin and Child with Saints" (1634), was painted by Rubens a few years before his death specifically for his burial chapel. In the painting St George's features are said be those of Rubens himself while Isabella Brant appears as the Virgin and Hélène Fourment, Rubens' second wife, as Mary Magdalena.
Also to be seen in the church are paintings by, among others, de Vos, Seghers, Jordaens ("Healing of the Plague Sufferers", next to the Rubens

Sint-Jacobskerk

Opening times
Apr.–Oct.
Mon.–Fri.
2–5pm;
Nov.–Mar.
Mon.–Fri.
9am–noon

*Rubens Chapel
with **altar-piece

Rubens Chapel

Chapel), Venius ("Virgin", left aisle, fourth chapel) and Rockox (triptych "Last Judgement", left aisle, third chapel). On the high altar stands a marble statue by Kerricx and Artus Quellin the Younger, the "Transfiguration of St James" (1685).

Church treasury
Valuable liturgical accoutrements, books and vestments are displayed in the treasury.

Rockoxhuis
Nicolaus Rockox, art collector and burgomaster of Antwerp, was a friend and patron of Rubens. In 1603 he acquired Nos. 10–12 Keizerstraat, a street a little to the north of the Sint-Jacobskerk. Rockoxhuis, easily recognised by its white facade, became a museum in 1977. In addition to rare period furniture, porcelain, glass and ceramics, it is endowed with a magnificent collection of paintings. These include two by Rubens, "Mary Worshipping the Sleeping Infant Jesus" and a sketch of the "Crucifixion" which once belonged to George Sand, as well as works by Jordaens, Massys, Teniers, Snyders, van Dyck and others (open: Tues.–Sun. 10am–5pm).

Museum voor het Vlaamse Cultuurleven
The Flemish Cultural Museum and Archives at Minderbroedersstraat 22 trace the revival of Flemish culture since the 18th c. (open: Tues.–Fri. 10am–5pm).

Koninklijke Academie voor Schone Kunsten
Minderbroedersstraat leads at its eastern end into Mutsaertstraat where, since 1662, the Koninklijke Acadamie voor Schone Kunsten (Royal Academy of Fine Arts) has occupied the buildings of a former Minorite monastery. Archways and other architectural pieces can be seen in the grounds.

Beguijnhof
Further east beyond the Academy the Béguinage in Rodestraat dates from 1542–46. The church was restored in the 19th c.

* Brouwershuis (detour)
Anyone with an interest in industrial archaeology should make a detour north from the Academy of Fine Arts, along Mutsaertstraat, across Falconplein and past the International Seamen's House to Adriaan Brouwerstraat. The former gildehuis (No. 20), built by the engineer Gilbert van Schoonbeke in 1553, used not only to be the headquarters of the brewers' guild but a working brewery and pumping station as well, supplying the water for other breweries. It remained in operation until 1930. The pumping mechanism, powered by horses until as short a time ago as 1873, can still be seen, together with rooms containing the paraphernalia of the coopers' and brewers' trades. A portrait of Gilbert van Schoonbeke, who contributed hugely to Antwerp's expansion beyond the confines of the old city, hangs in the council chamber (open: Tues.–Sun. 10am–5pm).

City centre – south

Sint-Andrieskerk
Viewing of the Gothic Sint-Andrieskerk in Sint-Andriesstraat is by appointment only (tel. 232 0384). Building started on the church in 1515. The interior boasts a fine choir stall (1821) with a depiction of St Peter's miraculous catch of fishes, a reliquary of "36 saints", and several splendid altars. One of the piers in the south transept bears a memorial to Mary Queen of Scots, erected by two of her exiled ladies-in-waiting.

In the course of only a short period during the 1890s, a connoisseur of the fine arts, Fritz Mayer van den Burgh, assembled a remarkable collection of more than 3,000 items. These are now displayed on four floors of a Neo-Gothic house at Lange Gasthuisstraat 19. The collection includes some superlative works of art, among them paintings by Pieter Bruegel the Elder ("Dulle Griet" and the earliest of the artist's signed works "The Twelve Proverbs", both in Room 26), Rubens, Jordaens, Bouts, van der Weyden, van Ostade, Lucas Cranach and Quentin Massys. Also of great interest are, in Room 20, the Flemish and French religious statues, the outstanding collection of ivories, and a unique 16th c. Flemish breviary, and in Room 14, a polychrome group "Christ with St John" (1300) by Henry of Constance and a Netherlands diptych (c. 1400). The second floor features a collection of porcelain, while 17th c. furniture and paintings occupy the third.

Museum Mayor van den Bergh

Opening times
Tues.–Sun.
10am–5pm

A few doors further along Lange Gasthuisstraat part of a 17th c. former orphanage for girls known as the Maagdenhuis (the Maidens' House, No. 33) has also been turned into a museum and archive. In addition to tracing the history of the orphanage and its orphans the museum possesses important paintings by Jordaens, Venius and van Dyck and a rare collection of Antwerp faience bowls (open: weekdays except Tues. 10am–5pm, Sat., Sun. 1–5pm, closed on public holidays).

Maagdenhuis

The Elisabeth Gasthuis (Lange Gasthuisstraat No. 41) was a hospital founded in the 13th c. Its 16th c. chapel has an ornately carved high altar by A. Quellin the Younger (1682).

Elisabeth Gasthuis

Antwerp's botanic garden, the Kruidtuin, is situated approximately level with and behind the Maagdenhuis, on Leopoldstraat, which runs parallel to Lange Gasthuisstraat and just to the east (open: daily 8am–6pm).

Kruidtuin

**Koninklijk Museum voor Schone Kunsten

The Koninklijk Museum voor Schone Kunsten (Royal Museum of Fine Arts) celebrated its centenary in 1990, having opened its doors eleven years after work began on its Neo-Classical building in 1879. The nucleus of the museum's collection belonged originally to the Lucas Guild of Painters and Sculptors, founded in 1442. Following the winding up of the guild in 1773 the works of art accumulated over the years passed into the possession of the Academy of Fine Arts and were housed in the Academy's premises in the old Minorite monastery. In the mid 19th c., however, the collection was swollen by a substantial number of new acquisitions, particularly gifts, mainly of 15th and 16th c. paintings, from Florent van Ertborn, a former burgomaster of Antwerp. The Academy found itself with insufficient space to accommodate the enlarged collection and the decision was taken to build a new museum.

Address
Leopold de Wael-plaats 1–9

Tram
Nos. 4, 8

Opening times
Tues.–Sun.
10am–5pm

The collection is housed on two floors. The ground floor is largely devoted to modern, i.e. 19th and 20th c. paintings and sculpture, some 1500 items in all, providing among other things an excellent overview of the development of the plastic arts in Belgium since 1830. The exhibition of Old Masters on the first floor comprises more than 1000 works, mostly from the Flemish and Dutch schools. Although visitors will wish to be guided by their own preferences aided by the plan of the museum provided here, some of the most important of the works on view are mentioned below: Specially noteworthy in the exceptionally well represented Old Netherlands school of 15th c. painting are Rogier van der Weyden's triptych with the Seven sacraments, two small pictures (a Madonna and a St Barbara) by Jan van Eyck, and a large triptych and portrait of Jehan de Candida, both by Hans Memling. Quentin Massys triptych with the Entombment, one of the artist's major works, dates from the early 16th c. Some supreme examples of Rubens' religious paintings hang in the museum, among them his "Last Communion of St Francis", "Adoration of

Tour

Old Masters

GROUND FLOOR

19th and 20th c.

- 4–10 Abstract art, Surrealism
- 13 Gustave van de Woestyne, Constant Permeke
- 14 Albert Servaes
- 15 Gustave de Smet, Frits van den Berghe, Edgard Tytgard, Jean Brusselmans
- 16–18 Temporary exhibitions
- 19 Henry de Braekeleer, Rik Wouters, Jacob Smits
- 21 James Ensor
- 24–29 Romanticism, Realism, Impressionism

UPPER FLOOR

Old Masters 14th–17th c.

- A Maarten de Voos
- B Marinus van Reymerswael
- C David Teniers, Adriaan Brouwer
- D Ambrosius Francken, Maarten Pepijn
- E Franz Hals, Abraham von Beieren, Rembrandt van Rijn
- F Jacon Jordaens
- G Jan Fyt, Franz Snyders, Jan Siberechts
- GA Abraham Janssens, Theodor Rombouts
- H Anton van Dyck, Jacob Jordaens
- I–J Pieter Paul Rubens
- K Titian
- L Lucas Cranach, Jean Clouet, Pieter Pourbus
- M Cornelius de Vos, Erasmus Quellin
- N Hans Memling
- O Masters of Frankfurt
- P Frans Floris de Vriendt
- Q Jan van Eyck, Rogier van der Weyden, Antonella da Messina
- R Quinten Metsys, Joachim Patinir, Barend van Orley
- S Simone David
- T Bruegel Family

the Magi", "Education of the Virgin" and "Virgin with Parrot". There are also numerous works by the Master's predecessors, pupils and imitators. The paintings by Jordaens and van Dyck are well executed, though perhaps not quite up to the standard of their finest. In addition, be sure not to miss the very typical examples of 16th and 17th c. Flemish sculpture, the animal paintings and still lifes by 17th c. artists such as Snyder and, from

the 17th c. Dutch school, the "Young Fisherman" by Frans Hals and a
portrait by Rembrandt.
Of the Italian paintings three are particularly outstanding: the series of
small panels by Simone Martini, Antonello da Messina's "Christ on the
Cross", and a Titian.
The pick of the 19th and 20th c. artists exhibited include Henri de Braeke-   19th and 20th c.
leer, James Ensor, Rik Wouters ("Woman Ironing") and René Magritte.

Scheldt embankment and quays – south-west

The area to the west of the Koninklijk Museum voor Schone Kunsten,
especially the unprepossessing square bounded by Waalsekaai and
Vlaamsekaai, forms one of the major sites for redevelopment under the
"City on the River" project. Already two rather unusual museums have
been established in waterfront buildings.

Opened in 1987 the Museum voor Hedendaagse Kunst (Museum of Con-   Museum voor
temporary Art) occupies an old corn silo with a lovely Art Déco façade at   Hedendaagse
Leuvenstraat No. 32, off the Waalsekaai. The museum promotes the latest   Kunst
in modern art, not just through its own collection but also by inviting artists
to exhibit their work. Nor are the works on show the only items of interest;
equally worth seeing is the cafeteria wall sprayed by the New York graphic
artist Keith Haring (open: Tues.–Sun. 10am–5pm).

Aficionados of the camera will also find a treat in store at Waalsekaai No.   Provinciaal
47, an old warehouse recently given a new and rewarding lease of life as   Museum voor
the Provinciaal Museum voor Fotografie. The museum charts the history of   Fotografie
photography with the help of an important collection of cameras and old
photographs (open: Tues.–Sun. 10am–5pm).

An old hangar on Cockerillkaai beside the Scheldt is the location of Ant-   Antwerpen
werpen Miniatuurstad, the city in miniature (open: daily 10am–8pm).   Miniatuurstad

The Avenues and the New Town

Between 1540 and 1543 massive ramparts incorporating ten bastions and   The Avenues
walls up to 10m/33ft high were constructed to form a defensive ring around
the city on its eastern side. These have since been replaced by broad
avenues (the Flemish for avenue is "lei") which separate Old Antwerp from
the New Town. The northernmost of these avenues, Italiëlei, extends from
the docks in the north to Franklin Rooseveltplein, passing the entrance to
the Scheldt road tunnel at Tunnelplaats en route. On the south side of
Franklin Rooseveltplein Italiëlei becomes Frankrijklei, crossed at Tenierplaats by the road linking Centraal Station to the city centre. Near the
intersection stands the Koninklijke Vlaamse Opera (Royal Flemish Opera
House) built in 1907. Next comes Britselei with the Gerechtshof (Law
Courts; 1871–75) at the city end, and then finally the Amerikalei. The latter
passes quite close to the Koninklijke Museum voor Schone Kunsten before
terminating at Bolivarplaats.

Keyserlei, a particularly lively place in the evenings, lined with cafés,   Centraal
restaurants, cinemas and hotels, runs from Tenierplaats to Centraal Sta-   Station
tion, Antwerp's main railway terminal. The "Middenstatie" (the middle
section of the station building) with its imposing steps and impressive
dome was built between 1895 and 1905. All the materials used in its
construction came from Belgium itself. To the north the station opens onto
Koningin Astridplein, again a popular focus of city life and site of a branch
of the Antwerp Tourist Office.

**Dierentuin (Zoo)

Located right in the midst of the city, immediately behind Centraal Station,
the 10ha/25 acre Antwerp Zoo was founded in 1843. It is widely regarded as

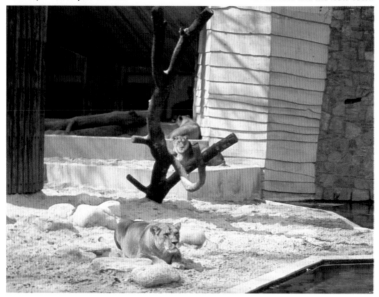

In the Antwerp Zoo

Entrance
Koningin
Astridplein

Opening times
Summer: daily
8.30am–6.30pm;
Winter: daily
8.45am–4.45pm

one of the finest zoos in Europe on account of its variety of species, its success in breeding, the care bestowed on the animals, kept in the most natural environment possible, and, last but by no means least, its architecture. While the Art Déco façades of the entrance area are the first features to catch the eye, inside the zoo there are several buildings of note, among them the giraffe and elephant house (1855) in the style of an Egyptian temple.

More than 6,000 animals of 950 species live in the zoo, including rare breeds such as white rhino, okapi and mountain gorilla. In the cleverly designed aviary occupants and visitors are able to mingle freely. The terrarium and aquarium are filled with many interesting animals, among them the komodo dragon and exotic fish from the Zaïre River. A nocturnal house, a dolphinarium seating over 1000 (performances: summer 11.30am, 2, 3, 4, 5pm; winter 11.30am and 3pm only) and a planetarium (presentations: Wed. and Sun. 2pm) have recently been added.

Natural history museum

The zoo also has a natural history museum concentrating mainly on native fauna. One rather unusual section is devoted to a collection of old microscopes and specimens.

Jewish Quarter

Metro stations
Diamant, Plantin

Antwerp's Jewish Quarter, home to the largest and most influential Jewish community in Europe, extends from Frankrijklei south as far as Koning Albertpark and eastwards to beyond the main railway line. Most of the Jews are orthodox and there are several synagogues in the area.

Pelikaanstraat

Busiest thoroughfare in the district and centre of the diamond trade, Pelikaanstraat runs south from Centraal Station, alongside the railway line. In addition to the principal Diamantbeurs (Diamond Exchange), numerous

jewellers, diamond merchants and cutters have premises on Pelikaanstraat
or in the side streets leading off it.

The Provinciaal Diamantmuseum (Lange Herentalsestraat 31–33) explores
all the different aspects of the trade in diamonds, including sections on
their extraction, processing and industrial use. Diamond cutters can be
seen at work. There is also a display of cut and uncut diamonds (genuine)
together with copies of the more famous stones (open: daily 10am–5pm;
guided tours Sat. 2 and 5pm).

Provinciaal
Diamantmuseum

Immediately south of the diamond museum lies the triangular Stadspark
(City Park), on the site of one of the Antwerp's old defence works. Stocked
with a fine range of plants the park is attractively laid out with an ornamental lake, footpaths, and several monuments.

Stadspark

From the south-east corner of the Stadspark Charlottalei continues to its
junction with Belgiëlei, on the opposite side of which No. 19 houses the
delightfully unmuseumlike Ridder Smidt van Gelder Museum. With its fine
period furniture and collection of fine porcelains the 18th c. mansion
retains the atmosphere of a patrician house of the day (open: Tues.–Sun.
10am–5pm).

Museum Ridder
Smidt van Gelder

**The port

The Port of Antwerp is second only to Rotterdam among the major seaports of Europe, fully justifying its claim to be one of the largest in the
world. The harbour installations alone cover an area of more than
10,000ha/25,000 acres, with a further 3400ha/9300 acres of land in industrial use. A total of 124km/77 miles of wharves provide berthing for sea-
going ships and inland craft, while 387 quayside cranes, twelve floating
cranes, nineteen loading gantries and 20 container hoists handle their
cargoes. Access to the harbour basins from the Scheldt is via six sea-locks
on the east bank and one on the west, among the former being the 500 ×
57m/1640 × 187ft Zandvlietsluis (cubic capacity 613,000cu.m/
733,150cu.yds) and the Berendrechtsluis (765,000cu.m/914,940cu.yds), the
largest lock in the world, opened in 1989.
Approximately 20,000 vessels from 70 nations enter the port each year
carrying between them some 95.4 million tonnes of freight (1989), mainly
oil, foodstuffs, raw materials for the chemical industry, mineral ore and
manufactured goods such as vehicles. There are 300ha/740 acres of
covered storage, including grain silos with a total capacity of 238,000
tonnes. Storage tanks with a combined capacity in excess of 10 million
cu.m/350 million cu.ft hold the oil and oil-based products (about 28 million
tonnes annually) which together make up a significant proportion of the
goods brought into the port for onward shipment. In recent years the
container handling facilities have been steadily enlarged. Efficient modern
industries, mainly petrochemicals, metal (motor car assembly) and food
processing, have grown up on sites around the port.

International
port

A flourishing port from the late Middle Ages onwards, Antwerp's earliest
harbour installations were built on the city's old waterfront along the
Scheldt. The first docks, the Bonapartedok and Willemsdok, were constructed during the period of French occupation, largely for military purposes. Commercially speaking it was only after 1863, when Belgium
bought back from the Dutch the right to levy dues on shipping in the
Scheldt, that the port took on a new lease of life. Since that time the facilities
have been developed systematically and with great success. The initial
stage of expansion was accomplished in 1913 with the completion of
eighteen docks for sea-going ships and seven for barges. Following the

History

First World War priority was given to improving the storage and loading facilities of the existing port, but in 1956 a huge building programme was embarked upon, bringing the Haven to its present size. The Churchilldok and the 10km/6 mile long Kanaaldok, through which the port is linked to Rotterdam via the Scheldt-Rhine Canal, were among the projects completed at this time. The process of expansion and development is still continuing, concentrated now around Kallo on the river's west bank. Four docks and the Sluis van Kallo are already in operation.

Docklands tour

The enormous size of the port rules out any attempt to explore it on foot. This leaves the option of joining one of the boat tours or resorting to bicycle or car.

Given sufficient time public transport offers another possibility, though not all parts of the port area can be reached in this way. The No. 37 bus goes as far as the Van Cauwelaertsluis and back, the No. 76 much further north to the Zandvlietsluis. But travelling by bus does not always guarantee a close look at the harbour installations.

By boat

The Flandria Shipping Co.'s boat tours of the Port of Antwerp depart from Kaai 13 (Londenbrug) on the northern extremity of the Old City. The same company also runs excursions on the Scheldt from the Vlotbrug near the Steen. These, however, are river trips and the entrance to the Sluis van Lallo is as close as they get to the docks themselves.

"Havenroute"

Lillo

The "Havenroute" is an approximately 50km/30 mile long sightseeing tour of the port area, marked out by the Antwerp Tourist Office. Start from the Loodsgebouw (Pilot House) on the embankment north of the Steen, from where the route heads northwards, passing almost immediately the two oldest docks, the Bonapartedok and Willemsdok, at the far end of which can be seen the massive Koninklijk Stapelhuis. Continue through the Kattendijkdok, built between 1853 and 1860, crossing the Kattendijksluis linking the dock to the river. Adjoining it to the east and north are a number of smaller docks, including the Straatsburgdok – off which leads the Albert Canal – and the Lefebvredok with access to the Scheldt via the Royerssluis. Beyond the Royerssluis the Havenroute turns westwards along the Scheldelaan, following the river as it makes its way past an apparently endless series of oil refineries. Eventually it bends rightwards again to the Van Cauwelaertsluis and Boudewijnsluis, continuing past the 17th c. Eenhoorn windmill to Lillo, one of the few polder villages to have at all survived engulfment by the port. The Polder Museum and the remains of Lillo's 16th c. fort are both well worth visiting, the latter having been part of the great fortifications which once surrounded Antwerp, the former documenting life as it was on the Antwerp polders prior to their being swallowed up by industrial development (open: Easter–Oct. Sun. and public holidays noon–6pm).

Berendrechtsluis

At Lillo there is a choice between driving on to inspect the huge Berendrechtsluis, the world's largest lock, or shortening the tour by turning round and following the Havenroute south again towards Antwerp, via the Frans Tijsmanstunnel beneath the Kanaaldok and then along the Noorderlaan. On the way the vast General Motors plant will be seen at the Churchilldok, beyond which a short detour to the left leads alongside No. 6 Havendok and back, passing the container terminals, the giant grain silos and the UK ferry terminal. From there the city centre can be reached by either of two routes, directly by continuing along the Noorderlaan and across the Albertkanaal or more circuitously via the Oosterweel Steenweg between Albertdok and Leopolddok, thence through No. 5 Havendok and Amerikadok to rejoin the Scheldelaan and so return to the Steen.

Kalmthoutser Heide

Port and Industrial Area ☐ Port Extension – – – – – Havenroute

1 Petroleumrichtingen Zuid
2 Vlotbrug (landing-stage for Scheldt trips, quays for visits to the fleet)
3 Bonapartedok and Willemdok
4 Kempschdok
5 Asiadok
6 Houtdok
7 Statsburgdok and Albetkanaal
8 Kattendijkdok
9 Royerssluis (1907) Amerikadok (grain silos, Marine Academy)
10 Albertdok, with 1–3 Havendok
11 Ford works (tractors)
12 Leopolddok
13 Hansadok (Esso Belgium, second largest refinery in Belgium) with 4 and 5 Havendok (chemical products, timber)
14 Marshalldok (Fina, largest refinery in Belgium)

15 Kallo thermal power station
16 Petrochemical plant (BP, Texaco, Fina, Exxon, Ucar)
17 Vrasendok
18 Bayerwerk
19 Bayerwerk
20 Degussa
21 Solvay
22 Container terminal
23 Doel nuclear complex works
24 Planned container terminal
25 BASF
26 Scheldt-Rhine Canal
27 Delwadedok (container, bulk goods, civic towing service)
28 Churchilldok (1967; container, vehicle loading)
29 6 Havendok (grain silos, cold-stores parcel service, timber, General Motors, Opel)

The Schldt Quay and pilots office·

Outlying places of interest

*Nachtegalenpark and Middelheim Open-air Sculpture Museum

Location
South of the
motorway ring

Entrance
Beukenlaan

Bus
No. 17

Nachtegalenpark (Nightingale Park), on the southern side of the city, was laid out in 1910 on land formerly belonging to three estates: Den Brandt, Vogelenzang and Middelheim.

The gardens of the Middelheim mansion have been made into an open-air sculpture museum (Openluchtmuseum voor Beeldhouwkunst), a sylvan setting for more than 300 works of art by well-known sculptors including Auguste Rodin, Aristide Maillol, Henry Moore, Rik Wouters, Louise Nevelson and Alexander Caldin. Smaller items are displayed in the pavilion (open: daily 10am–dusk). A biennial festival of sculpture is held from July to September every odd-numbered year in the section of the Nachtegalenpark adjoining the Middelheimpark.

Zurenborg district

Location
Suburb of Berchem

Tram
Nos. 8, 11

Located to the east of Berchem's railway station in Antwerp's south-east suburb of that name, the district known as Zurenborg is something of an architectural curiosity. Built around the turn of the century in a medley of Neo-Classical, Neo-Renaissance and Art Nouveau styles, it was designated a conservation area in 1970.

Cogels-Osylei with its splendid houses is the pick of several very attractive streets.

Te Bolaerpark and Boekenbergpark

Location
Suburb of Deurne

Both these parks, popular recreation areas for the people of Antwerp, are in Borgerhout, a district in the southern part of the suburb of Deurne where, every year in September, the "Parade of the Little Giants" is held, as it has been since 1712.

Tram
Nos. 8, 11

Te Bolaerpark is planted with several rare species of tree and also has an arboretum.

The mansion belonging to Boekembergpark has been converted into a home for the elderly. The park itself boasts an intriguing natural history museum complete with fossil and mineral collections, all housed in an artifical grotto (open: May–Sept. Sun. and public holidays 2–6pm).

Rivierenhof and Provinciaal Museum Sterckshof

The 87ha/215 acre Rivierenhof, another park also in Deurne, possesses a large lake and open-air theatre. It is also noteworthy for the great size of some its trees.

Location
Suburb of Deurne

In the south-west corner of the park stands the Renaissance château Sterckshof, now the Provinciaal Museum voor Kunstambachten (Provincial Craft Museum). Among the items on display are furniture, silver- and glassware, costumes and the fittings from an old apothecary's shop (open: Mar.–Nov. Tues.–Sun. 10am–5pm).

Tram
No. 10

Surroundings

Doel

D 3

Despite being situated in the shadow of a huge nuclear power station Doel, on the west bank of the Scheldt opposite Lillo, still retains something of the character of a Zeeland polder village. Protected from the Scheldt by a dyke Doel is the last community on the Belgian side of the border with Holland. Old milling equipment can be seen in the windmill (1615) on the dyke.

Bus
No. 293

*Kalmthoutser Heide nature reserve

E 3

Also close to the Dutch border, but in this case some 25km/16 miles north of Antwerp near the small town of Kalmthout, the Kalmthoutser Heide nature reserve covers 732ha/1800 acres of dunes and heathland. Within the reserve Putse Moer is a breeding ground for gulls, woodcock, curlew and lapwing. Visitors must not stray from the marked footpaths.

South of Kalmthout there is a 10ha/25 acre arboretum with rare species of tree.

Brecht

E 3

The Kempenland town of Brecht lies 18km/11 miles north-east of Antwerp, near the Dutch border. The town's grammar school, founded by Jan de Coster (Johannes Custos) in 1515, grew to be a centre of humanist learning. Among its notable pupils was the Jesuit Lenaart Leys (Leonardus Lessius), a statue of whom stands beside the church. Brecht was also the birthplace of the great Netherlands Renaissance poet Jan Baptista van der Noot (Jonker Jan), born in 1540.

Sint-Michielskerk provides a fine example of Kempenland church architecture in the late Gothic period. Except for some Baroque sculptures, however, all the interior furnishings are modern.

Sint-
Michielskerk

The Kempen Museum (Mudaeusstraat 1–2) traces the history of the town and Kempenland, including a section devoted to the humanist tradition (open: Apr.–Sept. every 3rd Sun. 2–6pm).

Kempen
Museum

Hoogstraten

Hoogstraten, 6km/4 miles north-east of Brecht, is famous for its vast straw-berry fields.

Sint-Catharinenkerk

Sint-Catharinenkerk was built in the 16th c. by Rombout Keldermans, its 105m/345ft high tower making it a landmark for miles around. The sixteen stained glass windows in the choir and transepts are by Bernard van Orley. Inside the church the splendid mausoleum of Antoon van Lalaing and his wife Elisabeth van Culembourg, a masterpiece of Renaissance sculpture by Jean Mone, stands out amongst the other tombs. The superb choir stalls with their life-like figures were the work of Albrecht Gelmers and date from between 1532 and 1548.

Begijnhof

The small 15th c. béguinage is a secluded haven of tranquility. Its Baroque church has a fine portal.
Works by the Flemish painter Alfred Ost can be seen in the Alfred Ost Museum at No. 21.

Arlon · Aarlen

Province: Luxembourg
Altitude: 450m/1475ft
Population: 23,000
Intercity Station

Location

Situated in the far south-east corner of Belgium wedged between France and Luxembourg, Arlon (Flemish Aarlen) is one of the country's oldest towns. Now the capital of the Belgian province of Luxembourg, it lies on the plateau of the Ardennes at the intersection of two Roman roads, Reims to Trier and Tongeren to Metz. Having founded the settlement (Orolaunum), the Romans also later fortified it in the 3rd c. A.D. The town is built on the slopes of a conical hill once topped by the castle of the counts of Arlon.

Maitrank

Among Arlon's special attractions is a drink called Maitrank, a traditional wine cup the origins of which can be traced to medieval Germany – to the monks of Prüm Abbey in the Eifel who used to sweeten their wine with fruit or aromatic plants. The custom has survived and is celebrated annually at Arlon's Maitrank festival, held on the third or fourth Sunday in May.
Arlon Maitrank is a Moselle wine flavoured with woodruff buds and forti-fied with brandy. It is served chilled, garnished with a slice of orange.

Sights

Grand'Place

The square known as the Grand'Place with its medieval cross, symbol of civic freedom, is the centre of the old part of Arlon.

Tour romaine

Reached by an alleyway leading off the south-east corner of the square, the Tour romaine (Roman tower) is a relic of the 3rd c. Roman ring walls. Today it is a museum (open: daily except Sun. 9am–6pm).

Saint-Donat

From the Grand'Place the road climbs to the top of the hill, where Saint-Donat's church now occupies the site of the counts of Arlon's medieval stronghold. Capuchin friars built a monastery on the ruins of the old castle in 1626, only for it to be converted into a fortress again by Louis XIV. The erstwhile chapel became a church in 1807, undergoing considerable alter-ation later in the 19th c.
On the west side of the hill stone steps lead up in an impressive arc to the church, and near their foot is a statue (1987) of the "Helleschman", an Arlon carnival figure. The interior of the church is embellished with 17th and

18th c. frescos of the life of St Donatus. There are also a number of other treasures well worth seeing.

The tower affords a splendid panoramic view encompassing four countries – France to the south, the Belgian Ardennes to the north and west, and to the east Luxembourg with Germany beyond.

*View

Down the hill from Saint-Donat's, below the Grand'Place, Arlon's provincial government building (1845), Palais de Justice (1864) and main post office stand grouped around Place Léopold. At the southern corner of the square an American tank commemorates the liberation of the town by General Patton's forces in December 1944.

Place Léopold

Beyond Place Léopold, on the far side of Square Albert I, the 97m/318ft tower of Saint-Martin's church (1907) rises high above the roofs of the new town.

Saint-Martin

*Musée Luxembourgeois

Leaving the Place Léopold by the Rue des Faubourgs and turning left into the Rue des Martyrs leads us to Arlon's exceptionally interesting Musée Luxembourgeois, three rooms of which are taken up by a collection of Roman tombstones and sarcophagi unique in Belgium.

Opening times
Mon.–Sat.
9am–noon and
2–5pm;
Sun. and public
holidays
10am–noon and
2–5pm;
Sept. 15–
June 15
closed Sun. and
public holidays

Particularly noteworthy among the sculptures are a relief showing travellers in the course of their journey (A.D. 170–180), statues of a divine horseman and various other gods, a satyr-decorated stele, and a large fragment found only recently, in 1980, carved with scenes from ancient mythology. The room devoted to ceramics and Roman artefacts contains vases, glassware, bronzes, weaponry, etc.

127

Saint-Donat and "Helleschman" monument

There is much to see apart from the Roman finds. One room concentrates on the Merovingian period with a collection of weapons, Damascene work, glass and items of everyday use.

Folk art is also well represented, with displays of furniture and domestic items such as kitchen utensils and jewellery. Exhibits include some from the Luxembourg Ardennes and range in date from the Middle Ages to the recent past.

Among the museum's many examples of religious art the most notable is the Fisecne retable, made in Antwerp in the 16th c.

Thermal baths

Also part of the museum are the remains of a 1st c. A.D. Roman bathhouse in the Rue des Thermes Romains.

Basilique romaine

Next to the thermal baths lie the ruins of the oldest Christian church in Belgium, originally a Roman building converted in the 5th and 6th centuries into a basilica and around which, in the 6th and 7th centuries, the Franks buried their dead.

Surroundings

Victory Memorial Museum near Hondelange

The Victory Memorial Museum, just off the E411/E25 motorway near the Hondelange Service Station about 7km/4 miles from Arlon, was opened in February 1990. Claiming to be the biggest Second World War museum in the world, its aim is to provide a lasting record of the Allied campaign. On display are a collection of 150 vehicles, weaponry and uniforms, augmented by dioramas, films and documentary material (open: daily 9am–6pm).

Habay-la-Neuve

Until the late 18th c. demand for the iron smelted in its furnaces made Habay-la-Neuve, a small town 14km/9 miles north-west of Arlon on the banks of the Rulles, a place of some importance. In the wooded countryside around it, houses such as Château Pont d'Oye (1742), 2km/1¼ miles east on the Martelange road, still testify to the prosperity of those days. Later, in the 19th c., the château was the meeting place of an intellectual circle which formed around the writer Pierre Nothomb.

Ath · Aat   C 6

Province: Hainaut
Altitude: 30–75m/98–246ft
Population: 24,000
Intercity and Inter-regional Station (bicycle rental at station)

The little town of Ath (Flemish Aat) situated at the confluence of the two rivers Dender (East and West), boasts some modest industry, mainly furniture manufacture and silk processing. In addition it serves as a market town for the surrounding villages. Ath's Parade of Giants – with the Wedding of Goliath one of the highlights – is among the oldest manifestations of this folk tradition in Belgium.

Location

The town was founded in the 12th c. when Baldwin IV, Count of Hainaut, purchased the title to the area. Because of its strategic importance he fortified it by building several castles, including one at Ath. War has principally shaped Ath's history ever since. Following capture by Louis XIV in 1667 it became the site of one of Vauban's earliest exercises in military engineering. Ironically enough it was the French who also later razed Vauban's fortifications during the War of Austrian Succession.
The humanist scholar Justus Lipsius (1547–1606) was brought up in Ath.

History

Sights

In addition to the 17th c. town hall, built between 1614 and 1624 by Wenceslas Cobergher, a number of fine 18th c. houses line Ath's central Grand' Place. These include the Maison Espagnole, a reconstruction of an earlier house dating from 1564.

Grand'Place

The 23m/75ft high Tour de Burbant (Burbant Tower) is a relic of Baldwin IV's original stronghold, built in 1168. Walls up to 3.7m/12ft thick leave little room actually inside the tower. The rest of the castle was demolished in the 16th c., to be replaced by another in the 17th c.

Tour de Burbant

Reached via the main thoroughfare running through the market-place, the 12th c. church of Saint-Julien had to be substantially rebuilt after a fire. Standing out from the rest of the church today the sturdy tower (1462) with its four turrets and carillon of bells was one part of the building to survive.

Saint-Julien

The Musée du cercle royal d'histoire et d'archéologie in the Rue Bouchain is dedicated to the history of the region. Well worth seeing are two paintings from the 14th and 16th c. respectively, both showing scenes of the Entombment.

Museum

Surroundings

An old quarry near Maffle, 3km/2 miles south-east of Ath, has been turned into the rather unusual Musée de la Pierre (open: July and Aug. Tues.–Fri. 2–5pm; Apr.–June. and Sept.–Oct. weekends 2–6pm).

Maffle

Built in the 18th c. for the Comte de Gomegnies, replacing a medieval castle, the Louis XV style Château d'Attre, situated 5km/3 miles south-east

Château d'Attre

129

Ath: Apse and tower of Saint-Julien

of Ath, was a favourite with Maria Christina, daughter of Empress Maria Theresa of Austria and Governor of the South (Austrian) Netherlands. The château's interior furnishings are almost entirely original, providing a unique glimpse into the life of the aristocracy in the 18th c. The fine parquet floors are by Dewez and the stucco work in the great salon by the Italian Ferrari. The paintings include works by Snyders, Hubert Robert and Watteau ("Les plaisirs d'été"). The wall-coverings are a particularly noteworthy feature of the house. They exemplify the many different materials in vogue at the time, from rice-paper and Chinese silk to the painted wallpaper (1760) of the Archduke's salon, the first such paper to be used in Belgium (open: Easter–end of June and Sept.–end of Oct. Sat., Sun. 10am–noon and 2–6pm; July and Aug. daily except Wed. 10am–noon and 2–6pm).

The park

The château overlooks a park laid out in the English manner, through which flows the river Dender. In addition to ruins and e.g. a dovecot and bathing pavilions in the style of the period, there is also a curious 24m/80ft high artificial hillock complete with grottoes and caves. This seems to have been intended partly as a vantage point for the Archduchess Maria Christina when out hunting.

Chièvres

Chièvres, another small town, 6km/4 miles south-east of Ath, began as a Roman settlement, later being a possession of, among others, the Counts of Gavre, Egmont and Croy. In the Middle Ages Chièvres grew to some importance on account of its manufacturing but subsequently proved unable to compete with Ath. The late Gothic church beside the Tour de Gavre dates from this period of prosperity, as does the Hotel de Croy or "Maison Espagnole" (1560) in the Grand'Place, the residence at one time of Count Lamoraal van Egmont. The tombs of the Gavre, Croy and Egmont families can be seen in Saint-Martin's church, built in the 14th c. and renovated in the 16th c.

Gardens of the Château d'Attre

Not far outside Chièvres, on a farm estate in the valley of the Hunnelle, stands the even older Romanesque chapel of La Ladrerie. In the 12th c. it belonged to a hospice for lepers.
The airfield serving SHAPE, the NATO headquarters in nearby Casteau (see Mons), lies to the south-east of Chièvres.

Ruins are all that remain of the 12th c. abbey at Cambron-Casteau, 12km/7½ miles south-east of Ath. The adjacent land on the banks of the Dender has been turned into a leisure park.

Cambron-Casteau

The church at Tongre-Notre-Dame, 6km/4 miles south of Ath, owes its status as a pilgrim church to a Romanesque statue of the Virgin, said to have undergone a miraculous transformation in 1081.

Tongre-Notre-Dame

See entry

Belœil

Bastogne · Bastenaken

H 8

Province: Luxembourg
Altitude: 515m/1690ft
Population: 12,000
Local Rail Station (bicycle rental at station)

The small town of Bastogne (Flemish Bastenaken), known for its tasty smoked ham and its nuts, is situated on the plateau of the Ardennes not far from the Luxembourg border. Today the town's name is inseparably linked with the Battle of the Ardennes, the final German counter-offensive of the Second World War mounted late in 1944 and early 1945. The "Road to Freedom" (French "Voie de la Liberté") which, with its kilometre-stones,

Location

marks the route of the 1944 Allied advance from Normandy to near Bastogne, passes through the town.

History

Bastogne's medieval fortress, strategically sited at the intersection of two great military roads (Reims to Cologne and Arlon to Tongeren), caught fire in the 13th c. and was eventually destroyed by the French in 1688.

On 16th December 1944 German forces launched their last great offensive of the Second World War in the Ardennes, with the intention of advancing on Antwerp. The initial swift German push succeeded in surrounding Bastogne, trapping US troops commanded by General McAuliffe. Called upon to surrender McAuliffe refused, holding out for a further four days. General Patton's tanks finally broke the German siege, so liberating Bastogne for the second time. The Battle of the Ardennes ended on 25th January 1945 with the Allies poised to advance into Germany.

Sights

Place McAuliffe

Bastogne's town centre, the old Grand'Place, is now called Place McAuliffe in honour of the man who ended the German occupation. The events of those days are further commemorated by a US Sherman tank and a monument to the general, both of which stand in the southern corner of the square.

Musée original au pays d'Ardenne

The Musée original au pays d'Ardenne, just off the square, about 50m/55yds along the Route de Neufchâteau, focuses on all the multifarious aspects of life in the Ardennes. As well as displays of farm implements and stuffed animals, etc. there are weapons and other equipment from the Battle of the Ardennes (open: daily 10am–5pm; July and Aug. 9am–6pm).

Monument Patton

A monument in the form of a relief dedicated to the US General Patton can be seen in the Rue Joseph Renquin, also quite near the square.

Saint-Pierre

The founding of the church of Saint-Pierre (Place Saint-Pierre) can be traced back to the 7th c., though nothing from that time survives. The tower of the present church dates from the 12th c. while the nave, damaged by fire in the 13th c., was later completed in the Meuse Gothic style in the 15th c. The church interior has several interesting features, chief among which is the nave vaulting, colourfully decorated with scenes from the Old and New Testaments by Renadin de Wicourt. Also noteworthy are the Romanesque fonts, the 12th c. altar, and the Baroque pulpit by Georges Scholtus from Bastogne.

Porte de Trèves

The Porte de Trèves (Trèves Gate), a massive, square, sandstone tower near the church, is all that remains of Bastogne's late medieval ramparts razed by the French in 1688 (open: July and Aug. daily 9am–6pm).

Maison Mathelin

Only a short distance from the church and gate, archaeological finds and other artefacts can be seen displayed in the Maison Mathelin, the town's historical and archaeological museum. Spanning a period from Gallo-Roman times, through the Middle Ages up to the Second World War, the collection covers the early as well as the modern history of Bastogne and the surrounding region. One section is specifically devoted to the rural life of the Ardennes (open: July and Aug. daily 9am–6pm).

Musée en Piconrue

Housed in fifteen rooms of a 17th c. Bethlehemite monastery at Place Saint-Pierre 24, the rather unusual Musée en Piconrue is a celebration of popular religion in its various forms, including its expression in folk art (open: Mon.–Fri. 1.30–6pm, Sat., Sun. 10am–noon and 1.30–6pm).

*Mardasson Hill

American Memorial

From Bastogne the kilometre-stones of the "Road to Freedom" lead 3km/2 miles north-east to Mardasson Hill with its broad vista over the countryside

Mardasson Hill: Monument

around. Here in 1950 an impressive memorial was erected in honour of the US soldiers who lost their lives during the Battle of the Ardennes. Built in the shape of a five-pointed star the monument bears the names of the units which took part in the battle, as well as recording details of the principal events. The crypt, decorated with mosaics by Fernand Léger, contains three altars, one Catholic, one Protestant and one Jewish.

The Bastogne Historical Center describes itself as "the finest war museum in the world", a claim which some might feel to be somewhat less than justified. Like the nearby American Memorial, the Center is built in the shape of a five-pointed star. Presentation takes three different forms. The central display consists of an amphitheatre-like model of the battle illustrating the different phases of the action. This is surrounded by screens featuring authentic still photographs with commentaries in six languages. Next come collections of weaponry, tanks, military vehicles and uniforms, all fully authentic, together with groups of uniformed figures representing the main protagonists.

Bastogne Historical Center

Finally there is a cinema which shows films of the Ardennes offensive made by the two sides (open: Mar.–Apr. and Oct.–mid Nov. daily 10am–4pm; May, June and Sept. daily 9.30am–5pm; July and Aug. daily 9am–6pm).

Surroundings

The 6,785 German soldiers killed in the Ardennes lie buried in the German War Cemetery at Recogne, 6km/4 miles north of Bastogne (see Practical Information, Military Cemeteries).

Recogne

Beaumont

Province: Hainaut
Altitude: 230m/755ft
Population: 6000

Location

Beaumont lies surrounded by woods on a hill above the river Hantes, close to the French border. As early as the 12th c. it was defended by a 2.4km/1½ mile long wall with 30 towers, later demolished in the 16th c. During the 18th and 19th centuries the town experienced a modest upturn in fortune, boosted by its cloth industry.

Sights

Tour Salamandre

The Tour Salamandre (Salamander Tower) on the southern edge of the hill is the main survival from the old ramparts. Built in the 16th c. it is now a museum, its five floors given over to documents and other items of local history as well as a display of regional arts and crafts. The former include memorabilia of Napoleon I (who made a stop here en route to Waterloo). The top of the tower affords a lovely view of the Hainaut countryside. (Open: May–Sept. daily 9am–noon and 2–5pm; Oct. Sun. 10am–noon and 2–5pm.)

Surroundings

Montignies-
Saint-Christophe

In Montignies-Saint-Christophe, 5km/3 miles to the north-west, the Hantes is spanned by a 25m/82ft bridge with thirteen arches. Lying as it does on the route of the Roman road to Trèves, the bridge is often referred to as a "pont romaine" (Roman bridge) but in fact almost certainly dates from the 15th c.

Beaumont: Tour Salamandre

Soire-sur-Sambre: the castle tower

Some 10km/6 miles north-west of Beaumont, just off the road to Merbes-le-Château (which bypasses the village), the moated château at Solre-sur-Sambre is one of the less well-preserved of Hainaut's feudal castles. It is entered through the 13th–14th c. keep on either side of which high walls extend in a square with two round corner towers. The right-hand tower and knights' hall, the latter with a magnificent fireplace, are open to visitors (open: daily 10am–noon and 2–6pm).

Solre-sur-Sambe

Sivry's natural history and toy museum boasts a collection of more than 5,000 animal specimens (11km/7 miles south-west of Beaumont; open: Mon.–Fri. 10am–5pm; Easter–Sept. also Sat., Sun. 2–6pm).

Sivry

The area around Rance, a small town 12km/7½ miles south of Beaumont, is noted for its red marble, Rance itself being the location of the Musée National du Marbre (National Marble Museum, Place Albert I).
Despite the dust and the appearance of chaos, the museum is unique and utterly fascinating, demonstrating the techniques of marble extraction and processing. The museum also maintains a collection of all the different kinds of marble found anywhere in the world (open: Apr.–Oct. Mon.–Fri. 9.30am–6pm, Sun. and public holidays 2–6pm; Nov.–Mar. Mon.–Fri. 8.30–5pm).

Rance

*Musée National du Marbre

Beauraing

See Dinant, Surroundings

Belœil

C 6

Province: Hainaut
Altitude: 28m/92ft
Population: 13,500

The little town of Belœil is situated about 30km/19 miles north-west of Mons (see entry). Belœil's Baroque château and park have the reputation of being the finest of their kind in Belgium.

Location

**Château de Belœil

For almost seven hundred years the Château de Belœil has been in the possession of the aristocratic de Ligne family. The most brilliant member of this noble line was Charles-Joseph Lamoral, Prince de Ligne (1735–1814), diplomat, officer in the Austrian army, writer, and friend of many of the great figures of his time including Marie-Antoinette and Catherine the Great. Such was his character he earned himself the sobriquet "Prince Charming".
In the 16th c., and in the 17th and 18th centuries in particular, the small 12th c. castle which originally stood on the site was progressively altered to the taste of successive generations of the de Ligne family until finally completely transformed. The main house burnt down in 1900, being rebuilt in its present 18th c. style in 1920. Only the two free standing wings and the entrance pavilions survive substantially unchanged from 1682. The latest in the long and distinguished line of the princes of Ligne lives with his family in the left-hand wing.

Opening times
Apr.–Nov.
daily 10am–6pm

The rooms of the château are superbly furnished with a wealth of period furniture, Gobelin tapestries, glass and porcelain, etc. belonging to the de Ligne family. Especially noteworthy are Prince Charles-Joseph's apartment with its series of paintings depicting episodes in his life, the Salle des

Interior

In the park of the Château de Belœil

Médailles with its valuable coin collection, the library which has over 20,000 volumes (including an hour-book dated 1532 and said to have belonged to Charles V), the dining-room hung with superb Gobelins, the Salon des Ambassadeurs with its magnificent painting by Canaletto ("Canale Grande in Venice"), and the Tour Maria-Antoinette where some locks of hair from the head of the French queen, executed in 1793, are preserved in a pouch knitted from gold yarn.

Chapel

Precious items of religious art, e.g. coral sculptures and enamel work from Limoges, can be seen in the chapel created in 1950 in the right-hand wing.

** The park

Opening times
Apr.–Nov.
daily 10am–6pm

The 120ha/296 acre park of Belgium's "Little Versailles" was designed and laid out in the 18th c. by Prince Claude Lamoral II, with the aid of the French architect Chevotet. A series of small hedged gardens, several with pools, are arranged in typical Rococo fashion around the 460m/1500ft long ornamental lake known as Le Grand Pièce d'Eau, at the far end of which stands a Neptune group by Henrion. The splendid 5km/3 mile Allée Grande Vue extends beyond the boundaries of the park itself.

Jardins Anglais

With English-style gardens very much in fashion at the end of the 18th c., Prince Charles-Joseph had one laid out to the side and rear of the left-hand wing. This part of the park remains private and is not open to the public.

Parcs des
Attractions

Some years ago various attractions were added, utilising land on the west side of the estate (orangery and kitchen garden). They include a restaurant, a childrens' playground, and "Park Minibel", a 1:25 scale reconstruction of some of Belgium's most famous sights and buildings – the Huy Collégiale, Liége railway station, Brussels Town Hall, the Bruges Belfry, Zeebrugge

Beloeil

© Baedeker

harbour, and much more. A miniature train ferries tourists between château and amusement area.

Beveren

See Sint-Niklaas, Surroundings

Binche   D 7

Province: Hainaut
Altitude: 110m/360ft
Population: 32,600
Inter-regional Station

Situated between Charleroi and Mons (see entries) not far from the French   Location
border, Binche takes great pride in being the only town in Belgium – and
indeed in the Netherlands – to retain intact a substantial proportion of its
medieval ramparts including 27 towers. Now serving primarily as the
market town for the surrounding region, little remains of Binche's once
quite considerable textile industry apart from the manufacture of carnival
costumes.

Throughout its long history those who have held the fate of Binche in their   History
hands have frequently been women – Joanna of Constantinople, Margaret
of York, and especially Mary of Hungary under whom the town enjoyed its
heydey. Mary, sister of the Emperor Charles V, played host to her brother,
his son Philip and the flower of Europe's nobility at a great celebration held

at her Renaissance palace in 1549. Only five years later Binche was occupied by troops of the French King Henry II and the palace was destroyed. Apart from the 19th c. when it had a thriving textile industry, the town has remained something of a backwater ever since.

**Carnival

Once a year, however, Binche reclaims its place in the national limelight with the holding of its carnival, probably the most famous event of its kind in Belgium. Hundreds of "Gilles" (carnival jesters) in brightly coloured costumes dance in the streets. This custom may in part have originated with the great fête organised by Mary of Hungary in 1549 for Charles V in celebration of Pizarro's conquest of Peru, when many of those attending were dressed as Incas. The carnival itself is older, however, being mentioned in documents from as early as the 14th c., while the figure of the "Gille" goes back only to the 18th c.

Sights

Hotel de Ville

The Hôtel de Ville (Town Hall) in the Grand'Place is emblazoned with the coats of arms of Charles V and Mary of Hungary as well as those of the town itself. The belfry has a carillon of 27 bells.

Town walls

To the right of the town hall a narrow alleyway joins a path running along the old town walls as far as Rue de Posty. This latter in turn leads up to the Rue Haute.

Chapelle
Saint-André

On the left-hand side of the Rue Haute stands the Chapelle Saint-André (1537). Inside the chapel the heads of the rafters are interestingly carved, two with scenes from a Dance of Death.

Chapelle
Saint-Ursmer

At the end of the street the large votive church of Saint-Ursmer (12th–15th c.) has a very fine Renaissance gallery directly behind the main portal.

Carnival figures greet the visitor to Binche

Noteworthy in the interior are a wooden pietà dated 1511 and a 15th c. polychrome Entombment.
Mary of Hungary's palace once occupied the site behind the church, now a park. The bronze statue at the entrance is of a carnival "Gille".

Housed in a former Augustinian monastery immediately adjacent to the church, the Musée international du Carnaval et du Masque (International Museum of Carnival and Mask) is surely unrivalled anywhere. Its collection comprises some 15,000 costumes, masks and other carnival items, and the museum features carnival customs from all over the world.

°Musée international du Carnaval et du Masque

The first floor concentrates on costumes and masks from European countries, ranging from Russia to Italy and from the Balkans to the extreme north. The comprehensiveness of the collection can be judged from its inclusion of, e.g. masks from the Swabian-Alemannic shrovetide carnival. The second floor focuses on the carnival traditions of Africa, America, Asia and Oceania, many of whose customs are quite different from those of Europe. The story of Binche's own carnival is told on film in a special display hall (open: mid Jan.–Mar. daily except Fri. 9am–noon and 1–5pm. Sat. and Sun. 2–6pm; Apr.–mid Nov. daily except Fri. 9am–noon and 2–6pm, Sat. and Sun. 10am–1pm and 2–6pm).

Surroundings

°Hydraulic-lift locks near La Louvière

About 12km/7½ miles north of Binche the Canal du Centre passes by the industrial town of La Louvière. Although the town itself has little to offer in the way of sights, anyone with an interest in industrial archaeology should make a point of visiting it, if only to see the four hydraulic barge lifts on the canal at Houdeng Goegnies and Bracquenies on the outskirts. These steel monsters were constructed between 1888 and 1917 to overcome a height difference of 68m/225ft in the space of just 7km/4 miles. The four lifts are due to be replaced by the modern hydraulic-lift locks at Strépy-Thieu, but a campaign has recently been launched aimed at preserving the old installations.

One of the best ways of seeing the locks in operation is by taking a boat trip on the canal (from Bracquenies, Rue Noulet). If a more leisurely kind of canal excursion is prefered, there are also rides aboard an old horse-drawn barge (from the "Cantine italien").

Boat trips

Near lock No. 1 (Houdeng Goegnies, Rue Tout-y-Faut) an exhibition of models and photographs has been set up under the title "Ship-lifts of the World", illustrating the history of these and other similar installations around the world.

Museums

The industrial history of the area more generally is also explained in the "Cantine italien" close by. Lastly, all the different kinds of craft used on the inland waters of Wallonia can be seen in the open-air museum on the Canal du Centre quay at 120 Rue G. Boel (opening times for all the museums: May–June, Sept. daily 10am–4pm; July and Aug. until 6pm).
In the suburb of Bois-du-Lac, south of Houdeng-Goignies, the Mining Museum highlights the life of the miners of the region (open: Mon.–Fri. 8.30am–5pm; Sat., Sun. and public holidays 2–5pm).

A detour west of La Louvière to the enormous, modern hydraulic-lift locks at Strépy-Thieu provides an interesting comparison with the old barge locks. The new locks overcome a difference in level of 73m/240ft (open: daily 10am–6pm).

°Strépy-Thieu hydraulic-lift locks

**Domaine de Mariemont

Situated near the village of Morlanwelz about 8km/5 miles from Binche, the Domaine de Mariemont is named after Mary of Hungary who built a hunting lodge there in 1546. Eight years later the lodge was to suffer the same fate at the hands of the French as Mary's palace in Binche. The Austrian Archdukes Albert and Isabella rebuilt and enlarged it, only for French revolutionaries to set fire to the palace again in 1794. Later, one of the administrators of Mariemont, Nicolas Warocqué, acquired part of the estate, and in 1831 built himself a small château. This was subsequently expanded by Warocqué's grandson Raoul in order to house his extensive private art collection. In 1960, however, the greater part of this château was also burnt down and since 1975 the art collection has occupied a modern purpose-built museum.

The park
The museum and palace ruins are set in an English-style park adorned with some very fine sculptures. These include several works by the Belgian sculptor Victor Rousseau, as well as Auguste Rodin's "The Burghers of Calais".

Museum
The first floor of the new museum building designed by Roger Bastin contains extensive collections of Egyptian, Greek and Roman antiquities as well as precious jade and lacquer work from China and Japan. On the lower ground floor there are archaeological finds from Gallo-Roman and Mero-vingian times, although the most exciting section here is the extraordinary collection of Tournai porcelain with pieces representing four stylistic periods from between 1750 and 1799 (open: Tues.–Sun. 10am–6pm).
The museum also has a library with some very valuable manuscripts and other items.

Abbaye de Bonne-Espérance

The Abbaye de Bonne-Espérance, just 4km/2½ miles south of Binche near the village of Vellereille-les-Brayeux, was founded in the 12th c. by Premon-statensian friars. Apart from its 15th c. Gothic tower, however, the present church is largely 18th c., the work of Laurent Dewez. Many visitors are drawn to the Abbaye by a reputedly miraculous statue of the smiling Madonna and Child (stone, 14th c.). The cloisters adjacent to the church also date principally from the 18th c., though one or two arches are survi-vals from the 13th c.

Blankenberge   B 3

Province: West-Vlaanderen
Altitude: sea level
Population: 15,000
Intercity Station

∘ Seaside resort
Blankenberge, with its 3km/2 mile stretch of beach on Belgium's North Sea coast, first began to attract holidaymakers as long ago as 1860. Despite having been somewhat eclipsed of late by Knokke-Heist (see entry), it remains one of the country's best known seaside resorts, popular espe-cially with families and offering a wide range of sporting and leisure activities. Today the tourists who throng the town in summer are the primary source of income, the small fishing fleet contributing only mod-estly to the economy.

Flower
parade
The very colourful flower parade held annually on the last Sunday in August always attracts many visitors.

Sights

Kerkstraat
Kerkstraat, Blankenberge's main thoroughfare, runs past the station, lined with shops and restaurants. Steps at its northern end lead up to the Zeedijk.

Blankenberge: the beach

No. 31 Kerkstraat, the former town hall built in 1680, is used for art exhibitions.

Opposite the station stands the Gothic Sint-Antoniuskerk, first consecrated in 1358. Restored in the 17th c. its furnishings are mainly 18th c. pieces.

Sint-Antoniuskerk

Majuttehuis, in the Breydelstraat, a little to the west of Casinoplein, is now the only survivor from among Blankenberge's once numerous fishermans' cottages.

Majuttehuis

Two monuments adorn the Grote Markt, one a memorial to the writer Hendrik Conscience, the other a war memorial.

Grote Markt

Further west lies a modern yacht marina, its entrance protected from silting by a 300m/330yd long pile breakwater. There are berths for 900 boats.

Marina

*Zeedijk

Blankenberge's promenade, the more than 2km/1¼ mile-long Zeedijk, runs along the seafront 10m/30ft above the level of the beach. Interspersed with somewhat unattractive modern hotels, restaurants, cafés and shops, are one or two pleasing older buildings from the town's early days, as well as a number of villas.
Ever since its opening in 1933 the "Lustige Velodroom", a "fun" cycling track at the eastern end of the promenade, has been one of the resort's most popular attractions.
Also at the eastern end of the Zeedijk is a 350m/380yds long seaside pier with an excellent "Aquarama" spotlighting the coast's marine life.
The cinema, located just before the steps up from Kerkstraat, was built in 1932; the Kursaal, just after the steps, once housed Blankenberge's first casino.

Surroundings

Wenduine

Wenduine, 4km/2½ miles east of Blankenberge, is a small seaside resort, considerably more sedate in atmosphere than its larger neighbour.

Fonteintjes

Extending all the way along the coast between Blankenberge and Zeebrugge (see entry), the Fonteintjes dunes offer excellent walking.

Bokrijk (Provincial)

See Hasselt, Surroundings

Bouillon   F 9

Province: Luxembourg
Altitude: 221m/725ft
Population: 5,000

**Location

In the south of the Belgian province of Luxembourg, close to the French border, Bouillon nestles prettily in a loop of the River Semois, encircled by the wooded heights of the southern Ardennes. Dominated by its imposing castle, the small town is a popular summer resort and makes a lively centre for excursions into the surrounding countryside.
Bouillon is closely linked in name and by history with Godfrey of Bouillon (Godefroy de Bouillon), the "most Christian of all knights".

Because of its favoured location Bouillon, principal town of the old Duchy of Lower Lotharingia, was for hundreds of years an important link between the Eifel and Champagne. It began life as a village which grew up in the shadow of Godfrey the Bearded's castle (started 1050). When, almost half a century later, the famous Godfrey of Bouillon left home to lead the First Crusade (1095), he mortgaged the castle to the Prince-Bishops of Liège who retained it, with one or two interruptions and in the face of challenges to their title by local noblemen, until the 17th c. After the French took over the region in 1676, Louis XIV gave the castle to the La Tour d'Auvergne family. Under their liberal patronage Bouillon developed in the 18th c. into a centre of Enlightenment where the printer Pierre Rousseau was able to publish numerous avant-garde journals, as well as works by Mirabeau and Diderot which had been banned in France. The town eventually became part of Belgium in 1830.

Sights

Starting at the lower bridge, the Pont de Liège or Vieux-Pont, go

Approaching the Château de Fort of Bouillon

along the left bank of the river past the church and up to the castle square from where there are some fine views. To the right is the entrance to the Château Fort (Fortified Castle), enthroned on its elevated "island" of rock overlooking the looping Semois on two sides. Built by Godfrey the Bearded between 1050 and 1067 on the remains of a still older fortress, the Château is the earliest and best preserved example of medieval feudal architecture in Belgium. After Louis XIV's troops had taken over the castle, the fortifications were strengthened by Vauban. Further alterations were also made by the Dutch at the beginning of the 19th c.

**Château Fort

Tour:
The castle, which contains some fine paintings, is entered over three drawbridges. The main courtyard then leads to the ducal palace with its 13th c. Salle Godefroy de Bouillon. From there visitors climb up to the top of the 16th c. Tour d'Autriche for a breathtaking panorama of the town and river, before making their way back via the torture chamber, cisterns and dungeons, and past the 65m/213ft deep well shaft (open: Jan., Feb. Sat., Sun. 10am–5pm; Mar., Oct., Nov. daily 10am–5pm; Apr.–June, Sept. daily 10am–6pm; July, Aug. daily 9.30am–7pm; Dec. Wed.–Sun. 10am–5pm).

The Musée Ducal (Ducal Museum), in a delightful 18th c. town house below the north side of the castle square, has a refreshingly old-fashioned charm. The section on local history and folklore includes displays of craftwork, old furniture and kitchen fittings as well as memorabilia relating to Bouillon's noble families and the printer Pierre Rousseau. There is also a section entitled "Godefroy de Bouillon" which, being devoted principally to the First Crusade, has among its exhibits some exceptionally lovely examples of Islamic craftsmanship. Works by the painter Albert Raty are exhibited in two side rooms (open: Apr.–June daily 10am–6pm; July, Aug. daily 9.30am–7pm; Oct. daily 10am–5pm; Nov., Dec. Sat. and Sun. 10am–5pm).

Musée Ducal

Brecht

Riverside promenade	An attractive riverside promenade with a good selection of restaurants, cafés and shops follows the bend in the River Semois. Several establishments have rowing boats and pedallos for rental.

Surroundings

Abbaye de Cordemoy	Picturesquely situated on the right bank of the Semois, the Abbaye de Cordemoy (Notre-Dame de Clairefontaine) is reached by taking the tunnel under the castle hill from the Porte de France, crossing the old Pont de Poulie and continuing westwards for about 3km/2 miles. Founded in the 13th c. the abbey was burned down in 1794 and acquired its present Neo-Gothic character when last rebuilt in 1935.
More trips around Bouillon	See Vallée de la Semois

Brecht

See Antwerp, Surroundings

Breendonk (Fort)

See Mechelen, Surroundings

Bruges · Brugge   B4

Province: West-Vlaanderen
Altitude: 9m/30ft
Population: 120,000
Intercity Station (bicycle rental at station)

Location	Bruges (Flemish Brugge, French Bruges), the old capital of Flanders and an archbishopric since 1559, is located on the little river Reie 12km/7½ miles south of the port of Zeebrugge (see entry) to which it is linked by the Boudewijn-Kanaal. Other canals connect Bruges with Ostende, Nieuwpoort, Veurne, Ghent (see entries) and Sluis.

Despite the addition of new building and the loss of its old town walls (all but four towers having been demolished since the mid 19th c. to make way for traffic), Bruges with its perfectly preserved medieval town centre remains a tourist dream, a magnet drawing more than two million visitors a year. But the town does have thriving industries as well – steel works, calico mills, furniture factories, breweries, gin (jenever) distilleries, prefabricated cement works and yeast, paint, television set and outboard engine manufacturers. Bobbin lace, for which Bruges has long been famous, continues to be important. Complementing all this industry is a strong service sector which makes a significant contribution to the local economy. The chief commodities passing through the port of Zeebrugge – the second largest fishing port in Belgium – are crude oil, coal, iron ore, packaged goods and meat.

In addition to its Academy of Fine Arts and its Chamber of Commerce and Industry, Bruges is also proud to play host to the College of Europe.

Festivals	Bruges's major festival is the annual Procession of the Holy Blood, celebrated in May. The superb historical Pageant of the Golden Tree which commemorates the marriage in 1468 of Charles the Bold and Margaret of York takes place every fifth year (the next being in 1995). Canal festivals

during which the waterways are attractively lit are held from time to time in
August at no particular intervals.

History

Surprisingly little is known about the early history of Bruges. There is
mention of a "Municipium Brugense" in documents dating from the 7th c.
but the name itself seems to have originated with the Vikings who landed at
the mouth of the Reie ("bruggja" = place of embarkation). Rather more
certain is that Baldwin I (Iron Arm), who died about 879 and who was the
founder of the powerful dynasty of Flemish counts and a son-in-law of
Charles the Bald of France, built himself a castle here. Trade gradually
flourished until Robert the Frisian (died 1093) made the town his capital.

Unknown origins

During the 12th and 13th centuries, when still linked by the Reie to the
North Sea via the inlet known as the Zwin, Bruges evolved into one of the
principal trading cities of the medieval world. Banking and commercial
houses representing seventeen different nations became established in
the city, trading in commodities as various as fabrics from Italy and the
Orient, fish from Scandinavia, furs from Russia, wine from Spain and
spices from Arabia. As the headquarters of the "Flemish Hanse in London"
Bruges held a virtual monopoly of trade with England, including the wool
trade so vital to the Flemish cloth industry. At the same time it served as the
commercial entrepot for the cities of the German Hanseatic League. The
city reached a pinnacle of prosperity in the 14th c. when work began on
building the town walls. Its wealth at that time can be judged from the
remark attributed to Joanna of Navarre, wife of Philip the Fair of France.
Arriving in Bruges in 1301 and catching sight of the burghers' wives with
their sumptuous clothes and unmistakable trappings of luxury, she is said
to have exclaimed indignantly: "I thought I was the only queen, but here I
am surrounded by hundreds".

Cosmopolitan
medieval city

In the 13th c. passions in the rich Flemish cities were inflamed by disputes
between the francophile "Leliaerts" (so-called after the French Lily) and the
"Clauwaerts" (after the claws of the Flemish lion), the latter being determined to maintain their traditional independence from France. Exploiting
this dissension the French king Philip the Fair seized control of Flanders,
appointing Jacques de Châtillon governor. Châtillon's suppression of the
Bruges guilds was so harsh that on the night of 17th–18th May 1302 the
inhabitants rose up in a revolt known as "the Bruges Matins". Led by Pieter
de Coninck and Jan Breydel they put to the sword anyone suspected of
being French. In the same year an army of Flemish burghers triumphed
over the French nobility at the Battle of the Golden Spurs near Kortrijk,
ensuring thereby the continued independence and success of the Flemish
cities.

"Bruges Matins"

The fruits of victory over the French were dissipated, however, by growing
rivalry between Bruges and Ghent. Partly for this reason, but mainly due to
the silting up of the Zwin, in the 15th c. Bruges's fortunes fell into decline. At
first the signs of impending disaster remained obscured by the outward
brilliance of the city under by the Dukes of Burgundy, rulers of the County of
Flanders since 1384. The marriages of Philip the Good to Isabella of Portugal in 1430 and of Charles the Bold to Margaret of York in 1468 were both
celebrated with great splendour in Bruges. But from 1500 onwards the
city's wealthy merchants gradually forsook Bruges for Antwerp and the
religious turmoil of the second half of the 16th c. finally brought the era of
prosperity to an end.

Decline

It was only in the 19th c. that the city roused itself again from the long
period of dormancy vividly described by Georges Rodenbach in his melancholy novel "Bruges la Morte". The construction of the Boudewijn-Kanaal

Recent revival

in 1907 gave renewed access to the sea, leading, especially after the Second World War, to the siting of major industries along the waterway. Then an ambitious restoration programme was undertaken, rescuing much of the town centre from dereliction.

Old Flemish painting in Bruges

Bruges was the centre of the Old Flemish School of painters. Here Jan van Eyck painted his famous "Adoration of the Mystic Lamb", the centrepiece of the polyptych for Sint-Baafskathedraal in Ghent, and near here Hugo van der Goes (1440–82), a native of Ghent, lived and died, leaving his most famous work "The Death of the Virgin" to the city. Together with van Eyck's "Madonna and the donor, Canon van der Paele", it now hangs in the Groeninge Museum.

The painter most closely associated with Bruges, however, is Hans Memling (1435–94). Born near Mainz he settled in the town from 1465 onwards. Some of his greatest works can be seen in the Memling Museum housed in the 12th c. Sint-Jansspitaal. Gerard David (1460–1523), a pupil of Memling's, came to Bruges in 1483. Fine pictures by him and by Pieter Pourbus from Gouda can also be seen in the Groeninge Museum.

Tour of the city

Townscape

With its wealth of interesting old buildings and its canals Bruges still retains a medieval air, more so perhaps than anywhere else in Belgium. Anyone taking a walk through the narrow streets or a boat trip on the canals falls immediately under its spell, charmed by the atmosphere of what is for many the most delightful of all the cities of Flanders. This together with its remarkable state of preservation makes Bruges a tourist destination almost without rival in Europe.

The style of the medieval brick houses is thoroughly distinctive. Above many of the windows are recessed shallow arches, and the windows themselves are often found bracketed together by a continuous cill running the length of the frontage.

Equally distinctive of Bruges are the godshuizen, almhouses for the elderly and infirm paid for by the guilds or in some cases prosperous burghers. Most are groups of whitewashed brick houses with a communal entrance gate and janitor's window. Examples can be seen in e.g. Gloeribusstraat, Moerstraat, Zwarte Leertouwersstraat, Sint-Katelijnstraat and Nieuwe Gentweg. The Folklore Museum, the Kant Centre (Lace Centre) and the Pelicaanhuis are also former godshuizen.

Restoration programme

The loveliness of Bruges today is the result of a massive programme of restoration. The first and most pressing problem was to deal with the sewage and other effluent which flowed untreated into the canals, creating a smell obnoxious enough to spoil any stay.

Thanks to the construction of a proper sewage system and efficient purification plant the canals are now clean and free of smell. The task of saving the houses from crumbling into ruin also called for radical measures. Most of the 8000 buildings in the city centre were taken into civic ownership, responsibility for their restoration being placed on the shoulders of the municipal authorities. Few houses now remain in private hands, the vast majority being leased to their occupants.

What to see

Because the centre of Bruges is comparatively small, even those with only a day to spend looking around can expect to take away a good idea of all the major sights. Essential viewing includes the Markt with the Belfry, the Burg and Stadhuis, Onze Lieve Vrouwkerk, the Memling Museum, the picturesque Minnewater, and the Béguinage. A trip on the grachten is a never-to-be-forgotten experience.

Knokke-Heist

400 m

Brugge
Bruges

1 Provinciaal Hof
2 Halls and Belfry
3 Huis Bouchoute
4 Craenenburg
5 Former Provost's House
6 Oude Griffie
7 Paleis van het
  Brugse Vrije
8 Stadhuis
9 Heiligbloedkapel
10 Burg
11 Schouwburg
12 Oud Tolhuis
13 Geneose Lodge
14 Huis ter Beurze
15 Pelicaanhuis
16 Folklore Museum
17 Kantcentrum
18 Hof van Watervliet
19 Bisschopspaleis
20 Blindenkapel
21 Organ Museum
22 Waterhuis
23 "Straffe Hendrik" Brewery

Bruges: one of the canals in the city

Having two days available for sightseeing allows the pleasures of the city to be complemented by those of its museums, with visits to, for example, the Gruuthusemuseum, the Groeninge Museum, the Chapel of the Holy Blood, or any of several more. The descriptions below are intended to be of help in making a choice.

*Trips on the grachten (canals)
: The tours of the grachten last half an hour, passing under bridges so low that passengers must duck their heads and with one delightful view following another. Boats leave from the landing stages at Huidenvetterplaats and Rozenhoedkaai.

Town tours and guided walks
: The Bruges Tourist Office organises minibus tours but it is more fun to take one of the horse-drawn carriages starting from the Burg. Throughout July and August guided walks set out daily at 3pm from in front of the tourist office in the Burg (and at other times by arrangment).

Multi-storey car park
: Avoid driving right into the centre of Bruges unless it is absolutely essential. The underground car park below t'Zand on the south-western perimeter of the city centre is a convenient place to leave a car.

Between the Markt and the Burg

**Markt

The Markt is Bruges's main square and traffic hub at the very heart of the city. Surrounded on all sides by fine buildings from a variety of different periods it also boasts a large monument erected in 1887 to the guildmasters Jan Breydel and Pieter de Coninck who led the rebellion against the French in 1302.

*Halle and
**Belfry
: The Halle, begun in 1248 and twice enlarged, first in the 14th c. and then again in the 16th c., occupies the south side of the Markt, a large rectangular

148

brick building 85m/278ft long and 43.5m/142ft wide enclosing a pictur-esque courtyard. It was once Bruges's main market and the city fathers used to promulgate their statutes from the balcony above the entrance, reading them out to the populace assembled beneath.

Above the Halle soars Bruges's most distinctive landmark the Belfry, 83m/272ft high and with a slight lean towards the south-east. It is one of the finest bell towers in Belgium and there can surely be few more impressive symbols of civic pride. Work started on the tower in 1282, the crowning octagonal upper section being completed two centuries later (in 1482). A carillon of 47 bells hangs in the tower (chimes: Oct.–mid June Wed., Sat. Sun. 2.15pm; mid June–mid Sept. Mon., Wed., Sat. 9pm, Sun. 2.15pm). The tower is entered from the inner courtyard of the Halle and the top (366 steps) affords a superb panorama of the town and surrounding country-side. On the way up the old Treasure Room where civic documents are kept behind wrought-iron grills can be visited on the second floor (open: Apr.–Sept. daily 9.30am–12.30pm and 1.30–6pm; Oct.–Mar. until 5pm only).

The east side of the Markt is dominated by the Neo-Gothic Provinciaal Hof (1887–1921), seat of the West-Vlaanderen provincial government. Adjacent to it on the south side is the post office. Until the end of the 18th c. cloth halls dating back to the 13th c. stood on both sites. The cloth stored in them was brought into the city by water, the Reie at that time flowing close by.

Provinciaal Hof

Over on the west side of the Markt the attractive brick 15th c. Huis Bou-choute occupies the left-hand corner of Sint-Amandstraat. On the opposite corner stands the Craenenburg where, in 1488, at the instigation of Ghent, the burghers of Bruges kept the future Habsburg Emperor Maximilian imprisoned for eleven weeks. He was freed only after agreeing to respect the authority of the ruling Regency Council and to order the withdrawal of all foreign troops.

Craenenburg and Huis Bouchoute

Huis Bouchoute and the Craenenburg

149

**Burg

From beside the Halle Breidelstraat leads eastwards to the square known as the Burg. Encircled by some of the finest buildings in Bruges it takes its name from the former Grafenburg, the original seat of the Counts of Flanders built by Baldwin Iron Arm but demolished in 1434.

Proosdij

The corner of the Burg and Breidelstraat was once the site of Sint-Donaas, a cathedral church of Carolingian origin, built in 900. The lovely Baroque building standing there today is the former Provost's House (1665–66), the cathedral itself having been demolished in 1799. A few remnants of the walls of the choir are still visible in the garden adjacent to the house.

Paleis van het Brugse Vrije

Across on the east side of the square the Bruges Tourist Office occupies part of what was, up until 1984, the Law Courts, built between 1722 and 1727 on the site of the former Paleis van het Brugse Vrije (Liberty of Bruges) from where independent magistrates exercised jurisdiction over the country area around Bruges. Some fragments of the older building have survived, including the pretty 16th c. façade overlooking the canal at the rear. One or two of the more historic rooms now make up the Brugse Vrije Museum (open: daily 10am–noon and 1.30–5pm).

*Chimneypiece

In the Schepenzaal ("vierschaar" or lay magistrates court) can be seen the famous chimneypiece (1529) designed by the painter Lanceloot Blondeel and executed in black marble and oak by Guyot de Beaugrant and others, a magnificent piece of Renaissance craftsmanship which in the imaginative quality of its ornamentation anticipates Baroque art. Above an alabaster frieze depicting the story of Suzanna and the Elders are carved oak figures of the Emperor Charles V and his parents, Ferdinand and Isabella of Castille, Mary of Burgundy and Maximilian. The hand holds were for the magistrates' use while drying their boots.

*Civiele Griffie

To the right of the Paleis van het Brugse Vrije stands the Civiele Griffie (Old Recorder's House). Richly decorated in gold and adorned with statues it was built between 1534–37 in typical Renaissance style.

*Stadhuis

On the south-east side of the square the Stadhuis is one of the oldest town halls in the Netherlands, having been constructed between 1376 and 1420. The façade of the delicate Gothic building displays the strong vertical emphasis characteristic of the style, with soaring pilasters, three of which end in octagonal turrets, separated by tall Gothic arched windows. Statues of the counts of Flanders from Baldwin Iron Arm onwards fill the 49 niches.

Inside are two rooms which should not be missed: the great Gothic Hall on the first floor with its beautiful timber vaulting (1402) and its murals recording events in the town's history by A. and J. de Vriendt (1895–1900); and the Historical Room containing documents which again relate to the history of Bruges (open: daily 9.30am–noon and 2–6pm; Oct.– Mar. until 5pm only).

The City Hall

*Heiligbloed-basiliek

In the southern corner of the square, to the right of the town hall and adjacent to it, stands the two-storeyed Heiligbloedbasiliek (Basilica of the

Holy Blood). Kept inside the church is a crystal phial reputed to contain a drop of Christ's blood brought back from the Holy Land by Dietrich of Alsace in 1149 on his return from the Second Crusade. From this has originated the traditional Procession of the Holy Blood when each year in May the sacred relic is carried through the streets of Bruges.

The façade of the basilica with its three Flamboyant-style arches and gilded statues was erected between 1529 and 1534. The basilica itself consists of a Romanesque lower chapel and late Gothic upper chapel. The lower chapel (1149) houses relics of St Basil brought from Palestine by Robert II, Count of Flanders. An elegant spiral staircase leads to the upper chapel (1480) where every Friday the phial containing the Holy Blood is brought out and shown to the faithful. Next to the upper chapel a small museum has been established, its most precious possession being the reliquary (1614–17) in which the Holy Blood is borne through the streets. Among the 15th and 16th c. paintings beside the reliquary are two wings of a triptych by Pieter Pourbus showing members of the Brotherhood of the Holy Blood (open: Apr.–Sept. daily 9.30am–noon and 2–6pm; Oct–Mar. daily 10am–noon and 2–6pm).

To the left of the Stadhuis Blinde Ezelstraat passes under a pretty Renaissance arch between the town hall and the Civiele Griffie before crossing Blinde Ezelbrug to the Vismarkt (1821). Here each morning from Tuesday to Saturday fishmongers sell their wares laid out on stone counters.

Blinde Ezelstraat and Vismarkt

Running alongside the Reie are Steenhouwersdijk and Groene Rei, two streets lined with picturesque buildings. Note in particular the rear facade of the Palais de Justice and also Pelicaanhuis.

Pelicaanhuis

From the Vismarkt cross Huidenvetterplaats (Tanners' Square) with its guild-house dating from 1630, to Rozenhoedkaai, one of the departure points for boat trips on the canals. From Rozenhoedkaai an exceptionally fine view is obtained of the old houses bordering the canal, with the Belfry rising high above the rooftops in the background.

Rozenhoedkaai

**View

Dijver to Minnewater

Skirting the south bank of the canal beyond Rozenhoedkaai is the tree-lined quay known as the Dijver. One of the row of superb old patrician houses (No. 31) is now occupied by the College of Europe, a post-graduate institute for the study of greater European integration.

Dijver

**Groeninge Museum

To the left of No. 12 Dijver an entrance leads from the quay to the Groeninge Museum (Stedelijk Museum voor Schone Kunst) tucked away behind. In addition to its excellent endowment of Old Flemish paintings the museum incorporates a gallery of modern art and a superb collection of views of old Bruges.

Opening times
Apr.–Sept.
daily 9.30am–6pm;
Oct.–Mar.
daily 9.30am–noon
and 2–5pm

The first five rooms of the museum are the ones most likely to claim the visitor's attention, however, containing as they do some quite exceptional paintings by Old Flemish masters.

Old Flemish painting

In Room 1 hang two major works by Jan van Eyck: "Madonna and the donor, Canon van der Paele" (1436) and the portrait of Margarete van Eyck, the artist's wife, painted when she was 33 years of age (1439). Both illustrate the extraordinary realism of his style. Room 2 has paintings by Hugo van der Goes ("Death of the Virgin"), Hans Memling (the Moreel Triptych, 1484; altar wing with Annunciation) and Petrus Christus ("Annunciation and Birth of Christ"; altar wing depicting Isabella of Portugal). In Room 3 are panels illustrating the legend of St Ursula and a portrait of Luis Gruuthuse, both famous works by unknown Bruges masters. Hanging in Room 4

1–5 Flemish painting 15th c.

6 Mannerism, Jan Provoost, Lancelot Blondeel, south Netherlands painting 16th c.

7 Pieter and Frans Pourbus, Marcus Gerards

8 Jacob van Oost, 17th c. painting in Brugge

9 Flemish and Dutch historical painting, 17th and 18th c. chef d'œuvres

10 Classicism in Brugge

11 Romantic and Realist genre painting, Symbolism

12 19th c. landscape painting

13–14 Fauvism, Flemish Expressionism, Surrealism

15 Art since 1945

are two large pictures entitled the "Judgement of Cambyses" (1498) and a triptych showing the Baptism of Christ, all by David Gerard, while the "Last Judgement" by Hieronymus Bosch is among the paintings in Room 5.

t'Leerhuys

Over in the Arentspark adjacent to the museum an art gallery (t'Leerhuys) has been established in the intriguing surroundings of an old tannery.

*Gruuthusemuseum

Opening times
Apr.–Sept.
daily 9.30am–noon
and 2–6pm;
Oct.–Mar.
daily 9.30am–noon
and 2–5pm

On the left at the far end of the Dijver stands an attractive ensemble of 15th c. buildings comprising what was once the mansion of the "Heren van Gruuthuse". Here in 1471 the fugitive English king Edward IV took shelter. The original "heren" were not noblemen at all but merchants with a monopoly on the trade in "gruut", the dried herbs, etc. used to flavour beer before the introduction of hops. In summer the charming courtyard with its vine covered colonnades and neighbouring Onze Lieve Vrouwkerk for a backcloth, becomes the venue for an atmospheric son-et-lumière show. The courtyard can also be reached direct from the Groeninge Museum by first crossing Arentspark and then the picturesque Bonifatiusbrug, beside which can be seen a bust of Juan Luis Vivés, the Spanish humanist.

The mansion itself, beautifully furnished in different period styles, now houses the quite exceptional Gruuthusemuseum, a superb collection of antiques and applied art occupying in all 22 rooms. Particularly eye-catching are the lace-work, carvings, tapestries and weaponry, also the delightfully restored and completely authentic old Flemish kitchen and the dispensary.

Brangwyn-
museum

The Brangwyn Museum, in the 18th c. Arentshuis next door to the Gruuthusemuseum, has porcelains, pewterware, ceramics, mother-of-pearlware and a charming collection of views of old Bruges as well as an exhibition of paintings and drawings, etc. by the Bruges-born English artist Frank Brangwyn (1867–1956) (opening times as for the Gruuthusemuseum).

*Onze Lieve Vrouwkerk

Immediately south of the Gruuthusemuseum towers the 112m/368ft spire of the Onze Lieve Vrouwkerk (Church of Our Lady), the tallest in Belgium.

The courtyard of the Gruuthusemuseum   *A Michelangelo Sculpture*

Work began on the nave and aisles around 1230, the outermost aisles and chapels being added in the 14th and 15th c.

The church is of interest chiefly for its wealth of art treasures, among which is a sublime sculpture by Michelangelo, "Virgin and Child" (1503–04). The sculpture stands on the altar of the chapel at the end of the south aisle and was a gift from the Bruges merchant Jan Moscroen who personally acquired it from the master in 1506. Dürer, who visited the church in 1521, was filled with admiration.

Interior
**Michelangelo sculpture

The Calvary on the high altar is by Bernaert van Orley, the triptych "Adoration of the Shepherds" is by Pieter Pourbus and the "Transfiguration of Christ" is by Gerard David.

Choir and ambulatory

Positioned adjacent to one another in the choir are the tombs of Mary of Burgundy (who married Maximilian, later Holy Roman Emperor; died 1482) and her father Charles the Bold (died 1477). Mary's tomb (1502) by Jan Borman is pure Gothic in style and of considerably greater interest from an artistic point of view than her father's, which dates from 1559. The black sarcophagi on which the copper gilt figures of father and daughter lie are colourfully emblazoned with coats of arms (viewing: Apr.–Sept. Mon.–Sat. 10–11.30am and 2.30–5pm, Sun. and public holidays 2.30–5pm; Oct.–Mar. Mon.–Sat. 10–11.30am and 3–4.30pm, Sun. and public holidays 2.30–4.30pm).

*Tomb of Mary of Burgundy

Mary of Burgundy's actual burial place is now believed to be one of a group of tombs discovered in the choir in 1979. All are notable for their mural decoration and can been seen behind a protective glass screen.

Pieter Lanchals, an adviser to Maximilian of Austria, lies buried in the Lanchals chapel off the south ambulatory. He was murdered in Bruges in 1488 at the time of Maximilian's "imprisonment". A number of fine paintings hang in the chapel including Adriaan Isenbrant's "Mater Dolorosa" (1530), a "Last Supper" by Pieter Pourbus and two panels by the Cologne artist Stefan Lochner ("Birth of Christ" and "Adoration of the Magi"). From the north ambulatory an elegant wooden gallery (15th c.) links the church to the Gruuthuse.

**Memlingmuseum in the Sint-Jansspitaal

Opening times
Apr.–Sept.
daily 9.30am–noon
and 2–6pm;
Oct.–Mar.
daily 9.30am–noon
and 2–5pm

Immediately opposite the west door of the Onze Lieve Vrouwkerk stands the oldest building in Bruges, the Sint-Jansspitaal founded in the 12th c. The tympanum over the bricked up gate to the left of the Mariastraat entrance, embellished with reliefs showing the Virgin, bears the date 1270. Inside the ancient building, in what were once wards, an exhibition of documents, surgical instruments, etc. charts the hospital's history. The old dispensary adjacent to the wards has also been preserved.

Museum

Occupying the former chapel is the Memlingmuseum where six exquisite masterpieces by Hans Memling (c. 1430–94) are on view, each a pearl of Old Flemish art. Outstanding even among these is the Reliquary of St Ursula (1489), recognised to be one of the master's most important works. Six scenes from the legend of the saint decorate the reliquary: the arrival in Cologne; the entry into Basle prior to crossing the Alps; the Pope's welcome in Rome with the baptism of Ursula's companions; the re-embarkation at Basle for the return to Cologne; the massacre of the 11,000 virgins by the Huns; the Hun chieftain's proposal of marriage and Ursula's death. Scarcely less famous is the "Mystic Marriage of St Catherine", painted for the so-called St John altar. Completed in 1479 it depicts Saints Barbara and Catherine (portraits it is thought of Mary of Burgundy and Margaret of York) flanked by St John the Baptist and St John the Evangelist. The four other works by Memling in the museum are the Maarten van Nieuwenhove diptych of 1487 (with on one wing the Virgin handing the Christ child an apple and on the other a superb portrait of the donor), a triptych (1479) with

Sint-Jansspitaal

the "Adoration of the Magi" and the donor Jan Floreins, another triptych with the "Descent from the Cross" (1480) and finally the portrait of Sibylla Zambetha (1480).
The museum also contains works by other Old Flemish masters (e.g. Blondeel and Van Oost) as well as items of applied art (antique).

To Minnewater

South of Sint-Jansspitaal, along Katelijnestraat, Walstraat branches off to the right, a street of tiny, exceptionally pretty, gabled 16th and 17th c. houses in which lace-makers still practise their craft.

Walstraat

South again, beyond the bustling Walplein, the "Straffe Hendrik" brewery has been producing its fairly strong light beer in Bruges since 1546 (guided tours; daily 11am–3pm).

"Straffe Hend-rick" brewery

In medieval times Minnewater (the "Lake of Love"), on the far side of Wijngaardplein, was part of Bruges's busy outer harbour. Nowadays only the Gothic sluishuis (lockhouse) at the north end provides a clue to its far from tranquil past and few of today's visitors think twice about how this enchanting little stretch of water came by its romantic name.

*Minnewater

From the bridge which crosses the southern end of the basin delightful waterside paths follow the line of the old town moat. The Poedertoren to the right of the bridge was built in 1398.

*Begijnhof

Standing by the lockhouse there is a lovely view of the bridge over to the Béguinage.

Minnewater, a rendezvous for lovers

The béguinage

The Prinselijk Beguijnhof ten Wijngaarde, its white 17th c. houses grouped around a grassy, tree-shaded court, was founded in 1245 by Margaret of Constantinople. Today the Béguinage is the home of Benedictine nuns. No. 30 was the Grootjuffrouw's house. To the left, between the entrance gate and church (founded 1245, restored 1605), one of the former béguine houses has been turned into a museum. It offers a fascinating insight into life in the béguinage as well as providing an outlet for the sale of lace (museum open: Apr.–Sept. Mon.–Sat. 9.30am–noon and 1.45–5.30pm, Sun. and public holidays 10.45am–noon and 1.45–6pm; Oct.–Mar. Mon.–Sat. 10.30–noon and 1.45am–5pm, Sun. and public holidays 10.45am–noon and 1.45–6pm).

Town centre – south-west

Sint-Salvatorskathedraal

From the Onze Lieve Vrouwkerk the short Heilige Geeststraat makes its way past the Bishop's Palace (16th–18th c.) to Sint-Salvatorskathedraal, the oldest parish church in Bruges and a cathedral since 1834. Originally founded in the 10th c. most parts of the present building date from the 12th and 13th centuries.

The fortress-like 99m/325ft-high west tower was constructed in several phases, the lower Romanesque portion between 1116 and 1227 and the brick section between 1183 and 1228. Building continued in the 15th c. and again in the 19th c., the Neo-Romanesque upper part being added between 1844 and 1846 and the steeple in 1871. Over the centuries the cathedral has survived four fires as well as the iconoclastic fury.

*Interior

The 101m/331ft-long interior, distinguished by its harmonious proportions, contains some noteworthy furnishings. Outstanding are the Baroque rood-screen with a figure of God the Father by Artus Quellin the Younger, the 15th c. choir stalls embellished with the coats of arms of Knights of the Golden Fleece and, above the stalls, Brussels tapestries made in 1731. The cathedral organ is famous for its magnificent case.

Even more priceless, however, are the art treasures in the cathedral museum off the right transept. In the cloister are six fine brass 14th–16th c. tomb plates. Displayed in the various rooms are liturgical accoutrements and several superb Old Flemish paintings including a triptych "Martyrdom of St Hippolytus" by Dirk Bouts, the left wing of which is thought to be by Hugo van der Goes, and a polyptych by Pieter Pourbus with a Last Supper on the centre panel (open: Apr.–Sept. Mon.–Sat. 10am–noon and 2–5pm, Sun. and public holidays 3–5pm; Oct.–Mar. Mon.–Sat. 2–5pm).

*Cathedral museum

Around Sint-Salvatorskathedraal

Running between the cathedral and the Markt, Steenstraat with its row of typical Bruges gable gildehuizen is one of the loveliest of the city's streets.

*Steenstraat

About halfway along towards the Markt Steenstraat opens onto Simon Stevinplein, named after the mathematician Stevinus, born in Bruges in 1548 and sometime adviser to Maurice of Nassau. Branching off from the south side of the square is Oude Burg, at the near end of which stands the Hof van Watervliet, a complex of restored old buildings dating from the 16th c. Over the years the Hof's illustrious residents have included Erasmus of Rotterdam and the exiled Charles II.

Hof van Watervliet

West of the cathedral lies the large square known as t'Zand with, a short distance north, the Blindenkapel. Erected in the 14th c. the chapel boasts a magnificent pulpit (1659) and a gilded statue of Our Lady of the Blind.

Blindenkapel

The 14th c. Smedenpoort was medieval Bruges's south-west town gate. The bell would be rung when the gate was to be shut.

Smedenpoort

Following the moat south from the Smedenpoort leads to the 14th c. Waterhuis on which the town used to rely for its water supplies.

Waterhuis

Hanseatic Bruges

The districts north of the Markt and to the north-east of the city centre were the commercial heart of Hanseatic Bruges where the city's merchants lived and carried on their business.

North of the Markt

From the north-west corner of the Markt Sint-Jacobstraat continues beyond the Eiermarkt to the Gothic Sint-Jacobskerk, passing on its way the 18th c. Musical Academy (left) and Boterhuis (Cultural Centre; right). Gifts from the dukes of Burgundy, whose palace was near by, transformed the 13th–15th c. church from its relatively modest beginnings to its present size. The richly ornamented interior contains a number of fine 16th–18th c. paintings by local artists as well as some interesting tombs. Among the latter, to the right of the choir, is the twin-tiered tomb of Ferry de Gros (a treasurer of the Order of the Golden Fleece; died 1544) and his two wives.

Sint-Jacobskerk

In 1440 Pieter Bladelin, also a treasurer of the Order of the Golden Fleece, built himself a house in Naaldenstraat, which branches right off Sint-Jacobsstraat. In addition to its exceptionally picturesque courtyard Hof Bladelin is distinguished by the portraits of subsequent owners embellish-

*Hof Bladelin

ing the facade, among them Lorenzo di Medici who gave the house to his Bruges agent and banker Tommaso di Portinari.

Naaldenstraat terminates in Grauwwerkersstraat, at the east end of which stands the Huis ter Beurze, now a bank. In the 15th c. when the house was built it was common practice for merchants to do business in their lodgings. Many took rooms here in the home of the van der Beurze family, as a result of which the word "beurs" or "bourse" has found its way into numerous languages as the term for a commercial exchange.

Huis ter Beurze

The Natiehuis van Genua (1399–1441) opposite the Huis ter Beurze was where Bruges's Genoese merchants carried on their business.

Natiehuis van Genua

Not far from the Huis ter Beurze the delightful Jan van Eyckplein adjoins the Spiegelrei, Bruges's busy inner harbour during the city's heyday. A statue of Van Eyck adorns the square.

*Jan van Eyckplein

Dominating Jan van Eyckplein is the Poorters Loge, a striking 14th c. building with a slender tower. Once a sort of club for the merchant burghers of Bruges it now houses the city archives. Several figures decorate the façade, most notably that of the bear, "Beertje van de Logie", which dates from 1417. (A bear also appears on Bruges's coat of arms.)

Poorters Loge

Across the Academiestraat stands the Oud Tolhuis (customs house; 1477) where merchandise was inspected. It now houses the city's library of 100,000 volumes and 600 manuscripts, the latter including 13th and 14th c. missals.

Oud Tolhuis

In the Woensdagmarkt, just to the north of Jan van Eyckplein, are a statue of Hans Memling and, near by, the Convent of the Black Sisters founded in 1561. The Oosterlingenplein beyond owes its name to the fact that the German Hanse had premises there (oosterling = easterling).

Woensdagmarkt and Oosterlingenplein

Sint-Gilliskerk, a hall church (1275) across on the north side of the canal from Oosterlingenplein, has a number of excellent paintings. Hans Memling and Lanceloot Blondeel are among those buried in the churchyard.

Sint-Gilliskerk

In the opposite direction from Sint-Gilliskerk, a little to the south of the Spiegelrei, stands the magnificent Baroque church of Sint-Walburga (1619–42). Built by Pieter Huyssens, a Jesuit from Bruges, its furnishings include a superb pulpit by Artus Quellin the Younger and a similarly fine marble communion rail.

Sint-Walburgakerk

Town centre – north-east

Sint-Annakerk, a short way east of Jan van Eyckplein, was erected in 1624 in place of an earlier Gothic church demolished in 1561. The Baroque choir stalls, rood-screen and pulpit are notable for their unity of style.

Sint-Annakerk

The distinctive oriental-looking tower visible behind Sint-Annakerk belongs to the Late Gothic Jeruzalemkerk in Peperstraat. Dating from 1428 it was modelled on the Church of the Holy Sepulchre in Jerusalem, the builders, members of the Adorne family, having made a pilgrimage there. The church boasts very fine 15th–16th c. stained glass windows and a copy of Christ's tomb.

Jeruzalemkerk

The 15th c. "Jeruzalemgodshuizen" adjoining the church is now the Kantcentrum (Lace Centre), a museum cum studio/workshop where the art of bobbin lace making is preserved and handed on. In the afternoons the skilled craftswomen and their young pupils can be watched at work (open: daily 10am–noon and 2–6pm).

Kantcentrum

The Stedelijk Museum voor Volkskunde occupies a group of 17th c. houses opposite the Kantcentrum. It comprises a collection of West Flemish folk

Stedelijk Museum voor Volkskunde

◄ *View of the Poorters Loge from the Spiegelrei*

art, costumes and items of an everyday kind, as well as interiors furnished in contemporary style. These include a hatter's workshop, a grocer's, a confectioner's, a kitchen, and an ale house known as the "Zwarte Kat" (open: Apr.–Sept. Mon.–Sat. 9.30am–noon and 2–6pm; Oct.–Mar. until 5pm only).

Goude Boom Brewery

Spurred on by their visit to the "Zwarte Kat" (see above) beer drinkers may care to make a short detour south from the Jeruzalemkerk to see the 1902 maltings at the Gouden Boom brewery in Langestraat.

Kruispoort and Kruisvest

The white limestone Kruispoort (town gate) at the end of Peperstraat dates from 1402. Running north from the gate, Kruisvest follows the line of the old ramparts. On the canal side are three windmills one of which, the Sint-Janshuysmolen (1770), can sometimes be seen working.

Sint-Joris Guild of Archers

The guild-house of the Sint-Joris Guild of Archers opposite the first windmill contains a collection of crossbows, paintings and documents (open: Mon.–Sat. 2–6pm).

Guido Gezelle-museum

The Flemish poet Guido Gezelle was born in a house in Rolweg which runs citywards off Kruisvest. The house is now a museum (open: Apr.–Sept. Mon.–Sat. 9.30am–noon and 2–6pm; Oct.–Mar. until 5pm only).

Sint-Sebastian Guild of Archers

The Sint-Sebastian Guild of Archers, which counted English royalty among its members, used to meet in the delightful turreted house (1562) in the Carmersstraat. Inside the house the history of the guild and its illustrious membership is documented and there are displays of weaponry and gold and silver work (open: Mon.–Sat. 2–5pm).

Engels Klooster

The lovely domed chapel (1736–39) on the right-hand side a little further up Carmersstraat belongs to the Engles Klooster, an English nunnery.

Museum Potterie

The Potteriespitaal, on the extreme northern edge of the city centre near the Episcopal Seminary on the Potterierei, was founded in 1276, though most of the present buildings date from the 15th c. Today it is still in use as a pleasant home for the elderly. The interesting Baroque chapel of Onze Lieve Vrouw van de Potterie and the even more interesting Museum Potterie in the old building are open to visitors, the latter comprising various items of ecclesiastical art including furniture, Gobelins, gold and ivory work and paintings (open: Apr.–Sept. Mon.–Sat. 9.30am–noon and 2–6pm; Oct.–Mar. until 5pm only).

Surroundings

The Tillegembos estate 2km/1¼ miles south of the city centre in the suburb of Sint-Michiels comprises a 83ha/205 acre woodland park with footpaths and bridleways, a lake with a mill and a 14th c. moated château.

Boudewijnpark and delphinarium

See Practical Information, Leisure Parks

Zedelgem

The church in Zedelgem, 8km/5 miles south-west, is justifiably proud of its extremely rare 11th–12th c. Romanesque font in the style of the Tournai school with reliefs illustrating the legend of St Nicholas of Myra.

Jakkebe

Jakkebe (11km/7 miles west of Bruges) was for 20 years the home of the painter and sculptor Constant Permeke (1868–1952). His house and studio in Bruggerstraat, designed by the artist himself, have been turned into a museum containing fine examples of his work from various creative periods. These include sculptures in the garden studio (open: May.–Sept. daily 10am–6pm; Nov.–Apr. until 4pm only).

Assebroek

Children in particular will enjoy a visit to "Zeven Torenjes", a farm at Assebroek 5km/3 miles east of Bruges. Here there is a chance to experience life on the farm and to encounter the various animals.

Bruges offers several opportunities for boat trips. All are a delight, particularly the excursion aboard the "Lamme Goedzak" along the Brugge-Sluis-Kanaal to Damme (see entry; daily from Easter–Sept.; from the Noorwegse Kaai). Excursion launches also run to Ghent (see entry; every Thur. in July and Aug.; from Bargeweg) and Ostende (see entry; every Tues. and Wed. in July and Aug.; from Houtkaai). Further information from the Benelux-Damme-Rederij, Sint-Salvatorstraat 6, B-9000 Ghent; tel. 350285 (Bruges).

Boat trips

See entry

Zeebrugge

Brussels · Bruxelles · Brussel　　　　　　　　　　　　　　　　　　　E 5

Province: Brabant
Altitude: 15–100m/50–330ft
Population: 970,000 of whom some 140,000 live in the inner city
Intercity and Inter-regional Station

The Baedeker AA series already includes a separate, fully comprehensive guide to Brussels. The descriptions given below are therefore somewhat abbreviated.
Where appropriate, names are given first in French and then in Flemish.

N.B.

**Royal capital

Brussels, capital of Belgium and principal seat of the Belgian Royal Family, is situated at the geographical centre of the country. It occupies rising ground on the edge of the valley of the Senne, a tributary of the Scheldt, at a point where the hills drop away to the plain of Flanders. The city is capital of the province of Brabant, and Greater Brussels ("L'Agglomération de Bruxelles") forms one of the country's three autonomous regions, the others being Flanders and Wallonia. Brussels is part of an archbishopric which also includes Mechelen (see entry).
Numerous international organisations and authorities are based in Brussels, in particular the European Community (EC). As the home of the Ministry for Europe and the European Commission, the city prides itself on being the de facto capital of Europe. Since 1967 it has also been the headquarters of NATO, the western defence alliance (General Secretariat and NATO Council; military supreme command headquarters SHAPE at Casteau near Mons (see entry)). The European space agency ESA also has its base here.

Location

The municipality of Brussels proper comprises only the area formerly enclosed by the old ramparts – long since replaced by the broad boulevards of the so-called "Pentagon". It is made up of the Lower Town, through which flow several branches of the Senne (now canalised underground), and the smaller Upper Town on a ridge to the east. Clustered around the city centre and today continuous with it are eighteen separately administered suburban districts. Thus Brussels as a whole is an agglomeration of nineteen different municipalities, each with its own local government. That this has been an obstacle to the coherent development of the city is all too obvious from the many dilapidated areas and failed or poorly executed building projects.

Urban district
and administration

Nowhere in Belgium do Flemings and Walloons live in quite such close proximity as in Brussels, the linguistic frontier running only a few kilometres south of the city. While Brussels itself is officially bilingual, Francophones in fact predominate (80%) in the central district and Flemish speakers in the suburbs. It is Brussels' fate therefore to be at the mercy of often opposing ethnic group interests, the paralysing effects of which have frequently proved to the city's disadvantage.

Population

Nevertheless, few if any European cities have such an international feel as Brussels. A quarter of the approximately one million inhabitants are foreigners and they could hardly be a more varied mixture. On the one hand there are the army of people employed by the international organisations, and on the other hand guest workers and immigrants from North and sub-Saharan Africa, many of whom live in the country illegally.

Brussels is an entirely modern city, extensive replanning and redevelopment since the early part of the century having profoundly altered the character of the old Brabant capital except in one or two places. Even now several major projects are in progress. Work is almost complete in re-shaping the area in front of the Gare Centrale to create a more fitting "entrée" to the historic heart of the city. And an ambitious plan exists to redevelop the area around the headquarters of the European Commission in the Palais Berlaymont – due for demolition because of the asbestos risk. Amid all this redevelopment those with an eye for such things will spot many an architectural disaster, as well as districts still badly in need of revitalisation. At the same time, speculative fever combined with the already mentioned ethnic rivalry and fragmented administrative responsibility threatens to destroy the vernacular character of attractive quarters like Les Marolles.

Architecture

As Belgium's main cultural and scientific centre Brussels is home to the Belgian Royal Academy as well as to a university, a polytechnic, numerous technical colleges and art schools and a variety of other cultural institutions. It is also the country's financial capital (National Bank) and economic hub, lying as it does at the intersection of some of western Europe's primary transport routes. Second only to Antwerp (see entry) as the largest industrialised area in Belgium light industry predominates, in particular the manufacture of "Brussels lace", woollen, cotton and silk goods, carpets and porcelain. The metal, automobile and chemical industries are also well represented, as too is brewing. Even so, the commercial and service sectors outweigh manufacturing in importance to the economy, owing in no small measure to the presence of the big international organisations employing about 100,000 people. The EC alone has a staff of 14,000. Most of the latter however are nationals of other EC countries who not only earn considerably more than local people but also pay no tax.

Culture, Science, Economy

Not surprisingly Brussels is also the country's gastronomic capital, plentifully provided with restaurants of high repute catering for a discriminating clientèle. Brussels chocolates are famous and, as is only to be expected in the city where Gambrinus was born, the art of brewing is cherished and cultivated.

Food

The city's foremost festival, the marvellously colourful parade known as the "Ommegang", is celebrated in July on the Grand'Place where it was held for the first time in 1549 in the presence of Charles V. The prestigious "Concours Reine Elisabeth", an international music competition, takes place in the spring. The ambitious biennial "Europalia" festival, held in June, takes each European country in turn as its theme.

Festivals and events

At the beginning of this century Brussels became a focal point for the Art Nouveau movement, Victor Horta, Henry van de Velde and Philippe Wolfers being among the architects and artists whose genius enriched the city with houses and objets d'art. The Brussels Tourist Office (see Practical Information, Information) arranges tours of the most beautiful Art Nouveau buildings, as does the Organisation ARAU (Atelier de Recherche et d'Action Urbaines, tel. 5134761) and Arcadia (tel. 6483541; in English too).

**Art Nouveau in Brussels

◄ Brussels: a floral carpet in the Grand'Place outside the Maison du Roi

History

Modest beginnings

The founding of Brussels is usually attributed to St Goorik (or Géry), Bishop of Cambrai, also credited with introducing Christianity into Belgium. He is thought to have established the original settlement here in about 580, on an island in the Senne. In 977 Charles, Duke of Lower Lotharingia, took up residence on the island, thereby attracting craftsmen and tradespeople to it. As a result the name "Bruocsella" (from "broec" = breach or marsh and "sele" = village) appears for the first time in 979 in a document of Otto the Great. Later, in the 12th c., the counts of Louvain, forerunners of the dukes of Brabant, built anew on the more elevated site of the Coudenberg. Standing as it did at an important crossing on the great trade route between Bruges and Cologne, subsequent expansion was rapid, and between 1357 and 1379 new ramparts were built around the much enlarged town. From then on Brussels ceased to be in the shadow of the hitherto more powerful Louvain.

Heyday

At the end of the 14th c. Brussels became the capital of Brabant, consequently falling in 1430 into Burgundian hands. By 1455 the population had reached 43,500 inhabitants. The dukes of Burgundy occasionally held court in Brussels and the French nobility who gathered there and who were already making the French language fashionable among their Netherlands counterparts, were responsible for a first flowering of the arts and sciences. At the same time trades and crafts increasingly flourished, leading to the emergence of a prosperous middle class and a new pride and self-confidence which soon found expression in the building of the splendid guild-houses and town hall on the Grand'Place.

When the country became a Habsburg possession in 1477, and especially following Charles V's accession in 1515 and the elevation of Brussels to capital of the Spanish Netherlands in 1531, a brilliant court life evolved in the city attracting a bevy of artists. It was during this time also that, in 1490, Franz von Taxis organised a permanent postal link between Brussels and Innsbruck. Charles V's abdication in 1555 however presaged the ending of Spanish rule.

Many masters

The year 1566 saw the first rebellion in the Netherlands against Spanish oppression, culminating in the execution of Counts Egmont and Hoorn on the Grand'Place. For the time being the Spanish hold remained unbroken, but economically the city was weakened by an exodus of its citizens to the free Netherlands. In 1695, during Louis XIV's wars, Marshal DeVilleroy's bombardment set fire to the Lower Town, destroying more than 4000 houses including the magnificent buildings around the Grand'Place. Although with the end of the War of Spanish Succession the Spanish Netherlands and with them Brussels passed to Austria, the struggle

Metro

obahn Gent   Antwerpen

Place de l'Yser
Boulevard Baudouin
Quai au Foin
Théâtre Flamand

World Trade Center
Centre Int. Rogier
Place Rogier

Gare du Nord

Ste-Marie

Bruxelles/Brussel
300 m
© Baedeker

SCHAERBEEK

Place de Brouckère
Église du Béguinage
Église du Finistère

Jardin Botanique
Église de Jésu
Prévoyance Sociale

Rue du Moulin

Ste-Cathérine
Tour Noir
Place de la Monnaie
Opéra National

Place des Martyrs
Comic-Museum
Cité
P
Administrative

ST-JOSSE

Col. du Congrès
Banque Nationale
Cathédrale St-Michel
Cirque Royal
Palais de la Nation

Place de la Liberté
Pl Surlet de Chokier

St-Nicolas
Bourse
Place de la Bourse
Maison des Corporations
Galeries St-Hubert
Hôtel de Ville
Grand Place
Maison des Ducs de Brabant
Chapelle Madeleine
Place St-Jean
Manneken-Pis
Air Terminus
Gare Centrale
Parc
Théâtre Royal du Parc

Halles
re-Dame aux Riches Claires
adémies s aux Arts
Notre-Dame de la Chapelle
Minimes
UARTIER DES
e Jeu Balle AROLLES

Bibliothèque Albert I.
Musées d'Art Moderne
Musées Royaux des Beaux-Arts
Notre-Dame du Sablon
Conservatoire de Musique (Musée)
Place Poelaert
Palais de Justice
Église des Carmes
Église Anglicane

Palais de la Dynastie
Palais des Congrès
Hôtel Ravenstein
Belle-Vue
St-Jacques-sur-Coudenberg
Palais Royal

Palais des Beaux-Arts
Bruxelles
Place des Palais
Palais des Académies
Place du Trône

Palais d'Egmont
Porte de Namur

St-Boniface

Palais d'Assche
St-Joseph

Gare du Quartier Léopold

IXELLES

Place Fern. Cooq
Maison Communale d'Ixelles

U.L.B.

of the people of Brussels for their freedom continued. In 1719 Frans Anneessens, leader of the Brussels guilds, was beheaded on the orders of the Austrian-appointed Governor, Prince Eugène.

Under Maria Theresa and her Governor Charles of Lorraine (1744–80) more peaceful times ensued, the population rising again to reach 74,000. Then came the French Revolution, Brabantine supporters of which led a new revolt against the Austrians. In 1794 the French themselves marched in, Brussels remaining in French hands until 1814. Possession then passed to the Dutch under whom Brussels became the Netherlands' second city. Finally a popular riot in Theatre Square on August 25th 1830 was the signal for the start of the revolution out of which Brussels was to emerge as the capital of the newly created Kingdom of the Belgians.

The Belgian capital

The new capital now developed rapidly. In 1834 the university was founded, and a year later continental Europe's first rail service began operating between Brussels and Mechelen. Subsequently, under King Leopold II and Burgomaster Ansprach, the great boulevards were built. Although occupied in both World Wars the city was fortunately spared the worst destruction. The 1958 World Exhibition brought a new landmark in the form of the Atomium while the arrival of the EEC and EURATOM in 1959 followed by NATO in 1967 marked Brussels' elevation to unofficial "Capital of Europe". The 1980s saw the first steps towards the city's becoming an autonomous region alongside Flanders and Wallonia, a process which should come to fruition in the 1990s. Sadly, in 1985, the Heysel Stadium was brought to the attention of the world when, before the European Cup Final between Liverpool FC and Juventus of Turin, British football hooligans caused panic in the course of which 38 spectators were killed.

Famous people

Brussels was the birthplace of, among others, the painters Bernard van Orley, Pieter Breugel the Elder and René Magritte, the Art Nouveau architect Victor Horta and the cabaret singer Jacques Brel.

Sightseeing

What to see

All the most important sights in Brussels are comfortably within the scope of a single day's sightseeing on foot. The best place to start is at the Grand'Place with its Hôtel de Ville, guild-houses, and the Maison du Roi. Then the part of the Old Town around the Place can be explored, including the mandatory visit to the world-famous Manneken Pis and a tour of the shopping arcades of the Galéries Saint-Hubert. From there it is only a short step uphill to the venerable old Saint-Michel Cathedral, to be followed by a walk through the green Parc de Bruxelles to the Palais Royale. Next stop should be at the Place Royale to the right of the palace, from where the Mont des Art (literally Hill of the Arts) descends to the Lower Town and where the Royal Museums of Fine Arts beckon those equipped with both time and patience. Afterwards the Place du Grand Sablon demands inclusion in the route back to the Lower Town.

Visitors with more time to spend in Brussels should be sure to visit the Atomium located in the north of the city. The next priority should be the museums, the main ones, apart from those on the Mont des Arts, being located in the Parc du Cinquantenaire – Autoworld, the Military Museum, and the Museum of Art and History. Any visits further afield should certainly include Waterloo (see entry) and the Central Africa Museum.

Guided walks and tours

For information about guided tours apply to the Brussels Tourist Office in the Grand'Place. Horse-drawn cabs are available for hire in the Place and the taxis marked "Taxi-Tour" likewise undertake city tours. The "Rose des Vents" ("Compass Card") is a list of suggested excursions by public transport compiled by the Brussels transport authority (information from e.g. the Midi, Porte de Namur and Rogier Metro Stations).

Art in the Brussels Metro

© Baedeker

NUMBER on plan	STATION NAME French/Flemish	WORK *Name* (Category and year of execution)	ARTIST Name
● 1	Osseghem/Ossegem	*Stop the run* (copper relief; 1982)	Reinhoud (D'Haese)
		Driehoek in beweging (marble sculpture; 1980)	Hilde Van Sumere
● 2	Gare de l'Ouest/ Weststation	*Composite* (painting on glass; 1982)	Guy Vandenbranden
● 3	Jacques Brel	*Coming up for air* (acrylic picture; 1982)	Maurice Wyckaert
● 4	Aumale	*Metrorama* (photos on the wall; 1982)	Jean-Paul Laenen
● 5	St-Guidon/St.-Guido	*Wij leven* (metal wall relief; 1981)	Frans Minnaert
● 6	Etangs Noirs/ Zwarte Vijvers	*De zwarte Vijvers* (wall painting in oil colours; 1980)	Jan Burssens
● 7	Comte de Flandre/ Graaf van Vlaanderen	*16 × Icarus* (suspended bronze figures; 1978) and ceiling relief in plaster; 1978)	Paul Van Hoeydonck
● 8	Rogier	*The Fall of Troy* (wall picture in oils; 1978)	Jan Cox
● 9	Bourse/Beurs	*Moving ceiling* (steel cylinder; 1976)	Pol Bury
		Nos vieux trams bruxellois (oil picture; 1978)	Paul Delvaux
● 10	Anneessens	*Sept écritures* (word painting; 1976)	Pierre Aléchinsky und Christian Dotremont
● 11	Botanique/Kruidtuin	*Les Voyageurs* (21 coloured wooden figures; 1979)	Pierre Caille
		The last migration (copper sculpture; 1977)	Jean-Pierre Ghysels
		Tramification fluide – Tramification syncopée (coloured steel tubes; 1978)	Emile Souply
● 12	Parc/Park	*La ville* (wall mosaic; 1972)	Roger Dudant
		Happy metro to you (coloured wooden figures; 1972)	Marc Mendelson
● 13	Arts-Loi/Kunst-Wet	*Isjtar* (lacquered wooden reliefs; 1980)	Gilbert Decock
		Ortem (coloured ceramic tiles; 1976)	Jean Rets
● 14	Porte de Namur/ Naamse Poort	*Het uiteindelijk verkeer* (four round enamelled ceramic reliefs; 1976)	Octave Landuyt
● 15	Mérode	*Carrelage cinq* (coloured ceramic tiles; 1976)	Jean Glibert
		Ensor: "Vive la Sociale (?)" (oil painting; 1976)	Roger Raveel
● 16	Thieffry	*Aequus Nox* (tinted mirror glass; 1976)	Vic Gentils
		Sculptures (bronze and steel; 1976)	Félix Roulin
● 17	Pétillon	*Que la mer épargne* (aluminium chrome relief; 1976)	Lismonde
● 18	Hankar	*Notre temps* (acrylic colour on concrete; 1976)	Roger Somville
● 19	Herrmann Debroux	*L'aviateur* (bronze sculpture; 1967)	Roel D'Haese
		Ode aan een bergrivier (bronze; 1982)	Rik Poot
● 20	Montgomery	*Rythme bruxellois* (coloured ceramic tiles; 1975)	Jo Delahaut
		Magic city (wall painting in oils; 1975)	Jean-Michel Folon
		Thema (six oil paintings; 1975)	Pol Mara
● 21	Joséphine-Charlotte	*La fleur uniqe ou les oiseaux émerveillés* (coloured wooden relief; 1979)	Serge Vandercam
● 22	Gribaumont	*Le Tropolitain* (wall painting in oils; 1976)	Frans Nellens
● 23	Roodebeek	*Intégration Roodebeek* (steel and glass; 1981)	Luc Peire
● 24	Vandervelde	*La grande taupe et le petit peintre* (huge wall painting in acrylic colour; 1981)	Paul De Gobert
● 25	Bockstael	Comic pictures from Tintin	Atelier Hergé

167

Traffic

In Brussels as in all major cities visitors are well advised to dispense with their own cars. The city's extensive and dependable public transport system brings everything of interest within easy reach.

*Art in the
Metro

The 33km/20 mile combined network of the Metro and Prémétro provides the quickest and most convenient method of transport, trains running from 6am to midnight. The Brussels Metro is quite exceptional. Many of the stations have been decorated by well-known contemporary artists, the most recent being Bockstael, now enlivened with characters from "Tintin" by Hergé. In addition to the Metro there is a tram service operating mainly outside the "Pentagon" and a very extensive bus network. Tram stops have red and white signs, bus stops blue and white ones. "Request only" stops are marked "Sur demande". Tickets can be bought at ticket machines in Metro stations or on the trams and buses themselves. Timetables are available from tourist information offices.

City centre

Metro
Gare Centrale
De Brouckère

Many of Brussels' chief sights are located within the comparatively small area enclosed by the "Pentagon", the ring of great boulevards following the line of the old 14th c. walls.

** Grand'Place · Grote Markt

The 110m/120yds by 68m/75yds Grand'Place (Grote Markt) lies at the very heart of Brussels Old Town, its sublime stylistic unity making it one of the loveliest squares in the world. Delightful at any time it is especially so when lit up in the evening and when filled with the additonal colour of the Sunday bird market and daily flower markets. First established on a marsh in the 11th c. the market soon evolved to become the city's political, economic and social nerve centre. The bombardment by the French on August 13th–14th 1695 wrought havoc with its buildings, nearly all of which were subsequently rebuilt. The Place has thus preserved all its old magnificence and its original happy blend of Gothic and Baroque. Across the years, from the 14th and 15th centuries to the revolution of 1830, the square has witnessed many a dramatic political moment, including in 1568 the execution of Counts Egmont and Hoorn, beheaded in front of the Maison du Roi. It has also been the scene of much celebration and a stage for the city's major festivals. The "Ommegang" is held here every year and every second August the square is carpeted with flowers.

** Hôtel de Ville
· Stadhuis

Viewing
Apr.–Sept.
Tues.–Fri.
9.30am–12.15pm
and 1.45–5pm;
Sun. and public
holidays 10am–
noon and 2–6pm;
Oct.–Mar.
until 4pm

The Place is dominated by the Hôtel de Ville (Town Hall), one of the biggest and finest buildings of its kind in Belgium. It was begun in 1450 with the intention of upstaging the Stadhuis in the rival city of Bruges (see entry). At first the plan was to build only what is now the left wing (1402–10); but in 1444 the right wing was also completed, followed in 1455 by Jan van Ruysbroek's 96m/315ft high belfy surmounted by the figure of St Michael. Although the French bombardment left only the walls and tower standing, rebuilding started almost at once. Both wings are embellished with very fine Gothic sculptures beneath which, under the arcades on the right, are the signs of inns demolished to make way for the town hall.

Inside are several magnificent rooms. Among the most impressive are the Maximilian Chamber hung with Brussels tapestries (historical scenes from the life of Clovis), the large Council Chamber with a superb ceiling by Victor Janssens and tapestries to his designs, the great banqueting hall and the Marriage Chamber, both beautifully panelled, and the Escalier d'Honneur with murals by Lalaing (1893) illustrating the history of Brussels.

The imposing City Hall of Brussels ▶

A carriage ride across the Grand'Place

*** Maison du Roi ·
Broodhuis**

Opposite the Hôtel de Ville stands the Maison du Roi which, despite its name, was never a royal residence. The king in question was the king of Spain and the "maison" was in fact the law courts. Directly in front is the spot where executions were carried out. The Maison's 13th c. predecessor was a building known as the Broodhuis (Bread House), appropriately enough since bread was indeed sold there for a time. Later it became a ducal law court before being replaced in 1515. By now rechristened the Maison du Roi, it was destroyed in 1695. The post-bombardment reconstruction was never very satisfactory and in 1873 rebuilding started yet again, based this time on the 1515 plans. The house as seen today was completed in 1895. The statues above the central arcade are those of Mary of Burgundy, Charles V and Duke Henry I.

Musée
Communal ·
Stadmuseum

The Maison du Roi is now Brussels' civic museum. The ground floor rooms to the left of the entrance contain 14th–18th c. sculptures, including some of the original ones from the Hôtel de Ville. In the rooms to the right of the entrance are 15th and 16th c. paintings, Brussels tapestries, porcelain and faience. The city's own development is the subject of a display on the first floor while on the second floor the emphasis is on social history – popular art, religion and other social themes. Also on the second floor is the wardrobe of Manneken Pis, a collection of costumes presented to "Petit Julien" by the rich and famous over the centuries, among them the French King Louis XIV (open: Apr.–Sept. Mon., Tues., Wed., Fri. 10am–12.30pm and 1.30–5pm, Thur. 10am–5pm, Sat., Sun. and public holidays 10am–1pm; Oct.–Mar. until 4pm).

* Guild-houses

Grand'Place owes much of its character to its elegant gildehuizen, with their magnificent gables, pilasters and balustrades, their ornately carved stonework and rich gold decoration. Most were built between 1696 and 1700 in the style of the Italian Baroque but with some Flemish influences. As well as bearing the name of the guilds, all the houses have individual names. Only some of the most splendid are mentioned below.

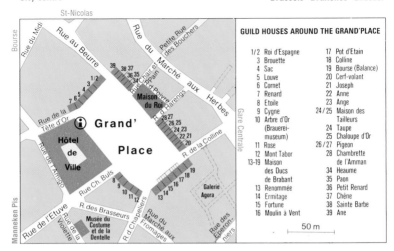

GUILD HOUSES AROUND THE GRAND'PLACE

1/2	Roi d'Espagne	17	Pot d'Etain
3	Brouette	18	Colline
4	Sac	19	Bourse (Balance)
5	Louve	20	Cerf-volant
6	Cornet	21	Joseph
7	Renard	22	Anne
8	Etoile	23	Ange
9	Cygne	24/25	Maison des
10	Arbre d'Or		Tailleurs
	(Brauerei-	24	Taupe
	museum)	25	Chaloupe d'Or
11	Rose	26/27	Pigeon
12	Mont Tabor	28	Chambrette
13–19	Maison		de l'Amman
	des Ducs	34	Heaume
	de Brabant	35	Paon
13	Renommée	36	Petit Renard
14	Ermitage	37	Chêne
15	Fortune	38	Sainte Barbe
16	Moulin à Vent	39	Ane

50 m

The row of houses on the north-west side of the square are the most elegant of all. No. 1–2, known as "Au Roi d'Espagne" and now the premises of a famous café of that name, belonged to the bakers' guild. Then, from right to left, come No. 3 "La Brouette" ("The Wheelbarrow"; the grocers' house), No. 4 "Le Sac" ("The Sack"; the joiners' and coopers' house), No. 5 "La Louve" ("The She-Wolf"; the archers' house), No. 6 "Le Cornet" ("The

North-west side

Guild-houses on the north-west side of the Grand'Place

171

Cornucopia"; the bargees' house) and No. 7 "Le Renard" ("The Fox"; the shopkeepers' house).

South-west side   The five houses to the left of the Hôtel de Ville are also very splendid. No. 8, "L'Étoile" ("The Star"), was not a guild-house but seat of the ducal judiciary. No. 10, "L'Arbre d'Or" ("The Golden Tree"), was the brewers' house and now contains a small brewing museum (open: Mon.–Fri. 10am–noon and 2–5pm; in summer also Sat. 10am–noon).

South-east side   Making up the south-east side of the Place is the large building known as the Maison des Ducs de Brabant, its façade reminiscent of an Italian palazzo. It is adorned with the busts of nineteen dukes of Brabant – hence the name.

South-west side   Of the houses on either side of the Maison du Roi the most interesting is No. 24–25, "La Chaloupe d'Or" ("The Golden Sloop") which belonged to the tailors' guild.

Around the Grand'Place

Musée du Costume et de la Dentelle   A narrow street off the south side of the Grand'Place just to the left of the Hôtel de Ville leads in a few steps to the Musée du Costume et de la Dentelle (Museum voor de Kleedertracht en de Kant) on the left-hand side a short way down the hill. As well as documenting the history of fashion from the 17th to the 19th c. the museum is a shrine to the art of Brussels lace making (open: Mon.–Thur. 10am–5pm, Fri. 10am–12.30pm and 1.30–5pm, Sun. and public holidays 2–4.30pm).

**Manneken Pis   Along the Rue de l'Etuve (Stoofstraat) from the Musée du Costume is by far the best-known landmark in Brussels, the Manneken Pis, usually beseiged by a throng of tourists. Although he can be traced back to at least 1388, nothing much is known about the origin of the figure of a little boy urinating, popularly referred to as "the oldest citizen of Brussels". The Manneken is however surrounded by various legends. According to one the fountain is a memorial to a courageous infant who averted a conflagration, according to another it commemorates the son of a count who succumbed to a pressing urge while taking part in a procession. The present statue was made in 1619 by Jérome Duquesnoy the Elder and has been stolen on several occasions though always recovered. During the War of Austrian

Manneken-Pis, the best-known monument in Brussels

Succession (1741–48) it was removed and smashed. Found in pieces it was restored and replaced. Even in recent times attempts have been made to steal it. During major Brussels festivals wine or beer spurts from the fountain instead of the usual 70 litres/15 galls of water per hour. The Manneken has been presented with more than 450 costumes, which he wears on certain appointed days (see above, Maison du Roi).

Ilôt Sacré, the district extending north of the Grand'Place as far as the Place   Ilôt Sacré
de la Monnaie, was the original Senne island on which St Géry founded his chapel. Nowadays it is known for its numerous, always busy, restaurants and bars in the Rue des Bouchers (Beenhouwerstraat) and the streets round about. Tucked away in a narrow cul-de-sac called the Impasse   Toone Puppet
Schuddeveld is one of Brussels' oldest institutions, the "Toone Puppet   Theatre
Theatre", carried on by the Toone family for seven generations.

Situated only a short distance from the north-east corner of the Grand-   *Galéries
'Place is one of the first covered shopping arcades to be built in Europe, the   Saint-Hubert
Galéries Saint-Hubert completed in 1846. There are two main arcades, one either side of the Rue des Bouchers, the nearer of the two being the Galérie de la Reine (Queen's Gallery) with, on the other side of the road, the Galérie du Roi (King's Gallery). Off the latter runs the little Galérie des Princes (Princes' Gallery). The motto "Omnibus omnia" ("Everything for everyone") above the entrance is all that remains of the silversmiths' guild-house demolished when the Galéries were built. The three-storeyed arcade is a shoppers' delight with luxury boutiques, cafés, restaurants and chocolate shops.

Turning left at the end of the Galéries leads to the Place de la Monnaie and   Théâtre Royal de
the Théâtre Royal de la Monnaie, both of which take their name from the   la Monnaie ·
15th c. Hotel de la Monnaie, the Duchy of Brabant's mint, which originally   Muntschouwburg
stood there. Designed by the architect Damesme the Neo-Classical theatre,

Galéries Saint-Hubert   *Place des Martyrs*

its façade embellished with Ionic columns and gable relief, was built in 1819 to replace an earlier building, also a theatre. It was here on August 25th 1830 that the Belgian Revolution began. During a performance of the opera "La Muette de Portici" (by D. F. Auber) the audience, stirred by the duet "Sacred Love of the Fatherland", rushed out onto the streets sparking off the rebellion against the Netherlands. The theatre burned down in 1855 and was then rebuilt with the original façade. It was here also that Maurice Béjart founded his world-famous ballet company "Ballet du XXme Siècle" (now based in Lausanne).

Place de
Brouckère ·
Brouckèreplaats

Across the square towers the Centre Monnaie (Muntcentrum), a shopping precinct and office block facing onto the large and busy Place de Brouckère (Brouckèreplaats) with its restaurants, cinemas and shops.

Saint-Nicolas ·
Sint-Niklaas

A block or two south of the theatre, hidden away behind the Bourse, stands one of the city's oldest churches, Saint-Nicolas, built originally by merchants in the 11th or 12th c. in honour of their patron saint, and from which, as was the custom, they marketed their wares. Inside the church, which has since undergone alteration several times, is an interesting 15th c. Madonna.

Bourse · Beurs

Saint-Nicholas faces the rear of the Bourse (1871), the country's leading stock exchange. The main façade, overlooking the Place de la Bourse, has wonderfully rich figurative ornamentation with a crowning figure symbolising Belgium itself.

City centre – north

Sainte-Catherine
· Sint-Katelijne

Not far west of the Théâtre Royal lies the majestically proportioned church of Sainte-Catherine, built in 1850 in a blend of Romanesque, Gothic and Renaissance styles to replace an earlier building. Of particular interest in the interior are the 14th or 15th c. figure of a black Madonna and a painting by de Crayer. The Tour Noire (11th–12th c.) which stands behind the church is a remnant of the old city wall while, on the west side, the delightful fish market is a reminder that this was once one of the old town quays.

*Saint-Jean ·
Sint-Jans

Even when seen at a distance along the Rue du Peuplier (Populierstraat) from the fish market, the magnificent façade of Saint-Jean-Baptiste au Béguinage is an impressive sight. The church, all that remains of a Béguine convent founded in the 13th c., was built between 1657 and 1676. Designed by Luc Fayd'herbe it is one of the finest Flemish-Italian Baroque churches in Belgium. Among the items of note in the light and spacious interior are the beautiful pulpit and the many paintings, including seven by the Brussels artist Van Loon.

Place des
Martyrs ·
Martelaarsplein

The dilapidated state of the Place des Martyrs, situated to the east of the pedestrianised Rue Neuve (Nieuwstraat) running north from the Théâtre Royal, is a sad commentary on the inactivity of the Brussels city council. The square, encircled by buildings dating from 1775, has in its centre a monument to the martyrs of the 1830 rebellion.

*Comic Museum

Housed in a building which is well worth seeing in its own right – the Maison Waucquez in the Rue de Sable (Zandstraat), a 1906 department store designed by Victor Horta – the diverting Comic Museum (Centre Belge de la Bande Dessinée/Belgisch Centrum van het Beeldverhaal) is one of Brussels' more unusual museums, being devoted to the art of the cartoon and the comic strip. On view is a constantly rotated exhibition of 200 original drawings by Belgian and French comic artists. In addition the museum documents the rise in popularity of Belgian and French comic strips through its collection of original manuscripts, draft sketches, and imaginatively reconstructed sets – of which Gaston Lagaffe's office, Lucky

Luke's saloon and Tim, Struppi and Captain Haddock's moon rocket are only three (open: Tues.–Sun. 10am–6pm).

Half way up the hill on the way from the Grand'Place to the Upper Town stands the Cathédral Saint-Michel (Sint-Michielskathedraal). Dedicated to St Michael and St Gudula, the patron saints of Brussels, it has been the episcopal church of the Mechelen-Brussels diocese since 1962. First founded in 1225 the white building in plain Brabant Gothic style was to all intents and purposes complete by the end of the 15th c. The façade is impressive, rising majestically above a broad flight of steps and crowned with twin 69m/226ft high towers designed by Jan van Ruysbroeck.

Saint-Michel · Sint-Michiel

The beautifully proportioned interior (108m/354ft by 50m/164ft) is exceptionally pleasing to the eye. As well as being lavishly furnished the church has some outstanding 16th–17th c. stained glass windows, the finest – all by Bernard van Orley – being those in the transepts (1537–38) depicting Charles V and Isabella of Portugal (south) and the Hungarian royal pair Louis II and Mary (north), and in the Chapel of the Holy Sacrament to the left of the choir illustrating the story of the "Miracle of the Host" (1534–39). The piers of the nave are adorned with figures of the Twelve Apostles by Fayd'herbe and Duquesnoy the Younger while towards the right aisle is a projecting carved wooden pulpit by Verbruggen (1669). Under the very beautiful triforium in the choir (1215–65) are the tombs of John, Duke of Brabant and his wife Margaret of York (left), and of Archduke Ernst of Austria. During July and August six magnificent tapestries by van der Borght (1785) are usually hung in the choir. In the ambulatory to the right of the choir there is a statue of the Virgin by Quellin the Elder (1645), and to the left of the choir, beside the Chapel of the Holy Sacrament, a memorial tablet to the Brussels artist Roger van der Weyden who is buried here.

Interior

Behind the cathedral the Treurenberg (Hill of Mourning) ascends to the Rue Royal (Koningstraat) in the Upper Town. To the left, a little way along the Rue, the Colonne du Congrès (1859), surmounted by a statue of Leopold I, commemorates the National Congress of 1831. At its foot an eternal flame burns on the Grave of the Unknown Soldier. A good view of the Lower Town can be had from the esplanade around the column.

Colonne du Congrès · Kongreszuil

Beyond the Colonne, across the boulevard at the north-east extremity of the city centre, the conservatories of the former botanic garden (1826–29) have been put to new use as a cultural centre for the city's French-speaking community.

Botanique · Kruidtuin

Quartier Royal

On the way up from the cathedral to the Rue Royal the west elevation of the 18th c. Palais de la Nation can be seen ahead. The façade of the Neo-Classical building, seat of the Belgian Senate and Chamber of Deputies, overlooks the Parc de Bruxelles.

Palais de la Nation · Paleis der Natie

The Parc de Bruxelles, one time hunting preserve of the dukes of Brabant and the scene in 1830 of much bloodshed during the rebellion against the Dutch, is laid out geometrically with its main axis towards the Palais Royal at the southern end. In the north-east corner stands the Royal Park Theatre.

Parc de Bruxelles

The Coudenberg Palace, historic seat of the dukes of Brabant, was destroyed by fire in 1731, later being replaced by the present Palais Royal. Used for state occasions the palace is the Belgian Royal Family's official residence rather than their home. The Belgian flag, flown from the roof, signals the sovereign's presence. A ceremonial Changing of the Guard takes place every day at about 2.30pm. The palace originally comprised two separate buildings which were made into one in 1827–29. Further

Palais Royal · Koninklijk Paleis

Place Royale and Saint-Jacques-sur-Coudenberg

alterations continued until 1904. (The state apartments are opened to the public in Aug. and Sept.; further information from tourist offices.)

Musée Bellevue
The Musée Bellevue in the west wing of the palace contains 18th and 19th c. furniture, glass and other objets d'art.

Palais des Académies
A square extends in front of the palace, on its east side being the Palais des Académies, home of the Royal Academy of Sciences and once the residence of the Crown Prince of Orange.

Palais des Beaux-Arts
The Palais des Beaux-Arts (Paleis voor Schone Kunste) on the opposite (west) side of the square was designed and built in the 1920s by Victor Horta. Cleverly integrated into its sloping site the Palais houses several cultural institutes, a concert hall and theatre and cinema museum.

*Place Royale · Koningsplein
Behind and to the west of the palace stand an exceptionally attractive ensemble of Neo-Classical buildings grouped around the Place Royale. In the 18th c. the French architect Barnabé Guimard was commissioned to produce a design for this important site on the Coudenberg, resulting in the construction of the Place between 1773 and 1780. The principal building in the square is the church of Saint-Jacques-sur-Coudenberg – the Chapel Royal – with its imposingly spacious interior.

Saint-Jacques-sur-Coudenberg

*Mont des Arts · Kunstberg

The Mont des Arts was created between 1956 and 1958, occupying the elevated site between the Place Royale (above) and the Place de l'Albertine (lower down). The architecturally imposing complex of large buildings includes the Bibliothèque Albert I and the strikingly modern Palais de la Dynastie and Palais de Congrès. From the square between them a fine view can be obtained of the Lower Town.

Although named after King Albert I the library is actually of much older origin, having been founded during the period of Burgundian rule. Its stock now comprises more than three million volumes together with a valuable collection of manuscripts. The library incorporates several interesting museums; also the Chapelle St Georges (1520), part of an earlier mansion belonging to the Nassau family.

Bibliothèque Albert I · Bibliotheek Albert I

The museums are: the Musée du Livre (Book Museum) which, in addition to outlining the history of books from Antiquity to the present day, has exhibitions of manuscripts, reconstructed interiors of the studies used by e.g. Emile Verhaeren and Michel de Ghelderode, and several very fine private collections built up by the Van de Velde family among others (open: Mon., Wed., Sat. 2–5pm); the Musée de l'Imprimerie (Printing Museum) illustrating the history of printing and bookbinding (open: Mon.–Sat. 9am–5pm); the Musée de la Littérature (Literature Museum) containing literary manuscripts by mainly French-speaking authors; and the Graphics Room with a collection of more than 5,000 engraving plates, etc. (open: Mon.–Fri. 9am–noon and 2–5pm).

Museums

Just up the hill from the Palais de la Dynastie, at the end of the Rue Ravenstein in what was once the Jewish Quarter, the 15th c. Hôtel Ravenstein is the city's sole building of any size surviving from the Burgundian period.

Hôtel Ravenstein

⁎⁎Musées Royaux des Beaux-Arts en Belgique · Koninklijk Musea voor Schone Kunsten van België

Belgium's Royal Museum of Fine Arts (1875–81), one of the largest and best art galleries in the world, extends for some distance along the Rue de la Régence (Regentschapsstraat) from the west side of the Place Royale. The museum grew out of a collection first set up in 1797 and originally housed in the former palace of Charles of Lorraine. This was transferred to the newly established Musées Royaux in 1846. In 1978 a major programme of modernisation was undertaken involving enlargement of the museum by the addition of an underground extension. The entire collection was reorganised and divided into two parts, the Musée d'art ancien (15th to 18th c.) occupying the old building, and the Musée d'art moderne (mainly 19th and 20th c. Belgian works) in the new section lit by a shaft opening onto the Place du Musée. The main entrance is in the Rue de la Régence.

The museum is world famous for its collection of Flemish and Dutch Old Masters. This includes works by Petrus Christus ("Pietà"), Rogier van der Weyden ("The Mourning of Christ"), Dirk Bouts ("Judgment of the Emperor Otto"), Hans Memling, and a fine "Adoration of the Magi" by Gerard David. Also on view are Quentin Massys' triptych with the Life of St Anne (one of the best examples of the work of the man regarded by many as the supreme artist of the transitional period from the 15th to the 16th c.), a triptych with the Trials of Job by Bernard van Orley, an "Entombment" by the same artist, and a portrait by Lucas Cranach. Among the highpoints of the collection are two works by Pieter Breugel the Elder, "Census at Bethlehem" and "The Fall of Icarus". Among paintings of the 17th c. Flemish school are a number by Rubens himself ("Adoration of the Magi", "Calvary", and an unusual landscape painting) and several large altar pictures from his workshop. Jordaens is represented by a number of his very best works of which the finest is his "Allegory of Fertility". There are also paintings by van Dyck and by David Teniers, the latter's "Flemish Fair" being outstanding. Although the quality of the paintings from the 17th c. Dutch school is generally speaking not so high, among the more notable are pictures by Frans Hals, Rembrandt, van der Helst, Thomas de Keyzer and Nicolaus Maes, also the genre paintings by Jan Steen and Gabriel Metsu and a number of delightful landscapes.

Musée d'art ancien

Opening times
Tues.–Fri.
10am–noon and
1–5pm

The collection also includes other works mainly of the Italian, Spanish and French schools.

■ **15th and 16th c.**
(First floor)

10–17　Flemish primitives
　　11　Van der Weyden
　　13　Bouts
　　14　Memling
　　17　Bosch
21–34　Flemish school of
　　　　the 16th c.
　　22　Metsys
　　24　Mostaert
　　25　Gossart
　　26　Van Orley
　　31　Bruegel
　　32　Moro
　　34　Heulen bequest
17, 24, 25　North Dutch school
18–20　German school
　　20　Cranach
11, 12, 15, 16　French school
37–45　Delporte legacy

© Baedeker

**Art from
15th to 19th c.**

Rue de la Régence　Regentschapsstraat

■ **17th and 18th c.**
(Second floor)

52–54
57, 60, 62 } Flemish school
　　62　Rubens
　　50　Spanish school
　　61　French school
　　60　Dutch school
50–51　Italian school (14th–18th c.)
55–56　Faille bequest

**Musées Royaux des
Beaux-Arts en Belgique**

■ **19th c.** (ground floor)

68–71　Neo-Classicism, Romanticism
71–80　Realism
　　79　Meunier
82–84　Watercolours, drawings
80–85　Symbolism
　　87　Luminism
　　88　Evenepoel
　　89　First school of Laethem
90–91　Impressionism
　　91　Hess-Vandenbroeck legacy

**Koninklijke Musea voor
Schoone Kunsten van België**

■ **20th c. Art**
(basement)

　–8　Cobra, Surrealism after 1940
　　　lyric abstraction
　　　geometric abstraction
　　　new figuration
　–7　Realism, Animism
　　　recent Belgian painting 1945–1948
　–6　Expressionism, Cubism
　　　pure sculpture, Surrealism
　–5　Nervia, Expressionism
　–4　Ensor-Spilliaert
　　　Neo-Impressionism
　　　Nabis, Fauvism
–2, –3　Entrance area
　–1　Contemporary tendencies

20th c. Art

© Baedeker

■ **Temporary exhibitions**

Entrance

The museum of modern art occupies the ground floor of the old building and the new below ground extension contoured into the slope of the hill. Most of the works displayed are by Belgian artists. Neo-Classicism (Navez) and Romanticism (Wappers) are well represented, while among other 19th c. works on view is the very famous "Assassination of Marat" by the French artist Jacques-Louis David. The collection of 20th c. painting includes works by James Ensor, Paul Delvaux, René Magritte, Fernande Khnopff, Rik Wouters, Frits van den Berghe and the non-Belgian Henri Matisse, Paul Gauguin and Salvador Dali.

Musée d'art moderne

Opening times
Tues.–Fri.
10am–1pm and
2–5pm

The former palace of Charles of Lorraine abuts the north-west side of the Place du Musée as it runs down to the Mont des Arts. The palace is part of a larger building which, in the 18th c., was the residence of the governor of the Austrian Netherlands and which has recently been very well restored.

Palais de Charles de Lorraine

Sablon · Zavel

The area to the south-west of the Place Royale, the Sablon (Sands), was originally a barren and desolate piece of ground used as a cemetery for the poor. In the 16th c. members of the Brussels gentry began to build themselves houses there, with the result that it gradually developed into an elegant residential district.

In the Place du Petit Sablon (Little Sand), a block or two along the Rue de la Régence from the Place Royale, the small garden is surrounded by an unusual railing with 48 small columns, each topped by a statuette representing one of the Brussels guilds. Statues of Counts Egmont and Hoorn and some of the humanist scholars adorn the centre of the Place.

Petit Sablon · Kleine Zavel

South-east of the Place stands the Palais d'Egmont (Palais Arenberg), now used for state receptions.

Palais d'Egmont · Egmontpaleis

Palais de Charles de Lorraine

*Musée
Instrumental ·
Instrumenten-
museum

The museum in the Conservatoire de Musique on the south-west side of the square boasts one of the finest and most comprehensive collections of musical instruments to be found anywhere. More than 5000 exhibits gathered from down the centuries and all over the world testify to mankind's love affair with music. (Open: Tues., Thur., Sat. 2.30–4.30pm, Wed. 4–6pm, Sun. 10.30am–12.30pm.)

*Église du Sablon
· Zavelkerk

The 15th–16th c. church of Notre-Dame du Sablon (Onze Lieve Vrouw op de Zavel), generally considered one of the loveliest Late Gothic churches in Belgium, was built as a replacement for a small chapel first erected on the sandy expanse of the Sablon by the Crossbowmen's Guild in 1304. The interior of the church is breathtaking, in particular because of its marvellous stained glass. Also of interest is the burial chapel of the Tourn und Taxis family, partly the work of Luc Fayd'herbe. Kept in the sacrarium is a figure of the Virgin, a copy, so legend has it, of a Madonna brought to the chapel in 1348 by an Antwerp woman, Baet Soetens, to whom the Virgin had appeared.

Grand Sablon ·
Grote Zavel

Below the church the Place du Grand Sablon (Grote Zavel) slopes down to the Lower Town. The area is dotted with antique shops and antiquarian bookshops. Brussels' best-known flea market is held on the square itself every Saturday.

*Quartier des Marolles

Metro
Porte de Hal

The Quartier des Marolles occupies a triangular area on the south side of the city centre between the Gare du Midi, Porte de Hal and, towering high above everything, the Palais de Justice. Up to now the district has always been the preserve of the under-privileged, living by their wits and deeply distrustful of "the authorities". This distrust has been fuelled anew now

Notre-Dame du Sablon, seen from the Petit Sablon

that the very survival of the quarter is threatened by a wave of speculative building and an influx of EC employees for whom the Marolles is the "smart" place to have an apartment – after it has been luxuriously restored that is! About 10,000 people live in the area, mainly low wage earners, shopkeepers and tradespeople, often speaking a patois incomprehensible to outsiders by whom they tend to be regarded as loud-mouthed and uncouth. Even in the Middle Ages the Marolles was a refuge for the persecuted and today as many as a third of its inhabitants are thought to be illegal immigrants. The quarter's most famous son was Pieter Breugel the Elder whose house stands in the Rue Haute (Hoogstraat; No. 132).

The Place du Jeu de Balle at the heart of the Marolles has a very colourful street market selling all kinds of merchandise.

Place du Jeu de Balle · Vossenplein

The modest houses of the Quartier des Marolles cower in the shadow of the huge Palais de Justice (1866–83), designed by Joseph Poelaert and built on the Galgenberg, the hill where the gallows stood in medieval times. Its massive dimensions, 104m/341ft high and 26,000sq.m/31,096sq.yds in area, make it the largest building to be erected in Brussels in the 19th c.

*Palais de Justice Justeipaleis

This gate at the southern extremity of the city centre is the sole remnant of the 14th c. ring walls.

Porte de Hal · Hallepoort

Except for the west tower which was completed in 1699, the Brabant Gothic church of Notre-Dame de la Chapelle on the northern edge of the Marolles dates from the 13th–15th c. Inside are figures of the apostles by Duquesnoy and Fayd'herbe, but the church is best known as the burial place of Pieter Breugel the Elder whose tomb can be seen in the fourth chapel along on the right from the main door. The black marble memorial with a painting by Rubens (now a copy) was erected by the artist's younger son Jan, known as "Velvet". The frame and inscription were added later by Breugel's grandson David Tenier III. To the right of the choir is the burial chapel of the Spinola family.

N.-D. de la Chapelle · Kapellekerk

*Breugel's tomb

Eastern districts

The Rue de la Loi (Wetstraat), running east from the city centre towards the Parc du Cinquantenaire, terminates at the Rond Point Schuman (Schumanplein), around which is grouped the Cité Européenne, headquarters of the EC. The European Commission and its vast administrative staff occupy the Palais Berlaymont, the largest of the 43 buildings and shaped like an irregular cross. Erected between 1963 and 1969 the Palais now faces demolition because of the asbestos used in its construction. The people of Brussels favour moving the EC headquarters to a green field site outside the city.

Cité Européenne

Metro Schuman

One street south of the EC building lies the attractive Parc Léopold, at the southern end of which are the Natural Science Museums (Musées des Sciences Naturelles/Musea voor Natuurwetenschapen). The biggest attraction in the museums are the partially reconstructed skeletons of 29 iguanodons discovered in 1878 at Bernissart in western Belgium (opening times: Tues.–Sun. 9.30am–4.45pm).
The Musée Wiertz immediately next to the science museum contains a large number of paintings by the Belgian Romantic painter Antoine Wiertz.

Musées des Sciences Naturelles
*Dinosaur skeletons

Musée Wiertz

*Parc du Cinquantenaire · Jubelpark

The Parc du Cinquantenaire, the entrance to which is just a short walk from the Metro station Schuman, was established in 1880 to commemorate the country's 50th anniversary. Its centrepiece is the monumental Palais du

Metro Schuman, Merode

A Corinthian vase

Stained-glass: William II, Count of Namur

Cinquantenaire, the two wings of which, linked in 1905 by a massive triumphal arch designed by the French architect Charles Girault, house two of Brussels' most interesting museums.

** Musées Royaux d'Art et d'Histoire

The Royal Art and History Museum (Musées Royaux d'Art et d'Histoire/ Koninklijk Musea voor Kunst en Geschiedenis) occupying the south wing of the Palais is split into two main sections: Mediterranean culture from early history to Antiquity (in the new Kennedy Wing) and Belgian pre- and early history, the history of Christian Europe from the Middle Ages, and Asian and American culture (in the older Nerviens Wing).

Opening times

Generally speaking the museum is open from Tues.–Fri. 9.30am–12.30pm and 1.30–4.45pm, Sat., Sun. and public holidays 10am–4.45pm. Some departments are only open on certain days however: antiquities, Islam, Oriental and Christian art on even dates; sculpture and decorative art on odd dates; early Belgian history on Wed. only. In addition the opening times of other departments, e.g. Asia, Oceania, the Americas and Glass, may vary.

Kennedy Wing

Ground floor: archaeological finds from, e.g. Luristan and Jericho. First floor: Etruscan, Greek and Roman cultures including a 2nd c. A.D. street and very large 5th c. A.D. mosaic from the town of Apamea in Syria. Second floor: Egyptian artefacts.

Nerviens Wing

Only the most interesting rooms can be listed. Rooms 1–6: Belgian settlement up to Roman times; Rooms 16–31: art and applied art from the 14th to 17th c., including Paris, Tournai and Brussels tapestries (legend of the Sablon Virgin, Battle of Roncevaux) and, in pride of place, a carved altarpiece of St George by Jan Borman; Room 36: large narthex with eight Brussels Gobelins from cartoons by Bernard van Orley illustrating the story of Jacob; Rooms 45–46: Oriental and Islamic art; Rooms 48–53: European applied art from the 17th to 20th c. including, Room 51, Art Nouveau;

Rooms 55–67: South-east Asia, America and Oceania; Rooms 76–83: 15th
to 20th c. European costume and lace; delftware; Room 96: China.

The Belgian Army Museum and Museum of Military History (Musée Royal   ***Musée Royal de**
de l'Armée et d'Histoire Militaire/Koninklijk Museum van het Leger en van   **l'Armée**
de Militaire Geschiedenis) occupies the north wing of the Palais Cinquantenaire. It provides an overview of the development of military technology   **Opening times**
and of the major campaigns fought on Belgian soil.   Tues.–Sun.
                                                                       9am–noon and
                                                                       1–4.45pm

The museum has three principal sections: Belgian military history (docu-   Departments
ments, uniforms and weaponry from the Middle Ages to the present day,
including a most comprehensive collection of medieval arms and armour);
the Armoured Vehicle Hall with artillery, tanks, etc. from the two World
Wars; and the Air Section with a collection of aircraft from the First World
War onwards.

Established in 1986 and housed in the imposing Palais Mondial (1880)   ***Autoworld**
where, between 1902 and 1934, the famous Brussels motor car and motor
cycle exhibitions were held, Autoworld comprises a display of some 550   **Opening times**
vintage cars and other vehicles. Most come from private collections and   daily 10am–6pm,
span the whole range of marques starting from the very earliest days of   Nov.–Mar.
motoring. Among them are all the best known names including Mercedes-   only until 5pm
Benz, Horch, Opel, Minerva, Cadillac, Rolls Royce, Hispano Suiza, Ford,
Humber, Bentley, Packard and Oldsmobile. A collection of American presi-
dential limousines is one of Autoworld's special attractions.

Northern districts

Laeken

Although the Château Royal, home of the Belgian Royal Family, is not itself   **Château Royal ·**
open to the public, the park surrounding it at Laeken is (Metro to Bockstael,   **Koninklijk**
then bus No. 53). There are delightful footpaths and a number of things   **Kasteel**
worth seeing such as the monument to Leopold I at the centre of the
circular flowerbed in front of the palace. The Japanese Tower in the northernmost corner of the park was originally built for the Paris Exhibition of   *Royal hothouses
1900. The hothouses, erected in Leopold II's time, are the highlight of the
gardens and open to the public during April and May when many of the   Chinese Pavilion
plants are in flower. The Chinese Pavilion, facing the Japanese Tower, on
the opposite side of the road, was likewise brought to the park from the
Paris Exhibition. It now houses a good collection of Chinese and Japanese
porcelain (open: Tues.–Sun. 9.30am–12.30pm and 1.30–5pm).

On the far side of the wide avenue skirting the western edge of the park   Notre-Dame
stands the extremely large church of Notre-Dame de Laeken (Onze Lieve   de Laeken
Vrouw te Laeken), burial place of Belgium's kings and queens. Commissioned in 1851 by Leopold I following the death of his wife Louise-Marie,
the building was designed by Josef Poelaert, architect of the Palais de
Justice. It was completed in 1872. Inside the church a much revered 13th c.
Madonna adorns the high altar and behind the choir can be seen the
entrance to the royal crypt. The graves of many an important Belgian public
figure are to be found in the churchyard.

** Atomium

Apart from Manneken Pis the Atomium is Brussels' best-known landmark.   **Metro**
Designed by the architect André Waterkeyn for the 1958 Brussels World   Heysel
Exhibition, the 102m/326ft-high steel and aluminium structure represents

a molecule of iron magnified 165 million times. Four of the nine spheres are now used for the presentation of a show about human life called "Biogenium". The topmost sphere contains a restaurant and a viewing platform (open: 6.30pm–10pm).

Opening times
Daily 9.30am–6pm, summer till 10pm

Bruparck, a popular leisure park immediately adjacent to the Atomium, incorporates four principal attractions: "Mini-Europe", a collection of 1:25 scale models of the continent's most famous historic and modern monuments; the "Oceadium" in the Parc Aquatique, a 7000sq.m/8375sq.yds swimming pool with all kinds of additional features; the "Kinepolis", a 24-auditorium cinema complex; and "Le Village", with restaurants, bars, etc. and a place to sit down!

Bruparck

A short distance beyond Bruparck lies the Heysel Stadium, made tragically familiar by the events of May 1985.

Heysel Stadium

The Palais du Centenaire (Paleis van het Eeuwfestwijk) north of the Atomium was completed for Belgium's centenary celebrations in 1930. It now forms part of the Brussels trade fair and exhibition centre also incorporating the big International Trade Mart (1975).

Palais du
Centenaire

Western districts

Koekelberg

The Koekelberg district is dominated by the massive Basilique National du Sacré Cœur (Nationale Basiliek van het Heilig Hart), the brainchild of Leopold II and begun in 1905 to mark the country's 75th anniversary. The building was only completed in 1970. Not surprisingly therefore it displays something of a mixture of styles, impressing nevertheless by its sheer size (141m/463ft × 107m/351ft). The picture of Christ giving His blessing which hangs above the altar is by Georges Minne. The dome affords a magnificent view over the city.

Basilique National
· Nationale
Basiliek

Metro
Simonis

Anderlecht

The Anderlecht district to the west of the city centre is the home of Brussels' most famous football club, RSC Anderlecht.

Metro
Gare du Midi,
St Guidon

A short distance north of the Gare du Midi Metro station, in the Rue Gheude (Gheudestraat), one of the most unusual of all the city's museums, the Musée de la Gueuze (Gueuze-Biermuseum), can be visited in the only Brussels brewery still producing this bitter-sweet speciality beer (open: Mon.–Sat. 10am–5pm).

Musée de
la Gueuze

In 1521 the humanist scholar Erasmus of Rotterdam (1469–1536) lodged for five months in the early 16th c. house still standing today in what is now the Rue du Chapitre (Kapiteelstraat) near the Metro station St-Guidon. In addition to Gothic and Renaissance furnishings the rooms of Maison d'Erasme contain a number of items belonging to the great man. Visitors can see his study and his bedroom, in the latter a first edition of "In Praise of Folly" is displayed. On the ground floor are several interesting paintings, including one by Hieronymus Bosch (open: Mon., Wed., Thur., Sat., Sun., 10am–noon and 2–5pm).

·Maison
d'Erasme ·
Erasmushuis

The fine Gothic building seen not far from the Maison d'Erasme is the 14th–16th c. collegiate church of St Peter and St Guido, the distinctive spire of which is a 19th c. addition. As well as a 14th c. arch and some reasonably

Saints Pierre et
Guidon · Sint-
Pieter en Guido

◀ *The Atomium, an iron molecule exaggerated 165 thousand million times* well preserved medieval wall paintings, the interior boasts an 11th c. five-aisled crypt below the choir, probably originally part of a church above ground. The crypt contains a stone sarcophagus, the tomb of St Guido, patron saint of horses.

Béguinage

Anderlecht's béguinage, founded in 1252, used to be situated near the church. Four surviving 17th c. buildings have been converted into a museum (open: Mon., Wed., Thur., Sat., Sun., 10am–noon and 2–5pm).

Southern districts

Forest · Vorst

Tram
19, 52

The suburb of Forest lies sprawled across the slope of the Senne valley 3km/2 miles south of the city centre. The Parc de Forest and Parc Duden are the remains of a large forest which was once Charles V's hunting preserve.

Saint-Denis ·
Sint-Denijs

Built in 1250 on the site of an earlier (7th c.) chapel, the small church of Saint-Denis (Square Omer Denis) contains the 11th c. tomb of Alène, daughter of a non-Christian nobleman from Dilbeek. Incensed by learning of his daughter's secret baptism he is said to have beaten her to death, only to become a convert to Christianity himself as a result of miracles witnessed at her grave.

Saint-Gilles · Sint-Gillis

* Musée Horta

Tram
92

Victor Horta's house (Rue américaine/Amerikaansestraat), itself a masterpiece of Art Nouveau architecture (1898–1900), has been turned into a museum celebrating the life and work of the movement's leading Belgian exponent. The staircase is magnificent (open: Tues.–Sun. 2–5.30pm).

Ixelles · Elsene

Tram
81, 93, 94

The suburb of Ixelles extends south of the ring boulevard, its main shopping street being the Chaussée d'Ixelles (Elsenesteenweg), a busy thoroughfare.

* Musée
communal des
Beaux-Arts

The Musée communal des Beaux-Art (Gemeendemuseum voor Schone Kunsten) in the Rue Jean van Volsem off the east side of the Chaussée possesses an excellent collection of Belgian and French paintings and of Belgian Impressionist paintings in particular.

Abbaye de la
Cambre · Abdij
ter Kameren

In 1200, in what was then a small valley between the Etangs d'Ixelles (the little lakes now situated at the end of the Chaussée d'Ixelles) and the Bois de la Cambre which today forms an oasis of tranquillity amidst the city traffic, Cistercian nuns founded an abbey. It was destroyed in the 16th c. but then rebuilt. Now, set in lovely French gardens, it houses the National Geographical Institute and an art college.

The former abbey church (14th c.) is a slender, elegant building with Baroque vaulting. Inside can be seen a painting by Albert Bouts ("The Mocking of Christ") and the shrine of St Boniface, a 13th c. Bishop of Brussels. The windows of the cloister are decorated with the arms of over 40 abbesses and nuns.

Bois de
la Cambre ·
Kamerenbos

The Bois de la Cambre in the very south of Ixelles is one of the favourite recreation areas close to Greater Brussels. The 24ha/59 acre park has a lake, restaurants and broad expanses of grass for games or merely for resting. The wide and splendid Avenue Louise (Louizalaan) links the park directly with the city centre.

Located at the east edge of the park are administrative buildings and lecture halls belonging to the Université Libre de Bruxelles (Free University of Brussels), the larger and more modern part of which occupies a site a little further east still, in Etterbeek.

University

Charles de Coster (see Famous People) lies buried in the cemetery on Ixelles' boundary with Etterbeek. A figure of Till Eulenspiegel decorates his grave.

Cemetery

Uccle · Ukkel

The museum at Avenue Léo Errera No. 41, home of art collectors David and Alice van Buuren, is of great interest on two counts, the first being the house itself with its genuine Art Déco furnishings. The second of course is the superb art collection complementing the furniture. Among the finest items are Pieter Breugel the Elder's "The Fall of Icarus", paintings by Patinir, Fantin-Latour, Permeke, and van de Woestyne, sculptures by Minne and the collection of delftware (opening times: Mon. 2–4pm).

*Musée van Buuren

Tram 92

Auderghem · Oudergem

This south-eastern district of Brussels borders the Forêt de Soignes (see below). The Etangs de Rouge Cloître (Rood Klooster) are a reminder of the priory which once stood here, where in 1482 the painter Hugo van der Goes died. The Château de Val Duchesse in the large park just to the north is best known for being the place where the original Treaty of Rome setting up the EEC (now the EC) was made ready for signing.

Tram 44

Surroundings

*Forêt de Soignes · Zoniënwoud

Beyond the Bois de la Cambre south-east of Brussels stretches one of the finest woodlands in Belgium, the 4000ha/9900 acre Forêt de Soignes. With its magnificent beech groves the Forêt is a popular recreation area for the capital and in summer old trams from the urban transport museum (Musée du Transport Urbain Bruxellois) in Woluwe-Sint-Pieter (364b Ave. de Tervuren) trundle through the woods.

Tram 44

Some 13km/8 miles south-east of the city centre, tucked away in a pretty valley in the midst of the forest, the little hamlet of Groenendael was once the site of a famous Augustinian abbey founded in 1343 by the mystic Jan van Ruysbroek. The only abbey building to survive (18th c.) is now in use as a high-class restaurant. The interesting Groenendael arboretum on the valley's south-facing slope has over 500 exotic tree and shrub species as well as a forest museum.

Groenendael

Tervuren

A visit to Tervuren, 12km/7½ miles east of Brussels, should be high on any list of excursions outside the capital simply on account of its quite exceptional museum.

Tram 44

The Musée Royal de l'Afrique Central is housed in a palatial building designed by the French architect Charles Girault. Completed in 1910 the project was yet another brainchild of King Léopold II. The museum's

*Musée Royal de l'Afrique Centrale

extremely comprehensive collection, deriving mainly from the former Belgian Congo, embraces the wildlife, archaeology, minerology, ethnography and art of the peoples of Central Africa. The minerals section in particular, and also the collection of masks and carved wood and ivory figures, are unique (open: mid Mar.–mid Oct. daily 9am–5.30pm, mid Oct.–mid Mar. daily 10am–4.30pm).

Well stocked with fine old trees, the large and pleasant Tervuren Park extends south from the museum.

Arboretum

More inviting even than the Park is a stroll through the Tervuren arboretum in the delightful woodland setting of the Bois de Capuchins (Kapucijnenbos).

Jezus Eik

Plentifully supplied with restaurants, including many which serve the local cherry-flavoured beer called kriek, Jezus Eik, a small commune immediately south of the Arboretum, offers welcome respite for tired legs.

*Kasteel van Gaasbeek

Bus
LK

Ensconced in a charming park 14km/8½ miles south-west of Brussels (leave by Anderlechtsepoort, thence via Viezenbeek) stands the medieval Kasteel van Gaasbeek. Parts of the château are 13th c. but the main Renaissance-style building dates from the 16th c.

The magnificent interior contains superb furniture, carpets, glass, porcelain, paintings, gold and silverware and armour. Most remarkable of all however are the priceless 15th–17th c. Brussels and Tournai tapestries. Rubens' will can also be seen, on display in the archive room.

The terrace has a lovely view of the gently undulating countryside which Bruegel so often captured in his paintings and which today remains a delightful place to walk (open: Apr.–Oct. Tues.–Thur., Sat. and Sun. 10am–5pm; July/Aug. also open Mon.).

The Kasteel van Gaasbeek, popular for outings with the people of Brussels

*Nationaal Plantentuin van Bouchout

Belgium's national botanic garden in the suburb of Meise 14km/8½ miles north of Brussels opened in 1958. The nurseries and hothouses are grouped around the castle (12th c.) and lake of the Domaine Bouchart, where Leopold II's sister the Empress Charlotte of Mexico lived after fleeing the Mexican Revolution. More than 10,000 plants are arranged according to geographical origin. Among the highlights are the collection of water and wetland plants in the "Victoria" hothouse and the tropical and subtropical plants in the so-called "Palais des Plantes" (open: park 9am–one hour before sunset; hothouses Mon.–Thur. 1–4pm, Easter–Oct. also the last Sun. 2–6pm).

Bus
L (to Meise)

Grimbergen

Grimbergen, 12km/7½ miles north of the city centre, could once lay claim to an abbey founded in the 12th c. It still takes pride in its impressive abbey church (1660–1700), the Baroque interior of which is one of the most sumptuously ornate in Belgium. Particularly noteworthy are the four confessionals by Verbruggen.

Bus
G, H

See Halle, Surroundings

Beersel

See entry

Waterloo

Charleroi

E 7

Province: Hainaut
Altitude: 40–200m/130–656ft
Population: 220,000
Intercity and Inter-regional Station

The modern industrial city of Charleroi and its environs lie at the heart of one of Europe's oldest industrial regions. This part of southern Belgium is almost synonymous with coal and steel production, both of which industries have been in crisis in recent years but now show signs of recovery. Such is the scale of industrialisation hereabouts that the area is known as the Pays Noir (the Black Country). More than 450,000 people live in the conurbation around Charleroi, a pool of skilled labour for the 200 companies engaged in iron and steel (Cockerill-Sambre) or chemical production, various types of manufacturing (farm machinery, electrical goods, medical appliances), aircraft assembly and publishing (Dupois). Charleroi is famous too for its glassworks, carrying on a tradition going back more than 400 years. The city is an important crossroads served by the Charleroi-Bruxelles Canal which forms a vital link between the Sambre and the Scheldt. It has a technological university (Université de Travail) and a number of other scientific institutes. Even though separated from the industry dominated lower town, the upper town with its pedestrian zone has little in the way of sights apart from one or two interesting museums. Charleroi however is a big, lively, enterprising city. Every year thousands of visitors are attracted to its various trade fairs, one of which, the Salon de la Bande Dessinée (Comic Strips), is unique in Europe.

Location

Charleroi began as an ordinary medieval rural village called Charnoy the inhabitants of which also engaged in a little mining. This changed in 1659 when much of Hainaut was captured by the French and Charnoy suddenly found itself a Spanish frontier post. As a check on the ambitions of the French King Louis XIV, Charles II of Spain expanded the village into a fortress, renaming it at the same time. For the next 30 years Charleroi lay at the centre of a battlefield, being taken by the French in 1667 – after which

History

189

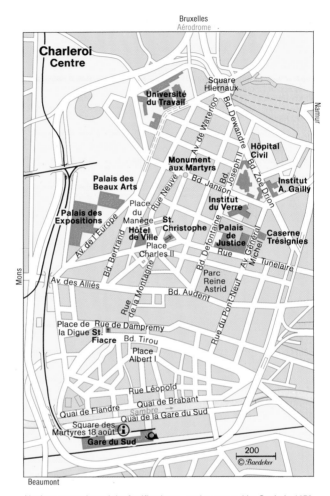

Bruxelles
Aérodrome

**Charleroi
Centre**

Square
Hiernaux

**Université
du Travail**

Bd. Dewandre

Namur

Av. de Waterloo

**Hôpital
Civil**

**Monument
aux Martyrs**

Bd. Joseph II

Bd. Zoé Drion

**Palais des
Beaux Arts**

Rue Neuve

Bd. Janson

**Institut
A. Gailly**

**Institut
du Verre**

**Palais des
Expositions**

Place
du
Manège

**St.
Christophe**

**Hôtel
de Ville**

Bd. Defontaine

**Palais
de
Justice**

**Caserne
Trésignies**

Av. de l'Europe

Bd. Bertrand

Place
Charles II

Rue

Av. Général Michel

Tunelaire

Mons

Av. des Alliés

Rue de la Montagne

Bd. Audent

Parc
Reine
Astrid

Rue du Pont Neuf

Place de
la Digue

Rue de Dampremy

**St.
Fiacre**

Bd. Tirou

Place
Albert I

Rue Léopold

Quai de Brabant

Sambre

Quai de Flandre

Quai de la Gare du Sud

Square des
Martyres 18 août

Gare du Sud

200

© Baedeker

Beaumont

Vauban strengthened the fortifications – and recovered by Spain in 1679. The Peace of Rujswijk in 1697 brought a period of respite, which ended when hostilities were renewed following the French Revolution. Industrialisation proper began in the first half of the 19th c., accompanied by the construction of a canal link with Brussels in 1832. The old walls were demolished in 1868 being replaced by boulevards which can still be seen today. In the First World War, after heavy fighting, German troops occupied the city in August 1914.

**Military
processions**

The region around Charleroi is unique in Belgium for its tradition of "marches militaires", a form of religious cum military festival in which the members of various local societies and brotherhoods don colourful military uniforms and parade to the music of brass bands and the noise of guns. One of the best-known is the Marche de la Madeleine (end of July) when 1500 "infantry", 150 horsemen and 30 bands set off from Jumet on a 20km/12 mile "march".

Sights

The heart of Charleroi's upper town is the Place Charles II, dominated by the Hôtel de Ville (Town Hall; 1936) and its towering 70m/230ft-high belfry with a carillon of 47 bells.

Hôtel de Ville

Housed in the Hôtel de Ville the Musée des Beaux-Arts (Museum of Fine Arts) consists primarily of a collection of works by Hainaut artists. Another whole section (Musée Jules Destrée) is devoted to the lawyer, statesman and writer Jules Destrée (1863–1936; open: Tues.–Sun. 9am–5pm).

Musée des Beaux-Arts

Across the square from the Hôtel de Ville can be seen the cupola of the Basilique Sainte-Christophe (1801; fine mosaic in the choir).

Sainte-Christophe

The Palais des Beaux-Arts in the Avenue de l'Europe (west of the Hôtel de Ville on the far side of the Place de la Manège) is the home of the well-known Ballet Royal de Wallonie.

Palais des Beaux-Arts

The Musée du Verre (Glass Museum) occupies part of the Institut National du Verre on the Boulevard Defontaine to the east of the Hôtel de Ville. The museum comprises two large departments, one concerned with the history and production of glass throughout the world, the other with the development of the Belgium glass industry in particular. On display are some quite exceptional examples of the glass-maker's art from Antiquity to the present day. A permanent exhibition on the ground floor provides a showcase for the glassware manufactured in Belgium today (open: Tues.–Sun. 9am–5pm).

*Musée du Verre

The Musée Archéologique occupies the basement of the Institute National du Verre. As well as archaeological finds mainly from the Roman and Merovingian periods there are interesting exhibits from the early modern and industrial eras (open: Tues.–Sun. 9am–5pm).

Musée Archéologique

Surroundings

In the western suburb of Marchienne-au-Pont, part of an old ironworks (134, Rue de la Providence) has been converted into the Musée de l'Industrie. Sections of an old rolling mill, forges, a machine workshop and a print-works are among the many intriguing exhibits (open: daily 9am–4pm. Sat. on request).

Marchienne -au-Pont

Musée de l'Industrie

Also in Marchienne-au-Pont (Place des Martyrs) the Musée d'Histoire, de Folklore et d'Archéologie Industrielle (Museum of Local History and Industrial Archaeology) traces the history of industrial development in and around Charleroi (open: Wed. and Fri. 5–7pm).

Musée d'Histoire, de Folklore et d'Archéologie Industrielle

Marchienne-au-Pont's 17th c. château was the family seat of the writer Marguerite Yourcenar.

Château

The south-western suburb of Mont-sur-Marchiennes also has a surprise in store in the shape of its remarkable Musée de la Photographie in the former Carmelite convent. Here, in one of the best museums of its kind, there are excellent displays explaining the development of photography as well as collections of cameras and photographs old and new (open: Tues.–Thur., Sat., Sun. 10am–6pm).

Mont-sur-Marchiennes

Gerpinnes, 8km/5 miles south of Charleroi, is a traditional stronghold of the marche militaire, well-known for its big Easter Monday Marche de Saint-Roland.

Gerpinnes

191

°Abbaye d'Aulne   Some 12km/7½ miles west of Charleroi stand the impressive ruins of the
                   Abbaye d'Aulne, founded in the 7th c. by St Landelin of Lobbes. It was taken
                   over by the Cistercians in 1147 and burnt down by French revolutionaries in
                   1794.
                   The abbey remains are well worth seeing. They include the great court and
                   Prince-Bishops' reception hall, also the 14th–15th c. choir and transepts of
                   the ruined abbey church.

Claire-Fontaine   The Claire-Fontaine leisure centre in the small town of Chapelle-lez-Herlai-
                   mont, 11km/7 miles north-west of Charleroi, offers an extensive range of
                   amusements including boating, swimming, dry tobogganing and
                   mini-golf.

Chimay   E 8

                   Province: Hainaut
                   Altitude: 100–270m/328–885ft
                   Population: 10,000

Location   Surrounded by extensive woods the small town of Chimay is situated in the
                   province of Hainaut, near the French border. Jean Froissart, chronicler of
                   the Hundred Years' War, spent his last years in Chimay; another famous
                   inhabitant of the town was Thérése Tallien (1773–1835), an enigmatic
                   personality, who went down in history as "Notre-Dame de Thermidor". As
                   the wife of the proconsul of the French republic, Tallien, she encouraged
                   him to resist the tyrant Robespierre, which later led to his downfall. Follow-
                   ing her divorce from Tallien she married François-Joseph de Caraman,
                   Prince of Chimay, and turned the château at Chimay into a meeting place
                   for lovers of music and theatre.

Sights

Grand-Place   The attractive small Grand-Place is surrounded by several old manor
                   houses and the 17th c. town hall.

Sts-Pierre-et-Paul The collegiate church of Saints-Pierre-et-Paul stands directly in the centre
                   of the Grand-Place. Building of the choir started in the 13th c. but the tower
                   was not completed until the 18th c.
                   The church interior contains Baroque choir stalls (1702) and the tombs of
                   Charles de Croy, the chamberlain of Charles V, Madame Tallien and Jean
                   Froissart. Among the church treasure is a small chest decorated with
                   Byzantine mosaics which belonged to Philippe de Croy.

°Château   A few yards to the west of the Grand-Place is Chimay Château, built on
                   a rocky promontory over the Eau Blanche River by the Croy family in the
                   16th c. Madame Tallien commissioned the construction of a theatre in the
                   courtyard but it was partly burnt down in 1935 together with the château.
                   The tour leads through rooms furnished in contemporary style to the
                   Grand Hall with an interesting 14th c. fireplace and into various drawing
                   rooms where keepsakes of Madame Tallien and her visitors can be seen,
                   including a portrait of Princess Gérard; in the Napoleon Room the christen-
                   ing dress of Eugène, son of Napoleon III is displayed.

Surroundings

Abbaye de   Founded in 1850 the Trappist monastery of Scourmont is idyllically situ-
Scourmont   ated in the forest of Chimay 9km/6 miles south of the town. The monastery

The cloister garth of Scourmont, near Chimay

is widely known for its own beer, "Trappiste de Chimay", brewed in three different strengths, and its cheese.

In the small town of Couvin 11km/7 miles to the east the first coking plant in Europe was erected. The Cavernes d'Abîme, inhabited in prehistoric times, as illustrated by a slide show on early history, are worth visiting as are the Grottes de Neptun, cut into the limestone rocks by the Eau Noire river. The tour finishes with an underground boat trip (open: Apr.–Sept. daily 9.30am–noon and 1.30–6pm; Oct. at weekends).

Couvin

Nismes, 15km/9 miles east of Chimay, is a popular venue for summer holidays. A small tourist train calls at the sights: the ruins of the magnificent castle, the neo-Gothic town hall and the Museum of Folklore and History.

Nismes

On the instructions of Charles V Mariembourg, 16km/10 miles north-east of Chimay, was fortified in 1546 in the shape of a star. The town gets its name from Maria of Hungary. Mariembourg is the departure point of the nostalgic steam railway "Trois Vallées", which chugs through the protected area of Viroin via Chimay to Momignies (Mar.–Oct. Sat., Sun., public holidays; July and Aug. also Tues., Wed., Thur.). There is a 600m-long go-karting track, the "Karting des Fagnes" with go-karts available for hire in Mariembourg.

Mariembourg

The Étang de Virelles, 3km/2 miles north of Chimnay, is a popular venue for excursions.

*Étang de Virelles

Damme

B 4

Province: West-Vlaanderen
Altitude: 8m/26ft
Population: 10,500

Damme

Location

The charming little Flemish town of Damme lies about 7km/4 miles north-east of Bruges (see Bruges). Up until the silting of the Zwin inlet it served as the customs point and outer port of Bruges, in which capacity it enjoyed great importance and prosperity. Its heyday only lasted about 200 years but

*Townscape

several significant buildings still remain from this period which give the town a contented atmosphere and have kept the image of a medieval Flemish town alive. In addition its highly-praised and excellent restaurants make Damme a popular destination for many gourmets.

In the second half of the 13th c. the "Vader der Dietsche Dichters" (Father of Dutch poets) Jacob van Maerlant lived in Damme where he wrote his most significant works. However, the town was immortalised as the home town of Thyl Ullenspiegel and Lamme Goedzak, the famous characters in the novel by Charles De Coster (see Introduction, Famous People).

History

850 years ago, when the Zwin, a wide inlet, penetrated far into the coastal plain Bruges began to gain importance as a port. A terminal dyke was built up at the end of the Zwin on which a small town, which is now Damme, developed. It became the outer port of Bruges and received its town charter in 1180 but was burnt down in 1213 together with its fleet of 400 ships by the troops of the French king. Undeterred the citizens of Damme set about rebuilding so that it retained its function as port and commercial centre with important nations and trading companies being represented here until the beginning of the 15th c.; in its heyday Damme was the chief trade centre in northern Europe for wine and the most important market in Europe for Swedish herring. Silting up of Bruges harbour was already noticeable by the end of the 13th c. finally reaching the harbour basin at Damme. A final high point before its eventual decline was the marriage of Charles the Bold with Margaretha of York.

The Stadhuis in Damme

194

Sights

The central point of Damme is the Grote Markt surrounded by some interesting buildings. A monument to Jacob van Maerlant stands in the centre of the square.

The magnificent Gothic town hall (Stadhuis) built by Gottfried von Bosschere in 1464–68 has six statues of Flemish counts and countesses decorating its façade: Philip of Alsace, Johanna and Margaretha of Constantinople, Philipp of Thiette, Charles the Bold and Margaretha of York. The entrance loggia was added in 1860. The interior houses original doorways carved with historic scenes.

To the right of the town hall stands the "De Grote Sterre" (Great Star) House, a 15th c. patrician's house and later seat of the Spanish governor. It is at presently undergoing refurbishment so that the Ullenspiegel Museum inside is also at present not accessible.

The semi-detached house next to the Grote Sterre was where the wedding party of Charles the Bold and Margaretha of York took place in 1468.

Not far from the Grote Markt in the Kerkstraat, Damme's main street, is the Sint-Janshospitaal. It was founded in 1249 by Margaretha of Constantinople and has been a home for the elderly since the 19th c. Part of it, however, serves as a museum with exhibitions of paintings, enamel, silver and books from the monastery library (open: Apr.–Oct. Mon. 2–5pm, Tues.–Sat. 10–noon and 2–6pm, Sun. and public holidays 11–noon and 2–6pm; Nov.–Mar. daily 2–5.30pm).

The impressive 45m/147ft-high tower of the Onze-Lieve-Vrouwkerk (Church of Our Lady) is visible from afar, a brick building begun in 1230 in the Schelde Gothic style. At the beginning of the 14th c. the choir which was completed in 1250 was converted into an interesting hall choir. In 1578 the church was set on fire by troops belonging to the Prince of Orange; in 1725 when Damme was becoming increasingly impoverished the top of the tower, the transept and parts of the nave were demolished. The interior houses valuable figures of the apostles carved in oak from 1400, the St Anne altar dated 1555 and the Baroque Holy Cross altar of 1636. Jacob van Maerlant is buried under the former main portal below the tower. From the top of the tower there is a marvellous view of the Flemish countryside, sometimes as far as the coast.

In the nearby Burgstraat the Museum Delporte was opened in 1990 in the pretty whitewashed old schoolhouse. Modern paintings and sculptures by the Belgian artist Charles Delporte are on display (open: Easter–Autumn daily 2–6pm).

Charles Deporte is both painter and sculptor, known primarily for his portraits. He uses a variety of material in his work. Typical of his sculpture are heads looking into the light as in this example.

Erected in 1979 the Ullenspiegel monument on the canal bridge commemorates the 100th anniversary of the death of Charles de Coster.

On the other side of the canal, to the east of the town centre, stands the Schellemolen, erected in 1867, a popular subject for photographs.

In a typical Flemish house near the mill copper casting in an artist's forge can be seen at the Frans Wiro van Hinsberg Museum (open: Sat. and Sun. 2–5pm; June–Sept. also Wed. 2–5pm).

Surroundings

In 1846 work commenced on the branch canal for the Leie (Afleidingkanaal van de Leie), also known as Schipdonkkanaal. It leads north of Damme in a north-west direction to Zeebrugge. Road 374 crosses the canal at Oost-kerke where there is a small guest house with a terrace. The two straight courses of the canal flowing past with the apparently endless rows of poplars provide a wonderful scene of peace and tranquillity.

Boat trips

In summer there are daily boat trips from Damme to Bruges (see Bruges) on the "Lamme Goedzak" (Information: Benelux-Damme Shipping Company, Stadhuis Damme, tel. (050) 35 33 19).

Dendermonde · Termonde   D 5

Province: Ooost-Vlaanderen
Altitude: 25m/82ft
Population: 42,000
Inter-regional Station (bicycle rental at station)

Location

On the right bank of the Scheldt, which joins the Dender lies Dendermonde (French Termonde; mouth of the Dender). The town's prosperity, still apparent from the magnificent buildings, stems from the textile industry. A large number of interesting historical monuments and art treasures have been preserved from its long history.

History

The first building on this site at the mouth of the river was a castle in the 10th c. under the protection of which a small town developed and received its charter in 1233. Owing to its strategic position Dendermonde was fortified and often besieged, as in 1667 when the 50,000 soldiers of Louis XIV had to retreat when the townspeople opened the locks thereby flooding the land. Parts of the town were badly damaged in 1914 when it was captured by German troops.

Festivals

On the fourth Sunday in August a giant procession takes place annually in Dendermonde where the giants Indiaan, Mars and Goliath dance. A more unusual event is the procession of the Bayard steed with the four children of Haimon on its back. This takes place every ten years (next date: 2000). Every year at the beginning of September Dendermonde stages a busy international jazz festival.

Sights

*Grote Markt

The buildings of the Grote Markt in the centre of the town provide the picture of an attractive enclosed Flemish market square towards the end of the Middle Ages.

Stadhuis

The stadhuis (town hall) was built between 1336–50 as a textile hall and converted in 1600. It was almost competely destroyed by fire in 1914, only the belfry (1378) with its carillon remained undamaged. Rebuilding took place in the Twenties. The rooms contain some interesting paintings among which are works by the painter Jan Verhas (1834–96) who came from this town.

Vleeshuis

The former vleeshuis (meat market) is another notable building in the market square, easily recognisable by its octagonal tower. This Gothic hall was built in 1460–62. Until 1862 the benches still stood on the ground floor where the butchers offered their products for sale. The Sint-Joris-Gilde used to meet on the first floor and under the roof the rhetoric guild "De Leeuwerckenaers". From 1715 both these rooms were used as the main police station. Since its restoration in 1899 the vleeshuis houses the Stede-lijk Oudheidkundig Museum (Municipal Museum) of the town's history (open: daily 9am–noon and 2–4pm; Easter–Sept. also Sat., Sun. and public holidays 10am–noon and 2–4.30pm).

Onze-Lieve-Vrouwkerk

From the market square the Kerkstraat leads west to the Kerkplein where stands the Gothic 14/15th c. Onze-Lieve-Vrouwkerk (Church of Our Dear Lady); the octagonal crossing tower was completed in 1388.

Dendermonde: the Vleeshuis in the Grote Markt

Viewing of the church interior is highly recommended. The Romanesque limestone font from the first half of the 12th c. was made in Tournai and depicts the Last Supper together with the Vision of SS Paul and Peter before paradise. Among the many paintings are two noteworthy works by van Dyck ("Crucifixion", 1630; "Adoration of the Shepherds", around 1632), three by Gaspar de Crayer ("Virgin of the Canon van Calandries", 1634; "St Roch and the Plague Victims", 1650; Virgin of the main altar, 1634–36) and an "Adoration of the Shepherds" credited to Blès.

*Interior

The magnificent high altar with marble columns is the work of Hubert van den Eynde from 1683. The church also possesses many works of sculpture by A. Fayd'herbe (the figure of the Madonna in the west doorway) and Artus Quellin (parts of the choir screen) among others.

To the south of the market square over the Dender is the Vlasmarkt where the Benediktijnabdij (Benedectine Abbey), destroyed in 1914 and rebuilt in Flemish style 1919–24, and the neo-Gothic church Sint-Pieters-en Paulus-kerk (1901/1902) are situated.

Vlasmarkt

Not far from the Vlasmarkt an alley in the Brusselsestraat turns off right to the Sint-Alexiusbegijnhof, where the last béguines lived until 1975. The béguinage was established in 1250; in 1597 the buildings were devastated by the Geuzen. Most of the 61 brick houses now grouped around the peaceful courtyard were rebuilt at the beginning of the 17th c. House No. 11 is today the Béguinage Museum and a small béguine house equipped in the original 19th c. style with furniture and two bedrooms containing typical béguine beds is on display. In No. 25, the former house of the Grootjuffrouw (oldest béguine) the Museum voor Volkskunde (local museum) has been set up. The institution dates back to the 17th and 18th c.; the brewery is of particular interest (open: April–Oct. first Saturday in the month 10am–noon and 2–6pm).

Begijnhof

Surroundings

Sint-Amands	Sint-Amands, 15km/9 miles north-east of Dendermonde, is the birthplace of the great Flemish poet Emile Verhaeren (1855–1916). The town is situated on the Scheldt, which is 225m/738ft wide at this point and can be seen from the riverside promenade. The marble tombstone of the poet and his wife stands behind the church on the bank of the Scheldt.
Emile-Verhaeren-Museum	The poet's birthplace at Verhaerenstraat 69 is open to the public as a museum (open: Tues.–Sun. 10am–noon and 2–6pm).
Molenmuseum	The Molenmuseum (Mill Museum) at Verhaerenstraat 7 has everything there is to know about wind mills (open: Mon.–Fri. 8am–noon and 1–6pm).

Diest   F 5

Province: Brabant
Altitude: 23m/75ft
Population: 21,600
Inter-regional Station

Location	Diest, situated on both banks of the Demer in the transition zone between the fertile and hilly Hageland and the wooded Kempenland, is the market centre of an intensively farmed area. The main products grown here are asparagus, early potatoes and vegetables. Diest, which received its charter in the second half of the 13th c., ranked among the most important towns in Brabant because of its famous cloth-making, but which has long since disappeared. It has been replaced by flour-milling and other branches of the food industry. Diest is also well known for its special beers (gildebier). From its rich history remarkable buildings and parts of the fortifications have been preserved. Diest is closely associated with the House of Orange-Nassau, to which the present day Queen of the Netherlands belongs. Like Breda in the Netherlands, Dillenburg in Germany and Orange in France Diest was the seat of the royal house. Its most important representative was Prince William I of Orange-Nassau, called William the Silent, who led the Dutch revolts against Spanish domination. St Jan Berchmans (1599–1621), patron saint of youth, is a native of Diest. The room in which he was born in the "Gulden Maan" house in Sint Jan Berchmanstraat near the Grote Markt has remained unchanged and is open to visitors.

Sights

°Grote Markt	The Grote Markt, the picturesque centre of the Old Town, is framed by several beautiful patrician houses of the 16–18th c. In the south-west of the square is the pre-Classical Stadhuis (town hall) built in 1728.
°Stedelijk Museum	The cellars of the town hall house the Stedelijk Museum (municipal museum) which is impressive not only because of its valuable collections but also because of its medieval premises. The Gothic hall has a collection of weapons, a fine painting on wood of the "Last Supper" (around 1450) and goldsmiths' work belonging to the guilds. In the Romanesque room are paintings depicting scenes from the life of William the Silent's son, Prince Philipp of Orange-Nassau, who was born in Diest. The Van der Linden room is named after the museum's founder and contains prehistoric finds from the surrounding area of Diest (open: Apr.–Oct. Mon.–Sat. 10am–noon and 2–5pm; Sun. and public holidays until 6pm).
Refuges	In the Demerstraat which leads away from the right of the town hall are the refuges of the abbeys of von Tongerlo ("Het Spiker"; 16th c.) and von Averbode (15th c.)

The Town Hall of Diest, housing the municipal museum

In the midst of the market stands the noteworthy collegiate church of Sint Sulpitius, one of the finest examples of Brabant Gothic (Demer Gothic). It was built mainly in 1417–1534 using the characteristic reddish brown brick. The choir dates from 1320. The small tower, known as "mostaardpot" (mustard pot), has a carillon with 43 bells. **Sint-Sulpitiuskerk**

The church houses interesting works of art including superb carvings on the pulpit, altars and confessionals. In the choir can be seen magnificent Late-Gothic choir stalls dated 1491 and the tomb of Philip of Orange-Nassau, who died in 1618; the font of St Jan Berchmann in the right side aisle and the treasure in a room adjoining the choir also warrant close examination. The main altar (18th c.) is by Michael van der Vorst; before it on the right is a work of the Antwerp school "Worship of the Kings". *Interior

Behind the church to the right in Ketelstraat is the Lakenhalle (cloth hall) from 1346, where the products of the Diest cloth industry were traded. Next to the hall stands the "Holle Griet", a 15th c. catapult. Lakenhalle

Also behind the church Koning Albertstraat heads north, off which branches Schaffensestraat where the 16th c. Watermolen van Oranje (water mill) presents a charming scene by the canal. Watermolen van Oranje

In Begijnenstraat is the begijnhof founded in 1252 together with the Gothic Sint Katharinakerk. The béguinage of Diest is one of the oldest and most important in Belgium. Its well-preserved 17th c. houses stand around a square and in five small streets. The houses are separated from the street by a magnificent Baroque portal with a likeness of the Madonna and Child. Today the béguinage is used chiefly as a youth and cultural centre; house No. 5 in the Engelen Conventstraat is still furnished in keeping with the béguinage period. *Begijnhof

The Sint-Katharinakerk (14th c.) in Brabant Gothic style has a brilliantly carved pulpit dating from 1671. Former monasteries, spitals and a hospital surround the church, all built between the 16th and 18th c. Sint-Katharinakerk

Town fortifications	Behind the béguinage extend the former 19th c. double fortifications of Brialmont with the Schaffense Post gate on the left. Leopoldsvest street follows the line of the fortifications with a good view of the béguinage. To the south it leads to the 18th c. Lindenmolen.
Warandepark	Within the ring of the Leopoldsvest lies the Warandepark, part of the former hunting lodge of the Princes of Orange-Nassau. Opposite the main entrance of the park stands the Nassau residence (1516), a brick building with a typical gable and octagonal tower.

Surroundings

*Abdij Averbode	An excursion to the picturesque Premonstratensian Abbey of Averbode, 6km/4 miles north-west of Diest, is well worth while. The monastery was founded in 1134. The oldest part of the building, which dates from the 14th–18th c., is the entrance gate which stands at the point where the three provinces of Brabant, Limburg and Antwerp meet. A large number of monks still live in the abbey and their activities include the operation of a large printing press for daily newspapers.
Abbey church	The Baroque abbey church built by Jan van Eynde in 1664 has rich interior furnishing (pews from 1672, high altar from 1758, beautiful organ) and noteworthy paintings by P. J. Verhaghen. The size of the interior is surprising. The monastery building, which was set on fire in 1942, cannot be visited. The 18th c. cloisters, chapter house and sacristy survived the fire.
Scherpenheuvel	Scherpenheuvel, 6km/4 miles west of Diest is a popular place of pilgrimage. Seven paths lead to the Onze-Lieve-Vrouwkerk (Church of Our Lady) standing on high ground. This Baroque building shows strong Italian influence with an oriental cupola. It was built in 1609–27 according to plans by W. Coebergher and marks the beginning of the Baroque style in present day Belgium. The interior houses beautiful paintings by Th. van Loon, a marble relief by F. Duquesnoy and a rich treasury.

Diksmuide · Dixmude   A 4

	Province: West-Vlaanderen Altitude: 0–10m/0–32ft Population: 15,000 Inter-regional Station
Location	The small Flemish town of Diksmuide (French Dixmude), 20km/12 miles inland from the coast on the IJser, was flattened to ground level by week-long German artillery fire during the First World War. Like Ypres (see entry) the town has been rebuilt in the old Flemish style and is now an important market centre for intensive dairy farming. The fact that the ordinary soldiers who died along the IJzerfront on the Belgian side were chiefly Flemish – whereas the officer corps was made up primarily of Walloons and French was the language of command – makes Diksmuide with the IJzer monument a place of great symbolic importance for Flemish political consciousness.
History	Diksmuide grew up in the 9th c. around a wooden castle built to combat the threat of Norman invasion. In 985 Count Balduin III awarded the town its charter and market rights. In the Middle Ages Diksmuide was a sea port and achieved considerable prosperity through its cloth trade with England. With the silting up of the IJser and sea-going vessels no longer able to reach the town Diksmuide declined. From 10th October to 10th November 1914 6000 Belgian and 5000 French soldiers defended the town, then withdrew over the IJser and abandoned

the totally destroyed town to the German troops. Following its rebuilding Diksmuide was bombed again in 1940.

Sights

At the Grote Markt stand the Sint-Niklaaskerk, which was rebuilt in 1940 in accordance with 12th c. plans, the town hall with a belfry and carillon dated 1923 and the butter hall.
There is a monument to General Baron Jacques, commander of the Belgian army.

Grote Markt

North of the market across the Handzamekanaal is a béguinage originating from the 12th c. with houses which were rebuilt in the Twenties in 17th c. style. In the entrance can be seen a small figure of Thomas Becket who is said to have taken refuge here when fleeing from Henry II. Some of the treasures which survived the destruction are in the Godelieve chapel.

Béguinage

To the west of the market in the General Baron Jacquesstraat is the handsome building of the Stedelijk Museum (municipal museum). Together with works of art and documents relating to the history of the town there is a room dedicated to the First World War on the IJser (open: Easter–Oct. daily 10am–noon and 2–6pm).

Stedelijk Museum

The IJserlaan leads a short distance out of the town to the IJser gate memorial, clearly visible on the left bank of the river. The 84m/275ft-high memorial commemorates the 40,000 Flemish soldiers killed during the First World War. At the same time it is a peace memorial with its appeal "No more war". It is also symbolises the pride of the Flemish people who made up nearly 90% of the ordinary soldiers in the First World War and had to bear the brunt of the fighting. Today many Flemish still see the letters A.V.V. and V.V.K. (Alles voor Vlaanderen and Vlaanderen voor Kristus) inscribed on the memorial as a symbol of resistance and the struggle against the cultural and linguistic domination of the Walloons at the beginning of this century, which also finds expression in the added French inscription

* IJser gate

IJertoren Monument

"Et pour les Flamands la même chose". There is an annual remembrance service every August at the foot of the memorial which in recent years has been accompanied by right-wing extremist marches. The first memorial, erected in 1928, was blown up by unknown persons with only the Paxpoort (peace gate) remaining. The present tower was completed in 1965. The first floor houses a commemorative museum; from the tower there are far-reaching views over the Flemish battlefields.

Surroundings

About 2km/1 mile north-west of Diksmuide the Dodengang runs along the left bank of the IJser. This trench with numerous dugouts was part of the

Dodengang

front line of the fighting in the Battle of Flanders. The German lines lay just a few yards away on the opposite bank. Visitors can enter the reconstructed trenches; a pavilion houses an information centre.

Military cemetery Vladslo

Around 4km/2½ miles north-east of Diksmuide 25,644 German soldiers are buried in the Vladso military cemetery. Among them is Peter Kollwitz, killed in 1914, son of the sculptress Käthe Kollwitz, whose gripping work "Trauernde Eltern" (Grieving Parents) was exhibited here in 1932.

IJser Museum

Castle Esen, 2km/1 mile east of the town, contains the IJser museum with documents and items from the First World War.

Torhout

Torhout, 23km/14 miles north-east of Diksmuide, was an important market town in the Middle Ages. Sint Petersbandkerk with its typical octagonal tower, blown up in 1918 and again destroyed in 1940, has been rebuilt. The Stadhuis (1713) houses the Amand Maes Museum for faïences.

Kasteel van Wijnendale

Kasteel van Wijnendale, a moated castle surrounded by splendid parkland, situated 3km/2 miles west of Torhout by a town of the same name, was the favourite retreat of the Counts of Flanders. In 1482 Maria of Burgundy died in a riding accident nearby.

Dinant   F 7

Province: Namur
Altitude: 90m/295ft
Population: 12,000
Intercity Station (bicycle rental at station)

*Location

Dinant is the second largest town in the Belgian region of Condroz and one of the most important tourist centres in the Ardennes. Thanks to its delightful situation in the Upper Meuse valley (see Vallée de la Meuse) below precipitous limestone rocks, crowned by a mighty citadel, Dinant has become a very lively tourist resort, especially at weekends when the Meuse is dotted with pleasure boats and canoeists.
The town's culinary specialities are "coques", shaped biscuits made with honey, and "flamiches", a spiced cake made from bread, eggs and cheese. The painter Joachim Patinier (1485–1524) and Adolphe Sax (see Introduction, Famous People), the inventor of the saxaphone, were born in Dinant.

History

From the time of the Hohenstaufen dynasty the town belonged to the diocese of Liège and was highly prosperous as early as the 13th–15th c. It was famous throughout the Middle Ages for its brass and copperware, the so-called dinanderies.
Unlike any other town in Belgium Dinant has been destroyed by war throughout its history. The town was conquered and burnt by Charles the Bold in 1466; Philip the Good had 800 townspeople tied together in pairs and drowned in the Meuse. In 1554 the French laid siege to the town and destroyed it; under Louis XIV they conquered the town and fortress occupying it until 1703.
In the First World War Dinant was an important bridgehead on the Meuse and, therefore, the focus of heavy fighting, in which 674 of its citizens lost their lives. In the Second World War the Meuse Bridge was bombed in the 1940 air raids and the town suffered heavy damage in 1944, so that hardly anything remains of old Dinant.

Dinanderies

The famous medieval art of dinanderies has been revived in recent years and can be observed in two workshops:
Monsieur de Marco, 64, Rue Grande (daily by appointment) and Dinanderie Mecap, 13, Rue de Moulin (Mon.–Thur. 3pm, Fri. 10am).

Trips on the Meuse

Pleasure boats depart from Dinant to Anseremme, Freÿr (see Vallée de la Meuse), Namur and the French border.

Dinant
300 m

Givet   Rocher Bayard

Sights

In the Place Reine Astrid at the foot of the citadel hill the collegiate church of Notre-Dame stands at the end of the Meuse bridge. It is a beautiful early Gothic building from the 13th c. standing on the sight of a Romanesque basilica which was destroyed by falling rocks in 1227. Following the devastation of 1466 the arches had to be reconstructed. The central tower with a pear-shaped dome (1566) provides a harmonious contrast to the dominating citadel high above the town. The only remains of the Romanesque church is the sandstone doorway on the north side. Inside the church examples of dinanderies can be seen in the form of the font, the Easter candles and the lectern. In the left transept is the tomb of Gérard de Blanmostier dated 1356. The light shines through a beautiful Gothic arched stained window above the south doorway.

Collégiale
Notre-Dame

The Musée de la Photographie is situated directly next to the church at the valley station of the cable railway up to the citadel. It contains over 300 old cameras and a reconstructed dark room from 1920 (open: mid March–April Sat. and Sun. 10am–6pm).

Musée de la
Photographie

The busy main street in the elongated town, the Rue Grande, runs parallel to the right bank of the Meuse from the Place Reine Astrid to the bridge heading south. Through traffic is concentrated on the left bank.
Further south of the Place Reine Astrid is the Hôtel de Ville (town hall) with a monument to the citizens who lost their lives in 1914. Continuing south Dinant casino is on the left.

Rue Grande

Behind the casino a narrow path leads up to the cableway to Mont-Fat. This ascends to the Mont-Fat viewing tower and children's playground. Prehistoric discoveries were made in the Grotte de Mont-Fat; it was a Roman temple to the goddess Diana (open: April–Oct. 10.30am–7pm).

Grotte et
Tour de Mont-Fat

Dinant

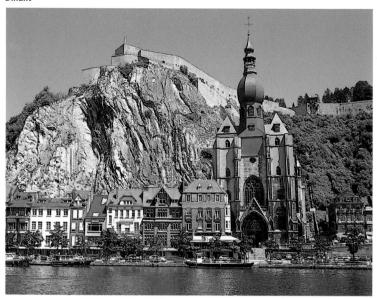

Dinant: Above the Collégiale Notre-Dame towers the Citadel

°Rocher Bayard

The Rue Grande continues southwards as the Rue Léopold and, at the end of the town, passes between the rocks of the high plateau and the famous Rocher Bayard, a rocky needle some 40m/131ft high, rising steeply up from the river. Bayard was the name of the horse of the legendary four sons of Haimon. Fleeing from Charlemagne they all crossed the river in one mighty jump, thereby splitting the rocky needle with its hooves. In fact a thoroughfare was blown through the rocks in 1698.

Rocher Bayard

Birthplace of Adolphe Sax

The northern continuation of the Rue Grande from the Place Reine Astrid is the Rue Adolphe Sax, named after the inventor of the saxaphone who was born here. A window in the house (No. 31) commemorates the instrument maker.

Abbaye de Leffe

Further north in the suburb of Leffe at the entrance to the rocky cleft Fonds de Leffe is a former Premonstratensian abbey. It was founded in 1152 and suffered during the besieging of Dinant. Only the guest house, prior's house and refectory, all from the 17th and 18th c. remain.

Grotte "La Merveilleuse"

The suburb of Saint-Médard which includes the railway station and numerous hotels extends along the left bank of the Meuse. West of the bridge, 500m from the railway station on the Route de Philippeville, is the entrance to the Grotte de Raimpaine ("La Merveilleuse"). The 500m-long cave has beautiful stalactite formations (open: Apr., May, June, Sept. daily 11am–4pm; July and Aug. 10am–6pm).

* Citadel

The citadel of Dinant towers high above the town. There are four ways up to it: the cabin cable railway (télépherique) behind the collegiate church, a difficult route consisting of 400 steps next to the cableway, the chair-lift to Mont-Fat and a short walk or via the Rue Adolphe Sax and then to the right by the Rue de Saint Jacques. The present-day citadel was built by the Dutch government in 1821 on the site of the episcopal fortresses which had often been destroyed. A tour through the citadel leads along battlements heavily contested by the Germans and French in 1914, through a bakery and a weapons museum. There is a reconstructed dugout, riddled with bullets, from the First World War. From the ramparts projecting over the town there is a magnificent view over the Meuse. At the top are a cemetery for French soldiers (see Practical Information, Military Cemeteries) killed in action and a monument to the German soldiers.

Opening times
daily 10am–4pm, from Easter until 5pm, June until 6pm, July and Aug. until 7pm; Dec.–Feb. closed Fri.

** View

Surroundings

Situated 2km/1 mile north of Dinant on the left bank of the Meuse, Bouvignes, dating back to the 7th c., was a former rival of Dinant but is now incorporated. The fortifications of the 15th c. Château de Crèvecoeur used to tower above the town but today only the ruins remain. There is a splendid view from the top. The remains of Poilvache and Géronsart castles (see Vallée de la Meuse) are visible to the north high up on the opposite bank.

Bouvignes

Built in the Meuse Gothic style the church of Saint-Lambert has two choirs: the east one dated 1247 and the 16th c. west choir.

Saint-Lambert

The Renaissance building "Maison Espagnole" in the market place of Bouvignes houses the Musée de l'Eclairage (Museum of Lighting), which describes mankind's technical efforts to create light (open: May–Sept. Tues.–Sun. 1–6pm).

Musée de l'Eclairage

The Château de Spontin, an impressive moated castle, one of the finest in Belgium, is situated in the Bocq valley near the small town of Spontin 11km/7 miles north of Dinant. It was built on the site of 12th c. keep which was extended into a fortified castle in the 14th c. and rebuilt in Renaissance style in the 16th c. In 1622 the working quarters were added adjoining the courtyard in which there are beautiful 19th c. wrought-iron fountains.

* Château de Spontin

A tour through the castle rooms shows how styles have changed with time. The keep has two bare rooms with Gothic chimneys, the library a chequered floor, the Renaissance salon and the neo-Gothic south wing with the dining room and staircase (open: July and Aug. daily 10am–5pm).

The village of Anseremme, not far south of Dinant where the Lesse enters the Meuse, is a good place for walking and hill-climbing. Both train and bus operate to the village of Houyet on the Lesse, the starting point of a boat trip along the scenically beautiful lower reaches of the Lesse (Descente de la Lesse). It is possible to hire canoes or take a guided boat tour along the 21km/13 miles stretch through the Furfooz nature reserve, past Walzin (13th c.) and Pont-à-Lesse castles back to Anseremme with its 16th c. bridge Pont Saint-Jean across the river (departures daily between 9 and 11.30am; journey time about 4½ hours).

* Lower reaches of the Lesse

The Furfooz nature reserve (Parc Naturel de Furfooz) extends around the lower reaches of the Lesse. In the caves of this limestone plateau above the meandering river Stone Age relics such as tools and bones have been found together with remains of Roman baths.

* Parc Naturel de Furfooz

Dinant

Spontin Castle

Falmignoul

At Falmignoul, 8km/5 miles south of Dinant, centre for climbing in the nearby cliffs at Freÿr, there is an interesting bicycle, motorcycle and poster museum (Musée du Cycle et de la Moto et de l'Affiche). Its exhibits range from the 1818 dandy horse to the racing bike on which Eddy Merckx won the Tour de France, old motorcycles and posters from before 1914.

Celles

The village of Celles, 10km/6 miles south-east of Dinant, is famous for its Church of St Hadelinus, built in the Mosan Romanesque style with a beautiful 9th c. crypt and squat fortress-like towers. The triple-naved interior houses a stone pulpit, a beautiful marble memorial slab for Louis de Beaufort and his wife and early Gothic 13th c. choir stalls, the oldest in Belgium (open: Easter–Nov. daily 10am–6pm).

At the entrance to Celles a German tank marks the furthest point reached by the German troops during the Ardennes offensive.

°Château de Veves

Not far south-west of Celles stands the Château de Veves, seat of the Lords of Beaufort, a fine 15th c. building with a large keep and smaller side towers with pointed roofs. The rooms are furnished with family heirlooms from various periods.

Foy-Notre-Dame

Situated almost 10km/6 miles east of Dinant Foy-Notre-Dame is a popular place of pilgrimage. The object of veneration is a miracle-working Madonna figure which was reputedly found in an oak tree in 1609. It is now housed in an outwardly apparently unassuming church but which has a splendid interior: outstanding wood carving and a highly impressive coffered ceiling with 145 biblical scenes, painted in the 17th c. by the Goblet brothers from Dinant.

Beauraing

20km/12 miles south of Dinant the small town of Beauraing became famous in 1932 and 1933 for several alleged appearances of Mary before five children. These events dominate the character of the town. Various consecrated shrines, the chapel built in 1954 and a large pilgrimage church with over 7000 seats (1968) are frequented by believers and those seeking cures.

See Vallée de la Meuse

Other places in the surroundings

Ecaussinnes

D 6

Province: Hainaut
Altitude: 40–159m/131–521ft
Population: 9500
Inter-regional Station

The twin parish of Ecaussinnes, about 45km/28 miles south of Brussels, consists of both towns of Ecaussinnes-Lalaing and Ecaussinnes-d'Enghien. The names originate from the noble lines to which the town belonged in the Middle Ages.

Location

The castle of the Enghiens, the Château de la Folie, dates back to a 13th c. building, which was demolished in 1506. The new building of 1528 was enlarged by a late-Gothic chapel. This was again converted in the 18th c. to the country house which the visitor can see today (visits only by arrangement). Some of the chapel windows are the work of Bernard van Orley who is buried together with his wife in the church of Saint-Remy.

Ecaussinnes-d'Enghien

Ecaussinnes-Lalaing is situated in region rich in granite quarries. On Easter Monday every year it is the scene of a marriage market where those wanting to marry are fed in the Grand-Place. In the local church Blandine

Ecaussinnes-Lalaing

Chateau d'en Haut in Ecaussinnes-Lalaing

Rubens, the sister of the great painter and Michel de Croy (fine reclining figure) are buried.

*Château
d'en Haut

The first building of Château d'en Haut on a rocky promontory not far from the Grand-Place originates from the 12th c. In the 14th c. a new, larger construction followed which has remained almost unchanged to the present day and is one of the best preserved medieval castles in Belgium. The gate tower of 1372 was altered in the 17th c., other alterations have not made such an impression on the overall picture such as the extension of the castle chapel around 1600. Under the French (around 1800) and in the 19th c. when the building was being used among other things as a factory, it collapsed. Restoration work began at the beginning of this century; since 1928 the château has been under the ownership of the Counts van der Burch, who inherited it in the 17th c.

The tour of the rooms takes in the weapons hall, kitchen, sick room, state room and dungeon; some rooms have exhibitions of glass, sculpture, ceramics and porcelain (open: Mar., Apr., June, Sept., Oct. Sat., Sun. and public holidays, July/Aug. daily except Wed. 10am–noon and 2–6pm).

Surroundings

**Sloping lock of Ronquières

**Opening times
Tower:
May–Aug.
daily 10am–6pm

Just 4km/2½ miles north-east of Ecaussinnes is the technical spectacle of the sloping lock of Ronquières (Plan incliné de Ronquières), a gigantic barge lift on the canal from Charleroi to Brussels.

The difference in height between the Sambre Valley at Charleroi and the Senne south of Brussels was for a long time an insuperable obstacle to linking the canal network between north and south Belgium. The first canal project completed in 1832 involved 55 locks over a distance of 60km/37

Lower lock of the ship-lift of Ronquières

Ronquières sloping lock

(section through the machinery
and the upper lock)

1 Safety gate
2 Canal gate
3 Lock gate

Total length: 1432m/1567yds   Maximum permitted weight: 5700 tonnes
Height difference: 88m/289ft   Counterweight: 5200 tonnes

Galerie

Canal Bridge

Carrying basin

Machine House

5%

Counterweight

© Baedeker

miles. This canal soon proved to be too small and following further enlargements in the 19th c. it was decided to modernise the waterway in 1937. The work lasted from 1947 to 1968 and reduced the number of locks to ten. The centrepiece of the canal is the sloping lock of Ronquières.

Barges up to a total of 1350 tonnes enter one of two tanks up to 91m/298ft long and 12m/39ft wide (water depth 3.7m/12ft; max. weight 5700 tonnes), which are pulled or lowered on rails on 59 axles with 236 rollers by 8 steel cables (55mm diameter). The basins are moved independently of each other as they are counterbalanced by 5200 tonne weights. The height difference of 68m/223ft is resolved over a distance of 1432m/1566yds in about 90 minutes. The entire complex is dominated by a 154m/505ft-high control tower with a viewing platform at 139m/456ft. There are boat excursions to the lock (departures: Mon., Tues., Thur., Fri. noon, 3 and 5pm; Sun. and public holidays noon, 2, 3.30 and 5pm).

Eeklo

See Ghent, Surroundings

Eupen · Néau

H 6

Province: Liège
Altitude: 300m/984ft. Population: 17,500
Intercity Station (bicycle rental at station)

Eupen (French Néau), the largest town in the German-speaking part of Belgium, lies at the confluence of the Vesdre (Weser) and the Helle (Hill). In the south and south-west the wooded hills of the Hohe Venn (see German-Belgian Nature Park) reach almost to the edge of the town, whereas in the north and west the green carpet of a continuous belt of meadow and pasture stretches from the hills of the Aachener Wald to the banks of the Meuse. Eupen has, despite its modest altitude of 300m/984ft, a cool highland climate which has contributed to its reputation as a popular health resort. Visitors can among other things enjoy the Kneipp water cure. Most of the inhabitants of the town are employed in the textile industry and manufacture of man-made fibres, with 25% of the workforce commuting from the surrounding countryside. Eupen is the headquarters of the council, the executive and administration of the German-speaking part of Belgium and the German language Belgian radio station is here.

Location

History

Eupen, which once belonged to the Duchy of Limburg, is first mentioned in the Chronicles in 1213. The Duchy's location proved to be a frequent drawback for the town. As a result of the Battle of Worringen (1288) Limburg, and therefore Eupen, became part of the Duchy of Brabant. But in 1387 Joanna of Brabant handed over Limburg to Burgundy. Only 90 years later (1477) the Duchy of Limburg was acquired by the Austrian Habsburgs, but their domination only lasted until 1555. The Duchies of Limburg and Brabant were then taken over by Spain. In 1674 Eupen received its town charter. After the Peace Treaty of Utrecht (1713) the Austrian Habsburgs became its rulers for the second time. Eupen became prosperous during this period and by 1721 had a population 13,000. The famous cloth industry of Eupen exported its products to the whole world. In 1795 the district of Eupen was annexed by France, but after the defeat of Napoleon it became part of Prussia (Congress of Vienna 1815). Until 1920 Eupen was the westernmost district of Germany. In the Treaty of Versailles the town was given to the Kingdom of Belgium, but was again part of Germany between 1940 and 1945.

Carnival

Eupen is famous for its Carnival which is similar to those in the Rhineland.

Sights

*Patrician houses

Eupen is clearly divided into the more industrial lower town and the upper town characterised by buildings from its period of prosperity (18th c.). Superb patrician houses stand in the market place, Gospertstrasse and in the Werthplatz.

Saint-Nicholas

The Church of Saint-Nicholas in the market square was built between 1724–29 according to plans by the city architect of Aachen, Mefferdatis as a triple-aisled hall church; the towers were completed in 1898. Of interest inside are a Baroque high altar by Couven (1750), pulpit of 1730, confessionals and apostle figures from the Minorite church in Cologne.
In the market place is the Column of St Mary, 1857.

Town hall

Until the French Revolution the town hall in Aachener Strasse was part of a Capuchin monastery. The former Baroque church of this monastery is worth visiting.

The municipal museum is in at 52 Gospertstrasse. It is housed in the former house of a cloth handler (1697) and documents the changing history of the Eupen region. It contains a clock collection, Raeren stoneware, clothing and a completely equipped goldsmith's forge (open: Wed. 6–8pm, Sat. 2–5pm, Sun. 10am–noon and 2–5pm). — Municipal museum

Surroundings

The surrounding countryside is ideal for walking in the Hertogenwald, around the Barrage de la Gileppe dam (8km/5 miles south-west) and in the Hohe Venn nature reserve (see German-Belgian Nature Park). — Walking

A nostalgic and peaceful way to get to know the surroundings of Eupen and the Hohe Venn (see German-Belgian Nature Park) is a trip on the 106-year-old Venn railway. A train departs at 10am every Sunday from Eupen and puffs past Raeren into Roetgen in Germany, continues to Monschau through the border town of Kalterherberg in the Hohe Venn and back into Büllingen in Belgium, near the Bütgenbach dam (see Malmédy, Surroundings). — °Venn railway

It is worth a visit to the Vesdre dam (Barrage d'Eupen), 5km/3miles east, with a capacity of 25 million cu.m and an area of 126ha./311 acres the largest reservoir in Belgium. The wall is 58m/190ft high and 410m/1345ft long; the base of the wall is 55m/180ft wide. The reservoir serves the Herver Land and the surroundings of Liège. There is sailing on the lake. — °Barrage de Vesdre

9km/5 miles to the north Raeren is a centre of pottery and stoneware, with a tradition stretching back to 1400. Pottery from Raeren was valued throughout the world. A pottery museum in the magnificent château shows the development of Raeren pottery in seven rooms (open: Tues.–Fri. 2–5pm, Sat. and Sun. 10am–5pm). — Raeren

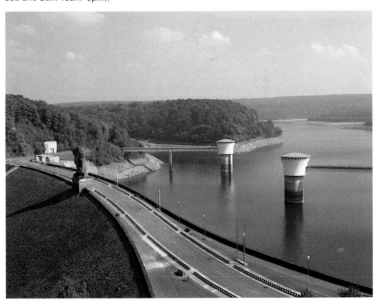

The Gileppe Dam

Gaasbeek

Henri-Chapelle	In the military cemetery at Henri-Chapelle (5km/3 miles north-west) are buried 7989 American soldiers who died in 1944/45.
Kelmis	Kelmis, 12km/8 miles north of Eupen, is an ideal starting-out point for walks, but is more interesting for its curious history: at the Congress of Vienna agreement could not be reached over which country Kelmis belonged to. Moresnet became Dutch (then Belgian), Neu-Moresnet German, and the zinc-quarrying area in between neutral under joint administration. Out of this Kelmis developed but did not become Belgian until 1919.
* Drielandenpunt	A few kilometres north of Kelmis the borders of Belgium, Holland and Germany meet. In clear weather the Eifel, Aachen and Maastricht can be seen from the 321m/1053ft-high Drielandenpunt. Just inside the Dutch border is the highest point in Holland.

Gaasbeek (Château)

See Brussels, Surroundings

Geel

Province: Antwerp
Altitude: 20m/66ft
Population: 32,000
Inter-regional Station

Location	The town of Geel is situated in the centre of an agricultural region in Kempenland in the eastern part of the province of Antwerp. It is well known for its pioneering method of treating psychiatric patients and the mentally ill. They receive treatment at a large psychiatric hospital but live in the community with families, taking part in everyday life. There are about 1400 patients living in Geel. This tradition is derived from the legend of St Dymphna or Dimpna, the patron saint of the possessed and insane. Dymphna was an Irish princess from the 6th c. who fled from her father who wanted to marry her after the death of his wife. With her confessor Gerebernus Dymphna sought refuge in Geel, but she was discovered by her father who, in a frenzy, is supposed to have decapitated her. The town soon became a place of pilgrimage for the mentally ill. The pilgrims who came to visit the tomb were accommodated by the townspeople, a custom which has remained, although in a different form, until the present day. An annual fair, the oldest in Belgium, resulted from the pilgrimages.

Sights

Sint-Dimpnakerk	Situated on the road to Mol, Sint-Dimpnakerk is late Gothic, built 1349–1479. The massive tower (16th c.) made of alternating white sandstone and brown ironstone was never finished. The church's art treasures include the Sint-Dimpna retable of 1515 on the main altar with fine wood carving, a Brabant retable of the Passion in the right transept (wood; 1490), a stone retable depicting the twelve apostles (14th c.) and the silver reliquaries of St Dymphna and her confessor, Gerebernus. In the choir the Renaissance mauseoleum in marble and alabaster of Jan III de Merode and his wife was the work of Cornelis Floris de Vriendt in 1554. From 1484–1601 Geel was owned by the de Merode family. The so-called "sick room" built against the church tower housed the sick during the nine day pilgrimage and from here they were carried into the church three times a day to pray.

The first hospital was founded in Geel in 1280; the present day buildings are primarily from the 17th c. and have been converted into a local museum with collections of furniture, paintings and church exhibits (open: mid May–Aug. Wed., Thur. and Sun 2–5.30pm).

Sint-Dimpna Gasthuis

Surroundings

Herentals

F 4

14km/9 miles west of Geel is Herentals which was awarded its town charter in 1209 and was a flourishing cloth-making town in the 14th and 15th c. During this period the town walls were built, of which two towers remain.

The town hall in the centre of Herentals is the former cloth hall dating from the beginning of the 15th c. and rebuilt in 1534 following a fire. A niche on the north façade houses a Madonna statue from 1616. The narrow belfry contains a carillon with 50 bells (1590). On the top floor is a museum in honour of the sculptor Karel August Fraikin who was born in the town (open: June–Sept. daily 10am–noon and 2–5pm).

Stadhuis

Sint-Waldetrudiskerk is a fine example of Brabant High Gothic, its oldest parts being the lower part of the tower and the transept (14th c.). The choir and nave were built in the 15th c.
Inside is the retable depicting the martyrdom of Sts Crispinus and Crispianus, the patron saints of shoemakers and tanners, an outstanding work by Pasquier Borreman (16th c.). Among the numerous paintings are works by Frans Francken the Elder of Herentals; choir stalls and confessionals survived the iconoclastic fury.

Sint-Waldetrudis-kerk

The béguinage was founded in 1266 and is the oldest in Kempenland. It was destroyed by the Geuzen in 1578, but rebuilt in 1590; in 1614 the late Gothic béguinage church, Sint Catherinakerk, was completed. Other interesting buildings around the landscaped inner courtyard are the fondatiehuis (1647) and the sick hall (1715).

Begijnhof

At Grobbendonk, 6km/4 miles west of Herentals, a diamond museum informs the visitor of all there is to know about the mining and working of these precious stones. Reproductions of the most famous diamonds are on display (open: Mon.–Fri. 10am–4pm, Sat. 10am–1.30pm and Sun. 10am–noon).

Grobbendonk

Abdij van Tongerlo

F 4

The abbey of Tongerlo, 9km/5 miles south-west of Tongerlo, was founded by the Premonstratensians of Sint-Michielsabdij of Antwerp in 1130, who set about converting the heathens. Following the French Revolution the abbey was abandoned and only reinhabited and restored in 1840. The oldest parts of the building are the 14th c. tower and a barn dating from the 15th c.; the remaining buildings originate from various later epochs to the neo-Gothic Onze-Lieve-Vrouwkerk (1851–58). A splendid avenue of lime trees, planted in 1676, leads up to the entrance.

In the abbey is the Museum da Vinci, which has a remarkable copy of "The Last Supper", painted barely 20 years after Leonardo had finished the original for the Santa Marie delle Grazie church in Milan. The copy in Tongerlo was acquired for the abbey church in 1545. Other paintings include a small Pietà by Roger van der Weyden (open: Sun. 2–5pm).

* Museum da Vinci

The small town of Westerlo, situated in woodland only 2km south of Tongerlo, is famous for the two châteaux of the van Merode family, who

Kasteel van Westerlo

Kasteel van Westerlo

lived here from the 14th c. and were engaged in Belgian politics from time to time.

The right-angled keep of the château surrounded by parkland belonged to the van Merode princes and was built around 1300 as part of the new château, which replaced the first 11th c. house. Further extension and conversion work took place from the 16th c. and during the next two centuries. A second château was built along the Boerenkrijglan in 1910. Since 1972 the neo-Gothic building has been the parish house of Westerlo.

Lommel   G 4

German
military
cemetery

South of Lommel which lies 30km/18 miles north-west of Geel is a military cemetery where all the German soldiers killed in Belgium during the Second World War are buried. 20,000 crosses represent the 40,000 graves.

Gembloux-sur-Orneau · Gembloers   E 6

Province: Namur
Altitude: 230m/143ft
Population: 18,000
Intercity Station

Location

Situated between Brussels and Namur the small town of Gembloux (Flemish Gembloers), which dates back to a Roman settlement on the military road from Bavai to Cologne, received its town charter in the 12th c. The town walls, parts of which are still standing, were constructed in the same period. From the 17th to the 19th c. Gembloux was famous for its steelware but this was only small scale and was superseded by other metal-working

industries. Together with several surrounding districts Gembloux forms the administative district of Gembloux-sur-Orneau.
Sigisbert of Gembloux (1030–1112) wrote a world chronicle of the years 381–1111 in the Benedictine abbey.
During the Dutch Wars of Independence the Spanish commander Don Juan d'Austria defeated a Spanish army here in 1578.

Sights

The abbey was founded in the 10th c. by St Guibert but the buildings from this period were demolished between 1762 and 1779. The new building including restoration of the old cloisters began in 1779 according to plans by the architect Dewez on a rocky outcrop above the Orneau. The former abbot's palace with an Ionic portal with columns stands in the impressive courtyard. The former abbey church, a parish church from 1812, is built above a 12th c. Romanesque crypt. Since 1861 the monastery buildings have been occupied by the National Agricultural Institute.

Benedictine abbey

The Maison du Bailli (Bailif's house) is known to date back to the 12th c. The present day building is 16th c. and is used as a town hall; it houses a small museum about the production of steelware.

Maison du Bailli

Surroundings

Corroy-le-Château 6km/4 miles south-west owes its name to the 13th c. castle, one of the best preserved medieval castles in Belgium. This moated fortification with its massive gate building, drawbridge and seven massive round towers was commissioned by Philipp of Vianden and was part of a defensive ring around Brabant. The 18th c. conversions have not had a major effect on the overall appearance.
A visit to the castle, which is still inhabited, passes through the 13th c. chapel, refurbished in the 19th c. The remaining rooms contain furniture and paintings from the 16–18th c.; one hall has a collection of old-fashioned clothing (open: May–Sept. daily 10am–noon and 2–6pm).

Corroy-le-Château
*Castle

Near Onoz, 8km/5 miles south of Gembloux, the 12th c. Château de Mielmont towers over the Orneau on a steep cliff.

Château de Mielmont

Ligny, 12km/7 miles south-west, is the site of Napoleon I's last victory, where two days before the Battle of Waterloo he defeated a Prussian unit. The battlefields of Waterloo are visible from a viewing platform.

Ligny

In Grand-Leez, 6km/4 miles east of Gembloux, numerous Roman finds were made. The Moulin Defrenne from 1830 is still in use today but driven by electricity.

Grand-Leez

Genk

See Hasselt, Surroundings

Geraardsbergen · Grammont

D 5/6

Province: Oost-Vlaanderen
Altitude: 14–110m/45–360ft
Population: 30,000
Inter-regional Station (bicycle rental at station)

Geraardsbergen (French Grammont) lies in the hilly countryside of the Flemish Ardennes on the Dender, close to the border. The town, which

Location

received its charter as early as 1068, had a flourishing textile industry. The highest point of Geraardsberg is the 110m/360ft-high Oudenberg, which, on account of its steep cobblestone incline, is known to cyclists as "The Geraardsberg Wall" and is the most difficult stretch of the Tour de Flandres.

Sights

Grote Markt

By the steps of the stadhuis (town hall), which is of 15th c. origin and was rebuilt in neo-Gothic style at the end of the 19th c., is a fountain with a Manneken Pis from 1455 making it the oldest monument of its kind in Belgium.

The "Marbol" stands in front of the town hall, an octagonal Gothic fountain (1495), the only Gothic fountain in East Flanders.

In the square is the Church of Sint-Bartholomeus (15th/19th c.). Interesting features include a stone font (1620), a wrought-iron communion rail, choir stalls, 18th c. confessionals and the choir lectern.

Onze-Lieve-Vrouwhospitaal

The Onze-Lieve-Vrouwhospitaal in Gasthuisstraat is one of the oldest hospitals in Belgium. It was founded in 1100, but the monastery wing with the bishop's room, refectory and council chamber are from 1763. A small museum with objets d'art and paintings has been set up in the hospital.

Sint-Adriaans-abdij

In Abdijstraat is the site of former Sint-Adriaans-abdij, a Benedictine monastery founded in 1100 but of which only a few 18th c. buildings have been preserved. These house a small museum with craftwork and paintings. The rest of the site is a recreational park with a small zoo.

Oudenberg

Every year the famous Oudenberg is the destination of the "Krakelingen-worp" pilgrimage, a curious custom which finishes at the Onze-Lieve-Vrouwkapel on the hill.

View

Extensive views of the countryside are to be had from the top. An information board explains the view.

Surroundings

Lessines

Across the linguistic divide 8km/5 miles south of Geraardsbegen in Lessines, known for its porphyry quarries, the surrealist painter René Magritte (see Facts and Figures, Famous People) was born.

The Hôpital Notre-Dame à la Rose was founded in 1242 by Alix de Rosoit, widow of the Lord of Lessines, Arnold IV of Oudenaarde. The first floor of the monastery is now a museum with furniture, paintings, old instruments and household goods. The Musée Communal in the hospital documents the history of the quarrying of porphyry .

German-Belgian Nature Park   H/J 6/7

Province: Liège

Location and origin

The German-Belgian Nature Park was created in 1971 by the amalgamation of the Belgian Parc Naturel Hautes Fagnes with the German Nordeifel nature reserve. The area which comprises 2,485sq.km/959sq.miles stretches east of the Eupen-Malmédy line between the North Rhine Westphalian town of Aachen and the Luxembourg border to Euskirchen in Rheinland Pfalz in Germany. 722sq.km/278sq.miles are in Belgium, 1359sq.km/524sq.miles are in North Rhine Westphalia and 404sq.km/156 sq.miles in Rheinland Pfalz.

** Landscape

The characteristic landscape of this sparsely inhabited, undulating range of rounded hills is that of the Hohe Venn (corresponding to the Dutch "Fehn"

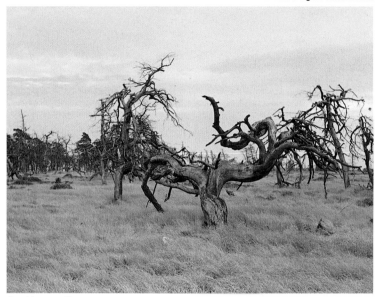

Dead trees on the moor

= fenland; French Hautes Fagnes). Its average altitude is around 400m/1312ft with the highest point being the Signal de Botrange at 694m/2277ft, which is also the highest point in Belgium. This region consists of extensive moor and heath, which gives it its name and forms a giant natural reservoir of water providing the source of several rivers, which have in turn been dammed to create large lakes. This remote moor with its flora provides unique evidence of the preglacial climate and is crossed only by very few footpaths.

There are impressive all-round views from the tower on the Signal de Botrange, to the north of Malmédy (see Malmédy), and from Mont Rigi (672m/2205ft) near Baraque-Michel. **** Viewpoints**
About 1km/½ mile east of Baraque Michel is the Fontaine Périgny, where the Helle (Hill) has its source. Here, too, there are fine views of the surroundings.
A few hundred yards from the source remains of the Via Mansuerica were discovered, according to recent research a 7th c. military road. Via Mansuerica

On the Belgian side comprehensive information about the Hohe Venn nature reserve is available from the Botrange Nature Park Centre. A permanent exhibition features a relief model of the moor landscape and a slide show of the most beautiful views. A 5km/3 mile long educational nature walk leads through the countryside and is marked with seven observation posts giving facts about the flora and fauna. The centre also organises walks, photography courses and introductions to herbal medicine (open: daily 10am–6pm; closed in Nov.) Botrange Nature Park Centre

A total of 4000km/2485ft of footpaths and walkways cross the reserve; citizens of EC countries may, if necessary, cross the green border. Main footpaths are marked by a red and a white post; double horizontal stripes indicate a change of direction, crossed stripes inform the walker that he/she Walks

The Helle stream

Peat-digging

has taken the wrong direction. Minor walks are marked by numbers, letters or symbols (see Practical Information, Sport).

Riding, long-distance skiing

Horse riding is permitted in Belgium only in the Eupen area on clearly marked bridleways. In winter 23 long-distance ski runs (13 in Belgium) are marked out (see Practical Information, Sport).

Behaviour in the nature reserve

The visitor to the protected nature reserve should not interfere with the animals and plants in their habitat and should enjoy nature quietly. Under no circumstances should the marked paths and trails be left. Litter must not be thrown away but taken home; dogs must be kept on a lead. The picking of wild flowers is not allowed, neither are camping, radios, walking at night nor camp fires.

Fire is a particular threat to the ecologically sensitive moorland so that in the warmer months it may not permitted to enter certain areas including signposted footpaths. These areas are marked by by red warning flags.

Ghent · Gent · Gand

C 4/5

Province: Oost-Vlaanderen
Altitude: 5–29m/16–95ft
Population: 235,000
Intercity and Inter-regional Station (bicycle rental at Sint-Pieter station)

Location

The old city of Ghent (Flemish Gent; French Gand), capital of the province of Oost-Vlaanderen and seat of the university, is situated on the confluence of the Scheldt and the Leie, the many branches of which intersect the city. With the surrounding communities Ghent is the third largest urban region in Belgium.

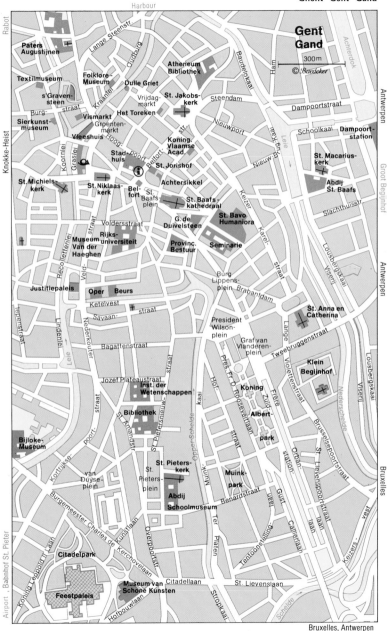

Harbour

Rabot

Paters
Augustijnen

Textilmuseum

s'Graven-
steen

Burg

Sierkunst-
museum

Knokke-Heist

Lange Steenstr.

Oudburg

Folklore-
Museum

Dulle Griet

Kraanl

straat

Vismarkt

Vleeshuis

Koornlei

Graslei

St. Michiels-
kerk

Gent
Gand

Achterdok

300m
© Baedeker

Antwerpen

Atheneum
Bibliothek

Steendam

Dampoortstraat

Vrijdag-
markt

St. Jakobs-
kerk

Het Toreken

Groenten-
markt

Hoog-

Nieuwport

poort

Belfort

Stad-
huis

St. Niklaas-
kerk

Bel-
fort

St. Niklaas-

Koning.
Vlaamse
Acad.

St. Jorishof

St.
Baafs-
plein

Achtersikkel

St. Baafs-
kathedraal

G. de
Duivelsteen

Keizer

Nieuw B.

Schoolkaai

St. Macarius-
kerk

Abdij
St. Baafs

Slachthuisstr.

Dampoort-
station

Groot Beginhof

Antwerpen

Lousbergskaai

Viserij

St. Bavo
Humaniora

Voldersstraat

Museum
Van der
Haeghen

Recolletten

Rijks-
universiteit

Veld-

Provinc.
Bestuur

Seminarie

Burg
Lippens-
plein

Brabantdam

Karel-

straat

Justitiepaleis

Iependal-

straat

Oper Beurs

Ketelvest

Savaan-

Nederkouter

straat

Lindenlei

Leie

Bagattenstraat

President
Wilson-
plein

Graf van
Vlanderen-
plein

Lange

Violettenstr.

Tweebruggenstraat

St. Anna en
Catharina

St.
straat

Jozef Plateaustraat

Inst. der
Wetenschappen

Bibliothek

St. Amandstr.

St. Pietersnieuw

Hor-

Pres. Fr. D. Roosevelt

Koning

Albert-

park

Zuid-

Frère

Orban-

Klein
Beginhof

Nederschelde

Lousbergskaai

Viserij

Brusselsepoortstraat

St. Lievenspoortstraat

Bruxelles

Bijloke-
Museum

Kortrijkse-

poort-

straat

van
Duyse-
plein

St.
Pieters-
plein

St. Pieters-
kerk

Abdij

Schoolmuseum

Opper-Schelde

kaai

Muink-

Ter

Muink-
park

Benardstraat

station

Gust.

Callier-

laan

Tentoonstelling

Citadelpark

Feestpaleis

Koning Leopold II

Bahnhof St. Pieter

Airport

laan

Burgemeester Charles de Kerchovelaan

Kunstlaan

Overpoortstr.

Museum van
Schoné Kunsten

Citadellaan

Hotbouwlaan

Strobkaai

Platen

St. Lievenslaan

Keizers-

vest

Economic
centre

Ghent is the largest industrial conurbation in West Belgium. For centuries the most important industry was textiles which made Ghent into a "Manchester of the European mainland". Today the city still has large cotton spinning mills and linen weaving mills where the world famous Flemish cloth is produced, but the decline of the textile industry has forced the establishment of new areas of economic activity. Thus today factories in and around Ghent produce paper, chemicals, cars, optical, engineering, electrical and electronic components with a large steelworks being the major industry. Many of these companies are on the Ghent-Terneuzen canal, exploiting the advantages of the waterway network.

Together with Antwerp and Zeebrugge (see entries) Ghent is one of the three most important sea ports in Belgium. The harbour is linked by various canals with the Westerschelde (Gent-Terneuzen canal) and with the North Sea (Bruges-Ghent canal, Bruges-Zeebrugge canal and Bruges-Ostend canal) and can accommodate vessels up to 60,000 tonnes. The annual turnover of goods handled amounts to about 25 million tonnes; Ghent being an important trade centre, especially for the import and export of cereals. In addition the city and its environs are the heart of the garden and cut flower growing area: 80% of all foliage plants in Belgium are grown here, chiefly for export. The ultra-modern exhibition site "Flanders Expo" in Sint-Denijs-Westrem has been instrumental in gaining Ghent prestige as a venue for trade fairs and exhibitions.

Festivals

Every five years (next in 1995) the Ghent Floralien is held with the gardeners of the region showing their produce. The Ghent Festival Week takes place in mid-July with music and theatre literally on every street corner and stands selling food and drink set up everywhere. The Flanders Festival (series of concerts of predominantly Baroque music) which is celebrated throughout Flanders focuses on Ghent.

History

Beginnings

As far back as the Romans a settlement had been established on the small island at the confluence of the Scheldt and the Leie. In the 7th c. the missionary St Amandus came to this area and founded two abbeys dedicated to St Petrus, in between which Ghent itself developed. The Norman threat led to the first fortifications being built, with the Gravensteen around 1000.

Powerful
guilds

Around 1000 a council of 11 jurors governed the city, where the cloth industry was gaining more and more in importance. After Paris Ghent became the most powerful city north of the Alps. In 1228 34 patricians took over the further fate of the town. The oligarchical rule of their successors, who together with the Counts of Flanders followed the French king, increasingly aroused the anger of the powerful guilds that were seeking independence.

When the import of English wool, upon which the Ghent cloth industry depended, was stopped, the citizens of Ghent united in 1337 behind Jacob van Artevelde with England and led other Flemish towns in opposing France. Artevelde ruled for years with dictatorial powers until he was murdered in 1345 by the head of the weavers' guild. The defeat of the Flemish army under Artevelde's son Philip near Rozebeke put a temporary stop to the Ghent citizens' desire for self-government.

Burgundian
rule

The marriage of the heiress of Count Louis II of Flanders to Duke Philip the Bold brought Flanders under Burgundian domination. His attempts to curb the power of the guilds again led to resistance. After the Battle of Gavere on the Scheldt on the 23rd July 1453, when thousands of Ghent citizens lost their lives, the most prominent burghers and the Council had to come out beyond the town gates wearing only their shirts and beg the victor for mercy. Following the death of the Duke in 1477 his daughter Maria of

Ghent: Belfry and Cloth Hall ▶

Burgundy was forced to grant the citizens of Ghent greater rights. The Burgundian period of the 15th c. was a time of prosperity for Ghent when culture and the arts flourished. The van Eyck brothers (Altar of Ghent) were active here at this time.

Habsburg rule

Ghent fell to the Habsburgs on Maria of Burgundy's marriage to the future Emperor Maximilian. In the 16th c. under the government of Emperor Charles V (born 1500 in the Prinsenhof in Ghent) Ghent tried to make up for the decline of the cloth industry as river navigation developed. Time and again the citizens of Ghent opposed the ruling dynasty; the climax was reached when the Protestant Geuzen rose up against the Spanish who reacted by sending troops in 1567, commanded by the Duke of Alba who exacted terrible revenge. In 1576 the "Pacification of Ghent" was signed in the city, a peace and friendship league between the general states and the southern provinces of the Spanish Netherlands. After Alexander Farnese, the Spanish governor of the Netherlands, had finally subjected Ghent to Spanish rule again in 1584, the town's downfall was sealed.

Revival

The establishment of the cotton industry brought a new revival in the 18th c. under Austrian rule; in 1800, under French occupation, Lieven Bauwens brought in English cotton looms and revolutinised the trade. In the course of the 19th c. the town experienced real prosperity with the rapid growth of industry and trade.

Ghent was occupied by German troops in both world wars but mostly escaped damage.

The Belgian-French poet and Nobel prize winner Maurice Maeterlinck (see Facts and Figures, Famous People) was born in Ghent in 1862.

Tour of the town

Townscape

Ghent's historic inner city offers a superb collection of splendid buildings along picturesque canals, only superseded by Bruges. A walk through the town on a summer's evening, when the most important buildings are illuminated, is a particularly unforgettable experience. In high summer the canals, almost at a standstill, have their own distinctive aroma which permeates the city in the heat. However, this hardly mars the overall impression of this unique city.

Programme

As the historic Old Town is quite compact it can be taken in on one day and still include a detailed visit to the Sint-Baafskathedraal, the Gravensteen and the Museum of Ethnography. A visit to the Museum voor Schone Kunsten requires more time.

Round trips and tours

Two organisations offer guided tours around the city on foot: Gidsenbond van Gent en Oost-Vlaanderen (tel. 25 83 02) and Sightseeing Service (tel. 23 52 26). Boats depart continually from berths on the Korenlei and the Graslei from April to the beginning of November for canal trips through the centre. Horse-drawn carriages depart from Sint-Baafsplein from Easter to October. It is also possible to tour the city by minibus (departing from the Belfry) or by taxi.

Car parks

Cars should not be driven into the city centre. There are car parks at Vrijdagmarkt, at the University, at Kouter Square, at Sint-Pieterskerk and at Sint-Pieter station (tram to the city centre).

Historic Inner Town

The Inner Town is encircled by the Leie and the western branch of the Scheldt, the Opper Schelde. The central point of Old Ghent is Sint-Baafsplein.

** Sint-Baafskathedraal

On the eastern side of Sint-Baafsplein stands Sint-Baafskathedraal (Cathedral of St Bavon), a majestic building of brick and granite with a Romanesque crypt of its predecessor, Sint-Jans church. Charles V gave the cathedral its present name after he destroyed the old Sint-Baafsabdij (see p. 232) to build a fortress.

The High Gothic cathedral choir is 13/14th c., the late Gothic tower and the main nave are 15/16th c., whereas the transept and the nave were only completed in 1539–59. The tower, which lost its roof in a fire in 1602, has a carillon and there is a good view from its platform.

The light interior of the cathedral is richly decorated with some unique paintings. These include "The Conversion of St Baaf" by Peter Paul Rubens (1624) and "Christ among the Doctors" by Frans Pourbus (1571), in which the artist painted well known people of his time such as Philip II, the Duke of Alba, Thomas Calvin, Pieter Breughel the Elder and Charles V, who can be seen in the bottom left corner. There are other important works by Gaspar de Crayer, Maarten de Vos and Otto Venius.

The Altar of Ghent, also known as "The Adoration of the Mystic Lamb" after the centre panel, is by far the greatest masterpiece of old Flemish painting. The panels, commissioned by the Ghent patrician Josse Vijd for an ambulatory chapel, were allegedly begun about 1420 by Hubert van Eyck (around 1370–1426) and completed by his brother Jan (around 1390–1441) in 1431/32. It has never been known to what extent each of the brothers was involved in the genesis of the painting. It is generally accepted that in the representation of the Knights of Christ the fourth rider has the features of Jan and the front rider those of Hubert van Eyck.

The large winged altar, which is regarded as the most monumental example of medieval altar painting and as the most important step away from the iconic painting of the Middle Ages towards a realistic style, illustrates in vivid sequential panels the story of Salvation from the Fall of Man to the Redemption (see diagram of panels p. 224). Albrecht Dürer on visiting the altar during his travels through Flanders called it " a magnificent realistic painting".

Opening times
Apr.–Sept.
Mon.–Sat.
9.30am–noon
and 2–6pm,
Sun. 1–6pm;
Oct.–Mar.
Mon.–Sat.
10am–noon
and 2.30–4pm,
Sun. 2–5pm

Interior
* Paintings

** Altar of Ghent

Sint-Baafskathedraal

1 Gaspar de Crayer
   "Assumption"
2 Maarten de Vos: "Ecce Homo"
3 Frans Pourbus or Michiel or
   Rafael Coxie: "The Seven
   Works of Mercy"
4 Peter Paul Rubens:
   "The Summoning of St Bavo"

5 Otto Venius:
   "Raising of Lazarus"
6 High Altar
7 Tomb of Bishop Antonius Triest
8 Tomb of the Bishop d'Allamont
9 Frans Pourbus: "Christ among the
   Scribes"
10 Baroque pulpit

Altar of Ghent (Hubert and Jan van Eyck: 1420?–1432)

OPEN

1 Adoration of the
  Lamb of God
2 Christ
3 John the Baptist
4 Mary
5 Singers
6 Knights
7 Righteous knights (copy)
8 Adam
9 Abel's sacrifice

10 Cain slays Abel
11 Eve
12 St Christopher
13 Hermits
14 Musicians and
   pilgrims

CLOSED

15 Josse Vijd
   (donor of the altar)
16 John the Baptist

17 John the Apostle
18 Elizabeth Boorlut
   (wife of Josse Vijd)
19 The Annunciation
20 Room with washbasin
21 Room with a view of the town
   through the window
22 The Angel Gabriel
23 Zacharias
24 Sibyl of Eritrea
25 Sibyl of Cuma
26 Micheas

The work became famous shortly after its completion and had a chequered history. After Philip II coveted it, in 1566, it narrowly escaped destruction by the iconoclasts and was saved from a fire in 1640. The Austrian Emperor Joseph II had the panels with Adam and Eve removed in 1794, objecting to their nakedness – an illustration of the work's striking realism. They were replaced by "clothed" copies. In 1794 the centre panels were taken to Paris and exhibited in the Louvre; six panels found their way onto the art market and were bought by the Prussian king, who displayed them in the Berlin Museum. In 1815 the centre panels were returned from France, in 1861 the panels of Adam and Eve were acquired by the Brussels Museum. Under the Treaty Of Versailles Germany had to return the wings from Berlin and in 1920 the entire work, with the exception of the Predella (socle) lost in 1550, was put on display again in the cathedral. In 1934 two panels of the left wing were stolen. "John the Baptist" was returned but the inner panel ("The Righteous Judges") was never rediscovered and was replaced by a copy by van der Veken. During the Second World War the altarpiece was hidden in Pau, in southern France, but it was found by German troops and stored in a salt mine near Lake Altau in Styria, Austria. Here it was discovered by American troops and returned to the cathedral. Since 1986 it has been housed in its own room on the left side of Sint-Baafskathedraal and can be seen from all sides.

Sculpture

Among the splendid works of sculpture in the cathedral are the pulpit by Laurent Delvaux (1741), the tomb of Bishop A. Triest by Jerome Duquesnoy (1652), the Baroque organ case (1653) and the bronze door (1633) of the chapel of Bishop A. Triest.

Crypt

The extensive crypt contains numerous 15th and 16th c. tombs of bishops, a rich treasury including a 9th c. gospel and the shrine of St Macarius by Hugo de la Vigne (1616).

The outstanding Calvarian triptych of 1464 by Joos van Wassenhove (Justus van Ghent) is shown in one of the chapels. To the left of the choir steps lead down to the crypt of the earlier 10th c. church.

* Calvarian triptych

Sint-Baafsplein

Sint-Baafsplein opens out in front of the cathedral with the Koninklijk Vlaams Theater (Royal Flemish Theatre) on the north side and the memorial to Jan Frans Willems (1793–1846), the founder of the Flemish movement, on the south side.

Among the surrounding houses No. 10 stands out, a very handsome patrician house of 1739 with a bust of the goddess Juno in the gable. It is the house of the Hamelinck family, who built the house on the site of the "Roosecransche" guest house which belonged to the van Branteghem family. It once housed the oldest theatre in Ghent.

Hotel van Branteghem/ Hamelinck

** Belfry

On the west side of Sint-Baafsplein stands the 91m/298ft-high belfry, symbol of the city's independence, where the charters of the privileges of Ghent were kept. The tower was begun about 1300 and by 1338 was mainly completed. The present-day spire was restored to its original 14th c. form at the beginning of this century and replaced the wooden bell tower of 1380. It is crowned by a gilded copper dragon, which was first installed in 1377. Today it is a replica as are the four armed figures at the corners of the platform. Only one of the originals of these survives and can be seen on the ground floor.

Opening times
Jan.–Mar. and mid Nov.–Dec. daily 10.30am –4.30pm
Mar.–mid Nov. daily 10am–6pm

The Roeland bell was cast in 1315 and installed ten years later in the tower. It has often called the population of Ghent to arms; in 1659 it was melted down and from the metal Peter Hemony cast a carillon of 37 bells. At the same time three large bells, the Triomfanten, were made, the largest of which, again being called Roeland, cracked in 1914 and was removed in 1950. It now stands west of the belfry on the Burgermeester Braunplein. Next to the bell is a fountain with kneeling figures, "Bron der Geknielden" (Youth Fountain) by George Minne (1892). The new Roeland weighing 5000kg was put in place in 1948.

Roeland bell

At the entrance to the tower platform, from where there are good views of Ghent, on the ground floor is the room, called "Secreet", where the privileges of the city were kept in an iron chest. On the fourth floor the workings of the clock (1670), the oldest in Belgium, and the 52-bell carillon can be seen.

Interior

* Lakenhalle

The splendid Cloth Hall directly adjoins the Belfry. This building (1426–41) by Simon van Assche, restored in 1900–03 was the meeting place of the wool and cloth traders, the "Halleheeren". The Gothic ground floor, partly below ground, is divided into three by 20 columns. In 1741 it housed the town prison, today it has a café-restaurant which is popular with tourists.

An audio-visual display about Ghent of 30 minutes duration is held in the Cloth Hall (performances: Apr.–Nov. from 9.30–11.30am and 2–5.20pm every 40 minutes).

"Multivision"

The Louis XIV style gaoler's house of the former prison is built on to the north side of the Belfry. There is a relief known as "Mammelokker" above

Mammelokker

the doorway. It depicts the old man Cimon, who has been condemned to death by starvation, being suckled by his daughter.

*Stadhuis and surroundings

Tours
Apr.–Oct.
Mon.–Fri.
4pm English
2.20pm French
2pm Dutch
3.20pm German

North of the Lakenhalle on the Botermarkt stands the magnificent Stadhuis (town hall). It combines a variety of architectural styles, having been built over a long period of time. On the oldest parts of the building on the Hoogpoort, completed in the style of Bruges City Hall in 1482 and containing the council chambers, the architects Rombout Keldermans and Dominik de Waghemakere built a new wing in the finest late Gothic form richly decorated with statues. However, building work on this part, which is best seen from the corner of Hoogpoort and Belfortstraat, was suspended because of religious disputes in 1539. Only a quarter of the original plan was realised and only the Pacificatiezaal (Peace Hall; actually the court room for the Keure, the protectors of the town constitution) and the Marriage Chapel, both 1535, were built. Work only resumed at the end of the 16th c. so that the wing facing the Botermarkt is in Renaissance style as is the Throne Room on the upper floor (1635). Further building was carried out in the 18th c. on the Conciergerie (Flemish Baroque; corner of Hoogpoort/Stadhuissteeg) and the Armenkamer (Rococo, 1750; at the Poeljemarkt).

Sint-Jorishof

Directly opposite the town hall on the corner of Hoogpoort stands the former house of the Guild of Crossbowmen, Sint-Jorishof of 1477, where Maria of Burgundy granted greater freedom to the Flemish towns.

*Hoogpoort

There are many fine old houses in Hoogpoort which runs north of the Stadhuis.
On the Sint-Jorishof are No. 50 "Grote" or "Witte Moor" (15th c.) and No. 52 "Zwarte Moor" (15th c.), both fine examples of Brabant Gothic with

Ghent: Stadhuis

typical stepped gables. No. 54 "De Grote Sikkel" (14th c.) adjoins, once owned by the van Sikkeln family; today it houses the Academy of Music. Off the Biezekapelstraat is the "De Achtersikkel" (16th c.) with an attractive courtyard and small tower.

In Hoogpoort heading west are No. 33 "De Samson" (1481; the guild house of the Ghent goldsmiths until 1540), No. 15, "De Draecke" (15th c.) and finally house No. 10 (1732). It is called "De Ram" and was originally occupied by an apothecary. On the façade are an apothecary sign and a bust of the botanist Carolus Clusius, founder of the botanical gardens in Leiden, Holland.

From the Groentenmarkt to Sint-Michelskerk

At the western end of the Hoogpoort is the Groentenmarkt, originally a fish market and since the 18th c. a vegetable market. In the Middle Ages the pillory stood here. A mustard factory and shop are in one of the surrounding houses.

Groentenmarkt

On the west side of the market is the long Groot Vleeshuis, a medieval covered meat market with a guild house, chapel and numerous gables in the roof. The building originated in 1406–10 and was restored in 1912. At the south end of the Vleeshuis is the "Penshuizeken" (entrails cottage) where the poor were given the entrails of slaughtered animals.

* Groot Vleeshuis

At the south end of the Korenmarkt (corn market), surrounded by 16–18th c. buildings, the business centre of old Ghent, the lane known as Klein Turkije branches off. The oldest house is "De rode Hoed" (red hat) from the 13th c., where Albrecht Dürer lived during his stay in the town in 1523. The "Huis der Kruideniers", the guild house of the grocers, is in the same street.

Klein Turkije

The tower of the Sint-Niklaaskerk dominates the Korenmarkt, an excellent example of Scheldt Gothic. The first work began in the 13th c. and continu-

Sint-Niklaaskerk

Groot Vleeshuis

ed with interruptions until the 18th c. The Baroque west gateway to the Korenmarkt dates from 1681. The guilds of businessmen and the chamber of rhetoric 'De Fonteyne' had a chapel in the church. The house of the orators is in the Goudenleeuwplein No. 7 (1539) behind the church and is the oldest voluted building of its kind in Ghent with a Renaissance façade.

Postgebouw

Opposite the church doorway the architects Cloquet and Mortier attempted to harmonise the Postgebouw, completed in 1903, with the neo-Gothic style of the neighbouring historic gables.

Sint-Michielsbrug
*View

The Sint-Michielsbrug crosses the Leie. From the bridge there is a wonderful view of Sint-Niklaas, the Belfry and Sint-Baafs together with the Korenlei and the Graslei with the Gravensteen in the background.

Sint-Michielskerk

*Van Dyck
painting

At the far end of the bridge stands the Sint-Michielskerk. Work started on it in 1440 and reached the tower by 1648. It has a rich interior with paintings (de Crayer, van Oost, Otto Venius), the most impressive being "Crucifixion" (1629) by Anton van Dyck.

Het Pand

Along the Leie a group of buildings next to the church to the south in Onderbergen street are known as "Het Pand". This is a former 13th c. Dominican monastery and is one of the oldest buildings in Ghent. Today it is used by the university.

*Korenlei and **Graslei

This part of the town from the Sint-Michielsberg northwards along the Korenlei and Graslei was Ghent's oldest harbour where many of the guilds built their splendid, now famous, houses.

Korenlei

The Sint-Michielsbrug leads down to the Korenlei, itself lined by splendid façades but which offers the best view of the even finer houses on the opposite bank of the Graslei. No. 7 along the Korenlei, the "Gildehuis der Onvrije Schippers" (House of the Tied Boatmen), is a Baroque building from 1739. No. 9 is "De Zwane", a former brewery with beautiful swan motifs on the gable (16th c.). No. 15 is the site of the former "Hof van Gruuthuse", House of Duke Egmont (1352), now replaced by a building with a neo-Classical façade, which also encompasses Nos. 17–19, the "Hotel de Ghellink". Finally No. 24, "Lintworm en Krocht", was a Romanesque château from the 12th c., rebuilt at the beginning of this century.

Graslei

Some of Belgium's finest guild houses are to be found along the Graslei. Next to the rear façade of the post building is the "Gildehuis der Vrije Schippers" (House of the Free Boatmen), built in 1531 in the Brabant Gothic style. Adjoining it is the second "Gildehuis der Graanmeters" (House of the Grain Weighers), from 1698, a late Baroque building with a stepped gable. Almost squeezed in is the tiny "Tolhuisje" (Customs House), a Flemish Renaissance building of 1682, followed by the Romanesque "Spijker" or "Koornstapelhuis" (around 1200). The first "Korenmetershuis" (House of the Grain Weighers) was built in 1435; finally the "Gildehuis der Metselaars" (House of the Masons) from 1527 in Brabant Gothic style completes this unique row of guild houses.

North-west Inner City

*Museum voor
Sierkunst

At the end of the Korenlei, where the Lieve, the first sea canal of the 13th c., branches off from the Leie, Jan Breydelstraat turns off to the left. The splendid house, No. 5 dated 1754, was the town house of the de Coninck family who furnished it in grand style. The individual rooms of the house are open as a museum (Museum voor Sierkunst = Museum of Decorative

View of the Graslei from the Korenlei

Arts) and contain some later works of art, furniture, (including a sofa and two armchairs which belonged to the Tsarina Catherine II), porcelain, glass and paintings. The writing desk of the French king Louis XVIII, who had fled to Ghent in 1815 from Napoleon I, returned from Elba, is on display (open: Tues.–Sun. 9am–12.30pm and 1.30–5.30pm).

On the corner of Gewad/Burgstraat stands the "Huis der Gekroonde Hoofden" (House of the Crowned Heads) with a Renaissance façade of scrolled gables and portraits of the Counts of Flanders.

Huis der Gekroonde Hoofden

House No. 14 in the Gewad is the Museum voor Industriële Archeologie en Textiel (Museum of Industrial Archaeology and Textiles). As well as many tools and documents there is a Mule Jenny (spinning Jenny), one of the oldest still functioning spinning machines in the world that Lieven Bauwens introduced to Ghent at the beginning of the 19th c., thereby revitalising the textile industry (open: Mon.–Fri. 9am–noon and 2–5pm).

Museum voor Industriële Archeologie en Textiel

Gewad street comes to the Prinsenhofplein with the Donkere Poort (Dark Tower), remains of the Prinsenhof palace, inhabited by the Counts of Flanders from 1353, birthplace of Charles V, in 1500.

Detour

Further north-west is the Rabot, a lockhouse built in 1489 on the Lieve with stepped gables, flanked by two mighty round towers. On this spot the citizens of Ghent resisted the army of the German Emperor Friedrich III. Rabotstraat leads back to Burgstraat, past the ruins of the Sint-Elisabeth Béguinage (16th/17th c.). A monument to the poet Georges Rodenbach (1855–98) stands next to Sint-Elisabeth church.

Rabot

Sint-Elisabeth Béguinage

From the Rabot there is a footpath along the Lieve back to Burgstraat. It passes the Lievekaai, a romantic spot with small gabled houses.

*Lievekaai

**Gravensteen

Opening times
Apr.–Sept.
9am–7pm;
Oct.–Mar.
9am–5pm

Missing out the detour, on the right past Jan Breydelstraat is the rear façade of the castle of the Counts of Flanders, the Gravensteen, one of the strongest moated fortresses in Western Europe, surrounded by the River Lieve. It was built 1180–1200 on the orders of Philipp of Alsace, the former count of Flanders, on the foundation of a 9th c. structure in the style of Syrian crusader castles. Together with Bruges Castle it was the residence of the Flemish counts and still remains a unique example of the medieval art of fortification. In the 14th c. it ceased to have a military function and was used by the counts for administration of the land. In 1800 it came into private ownership and was converted into a cotton mill and flats for the workers; between 1894 and 1913 comprehensive restoration took place.

Tour

The tour of the castle leaves from the gatehouse into a large courtyard surrounded by a circular wall with 24 half towers and a defence gallery which encircles the main castle. This is dominated by a massive keep or "Meestentoren", its platform being reached by a narrow spiral staircase. Outstanding views of the castle and town are to be had from here. The tour continues through the palace (living quarters of the lords of the castle), where instruments of torture and court documents are now displayed, through the Great Hall, where Philipp the Good gave a huge banquet for the knights of the Golden Fleece in 1445, then through the torture chamber, finishing with the hole down to the dungeons.

Sint-Veerleplein

In front of the castle extends the ancient Sint-Veerleplein, possibly the oldest square in Ghent, although the neighbouring façades are of 17th c. origin at the earliest. This square was a market place but also the site of executions and burnings of the victims of the Inquisition.

Oude Vismarkt

The superb Baroque building at Sint-Veerleplein No. 5 is the old fish market, built in 1689 according to plans by Artus Quellin. Following a fire in

The fortified castle of Gravensteen

1872 it was extended and connected to the new meat market in Reke-lingestraat. The gateway depicts Neptune and allegorical representations of the Scheldt (male) and Leie (female).

*Kraanlei

To the north-east the Kraanlei adjoins Sint-Veerleplein, also lined with elegant houses. Immediately on the left is No. 1, the "Craenenburgh", then the row of houses "De Lelye" (Nos. 3–11), built around 1500 in Brabant Gothic style. No. 13, "In den Bliekenmarkt" (15th/16th c.) is a former fish shop.

No. 65, immaculately restored in 1962, Alijns Godhuis, a children's hospital founded in 1363 and one of the last remaining Godshuizen. These houses were founded by well-off families for the needy.   *Museum voor Volkskunde

In a picturesque courtyard are eighteen typical Flemish cottages, all in-terconnected. They house the extremely comprehensive Museum voor Volkskunde, which with its notable collection of equipment, documents and everyday objects provides a vivid picture of Flemish folk life around 1900. Of particular interest are the restored workshops and living rooms, a dining room, a barber's shop, a cobbler's workshop, an apothecary's shop, a confectioner's, bakery and a candlestick-maker's workshop.

The museum also has a puppet theatre with performances on Wednesday afternoons at 2.30pm and Saturday afternoons at 3pm (open: Apr.–Oct. daily 9am–12.30pm and 1.30–5.30pm; Nov.–Mar. Tues.–Sun. 10am–noon and 1.30–5pm).

Further along the Kraanlei is house No. 75, "De Klok", dating from the 17th c. with a spiral staircase and decorated with numerous allegorical reliefs. On the ground floor are care and temperance, love, faith and hope in the first floor with justice and strength above the roof window. No. 77, "De Zeven Werken van Barmhartigheid", and No. 79, "Het Vliegend Hert", are Baroque 17th c. town houses, decorated with exquisite reliefs.

Vrijdagmarkt and surroundings

From Kraanlei the Zuivelbrug crosses the Leie to Grootkanonplein, where stands the 5 metre-long and 16 tonne cast iron canon "Dulle Griet" (Mad Meg). It dates from the mid-15th c. and could fire, not very accurately, 340kg cannonballs.   Dulle Griet

Next is the Vrijdagmarkt (Friday Market), centre of political life in medieval Ghent. It was in this square that the Flemish counts had to swear their observance of the freedoms accorded to the citizens of Ghent. The guilds also fought each other here and in 1477 two advisers and envoys of the stadholder (governess) Maria of Burgundy were executed.   **Vrijdagmarkt**

In the centre of the square stands the monument to the hero of Ghent Jacob van Artevelds (see Facts and Figures, Famous People), by Petrus de Vigne-Quyo in 1863.   Artevelde-monument

Several guild houses surround the market: the House of the Tanners "Het Toreken", 1460, "Den Bonten Mantel" (No. 45) the furrier, 1675 and the "Lakenmetershuis" (No. 22) which was built on the site of the former tanners" guild house in the 18th c. The Art Nouveau "Ons Huis", belonging to the socialist workers' associations, was built about 1900.   Guild houses

To the east of the Vrijdagmarkt Sint-Jacobskerk stands in the Bij Sant-Jacobs square, one of the oldest religious buildings in Ghent. The crossing tower and both west towers are of the Romanesque period; the rest was finished between the 13th and 15th c. The church contains tombs and some fine paintings, especially in the ambulatory (Coxie, de Crayer, van Cleef).   Sint-Jacobskerk

The cannon known as "Dulle Griet" ("Mad Greta")

A colourful flower market takes place at weekends in the square in front of the church.

Nederpolder

The Hoogpoort (see p.226) is continued by the Nederpolder. No. 1 is the twin-gabled Palais Vanden Meersche dated 1547, an attractive inner courtyard with Rococo façades being added in the 18th c. No. 2 is "De kleine Sikkel", a Romanesque 13th c. patrician's house, which also belonged to the Van der Sickelen family.

Geraard de Duivelsteen

The Nederpolder ends at Bisdomplein. On the right on the bank of the Scheldt is the castle of the steward of the Flemish dukes, Geraard de Duivel. Over the centuries it has served many purposes – as a prison, a lunatic asylum and an arsenal – and it now houses the East Flemish State Archives. There is a memorial to the brothers Hubert and Jan van Eyck in the park.

East and South-east Ghent

* Ruins of Sint-Baafsabdij

Opening times
Tues.–Sun.
9am–12.30pm
and 1.30–5.30pm

In the east part of the city, across the Slachthuisbrug over the Leie, are the ruins of Sint-Baafsadbdij, one of the two abbeys still standing from the beginning of Ghent's development. It was founded in 630 by St Amandus and rebuilt after being destroyed by the Normans in the 10th c. Following the suppression of the revolt by the citizens of Ghent against Charles V. He dissolved the abbey and had a fortress built in its place in 1540, the Spanjards Kasteel, which was in turn destroyed in the 19th c.
A gallery of the late Gothic cloisters, the octagonal lavatorium and parts of the chapter house and the refectory still remain from the original abbey.

The refectory with its beautiful Romanesque frescoes (12th c.) has been the Museum voor Stenen Voorwerpen (Museum for Stonecutting and Sculpture) since 1882. It has an extraordinary collection of medieval tombstones, Ghent sculpture and architectural artefacts from the 12th–18th c. as well as mosaics.

Museum voor Steenen Voorwerpen

Klein Begijnhof

The smaller Béguinage (Klein Begijnhof van Onze-Lieve-Vrouw ter Hoyen) in Violettenstraat in the south-east part of the city dates back to 1234, when it was founded by Johanna of Constantinople and her sister Maria. The present day site with its cottages around a large tree-lined lawn has remained unchanged since the 17th c.

The Onze-Lieve-Vrouw ter Hoyen church which belongs to the béguinage was begun in 1658 and completed in 1720. It has a captivating Baroque doorway. In the interior are valuable paintings (de Crayer, van Cleef, polyptych by Horenbaut).

South City

Kouter and surroundings

The area south of the historic inner city, chiefly built in the 18th and 19th c., is, with its pedestrianised areas, the commercial and shopping centre of Ghent.

This square has played a major role over the centuries in the history of Ghent. It has been the site of meetings, festivals, tournaments, troop inspections and a shooting range. Since the 18th c. a flower and bird market is held every Sunday. Some of the old buildings have been preserved: the exchange built in 1738 as the main police station, the Hotel Faligan (1775) in French Rococo and the Koninklijke Opera (Royal Opera); (1837–40). The Municipal Library is on the southern side of the square.

Kouter

North of the Kouter in Korte Meer is the Museum Wetenschap en Techniek (Museum of Science and Technology), dedicated to the inventions and discoveries of scientists from Ghent and Flanders. Among these are Jan Palfijn, a famous Flemish surgeon, inventor of birth forceps and founder of anatomy and Leo Baekeland, the inventor of bakelite. There is an unrivalled collection of surgical instruments from all periods (open: Mon. and Wed. 2–5pm; 3rd week of July daily 9am–noon and 2–5pm; closed in Aug.). The museum is housed in the buildings of the university, founded by King Willem I in 1816.

Museum Wetenschap en Techniek

The Veldstraat, the oldest and best known shopping street, now pedestrianised, runs parallel to the Korte Meer in a westerly direction. The most striking building is the large 18th c. Palais D'Hane-Steenhuyse with a magnificent Rococo façade and an equally intact Classical façade facing the garden, where concerts are held. The French king Louis XVIII lived in the house in 1815 during the "Hundred Days" of further Napoleonic rule. Other guests included the King of Westphalia, Talleyrand, the Tsar of Russia and the Prince of Orange. Today the house is the information centre on restoration in the city.
In the houses opposite (today C&A department store) the American negotiators stayed who signed the Ghent Peace Treaty with the British in 1814, ending the war between the USA and Great Britain.

Veldstraat

The Museum Arnold van der Haeghen is to be found at Veldstraat No. 82. The building dates from 1741 and was first the residence of an industrialist;

Museum Arnold van der Haeghen

233

in 1815 the Duke of Wellington lived here. From 1836 it housed the printing press of the van der Haeghen family.

The Arnold van der Haeghen Museum comprises the Maeterlinck cabinet and the Stuyvaert cabinet. The Maeterlinck cabinet contains personal artefacts, the library and a manuscript collection of the writer and Nobel prize winner Maurice Maeterlinck (1862–1949). Victor Stuyvaert was a graphic artist from Ghent, part of his work is on show in a cabinet named after him (open: Mon.–Fri. 9am–12.30pm and 1.30–4.30pm).

Historische
Onderwijscollectie

The route along the Bartsoenkaai to the Bijlokemuseum to the south passes the Apotheekstraat. There is an interesting collection of original exhibits relating to school history (Historische Onderwijscollectie; open: Wed. 2–4pm).

* Bijlokemuseum

Opening times
daily 9am–12.30pm
and 1.30–5.30pm

The Bijlokemuseum is situated on the other side of the Leie in the Godshuizenlaan. It occupies the mainly brick buildings of the Cistercian abbey of Bijloke, founded at the same time as the hospital. The museum (Museum van Oudheden) is one of the richest of its kind in Belgium and shows remarkable ancient pieces in a unique historical setting. The numerous rooms contain works in glass, metal, pottery, leather, together with jewellery, weapons and paintings.
Some of the rooms are particularly noteworthy:

Armenkamer

The Armenkamer is a reproduction, true to the original, of the meeting room of this society (Governors of the Poor House), founded in 1531 by Charles V in the town hall. A painting by Jan van Cleef depicts the ruler at the founding ceremony.

** Refectory

Outstanding centrepoint is the 14th c. refectory, 31m/101ft long and almost 14m/46ft high, with an exceptional brick gable. The interior walls are painted with frescoes (around 1325), among which is a 10m-long painting of the Last Supper. In the centre of the room is the tomb of the castellan Hugo II of Ghent, who died in 1232.

Gildensaal

The former dormitory contains mainly artefacts of the Ghent guilds: coatsof-arms, insignia and procession lanterns.
The House of the Abbess is beautifully furnished with historic furniture. It contains the Ghent communal hall with the attractive silver insignia of Ghent music societies from the 15th–18th c.

* Museum voor Schone Kunsten
Museum voor Hedendagse Kunsten

Opening times
daily 9am–12.30pm
and 1.30–5.30pm

From the Bijlokemuseum the Charles de Kerchovelaan leads south-east to the De Liemaeckerplein, where the Museum voor Schone Kunsten (Museum of Fine Arts) is situated. The museum building with staircase and colonnaded doorway is dated 1904 and was enlarged in 1913. The main emphasis of the collections is painting covering the 15th–20th c.

Tapestries

The central hall adjoining the entrance hall has eight fine Brussels wall tapestries: three with motifs from the story of Darius (17th c.) and five with the theme "Triumph of the Gods" (1717).

Old Masters

Left of this hall are to be found the Old Masters. Prominent are two works by Hieronymus Bosch in Room B: "Bearing of the Cross" and "St Hieronymus". Other works are by Flemish and old Dutch masters such as Adriaan Isenbrant ("Seated Madonna and Child"), the Ghent miniaturist Gerard Horenbaut, Frans Pourbus the elder (Room D), Rubens ("Scourging

Hieronymus Bosch: "Christ carrying the Cross"

of Christ''; Room E), van Dyck, Jacob Jordaens (Room G) and Frans Hals ("Portrait of an Elderly Lady''; Room L). Representatives of Italian painters are Tintoretto and Magnasco (Room F); the English department has two paintings by Hogarth and one by Reynolds.

To the right of the Tapestry Room are paintings of the 19th and 20th c., especially Belgian artists. In Room 4 are Henri Evenepoel ("Spaniard in Paris"), Emile Claus and James Ensor; also Constant Permeke (Room 5) and among others the Sint-Martens-Latern group with Gustave de Smet (Room 13). In Room 6 there is a painting by Oskar Kokoschka; Camille Corot and Théodore Géricault represent the French school (Room 1).   **19th and 20th c.**

Since 1976 the Museum voor Hedendagse Kunst (Museum for Contemporary Art) has been an independent museum under the same roof. It shows modern art post-1945 with the main emphasis on the development of Belgian painting. The rooms of this museum in the left wing adjoin the Old Masters.   **Modern Art**

On display are the movements and schools COBRA, Hyperrealism. Minimal Art, Concept Art and Pop Art artists such as Andy Warhol, Frances Bacon, David Hockney, Panamarenko and Joseph Beuys; Belgian artists include René Magritte, Paul Delvaux, Karel Appel and Marcel Broodthaers.

Citadel Park

To the west of the museum the Citadel Park is laid out on the site of the citadel commissioned by Wellington. With its ponds and flower beds it is popular with Ghent citizens for taking a walk. Within the park is the Floralia-paleis (Feestpaleis), an exhibition and trade fair complex, which has now partly been replaced by the new trade fair "Flanders Expo" in Sint-Denijs-Westrem.

Plantenuin   On the other side of the Clauslaan, which borders the park in the south-east, Ghent University maintains botanical gardens (Plantenuin) with an exceptional collection of exotic plants (open: Mon.–Thur. 2–5pm; Sat., Sun. and public holidays 9am–noon).

Sint-Pietersabdij

North-east of Citadel Park is Sint-Pietersplein with Sint-Pietrsabdij on its western side. It was probably founded in the 7th c. and dissolved under the government of the French Revolution. Nowadays it is the Centrum voor Kunst en Kultur, which organises regular art exhibitions.

Schoolmuseum   The Schoolmuseum Michel Thiery is housed in the former sick room and
Michel Thiery   reception hall of the abbey. Contrary to its name its emphasis is not on school, but on school science subjects and displays fossils, stuffed birds and geological collections as well as computer technology (open: daily 9am–12.15pm and 1.30–5.15pm; closed Fri. afternoon).

Sint-Pieterskerk   Sint-Pieterskerk on the north side of the square was built in the 17th and 18th c. by the Huyssens brothers; it was based on St Peter's Cathedral in Rome and has an impressive 57m/187ft-high cupola. Inside are notable paintings by van Dyck and de Crayer.

Surroundings

Boat trips   As well as boat trips along the canals through the city centre there are boat excursions in the vicinity and further afield.
Boats leave from the Recolettenlei at the Law Courts for Deurle and back (departure 1.30pm, return 6.30pm; May and Sept.: Fri.; June: Mon., Wed., Fri.; July and Aug: Mon., Wed., Thur., Fri.; as well as public holidays in all these months). During July and August this trip also operates at night (depart 8pm).
Day trips to Bruges (see entry) leave from the same place (depart July and Aug. Thur. 9am).

Sint-Amandsberg   C 4

Nieuw Begijnhof   9km/5 miles north-east of the city centre the successor to the abandoned béguinage of Sint-Elisabeth (see p. 229) was constructed in an open field in 1873/74. The large, walled béguinage which attempts to recreate the medieval atmosphere is completely enclosed by the houses of the suburb of Sint-Amandsberg. The eighty cottages are still inhabited by béguines who earn their living by lace-making.
The béguinage has a museum with religious objects and household goods showing the lifestyle and development of a béguine (open: Apr.–Oct. Wed, Thur., Sat., Sun., public holidays 10–11am and 2–5pm).

Harbour   Sint-Amandsberg is well placed for a visit to the harbour (boat trips tel. 21 84 51; bus tours tel. 51 05 50).

Lochristi   Leaving Sint-Amandsberg in an easterly direction the N70 reaches Lochristi, a flower-growing centre, specialising in begonias. The begonia festival takes place during the last week in August.

*Kasteel van Laarne   D 5

Laarne castle is situated 11km/7 miles east of Ghent. The 11th/12th c. pentagonal fortress was built to defend Ghent and rebuilt in the 17th c.

Today it has two inner courtyards and a large keep on the right-hand façade and is surrounded by a moat. A stone arcaded bridge leads to the entrance. The interior is furnished in the French and Antwerp styles; with exceptionally beautiful Brussels tapestries (16th c.) depicting the Emperor Maximilian hunting, after cartoons by Bernard van Orley. On the first floor is a collection of silverwork of European class. It is the Claude Dallemagne Kollektion, which comprises chiefly French and Belgian silver from the 15th–18th c., including a plate designed by Rubens in 1628 which belonged to the Tsarina Catherine II and several splendid tankards.

Opening times
Tues.–Sun.
10am–noon and
2–6pm;
July and Aug.
also open Mon.

Leiestrek

C 5

The Leie meanders south-west of Ghent through delightful verdant countryside. There are numerous places of interest along its banks.

About 8km/5 miles south-west of Ghent is the town of Sint-Matrtens-Latem, the patron saint of one of the most important schools of Belgian fine arts. In 1897 a group of artists settled in the town around the sculptor George Minne, among whom were Gustav van de Woestijne and Valerius de Saedeleer. Their work was stopped by the First World War; during the Twenties a second group became known, including Albert Servaes, Constant Permeke, Gust de Smet and Frits van den Berghe, all of whom lived and worked in the town or nearby.
A large number of galleries still have collections of this period; the town church has many paintings by the above artists.

Sint-Martens-Latem

The small village of Deurle on the Leie, 12km/8 miles south-west of Ghent, consists of villas in the middle of gardens and parks. There are three interesting art museums dedicated to the various members of the Sint-Martens-Latem School:
The Ghent painter Gust de Smet (1877–1943) lived in Deurle from 1935 onwards. His house and studio have been maintained in their original condition (open: Mon. and Wed. 2–6pm).
Léon, the brother of Gust de Smet, (1881–1966), also lived in Deurle. His house has been reconstructed with his furniture and possessions (open: Tues.–Thur. and Sat. 2–6pm; Sun. also 10am–noon).

Deurle

Museum
Gust de Smet

Museum
Léon de Smet

Built on the Leie in 1969 this museum exhibits important works of the Sint-Martens-Latem School and 19th and 20th c. Belgian art in general, in chronological order.
Artists represented include Servaes, de Smet, Permeke, van den Berghe, Claus, Minne, de Saedeleer, Meunier, Evenepoel and Rik Wouters (open: Sat., Sun. and public holidays 10am–noon and 2–5pm, June–Sept. until 6pm; Thur.–Fri. only 10am–noon; closed Dec.–Feb.).

Museum
Mevrouw
Jules
Dhondt-Daenans

To the south, past Bachte Maria-Leerne, Deurle borders the park of the Château of Ooidonk. The original château was built in the 13th c. and burnt down in the 15th. The new building of 1595 was in Flemish-Spanish style with stepped gables and small towers finished with onion-shaped pinnacles. There are two wings off the main building, each ending in a side tower. The house, redesigned in the 19th c., is still inhabited by the Baron de Nevele but is open to visitors. Of interest are the paintings, including portraits of the Counts Hoorn and Egmont, and items belonging to the Royal Family (open: every Sun. from July–mid Sept.).

*Kasteel
van Ooidonk

The château stands in beautiful parkland which nestles in a bow in the Leie (open: daily 10am–noon and 2–6pm).

Park

The end of the Leiestrek is Deinze, 18km/11 miles from Ghent. It has a Gothic church with a painting by de Crayer and a local museum housing archaeological finds, exhibits from the town's history and paintings of the Sint-Marten-Latem School.

Deinze

Sint-Vincentiuskerk in Eeklo

Eeklo

Sint-
Vincentiuskerk

Eeklo is situated 20km/12 miles north-west of Ghent. The tower, over 100m/328ft high, of the neo-Gothic Sint-Vincentiuskerk from the end of the 19th c. is one of the highest church towers in Flanders.

Stadhuis

In front of the church in Grote Markt is the attractive red brick stadhuis (town hall) of 1609. A belfry was added in 1932.

Maldegem

Maldegem, 10km/6 miles west of Eeklo, provides an interesting diversion. The "Steam Centre" has a number of steam locomotives, steam rollers, steam tractors and industrial steam machines (open: May–early Oct. Mon., Tues., Fri., Sat., Sun. and public holidays 10am–6pm).

Halle · Hal   D 6

Province: Brabant
Altitude: 35m/115ft
Population: 32,300
Intercity and Inter-regional Station

Location

The neat town of Halle (French Hal) is 15km/9 miles from Brussels, not far from the linguistic border, on the Senne and on the canal which links Brussels with Charleroi. Blast furnaces, textile, leather and food processing plants make up the industrial base.
Halle is an important place of pilgrimage on account of its wonder-working black Madonna statue; donated by Aleydis of Avesnes, wife of the Duke of Hennegau in 1267.

*Onze-Lieve-Vrouwbasiliek (Sint-Martinuskerk)

North-west of the market is the Onze-Lieve-Vrouw-Basiliek (Basilica of Our Lady), also known as Sint-Martinuskerk or Sint-Martinusbasiliek. It is a notable buiding in Brabant Gothic, its elegant architecture showing French influence. Work began on the church in 1341; it was consecrated in 1410. The baptistry with its sturdy tower (around 1440) was the first onion-shaped roof in the Netherlands. The tower with its four Gothic spires was also started in the mid-15th c.; the Baroque lantern was not added until 1776. The tower houses a carillon with 54 bells. The large southern lateral aisle, next to the baptistry, is decorated with a row of simple wall formations, projecting columns and triangular gables in typical Brabant style and embellished with rich sculpture. There is a beautiful work of Mary with child, surrounded by angel musicians (14th c.) in the tympanum of the south portal; in the small south portal, which creates the impression of a transept, is the coronation of Mary. The north side portal has a Brabant picture of Madonna.

Exterior

Inside the church the sculptured decoration is remarkable. The Trazegnies chapel, added in 1467, has a beautiful alabaster altar by Jean Mone (1533), sculptor for Charles V, a Renaissance work with reliefs depicting the Seven Sacraments, together with statues of the four evangelists, the Church Fathers and the pelican motif.
In the chapel on the right is the marble memorial of the Dauphin Joachim, son of Louis XI of France, who died in 1460.
Particularly beautiful is the row of apostles over the arches of the choir, probably 14th c. and revealing similarities with the work of Claus Sluter. In the choir itself above the modern altar stands the 95cm-high Gothic Black Madonna, showing Mary seated on the Throne of Wisdom. It is thought to be from around 1200 and belonged to St Elisabeth of Hungary. The blackness is caused by oxidisation and not, as legend has it, from the gunpowder smoke of the 32 cannon balls which the Madonna caught during the siege of Halle in 1580 and which can be seen on the north wall.
The baptistry next to the tower has an impressive font, a Tournai work of 1446, with a brass cover depicting the apostles and other saints.

*Interior

The crypt houses the rich treasury; among which are gifts consecrated to the Black Madonna, a reliquary of Louis XI of France and a monstrance of Henry VIII of England.

Treasury

At the Grote Markt

In the market is the stadhuis (town hall) from 1616, restored in the 19th c. Both statues "Truth" and "Justice" are copies of original works by Jerome Duquesnoy.
In the middle of the square in front of the town hall is a memorial to the violinist Adrien Servais (1807–70), who came from Halle.

Stadhuis

Basiliek St-Martinus Halle

A Great South Doorway
B Small South Doorway
C North Doorway

1 Bell-tower (pre-1300; Carillon and Museum of bells)
2 Baptistery (c. 1440; font of 1461)
3 Trazegnies Chapel (1467; alabaster altar by J. Mone 1533)
4 Lady Chapel (pre-1335; marble tomb of the Dauphin Joachim, died 1460)
5 High Altar (above – the "Black Madonna" of Halle)

239

Sint-Martinuskerk in Halle

The moated castle of Beersel

Jesuit college	The former Jesuit college houses a music academy and the Zuidwest-brabants Museum (local history and art; open: May–Aug. Sat., Sun. and public holidays 10am–noon and 2–5pm).

Surroundings

Provinciaal Domein Huizingen	The 91ha/225 acre provincial domain of Hulzingen, 4km/2 miles north-east of Halle, is a popular recreational area near Brussels with a wide variety of attractions. The main attraction is the Botanical Garden with 1200 different species of plants. There is also a garden for the blind (open: daily 9am–sunset).
Beersel *Moated castle	Beersel, 7km/4 miles north-east of Halle, is already a suburb of Brussels. It is famous for its brick moated castle, built around 1300, on a triangular base. The three 17th c. towers, rounded on the outside but gabled on the side facing the inner courtyard, are linked by defensive walled walkways. One of the towers has a torture chamber (open: Mar.–Nov. Tues.–Fri. 10am–noon and 2–6pm; Dec. and Feb. Sat. and Sun. 10.30am–5pm).
Braine-le-Château	It is worth visiting Braine-le Château, 6½km/4 miles to the south-east, to see the tasteful castle built by the counts of Hoorn in the 17th and 18th c. A pillory decorated with ironwork, erected in 1521, stands in the market square. The grand tomb (1542) of Maximilian Hoorns, Charles V's chamberlain, in the local church is by Jean Mone.
Rebecq	The small town of Rebecq, 10km/6 miles south-west in the Senne valley, is the birthplace of the Solvay brothers, the founders of one of the largest industrial companies in Belgium. From Rebecq a small steam train operates along the 7km/4 mile-long route through the picturesque "Vallée des Oiseaux" (Valley of the Birds) to Rognon and back (departs May–Sept. Sun. 2.30pm).

These 18th and 19th c. buildings were part of an old industrial site from the 19th c. The machine room and forge are open to visitors. One of the rooms contains the porphyry museum, another is fitted out as a tavern.

Moulin d'Arenberg

Enghien is situated about 18km/11 miles south-west of Halle on the linguistic border. For a long time the town belonged to the Arenberg family, of whose estate only 342ha/845 acres of parkland remain.

Enghien

This large Gothic church on the Grand-Place has a beautiful font (15th c.) and modern church windows by Max Ingrand.

Saint Nicholas

The Renaissance alabaster tomb of Guillaume de Croy, archbishop of Toledo, was crafted by Jean Mone for the church of the former Capuchin convent. On the main altar is a sculptured group "Worship of the Kings" by Servay de Couls, its 51 figures representing members of the Arenberg family.

Eglise des
Capucins

Han-sur-Lesse

G 8

Province: Namur
Altitude: 120m/393ft
Population: 800

The village of Han-sur-Lesse in the south-east of the province of Namur is world-famous for its caverns and at weekends is overrun with tourists. The River Lesse flows through the stalactite caverns which have an amazing variety of rock formations caused by the porosity of the limestone found in this region.

Location

**Grottes de Han

The caverns were inhabited as far back as the Stone Age by people seeking refuge. Not until 1804 did four young men dare to venture further into the caves. During subsequent explorations over the following years the larger caverns with their stalagmites and stalactites were discovered: the grottos have been open to the public since 1856.

The system as it is known today consists of a series of intricate caverns with a total length of 10km/6 miles, only 3km/2 miles of which are accessible, some only since 1962. The dirt left on the ceiling in the oldest caves by the smoke and soot from torches is clearly visible but they remain extremely impressive thanks to the skilful illumination. Especially striking are the Salle des Scarabées, the Salle des Renards, the Salle du Vigneron, the Grotte du Précipice, Le Trophée, Le Styx, the Salle des Mystérieuses and the Salle des Draperies, all with superb stalactite formations. In the Salle d'Armes, a beautiful round cave where the Lesse reappears, a son-et-lumière show highlights the most impressive formations. The highpoint is the last cavern, the Salle du Dome, its vastness (length 154m/505ft, width 140m/459ft, height 129m/423ft) can be appreciated by the torchlight provided by an attendant. The exit to the Grottos is reached by boat where a cannon is fired. It is just a few minutes' walk back to the village.

A tour of the grottos takes about two hours. The temperature in the caverns is a constant 12°C/53°F and so warm clothing is recommended as are strong shoes.

Tour

The only access to the grottos is by the train which runs through the beautiful Ardennes countryside and departs from the information and ticket office opposite the local church.

Departure times: Easter–June every 30 mins. from 9.30–11.30am and 1–5pm; July and Aug. every 30mins. from 9.30–11.30am and 1–6pm; Sept.– Oct. hourly and Nov.–Easter every two hours 9.30–11.30am and 1–5pm.

At the exit to the caverns there is the Musée du Monde Souterrain (Museum of the Underground World) which explains the origin of the caverns and

Musée du Monde
Souterrain

Grottes de Han
Stalactitic caves
near Han-sur-Lesse

Constant temperature
in the caves 12°C/54°F

1 Salle des Scarabées	8 Salle Blanche	15 Salle des Mamelons	23 Salle des Draperies
2 Salle des Renards	9 Grotte du Cocyte	16 Grotte Centrale	24 Embarquement
3 Grotte	10 Grotte du Précipice	17 Le Trophée	(Abfahrt der Boote)
de la Grenouille	11 Salle d'Antiparos	18 Salle des Mystérieuses	25 Grotte des Petites Fontaines
4 Salle du Vigneron	12 Salle des Priapes	19 Grotte des Aventuriers	26 Grotte
5 Grande Rue	13 Grotte de	20 Le Capitole	de la Grande Fontaine
6 Petite Rue	l'Hirondelle	21 Le Styx	27 Débarquement
7 Salle de l'Escarpement	14 Labyrinthe	22 La Tamise	(Ankunft der Boote)

shows archaeological finds from the various expeditions ranging from the Stone Age to the Merovingian period (open: Apr.–Nov. daily 10am–6pm; July and Aug. until 8pm).

"Spéléothème"   The walk back to the village leads through grounds with a playground and restaurant and around a farm. Here an audio-visual show "Spéléothème" presents fantastic insights into the world of the Grottoes of Han (open: end Mar.–Nov. daily 11am–6pm, July and Aug. until 8.30pm).

*Wildlife reserve

The Grottes de Han are surrounded by a wildlife park which belongs to the Lesse et Lomme National Park. In the beautiful countryside indigenous animals such as stags and wild boars can be observed together with strains bred from extinct animals including bison, aurochs and tarpans in enclosures. The drive in the "safari car" passes by the Gouffre de Belvaux, where the Lesse disappears roaring into the mountain and does not reappear until Han.

Tour   The safari cars depart from opposite the local church.
Departure times: Easter–Oct. every 30 mins. 9.30am–5pm, May–June until 5.30pm and July–Aug. until 6pm.

Information   A combined ticket can be purchased for a visit to the grottos, the wildlife park and the museums.

Surroundings

Lavaux-
Sainte-Anne   Close to the E411 motorway Namur-Arlon, 6km/4 miles south-west of Han-sur-Lesse, is the village of Lavaux-Sainte-Anne. It has an interesting moated castle from the 14th and 15th c. with three corner towers and a keep, which replaced its predecessor from 1190. New Renaissance style residential wings were built between the towers in the 17th c. The castle which is partly furnished with contemporary furniture houses a hunting and conservation museum; agricultural equipment is displayed in the adjoining buildings. A film shows the reconstruction of the castle which was destroyed in 1795 (open: Mar.–Nov. daily 9am–6pm; Dec.–Feb. until 5pm).

Han-sur-Lesse: Leaving the "Underworld"

Near Lessive, 4km/2 miles north-west of Han-sur-Lesse at the confluence of the Lesse and Lomme, the satellite transmission station of the Belgium Post Office became operational in 1972. The giant 30m/98ft-high parabolic antennae weighing 53 tonnes is used for telecommunications with America. A tour through the grounds lasts around 1½ hours (open: mid Apr.–mid Oct. daily 9.30am–5pm; July and Aug. until 5.30pm).

Lessive

Hasselt

G 5

Province: Limburg
Altitude: 39m/128ft
Population: 66,900
Intercity and Inter-regional Station (bicycle rental at station)

Hasselt, the lively capital of the province of Limburg, is situated between Liège and Antwerp on the Demer, a tributary of the Dijle. To the south extend fertile fields and orchards, in the north is the Limburg coal basin. Hasselt, as well as being a market and commercial centre for the region, a role which was acknowledged by the establishment of the Economics Institute in 1968, is an important industrial town; its chief industries being food processing, chemical and electronics. The construction of the modern cultural centre in 1959, the biggest in Flanders, brought the town considerable cultural significance. Hasselt is known for the production of good quality Genever gin.

Location

Hasselt was already a market town in the Middle Ages in the county of Loon. In the 12th c. it received its town charter. In 1356 Hasselt was acquired together with County Loon by the Diocese of Liège and became the seat of local administration. In 1795 it was annexed by France and became capital

History

of the Département of Meuse-Inférieure, and later, in 1813 capital of the Dutch province of Limburg. On 8th August 1831 a battle took place to the west of the town between Dutch troops under Crown Prince Wilhelm and the Belgian army of the Meuse. In 1839 Limburg was divided between Belgium and the Netherlands and Hasselt became capital of the Belgian province of Limburg.

Festivals

Every seven years in August a procession for the Madonna Virga Jesse is held in Hasselt. The statue is kept in the Onze-Lieve-Vrouwkerk. On this occasion the "Langeman" is also carried, a 7m/23ft high figure in Spanish uniform, which goes back to the 15th c. (next date 1996).
On 30th April the "Meiavond" takes place, wherby a may tree is set up and the "Meiliedeken", known to date from the 17th c., is sung

Sights

Grote Markt

The busy Grote Markt is surrounded by several old patrician houses, the most attractive being the chemist shop "Het Sweert", built in 1659 in place of a guest house from 1452. A masked head with an arm holding a raised sword decorates the corner of the house.

Sint-Quintinus-kathedraal

Through the Kortstraat heading north-east is the Vismarkt with the 15th–16th c. Gothic Sint-Quintinuskathedraal, built on Roman foundations. Its 63m/206ft-high west tower (base 12th/13th c.) has one of the most attractive sounding carillons in Belgium with 47 bells; there is a small

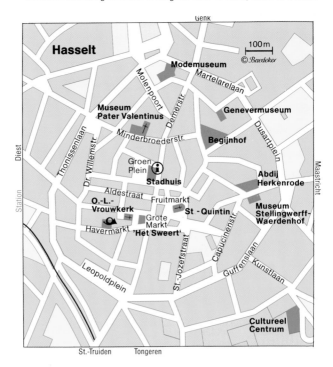

carillon museum (Beiardmuseum; open: June–Sept. Sat. and Sun. 2–6pm). The interior of the church contains Gothic frescoes on the columns of the main nave, fine Renaissance choir stalls from 1549, the pulpit and a Gothic triumphal cross below the crossing.

The church was elevated to the status of cathedral in 1967 when Belgian Limburg became a diocese and Hasselt the seat of the bishopric.

The Onze-Lieve-Vrouwkerk a short distance west of the market is as far as **Onze-Lieve-**
its art treasures are concerned, of greater importance than the Sint-Quinti- **Vrouwkerk**
nuskathedraal. It was built betwen 1728 and 1740 in a transitional style between Baroque and Classicism and rebuilt true to the original in 1950–52 following its bombardment in 1944.

In the interior some notable works of art from the former Cistercian abbey of Herkenkode near Hasselt have been preserved. The high altar (with the ˙High altar
14th c. Virga Jesse-Madonna statue) is an important work by Jean Delcour of Liège. In the transepts are the Baroque tomb of Anna-Catharina de Lamboy, abbess of Herkenrode 1653–75, by A. Quellin the Younger (1675) and the marble Rococo tomb of Barbara de Rivière d'Arschot, abbess of Herkenrode 1738–44, with the bas relief "Resurrection" by L. Delvaux (1744).

North of the Grote Markt on Groenplaats is the stadhuis (town hall), an Stadhuis
attractive patrician house from 1630, later converted in Classical style.

The Sint-Katharina béguinage north of Sint-Quintinuskathedraal was origi- Begijinhof
nally built 1245–1567 beyond the town wall south of the town as it was at that time and was called 'Extra Muros'. In 1567 it was completely de-stroyed; in 1571 work began on a new béguinage, this time within the town walls. At the beginning of the 18th c. the premises were extended and underwent conversion. The buildings from this later period stand in the southern part of the grounds. The Classical church was destroyed during air raids in 1944; the only evidence of it are some ruins .

In Minderbroederstraat leading from the béguinage is the Museum Pater Museum
Valentinus which documents the life and work of Father Valentin Paquay Pater Valentinus
(1828–1905; open: daily 9am–5.30pm).

The attractive and original Stedelijk Modemuseum (Municipal Fashion Stedelijk
Museum) is situated on the north side of the Inner Town. It has numerous Modemuseum
examples of 19th and 20th c. fashion and is arranged not only chronolog-ically but also thematically, for example, bridal dresses; underwear (open: Tues.–Fri. 10am–5pm; Sat., Sun. and public holidays 2–6pm).

In a town renowned for its genever it is fitting that there should be a National
museum dedicated to gin. It is in an old 19th c. steam distillery, not far from Genever Museum
the béguinage, that the production of this noble drink can be followed and the beneficial juniper gin sampled (open: Tues.–Fri. 10am–5pm; Sat., Sun. and public holidays 2–6pm).

On the east side of the Inner Town is the beautifully painted Maastrichter- Museum
straat with the Museum Stellingwerff-Waerdenhof, devoted to local and Stellingwerff-
town history. The most outstanding exhibit is the oldest known mon- Waerdenhof
strance in the world dating from 1286 (open: Tues.–Fri. 10am–5pm; Sat., Sun. and public holidays 2–6pm).

Opposite the museum is the refuge of the Abbey of Herkenrode from the 16th c.

Surroundings

˙Provinciaal Domein Bokrijk   G 5

Across the Albertskanaal, 8km/5 miles north-east of Hasselt, the 540ha/1334 acres of heath and woodland of the Domain Bokrijk offers a

Jugendherberge

Domäne Bokrijk bei Hasselt

Naturkunde-museum
Arboretum
Hirsch-gehege
Wander-park
Naturreservat Het Wiek
Cebolik
Autobus-station
Rosarium
Freilicht-museum
Schloß
Restaurant
Spielplatz
Autobus-station
Entrance to Open-air Museum
Bahnstation
Rijksweg 22
Genk
Genk

500 m
© Baedeker

——— Boundary of Estate
•••••• Boundary of Open-air Museum

Hasselt

Opening times
Open-air museum:
Apr.–Oct. daily
10am–6pm

widechoice of leisure activities. There is an enormous play area with round-abouts and pony rides for children together with facilities for various sports. Nature lovers can stroll through the arboretum, rose and herb garden. For variety the extensive open-air museum comes first with recon-structions of farmhouses and farmsteads from individual regions of the country. Old crafts such as milling, baking and lace making are demon-strated. A recent addition is a small town with a beer cellar where beer is served that has been brewed in Bokrijk. A total of seven cafés and restau-rants cater for the visitor.

Genk   G 5

The industrial town of Genk lies on the edge of the Kempenland coal mine 12km/8 miles north-east of Hasselt.

Molenvijver

Genk's town park known as the "Molenvijver" is a 21ha/52 acre walker's paradise by a lake.

Museum v. Doren

The painter Emile van Doren (1865–1949) settled in a villa in Genk. It is now a museum displaying some of his works in an unaltered setting.

Police museum

The Genk police museum has over 1000 police hats, 300 uniforms and numerous pieces of equipment.

Limburgse Zoo

6km/4 miles north of Genk the largest zoo in the province of Limburg is laid out on the site of the old coal mine Zwartberg. It has a remarkable bear collection (open: Easter–Oct. daily 9am–7pm).

*Mechelse Heide

Unspoilt heathland can be found on the Mechelse Heide nature reserve 7km/4 miles north-east of Genk.

Railway museum in As

A railway museum has been set up in the 1930s station of the district of As, 10km/6 miles north-east of Genk. It focuses on the history of Belgian Railways in general and coal transport on narrow gauge railways in particular.

Houthalen-Helchteren   G 4

Leisure parks

In the area around the twin community of Houthalen-Helchteren (13km/8 miles north of Genk) there are three leisure parks offering a variety of

Farmhouses in . . .

. . . Bokrijk Open-Air Museum

entertainment. The Domein Molenheide has water slides, swimming pools, sports grounds, a Robinson park and wildlife park and the Domein Hengelhoef and Kelchterhoef each with a zoo and numerous attractions.

Zolder   G 5

Race track

The 4½km/3 mile Zolder race track (Omloop van Terlamen) is famous outside of Belgium, 11km/7 miles north-west of Hasselt. The Formula I Grand Prix takes place alternating between here and Francorchamps (see Stavelot); other motor car and motorcycle races also take place.

Herentals

See Geel, Surroundings

Hoogstraten

See Antwerp, Surroundings

Huy · Hoei   G 6

Province: Namur. Altitude: 77m/252ft
Population: 17,000
Intercity and Inter-regional Station (bicycle rental at station)

Location

Marche–en–Famenne

The town of Huy (Flemish Hoei) is pleasantly set in an undulating landscape at the confluence of the Meuse and the Hoyoux, approximately half-way between Namur and Liège. Sugar refineries, paper industry and the Tihange atomic power station situated upstream make up the economic base of the town, which is dominated by the powerful citadel. The town's most important buildings are known as the "four wonders": Li Tchestia (the castle, destroyed 1717), Li Pontia (the bridge, its successor is the Pont Roi-Baudouin), Li Rondia (the window rose) and Li Bassinia (the fountain); only the last two still exist in their original form. The two best known masters of metal casting in the Meuse region Renier de

Huy and Godefroid de Claire, the latter also known as Godefroid de Huy, came from Huy. Father Dominique Georges Pire (1910–69), the founder of European Villages and winner of the Nobel Peace Prize in 1958, lived and worked in Huy.

Huy is one of the oldest towns in Belgium. It was mentioned in documents as far back as 636. It received its freedom charter from Prince Bishop Theoduin in 1066. During the High and late Middle Ages it achieved considerable prosperity because of its famous brassworks and wool industry and became a thriving market centre for wine, pewter and copperware. However, as a result of the numerous wars between the prince bishops of Liège and the dukes of Burgundy it gradually declined in importance.

History

The tourist office in Huy organises boat trips on the Meuse.

Trips on the Meuse

Sights

On the right bank of the Meuse stands the handsome Collégiale Notre-Dame, the most important High Gothic church in Belgium. Work began on the foundations of a Romanesque basilica in 1311 and was completed in 1377. The church has an unusual exterior with two towers flanking the crossing tower ("Hemony" carillon in the north tower) and the massive west tower, its spire being destroyed by lightning in 1803. The superb rose window "Li Rondia" is on this tower, diameter 9m/29ft.

*Collégiale Notre-Dame

The 72m/236ft-long church interior receives its light chiefly through the large rosette and the 20m/65ft-high lancet windows in the apse. The fan ribbed vaulting of the polychromic painted crossing is particularly beautiful. In the right-hand side aisle is the 12th c. entrance to the crypt, its floor covered in tiles decorated with coats-of-arms.

Interior

Behind the choir screen (1728) is the treasury with four exceptionally splendid shrines beautifully crafted in metalwork of the Meuse region. The most sumptuous are the shrines of St Mengold and St Domitian, both probably the work of Godefroid de Huy from around 1176; the shrine of Our Lady is from about 1260 and the shrine of St Mark with its rich enamelling from about 1200. Other treasures include the remains of the Holy Cross, brought back by Peter the Hermit from the first crusade, and a chalice and cross from the grave of Prince Bishop Theoduin of Bavaria.

*Treasury

Especially worth seeing is the tympanum (14th c.) of the Bethlehem portal on the east side of the church, where the entrance to the cloister once was. The splendid sculpture depicts the birth of Christ, the worship of the Kings and Shepherds and the murder of the children in Bethlehem, framed by some lively folk scenes.

Portail de Bethléem

Not far to the east of the church is the Grand-Place with the copper fountain "Li Bassinia" from 1406, the only surviving Gothic bronze fountain in Belgium. The town hall (hotel de ville) is here, a splendid Louis XV building from 1766. Inside is a small collection of paintings.

Grand-Place

From the Place Verte behind the town hall a narrow street passes St Mengold church, founded 1244, in its present form the 17th c. Couvent des Frères Mineurs (Franciscan monastery). It accommodates the Musée communal (district museum) which has twelve rooms displaying pewter, glass, porcelain, coins and medals, faiences, guild signs, archaeological finds, paintings and religious art.

*Musée communal

Particularly interesting are three rooms completely furnished with old Walloon furniture and household objects, the moving figure of Christ "Beau Dieu de Huy" in oak (13th c.) and a cast of the font from St Barthélemy in Liège by Renier de Huy (open: Apr.–mid. Oct. Mon.–Sat. 2–6pm; Sun. and public holidays also 10am–noon).

Diagonally opposite the museum is the 16th c. Tour d'Oultremont.

Tour d'Oultremont

View of Huy from the Meuse

Left bank of the Meuse	On the left bank of the Meuse approximately at the same height as the Collégiale Notre-Dame is the Maison de Batta from 1575, former refugium of the Abbey Val-Saint-Lambert. To the north is the church of St-Pierre with a 12th c. Meuse font.
Citadel	A cableway from the left bank and a lift on the Chaussée Napoléon at the base of the fortress on the right bank ascend to the citadel which was built by the Dutch in 1818 and later captured by the Belgians. During the Second World War it was used by the German occupying forces as a prison, with many of the 7000 prisoners being dragged off to concentration camps. On the tour of the fortress old guns, weapons and casemates can be seen and also the interrogation and torture rooms used by the Gestapo (open: May–Sept. daily 9am–6pm).
La Sarte	The cableway, built in 1957, with wonderful views continues up to La Sarte where there are playgrounds, sport areas and a cafeteria.

Surroundings

Amay

G 6

On the left bank of the Meuse, on the edge of the Hesbaye, is situated the little town of Amay 8km/5 miles north-east of Huy. A visit to the church of Saint-George-et-Saintr Ode is highly recommended. It was begun in 1089 in Mosan Romanesque; the nave and west porch are still from that period, with the other parts being 16th–18th c. additions. During restoration work a 7th c. sarcophagus was found below the choir with the inscription "Santa Chrodoara", possibly the coffin of Saint Ode. Also worth seeing are the magnificent high altar (17th–18th c.) and the treasury. The reliquary shrine

* Reliquary

of Saints Ode and George constitute a masterpiece of Mosan goldwork. The shrine (around 1230) made of gold-hammered copper has pictures of the two saints on its end wall and on its side walls the 12 apostles. The depiction of St George idealised as a medieval knight is particularly impressive. Below the sacristy, where further valuable religious works of art are on show, the remains of Roman building were found.

*Château de Jehay

G 6

The château of Jehay, 10km/6 miles north-east of Huy, has under its roof one of the most interesting archaeological collections in Belgium, in addition to noteworthy paintings. On the site of a Romanesque castle the present day château was built in the 16th c. in an L-shape with characteristic chequered façade, surrounded by parkland with ponds and lakes.

Opening times:
May–Sept.
Sat., Sun.
public holidays
2–6pm

The extensive art collection of the present owner Guy van den Steen is displayed in some rooms of the house. It includes tapestries (Brussels, Aubusson), paintings (Tintoretto, Bruegel, Murillo, Peter Lely), Mosan goldwork and much more; notable individual pieces are a clock by Porlaine, commisioned by Marie-Antoinette and the lace bridal veil of the wife of the Duke of Marlborough in a room devoted to this English commander.

Art collection

In the Gothic vaults of the château alongside a speleological collection is the impressive archaeological collection which features a unique bone ice-skate and a prehistoric pipe made of human bone.

Archaeological
collection

*Château de Modave

G 7

12km/8 miles south of Huy high above the Hoyoux is the Château de Mondave with its striking flecked main tower. Onto the part of the building projecting over the river the French architect Jean Goujon built a château in

Opening times:
daily 9am–6pm
tours on the hour

Château de Modave

the most attractive Louis XIV style with numerous water games. These are supplied by a hydraulic machine, invented by the carpenter Rennequin Sualem from Liège, which pumps up water from the Hoyoux. In 1669 Sualem constructed similar grounds for Louis XIV's château in Marly, near Versailles.

Château rooms The grand rooms of the château, twenty of which are included in the tour, are richly appointed with 17th and 18th c. furniture. The architect and sculptor Jean-Christian Haensche designed the multi-coloured stucco ceilings in the vestibule (heraldic family tree of the owners Comtes de Marchin) and in the Hercules room. The alcoves of the Duchess de Montmorency, the cousin of the French king, are especially splendid.

Bois-et-Borsu The church of Saint-Lambert in Bois-et-Borsu, 7km/4 miles south-east of the château, contains beautiful 15th c. frescoes representing scenes from the life of Christ and the Saints Lambert and Hubert. The small church was built in 911 and altered around 200 years later.

Jehay (Château)

See Huy, Surroundings

Knokke-Heist   B 3

Province: West-Vlaanderen
Altitude: sea level
Population: 31,000
Intercity Station (bicycle rental at Knokke station)

Knokke-Heist: the Casino

Together with Ostend, Knokke-Heist, situated near the Dutch border in an attractive landscape of dunes, is probably the most elegant seaside resort in Belgium. The broad beach is 12km/8miles long and comprises approximately one fifth of the Belgian coastline.

Seaside resort

Since 1880 the present tourist resort has developed very rapidly from the small fishing village of Knokke to merge with the residential suburb Het Zoute and the newer suburb of Albertstrand, and until the Thirties was one of the leading seaside resorts in Europe, patronized by the British. In recent years the coastal towns of Heist and Duinbergen have been absorbed into the growing built-up area. The entire agglomeration can accommodate five times its population in several thousand apartments, 120 hotels and guest houses and five campsites, which, during the high season, is not unproblematic. To the large amount of accommodation available in the town can be added an unusually wide range of entertainment and recreational facilities, with something to offer every visitor.

Among the best walks in and around Knokke-Heist are the "Bloemenwandeling" through the residential suburb of Het Zoute, the "Landelijke Knokke" and the "Polderwandeling" through the attractive dune landscape. The 7km/4 miles long Zeedijk which stretches from Heist past Duinbergen to Het Zoute across the wide beach, is lined with numerous hotels and villas. The tourist information office has brochures with a total of ten cycle tours in the surroundings of Knokke-Heist.

Walks and cycle tours

As well as the permanent choice of entertainment there are occasional important fairs and festivals which are mainly held in the Scharpoord cultural centre or in the casino. These include the Kartoenale (World Cartoon Exhibition), the Knokke European Song Contest and the folk festival in July and August.

Festivals

Heist

The western part of this agglomeration is Heist which is increasingly in danger of being swallowed up by the expanding town of Zeebrugge (see entry). The regional museum illustrates the history of fishing, local crafts and everyday life and the "Humorhall" has a collection of humorous photographs.

Visitors can get in trim at the "Meer van Heist", an indoor swimming pool with sea water and artificial waves, and the "Fit-o-meter" keep fit park.

Knokke and Albertstrand

Knokke's busy main street is the Lippenslaan, which, near the railway station, adjoins the Verweeplein with the town hall and monument to the animal painter A. Verwee.

To the west of Knokke is the new quarter of Albertstrand with the famous Casino situated alongside the dike. It is worth a look as it contains some fine works of art as well as offering roulette and other gambling games. The sculpture "Le poète" by Ossip Zadkine stands in front of the building. In the foyer hangs a 7 tonne chandelier made from 22,000 pieces of glass, considered to be the largest in Europe. The walls are hung with works by famous painters including René Magritte's "Le Domaine enchanté".

The Zegemeer is an artificial lake in the dunes. On its south bank was built the Scharpoord cultural centre with the modern Institute for Thalasso therapy.

Het Zoute

Het Zoute, with its elegant villas set back in the dunes and the evening meeting place of Albertplein, owes its reputation as a fashionable seaside resort to Knokke-Heist. The Royal Golf Club de Zoute, with two 18-hole courses, one of the largest in Europe, and the grounds of the Riding Club add to this.

A more recent attraction is the butterfly garden in the Bronlaan with exotic and indigenous butterflies under 425sq.m/4575sq.ft of glass (open: mid Apr.–mid Oct. daily 10am–5.30pm).

** Het Zwin Nature Reserve near Knokke-Heist

Opening times:
Apr.–Sept.
daily
9am–7pm;
Oct.–Mar.
until 5pm

Guided walks
Apr.–Sept.
Thur. and Sun.
10am

The Het Zwin nature reserve stretches from the end of Het Zoute over the Belgian-Dutch border. Some two fifths of the 150ha/370 acres are accessible to walkers.

Het Zwin is now the silted inlet that once made Bruges (see Bruges) one of the richest harbours in Europe. Today the countryside, bordered by dunes and the sea dyke and criss-crossed by rivulets subject to the tides, provides a unique habitat for plants and animals. Over 100 species of bird nest in Zwin, among which are waders, ducks, the silver plover and snipe. At the entrance to the nature reserve the indigenous species are kept on several ponds and in aviaries so that the visitor can see many of the birds at close hand without disturbing those in the wild. The best times to visit are in Spring, to see the birds, and in July and August when the ground is covered with sea of blossom, the "Zwinneblom".

Koksijde · Coxyde   A 4

Province: West-Vlaanderen
Altitude: sea level
Population: 10,000

Brugge

The seaside resort of Koksijde (French Coxyde), especially popular with families, developed from a small fishing village at the beginning of this century. Today the resort consists of Koksijde-Dorp, Koksijde-Bad and the residential suburb Sint-Idesbald to the south-west and caters for a wide range of leisure activities.

Location

Koksidje is famous for its flower market, the fishermen's festival and the flower-covered artists' procession.

Festivals

Sights

The highest and longest dune on the Belgian coast, the 33m/108ft high and 42ha/103 acre "Hoge Blekker", is here in Koksijde. Guided walks are organised through the Schipgat dunes with its flora and fauna, the north dunes and the "Doornpanne" and "Kerkepanne" nature reserves.

Natural Monuments

The ruins of the Duinenabdij of Koksijde are among the most notable sacral buildings on the Belgian coast. The abbey was founded in 1107 by the Benedictines and taken over by the Cistercians in 1138 who built dykes to reclaim sizeable strips of land from the sea and farmed large areas. The monks were driven away when the monastery was destroyed in 1578. The ruins of the building give an idea of the size of the abbey. The narthex, the 129m/423ft-long nave of the church of 1214, the cloisters, the refectory and parts of the monastery kitchen can still be seen.
Excavated finds on display in the museum comprise ceramics, architectural remains, glass, coins and documents on the history of the monastery (open: July–Sept. daily 10am–6pm; otherwise daily 9am–noon and 1.30–5pm).

Duinenabdij

The Onze-Lieve-Vrouw-ter-Duinen church is a remarkable modern creation by the Bruges architect Langsoght from 1965. Its wavy roof and blue paint express the sea, whereas the beige bricks symbolise the dunes formed

Onze-Lieve-Vrouw-ter-Duinenkerk

255

by the wind. The light interior houses in the crypt the tomb of St Iselbald, 12th c. abbot of the abbey. The statue of Onze-Lieve-Vrouw-ter-Duinen weighing 2.8 tonnes is by Brigitte Loire.

Paul Delvaux Museum

Paul Delvaux, after René Magritte the most well known Belgian Surrealist, spent a lot of time in Koksijde and painted many of his paintings here. An extensive collection of paintings and drawings by the artist are displayed in the museum dedicated to him in a villa in Sint-Idesbald (open: Apr.–June and Sept. Tues.–Sun. 10.30am–6.30pm; July and Aug. also Mon.; Oct.– Dec. Sat. and Sun. 10.30am–4pm).

Surroundings

Oostduinkerke

°Shrimp fishing on horseback

Oostduinkerke, 3km/2 miles east of Koksijde, used to be a quiet fishing town and seaside resort. A type of shrimp fishing, which is unique in Europe, is practised here. At the ebb tide the fishermen ride through the shallow water on sturdy cart-horses. The animals trail large nets behind them at a leisurely pace and from time to time the rider empties the catch into the baskets on the horse's back. This custom is celebrated in the annual shrimp festival held at the end of June, when a "Mieke Garnaal", a shrimp queen is chosen.

National Visserijmuseum

The National Visserijmuseum (National Fishing Museum) is dedicated to the history and technology of fishing and has a collection of model fishing boats, instruments and tools. There are even reconstructions of a fishermen's tavern and cottage (open: daily 10am–noon and 2–6pm).

Florishof in Oostduinkerke

The Florishof is a restored group of buildings which is now a folklore museum with exhibitions of furniture, lace and everyday objects.

Fishing for shrimps on the beach at Oostduinkerke

Sint-Niklaaskerk is an original building from 1954 with its pointed roofs and massive tower. Unusual are the absence of a choir and the columns in the yellowish interior which seem to sprout out of the ground.

Sint-Niklaaskerk

The SunAquaPark is a spacious swimming paradise.

SunAquaPark

4km/2 miles to the south of Koksijde, Hof Ten Bogaerde was the refuge of the monks who fled the destruction of the Duinenabdij. It was laid out as long ago as 1184 but today only ruins remain, the most noteworthy being the large 13th c. barn.

**Hof
Ten Bogaerde**

Kortrijk · Courtrai

B 5

Province: West-Vlaanderen
Altitude: 19m/62ft
Population: 76, 500
Intercity and Inter-regional Station (bicycle rental at station)

The town of Kortrijk (French Cortrai) is situated on the River Leie (French Lys), which is connected to the Scheldt by a canal. The economy of Kortrijk has been based on the textile industry which has its beginnings in the 14th c. The raw material flax is grown in the surrounding area of Flanders and is processed in several spinning, weaving and finishing mills. Kortrijk is also important for man-made fibres and has large flax treatment plants and other textile processing concerns (clothing, linen, carpets, canvas). In recent years efforts have been made to diversify from concentration on the single crisis-prone textile industry. New industries introduced include engineering, building materials, electronics, jewellery, rubber, furniture and printing. Polishing of precious stones is also a well known and economically important activity. In addition Kortrijk is the economic and cultural centre of an area encompassing 300,000 people and with a department of the Catholic University of Louvain (see Louvain) is also a

Location

257

university town. In the "Hallen" built in 1967 important trade fairs and
congresses take place.

History

Kortrijk was already an important junction of two roads in Roman times
when it was known as Cortoriacum. In Merovingian times it had the right to
mint coins. It became the seat of a Flemish burgrave and in 1189 was
elevated to the status of town. Its period of prosperity was in the late Middle
Ages, when it developed into a centre of the Flemish cloth industry. When
this declined in the 16th c. it was replaced by linen weaving based on the
local cultivation of flax, which is still dominant today. The prosperous
trading and industrial town was badly damaged during the wars of Louis
XIV and in both world wars. Rebuilding radically altered the townscape,
however, some architectural monuments have remained intact.

Battle of the
Golden Spurs

On 11th July 1302 close to Kortrijk the Battle of the Golden Spurs took place
on the battlefield on the Groeningekouter. Here the Flemish, mainly armed
men on foot from the towns of Bruges and Ypres, routed an army of French
knights under the command of Robert, Count of Artois. This battle was of
international importance for two reasons: firstly, this victory assured the
English allied to the Flemish towns important landing places in the
Hundred Years' War; secondly, it was the first time in history that an army
of knights had been conquered by foot soldiers, thereby severely deflating
the myth attached to the knights – their downfall had begun. After the battle
the victorious Flemish weavers collected over 700 knights' spurs and hung
them as a symbol of their triumph in the nave of the Onze-Lieve-Vrouwkerk
in Kortrijk. They remained there until 1382 when the French inflicted a
crushing defeat on the Flemish near Rozebeke, and one of their first acts
after the victory was to expunge the humiliation of 1302 and remove the
spurs from the church.
However, 11th July remained the most important day in Flemish history
and has been a national public holiday since the 19th c.

Sights

Grote Markt
Belfry

The Grote Markt is in the centre of Kortrijk. Standing in the middle is the
belfry with five small towers, the only remains of the cloth halls built in
1307. Two copper figures "Manten'" and "Kalle" strike the hour. On the
reverse of the tower is a memorial to those who died in the First World War.

°Stadhuis

In the north-west corner of the market is the Gothic stadhuis (town hall),
built 1418–20, enlarged in the 16th and 19th c. and restored in 1962. The
façade is decorated with statues of the Counts of Flanders. In the historic
Schepenzal on the ground floor is a magnificent Gothic fireplace (1527)
with statues of the Virgin, local saints and allegorical scenes of justice. A
similar fine fireplace adorns the old council chamber upstairs; depicted are
Charles V in the centre, the Vices and expressive scenes on the theme "The
unholy influence of women on men" with a representation of Aristotle and
a woman riding on his back. Two maps of Kortrijk and the surroundings
from 1641 hang on the walls of the hall.

Sint-Maartens-
hoofdkerk

Not far to the east of the market is Sint-Maartenshoofdkerk dating from the
second half of the 13th c.; it was destroyed by the French in 1382 and later
rebuilt. The original tower in Brabant Gothic with a carillon with 49 bells
was rebuilt following a fire in 1862. In the main nave of the triple-aisled
interior the main features are a carved late Renaissance pulpit and in the
choir a 6½m/21ft-high hexagonal tabernacle by Henrik Mauris (1585)
together with fine goldwork and paintings (de Crayer, Karel van Mander, J.
Ykens, F. Francken among others) of the 16–18th c.

°°Begijnhof

Immediately adjoining the church is the picturesque béguinage founded by
Joanna of Constantinople in 1242. With its 42 whitewashed cottages
closely grouped around the landscaped courtyard, an oasis of tranquillity,

The beautiful béguinage at Kortrijk

it is possibly the most attractive béguinage in Belgium. A stroll through the narrow lanes leads to the chapel of 1465, the bleachery and the Chapel of the Virgin of the Snow. The last béguine in Kortrijk died a few years ago. Her memory and that of all other béguines is preserved in the house of the Grootjuffrouw (oldest béguine). It differs from all other cottages in its size and the double stepped gable and is now a museum. Some of the rooms have been kept in their original condition; other rooms are filled with memorabilia on the history of the béguinage in Kortrijk (open: Sat. 2–5pm).

Further north in Begijnhofstraat in a quarter with narrow lanes stands the Onze-Lieve-Vrouwkerk founded by Baldwin IX. Its façade and towers are 13th c. and the choir was completed around 1300. The Flemish poet Guido Gezelle was chaplain of this church for a long time; he is commemorated by a memorial in front of the church. **Onze-Lieve-Vrouwerk**

In the left transept is the outstanding work "The Raising of the Cross" by Anton van Dyck in the style of Rubens. Another notable work of art is a statue of St Catherine wearing a martyr's crown (around 1380) by André Beauneveu in the Chapel of the Counts which was founded by Louis de Male, built in the shape of a parallelogram and decorated with the portraits of Flemish counts. The first 32 of these frescoes were completed in 1378 and are by Johann van der Asselt; the remainder by various artists were added later. *Van Dyck painting

From the church Guido Gezellestraat leads to the Broeltorens, two massive towers of a former fortification of the town of the 12th c. (south "Speyerto-ren") and 13th c. (north "Ingelborchtoren"). Broeltorens

On the opposite bank of the River Leie the Stedelijk Museum voor Schone Kunsten (Municipal Museum of Fine Arts) is at Broelkaai 6, one of the finest patrician houses in the town (17th c.). The museum has an art collection Stedelijk Museum

259

consisting primarily of Kortrijk painters, among them Roeland Savery (1576–1639), a good ceramics department, an archaeology department and a collection, unique in Europe, of 17th and 18th c. damask from Kortrijk's workshops, for which the town was famous (open: Apr.–Sept. daily except Fri. 10am–1pm and 3–6pm; Oct.–Mar. only until 5pm).

National
Vlasmuseum

Some distance from the centre the National Vlasmuseum (National Flax Museum) is housed in a 19th c. flax farmhouse at Etienne Sabbelaan 4. It illustrates the cultivation and processing of flax with 26 slides using life-size figures. There is an inn "In de Vlasblomme" providing refreshments (open: Mar.–mid Nov. daily except Tues. 9.30am–12.30pm and 1.30–6pm; Tues. 1.30–6pm only; Sat. and Sun. 2–6pm).

Battle of the
Golden Spurs
Memorial

To the east outside the town centre can be seen a memorial erected in 1906 in memory of the Battle of the Golden Spurs; it is reached from the Onze-Lieve-Vrouwkerk along Groeningstraat.

Surroundings

Menen

The industrial and commercial border town of Menen, 10km/6 miles south-west of Kortrijk, often changed hands between French and Dutch rulers and suffered many sieges. The town hall in the market was built in 1784 in Classical style; the adjacent octagonal belfry with a carillon of 47 bells is of 16th/17th c. origin.

Wervik

Wervik, 7km/4 miles west of Menen, has a tobacco museum documenting the history of snuff, smoking and chewing tobacco (open: Mar.–Oct., daily 1.30–5.30pm).

Mouscron

In the French-speaking area directly on the border with France is the town of Mouscron, situated on a hill, 7km/4 miles to the south. It is dominated by the 13th c. castle of the Counts of Mouscron.

Tielt

25km/15 miles north of Kortrijk is the small town of Tielt. The ruins of the cloth hall, the belfry and the town hall (stadhuis) together with the other buildings of the Grote Markt make a handsome scene. There is a small museum in the town hall chronicling the everyday life of the countryside around Tielt, the Hageland.

Ingelmunster

Ingelmunster, 11km/7 miles north of Kortrijk, once possessed a mighty fortress and was "the key to Flanders" of great strategic importance. The fortress was replaced in the 18th c. by a splendid château, but is not open to visitors.

Izegem

Izegem is only 3km/2 miles west of Ingelmunster. The National Shoe and Brush Museum in the stadhuis is worth a visit.

Ingooigem

The Flemish poet Stijn Streuvels (1871–1969) was born in Ingooigem, 10km/6 miles to the west. His birthplace in the street named after him is today a museum.

Roeslare

Roeslare, 21km/13 miles north-west of Kortrijk, is home of the poet Albrecht Rodenbach and the blind statesman Alexander Rodenbach. These and other sons of the town are commemorated in the arsenal building on Polenplein. Even the beer brewed here, a bitter "red" beer, is called Rodenbach.

Rumbeke

The Roeslare suburb of Rumbeke has a fine moated castle (16/18th c.) with seven octagonal towers. The Sint-Pieter-Paulskerk contains a Romanesque font of 1200.

Westrozebeke

At Westrozebeke, 8km/5 miles west of Roeslare, the Flemish were heavily defeated in the battle of Rozebeke in 1382.

The Grote Markt of Tielt

Leuven · Louvain

E 5

Province: Brabant
Altitude: 20–40m/65–131ft
Population: 85,000
Intercity and Inter-regional Station (bicycle hire at station)

Leuven (French Louvain) lies on both banks of the Dijle east of Brussels. Together with the suburbs, which were incorporated in 1977, the town is a conglomeration of over 85,000 inhabitants and is the commercial, cultural and administrative centre of East Brabant and southern Kempenland. The many different industries are based mainly in the north of the town along the canal which links the Dijle with the Rupel. Brewing is the chief industry and headquarters of the Stella Artois brewery, with an annual output of over 5 million hectolitres, the largest in Belgium. Despite heavy bombardment in both world wars the university buildings, which are dispersed throughout the town, provide a good impression of architecture from the 15th c. onwards.

Location

The Catholic university, which was founded in 1425 and rapidly became one of the most highly regarded universities in Europe, is world famous. Once the great humanist Erasmus of Rotterdam and Justus Lipsius taught here. The geographer Gerhard Mercator studied here and one of its chancellors was elected Pope Adrian VI in 1459. The university library was unparalleled yet was set on fire by the German occupying forces in 1914 and again in 1940 with the irretrievable loss of over a million volumes. Many regard the division of the university in 1968, following linguistic quarrels between the Flemish and Walloons, as the "Third Destruction": the Francophile teachers and students broke away and established the "Université Catholique de Louvain" in the new university town of Louvain-

**University town

261

la-Neuve (see Louvain-la-Neuve). The books were divided between them on the basis of odd and even shelf-marks – a really insane initiative. Today 24,000 students are matriculated at the university to soak up knowledge as amusingly demonstrated by the statue on the fountain "Fons Sapientiae", known as "Fonske", in the Grote Markt.

History

The first settlement to develop around the castle derived its name from the Low German Loo (bushy hill) and Veen (swamp). It was taken by the Normans, who were in turn driven away at the end of the 9th c., and from the 11th c. onwards a town grew up around the castle of the counts of Leuven. In 1106 the counts became dukes of Lower Lothringia and from 1190 called themselves the Dukes of Brabant. Owing to its position on the main trading route from Cologne to Brussels the town underwent rapid expansion and became the capital of Brabant and centre of cloth-making. Fortified walls were built; their course still visible where the ring-road encircles the inner city. In the 14th c. Leuven with over 100,000 inhabitants was one of the largest cities in Europe and is said to

Leuven: the Fonske Fountain

have had 2500 looms. Internal disputes, in the form of the uprising of the guilds against the patricians in 1379 and resulting in the leaders of the patricians being thrown out of the town hall windows onto upright pikes ending with severe punishment by the Duke of Brabant, the gradual shifting of trade routes and the transfer of the Brabant court to Brussels all led to a decline in trade and crafts. However, at this very time the greatest manifestation of bourgeois pride in the Netherlands took shape in the form of the town hall. In the 15th and 16th c. the university, founded in 1425, a bulwark of Catholic orthodoxy, brought a new impetus for revival. A new period of growth took place in the 19th c. under the Kingdom of Belgium. The town was heavily damaged in both world wars, yet the destruction of the Second World War caused by the German troops and British bombing in 1944 has been rectified.

From 1450 onwards Dirk Bouts, one of the greatest late-Gothic painters of the Netherlands, worked in Leuven. His major work "The Last Supper" can be seen in Sint-Pieterskerk. The painter Quentin Mayssys was born here in 1466.

**Stadhuis

Tours
Mar.–Oct.
Mon.–Fri.
11am and 3pm
Sat., Sun.,
public holidays
3pm

The south side of the Grote Markt, a traffic junction where all the main streets converge in the middle of the town, is dominated by the stadhuis (city hall), built to plans by Sulpitius van Horst, begun by Jan Keldermans II and completed by Matthaeus de Rayens 1448–63. It is one of the most magnificent secular buildings of late Gothic style in Europe and is decorated more lavishly than the city halls of Bruges, Brussels, Ghent and Oudenaarde (see entries). The building, which resembles a shrine, bears De Layens' distinctive architectonic trademark in the form of three narrow smaller towers at each gable end instead of a single tall central tower. Three rows of sculpture adorn the main façade and both side façades. The 236 figures which were only installed at the end of the 19th c. represent eminent personalities from the history of the town, whereas the consoles

Antwerpen   Mechelen   Turnhout

Leuven Louvain

300 m
© Baedeker

laan · Vaart-
Mechelse-
poort
Abdij Keizersberg
Burchtstr.
vest
Vaart
Diestsevest
Vaart

Museum van
Humbeeck-Piron

Mechelse
straat

Dijle

J.-P. Minckelerstraat

Klein Begijnhof

St. Gertrudis
St. Gertrudis-abdij

Scoutsmuseum

Station
straat
Martelaren-plein

St. Pieter
Diestse-

Bondgenotenlaan

Justus Lipsiusstr.

Theresia str.

Tiense-

Diest

Grote Markt
Foch-plein

Museum Vanderkelen Mertens

Stadhuis

Universiteits-bibliotheek

Oude Markt

Tiense

Drievuldig-heidscollege

Universiteits-halle

H. Hoover-plein

Heilige Geest College

St. Michiel

St. Donatus-park

Konink. Atheneum

Frederik Lintsstraat

Vesaliusstraat

Maria Blijde Inkomststr.

straat

Deken-

Brabançonne-

Leo

Geldenaaksevest

Scheursvest

St. Antonius

Naamsestraat

Schapenstraat

Park-

vest

Groot Begijnhof

Redingen-

Tervuurse-

St. Kwinten

Naamse-poort

Naamsevest

Erasme

Ruelensvest

Ronde-

Oude
Mechelse-

Wijnpersstraat

Ridders

Brouwersstr.

Brusselse-

Kaboutermansstr.

Remy-vest

Edward

straat

St. Jakob

Geeststr

Kapucijnenvoer

Tervuurse-poort

Tervuursestraat

Bankstraat

Heilige

Groenveld-

IJzermolenstraat

Broek-

Tervuurse

Bruxelles

Tervuren

Bruxelles, Kasteel van Arenberg

Namur   Abdij van 't Park, Liège

and bases of the niches were carved with reliefs from the Old and New Testament, some of them with medieval coarseness, when the stadhuis was built. Even the roof is richly decorated with small turrets.

Inside the entrance hall are flags of the seven noble families of Leuven. This leads to three rooms newly furnished in the 18th and 19th c. The Great Gothic Council Chamber with its carved beamed ceiling (15th c.) and Gothic fireplace and the Small Gothic Hall with a Gothic vaulted wooden ceiling are noteworthy.

The cellar of the town hall houses the Stedelijk Brouwerijmuseum (Municipal Museum of Brewing) which documents the production of beer and Leuven's history as an important brewing town (open: Tues.–Sat. 10am–noon and 2–5pm; Easter–Sept. also Sun. and public holidays 2–5pm).

Stedelijk Brouwerijmuseum

The building to the left of the town hall is a reconstruction of 1921. Named the Tafelrond, it is the meeting house of the rhetoricians' guild, built at the end of the 15th c. by de Layens.

Tafelrond

** Sint-Pieterskerk

Standing in the middle of the Grote Markt Sint-Pieterskerk is a prime example of Brabant Gothic. Begun in the 15th c. by van Vorst, continued by Keldermans and de Layens, it was more or less completed by Joost Massys. Original plans envisaged three towers on the west side and a main tower of 165m/541ft. This work was abandoned as the foundations were on sand and previous buildings had collapsed.

The Romanesque "Head of Christ"

Interior

The main nave's notable features are its straight line of sheaf pillars and high pointed arch windows. Among the treasures in this part of the church are the late Gothic brass font in the chapel to the left of west gate and the splendidly carved Baroque pulpit of 1742. In the left transept is a Madonna "Sedes Sapientiae" (1441), the patron saint of the Catholic University. The choir is separated from the nave by a richly decorated late Gothic rood screen (1488) depicting a crucifixion scene by Jan Borreman (around 1500). During restoration work the octagonal Romanesque crypt of the original 10th c. church was discovered below the choir.

Choir

The choir and ambulatory have been converted into the Stedelijk Museum voor Religieuze Kunst (Museum of Religious Art). The late Gothic choir stalls have the original carvings; to the left is the impressive 12½m/41ft-high stone tabernacle by de Layens (1450). In the chapels to the right and left of the choir are the tombs of Duke Henry I of Brabant (d. 1235), his wife Mathilde (d. 1211) and his daughter Maria (d. 1260). All that remains of a 12th c. wooden cross, burnt in 1914, is a head of Christ with a pitiful expression. Outstanding is the "Last Supper" the chief work of Dirk Bouts, painted 1464–68 and still well preserved. The supper takes place in a Gothic hall and the figures are arranged around Christ; unlike many representations the betrayal of Judas is not in the foreground, instead it is the symbolic Eucharist, as also portrayed in the side panels. The triptych with the "Martyrdom of St Erasmus" as the centre panel (1465) is also by Bouts; the "Descent from the Cross" is a copy of a masterpiece by his teacher, Rogier van der Weyden.

Along Naamsestraat

To the right of the town hall is Naamsestraat where many university buildings are to be found either in this street or nearby, in particular the college buildings funded by various patrons in the 15th–18th c. to accommodate students and institutes.

Just to the right are the main buildings of the Catholic University, formerly the Lakenhalle (Cloth Hall) built in 1317–45, which became the seat of the university following the decline of the cloth industry. An upper storey was added in the 18th c. and it housed the university library until it was set on fire by the German occupying forces in 1914 destroying the most valuable books. Today it serves as the administrative centre of the university. Items

Lakenhalle/ Universiteitshalle

◀ *The magnificent Stadhuis of Leuven*

from the university's art collection are exhibited in the Jubilee Hall (visits by request).

*Oude Markt

Not far to the west of Naamsestraat is the Oude Markt, the bustling centre of Leuven, especially on summer evenings. Although its historic brick gabled houses were almost completely burnt down in 1914, they have been beautifully rebuilt and now accommodate many pubs and restaurants. A bronze sculpture commemorates the "Kottmadams" of Leuven, the landladies of the student rooms. On the narrow south side of the square is the Collegium Vauxianum (Heilig Drievuldigheidscollege; Holy Trinity College) with a Baroque façade of 1657.

*Sint-Michielskerk

Where Naamsestraat widens, diagonally opposite the Heilig Geest College (founded 1442, 18th c. building), stands Sint-Michielskerk, built 1650–66 by Willem Hesius. It has a splendid Baroque façade, one of the finest of its kind in Belgium. The lane in front of the church off to the left leads to Hogeschoolplein with the Pauscollege (Papal College), founded by Pope Adrian IV in 1523 and rebuilt in the 18th c.

Colleges

Beyond Sint-Michielskerk more colleges line both sides of Naamsestraat, many of which were built in the 18th c.: Koningcolleg (King's College, No. 59) founded by Philipp II of Spain in 1579; the College van Promonstreit (Premonstratensian College, No. 61), founded in 1571; Arras College (No. 63) founded in 1508 by the future Bishop of Arras; the Huis Van 't Sestich (No. 69, Gothic) with the adjacent College van de Hoge Heuvel; the College van Dale (No. 80), founded in 1579 and the oldest, since wonderfully restored, Renaissance building in Leuven; finally the American College (No. 100), founded in 1659 for Cistercians and occupied by American students since 1857.

*Groot Begijnhof

From Naamsestraat head west through the Karmelietenberg and left into Schapenstraat to the picturesque Groot Begijnhof. This romantic complex, traversed by a tributary of the Dijle, was founded in the 13th c. and today comprises over 1000 houses and a church; earlier it encompassed a hospital and a farmhouse. In the 18th c., when 300 béguines were still living in the béguinage, the houses were renovated with stepped gables, mullions and transoms, but the French Revolution brought a temporary halt. Only a few béguines returned afterwards. In 1962 the site was bought by the university and underwent extensive restoration to create student residences and lecture halls. Only the second cottage on the right past the entrance is still furnished as it was when the last béguine died in 1988. The early Gothic béguinage church Sint-Jan-de-Doper, built in the 13/14th c., serves the university community as a place of worship.

Sint-Kwintenkerk

At the end of Naamsestraat is Sint-Kwintenkerk, its towers begun around 1200 and only completed in the 16th c. The choir – possibly by de Layens – and transept were added in the 15th c. The interior houses some notable paintings of the Rubens School.

Other sights

Vlaams Filmmuseum

For the visitor interested in Flemish films there is the Vlaams Filmmuseum in Boekhandelstraat, a short street to left of the town hall from the market (open: Wed. 9am–noon and 1.30–10pm).

*Vanderkelen-Mertens Museum

Leaving the Grote Markt in the direction of the railway station and turning right into Vanderkelenstraat the Vanderkelen Museum, which has the Municipal Museum Collections, is on the right (Savoyestraat 6). It is in three departments: painting with good pictures from the Leuven School (Quentin Massys: "Mourning over Christ"; Pieter Coecke van Aalst "Holy Family"; Michiel Coxie) and other paintings from different periods up to the present; sculpture including a 12th c. Madonna "Sedes Sapientiae", an outstanding alabaster relief (16th c.) and a section of a Passion relief from Antwerp (around 1525); finally craftwork including glass painting from the

The Antwerp Retable of the Passion in the Vanderkelen-Mertens Museum

16–20th c., ceramics, faïences from Delft, porcelain from China and Japan, engravings, coins, goldwork and textiles (open: Tues.–Sat. 10am–noon and 2–5pm; Easter–Sept. also Sun. and public holidays 2–5pm).

Further along the Vanderkelenstraat is the Mgr. Ladeuzeplein. The University Library stands here, designed by the American architect Whitney Warren and built with American donations 1921–28 in Dutch Renaissance style. Above the belfry soars the 85m/278ft-high tower with a carillon worth listening to.
The library's most valuable collections were destroyed in 1914 in the fire and again in 1940, yet it still contains over a million books. The archive and Museum of Flemish Student Life can be found in the library and illustrate the efforts of students in Leuven (visit by request). There is a very original memorial to a balloonist on the neighbouring Hooverplein. — *Univeriteits-bibliothek*

To the north of Grote Markt, between Mechelstraat and the Dijle, set back is the 14th and 15th c. Gothic Sint-Gertrudiskerk. The tower and a chapel were destroyed in the 1944 air raids and the superb choir stalls, of a transitional style between Gothic and Renaissance, were buried under the rubble. They have been restored and are now in the new church built in 1953. — *Sint-Gertrudiskerk*

Sint-Gertrudiskerk belongs to the Benedictine Abbey of Sint-Gertrudis, which also suffered heavy damage in the Second World War. The former chapel houses the Scouts Museum, which illustrates the history of the Scouting Movement (open: May–Sept. Sun. 2–6pm). — *Scouts Museum*

North of the church stands the Smaller Béguinage, founded in the 13th c. The present day houses in traditional brick and sandstone were built in the 17th and 18th c. — *Klein Begijnhof*

The Keizersberg at the end of Mechelsestraat is crowned by the Keizersberg Abbey, built in neo-Romantic style in the last century on the site of the former castle of the Dukes of Brabant. — *Keizersberg*

The Museum van Humbeeck-Piron on the ring road west of the Keizersberg is dedicated to the work of the Leuven artists Pierre van Humbeeck (1891–1964) and Maria Piron (1888–1969) (open: daily except Tues. 10am–6pm). — *Museum van Humbeeck-Piron*

Surroundings

South-east of the town lies the Premonstratensian Abdij van t' Park, founded by Gottfried the Bearded in 1129; today most of the buildings date — **Abdij van t' Park* from the 16th and 18th c. The visitor is taken through two gateways and a long entrance, past the watermill and the estate to the courtyard of the prelate's house. The tour continues to the former abbots' palace, the chapterhouse with its mixture of Gothic and Renaissance styles, the library and the refectory, which both have fine stucco reliefs. The monastery church is of 12/13th c. origin, being redesigned in the 17/18th c.

Kessel-Lo
Abdij van
Vlierbeek

The town of Kessel-Lo is situated 4km/2 miles east of Leuven. The Abdij van Vlierbeek was founded here in 1127 and inhabited by the Benedictines. The troops of William of Orange destroyed the site in 1572 and it was several decades later before it was rebuilt. The main and adjoining buildings were built 1642–1730, the abbey church followed later in 1776–94.

Provinciaal-
domein

The provinciaal domein of Kessel-Lo offers numerous sporting and recreational facilities.

Kasteel van
Arenberg

2km/1 mile south-west of Leuven at Heverlee the Kasteel van Arenberg (16th c.) on the Dijle has fine grounds and is well worth a visit. The château with its two striking corner towers with gabled roofs was built in traditional late Gothic style with Renaissance features and today is the property of the Catholic University, which maintains several institutes here and in the grounds.

IJse Valley

The IJse, a tributary of the Dijle, flows through peaceful green countryside to the south-west of Leuven, where vegetables, especially chicory, are grown and grapes are pressed.

Korbeek-
Dijle

The church of Korbeek-Dijle has an outstanding carved altar representing the life of St Stephan from 1522.

t' Zoet Water

Only a few kilometres east of Korbeek-Dijle are the five lakes of the recreation area and park t' Zoet Water (Gentle Water).

Overijse

The IJse continues to the town of Overijse, the birthplace of the humanist Justus Lipsius (1547–1606).

Liège · Luik   G 6

Province: Liège
Altitude: 70m/230ft
Population: 205,000, with suburbs 490,000
Intercity and Inter-regional Station

Location

Liège (Flemish Luik), the third largest town in Belgium, is situated on the confluence of the Meuse (Maas) and the Ourthe. It is the capital of the province of the same name and of French-speaking Wallonia, seat of a university and of a bishop, and owing to its locational advantages and long tradition an important industrial centre with one of the largest inland ports in Europe. Liège was one of the first places on the continent to start mining coal, thereby creating the base for the coal and steel industry, to which has been added a range of other manufacturing industries. Today more than 200,000 workers are employed in mining, blast furnaces, steel (40% of Belgian steel production), textiles, food, electrical equipment, chemical products, glassware (famous glass production in Val Saint-Lambert), not forgetting weapons manufacture ("FN" small arms from the Fabrique Nationale in Herstal). Liège is the home of the author Georges Simenon (see Introduction, Famous People), who immortalised the town in his work, and enjoys increasing importance as a place of research and science (university, technical colleges and institutes). Liège is at the junction of important international roads and railway lines and an important trade centre for inland river traffic, which in recent years has suffered considerable losses: the waterways of the Rhine and Ruhr, the Albert Canal, which links the Scheldt with the Meuse, and canals crossing the Hainaut from France, unite in Liège and continue into the Netherlands. The inland port covers 97ha/239 acres and can accommodate ships up to 2500 tonnes.

There is also a yachting marina. Liège is not a particularly attractive town, considering the devastation it has suffered throughout its history and only has a few buildings of historic interest. However, the town's long history is documented in the many churches which avoided destruction and in its many museums, which range among the best in the country.

According to legend Liège developed around a chapel which St Hubert, Bishop of Tongeren-Maastricht, had built in 705 on the spot where his predecessor, St Lambert, was murdered. In 721 Hubert moved the seat of his bishopric from Tongeen to Liège, but it was under Bishop Notker (972–1008), who elevated the bishopric to the status of a principality, that the town and region began to prosper. In contrast to the Flemish towns the citizens of the Prince-Bishopric, which belonged to the Holy Roman Empire of the German Nation, were involved in bitter quarrels with the bishop over their freedom, as his first allegiance was to the Catholic church. The internal feuds of the 13th and 14th c. were characterised by revolts against the rulers who tried to compromise and called for calm; as did Johann of Bavaria, appointed bishop in 1390, leader of a ruthless régime until 1417. At this time of turmoil the metallurgical industry was beginning to develop. Catastrophe befell Liège when in the 15th c. the Dukes of Burgundy, who had already acquired the rest of Belgium, attempted to take the principality, but came up against heavy opposition from the population. In 1467 the troops of Charles the Bold took the city and its fortifications were razed. The city rose again, but not even the efforts of 600 Franchimontois to break the siege could prevent the town being stormed, plundered and set ablaze again. The city burned for seven weeks and Charles the Bold ordered that only the churches and monasteries should survive the fire. It was not until 1475 that the citizens of Liège received permission to rebuild their town. With his death in 1477 they regained their independence which they again had to defend against Guillaume de la Marck. Under the prince bishop, Erard de la Marck (1505–38), a new period of prosperity began coinciding

History

Liège: Market on the Quai de la Batte

with the work of Liège's greatest painter, Lambert Lombard (1505–66). In the same century, as well as later, there was new progress as a result of coal mining and weapons manufacture. Repeated power struggles between the guilds, made powerful by industry, and the prince bishops ended this time with the victory of the bishops; several mayors were sent to the scaffold in the 17th c. One of the most important sculptors of the 17th c., Jean Delcour (1631–1701), lived here at this time. Only 100 years later the French Revolution put an end to the ecclesiastical domination and for a short time Liège was the capital of the French département of Ourthe. In the 19th c., in particular since the founding of Belgium as an independent country, Liège began to develop into an important industrial city which found expression in its urban architecture. In 1889 the Fabrique Nationale was founded.

In the First World War Belgian regiments in Liège held off the advance of the German army long enough for the French and remaining Belgian troops to form. In 1939 the Albert Canal was opened. At first Liège sustained little damage during the Second World War, but following the withdrawal of the German occupying forces between November 1944 and January 1945 it was the target of over 1500 V2 rockets which damaged or destroyed over 23,000 buildings. In recent times Liège has been affected by the crisis in the steel industry; since the end of the Eighties the city has an enormous debt problem and is more or less bankrupt. Local government employees fearful of their salaries sought to bring attention to their demands by drastic action: firemen occupied public buildings and did not put out fires, civil servants threw mountains of files out of the offices onto the streets and the police supported it all by benevolent non-intervention.

Tour of the city

Tour programme

The sights of Liège are not very far apart so that the most important – Palais des Princes-Evêques, Musée Curtius, Musée de la Vie Wallone and the Church Saint-Barthélemy – can easily be visited on foot in one day. The museums on the right bank of the Meuse can be reached by bus (departure from Place Saint-Lambert).

Guided tours and trips on the Meuse

Guided tours are organised by the tourist office (see Practical Information, Information). A brochure is available here with a city walk following the steps of Georges Simenon and information on boat trips on the Meuse, including Visé (see entry).

Views

The best views over the city are from the Citadel and the Parc de Cointe to the south, where the Basilique du Sacré-Coeur (1936) and the immense Monument Interallié (Monument to the Allies in the First World War; 1937) can be seen.

Left Bank of the Meuse

Palais des Princes-Evêques and Surroundings

The central area of the city is formed by Place Saint-Lambert and the adjoining squares Place du Marché (Market Place) in the north-east and the Place de la République Française in the south-west. The Place du Maréchal de Foch joins the Boulevard de la Sauvenière. As all four squares are choked by traffic a new road system is being introduced. The district east of the Place Saint-Lambert is the oldest part of the city.

Place Saint-Lambert

Until 1796 the Cathédrale Saint-Lambert, the largest cathedral in the Netherlands at that time, stood in the Place Saint-Lambert. It was destroyed by the French revolutionaries and their supporters in Liège and the ruins moved in 1808. The excavations of the church foundations and the hypocaust of a Roman villa below the square are accessible by a staircase.

Citadelle

Place Hocheporte
Académie des Beaux-Arts
Musée de la Vie Wallonne
St-Barthélemy
Place Paul Janson
Quai St-Léonard

Rue de L'Académie
Gare du Palais
R. du Palais
St-Antoine
Féronstrée
Pont St-Léonard
Quai St-Léonard

R. Sainte Marguerite
R. de Bruxelles
Palais des Princes-Évêques
En
La Batte
Quai de Maestricht
Quai Godefroid Kurth

St-Martin
Mont Saint-Martin
Ste-Croix
Place du Marché
Musée d'Art Wallon
Quai des Tanneurs

VIEILLE
St-Lambert
Place Marché
Hôtel de Ville

la Sauvenière
Place Maréchal Foch
Rue Léopold

Théâtre Royal
Place de la République Française
Pont des Arches
St-Pholien
Boulevard de la Constitution
Rue des Bonnes Villes

R. de la Casquette
St-Jean
St-Denis
Place de la Cathédrale
Ch. des Prés
Théâtre de la Place
Place du Congrès

VILLE
Place Cockerill
Passerelle Saucy
St-Nicolas
Rue St-Nicolas
Maison Grétry

R. sur-la-Fontaine
Boulevard de la Sauvenière
Université
Rue d'Ourreuneuse

St-Cristophe
R. Pont d'Avroy
St-Paul
Musée Préhistoire
Musée Tchantchès
Rue Jean d'Entre 2 Ponts

Rue Saint-Gilles
Place du Roi Albert
Quai Ed. Van Beneden
Rue d'Pitteurs
Musée de Zoologie
Rue L. Jamme

Abbaye Bénédictine de la Paix N.-D.
Place St-Jacques
St-Jacques
Pont J. Kennedy
R. Méan
Quai de l'Ourthe
St-Remacle

Rue Darchis
Boulevard d'Avroy
Quai Marcellis
Rue de la Boverie
Grétry
Quai de Longdoz
Fort de la Chartreuse

Jardin Botanique
Boulevard Louvrex
Conservatoire
Quai de la Meuse
Rue d'Harscamp
Rue des Champs
Basse

Rue Fabry
Avenue Rogier
Boulevard Frère Orban
Parc d'Avroy
Pont Albert Ier
Rue Natalis
Grétry
Rue du Beau Mur

Meuse / Maas

Musée du Fer et du Charbon

Place de Bronckart
Av. Blonden
Jardin d'Acclimatation
Quai Mozart
Boulevard R. Poincaré

Guillemins Gare
Rue du Plan Incliné
R. des Guillemins
Rue de Serbie
Palais des Congrès
Tour
Musée des Transports
Rue de Fétinne

Point de Vue
Avenue Mandeville
R. Dartois
Paradis
Rue R. de Sclessin
Parc de la Boverie
Dérivation
Bd. de Froidmont

l'Observatoire
Rue Mandeville
R. de Kinkempois
Musée d'Art moderne
Quai de Rome
Mathiva
Rue de Fétinne
Vennes

Liège Luik
300 m
Varin
Fragnée
Pont de Fragnée
St-Vincent
Boulevard Émile de Laveleye

© Baedeker
Place du Batty
Basilique du Sacré-Cœur
Monument Interallié
Av. E. Digneffe
Quai Gloesener
Quai des Ardennes
Ourthe
Condroz

Namur, Flughaten, Bruxelles
Aachen
Luxembourg

1 Musée d'Ansembourg   2 Musée d'Armes   3 Musée Curtius   4 Fontaine du Perron

271

Georges Simenon was born at No. 24 Rue Léopold which leads from the square to the Meuse.

*Palais des
Princes-Evêques

On the north side of the Place Saint-Lambert stands the Palais des Princes-Evêques, the former palace of the prince-bishops. Notker had the first modest bishop's seat built here, which – after being extended – was destroyed at the end of the 15th c. Erard de la Marck was responsible for the rebuilding, which was completed 1526–40 according to plans by Arnold van Mulckens in the transition style betwen Gothic and Renaissance. 1734–40 the new (south) main façade was added. Today the building houses the Law Courts and is the seat of the Walloon government.

There are two picturesque courtyards with arcaded walkways and columns. The artists who carved the columns with fools' masks and grotesque faces were inspired by Sebastian Brants and Erasmus and news from the New World. The second courtyard is more peaceful with a fountain. The palace interior is not open to visitors.

Place du Marché

South-east of the palace of the prince-bishops stretches the tree-lined Place du Marché, the market square surrounded by Baroque houses. From here the narrow street En Neuvice, once the street of goldsmiths and today a pedestrian zone, leads down to the Meuse.

Perron

In the middle of the market square stands the Perron, which to the communities of the former prince-bishopric symbolized their much-fought for and documented liberty. The Perron, erected in 1697 on the site of a much older predecessor, stands in the centre of the fountain created by Jean Delcour and is crowned by the Three Graces.

Hôtel de Ville

The Baroque Hôtel de Ville (town hall), built 1714–18, stands on the south side of the market square, still referred to as "La Violette" after the first meeting hall of the town council. It was destroyed in 1468 by Charles the Bold, again in 1691 by the French. In the interior there is an interesting foyer.

Palais des Princes-Evêques: the main façade . . .

The onion-shaped cupola of the former church of Saint-André (1772), now a concert hall, dominates the market square.

Saint-André

The north-east corner of the palace of the prince-bishops overlooks the Court des Mineurs, the former Minorite monastery built in the 17th c. in the style of the Meuse Renaissance. It houses the Musée de la Vie Wallonne, where 350,000 exhibits and documents illustrate life and culture in the Walloon part of Belgium. The most modern technology and a presentation in four languages make it one of the best museums to visit in Belgium. In the former chapterhouse on the ground floor there are temporary exhibitions. The rooms on the first floor are each dedicated to a different theme, for example, national religion, magic, festivals, housework, heating and lighting and craftwork. On display are puppets, various workshops (chandlers, pipemakers, coopers, pewterers) and an unusual collection of old sundials. The upper floor is devoted to agricultural crafts such as cheesemaking and basketmaking and to coal mining in Wallonia; in the basement there is a reproduction of a coal mine tunnel around 1900. Traditional puppet shows using old puppets are performed in the adjoining Maison Chamart. A branch of the museum is the Musée du Fer et du Charbon (see p. 278).

** Musée de la Vie Wallonne

Opening times
Tues.–Sat.
10am–5pm,
Sun. and public
holidays
10am–4pm

Adjoining the Musée de la Vie Wallonne in the Rue Mère-Dieu is the Musée d'Art Religeux (Museum of Religious and Mosan Art). It was the former Diocesan museum and exhibits in nine rooms religious works from the churches of Liège and the Meuse region (open: Tues.–Sat. 1–6pm, Sun. 11am–4pm).

Musée d'Art
Religieux

From En Hors Château, which runs south of the above-mentioned museum complex, a short way on the left the Montagne de Bueren steps climb up to the Citadel. At the beginning of the steps the narrow alley Impasse des Ursulines leads into the quiet former monastery of the Holy Spirit and the

Musée
d'Architecture

. . . and the second courtyard

adjacent postal station which now accommmodate the Museum of Architecture. There are examples of Liège architecture but it is primarily a
document centre for the history of building in the town. In the postal station
the study of the Liège violinist Eugène Isaye (1859–1931) can be seen
(open: daily except Tues. and Thur. 1–6pm).

Detour to the citadel

The climb up the 374 steps of the Montagne du Bueren up to the Parc de la
Citadelle (158m/518ft) is rewarded with a fine view of the city. The park
incorporates the grounds and bastions of the 18th c. citadel (now a barracks). Either return the same way or continue along the path already
started, which finally leads back down to the church of Saint-Barthélemy.

Along the Féronstrée

Féronstrée

This street runs from the east side of the market square through the heart of
the Old Town to the church of Saint-Barthélemy. Its name is a reminder that
in the Middle Ages the forges, iron foundries and the offices of the metal
merchants together with the guilds' meeting houses were found here.
Most of the buildings which escaped demolition are from the 18th c.

Musée de l'Art Wallon

About halfway along this street is the Ilot Saint-Georges Complex with the
Musée de l'Art Wallon which houses paintings, sculptures and drawings by
Walloon artists such as Joachim Patinir, Lambert Lombard, Henri Blès and
Jean Delcour (open: Tues.–Sat. 1–6pm, Sun. 11am–4.30pm).

* Musée Ansembourg

Opening times
Thur.–Sun.
1–5pm

A short distance past the Ilot Saint-Georges is the beautiful façade of the
house built 1735–40 for Michel Willems, a patrician whose granddaughter
married a Count Ansembourg. Converted into a museum it is an eloquent
example of the bourgeois lifestyle of the nobility in the 18th c. It contains a
wooden Madonna from Delcour in the entrance hall, leather wall hangings
from Córdoba, a stucco ceiling and an exemplary china cabinet in the
dining room, tapestries in the Salon des Tapisseries from Oudenaarde (see
Oudenaarde) and a magnificent inlaid table from the Prince-Bishop's palace as well as a huge fireplace on the upper floor with the portrait of the
head of the house hanging above it and a large inlaid table from Liège.

Saint-Barthélemy

** Bronze font

The second street on the left past the museum leads to the church of
Saint-Barthélemy. It was built in the 11th–12th c. with three aisles and
extended in the 18th c. by two main aisles and a side aisle. The west front
with its two towers is characteristic of Rhine and Mosan Romanesque
church architecture. The late 11th c. choir is also of interest. The interior
houses paintings by Bertholet Flémalle (1614–75) and Englebert Fisen
(1655–1733), both from Liège; the most valuable treasure is the bronze font
cast by Renier de Huy between 1107 and 1118. It rests on twelve bulls,
symbolising the Apostles, and is splendidly decorated with five baptismal
reliefs (see p. 53 for a more detailed description). Originally the font stood
in the Notre-Dame-aux-Fonts church which was destroyed during the
French Revolution; it was brought to its present location for safety.

On the Meuse

La Batte

The return from Saint-Barthélemy and around the block of houses between
En Féronstrée and the Meuse leads to the quays Quai de Maestricht, Quai
de la Batte, Quai de la Goffe and Quai sur la Meuse. A market is held here
every Sunday at 9am offering everything from a flea market to food and
vegetables.

Museums

Two buildings on the Quai de Maestricht house three very interesting
museums.

* Musée d'Armes

First at No. 8 Quai de Maestricht is the Musée d'Armes (Arms Museum). It
has a magnificent collection of small arms (12,500 exhibits) documenting

the tradition of weapons manufacture in Liège dating back to the 14th c. Worth particular mention is a room containing splendid ornate weapons and a collection of hunting and blank guns (open: Mon., Thur. and Sat. and 1st and 3rd Sun. 10am–1pm, Wed. and Fri. 2–5pm).

The Musée Curtius (13, Quai de Maestricht) is in the former mansion of Jean Curtius (1551–1628), once supplier to the Spanish army. Between 1600 and 1610 he had this exemplary red brick house built on the river bank in the style of the Mosan Renaissance. The museum which now occupies the house contains in two departments exhibits from prehistoric, Roman and Frankish-Medieval periods together with furniture and decorative art collections from the Middle Ages to the French Revolution. Only the most notable pieces from its valuable collections are listed: on the ground floor Roman bronzes, a Roman ceramic mask and a unique Roman glass service, Merovingian everyday objects, wonderful early Romanesque ivory carvings including a figure of Christ from Amay and Bishop Notker's Evangelistery (around 1100), the museum's pièce de résistance; on the first floor the finely worked Madonna by Dom Rupert (around 1140), the wooden tympanum with the "Mystery of Apollo" (around 1150), lavishly decorated Renaissance rooms; finally on the second floor a collection of coins from Liège (open: Mon., Thur. and Sat. as well as every 1st and 3rd Sun. 2–5pm, Wed. and Fri. 10am–1pm).

* Musée Curtius

In an annexe of the Musée Curtius the Musée du Verre (Glass Museum) has a collection of over 10,000 glass exhibits from the 5th c. B.C. to the present, among them highly original Art Nouveau glasses and vases (opening times as for the Musée Curtius).

* Musée du Verre

Further along the river bank, with a view of the Pont des Arches, which was built 1858–62 to replace the oldest bridge (11th c.) over the Meuse, between the Rue du Pont and the Rue de la Halle aux Viandes stands the Meat Hall, built 1544–46. Behind it on the right on the corner of Rue de la Boucherie/

Return to
Féronstrée

Bishop Notker's Gospel . . .   *. . . in the Musée Curtius*

Potiérue is Maison Havart, a historic inn from 1594, dominated by the Cité Administrative, the City Administration building. From here it is a short distance back to Féronstrée.

Around the Place de la République

Théâtre Royal

Built 1818–22 and modelled on the Odéon in Paris the Théâtre Royal on the south-west side of the Place de la République is home to the Opéra Royal de la Wallonie.

Sainte-Croix

North of the square on the corner of the Rue Haute Sauvenière/Rue Sainte-Croix stands the church of Sainte-Croix (Church of the Holy Cross), consecrated in 979 by Bishop Notker and rebuilt several times. It is one of the few churches in Belgium with two apses: the Romanesque west choir is from 1175, the Gothic east choir (and the nave) are from the 14th c. The west choir contains the notable tomb of Canon Milleman, decorated with hieroglyphics (1558).

*Treasury

The treasury contains two exceptional pieces: one is the "Triptych of the True Cross", probably by Godefroid de Huy, into which four fragments of Christ's cross, a piece of John the Baptist's skull and a tooth of St Vincent were worked; the other is a 37cm/14½in. long "Clef de Saint-Hubert" (St Hubert's key) which Pope Gregory II gave to St Hubert in 722 in accordance with a custom of giving great churchmen a key to St Peter's tomb in Rome, into which a piece of Peter's chain had been inserted. The only other such key in Europe is in St Servatius' church in Maastricht.

Basilique Saint-Martin

From Sainte-Croix the Rue Mont Saint-Martin climbs up to the Basilique Saint-Martin, visible from afar, founded in the 10th c. and destroyed by fire in 1312 in disputes between the guilds and the nobility. It was rebuilt in its present form at the beginning of the 16th c. with a large star-covered choir.

Théâtre Royale

The church has stained glass windows dating from 1526–36, paintings by Englebert Fiesen together with 14 marble plaques in the first side chapel on the right by Delcour commemorating the initiation of the feast of Corpus Christi (Fête-Dieu). This was first celebrated in 1246 following a vision by St Juliana, a Liège nun, and was proclaimed by Pope Urban IV (former Archdeacon of Liège Cathedral Church) a church holiday throughout Christendom.

Not far beyond the Théâtre Royal stands the Eglise Saint-Jean, founded in 980 by Bishop Notker. It was modelled on the Pfalz chapel in Aachen as can be seen from the octagonal outline of the central building. In the 18th c. it fell into disrepair and was partly demolished, being rebuilt according to the original plans in 1754–60. It contains two beautiful sculptures, a Madonna "Sedes Sapientiae" (around 1230) in oak and from the same period "Mary and John the Baptist".

Saint-Jean

A second pedestrianised area lies to the south of the theatre around the triangular square Vinâve d'Ile (fountain by Delcour), off which leads the Passage Lemonnier, the first covered shopping arcade in Belgium (1839).

Vinâve d'Ile

The Vinâve d'Ile opens out onto the Place de la Cathédrale. Here stands the former Convent Church of Saint-Paul, founded by Bishop Heraclius in 971; since 1801 it has been the successor to the Cathedral of Saint-Lambert in the diocese. The 90m/295ft-high tower has a carillon from the old cathedral which plays the Walloon hymn "li Chant dès Wallons". The original Romanesque church was destroyed at the beginning of the 13th c. and replaced by the early Gothic church of 1232–89, which later underwent further expansion. The decoration of the expansive interior (85m/278ft long, 34m/111ft wide, 24m/78ft high) took place between the 16th and 19th c. and encompasses works such as the marble sculpture of the burial of Christ by Delcour in the left side aisle, a large glass window by Hans of Cologne (1530) in the right hand aisle and other examples of artistic stained glass from 1557–87 in the choir apse. The Treasury in the adjoining cloisters possesses two outstanding works together with two 11th c. ivory pieces. The 1.5m/5ft-high reliquary of St Lambert was made in 1506–12 by Hans von Reutlingen, the goldsmith of Emperor Maximilian and Charles V, resident in Aachen, and commissioned by Erards de la Marck. The gold reliquary of Charles the Bold depicts the Duke of Burgundy kneeling with St Lambert's reliquary, while St George standing behind him is also portrayed with the face of the Duke. This work of art by Gérard Loyet in 1467 was allegedly a gift to the city of Liège from Charles the Bold in 1471 as an expression of regret at the destruction of the city which he had ordered.

*Cathédrale
Saint-Paul

*Treasury

In a street running parallel to the Rue de la Régence from the theatre to the Meuse stands the Church of Saint-Denis, founded by Bishop Notker in 987 and consecrated in 1011. The tower is of 11th c. origin, the choir was built in the 14th c. In the right side aisle there is a fine carved Gothic altar with a representation of the Passion of Christ.

Saint-Denis

At the end of the Rue de la Régence is the Place Cockerill with the neo-Gothic main post office and the state university founded in 1817. As well as lecture halls the university building houses a library containing over a million volumes and a natural science museum with an important palaeontology department.

Université

Southern parts of the city

South of the cathedral the Rue St-Remy comes to the church of Saint-Jacques (St Jacob's Church), founded in the 11th c. and converted to a splendid example of late Gothic architecture in 1513–38. The Romanesque portico of 1170 on the west side has been preserved; the magnificent north

*Saint-Jacques

portal was remodelled by Lambert Lombard in Renaissance style in 1558–60, but leaving the relief below the arch of the Coronation of the Virgin (1380), a masterpiece of Mosan Gothic sculpture. Worth seeing inside the church are the superb vaulting, the rood-screen (17th c.) and the stained glass (1520–40).

Parc d'Avroy

Further south the Parc d'Avroy is laid out on the site of an old harbour. In the north of the park is a massive statue of Charlemagne on horseback (1868), a few yards to the east, on the Boulevard Piercot, stands the Royal Conservatory of Music (1881–86). Alongside the Meuse is an elevated terrace surrounded by a wall with four groups of bronze statues, among them the Bulltamer by L. Mignon and the Monument National de la Résistance (National Monument to the Resistance Fighters in the Second World War).

Right Bank of the Meuse

Outre-Meuse

"Tchantchès"

The Pont des Arches links the Old Town with the district of Outre-Meuse lying between the Meuse and a canal of the Ourthe. It is the most colourful and extrovert quarter of the city where in 1927 the not entirely serious République Outre-Meuse and the Commune de Saint-Pholien proclaimed themselves "free states", thereby keeping the custom alive. Pure dialect is still spoken here and this is the home of "Tchantchès" (Walloon for François), the hard-drinking symbolic figure of the population of Liège, allegedly born in 760, adviser to Charlemagne and companion of Roland, who firts appeared as a marionette in 1836 together with "Polichinelle" and "Guignol" in the puppet theatre. A monument to him was placed at the Place d'Yser in 1936.

Maison Grétry

Not far from the site of the monument the composer André-Ernest-Modeste Grétry was born (1741–1813). His birthplace is open to visitors on request.

Musée Tchantchès

To the south in Rue Surelet the Musée Tchantchès documents the history of this popular figure with over 200 of its costumes and a notable collection of puppets (open: Wed. and Thur. 2–4pm, puppet shows Sept.–Easter Sun. 10.30am).

Musée de Zoologie with Aquarium

On the Meuse near the Pont John F. Kennedy the Musée de Zoologie with an aquarium is part of the Zoological Institute of the University. There is a coral collection, a zoological collection and 26 ponds containing exotic fish (open: daily 10.30am–12.30pm and 2–6pm).

Parc de Boverie

South of the Pont Albert I (Pont de Commerce) is the Parc de Boverie with the Palais de Justice (1952–58) and the Tour spatio-dynamique et cybernétique, a 52m/170ft-high bizarre steel construction.

Musée d'Art moderne

In the southern tip of the park the Musée d'Art Moderne (Museum of Modern Art) awaits the visitor, an impressive collection of 19–20th c. paintings, including Picasso, Pissarro, Monet, Kokoschka, Chagall and primarily Belgian artists such as Evenepoel, de Smet and Delvaux. Adjoining it is the Cabinet des Estampes (copper engraving gallery), which has 26,000 items from all periods since the 19th c. (open: Tues.–Sat. 1–6pm, Sun. 11am–4.30pm).

Musée du Fer Charbon

On the other side of the Ourthe canal the Musée du Fer et du Charbon, a branch of the Musée de la Vie Wallone on the Blvd. Poincaré, specialises in mining and metal working in Wallonia and has a 17th c. melting furnace and 18th c. blacksmiths' hammers (open: Mon.–Fri. 9am–5pm).

Further along the same road the Musée des Transports exhibits vehicles and documents of the city's transport system.   Musée des Transports

Surroundings

The Château d'Aigremont lies on the left bank of the Meuse 16km/10 miles south-west of Liège and according to legend was built by the four children of Haimon. The present day château is of 15th c. origin and was rebuilt in the 18th c. The tour takes in the kitchen with over 1000 Delft tiles. It has a beautiful staircase with Italian idyllic landscape paintings in a trompe-l'oeil style.   Château d'Aigremont

The Fort de Loncin 8km/5 miles to the north played an important role in the resistance against the advance of the German troops in 1914. After incessant artillery fire it was destroyed when its magazine exploded.   Fort de Loncin

Domäne Sart Tilman (740ha/1829 acres), part of the university, extends along the right bank of the Meuse to the south of the city. There are Botanical Gardens, the Château de Colonster (17th c.) with the Georges Simenon Foundation and an open air museum with over 70 sculptures and works by Belgian sculptors.   Sart Timan

In the south-west suburb of Seraing the visitor can watch the famous glass being blown as it is manufactured in Val Saint-Lambert and purchase one of the beautiful crystal glasses on sale (open: Apr.–Oct. daily 10am–5pm, Nov.–Mar. Sat., Sun. and public holidays at the same times).   Val Saint-Lambert

At Neuville-en-Condruz, 20km/12 miles south-west, the largest American cemetery of the Second World War is situated (see Practical Information, Military Cemeteries).   Neuville-en-Condruz

From Neuville it is another 3km/2 miles (branch off to the right) to Saint-Séverin-en-Condroz, where there is a notable Romanesque church (12th c.), the former priory of the Cluny Convent. It is notable for its octagonal tower and a fine Romanesque font, formed by twelve lion-shaped figures.   Saint-Séverin-en-Condroz

Chaudfontaine, 10km/6 miles south, is an attractive thermal spa resort on the Vesdre.   Chaudfontaine

Blégny, 20km/12 miles north-east of Liège, is a traditional small mining town. There are guided tours of the old coal mines in Blégny-Trembleur (open: Apr.–Oct. daily 10am–4pm, July and Aug. 9.30am–5pm). A small old-time railway runs through the Herver Land to Montroux and back (departures daily between 10am and 3.30pm, July and Aug. also Sun. and public holidays until 4.30pm).   **Blégny-Trembleur**

The old railway station at Montroux houses a museum with agricultural equipment and horse-drawn carts.   Montroux

Lier · Lierre   E 4

Province: Antwerp
Altitude: 4–13m/13–43ft
Population: 31,000
Interregional Station (bicycle rental at station)

The town of Lier (French Lierre), birthplace of the popular Flemish author Felix Timmermans (1886–1947) and other well known artists including the   Location

Lier
Lierre

painter Isidoor Opsomer, is situated 17km/11 miles south-east of Antwerp at the confluence of the Grote and Kleine Nete. Lier is the gateway to the region of Kempen and is nicknamed "Lierke Plezierke" (Lively Lier), on account of its colourful folklore.

The economy of the town is based on the textile industry with its old and famous traditions of silk spinning, lace making and embroidery. Also important are some recently introduced industries including brewing, the manufacture of synthetic fibres and the production of building materials near the Nete canal, which provides a waterway between Lier and Antwerp for vessels up to 1350 tonnes. Many people commute daily between Lier and Antwerp. Culinary specialities of the town are Lierse Vlaaikes (sweet tarts with candy) and the light "Caves" beer.

The origins of the town can be traced back to a hermitage founded in 760. In the early Middle Ages the town was known for its cloth making and received its town charter as early as 1212. It was fortified in the late Middle Ages and its fortifications resisted all enemy attacks until 1784 when they were razed but rebuilt in 1830. During the First World War the town held a key strategic position and was often heavily shelled.

*Sint-Gummaruskerk

East of the Kleine Nete stands Sint-Gummaruskerk, a masterpiece of Brabant late Gothic, built in 1425–1540 by Keldermans and de Waghemakere. The octagonal tower with its carillon of 45 bells was begun in 1377 but only completed in 1702.
Philipp the Handsome married Johanna the Mad of Castille here in 1496.

Interior	The church contains some outstanding art treasures.
*Choir screen	Among them is the late Gothic choir screen carved out of light sandstone by the Mechelen sculptors Mynsheeren and Wischavens (1536–39) depicting the story of the Passion, evangelists and churchmen. The small turret was added in 1850.
*Windows	The late Gothic stained glass is of outstanding beauty: in the right side aisle the "Coronation of the Virgin" (15th c.), in the choir apse three windows presented by the Emperor Maximilian in 1516 representing himself and his wife Maria of Burgundy and in the same place a window of Sts Gummarus and Rumoldus (1475).
Paintings	Of the numerous paintings the most impressive are a triptych in the first ambulatory chapel, its side panels probably painted by Rubens; in the fourth chapel the Colibrant triptych (1517) representing the marriage of the Virgin in the centre and the Annunciation and Circumcision on the side panels, probably by Goswyn van der Weyden, the grandson of Rogier van der Weyden; finally in the right aisle a triptych by Otto Venius ("Coming of the Holy Spirit"; 1612).

In Sint-Gummaruskerk

The Baroque pulpit of 1642 by Artus Quellin is also noteworthy . The most important of the church treasures is the 800kg silver shrine of St. Gummarus which is carried through the streets in processions.

Opposite the church of St Gommarus stands the Romanesque Sint-Pieters-kapel, the oldest building in the town (1225).

Sint-Pieterskapel

Other sights

In the centre of the town is the Grote Markt, which was badly damaged during the German shelling of Antwerp, but its most important buildings survived.

Grote Markt

On the east side of the square is the 18th c. stadhuis (town hall) with an attractive Rococo staircase and beautifully decorated rooms. The adjoining Gothic belfry (1369) is all that remains of the medieval cloth hall.

Stadhuis and belfry

North of the stadhuis stands the Vleeshuis (meat hall) built in 1418, today an exhibition hall, and some notable guild houses such as the bakkerhuis (1717) and the Huis d'Eyckenboom (1721).

Vleeshuis and guild houses

Sint-Jacobskapel behind the town hall is also called the "Spanish Chapel" and originates from 1383.

Sint-Jacobskapel

Not far to the west of the market No. 14 Cauwenberghstraat houses the Museum Wuyts van Campen en Baron Caroly (Stedelijk Museum) which has a notable collection not only of Dutch and Flemish, but also of French and Spanish masters as well as contemporary works. Among the artists represented are Jan and Peter Bruegel the Younger, Rubens, van Dyck, Floris ("Berchem family"), Poussin, Lorrain and Murillo; the Modernists are represented by Permeke, de Vlaminck, de Braekeleer and Opsomer and de la Haye from Lier (open: Easter–Nov. Mon., Tues., Thur., Sat, Sun. 10am–noon and 1.30–5.30pm).

Museum Wuyts van Campen en Baron Caroly

Lokeren

° Begijnhof

From the Grote Markt Eikelstraat leads south through Gevangenpoort (1375) by the wall promenade (former moat) to the adjoining begijnhof (béguinage), one of the most picturesque in Belgium. With its low cottages, narrow alleys and crossroads it resembles a small town within a town. The béguinage was founded in the 13th c. and, together with most of the others, destroyed in the 16th c. The church dedicated to St Margaret is 17th c. and has a pulpit by Schneemaeckers.

° Zimmertoren

The Zimmerplein extends south-east of the Gevangenpoort. Here stands the Zimmertoren, once part of the town's defences and called the Corneliusturm, named after the astronomer and watchmaker Louis Zimmer (1880–1970). On its façade is his centenary clock from 1930 with 13 dials and scales: Greenwich Mean Time, day and night, zodiac, solar cycle, week days, the earth's meridian, months, date, seasons, tides, ages of the moon, phases of the moon and the metonic cycle. Every day at noon figures appear on the right façade. Inside the tower the clock mechanism and an astronomic studio with 57 dials can be seen.

In a pavilion near the tower is the clock which Zimmer featured in the 1939 World Exhibition in New York. It has 93 dials and made Zimmer world famous (open: daily 9am–noon and 1–6pm; in winter 9am–noon and 2–4pm).
Between the pavilion and the tower there is a wrought iron sculpture "Eagle and Chamois" by the Lier artist van Boeckel.

Museum
Timmermanns-
Opsomer

The Timmermans-Opsomer Museum, situated to the right of the bridge over the Nete next to the Zimmertoren, commemorates four artists born in Lier. The first is the author Felix Timmermans, who was also active as a musician and painter; several rooms are dedicated to him and his works such as "Pallieter".
Also on view is the studio of the painter Baron Opsomer, van Boeckel's forge and memorabalia of the Flemish composer Renaat Veremans, who also composed texts for Felix Timmermans (open: Apr.–Oct. Mon., Tues., Thur., Sat., Sun. 10am–noon and 1.30–5.30pm; Nov.–Mar. Sun. 10am–noon and 1.30–4pm).

Lokeren

See Sint-Niklaas, Surroundings

Lommel

See Geel, Surroundings

Louvain-la-Neuve

E 6

Province: Brabant
Altitude: 70m/230ft
Population: 4500 (permanent)
Local Rail Station

Location

The university town of Louvain-la-Neuve is a product of the conflict between the Walloons and the Flemish. When this confrontation reached another zenith in 1968 the Flemish expelled their Walloon colleagues from the Catholic University of Leuven (see entry) founded in 1425. The Walloons looked for a fresh place and found it 30km/19 miles south-east of Brussels in the French part of Belgium and Louvain-la-Neuve, "New Leuven'', was founded; it was the first newly set up town in Belgium since the foundation of Charleroi in 1666. Building went on from 1971, and between 1972 and 1979 all the French-speaking faculties moved out of Leuven with the exception of the medical faculty which was accommodated in the Brussels suburb of Woluwe-Saint-Lambert. Today in this town, which was conceived for 35,000 people, about 4500 permanent residents and 18,000 students live. It can be seen that the aim of a homogeneous structure of residence has not been achieved and as a consequence at weekends and in the university holidays it can be very quiet in the town.

*Townscape

In Louvain-la-Neuve it was intended to try out new forms of residence and living. More than 80 architects wanted to turn away from the idea of a large town and to recreate the intimate character of small areas as they were in a medieval town; therefore around the urban centre brick was the preferred material for the buildings in the narrow little streets. Here pedestrians have priority; the station access roads and car parks are sited underground and from them a system of passages, branching out in all directions, leads into the open air. The centre of the town is the main square with the concrete university hall, the Church of Saint-François d'Assise and the Museum of the Archaeological and Art History Institute in which sculpture from the 12th to the 18th c. is displayed. Around the centre are grouped the residential buildings of the parts of the town called Bruyères, Hocaille, Lauzelle and Biéreau; to the east towards the motorway lie the science park and the large buildings of the cyclotron. Relaxation from studies can be enjoyed in the provincial estate the ''Bois des Rêves''.

Surroundings

5km/3 miles west lies Céroux-Mousty where in May a festival of hot air ballooning is held, attracting many visitors. | Céroux-Mousty

In the township of Rixensart, 8km/5 miles north-west, the pretty red brick Château de Mérode was built between 1631 and 1632. It is square with four corner towers and many windows and is open to the public. It is impressive because of its tasteful furnishings which include Gobelin tapestries, Louis XV pieces, pictures (including some by Nattier and Tischbein) as well as a collection of weapons which the French mathematician Monge brought back from Napoleon's Egyptian campaign. (Open: Easter–Oct. Sat., Sun. and public holidays 2–6pm; July Tues.–Sun. 2–6pm.) | **Rixensart**

A little outside Rixensart lies the Lac de Genval which is a favourite rendezvous at weekends for the people of nearby Brussels; it has excellent facilities for angling and a considerable number of good restaurants. | Lac de Genval

A little further to the west of Rixensart lies La Hulpe where the Belgian paper industry had its beginnings. Today it is an elegant residential quarter of Brussels with eight little châteaux. A walk in the Domaine Solvay, named after the industrial family, who in the 19th c. owned the château in the middle of the park, is well worth while. Today the château is a culture centre. | La Hulpe

Wavre, 6km/4 miles to the north, has three attractions: the unusual open-air museum of living water plants in the suburb of Limal, with over 800 species of plants (open: Apr.–Oct. daily 10am–5pm); the Walibi Adventure Park and the Aqualibi aquapark (see Practical Information, Leisure Parks). | Wavre

La Louvière (ship lift)

See Binche, Surroundings

Maaseik

Province: Brabant
Altitude: 70m/230ft
Population: 21,000

Location

In the extreme north-east of Belgium right on the frontier with the Netherlands lies Maaseik, the birthplace of the Flemish painters Hubert and Jan van Eyck. There was a monastery here as early as the 8th c. around which arose a village which was later destroyed; a new village grew up around the castle, built in the 11th c., and from this developed Maaseik. Thanks to its favourable position on the Meuse the town had some importance as a commercial centre, but after the separation of Belgium from the Netherlands Maaseik became remote. However, the town has always been interesting because of its many examples of the Renaissance architecture of the Meuse area.

Sights

*Grote Markt

The extensive Grote Markt with its four fountains, a double row of lime trees and in the middle a monument to the van Eyck brothers, is surrounded by a number of examples of this architecture of which the houses "Stad Amsterdam" (1686) and "Drie Leliën" (1715) are the finest. In the Town Hall of 1827 is the only copy of the "Lamb of God" by the brothers van Eyck 1923 and also a collection of church-tower cockerels.

Bosstraat

Along Bosstraat are other examples of Mosan Renaissance architecture, including the brick built house "Verkerde Wereld" (No. 7), the half-timbered house No. 17 dating from 1600, No. 19 dating from 1620 and the "Stenenhuis" or "Drossaardhuis" (an official house; No. 21).

Museactron

At No. 5 Lekkerstraat, in the very fine building of 1704 and also in a new building are housed three museums under the futuristic name of Museactron. They are the Apothecaries' Museum with the oldest apothecary's shop in Belgium (17th c.), the regional Archaeological Museum with historic and Roman exhibits, an impressive ivory collection and many different examples of handwork; finally in the cellar can be found a bakery museum with an old bakery. (Museums open: Tues.–Fri. 9am–noon and 2–5pm, Sat. and Sun. 10am–noon and 2–5 pm.)

Sint-Catharinakerk

The 19th c. Sint-Catharinakerk has little of architectural merit, but possesses an extraordinary treasury, the masterpiece of which is the "Codex Eyckensis" – a gospel dating from the 8th c. (the Gospel of St Harlinde), which is the oldest book in Belgium – as well as a satin reliquary of the 10th c.

Sint-Annakerk

Sint-Annakerk in the north-west suburb of Aldeneik goes back to a former 8th c. monastic church. The present building is a pillared basilica of the 12th c. which was not erected until the monastery fell into ruins. It still has its Romanesque doorway and nave with the remains of paintings as well as Merovingian stone sarcophagi, among which beneath the altar is that of the saints Harlinde and Relinde who founded the monastery.

Surroundings

Bree

Bree is situated 16km/10 miles from Maaseik on the Willems Vaart canal. The little town belonged for a long time to the bishopric of Liège. Of interest are the five-aisled Sint-Michielskerk, the fine tombstones and especially a 15th c. calvary and a 16th c. burial group. The Stadhuis of 1754 also houses a local museum.

Bocholt, 4km/2½ miles north of Bree, has a 15th c. church with an interesting interior; of special note is a Christophorus statue of the 15th c. The Goolderheide Leisure Park with a camping site has an open-air swimming pool with water-chutes.

Bocholt

Maas Valley

See Vallée de la Meuse

Malmédy · Malmedy

H 7

Province: Liège
Altitude: 330m/1083ft
Population: 7000

The little town of Malmédy (Latin "malmundarium" = cleansed from evil ones) is in the province of Liège at the confluence of the Warche and Warchenne on the southern slope of the thickly wooded and scenically very charming Hohe Venn. About 90% of the inhabitants are Walloons who speak French or the local Walloon dialect; about 10% are German speakers. The varied history of Malmédy, which is due in no small measure to its situation in the frontier region of Belgium, has for a long time led to economic disadvantage of the area. This could only be improved after the Second World War. Several new industries arose so that today canneries, a paper factory, and a dairy are the most important industrial concerns of Malmédy. In addition the town developed into an important educational centre. The well-tended town and the wooded surroundings have also contributed to the prosperity of the place and tourism is now an important economic factor.

Location

For a long time Malmédy was a source of dispute between France, the Netherlands and the German kingdom, and has changed its national allegiance several times in the last 200 years. The town developed from an abbey founded in 648 by St Remaclus, the Bishop of Maastricht, and from the ecclesiastical town of Malmédy-Stavelot. Malmédy lived in constant rivalry with neighbouring Stavelot (see entry) for pre-eminence in this independent and self-governing principality. In 1690 French troops almost completely destroyed the town and in 1795 it was incorporated into France. After the defeat of Napoleon I it was annexed in 1815 to Prussia and not until 1925 did it become Belgian. In 1940 the town was occupied by German troops and in 1944 was attacked in error by US bombers when parts were destroyed, although it had by then been occupied by American forces.

History

"Cwarmê" (carnival) is renowned. For four riotous days known as "Grandes Haguètes" there are large processions and traditional figures, such as the "Haguètes" and the "Sotê", appear (see page 84).

Carnival

Sights

The townscape of Malmédy is characterised by houses with slates decorating their fronts. The slates are so arranged that on close inspection patterns and even inscriptions can be discerned. There are good examples in the street called Rue devant les Religieuses, in the Rue de la Tannerie and in the Place de la Fraternité.

Houses with slate facing

Maisons de Cavens	The centre of Malmédy is the Place de Rome. The most important building in the square is the Maisons de Cavens erected in 1830 as an orphanage. Today it houses the tourist office, the national paper museum (Musée National du Papier) and the carnival museum (Musée du Cwarmê; both museums open: Sat. and Sun. 2.30–5.30pm; in school holidays daily).
Cathédrale Saints-Pierre, Paul et Quirin	In the Place du Châtelet, not far east from the Place du Rome, rise the plain towers of the Cathedral of Saints-Pierre, Paul et Quirin. It was built between 1775 and 1784 as an abbey church and in 1921, when Malmédy became a bishopric (until 1925), it was raised to the status of a cathedral. The quite simple interior, designed by the architect Galhausen, has 18th c. choir stalls, a "Virgin with Child" ascribed to Delcour, and the reliquary of St Quirinus as well as a silver reliquary bust of St Gereon and his companion (18th c.).
Abbey	The abbey gardens and the abbey buildings (now a grammar school and law courts) adjoin the cathedral.
Église des Capucins	To the south of the cathedral in the Ruelle des Capucins can be found the Capuchin church dedicated in 1631; the interior mostly dates from the 17th and 18th centuries.
Pouhon des Iles	The Pouhon des Iles in the north-west on the far side of the Warche is a mineral spring rich in iron. On the bridge over the Warche which leads to the spring stands the oldest chapel in Malmédy, dedicated in 1544.

Surroundings

Walking	Malmédy is surrounded by beautiful woods and is an excellent place for invigorating walks. Almost adjoining the town lies the German-Belgium Nature Park (see entry) with its centre at Botrange. A short walk in the direction of Stavelot leads to the Rocher de Falize, an impressive rock pinnacle towering up over the Warche.
Bütgenbach	15km/9½ miles east of Malmédy lies the village of Bütgenbach once part of the dukedom of Limburg and the property of the Herren von Valkenburg. The fortress and the castle were destroyed in 1689 by the French; still to be seen is a fine estate which dates from the 18th c.
* Barrage	In 1932 near Bütgenbach the Warche was dammed by a 23m/75ft-high wall and turned into a lake of 120ha/297 acres containing 11 million cu.m of water (approx. 14 million cu.yds). Since the completion of the leisure centre of Worriken in 1979 the reservoir annually attracts numerous proponents of water sports and campers. The power station produces 2 million kwh of electricity.
Robertville	Robertville, 10km/6 miles north-east of Malmédy, is another popular holiday and leisure centre thanks to its reservoir, the Lac de Robertville, its close proximity to the German-Belgium Nature Park as well as to the skiing district of Ovifat. The lake which has an area of 63ha/156 acres contains 8 million cu.m of water (approx. 10 million cu.yds) was dammed between 1925 and 1919 by a wall 54m/177ft high and 120m/394ft long; it provides electricity and water for Malmédy. Less than a kilometre from the reservoir
* Burg Reinhardstein	rises the mighty and picturesque Burg Reinhardstein, surrounded by a park in the valley of the Warche into which a waterfall plunges down 50m/164ft. The castle was built in 1354 for Wenzel von Luxemburg and was for a long time owned by the dukes of Nassau until it came into the ownership of the ancestor of the Austrian statesman Klemens Wenzel, Prince of Metternich, through the marriage of Anna von Naussau with William von Metternich. In the 19th c. the castle fell into disrepair but was restored from 1969 according to the old plans. The interior of the castle is open to the public; the first room to be seen is the Knight's Hall in which there is a remarkable collection of weapons; in

Winter around Burg Reinhardstein

the castle chapel are religious works of art dating from the 14th to the 18th c. (open: mid June–mid Sept. Sun. and public holidays 2–5pm; July and Aug. also Tues., Wed. and Sat. 2–5pm).

Right on the German border, 22km/14 miles south of Malmédy, lies Sankt Vith. Founded in the 12th c., it was Prussian from 1815 to 1919 and almost completely destroyed in 1944 by an Allied bombing attack. The only remnant of the old buildings is the Büchelturn dating from 1350. The local museum in the Heckingstrasse has exhibits about the history and character of the countryside "between the Venn and Schneifel".

Sankt Vith,
Saint-Vith

Another 12km/7½ miles south from Sankt Vith is Burg Reuland; it owes its name to the castle from which the surrounding territory was controlled during the Middle Ages. The Paul-Gerardy Museum documents the life of this 19th c. author and painter.

Burg Reuland

Mechelen · Malines

E 5

Province: Antwerp
Altitude: 7m/23ft
Population: 75,800
Intercity and Inter-regional Station

The impressive town of Mechelen (French Malines) is situated between Brussels and Antwerp on the Dijle which here is still tidal. Since the 16th c. it has been the spiritual capital of the region as the seat of the Archbishop Primas (in common with Brussels) as well as the headquarters of an archiscopal seminar; it has the only carillon school in the world. Industry includes furniture and canning factories, a brewery, a railway workshop as

Location

well as many factories founded within the framework of the European Community by the countries of the Community. The products of lace, carpet and woollen concerns enjoy an excellent reputation. In addition Mechelen is a centre of market gardening (asparagus, peas, etc.).

History

There was a settlement on the right bank of the Dijle as early as the 6th c. B.C. In the 8th c. an Irishman named Rombout brought Christianity to Mechelen, which in the Middle Ages was called Machlina (Latin Mechlinia). In 915 it belonged to the bishopric of Liège and from 1213, thanks to its favourable situation from the point of view of communications, it gained almost complete independence. Bishop Adolf van der Marck sold it in 1332 to the dukes of Flanders. From 1369 it belonged to Burgundy and in 1473 it became the seat of the Great Council, the highest court in the Netherlands. After the death of Charles the Bold his widow Margarete of York chose Mechelen as her residence. From 1507 to 1530 Mechelen was ruled as Stadholder by Margarete of Austria, the aunt of Charles V. The town blossomed as a residence and many scientists and artists, such as Eramus of Rotterdam and Albrecht Dürer, came to stay for a time. After Margarete's successor Maria of Hungary moved her seat in 1546 to Brussels, Mechelen was compensated by the gift of the archbishopric with primacy over the whole of the Netherlands. The first archbishop was Antoine Perrenot de Granville, the confessor of Charles V and Philipp II. At this time lace, carpets and particularly gilded leather tapestry were especially prized. The War of Independence in the Netherlands brought destruction, yet the town flourished again in the Baroque era. In 1835 the first railway on the European continent ran from Mechelen to Brussels. Damage done in the First and Second World Wars has long been made good.

**Grote Markt

Near the centre of the old town, which was laid out in an almost circular manner with broad boulevards replacing the former surrounding ramparts, and which is in some respects well preserved its medieval appearance, lies the Grote Markt. Here can still be seen some fine gabled houses of the 16th to 18th c. and in the centre the statue of Margarete of Austria. In the pavement around the monument the sizes of the dials of Sint-Rombouts Cathedral have been introduced.

*Stadhuis

The south-east of the market is occupied by the Stadhuis which consists of two parts. On the right is the Lakenhalle (cloth hall), built in 1320–26 according to the models of the halls of Bruges and renewed after a fire in 1342. The central building is flanked by two turrets and over the Gothic doorway is the base of a belltower which, however, was never completed. The left part of the building was presented by Charles V to the seat of the Great Council and designed by Rombout Kelderman in 1529. In his time the building remained incomplete and was only finished in the 20th century.

Schepenhuis

The Schepenhuis on the southern edge of the market was erected in 1374 and until 1618 was the seat of the Great Council. Today it is the municipal library and archive.

Postgebouw

On the north-east side of the square stands the post office which was once the town hall (14th/18th c.) and has a restored Gothic façade.

*Sint-
Rombouts
Cathedral
**Clock tower

Behind the post office rises the metropolitan Sint-Rombouts Cathedral, begun in the 13th c. and completed as far as the choir in 1342 when a fire broke out. In 1375 reconstruction was finished. The beginning of the tower was made in 1452 which was intended to be 167m/580ft and the highest tower in Christendom. However, when William of Orange required building material for the fortress of Willemstad in 1546, work was stopped and never again restarted. However, the form of the tower which is

The Stadhuis of Mechelen

only 97m/318ft high is imposing on account of its clear vertical lines and Gothic decoration. The dials of the tower clock (1708) have a diameter of 13.7m/45ft. There are two carillons each with 49 bells, one dating from the 17th c., the other from 1981 and altogether weighing 17 tonnes. They are played in summer on Mondays from 8.30pm.

The interior of this spacious church has important works of art, including statues of the Apostles dating from 1774 on the pillars of the nave and the grave of Cardinal Mercier (1851–1926), who opposed German occupation forces in the First World War, which can be seen in the left aisle near the Lady Chapel. In the Chapel of the Sacrament at the base of the tower is a communion bench by Artus Quellin the Younger and in the second chapel on the left weapons of the Knights of the Golden Fleece who in 1491 maintained a chapter of their order in Sint-Rombouts. In the transepts are several pictures dating from the 15th–16th c. including, on the right, the remarkable painting "Christ on the Cross" by Anton van Dyck (1627). The Baroque high altar (1665) of white marble was created by Luc Fayd'herbe, a citizen of Mechelen. In the choir ambulatory are four Baroque tombs of archbishops, including von Granville, and pictures from the life of St Rombout.

Interior

There is a small archaeological museum in the churchyard open from Easter to October at weekends.

Museum

Round the Grote Markt

Not far from Sint-Rombouts can be found E-Wynants Museum dedicated to the works of this Mechelen sculptor. (Open: Apr.–Sept. Sat., Sun. and public holidays 10am–noon and 2–5pm; in July also on Mon.)

E-Wynants Museum

Sint-Katelijnestraat leads from the cathedral to the Gothic Sint-Katelij-nekerk north-west of the market. This church, which was created in the

Sint-Katelijnekerk

289

Mechelen
Malines

1 Paradijs, Duivelshuis
 St-Josefhuis
2 Klokkengietersmuseum
 (bell-foundry museum)
3 Horlogerie en -klokkenmuseum
 (clock and bell museum)
4 Gerechtshof (Palais van
 Margareta van Ostenrijk)

5 Palais van
 Margareta van York
6 St-Pieter en Pauluskerk
7 Hof van Busleyden
 (museum)
 and Beiaardschool
 (carillon school)
8 St-Janskerk

9 Refugie van de Abdij
 van Sint-Truiden
 (refuge)
10 Refugie van de Abdij
 van Tongerlo
11 St-Katelijnekerk
12 Begijnhofkerk
13 E. Wynants Museum

style of the Scheldt and Dender Gothic mainly between the 13th and 15th c.,
has a Joseph altar by Fayd'herbe and Baroque choirstalls.

Begijnhof

Sint-Katelijnekerk is situated between the Smaller and the Greater Béguin-
ages. The Greater Béguinage was set up in 1350 and the present houses
along the narrow streets date from the 16th and 18th c. In the Baroque
Béguinage church (1629–47) can be seen pictures by De Crayer, the
Baroque high altar by Jan van der Steen (17th c.) and two statues by
Fayd'herbe.

Refuges

To the east of the Smaller Béguinage we pass the Refuge of the Abbey of
Tongerlo and shortly afterwards on the right come to the Refuge of the
Abbey of Sint-Truiden. Just to the right of the Wool Market there is the most
secluded little square in the town, from which there is an attractive view of
the buildings of the refuges on the edge of a little canal.

Just right of the Refuge of Sint-Truiden stands the Gothic Sint-Janskerk (15th c.) which also houses notable works of art. Among these pride of place goes to a winged altar by Rubens ("The Adoration of the Kings") painted in 1617–19, one of his most beautiful works and for which his wife Isabella Brant sat as the model for the Virgin Mary. Also of note are various woodcarvings by Theodoor Verhaegen (17th c.) on the pulpit, in the choir and on the pews in the transepts, as well as a wall shrine for the Reliquary of St John by Fayd'herbe.

Sint-Janskerk

Not far from the church we come to the Hof van Busleyden, an attractive Gothic brick building of 1507 with a flower-decked inner courtyard and a belfry. The buildings, which were renovated after the First World War, house the Town Museum of Mechelen with departments of Civic History, Arts and Crafts and Customs, a selection of pictures and a carillon museum (open: daily except Tues. 10am–noon and 2–5pm). The little house in the corner is the carillon school.

Hof van Busleyden

The Biest road leading eastwards from the museum finishes at the Vee-markt. Here stands the Sint-Pieter-en-Pauluskerk the former monastic church of the Jesuits, who came to Mechelen at the beginning of the 17th c. and built their church between 1670 and 1677. The final portion of the façade was only added in the 18th c.

Sint-Pieter-en-Pauluskerk

To the right can be seen the Late-Gothic former palace of Margareta van York, the widow of Charles the Bold. It was erected in 1480 and later became the residence of Philip II and Charles V until 1516. It is now a theatre.

Paleis van Margareta van York

Opposite this palace extends a complex of buildings with a large arcaded courtyard which was once the Hof van Savoye, the palace of the Stadholder (governor) Margareta of Austria, then of the Cardinal de Granville. From 1616–1794 it was the seat of the Great Council and from 1796 onwards a Palace of Justice.

* Paleis van Margareta van Ostenrijk

Around the courtyard the oldest parts were built between 1503 and 1507 by Rombout Kelderman; the part along Keizerstraat was also the work of Kelderman and of Guyot de Beaugrant and is one of the earliest examples of Belgian Renaissance.

Further east on the far side of the railway line, the Speelgoedmuseum (Nekkerspoelstraat 21) exhibits old and new toys and objects of folk-art (open: Tues.–Sun. 2–5pm). On the arterial road to Leuven is a little regional railway museum (open: third Sat. in the month 1–5pm).

Other museums

Over the Dijle

Behind the Schepenhuis extends the long IJzerenleen Square. Its name comes from the iron railings (1531–34) which flanked a canal, now filled in, which flowed into the Dijle between the three-arched Grootbrug (13th and 16th c.) and the middle bridge over the river. Just before the bridge there lies on the right the little idyllic Vismarkt; to the left is the Clock and Bell Museum (open: Mon.–Sat. 10am–noon and 2–6pm).

IJzerenleen

On the left over the bridge stands the Huis de Zalm (No. 5), the guildhouse of the fishdealers, with a beautiful Renaissance façade. Today here in the art and craft museum can be seen the handmade products of Mechelen, such as gilded leather tapestry, pillow lace and pewter (open: daily except Fri. 10am–noon and 2–5pm).

* De Zalm

To the right of the bridge by the Haverwerf on the corner of Kraanstraat, stand several houses with very fine façades partly made of wood. Particularly attractive are the so-called Paradies (16th c.) with the representation of Adam and Eve on the arch of the door and nearby on the left the Duivels-huis (a 16th c. timber house) and at No. 20 the Huis Sint-Josef (1669).

* Houses on the Haverwerf

The Dijle at the Vismarkt

Brusselpoort

From the Dijle bridge we go straight ahead across the Korenmarkt (bell-foundry museum in Edwin-Michiels-Moeremanhuis; open: Mon., Tues., Thur. 6–8pm, Fri. 2–8pm., Sat. 2–6pm) and through Hoogstraat to the twin-towered Brusselpoort (rebuilt in the 18th c.), the only one of the twelve medieval town gates still remaining.

Onzwe-Lieve-Vrouw over de Dijle

The foundation stone of the church Onzwe-Lieve-Vrouw over de Dijle, to the east of Hoogstraat, was laid in 1255; in its present form the church dates mainly from the 14th and 15th c. Inside in the left side aisle can be seen Rubens painting "The Miraculous Draught of Fishes" which was a commission from the Fishmongers' Guild (1618–19).

Onzwe-Lieve-Vrouw van Hanswijk

Further east stands the Baroque basilica of Onzwe-Lieve-Vrouw van Hanswijk, designed by Luc Fayd'herbe between 1663 and 1678, who was also responsible for the large frescoes on the central dome. Inside the church a miracle-working statue of Mary, dated 986, is much venerated.

Surroundings

*Dierenpark Planckendael

Opening times
Summer: daily
8.30am–6.30pm;
Winter: daily
10am–5pm

In 1956 the Royal Zoological Society of Antwerp bought the Planckendael estate which lies 5km/3 miles south-east of Mechelen near the village of Muizen. Here the society wanted to set up a breeding station for endangered species for Antwerp Zoo (see entry). Now Planckendael has become a real zoo with over 1000 animals which live in open-air compounds in an attractive park.

Domein van Hofstade

Only a short way south of Planckendael a typical Belgian recreation centre has arisen around two lakes.

Fort Breendonk Eingang Ausgang

Arbeitsgelände

Hinrichtungs-stätte

© *Baedeker*

1 Tunnel	4 Mortuary	7 Studio	10 Reliquary chamber
2 Cells	5 Torture chamber	8 Sal Jacques Ochs	11 Dark cells
3 Dormitories	6 Barracks	9 Museum	12 Meditation room

*Fort Breendonk   E 4

To the south of the village of Willebroek, 12km/7½ miles from Mechelen, stands Fort Breendonk, the name of which many Belgians associate with the terror of the German occupation in the Second World War. The fort was built between 1906 and 1914 and was the last defensive position of Antwerp to surrender in October 1914. In the Second World War, when the German army moved in, the SS set up a concentration camp here which up to 1944 held about 4000 prisoners of war, of whom 370 died or were executed. An impressive tour of the fort leads first to the cells and torture chambers and is accompanied by recorded evidence from former detainees. Of the working areas it should be remembered that the walls of the fort were first blown up and the debris then shovelled away by the prisoners. In the former printing press ("Studio") a film is shown about the history of the camp, and this is complemented by the museum in the Saal Jacques Ochs where can be seen drawings by this Belgian painter who was incarcerated in Fort Breendonk from 1941–42.

Opening times
Apr.–Sept.
daily 9 am–5pm;
Oct.–Mar.
daily 10am–6pm

Modave (castle)

See Huy, Surroundings

Mons · Bergen   D 7

Province: Hainaut
Altitude: 29–105m/95–345ft
Population: 91,600
Intercity and Inter-regional Station

Mons (Flemish Bergen) stands on a ridge between the two rivers Haine and Trouille and owes its name to this situation. It is the administrative seat of the province as well as a commercial and supply centre of the Borinage, one of the largest mining and industrial regions of Belgium. Mons is also an important junction on the railway between Brussels and Paris, and has considerable cultural and scientific institutions including the University

Location

Centre, founded in 1965, the Royal Music Conservatory, an academy of fine arts, a mining academy and a research institute for nuclear technology. There are also a number of interesting museums and several large libraries.

Industry plays only a minor role in the economic life of Mons. There are factories producing textiles and leather goods and some smaller pharmaceutical and metal-working concerns. In the inland harbour of the town, which is linked with the Scheldt and the Charleroi-Brussels canal by a branch canal, the principal traffic is coal from the Borinage.

History

Mons owes its origin to a castle first mentioned in 642 and to the monastery founded a little later by the patroness of the town, St Waltrud (French Waudru). At this time it was called "Castri Locus" and kept this name until the 12th c. when the first town wall was built. After a period of great prosperity in the 13th–15th c. – in 1295 Mons became the capital of the county of Hennegau – the town suffered considerably in the wars of the 17th and 18th c. From the end of the 17th c. it came in succession under the domination of France, Spain and Austria and endured several sieges including one in 1691 by 80,000 French under Louis XV who, after his victory, gave Mons its present-day aspect. In nearby Jemappes the French revolutionaries beat the Austrians in 1792 and once more gained domination over the country. During both World Wars the town was on many occasions the target for heavy bombing attacks which caused great destruction. It was the first large Belgian town to be freed by the Allies in 1944. The best known citizen of the town is the composer Orlando di Lasso (1532–94), who became director of music in the court of Munich.

Le "Lumeçon"

On the Sunday after Whitsun a strange festival takes place in Mons; it is called "Lumeçon" and has its origins in a processional game which dates from the end of the 14th c. and which is associated with St George. The participants are St George in the uniform of a cuirassier and a dragon called "Doudou", ten so-called "Chinchins" who carry St George, as well as eight "devils", seven "wild men" and twelve "white men". They all form up in a procession which punctually at 12.30pm leaves the Collégiale Ste-Waudru for the Grand-Place to the sounds of the "doudou" folk song. The dragon, over 9m/30ft long, is carried by the "white men" and moves his tail over the spectators with the help of the "wild men". The fight between St George and the dragon begins when they reach the Grand-Place and the "Chinchins" also fight each other. Finally the saint is declared the winner by two pistol shots and the "Chinchins" drag the "dead" dragon into the courtyard of the city hall.

On the morning of the same day there is also a procession of the "Car d'Or" when the relics of St Waltrud are taken in procession in a golden coach.

Sights

Hôtel de Ville

In the centre of the town which is surrounded by a ring of wide boulevards is the Grand-Place. On the west side, where it is still flanked by some old houses, stands the impressive Hôtel de Ville, the façade of which was designed by Mattheus de Layens in 1458; the rest of the buildings which are grouped around the courtyard date from the 15th to 18th centuries. The City Hall is framed by the "Toison d'Or" house (1615) and the Chapel of St George (1604). To the left of the main entrance can be seen a bronze sculpture of a monkey with a polished head – stroking it is said to bring good fortune. Among the rooms of the City Hall (which can be seen on application at the door) should be mentioned the Salle des Commissions with Brussels tapestries of 1707, the Salle des Mariages with old wooden panelling, the Gothic Salle des Sacquiaux, so called because every evening the keys of the town are placed in a leather purse and guarded, as well as the Neo-Gothic Cabinet du Bourgmestre.

Jardins du Mayeur

Through the courtyard of the City Hall can be found the Jardins du Mayeur, the Burgomaster's garden which has a fountain representing a street

Mons
Bergen

Musée d'Histoire naturelle

Rue Compagnons · Rue Ferrer

Musée de la Vie montoise

Musée des Beaux Arts

Musées du Centenaire

Jardins du Mayeur

Musée du Chanoine Puissant

R.M.Berroets

Hôtel de Ville

Ste-Elisabeth

Station

Beffroi

Gr. Place

R des Clercs

Rue d'Hayré

Collégiale Ste-Waudru

Marché aux Herbes

R. du Hautbois

Charleroi

Grand'Rue

R. Notre-Dame

R. Grande Triperie

Université

R. de la Halle

R. de Archers

100 m

© Baedeker

Cuesmes

urchin of Mons. On the left is the Conciergerie, the old civic prison of 1512
with a torture chamber.

The landmark of Mons is the bell tower (French Beffroi) which stands on the
former castle hill above the town. The 87m/285ft high tower built in 1661 is
the only purely Baroque belfry in Belgium and contains a carillon of 47
bells. From the observation platform there is an extensive view over the
Hennegau; plaques explain the battle scenes of the First and Second World
Wars.
There are only a few remains of the old feudal castle, but the Romanesque
Chapel of Saint-Calixte (11th c.) with a few frescoes of this time is better
preserved.

*Beffroi

The Collegiate Church of Sainte-Waudru below the castle hill was built in
1450 to plans by Mattheus de Layens. The building was several times
interrupted, but in spite of this the church reveals a remarkable unity of
style in Brabant Gothic. The oldest part is the choir of four bays (1450–
1502); the transepts date from 1535–37 and the three-aisled nave with its
bays was built between 1529 and 1589. A tower was also planned which
was to be 187m/614ft high, but building was suspended in 1689 and consequently the roof of the nave is not overpowered. Altogether there are 29
chapels around this fine church.
The first thing to strike the visitor in the interior, which is 115m/377ft long,
32m/105ft wide and 24m/79ft high, are the pillars of the central nave which
reach up into the vault of the roof without any capitals. Near the main door
on the left stands the "Car d'Or", a processional carriage built in 1780 for

*Collégiale
Sainte-Waudru

*Interior

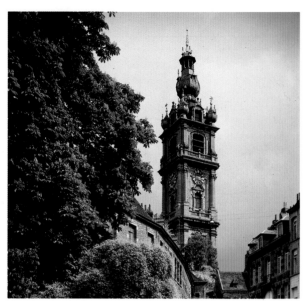

The Belfry, the landmark of Mons

the shrine of St Waltrude. The shrine can be found near the High Altar and was constructed in 1887 of gilded copper. It holds the body of the saint who died in 682 and was sewn up in a skin of a stag. Her head is kept in one of the chapels in a casket. At various points in the church (transept, choir, chapels 11, 14, 20, 24 and 28) are distributed the remains (reliefs and statues) of the choir screen which were made by Jacques Dubroecq of Mons between 1535 and 1548. This is one of the most important of Renaissance works in Belgium with a strong Italian influence. It was destroyed in 1792 by the French. Many other sculptures by the same artist include those in the right aisle (chapel 6) of "Christ on the Cross", an Annunciation group made of alabaster in the transept, in the choir ambulatory (chapel 12) an altar, and eight fine statues in the choir. Of note also are the ancient windows in the choir and transepts (16th c.) and in the nave (17th c.), as well as the considerable number of wall hangings.

Treasury

In the Treasury can be seen a number of valuable reliquaries including that of St Vincent by the school of Hugo d'Oignies (13th c.), as well as gold and silver work from Mons and district. A 15th c. book of hours has some fine miniature paintings.

Museums

Mons has several interesting museums most of which can be found near the City Hall. Unless otherwise indicated they have the same opening times, etc.

Musées du Centenaire

The Jardins du Mayeur which adjoin the City Hall have at their end a former pawnshop which now contains the Musées du Centenaire (civic museums) housing three museums under one roof.

Musée de Guerre

The War Museum occupies two storeys. On the ground floor the First World War is commemorated, especially the British regiments which near Mons on the 23rd and 24th August 1914 stopped the Germans who were proceeding in the direction of Paris. The museum on the third floor is dedicated to the Second World War and the liberation of Mons by American troops on September 2nd 1944.

The Ceramic Museum on the first floor has more than 3500 exhibits from all important European faience and porcelain manufactories such as Delft, Sèvres, Meissen, Ludwigsburg and local products from Mons and Nimy, dating from the 18th c. to the present day.

Musée de
Céramique

Almost 20,000 coins and medals from all epochs and countries fill the showcases of the Numismatic Museum on the second floor.

Musée de
Numismatique

Not far away from the Musées du Centenaire is the Musée des Beaux Arts where there is a collection of pictures primarily by French and Belgian artists from the 16th to 18th c., but there are no particularly fine works.

Musée des
Beaux Arts

The Musée de la Vie montoise on the left of the Museum of Art is a very beautiful museum which in a very vivid way describes the life of the people in Mons. It is housed in the Maison Jean Lescarts, a convent building of 1632 and in three rooms exhibits everyday objects and objets d'art.

*Musée de la
Vie montoise

This museum is situated a little north of the Collégiale Ste-Waudru and is in two buildings: the so-called "Vieux Logis" a brick building of 1550, and the Chapelle Ste-Marguerite (13th c.). On display is the art collection of Canon Edmont Puissant, who made this over to the town in 1930, with pictures, furniture and other interior items as well as the canon's library which includes a Gutenberg bible.

Musée du
Chanoine Puissant

The Natural History Museum is situated north-west of the City Hall in the Rue des Gaillers. Here can be seen numerous articles of geology, zoology, botany and other scientific disciplines. (Open: Mon.–Fri. 8.30am–noon and 1–5pm., Sat. 10am–noon and 2–6pm.)

Musée d'Histoire
naturelle

Surroundings

Casteau, 10km/6 miles north-east of Mons, has a 13th c. church and the remains of a castle. The place is well known as the seat of the headquarters of NATO in Europe, SHAPE (Supreme Headquarters of the Allied Powers in Europe).

Casteau

See entry

Belœil

See entry

Binche

See Binche, Surroundings

Strépy Thieu

Soignes · Zinnik

D 6

Soignes, 19km/12 miles north-east of Mons, arose around an abbey founded in 650 by St Vincentius. Its heavy reliquary, weighing 250kg/551lbs, is carried every Whitsun in a great procession through the town.

The building of this massive church dedicated to St Vincent and in the style of Scheldt Romanesque was begun in 965 and completed in the 13th c. Both bays of the choir contain the oldest cross-ribbed vault in Belgium (believed 11th c.). The interior of the church with its two rows of arcades and its gallery is similar to that of the cathedral at Tounai (see entry). The most impressive items are undoubtedly the sculpture, the Renaissance choir screen made of marble and stucco, an interment scene in the ambulatory (15th c.), a "Nursing Virgin" (14th c.), and the Baroque choirstalls and

* Collégiale
Saint-Vincent

pulpit. The great 19th c. shrine of the saint stands in the choir. In the Chapel of St Hubert in the south wall is kept the treasury.

The old cemetery, not far from the church, is a public park in which can be seen a Romanesque chapel which is now an archaeological museum.

Museums
In the Culture House of Soignes is an apothecary museum and a photography museum.

La Borinage
C/D 7

To the south and south-west of Mons stretches the coalfield of the Borinage. In spite of the decline of Belgian mining, there are still winding towers and a workers' settlement to be seen amid the high slag heaps, the so-called "terils".

Cuesmes
Vincent van Gogh lived in Cuesmes, 3km/2 miles south, as a worker-priest among the miners of the Borinage from the summer of 1879 to the autumn of 1880 before he finally turned to painting.

Van Gogh house
On the edge of the forest stands a little mining cottage where he occupied a room; this is filled with documents and reproductions of his paintings (no originals; open: daily except Monday 10am–6pm).

*Hornu
Hornu lies 10km/6 miles to the west and is the oldest mining village of the Borinage. Here between 1814 and 1832 the industrialist Henri de Gorge put into operation his ideas, which were revolutionary for that time, for the unity of work and residence. The working complex of "Grand Hornu", now a protected monument, consisted of the mine, iron foundry, engineering offices, schools, a hospital, public squares, and 400 houses for workers. with an elliptical central square, around which were grouped the offices. Each worker's house had its own garden and the whole complex was financed by Henri de Gorge. In 1829 there were 2500 people in "Grand Hornu". (Open: Mar.–Sept. Tues.–Sun. 10am–noon and 2–6pm; Oct.–Feb. only until 4pm.)

Roisin
Right in the south-western tip of the Borinage lies the village of Roisin and nearby in a house by the rock "Caillou-qui-bique" the poet Emile Verhaeren spent the last 15 years of his life. Mementoes of the poet can be seen in the house.

Spiennes
The finds in the "Camp à Cayaux", 6km/3¾ miles from Mons near Spiennes, which can be seen in the little museum, prove that coal was being dug in the Borinage as long ago as the Stone Age.

Namur · Namen
F 7

Province: Namur
Altitude: 83m/272ft
Population: 103,000
Intercity and Inter-regional Station (bicycle rental at station)

Location
Namur (Flemish Namen) is situated at the confluence of the Sambre and the Meuse and is the ideal base for visiting the picturesque Upper Meuse Valley. It is the capital of the province of the same name, the seat of a bishop, a university town and an important communications junction for railway, inland shipping and road transport. Industries include glass, porcelain, paper and steel factories which are principally located in the suburb of Jambes. Because of its strategic position Namur has had to suffer a number of sieges in the course of its history. During these large parts of the town were destroyed again and again, so that a coherent and attractive townscape no longer exists. However, the citadel is well worth a visit on account of its excellent museums.

The hill on which stands the citadel of Namur was already of military importance in Roman times and was fortified at a very early date. Many historians presume that this was the seat of the Germanic Aduatuker, of whom Caesar speaks in the "Gallic Wars". Below the hill a settlement arose on the banks of the Sambre which from the 10th c. was the chief place of the county. This was seized by Burgundy in 1421 and in 1559 was raised to the status of a bishopric. From the 15th c. the history of Namur consists of a sequence of sieges and destruction in war. The most famous siege occurred in 1692 under Louis XIV and Vauban and ended with the entry of the French; in 1695, however, they had to give way to William III of Orange. In 1746 the French were once again in Namur but were driven out two years later by the Austrians, who for their part had to withdraw in 1792 in the face of the French revolutionaries who won back the city in the same year and two years later surrendered it to the Austrians. The latter were succeeded in 1816 by the Netherlanders who extended the citadel. In the Kingdom of Belgium the advance forts which had been erected in 1889–1902 were strong points of the Belgian line from the Meuse which, however, was taken in 1914 and again in 1940 by German troops. | History

Trips on the Meuse as far as Dinant (see entry) and on the Sambre are organised from Namur. The landing stage is on the Pointe de Grognon, the tongue of land at the estuary of the Sambre. | River trips

Inner City

If the Pointe de Grognon is chosen as a starting point for a walk of discovery around the inner city, the Sambre must first be crossed on the Pont de | *Musée Archéologique

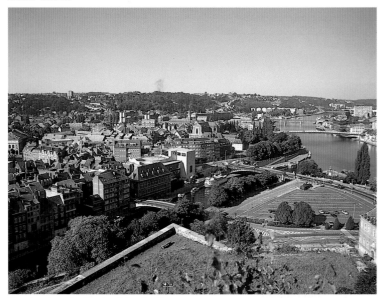

Namur, where the Sambre joins the Meuse

France and on the right will be seen the stately brick front of the former meat hall (1590). This now houses the Archaeological Museum which has a comprehensive collection of antiquities from the Province of Namur from Roman, Frankish, Merovingian periods (1st–7th c.); it is one of the best in Belgium. The goldsmith's work and glass work are valuable and unique. (Open: daily except Fri. 10am–noon and 2–5pm.)

Bourse

Beffroi

A short way from the museum is the Place d'Armes, the busiest square in the town, the north side of which includes the former exchange. To the rear rises the bell-tower, the foundations of which are a remnant of the Tour Saint-Jacques which was part of the second city wall in the 14th c.

Maisons des Sœurs de Notre-Dame
**Church treasury

The road in front of the exchange leading to the right comes into the square in front of the theatre. On the right in the Rue J. Billart lies the former Convent of the Sisters of Notre-Dame, in which one of the finest ecclesiastical treasuries in the country is kept. It consists of the treasure from the monastery of Oignies which came into the possession of the convent in 1818; its finest pieces were the work of the goldsmith Pater Hugo von Oignies. Hugo lived in the 12th/13th c. in the monastery of Oignies, and his work is in the tradition of the great masters of the Meuse district, Renier and Godefroid de Huy and Nikolaus of Verdun. Characteristic of his work is the extremely delicate chasing with foliage and sometimes little hunting scenes. There are two magnificent pieces exhibited in Namur: a cover of a gospel of 1230 from Trier decorated with enamel work, and the goblet of Gilles de Walcourt of 1238. (Open: Mon.–Sat. 9am–noon and 2–5pm, Sun. afternoons only; closed in March.)

The Church of Notre-Dame belonging to the convent lies further east. This Baroque church, restored between 1750 and 1756, contains in the crypt the funerary monuments of Counts Wilhelm I and Wilhelm II of Namur (died 1391 and 1418).

The belfry

The moat and Saint-Aubain

Returning and passing the theatre we come to Rue E. Cuvelier which leads into the Rue de Fer where can be seen the fine patrician residence the Hôtel de Gaiffier d'Hestroy dating from the 17th/18th c. It contains the Musée des Arts anciens du Namurois which exhibits artistic artefacts of the Middle Ages and the Renaissance from the region of Namur, especially goldsmiths' work, sculptures, copper utensils and ivory pieces. The department of painting contains four works by the painter Henri Blès (1510–50) who came from Bouvignes on the Meuse.

• Musée des Arts anciens du Namurois

On the far side of the Rue du Bruxelles the Rue d'Angle and the Rue de Fer continue. From here there is a turn to the right to the Baroque Church of Saint-Loup, architecturally the most interesting church in Namur because of its stucco façade with 12 Doric pillars. Peter Huyssens designed the plans for the church which was built in 1621–45; the College of Jesuits which now serves as a grammar school is richly furnished.

• Saint-Loup

Straight ahead the Place Saint Aubain opens out with the seat of the provincial government on its right side; this is the white shining former bishops' palace. In the middle of the square rises the Cathedral of Saint Aubain, a stately Classical domed building dating from 1751–67 which was built by Gaetano Pizzoni from Milan on the site of a previous 11th c. church. Particular features of the spacious interior are statues from Florette Abbey by Lauarent Delvaux, a choir screen of 1744, and behind the high altar a memorial plaque to Don Juan of Austria. who died in 1578 near Namur and whose body was taken in 1579 to the Escorial near Madrid. In the plaque a container was incorporated containing the heart of the victor of Lepanto.

Saint Aubain

On the right near the choir of Saint Aubain is the Renaissance building of the Diocesan Museum with the cathedral treasury. On display are liturgical vessels, vestments, sculpture and goldsmiths' work. Of special note are a portable altar of the Counts of Namur (12th c.) with ivory decoration, a

Musée diocesain et trésor de la cathédrale

Merovingian reliquary (8th c.) from Andenne and the reliquary crown of Philip the Noble of Namur which, it is said, bears thorns from Christ's passion crown; it was a gift from Philip's brother Henry of Constantinople. (Open: Easter–Oct. Tues.–Sat. 10am–noon and 2.30–6pm, Sun. and Mon. as well as Nov.–Easter afternoons only.)

* Musée de Croix

Going south from Saint-Aubain in the direction of the Sambre we come to the Musée de Croix. It is housed in the imposing town palace of the Groesbeck-Croix family which was built in the 18th c. in Louis XV style. In the interior the rooms are decorated in the fashion of the time, including hand-painted wallpaper, and contain magnificent objets d'art such as Chinese porcelain, paintings and sculptures. The kitchen, which has a huge chimney, is full of old household implements (guided tours: daily except Tues. 10 and 11am, 2, 3 and 4pm).

Musée Felicien Rops

Leaving the museum we turn right into the Rue des Brasseurs and immediately into a narrow street to the Musée Felicien Rops. Rops (1833–98), who was born in Namur, worked as a illustrator of literary and political books which had a satirical element. He was notorious as his works consisted, in the opinion of many of his contemporaries, of pure pornography. A selection can be seen in the museum (open: daily except Tues. 10am–5pm; Easter–Nov. until 6pm; July, Aug. also Tues.).

Musée africain

To the north-east just outside the inner city is the Musée africain which exhibits artistic objects of art and everyday life from the former Belgium colony of the Congo. (Open: Sun., Tues. and Thur. 2–5pm.)

* Citadelle de Namur

History

The citadel above the town, one of the mightiest fortresses of Europe can look back on a history of 2000 years. As early as Roman times the rocky outcrop between the Sambre and the Meuse was fortified, and the Counts of Namur chose this as the site for their castle. The extension of the citadel began in the 15th c. with subterranean defence passages which were completed in the 17th and 18th c. by Vauban and the Dutchman Coehoorn.

Access

There are several ways of reaching the citadel hill: by cable-way (téléphérique; lower station not far from the Pont de France near the Rue Notre-Dame; Apr.–mid Sept. daily 10am–6pm); by bus from the station; by car along the Route Merveilleuse behind the casino, over the steep bank of the Meuse or along the Route Panoramas through the citadel park; on foot on one of the paths along the bank of the Sambre also through the park. The entrance to the citadel is situated opposite the horseshoe-shaped stadium.

Tour
Apr.–Oct.
daily noon–7pm

A fine tourist trail leads through the citadel complex and this includes the subterranean passages. From the barracks a light railway covers the major attractions; there is also a film about the history of the fortress. The citadel can be clearly divided into four sections. Nearest the entrance is the "ouvrage à cornes" (earthworks in the shape of horns) and the powder magazine built by the Dutch. The path leads down to the Dutch barracks (which can also be reached along the subterranean "Galéries Boufflers"), the central point of the section called "terra nova", the "New Fortress" built by Vauban and Coehoorn.

Below the barracks the bridge, from which there is an impressive view of the town, leads across a deep ditch and links the "terra nova" with the section of the fortress called "Médiane" dating from the 16th c. From here the visitor can look down onto the bend of the Route Merveilleuse around the "donjon" (the site of the medieval castle). Only the detached Tour Joyeuse and two other towers (in one of which a military museum is housed) have remained from the fortress. A good view of the town can be enjoyed from a little platform near a halt on the way down from the citadel.

Citadelle de Namur

Ausfalltor
MEDIANE
DONJON
1
3
2
5
4
Graben
TERRA NOVA
6
7
Téléphérique
Centre
8
OUVRAGE
A CORNES
Stade
Entrance
des Jeux
50 m
© Baedeker

1 Tour des Guetteurs
2 Tour Joyeuse
3 Musée d'armes
4 Gun-carriage shed (1835)
5 Circuit des
   Caponnières
   (underground
   passages)
6 Barracks (1815)
7 Galéries Bouffiers
   (underground
   passages)
8 Powder magazine (1815)
---- Underground passages

From the top of the citadel hill extends the 65ha/160 acres wooded Parc de la Citadelle, a favourite rendezvous for the inhabitants of Namur at weekends. The attractions include the "Reine Fabiola" nature park and the Fort d'Orange, built in 1691 to protect the "terra nova". There are sports events in the stadium and performances in the open-air theatre. The forestry museum (Musée de la Forêt; open: Apr.–Oct. daily except Fri. 9 am–noon and 2–5pm) is devoted to the flora and fauna of the Ardennes forest; its principal attraction is a very fine large diorama with animals of the forest and a comprehensive collection of insects.

Parc de la Citadelle

Musée de la Forêt

Below the citadel on the left bank of the Meuse extends the oldest part of the town, of which, however, very little has remained. At the confluence of the Sambre and the Meuse, on a spit of land called Pointe de Grognon, stands an equestrian monument to King Albert (1955). To the right is the Hospice Saint-Gilles (16/17th c.) in the chapel of which can be seen the interesting tomb of the sculptor Colard Jacoris of 1395. Further downstream the Pont de Jambes (restored after war damage) links Namur with the suburb of Jambes. Still further to the south in the Avenue Baron de Moareau can be found the casino built in 1911 and the gardens called La Plante.

Below the citadel

Surroundings

10km/6 miles west of Namur lies the village of Floreffe where on a hill stands the great former Premonstratensian abbey, one of the best preserved examples of this order in Belgium. The abbey was founded in 1121 by St Norbert and extended in the 17th and 18th c. to its present size. The French Revolution put a stop to monastic life, but it is continued today in the form of a little seminar. Of the 90m/295ft abbey church only the transepts and sacristy still remain from the initial phase; the interior was restored at the end of the 18th c. by Dewez. Of particular interest are the choirstalls by Peter Enderlin. There are 74 seats richly carved including some with effigies of the founders of the order. The brewery which served

Floreffe

°Abbey

also as a mill dates from the 13th c. and from it the light and sweet monastery beer which is highly prized throughout Belgium can be obtained. The grottos of Floreffe are also worth seeing.

Fosses-la-Ville

It is another 10km/6 miles from Floreffe to Fosses-la-Ville which was already settled by the Celts and which in Roman times was called "Fossa". The Irish missionary Feuillen (or Follianus) founded a monastery here around 650 which was destroyed in the 10th c. However in the 11th c., when the relics of St Feuillen were brought here, a start was made with the building of a new church. Of this there remain only the tower, the choir and the crypt which is the oldest in Belgium. The remainder of the Church of St Feuillen was rebuilt in the 18th c. The oak choirstalls (1524) and the 16th c. reliquary of the saints are worth seeing.

Musée "Le Petit Chapitre"

Carnival

Highly unusual is the Musée "Le Petit Chapitre" in which more than 800 handmade puppets are exhibited representing the various type of Belgian people. Fosses-la-Ville is also well known for its carnival, in which the "Chinels" dance like marionettes, and for its military procession "Marche de Saint-Feuillen" which takes place every seven years (next in 1998).

Franc-Waret

Near Franc-Waret, 13km/8 miles north-east, stands the imposing castle of the same name dating from the 17th c. but which was considerably extended in the 18th c. in the style of Louis XV. The buildings are grouped around an inner courtyard reached across a drawbridge. During the guided tour visitors see the priceless furnished rooms with beautiful Brussels tapestries, a porcelain collection and Dutch-Flemish paintings. Around the castle extend a 17th c. French garden and an 18th c. English garden (open: June–Sept. Sat., Sun. and public holidays 2–5.30pm).

Marche-les-Dames

2km/1¼ miles before reaching Franc-Waret we pass through Gelbressée where Juan of Austria set up his headquarters during the siege of Namur in 1578. A narrow road leads south from here to Marche-les-Dames on the Meuse where a Cistercian abbey was founded in the 13th c. It is possible to return to Namur on the road along the bank of the river from Marche-les-Dames. Shortly after leaving the village can be seen the 70m/230ft high-rock, the Rocher du Roi Albert, or "Rocher Fatale", from which King Albert I fell to his death on February 17th 1934.

Other places in the vicinity

See Vallée de la Meuse

Nieuwpoort · Nieuport

A 4

Province: West Vlaanderen
Altitude: Sea level
Population: 9000

Location

The town of Nieuwpoort (French Nieuport) lies on the IJzer 3km/2 miles from where it flows into the North Sea. It is divided into Nieuwpoort Bad and Nieuwpoort Stad lying a little further inland, and is an important fishing port as well as the location of a fish processing industry. Other firms specialise in metalworking and chemicals which play an important part in the economy. The importance of tourism, which is concentrated in Nieuwpoort Bad, can be seen from the extensive yacht harbour, one of the largest in the North Sea. Its capacity is to be increased to 2600 moorings.

History

In the 12th c. when the IJzer had altered its course, Nieuwpoort was founded by Count Philip of Flanders as a fortified new harbour ("Nieuwpoort") for Ypres in place of Lombardsijde and in the course of time suffered seven sieges. In 1383 it was completely destroyed by the English. In July 1600 Mortiz of Orange defeated the Spanish on the dunes between

On the mole at Nieuwpoort

Nieuwpoort and Middelkerke, but this victory was of minor importance in the War of Independence of the Netherlands. In the First World War Nieuwpoort formed the key to the position on the IJzer to which the Allied armies withdrew. On October 29th 1914 the sluices on the IJzer were opened and the polders were flooded in order the prevent the advance of the German troops. However that did not prevent Nieuwpoort being almost completely destroyed in 1918. After the war the town was rebuilt according to the old plans.

Boat excursions as far as Diksmuide (see entry) can be made on the IJzer (May–Sept. daily 2pm; information tel. 23 67 66), and in July and August sea trips are operated by the fishing boat "Jean Bart IV" every Wednesday morning at 9am.

Boat excursions

Sights

Nieuwpoort Stad is a tranquil place and an attractive picture is presented by its extensive Grote Markt with its belfry, an old Renaissance house (rebuilt 1924; containing a small ornithological museum) and the corn hall, originally Late-Gothic of 1218 and rebuilt in 1923. The first storey of the hall houses the interesting K. R. Berquin Museum of History and Local History, in which can be seen among other things two views of Nieuwpoort which are attributed to Lancelot Blondeel.

Grote Markt

Behind the town hall stands the Onze-Lieve-Vroukerk which was destroyed in both World Wars but rebuilt in 1922 and 1946 in its original Gothic style. In the detached tower there is a carillon of 67 bells.

Onze-Lieve-Vroukerk

Six canals, which are regulated by many sluices, join the IJzer in Nieuwpoort. These are situated a little north of the Grote Markt near the IJzer bridge and are an interesting sight.

∗IJzer sluices

Koning Albert Monument	Near the bridge a large equestrian statue was erected in honour of the Belgian King Albert I; it is surrounded by a rondel supported by 20 pillars. From the top of the monument there is good view over the town and its surroundings.
Fishing and yacht harbour	In the fishing harbour on the Vismijnkaai the daily catch is still auctioned. A little to the north lie the basins of the yacht harbour.
Ijzermonding Nature Reserve	In the area of the IJzer estuary stretches the large Ijzermonding Nature Reserve (16ha/40 acres). Here many aquatic birds and waders have their nests. The reserve can only be visited on a guided tour (July and August on Sundays at 10.30am).

Surroundings

Lombardsijde	The little village of Lombardsijde has no attractions apart from the figure of the Madonna which was found on the beach and is now in the village church. The village is interesting on account of its history. In the 5th c. there was a large Anglo-Saxon settlement here which grew in the 11th c. into an important town with a large harbour. Storm floods in 1116 and 1134 devastated the town almost completely and altered the course of the IJzer so that Lombardsijde was divided from Nieuwpoort.
Middelkerke	Halfway towards Ostend (see entry) lies the quiet resort of Middelkerke which has a casino in addition to the leisure pursuits of water-sports, walking, riding and cycling.
Oostduinkerke	See Koksijde, Surroundings.

Nivelles · Nijvel   E 6

> Province: Brabant
> Altitude: 99m/325ft
> Population: 22,000
> Intercity and Inter-regional Station (bicycle rental at station)

Location	Nivelles (Flemish Nijvel) lies in the middle of an extensive fertile landscape south of Brussels. Although during the heavy bombing in the Second World War a great part of the town and buildings fell in rubble and ashes, including historical treasures of incalculable worth, the town very quickly recovered. Developed from a former agricultural centre to a modern industrial town the most important branches of industry, in addition to metal processing (railway equipment works, machine tools), is the production of paper.
History	The origins of the present town go right back to the early Christian centuries. Pippin the Elder, the chamberlain of the Merovingian king Dagobert I, owned considerable estates in this area. After his death his widow Itta and her daughter Gertrude moved here and founded a Benedictine convent around 650, the first convent on what is now Belgium territory. The first abbess was Gertrude, patroness of numerous medieval hospitals. She died in 659 and her grave soon became the object of pilgrimages around which the town developed. In the 11th c. the town had reached the height of its prosperity and this manifested itself in the building of the collegiate church. In the 12th c. Nivelles was surrounded by a wall 12km/7½ miles in length; at the beginning of the 16th c. it developed into a prosperous town with 20,000 inhabitants and eight guilds. Decline set in in 1789 with the dissolution of the convent with which the history of the town had always been connected. In 1815 Nivelles was besieged by Dutch troops. During the First

World War the town was spared, but a German bombing attack in May 1940 destroyed 50% of the old town and 20% of all the buildings.

Every year on the Sunday after St Michael's day a large procession attended by crowds of people takes place in honour of St Gertrude. The faithful, dressed in historical costumes, accompany the processional chariot which dates from the 15th c. and which is drawn by six horses carrying the reliquary of St Gertrude. During the 14km/9 mile tour around the town two meal breaks are taken. In addition to the faithful the giants Argayon and Argayonne accompany the procession, as well as their son Lolo and his horse Godet.

Procession

* Collégiale Sainte-Gertrude

The former Collégiale Sainte-Gertrude, a collegiate church dedicated in 1046 in the presence of the German emperor Heinrich III and which dominates the Grand-Place of Nivelles, is one of the most sumptuous examples of Romanesque architecture in Belgium. The origin of the church, built in Ottoman Romanesque style, was the monastic Church of Saint-Pierre dating from about 650 and rebuilt in four phases until the 10th c. The last church was burnt down at the beginning of the 11th c., and it was resolved to erect a new one, but this was badly damaged in the bombing attacks of 1940. The church treasury and two-thirds of the sumptuous shrine of St Gertrude were lost for ever. Rebuilding of the church was only decided upon in 1984. Today the Church of St Gertrude appears largely in the form in which it was conceived in the 11th c. The special nature of its architecture

Guided tours
Mon.–Fri.
10, 11am, 2, 3, 4pm
Sat., Sun. and
public
holidays
2, 3, 4 pm

lies in the plan of two transepts and two choirs opposite one another. The huge west front with its octagonal belfry and two 12th c. side doors is probably reminiscent of its Ottonian predecessor. In the right-hand tower a copper figure of Jean de Nivelles dating from the 15th c. strikes the hours with a hammer. Of the sculptures on the door of the west front only a doorpost with scenes of the legend of Sampson (north doorway) and the Angel Michael (south doorway) survive; the southern gable of the east transept is also artistically interesting.

The interior of the church is impressive, mainly because of its size (102m/335ft long, 20m/66ft high) but as a result of losses during the war, the simplicity of its decoration does not immediately strike the eye. Of note are the Baroque oak and marble pulpit by Laurent Delvaux with rich figurative decoration portraying the story of Jesus and the Samaritan, as well as Renaissance choir stalls in the northern part of the east transept. The famous shrine of St Gertrude, which was considered among the most valuable works of the Gothic goldsmith's art, was largely destroyed in a bombing attack of 1940. In the church can be seen a replica by Félix Roulina and a Late-Gothic brass container for the reliquary.

Interior

Above the choir at the west end of the church is the 19m/62ft-high Salle impériale, reached by a flight of 132 steps. It served the abbess for official receptions.

Salle impériale

The three-aisled crypt, c. 1100, is situated below the east choir. With an area of 230sq.m/2476sq.ft it is the largest in Belgium. From it the visitor can reach the excavations in which fragments of the predecessors of the present-day church were found in 1941–52, as well as the grave of Ermentrude (1001), the granddaughter of Hugo Capet, the first king of France.

Crypt

Cloister of the Collégiale Sainte-Gertrude   *Fontaine du Perron*

Cloister

The beautiful cloister of the church is a transitional work of the beginning of the 13th c.; only the north gallery in its original condition dates from this time. In the passages and in the courtyard gravestones and parts of the old bells are displayed.

Other Sights

Fontaine du Perron

At the junction of roads opposite the west front of the church can be seen the Fontaine du Perron, a fountain donated by the abbot Adrienne de Moerbeke in 1523 on which can be seen the effigy of the Archangel Michael (replica of 1922).

Tour Simone

From the fountain we pass along the Rue Seutin to the Tour Simone the last remaining of the 12 towers of the medieval town fortifications.

Musée d'Archéologie, d'Art et d'Histoire

The Museum of Archaeology, Art and History (Musée d'Archéologie, d'Art et d'Histoire) is housed in the vine-clad former refuge of the Trinity Brothers of Orval dating from 1763 (27 Rue de Bruxelles).
In ten rooms on two floors are art treasures saved from the Church of St Gertrude, including remains of the saints reliquary, Brussels wall-hangings, tombstones, sculptures, paintings, furniture and instruments of the 18th c., as well as finds from Gallo-Roman times. (Open: Mon., Thur., Fri., Sat., Sun. 9.30am–noon and 2–5pm, Wed. 9am–5pm.)

Chapelle de Recollets

The most important sacred building in Nivelles, apart from St Gertrude, is the Chapelle de Recollets in the Place de l'Abreuvoir, a beautiful Late-Gothic building in which the shrine of St Marie de Nivelles (Marie d'Ottignies) dating from the 17th c. is kept.

La Tourette

In the Avenue de la Tour de Guet, which passes the Parc de la Dodaine, stands "La Tourette", an original 17th c. brick tower.

Surroundings

17km/10½ miles east of Nivelles lies Villers-la-Ville where the most impressive ruins of the Cistercian abbey, the largest monastic ruins in Belgium, can be visited. The complex, founded in 1146 by Bernhard von Clairvaux after the model of the mother house in Citeaux, arose principally in the 12th and 13th c. and during its history was laid waste on several occasions, but until the 18th c. was again and again restored. Finally the French revolutionary troops destroyed the building which was then used as a quarry and was even further plundered. In the middle of the 19th c. a railway viaduct crossed the area.

Villers-la-Ville
Abbey ruins

The visit to the abbey, which, apart from a few local variations was erected in the Classical style of the Cistercians, follows a signposted route. In the court of honour opposite the entrance is a 13th c. watermill, now used as a restaurant, which is surrounded by 18th c. buildings among which on the right stands the monastery palace. Grouped around the large cloister, built in the 14th c. and restored in the 16th, are the Chapter House, with the dormitory of the monks over it, and in the south a thermal room, refectory and a kitchen. On the west are the dormitories of the lay brothers. The restored gallery of the cloister is now a lapidarium; among the remains can be seen the grave of Gobert d'Aspermont who died in 1263. The 13th c. monastery church follows the French model with the exception of the semi-circular apse which in Cistercian churches is usually straight, and the round window in the roof. The best preserved of the working quarters is the large 13th c. brewery.

In the parish church of Villers-la-Ville are two magnificent altar pieces from Brussels' workshops; both portray scenes from the life of Mary; the lower one was made in 1450 and the upper in 1538.

Parish church

Ophain-Bois-Seigneur-Isaac, 6km/4 miles north of Brussels, has a charming group of monastic buildings dating from the 14th–16th c. In the

Ophain-Bois-Seigneur-Isaac

Ruins of the Abbey of Villers-la-Ville

monastery church, which has an altar sculpture by Laurent Delvaux, can be seen a reliquary of 1555 containing a piece of linen said to be stained with the blood of Christ. The other monastery buildings, including the cloister of 1613 and the imposing monastery farm, are also well worth seeing. Opposite the abbey the lords of Ittre built a prestigious castle in Louis XVI style.

Seneffe

9km/5½ miles south of Nivelles stands the three-winged castle of Seneffe also in the style of Louis XVI and surrounded by a very fine park.

Ecausinnes

See entry

The sloping lock of Ronquières

See Ecausinnes

Oostduinkerke

See Koksijde, Surroundings

Orval (Abbey)   G 10

Province: Luxembourg
Altitude: 280m/919ft

*Location

Amid the quiet and picturesque forest of the Gaume, right on the French border, lies the most extensive and most beautiful monastery in Belgium, the Trappist abbey of Notre Dame d'Orval which has had a moving history. There is a legend about the name "Orval" (from the French "val d'or" =

The picturesque monastery ruins of Orval

golden valley). It tells that Countess Mathilde of Chiny, Duchess of Lower Lorraine, was one day resting near a spring and lost her ring which fell into the water. Saddened she prayed in a nearby chapel and a miracle occurred: a trout brought the ring back to her at which she cried out "this place must really be a golden valley"; the Romans had already described it as such. The arms of the monastery depict this legend by showing a blue stream on which the trout rises with the ring in its mouth.

The monks run a flourishing farm and the monastery is famous for its beer and its cheese.

The first monastery in the "golden valley" is said to have been founded in 1070 by Benedictines from Calabria in southern Italy. They were followed in 1132 by Cistercians who began building the Church of Notre-Dame. After a fire in 1251 it was rebuilt in the 15th and 16th c. and was extended around the monastery buildings. However in 1637 soldiers of the French Marshall Châtillon set fire to the complex. The monks began again and the building was successfully restored. Around 1700 the Abbey of Orval, which had adopted in 1683 the strict observance of the Trappist order, was one of the most prosperous monasteries in Europe. The architect Benoît Dewez was instructed to plan new buildings which were consecrated in 1732. However, once again it was French soldiers, this time the revolutionary troops

History

1 Fontaine Mathilde
2 Tomb of Wenceslas
3 Royal Chapel
4 Scriptorium
5 Chapter House
6 Museum

Abbaye Notre-Dame d'Orval

Florenville, Virton

of General Loison, who destroyed the monastery in 1793, and in 1797 the grounds were finally sold. It was not until 1926 that a new beginning was made and this on the foundations of Dewez' building. Finally in 1948 the present new monastery, planned by Henri Vaes, conforming to the architectural practices of the Cistercians but with Romanesque and Gothic elements, could be consecrated.

Visit

*New monastery buildings

The new monastery buildings can only be visited by previous arrangement and accompanied by a monk. From a little tower in the wall just behind the Court of Charity there is a fine view of the extensive complex. In the middle is the Court of Honour with a trapeze-shaped pond; from here a broad flight of steps leads up to the new monastery church, the façade of which is dominated by a monumental 17m/56ft-high statue of the Virgin Mary by Lode Vleeshouwers. Near the left aisle rises the 60m/197ft high belfry. On enquiring at the door visitors can attend services (Mon.–Sat. 11am, Sun. 9.30am), Vespers (daily 5.40pm) and Compline (daily 7.30pm).

*Abbey ruins

Opening times
Easter–Sept.
daily 9am–12.30pm
and 1.30–7pm;
Oct.–Easter
daily
10am–12.30pm
and 1.30–5pm;
closed Mon.
morning

From the entrance to the abbey grounds the Court of Charity and the guesthouse can be seen. Visitors pass through the shop where souvenirs, beer, cheese and bread are sold, and arrive in the old reception house where an audio-visual show (in French and Dutch) gives information about the life of the monks. From the ruins looking left is an equipment barn which was once the studio of the lay brother Jean-Henri-Gilson (1741–1809) known as the painter-monk Abraham of Orval; many churches in the vicinity possess one of his paintings. Nearby is the Mathilde Fountain about which is woven the legend of the lost ring. Next can be seen the remains of the early Gothic monastery church; the parts which have survived are the walls and arches of the nave, the choir and the apse, as well as the transepts; the great rose window in the left transept and the slender window arches are striking. Also noteworthy are the Gothic and Romanesque capitals of the pillars. In the choir stands the replica of the tomb of Wenceslas, the first duke of Luxemburg who died in 1383. The monastery buildings adjoin the right side aisle and are entered by way of a flight of steps, at the foot of which the best known abbot of Orval, Bernard de Montgaillard, was buried in 1628. Remains of his grave inscription can be seen on a pillar. The extremely long room was the reading room in which 15,000 books were available; from here we reach the arches of the ancient 18th c. vaulted cellar below the steps which now houses a museum on the history of the monastery. Returning to the entrance building a look should be taken at the herb garden and the old apothecary in which a museum of medicine has been set up.

Ostend · Oostende · Ostende   A 4

Province: West-Vlaanderen
Altitude: Sea level
Population: 68,400
Intercity Station (bicycle rental at station)

Location

Ostend (Flemish Oostende, French Ostende) on the North Sea coast is the home of the largest high seas fishing fleet in Belgium and the location of three technical schools of fishing. It is the most important ocean and ferry harbour in the country and deals with a large part of the ferry traffic to Great Britain. In addition Ostend is the largest Belgium seaside resort and one of the most popular in Europe and can look back on a fashionable past; since 1933 the town also is able to call itself a spa. Foreign trade is the lifeblood of Ostend, especially as fishing has suffered a decline, and the economy of the harbour is threatened by the building of the channel tunnel and with

*Seaside resort

competition from the very modern port facilities of Zeebrugge (see entry), so that industry (ship building and fish processing) is of increased importance. Since 1733 oyster farming has been practised in Ostend.

The town was originally a village at the east end of the spit of land Ter Streep which has meanwhile silted up. It is first mentioned in 814 and received its charter in 1267. A new harbour was built in the 15th c. and new defences in 1583. At the end of the 16th c. Ostend was the last bastion of the Dutch in the southern Netherlands and was violently attacked by the Spaniards. The archduchess Isabella vowed in 1601 to change her shirt only if this bastion fell. One can only hope that she did not comply with her vow for the siege lasted three years and caused 72,000 deaths. In the following centuries the town had various masters, Spanish, French and Austrian until it finally became Belgian. Shortly after that the first British arrived for a seaside holiday and Ostend began to develop into an extensive seaside resort of the Belle Epoque. In 1834 Queen Victoria and later the Belgian rulers also visited it. In the First World War Ostend like Zeebrugge was a German U-boat base and suffered greatly from the effects of the conflict; the Second World War brought several bombardments during which almost all the important buildings were damaged. The flood of 1953 also caused considerable damage when the dyke between Ostend and Knokke-Heist (see entry) gave way.

Festivals

The most celebrated festival in Ostend is the "Ball of the dead Rats" which takes place during the carnival. It was created by Ostend's greatest son, the painter James Ensor (1860–1949) and his friends who had seen it in Paris in the cabaret "Au Rat Mort" in Montmartre. In addition the carnival-like prawn and shrimp festival and the Blessing of the Sea in May attract many visitors.

Beaches and sports facilities

Ostend has five bathing beaches with all facilities such as showers, cabins, deck-chairs, etc.: the small beach between the dyke and the harbour entrance, the western beach between the kursaal and the racecourse, the beaches of Mariakerke and Raversijde west of the racecourse, and the beach to the east of the harbour. The facilities for sport are so comprehensive (including archery, sailing, riding) that almost every activity is catered for.

Sights

*Beach promenade
Casino

A good survey of beach activities can be had from Albert I promenade which is lined with restaurants and a few villas. Here is the casino, originally dating from 1745 and re-opened in 1953 after destruction in the Second World War. The first floor is decorated with frescoes by Paul Delvaux. The road continues on the 10m/33ft-high and 30m/98ft-wide Zeedijk which extends as far as the dunes near Westende, 15km/9½ miles. Here can be seen the royal residence, the spa complex and the Wellington racecourse.

*Harbour

Two so-called sea landing stages (Flemish Staketsel) extend out for a long way into the sea to protect the entrance of the harbour. The western

Ostend: View of the yacht-harbour

breakwater, 625m/684yds long, is popular as a viewpoint. The harbour installations include several large and small basins and extend 2km/1¼ miles inland as far as the mouth of the Ostende-Brugge canal. From the ferry terminal, where the first ferry to England left in 1846, jetfoils ply to Dover. In the yacht harbour the former training ship of the Belgian maritime marine the "Mercator" lies at anchor. This three-masted schooner is now a museum in which souvenirs of the 41 trips that the ship made are displayed (open: June and Sept. daily 9am–noon and 1–6pm; July and Aug. 9am–7pm; otherwise only at weekends).

North of the yacht harbour can be found the old fishing harbour and the Visserskaai. On the mole the North Sea Aquarium can be visited (open: June–Sept. 10am–12.30pm and 2–6pm; otherwise only at weekends). The new fishing harbour is located on the far side of the harbour basin by the Visserijdok. In the fish hall (vismijn) every weekday except Thursdays the fish auction begins at 7am. From 9am prawns and shrimps are auctioned. To the east, on the far side of the harbour entrance and the fishing harbour, rises the 56m/184ft-high Nieuwe Vuurtoren (new lighthouse). Further on stretch dunes with remains of defence works of both world wars and the Fort Napoléon which dates from Napoleonic times. There are trips round the harbour and to sea on the "Franlis" (west mole) from 10.45am (Easter–May at weekends; June–mid Sept. daily).

In the centre of old Ostend on the Wapenplein stands the Feestpalais which was built in 1957 in place of the old town hall of 1711 destroyed in the Second World War. On the first floor is the local museum "De Plate" where a great deal of interesting material about the resort and the fishing at Ostend can be seen (open: July–Sept. daily except Tues. 10am–noon and 2–5pm; otherwise only Sat.). On the second floor is the Museum of Fine Art which has a good collection of works by James Ensor, Constant Permeke and other Belgian artists (open: daily except Tues. 10am–noon and 2–5pm).

Feestpalais

North of the Wapenplein in Vlaanderenstrat No. 27 James Ensor was born. The house is now furnished as a museum, in which the old shop of his uncle and aunt, personal belongings and sketches, as well as the living-room and studio of the painter can be seen (open: June–Sept. daily except Tues. 10am–noon and 2–5pm).

James Ensorhuis

All the exhibits here also concern James Ensor but are about his religious themes (open: July–Oct. Thur.–Mon. 3–6pm).

Museum voor Religieuze Kunst

In Kapellestraat, leading south from the Wapenplein, stands the three-aisled Gothic Sint-Petrus-en-Pauluskerk (1905). Only the brick tower "Peperbus" from the first half of the 18th c. with relics of the 15th c. remains from the old church. The funeral chapel of the Belgian Queen Louise-Marie, who died in Ostend in 1850, was built on to the choir.

Sint-Petrus-en-Pauluskerk

The Provinciaal Museum voor Moderne Kunst is devoted to contemporary Belgian art (open: Apr.–Oct. daily except Tues. 10am–5pm; Nov.–Mar. daily except Tues. 10am–noon).

Provinciaal Museum

South of the centre extends Maria-Hendrike-Park with a prominent water-tower. Here visitors can walk or take boat trips.

Maria-Hendrike-Park

Surroundings

Remains of the Atlantic rampart can be seen in the suburb of Raversijde situated to the south-west of Ostend.

Raversijde

In Gistel, 10km/6 miles to the south, the saint Godelieve was born in 1045. Her husband had her strangled in 1070 and threw the body into a pond;

Gistel

from then on the water was thought to have miraculous powers. The church and the museum are dedicated to the legend of St Godelieve.

Abdij Ten Putte
The pretty whitewashed abbey of Ten Putte to the west outside Gistel was laid out around the wonder-working pond. Here can be seen the cellar where Godelieve was incarcerated, as well as the chapel on the spot of her first miracle.

**De Haan ·
Le Coq**
Situated in the dunes, 6km/3¾ miles to the north-east, is De Haan which is more tranquil than Ostend. Strict building regulations ensure that no concrete tower blocks are erected but only pleasant looking houses and villas in green surroundings. De Haan has today, therefore, something of the look of the Belle Epoque.

Oudenaarde · Audenarde   C 5

Province: Oost-Vlaanderen
Altitude: 14m/46ft
Population: 27,000
Intercity Station (bicycle rental at station)

Location
Oudenaarde (French Audenarde), in the south of East Flanders where the Flemish Ardennes give way to the coastal moorland (geest) and which is traversed by the Scheldt, is a quiet township which possesses a considerable textile industry and is known for its exceptional beer from Liefmans Brewery. For art lovers Oudenaarde is, after Ghent and Tournai (see entries), of the greatest interest because of its impressive buildings in the Scheldt Gothic style and its magnificent town hall. The town was once famous for its wall tapestries, the so-called Verduren, which differed by the colouring of their floral motifs from examples in Brussels where pictorial motifs were preferred. Oudenaarde is the birthplace of Margarethe of Parma (see Introduction, Famous People) the Stadholder of the Spanish Netherlands from 1559–67, and of the painter Adriaan Brouwer (1605–38) in whose honour an annual beer festival is celebrated.

History
Oudenaarde was first mentioned in the 11th c. when Count Balduin of Flanders built a fortress here. Around this a linen-weavers' town developed which, in the 13th c., was besieged and attacked on several occasions by the men of Ghent. After the decline of the linen industry in the 15th c. the people of Oudenaarde turned to the production of their celebrated Verduren which continued for some 300 years. Meanwhile Oudenaarde several times suffered destruction and siege during the quarrels of the Flemish towns, the Dutch War of Liberation and the campaigns of conquest of Louis XIV. Oudenaarde intervened conclusively in history in the battle of July 11th 1708 when troops of the Duke of Marlborough, supported by Prince Eugen, defeated the French under the Duke of Vendôme and the Duke of Bourgogne in the Spanish War of Succession.

Sights

Market
The market, which is surrounded by an impressive ensemble of historic buildings, is the centre of the life of the town. The most striking edifice is the Stadhuis in front of which can be seen a fountain adorned with dolphins, a present from Louis XIV in 1671.

** Stadhuis
The wonderful Stadhuis was built between 1526 and 1537 according to plans by the Brussels' civic architect Hendrik van Pede on the site of the courthouse (Schepenhuis) which had been pulled down. The architect followed the Late-Gothic city halls of Brussels and Leuven (see entries) and introduced Renaissance elements. Above an arcaded passage rises the

Station

Oudenaarde
Audenarde

Park
Liedts
Liedtskasteel

Kattestraat
De Paepestraat
Bekstraat

College
Nederstraat
Hoogstraat
Einestraat

Stadhuis (i)

Hospitaal

Markt
St-Walburga
Broodstraat
Tussenbruggen

Justitie-paleis

5 4
Burgstraat
Burgschelde
1
3
2

Huis de Lalaing

Begijnhof

Marlboroughlaan
Louise Mariekaai
Bergstraat

Schelde
✠ **O.L. Vrouw-van Pamele**

Abdij van Maagdendale
150 m
© Baedeker

Brussel, Aalst

Kortrijk   Tournai

25m/82ft-high elaborate main façade adorned with figures, pilasters and arches, and separated harmoniously by the introduction of a 40m/131ft-high clock-tower. On the top of this is the figure of "Hanske de Krijger" (Henry the victor) the symbolic protector of the city. The magnificence of the exterior is complemented by the interior. Passing through the vaulted halls on the ground floor we enter the Great Hall (Volkszaal) with a balcony overlooking the market, and which is heated by means of a great Late-Gothic fireplace by the Oudenaarde sculptor Pauwel van der Schelden. The same sculptor was responsible for the porch at the entrance door of the courtroom (Schepenzaal); here should be noted the original oak floor and the pictures: Charles VI, Louis XIV on horseback, Oudenaarde in the 18th c., and some examples from the school of Adriaan Brouwers. In the archive hall documents are kept concerning the history of the town.

Next to the City Hall stands the Cloth Hall dating from the 13th c. Its roof is borne by an unusual construction of beams.

The rooms of the City Hall and the Cloth Hall house the collections of the civic museums. These include excellent examples of Verduren from Oudenaarde on the walls of the Cloth Hall, pictures, especially those of Adriaan Brouwer, Gaspard Heuvick, Jan van Ruysdael and Jan Breugel the Elder, as well as historic documents and objects including cross-bows of the Sint-Joris riflemen's guild which had been known from the 12th c., and the famous twelve pewter "presentation tankards" which were filled with wine in honour of an important visitor: two for a prince, six for a king and all twelve for the emperor.

The second building which dominates the square is Sint-Walburgakerk with its east end facing the market. It is easy to recognise that it consists of two different parts. First the somewhat slender three-aisled choir with

Guided tours:
Apr.–Oct.
Mon.–Thur. 9, 10, 11am, 2, 3, 4pm;
Fri. 2, 3, 4pm;
Sat. Sun. and public holidays no tours at 9am.

Lakenhalle

Stadelijke Musea

*Sint-Walburgakerk

317

corner towers (the side choirs dating from about 1150, the choir apses from 1406) typical of Scheldt Gothic, and the massive main nave over which rises the mighty 90m/295ft-high tower. This was begun in 1498 and completed in 1620. It houses a carillon with 47 bells. Inside the church can be seen the figures of the apostles on the pillars on the nave, as well as a number of beautiful Verduren.

Behind the church stands the Bishop's Palace built about 1600, one of the finest Renaissance buildings in Belgium. The main part, however, dates from 1722 and is also furnished with beautiful Oudenaarde tapestries. Immediately adjacent is the Hospital of Our Lady which was built in 1382.

Bisschopskwartier, Onze-Lieve-Vrouw-Ziekenhuis

Returning to the market we see on the right the former Vleeshuis. The first meat-hall was built in 1338, a new building followed in 1584 and the present neo-Classical building, which now houses the town library, in 1779.

Vleeshuis

In the nearby Late-Gothic house it is said that Margaretha van Palma was born. Immediately adjacent arises the Boudewijntoren dating from the 12th c., probably a remnant of the town fortifications.

Huis van Margaretha van Palma

Leaving the market along Burgstraat in the direction of the Scheldt we come to the Béguinage which dates from 1367. The original buildings however were destroyed by the Iconoclasts. The 32 cottages which are here today were built in the 17th c.

Béguinage

The Tussenbruggen leads across the river to the district of Pemele. On the right stands the church of Onze-Lieve-Vrouw-van-Pamele another example of Scheldt-Gothic architecture in Oudenaarde built by Arnulf von Binche, the first Flanders' builder to be known by name; a replica of a bronze plaque on the outside wall of the choir indicates this with the date 1234. The church is distinctive for its tall narrow choir windows, the corner towers of the choir and the octagonal crossing tower; the northern transept was rebuilt in the 14th c. and both side chapels on the south were added in 1524. Inside can be seen the tomb of Philipp de Locquenghien, Baron of Pamele and Lord of Oudenaarde who died in 1620, as well as a triptych with panels by Jan Snellinck.

*Onze-Lieve-Vrouw-van-Pamele

By the churchyard stands the Zwartsuisterhuis, once the house of the black sisters who devoted their lives to looking after the sick. After the destruction of the old building by the French it was restored in the 17th c.

Zwartsuisterhuis

In 1232 Cistercians settled on the right bank of the Scheldt and soon their community became one of the richest in Flanders. As time went on the convent buildings were destroyed on several occasions and rebuilt; the present building dates from the 17th and 18th c. and only the Gothic chapel has survived the storms.

Abdij van Maagdendale

To the left of the Tussenbruggen can be found the Huis de Laiaing, a pretty Rococo dwelling. As well as an exhibition of works by Oudenaarde artists it houses a wall-hangings centre where the production of Verdüren is taught, as well as a workshop for restoring old tapestries, etc. (open: Mon.–Fri. 9am–4pm).

Huis de Laiaing

The Park Liedts is reached by recrossing the Scheldt and continuing north past the post office. In the middle of the park stands the Liedtskasteel built in 1883 in Neo-Renaissance style. The four rooms contain the Folk Art Museum (open: Apr.–Oct. Mon–Fri. 9am–noon and 2–5pm, Sun. 2–6pm).

Liedtskasteel

Surroundings

8km/5 miles north-west lies Kruishoutem with a museum which was the gift of Veranneman and contains an important collection of modern art,

Kruishoutem

◄ *The Stadhuis of Oudenaarde*

including works by Permeke, Vasarely and Niki de Saint-Phall. Here also can be seen a little 17th c. castle in the middle of a large park.

Waregem
7km/4½ miles east lies Waregem known for its annual equestrian jumping championship. The local museum has some works by well-known Belgian artists.

Maarkedal
Maarkedal, 7km/4½ miles south of Oudenaarde, is the heart of the Flemish Ardennes and an excellent place for walking tours.

*Zwalmstrek   C 5/6

The Zwalmstrek in the Flemish Ardennes is an attractive stretch of land to the east of Oudenaarde characterised by the valley of the little river Zwalm, a tributary of the Scheldt. There are excellent opportunities for walking in the area, a number of water-mills and neat little villages such as Brakel, Horebeke and Kortsele, the so-called "Geuzenecke".

Zottegem
On the extreme eastern edge of the Zwalmstrek lies Zottegem where Lamoraal, Count of Egmont (see Introduction, Famous People) is buried in the former estate of his family. His tomb and that of his wife Sabina of Beierens can be seen in the crypt of the church. Egmont's castle lies in a park with fine trees; in its present form it dates predominantly from the 19th c. The local museum has mementoes of the duke.

Grotenberge
There is another château in the suburb of Grotenberge in which a folk art and folklore museum is housed.

Leeuwergem
Leeuwergem, 3km/2 miles to the north, also has a castle. It was built in place of a moated castle of 1724 and is surrounded by a park laid out by Le Nôtre.

Velzeke
The Romans settled near Velzeke, 4km/2½ miles north of Zottegem. The Archaeological Museum has numerous finds of this and other epochs.

Ronse · Renaix   C 6

11km/7 miles south of Oudenaarde on the linguistic border is the town of Ronse (French Renaix) where a lively carnival "Bummelfeesten" takes place, and on the first Sunday after Whitsun the "Fiertelommegan" procession is held. In the procession the relics of St Hermes, a Roman martyr, are carried through the surrounding villages. They are kept in the Collegiate Church of Sint-Hermes which primarily dates from the 15th and 16th c. and has a notable large crypt. There is also an interesting local museum in the former house of the chief provost with a historical department and an exhibition concerning the history of textile production in Ronse, as well as the Art-Nouveau house "La Bruyère" built by Victor Horta.

Kluisberg
A few kilometres further west rises the 141m/463ft high Kluisberg on the border between Hainaut and East Flanders and therefore on the linguistic border. The viewing tower of the Hotond Mill, 150m/492ft high, is the highest point in East Flanders with an extensive panorama of the region.

Ourthetal

See Vallée de l'Ourthe

De Panne · La Panne   A 4

Province: West Vlaanderen. Altitude: Sea level
Population: 9500. Inter-regional Station

Strolling along the dunes of Westhoek

De Panne (French La Panne) is attractively situated in a sandy valley near   *Location
the French frontier. It was originally a fishing village, very popular with
artists, which quickly developed into a modern holiday centre. It is much
favoured by the French, and has many attractions and all kinds of leisure
activities. The township and its surroundings became famous during the
First World War as being the only unoccupied part of Belgium and the
residence of King Albert and Queen Elizabeth whose government had
moved to Le Havre. The king's military headquarters was in Veurne (see
entry).

Sights

At low tide De Panne has the broadest beach of the entire Belgian coast   *Beach
some 400m/440yds wide. This extends 12km/7½ miles to Nieuwpoort (see
entry) and in the other direction to Dunkerque in France, 17km/10½ miles
distant. It is not surprising that the brothers Dumont constructed their first
sailplane here more than 80 years ago. In doing so they instigated a sport
which is ideally suited to the beach of De Panne. From time to time a
spectacular sailplane race takes place here in November.

To the west of De Panne extends the 340ha/840-acre national nature   *Dunes of
reserve of the Dunes of Westhoek, probably the finest dune landscape in   Westhoek
Belgium, in which live ermine, martens, owls and rabbits, and the central
part of which is reminiscent of the Sahara. The nature reserve is crossed by
six signposted paths.

To the south-east stretch the 61ha/150 acres of dunes of Oosthoek, which   Dunes of
are adjoined by the wooded area of Calmeynbos, planted in 1903. In this   Oosthoek
area too there are well signposted walks to be enjoyed.

Surroundings

Adinkerke	3km/2 miles south of De Panne on the French frontier near Adinkerke lies the "Melipark" amusement park. Here is a fairytale garden, animal enclosures and, as the principal attraction, a huge waterway, 520m/570yds long, which passes through an imitation medieval knights' castle.
Dunkerque	On the far side of the frontier lies the French town of Dunkerque (English Dunkirk), heavily fought over in both world wars.
Veurne	See entry

Poperinge   A 5

Province: West-Vlaanderen
Altitude: 2–6m/6½–20ft
Population: 19,500
Inter-regional Station (bicycle rental at station)

Location

Poperinge, in the south-west of West Flanders a few kilometres from the French border, is the chief place of the "Hoppelandes", the most important Belgian hop-growing area. This is the excuse for an annual "Hopenfest" with the election of a hop queen (next in 1993). In the Middle Ages Poperinge was a member of the Hanseatic League and an important cloth-trading town. Although situated in the main battle area Poperinge was largely spared destruction during the First World War. The most important buildings in the town are three Gothic churches.

Sights

Hoofdkerk Sint-Bertinus	Hoofdkerk Sint-Bertinus near the Grote Markt is a 15th c. hall church built on the site of a Romanesque predecessor. It was rebuilt in 1436 after destruction by the English. Features of the interior are a 17th c. rood screen, the choir screen and the Baroque pulpit.
Onze-Lieve-Vrouwkerk	The Onze-Lieve-Vrouwkerk (14th c.) in Casselstraat is also a Gothic church with a massive west tower crowned with a spire. Striking features are the Renaissance west door, the choirstalls, and a very fine sculptured communion bench.
Sint-Janskerk	A third hall church and the oldest in Poperinge is Sint-Janskerk (c. 1300) in Sint-Janskruisstraat. It houses a figure of the Madonna believed to be wonder-working, which forms the central point of a procession in July. The interior of the church has beautiful 18th c. panelling.
Stadhuis	In the market stands the Stadhuis (town hall) of 1911 with a fine belfry.
National Hop Museum	The old weighbridge (Stadsschaal) of 1579 in Gasthuisstraat, in which hops and other produce used to be weighed, now houses the National Hop Museum. It exhibits the history, tools and techniques of hop-growing in "Hoppeland", and of course beer from Poperinge can also be sampled here. (Open: May, June and Sept. Sun. and public holidays 2.30–5.30pm; July and Aug. daily 2.30–5.30pm.)
Weeuwhof	Nearby in Sint-Annastraat a small doorway gives access to the Weeuwhof, a picturesque ensemble of 18th c. cottages which served as a hospital.

Surroundings

Lijssenthoek Military Cemetery	3km/2 miles south is a military cemetery where more than 10,000 British soldiers from the First World War are buried.

The Stadhuis of Poperinge, built in 1911

In the Abbey of Sint-Sixtus of Westvleteren, 10km/6 miles north of Pop-   Westvleteren
eringe, one of the five genuine Trappist beers of Belgium is brewed, the
"Abbot", the strongest beer of the country.

Rochefort   G 8

Province: Namur
Altitude: 120–190m/394–624ft
Population: 11,000

The pretty little town of Rochefort, about 30km/19 miles south-east of   Location
Dinant (see entry) near the Lesse and Lomme National Park (See Han-sur-
Lesse), was once the capital of a county the only witness to which are the
ruins of a 12th c. castle; now it is a summer resort visited especially by
walkers and anglers.
In the Abbey of Saint-Rémy, just outside the town, another one of the five
genuine Trappist beers of Belgium is brewed. A marble quarry in the
immediate vicinity once provided marble for St Peter's in Rome.
History touched Rochefort in 1792 when in Rue Jacquet No. 8 the Marquis
de La Fayette and Châteaubriand, both fleeing from Jacobin terror, were
arrested by Austrian troops.

Sights

Apart from its charming scenery Rochefort only has two small museums to   Museums
attract tourists: in one tower of the castle ruins can be found an historical
exhibition, and the Musée du Pays de Rochefort et de la Famenne in the
Avenue d'Alost has exhibits about the scenery of Famenne.

Grottes de Rochefort
Stalactitic caves
near Rochefort
(up to 180m/590ft below
ground level)

© Baedeker

Salle
du Sabbat

N

Val
d'Enfer

1 Grotte aux Fontaines
2 Palais de Bagdad
3 Passage des Soupirs
4 Cordillières
5 Obélisques
6 Passage de la Jonction
7 Passage du Lac
8 Marbres Coquillers
9 Cataclysme
10 Passage des Gros Blocs
11 Arcades
12 Salle aux Merveilles

Constant temperature
in caves 8°C/46°F

50 m

Entrance

The ruined castle of Rochefort

* Grottes de Rochefort

Opening times
Apr.–Sept.
daily 9.30am–
5.15pm; otherwise
by applying at the
tourist bureau

Rochefort is the base for visiting the grottos which were carved out by the waters of the Lomme thousands of years ago; they were discovered in 1865 and investigated throughout 1870. They rank almost equal to the grottoes of Han-sur-Lesse as far as their beauty and the number of visitors is concerned. Their stalactite formations are bizarre, the temperature of 8°C/46°F is less than that in Han so that warm clothing is necessary for the visit which takes about an hour.

The most impressive caverns and formations are those of the Val d'Enfer (valley of hell), the almost 90m/295ft high Salle du Sabbat – in which there is an impressive *son et lumière* show – the Salle aux Merveilles and the Les Arcades galleries which are located directly below the castle of Beauregard. Above the grottos stands the Loreto Chapel built in 1620, a copy of the chapel of the same name near Ancona.

Surroundings

Chevetonge

Chevetonge, 15km/9½ miles north-west of Rochefort, lies on the border between the regions of Condroz and Famenne. This village is the head-quarters of the Benedictine monastic brotherhood "Exaltation de la Sainte-Croix" (raising of the cross), founded in 1926 by Lambert Baudouin in Amay (see Huy, Surroundings), the main principles of which are the rap-prochement between the Catholic and the Russian orthodox churches. In 1939 the monks moved to Chevetonge where they occupied the buildings of a monastery which had been abandoned in 1902. Here in 1957 they built the oriental church after the pattern of the 11th c. Russian-Byzantine church in Novgorod which is a rectangular brick building with a large narthex, a central dome and a crypt. All the walls of the interior are decorated with frescoes by Greek artists, the religious representation of which corre-sponds to orthodox beliefs.

The Valéry Cousin provincial estate, a large area of 500ha/1235 acres with forests and lakes situated around a 19th c. castle, offers numerous leisure activities such as an open-air swimming pool, water slides and mini-golf.

Domaine provin-cial Valéry Cousin

About 18km/11 miles north of Rochefort near the N4 stands the Château de Jannée surrounded by a fine game park. It can be traced back to a 12th c. defence building which about 1600 was enlarged, and extended in 1850 to its present size. Grouped around a large courtyard bordered by towers are new buildings and the farm buildings which are of older date. Visitors are conducted through the kitchen with its old utensils, the bedrooms and bathroom as well as several reception rooms on the ground floor, all tastefully furnished and containing fine Louis XV furniture and porcelain (open: Apr.–Sept. daily 9.30am–6.30pm).

Château de Jannée

Marche-en-Famenne, 13km/8 miles to the north-east, is the chief place in Famenne and a centre of Wallonian pillow lace, the production of which is carried on in the village. It was here in 1577 that Don Juan of Austria signed the edict confirming the Peace of Ghent, which had been concluded a year before, and by which the Spanish left the provinces of the Netherlands. Features worth seeing in the village are the Musée de la Tourelle with a collection of lace work, the Musée de la Famenne, as well as the 14th Church of Saint-Remacle with its very fine font of the same date.

Marche-en-Famenne

The Church of Saint-Etienne in the suburb of Waha possess the oldest dedication stone of all Belgian churches. It can be seen on a pillar at the entrance to the choir, and states that on June 23rd 1050 the Bishop of Liège dedicated the church. The present building dates from the 16th c. and only the tower is still Romanesque. On the tower is a royal tablet with the arms of the Spanish king Philip II which is a memorial to the edict of 1577. In the three-aisled interior can be seen fine funerary monuments, a 13th c. reliquary, a 16th c. font, as well as fine statues of St Barbara and St Nicholas.

Waha

In the church of Nassogne which is situated on the Wamme, 13km/8 miles east of Rochefort, is buried St Monon, a Scottish missionary murdered here in 636. The present-day church, dating from the 18th c., stands on the site of a chapel erected in 661.

Nassogne

See entry

Han-sur-Lesse

Ronquières

See Ecaussinnes, Surroundings

Ronse · Renaix

See Oudenaarde, Surroundings

Saint-Hubert   G 8

Province: Luxembourg
Altitude: 436m/1431ft
Population: 5600

The little town of Saint-Hubert, which is visited by many pilgrims, lies in the centre of the Ardennes amid a wooded region full of game. According to legend Prince Hubert of Aquitaine was hunting in the surrounding forests in 683 when he saw a stag with a shining cross between its antlers, and a voice demanding that he dress as a priest and take up missionary work.

Location

Hubert became the first Bishop of Liège after he had renounced the bishopric of Tongeren on the Meuse. He died in 727 in Tervuren and his remains were brought in 825 to Andage which from that day was called Saint-Hubert.
The painter and botanist Pierre-Joseph Redouté was born in Saint-Hubert in 1759.

Processions and feast

As the place of pilgrimage for the patron saint of huntsmen Saint-Hubert has several processions in the time around Easter. On the Monday before Easter a procession of hunters, which had its origin in 1720 in Lendersdorf in the Eifel, enters the town. On Easter Sunday in even years an Ardennes pilgrimage takes place. The first Sunday in September is the International Day of Hunting which is marked by the traditional hunters' mass at 11 o'clock and a historical procession; and on the last Sunday of the year the Brotherhood of Butchers honours St Hubert as their patron saint for he also protects them. Annually in July the "Juillet musical" takes place under the aegis of the Festival du Wallonie.

Sights

* Basilique Saint-Hubert

In the Grand-Place, the centre of the town which is situated on a slope, stands the Basilica of Saint-Hubert with its 60m/197ft high towers. It has its origins in a Benedictine abbey church founded in the 7th c. which was destroyed by fire on several occasions. The present basilica was rebuilt between 1526 and 1564 and is a good example of Late-Gothic church architecture. However the façade, renewed in the 18th c., is in a mixture of Renaissance and Baroque work and shows the legend of St Hubert.

** Interior

The almost 25m/82ft-high light interior of the basilica is magnificently adorned with works of art principally of the 17th and 18th c. On either side of the entrance to the choir stand fine altars of Humain (Rochefort) marble. The choir stalls have scenes from the life of St Benedict and St Hubert (1733). The

Sant Hubert's Altar

statue of Mary on the high altar is probably by the sculptor Delcour from Liège. In the choir ambulatory in the Chapelle Saint-Laurent are 24 enamelled paintings in the style of Dürer by M. Didier (c. 1560). In the crypt underneath the choir a few remnants of the 11th c. building can still be seen. Notable in the right aisle are the lavish altars of St Hubert and St Lambert; the left aisle houses the mausoleum of St Hubert whose remains, however, disappeared after the French Revolution. Nearby is the church treasury which includes the saint's stole and his hunting horn, as well as relics of the maidens Hostia, Grata and Areapalis.

Palais Abbatial

On leaving the church the imposing buildings of the former Benedictine abbey, which was rebuilt in 1729, can be seen on the right. They are now used for art exhibitions. Opposite in the square is the local tourist bureau.

Saint-Gilles-au-Pré

The church of Saint-Gilles-au-Pré was built in the 11th c. and the four-cornered tower of the sanctuary still remains from this period. The choir and the ceiling date from 1567. After the Second World War the church was massively restored. On the high altar stands the figure of the saint who is accompanied by his hind.

Saint-Hubert

Basilique

1 Rosary Altar
2 Altar of the Martydom
   of St Agatha

3 High Altar
4 Altar of St Hubertus
5 Altar of St Laurentius

6 Mausoleum of
   St Hubertus
7 Church Treasury

Surroundings

2km/1¼ miles to the north on the road to Fourneau Saint-Michel we come to a 15ha/37 acre game park (Parc à gibier) which is attractive for walking. In the woods live stags, deer, mufflon and wild boar.

*Game park

In a sparsely wooded depression in the middle of the forest, 7km/4½ miles from Saint-Hubert, can be found the Musées Provinciaux Luxembourgeois (Museum of the Province of Luxemburg). It consists of two open-air museums: the Musée du Fer/Fourneau Saint-Michel with the Musée P.-J. Redouté, and the Musée de la Vie Rurale en Wallonie (open: Easter–mid Sept. daily 9am–5pm; July and Aug. until 6pm; mid Sept.–Nov. only at weekends and public holidays).

*Musées
Provinciaux
Luxembourgeois

The Ardennes Carthorse House in the open-air museum of the Province of Luxembourg

327

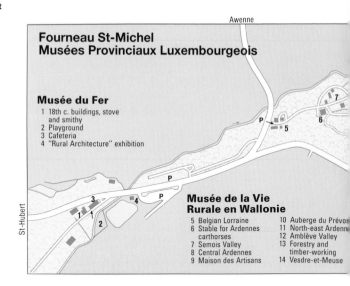

Fourneau St-Michel
Musées Provinciaux Luxembourgeois

Musée du Fer
1 18th c. buildings, stove
  and smithy
2 Playground
3 Cafeteria
4 "Rural Architecture" exhibition

Musée de la Vie Rurale en Wallonie
5 Belgian Lorraine
6 Stable for Ardennes carthorses
7 Semois Valley
8 Central Ardennes
9 Maison des Artisans
10 Auberge du Prévost
11 North-east Ardennes
12 Amblève Valley
13 Forestry and timber-working
14 Vesdre-et-Meuse

Fourneau Saint-Michel	The Musée du Fer is concerned with the former monastery smithy of Fourneau Saint-Michel of the 18th c. which was founded by Nicolas Spirlet, the last abbot of Saint-Hubert. Several buildings house tools, examples of forging, the smithy, the stove and the foundry. Adjoining are the exhibitions of rural architecture, the Museum of the Ardennes Forest and the Museum P. J. Redouté which is devoted to the life and works of the botanist.
Musée de la Vie Rurale en Wallonie	This museum is laid out on a large scale. Over an extensive area are various farmhouses and farms, a washing place, tobacco stores, a rural chapel and also a saw-mill. One of the most interesting buildings is the Maison du cheval du trait ardennais (house of the Ardennes cart horses), which documents the race of heavy cart horses from the Ardennes. Also available are a large playground with a cafeteria and the Auberge du Prévost restaurant in historic surroundings.
Château de Mirwart	Mirwart, 12km/7½ miles north-west of Saint-Hubert, has a large estate with a château begun in the 12th c. and extended in the 14th.
Redu	The village of Redu, about 18km/11 miles west of Saint-Hubert on the far side of the A4, is a mecca for bibliophiles. In 1984 a collector and a journalist set up the only book village on the continent of Europe in accordance with the predecessor at Hay-on-Wye in Wales. Nearly 30 antiquarians as well as bookbinders, a cooper and craftsmen offer their services. The books are chiefly of French literature and often quantity rather than quality prevails. The shops are open from Mar.–Dec. from time to time; at Easter a large bookmarket is held. Redu is also the home of a satellite communications base.
Euro Space Center Transinne	A full sized model of the European space glider can be seen from the motorway near the Euro Space Center in Transinne. Here all information about space travel, space science and the training of astronauts is available and there are models of various space vehicles. (Open: Apr.–Nov. daily 10am–5pm; Dec.–Mar. only Wed.–Sun.)

15 Hesbaye and Condroz
16 Condroz
17 Saw-mill
18 Cafeteria and playground
19 Famenne
20 Rièzes et Sarts

© Baedeker

Sint-Amandsberg

See Ghent, Surroundings

Sint-Niklaas   D 4

Province: Oost-Vlaaderen
Altitude: 5–30m/16–98ft
Population: 68,200
Intercity and Inter-regional Station (bicycle rental at station)

Sint-Niklaas, situated in the province of East Flanders between the rivers   Location
Scheldt and Durme, is the centre of the Waasland, the agricultural region to
the north-east of Ghent. The town has important industrial and trading
concerns and is a notable administration centre. The largest branch of
industry is textiles (weaving, knitwear and the production of carpets).
Metal, wood and tobacco also play a part in its economy.

Sint-Niklaas lies at the crossing of two old trade routes, one led from   History
Brabant to Zeeland, and the other linked Antwerp with Ghent and Bruges.
In 1217 the former trading place was raised to an independent parish with
St Nicolas as its patron saint. In 1248 Margarete of Constantinople,
Duchess of Flanders, gave the area of the present-day market place to the
newly formed parish with the instruction that the huge area should be free
of building for all time. In the 17th c. Sint-Niklaas grew to be an important
centre of textile working and extended its position in the following century.
In 1804 it was raised to the status of a town under Napoleon I. By reason of
its favourable position in the European economic area Sint-Niklaas developed in the 20th c. to one of the most important cities of Belgium.

Annually on the first Saturday in September balloonists from all parts of   Ballonfest
Europe meet in Sint-Niklaas to start a race from the Grote Markt.

Sights

<table>
<tr>
<td valign="top">

*Grote Markt

</td>
<td valign="top">

The imposing centre of Sint-Niklaas is the Grote Markt which has an area of 3.2ha/8 acres, the largest municipal town square in Belgium. Its north-west end is dominated by the Neo-Gothic Stadhuis (town hall) of 1878, the tower of which houses a carillon of 35 bells. Behind the Town Hall rises the tower of Onze-Lieve-Vrouwkerk of 1841 with a gilded dome and a statue (6m/20ft high) of Mary.

Opposite on the south-east end stand the Parochiehuis, a priest's house of 1663 later the town hall and now a commercial court, the Cipierage, originally a prison of 1662 and now a library, and the Landhuis, former law courts of 1637.

</td>
</tr>
<tr>
<td valign="top">

Sint-Niklaaskerk

</td>
<td valign="top">

Behind these three houses rises Sint-Niklaaskerk, the church of the patron of the town, dedicated in 1238 and extended on several occasions in the 16th c. Notable features of the interior include the Baroque side altars of Hubert and Norbert van de Eynden as well as sculptures by Luc Fay'dherbe and a figure of Christ by Duquesnoy. The church museum can be visited only by arrangement (tel. 7 76 37 18).

</td>
</tr>
<tr>
<td valign="top">

Museum

</td>
<td valign="top">

Zamanstraat branches off Statioonsstraat. Along it can be found the museum of the town and the Waasland (Museum van de Stad en van de Oudheidkundig Kring van het Land van Waas). It is divided into the Department of Fine Art (primarily Dutch and Flemish paintings of the 17–19th c.), the Archaeological Section (prehistoric and Frankish finds), the Folklore Section, the Mathys-Vanneste Collection (furniture, porcelain, silver, a painting by Rubens, Belgian paintings of the 19th c.) and of special interest the room devoted to the great geographer Geradus Mercator (see Introduction, Famous People). Mercator was born in Rupelmonde not far east. (Open: daily except Mon. 2–5pm, Sun. 10am–5pm.)

</td>
</tr>
<tr>
<td valign="top">

Branches

</td>
<td valign="top">

Three other collections belong to the museum and these are all housed in a building at Regentiestraat 65 (a little north of the museum). The collections

</td>
</tr>
</table>

Sint-Niklaas: the Grote Markt

include those concerned with the International Exhibition Centre with 90,000 exhibits and 150 relief plates, the "Barbierama", a collection of toilet articles and hairdressers' implements, and a collection of musical automata such as phonographs and gramophones (opening times as above).

The Castle of Walburg in the middle of the town park east of the Grote Markt was built in 1553 and considerably altered in the 19th c. The 5m/16½ft-high and 3.8m/12½ft-wide astronomical clock (Heirmanklok) adjoins the castle.

Walburg

In Oostjachtpark 15 can be found an organ museum with fair organs, barrel-organs and street organs (open only for groups, tel. 7 76 94 71).

Organ museum

Surroundings

The Waasland along the old Scheldt is a pleasant stretch of country crossed by canals and typical rows of poplar trees. Recently more modern industries have joined the old-established agricultural pursuits (including asparagus), traditional brickworks and cloth manufacturers.

Beveren

D 4

The parish of Beveren lies in the centre of the Waasland about 10km/6 miles east of Sint-Niklaas. This area with its little undulating fields, many lakes and poplar trees is a favourite place for walking.

In the Grote Markt stands the Sint-Martinuskerk (c. 1200), of which only the Late-Romanesque crossing-tower remains of the original building phase. The other parts of the church were added in the 15th c. (nave) and the 16th c. (choir). The interesting interior of the church has a high altar by Fayd'herbe (1622).

Sint-Martinuskerk

Kasteel Cortewalle in Beveren

Around 1840 the three-aisled nave was extended by two additional aisles.

Kasteel Cortewalle	Kasteel Cortewalle, a fine moated castle, dates from about 1600. The building in Flemish Renaissance style will serve after restoration as a culture centre and museum. Inside can be found 19th c. furniture and pictures (open: May–Sept. Sun. 2–6pm).
Hof Ter Saksen Oud Geestelijk Hof	The Hof Ter Saksen, now a ruined château was built in 1770 in a fine park. The moated castle Oud Geestelijk Hof or Hof Ter Welle (16th/17th c.) is now used as an orphanage.

Temse   D 4

Temse, 5km/3 miles south of Sint-Niklaas on the Scheldt, is known for its shipbuilding. The town was once a centre of the cloth industry particularly sail-cloth.

Onze-Lieve- Vrouwkerk	In the market stands Onze-Lieve-Vrouwkerk a Gothic 16th c. hall church which can look back to a predecessor dating from 770. In the church is the 16th c. tomb of the benefactors of the town, Roeland Lefebure and Hadewigis van Heemstede.
Stadhuis	The Stadhuis was erected between 1903 and 1906 in Neo-Renaissance style; it now houses the local museum (open: Sat. 1–7pm, Sun. 10am–noon and 2–7pm).

Lokeren   D 4

Lokeren lies 16km/10 miles from Sint-Niklaas on the Durme. The most important branch of industry in the town is textiles, especially the production of linen.

Grote Markt	Some typically fine Flemish houses of the 17th and 18th c. flank the Grote Markt; the elegant Stadhuis in Flemish Rococo style was designed by David t'Kindt the architect from Ghent.
Sint- Laurentiuskerk	The most striking feature of Sint-Laurentiuskerk is its white tower crowned by a dome. The church dates from the 16th and 17th c. and was destroyed in 1719 by fire. The reconstruction was in Baroque style. From this time dates the beautiful pulpit by the Mechelen artist Verhaegen. Also noteworthy are the confessionals (1655) and the Late-Gothic font.
Stedelijk Museum	The Stedelijk Museum (municipal museum) in the old cloth hall on the Grote Kaai exhibits pre-historic finds, furniture and folk art.

Sint-Truiden · Saint-Trond   F/G 5

Province: Limburg
Altitude: 34–106m/112–348ft
Population: 36,800
Intercity Station (bicycle rental at station)

Location	Sint-Truiden (French Saint-Trond) is the chief town of the Haspengouw (French Hesbaye), the market centre of an extensive fruit-growing area (principally cherries), and at the same time an important industrial base with a sugar refinery, distilleries, breweries and various other industries. The cherry blossom and the harvest are an excuse for lively festivals.
History	Sint-Truiden developed around an abbey which St Trudo had founded in 657. The town received a charter in the 11th c. and was surrounded by

Sint-Truiden
Saint-Trond

Guvelingen · Festraets-studio · Begijnhof · Speelhoflaan · Schurhoven · Diestersteenweg · Haardstr. · St.-Gangulfuskerk · Diesterstr. · Abdij · Station · Pr. Albertlaan · Rij-Schoolstr. · St.-Maarten-kerk · Stadhuis · Grote Markt · O.-L.-Vrouwkerk · Tienen · Stationsstr. · Tiensestr. · Ursulinen-klooster · Minder-broeder-kerk · Brustempoort · Spaansebrugstr. · Naamsevest · Ziekerenweg · Olympialaan · Naamsesteenweg · Lepelstr. · Luikersteenweg · Hasselt · Tongeren · St.-Pieterskerk · Namur · Tienen, Autobahn · Liège (Luik)

fortifications in 1086. At first the Benedictine abbey came under the jurisdiction of the abbot and bishop of Metz, whose place was taken in the
13th c. by the prince-bishop of Liège. In this period Sint-Truiden developed
into an important centre of cloth production on the trade routes between Bruges and Cologne. After the town had fallen to the French in 1795
the monastery was suppressed. From 1814 Sint-Truiden belonged to the
Netherlands until the founding of the Belgian kingdom.

Sights

In the centre of the town lies the Grote Markt, after Sint-Niklaas (see entry)
the largest in Belgium, in the middle of which stands the Classical 18th c.
Stadhuis (town hall). It was built on to the belfry (lower part 12th c.) which
had been erected in 1606 which rises above a side gable. The tower, in front
of which is a platform dating from 1596, houses a fine carillon of 41 bells.
Near the Town Hall can be found the Onze-Lieve-Vrouwkerk, the choir of
which dates from the 14th c. The nave of the church was completed in the
15th c. but the tower was only erected in 1847. The most valuable treasures
are a "Last Judgment" by van den Eenheu and the reliquary shrine of St
Trudo.

North of the Grote Markt are the buildings of the abbey founded in the 7th c.
by St Trudo. It was one of the largest monastic complexes in the Netherlands – the church alone was over 100m/328ft long and 24m/79ft wide – but

*Grote Markt
Stadhuis

Onze-Lieve-
Vrouwkerk

Abdij

333

during the French occupation almost everything was destroyed. The building to be seen today dates mainly from the 18th c.; notable are the archway and the Keizersaal on the left side of the courtyard which has fresco decoration. One part of the building serves as the Hoevemuseum where rural implements and machines can be seen.

Begijnhof

Further north is the Begijnhof (béguinage), founded in 1258, the cottages of which are grouped around a rectangular open space. The church is now the Provincial Museum of Religious Art (open: Tues.–Fri. 10am–noon and 1.30–5pm, Sat. and Sun. 1.30–5pm).

Festraets-studio

The Festraetsstudio opposite should be visited. It contains an astronomical clock assembled by Kamiel Festraets (1904–74) from over 20,000 individual parts. It is 6m/20ft high and the largest of its kind in the world. Also to be seen are other exceptionally fine examples of mechanical apparatus (open: Easter–Oct. Tues.–Fri. 9.45–11.45am and 1.45–4.45pm, Sat. Sun. and public holidays 1.45–4.45pm).

Sint-Maartenkerk

Not far west of the market place stands Sint-Maartenkerk the tower (1550) of which is one of the jewels of early Renaissance architecture. The nave was constructed in the 19th c. in Neo-Romanesque style.

Ursulinenklooster Minder-broederkerk

The former Ursuline convent, south of the Grote Markt, now houses an interesting museum of pillow lace, a craft once traditional in Sint-Truiden (open: Sun. and public holidays 10am–noon and 2–6pm). Opposite the convent is the Minderbroederkerk built in 1731, the interior of which is impressive because of its size (100m/328ft long, 16m/52½ft wide and 26m/85ft high).

Sint Pieterskerk

Sint Pieterskerk (12th c.) in the south of the old town is notable for its Romanesque architecture without any ribs.

Brustempoort

The Brustempoort at the end of Luikerstraat is a subterranean fortification dating from the 15th c. which was slighted under Louis XIV.

Surroundings

Guvelingen

In the north of the town the little Romanesque-Gothic church of Guvelingen occupies a lonely position. Here during the cherry blossom festival the orchards are blessed.

Zepperen

3km/2 miles north-east of Sint-Truiden lies Zepperen where the church of Sint-Genoveva (15th and 16th c.) has an interior which was painted in 1509 with frescoes illustrating the legend of St Genoveva and the Last Judgement. The tower dates from the 12th c.

Kortenbos

A visit should be paid to Kortenbos, 6.5km/4 miles east, to see the Basilica of Onze-Lieve-Vrouw, the interior of which retains its rich Baroque decoration.

Klooster van Kolen

12km/7½ miles to the east we come to Borgloon, once the chief town of the county of Loon, where just outside to the north lies the monastery of Kolen. It was founded in the 13th c. by crusaders and then taken over by the Cistercians. The reliquary of St Odile which was made in 1292 is kept in the sacristy; scenes from the life of the saint are painted on the wooden sides.

Zoutleeuw

See entry

Spa

Province: Liège. Altitude: 260m/853ft
Population: 9700. Local Rail Station ((bicycle rental at station)

The health resort of Spa lies 35km/22 miles south of Liège on the wooded slopes of the northern Ardennes in the charming valley of the Wayai or Spabach, which here is joined by the Picherotte. Within the town boundary are two springs and in the surroundings another seven which are alkaline and contain iron. It is to these springs that Spa owes its fame as the "town of waters" ("Ville d'Eaux") and it was for a long time an elegant health resort attracting visitors from all over Europe for the relief of circulatory diseases, stomach and intestinal disorders as well as gout and rheumatism. The word "spa" became synonymous for health resort in English. Now only the old baths and pump room and a few hotels remain. Today Spa gets its living from patients taking the cure, from individual visitors and coach tours, and offers its guests facilities for sports and for relaxing in the very pleasant surroundings.

*Location

Although the efficacious springs of Spa were already known to the Romans it was not until the 16th c. that a kind of tourism grew up which brought such illustrious guests as Christine of Sweden, Charles II of England, Peter the Great, Joseph II, Giacomo Meyerbeer and Victor Hugo to the little town. In the First World War Spa was occupied by German troops and served as a convalescent centre behind the lines. From March to November 1918 Kaiser Wilhelm II set up his headquarters with his General Staff in nearby Neubois. It was here on November 9th 1918 that he heard by telephone from Chancellor Max von Baden of his enforced abdication In Spa there were conferences between the victors and vanquished of the First World War about disarmament and questions of reparation.

History

Sights

The life of the spa is principally concentrated in the Place Royale around the baths and the assembly rooms built by Léon Suys in 1862–68. The baths are provided with water from the Marie-Henriette Spring outside the town. Adjoining is the building of the casino, first constructed in 1903–08 and renewed between 1919 and 1921 after a fire. When it was founded in the 18th c. by the prince-bishop of Liège it was the first gaming casino in the world combining the attractive with the useful.

Spa rooms

Casino

Just east of the casino in a pump room is the most efficacious of the springs of Spa named after Peter the Great.

Pouhon Pierre le Grand

Along the Avenue Reine Astrid to the west of the spa extends the Galérie Léopold II, a pump room built in 1878. Behind it lies the Parc de Sept

Galérie Léopold II

Spa: the Casino

Heures, a memorial to the composer Giacomo Meyerbeer and an armistice memorial.

Museums

Continuing along the Avenue Reine Astrid we come to a villa where Queen Marie-Henriette lived at the end of the 19th c. and where two museums are now housed. The Musée de la Ville d'Eaux is concerned with the history of the town and exhibits so-called "jolités", decorated wooden objects typical of Spa including boxes for various purposes, the oldest of which dates from the 16th c. The second museum is dedicated to horses and horse riding and includes the former royal riding school. (Both museums open: mid June–mid Sept. daily 2–5.30pm; mid April–mid June and mid Sept.–Dec. Sat., Sun. and public holidays 2–5.30pm.)

Spa monopole

Further to the south is the factory complex of Spa monopole where visitors can see bottles being filled with the famous water (Rue Auguste Laporte; open: Mon.–Fri. 9.30–11am and 1.30–5pm).

Surroundings

Walks

There are many fine walks to be had in the immediate vicinity of Spa, including the Promenade des Artistes along the Picherotte stream, paths along the Lac de Warfaaz and to the various springs.

Musée de la Forêt Berinzenne

A forest museum documenting plants and animals of the Ardennes has been set up in a farmhouse in Berinzenne 4km/2½ miles south of Spa.

La Reid

In the game park of La Reid, 8km/5 miles west of Spa, deer, wild boar and mufflon live in an area of 40ha/99 acres

*Theux

7km/4½ miles along the N62 leading north-east lies the little town of Theux which is characterised by 17th and 18th c town houses. The perron (raised platform) of 1768, the symbol of independence of the town, can be seen in the Place du Perron; outstanding, however, is the Church of Saints-Hermès-et-Alexandre which stands on the site of a Merovingian and Carolingian church. In its present form it goes back to the year 1091 and with its three aisles of equal height it is the only Romanaesque hall church between and Loire and the Rhine. The roof of the central aisle was provided in the 17th c. with 110 coffers with biblical scenes and personalities. The wooden figure of the Virgin of Theux on the left of the choir was created in the 15th c. To the right of the road to Theux just before reaching the town can be seen the ruins of the Château de Franchimont above the valley of the Hoëgne. It belonged to the prince-bishops of Liège and has witnessed numerous wars and sieges, including a massacre in 1468 in which 600 inhabitants of Franchimont, who had taken refuge here, were slain by the soldiers of Charles the Bold. During the course of the French Revolution the castle was destroyed. Visitors can see the remains and a small museum (open: Apr.–Sept. daily 10am–7pm; Oct.–Mar. Sat. and Sun. 10am–7pm).

Château de Franchimont

Not far north-west of Theux in the little pilgrimage chapel of Tancrémont is kept one of the best restored of early Romanesque wooden sculptures. The polychrome sculpture of "Christ on the Cross" was probably made in the 10th and certainly by the 11th c.

*Tancrémont

The N62 leads south-east to Francorchamps famous for its racecourse which runs through the forests (see Stavelot).

Francorchamps

See entry

Verviers

Stavelot

H 7

Province: Liège
Population: 6200
Altitude: 320–430m/1050–1411ft

the little town of Stavelot, 9km/5½ miles south-west of Malmédy on the Amblève, can look back on a great history as an independent princely abbey. The surroundings, especially the valley of the Amblève, are ideal for excursions on foot in the quiet woods on the southern edge of the Hohe Venn.

Location

In 648 and 650 St Remaclus founded in Stavelot and in Malmédy two abbeys which soon adopted the Benedictine rule, and from which the princely abbey of Stavelot-Malmédy was formed. Under the direct authority of the kingdom they experienced, between the 10th and 13th c. in the time of the prince-abbots Poppo and Wibald, the zenith of their spiritual and cultural development, and they produced unique articles of Maasland metal- and goldsmiths' work which can be seen today in many museums all over the world. Their decline was instigated by the destructive Normans, and in the 17th c. the soldiers of Louis XIV, and in 1794 French revolutionaries continued the destruction. The Second World War added to the tribulations of Stavelot

History

The carnival activities of Stavelot take place in mid Lent (Wednesday or Thursday before Mothering Sunday) in the form of a procession with more than 1000 participants. Several hundred "Blanc Moussis" in white hooded cloaks and masks with long red noses accompany the procession and pummel the spectators with blown-up sheep's bladders.

*Carnival

*Ancient Abbey

The Abbey of Stavelot was in existence until the French Revolution when it was dissolved. Afterwards the buildings had various functions and in the First World War were used as a military hospital. Today the premises,

Stavelot Abbey: the Remakus Reliquary "Mary and the Child Jesus"

principally of the 18th c., house the town administration and three museums. Remaining from the 16th c. are parts of the belfry, a beautiful spiral staircase and the doorway. In some of the rooms of the abbey a festival of concerts and plays takes place.

Musée d'Art religieux régional et de l'Ancienne Abbey

Opening times
Easter–Sept.
daily 10am–noon
and 2.30–5.30pm

The Regional Museum of Religious Art and of the Old Abbey is accommodated in the west wing which was built in 1714. The museum is divided into four parts. The Department of Local History shows the development of the princely abbey and the life of some of the great abbots by means of documents, paintings, etchings, sculpture and models of the abbey buildings, as well as a replica of the shrine of St Remaclus. A second section is devoted to craft work and especially to tanning, which was carried on in Stavelot from the 16th c. until the end of the 19th c.

The third and probably the most important part exhibits religious articles (14th–19th c.) from the church treasury, and is especially worth seeing for the many examples of goldsmiths' work. The Department of Art is especially concerned with Belgian painters including Degouve de Nuncques, and also with ceramic artists.

Musée Guillaume Apollinaire

In 1899 the French poet Guillaume Apollinaire (1880–1918) spent three months in Stavelot where he fell in love with Marie Dubois to whom he dedicated a number of poems. One night he left the town without paying his hotel bill; it was thought by the citizens of the town that this event justified a museum and this can be found on the first floor of the town hall (the east wing of the abbey) where notable documents and objects from the poet's property as well as a replica of his room can be seen. (Open: July–Aug. daily 10.30am–noon and 2.30–5.30pm.)

Musée du circuit National de Spa-Francorchamps

The Romanesque vaulted cellars of the abbey are an extraordinary place for a motor-car museum. Here more than 80 vintage vehicles and racing cars of more recent date, motor-cycles, documents, posters, etc., which illustrate the history of the celebrated motor-racing circuit of Francorchamps, are on show. (Open: Apr.–Sept. daily 10am–noon and 2.30–5.30pm; Nov.–Mar. only until 4.30pm.)

Saint-Sébastien

Crossing the Place Saint-Remacle, where a platform (1769) typical of the former bishopric of Liège stands, we reach the 18th c. Church of Saint-Sébastien. In the shrine of St Remaclus it possesses a unique example of Mosan metal work. The 2.7m/9ft-long and almost 1m/3½ft-high shrine was worked from gilded metal with enamel inlay; it received in 1268 the remains of St Remaclus which had been preserved since the 7th c. On the front are depicted Jesus giving a Blessing and Mary with the Child; on the long side on the left is a representation of Jesus and St Remaclus surrounded by six Apostles and on the right St Lambertus surrounded by another six Apostles. The lid bears another scene from the New Testament.

*Shrine of St Remaclus

The reliquary bust (17th c.) of St Poppo reveals the great artistry of its creator Jean Geosin. In the sacristy can be seen other religious works of art.

Surroundings

Not far east of Stavelot lies the Circuit National de Spa-Francorchamps one of the finest and most famous motor-racing circuits in the world. The circuit traverses the woods of the Ardennes with numerous curves and gradients. Every year international motor sports events are held here including Formula I meetings and motor-cycle master championships. Part of the circuit is on a public road and ordinary motorists can in fact drive on it. The stands for spectators are at the starting and finishing points.

Circuit National de Spa-Francorchamps

Vielsalm, 24km/15 miles south of Stavelot, is a resort for walking in summer and for skiing in winter.
Not far to the south lies Salmchâteau with the ruins of the princely castle. In the vicinity the so-called "razor stone" was mined which was used as a whetstone and grindstone. A little museum in the village documents the history and use of this stone.

Vielsalm

*Vallée de l'Amblève

The river Amblève rises in the Hohe Venn in the German-Belgium Nature Park (see entry). Its lower course winds its way through a pleasant and quiet valley towards the Ourthe (see Vallée de l'Ourthe). On its course it receives the little rivers Warche, Salm, Baleur, Lienne and Ninglinspo. There are picturesque walks in the valley and on its slopes, and in many places canoes can be rented for trips on the river.

Course

On the right bank of the river from Stavelot lies Trois-Ponts where the Salm flows into the Amblève. The village is a centre for walks and canoe trips in summer and in winter for skiing and skating (Wanne and Saint-Jacques). Trois-Ponts is also the starting point for two scenic drives by car: to the east along the stretch called "Boucle de Wanne", partly along the Salm and through the area of the old principality of Salm; to the west on the "Boucle de Basse-Bodeux" between the valleys of the Salm and the Baleur.

Trois-Ponts

Until the 18th c. the Amblève formed an enormous curve near the next village of Coo, where the arms of the river almost touched. The monks of Stavelot without ado pierced through this narrow place and there appeared

*Coo

The waterfalls of Coo

two raging picturesque waterfalls which have become a major tourist attraction. People come every year to see the illuminations of the cascades and to enjoy the restaurants, the canoe trips and the amusement park "Télécoo" with a chair-lift to the viewpoint of the Montagne de Lancre.

La Gleize

Only a little way away lies La Gleize which arouses memories of the Ardennes offensive. In December 1944 an SS Panzer group, stopped because of lack of fuel, drew the population into the bloody fights between Stavelot and Stoumont with over 2500 victims; 100 of the civilians were shot by the SS. The "king's tiger" German armoured car which was left behind and the museum "December 1944" are souvenirs of these events.

*"Le Congo"

There are several viewpoints on the road between La Gleize and the little town of Stoumont. The finest is "Le Congo", so-called because after Stanley discovered the river Congo at the end of the 19th c. the surrounding forests reminded the local people of the African jungle which had become popular. Above the right-hand bank of the river rises Froidecœur castle.

*Vallée de la Lienne

From Targnon onwards the road accompanies the river. Here the Lienne flows in, and in its picturesque valley are numerous springs such as those near Chevron; at the end of the valley, near Lienne, an extensive view of the Ardennes appears.

Fonds de Quareux

After passing through Lorcé the road bears sharply right and crosses the railway. Below the lines a footpath leads right down to the bank of the Amblève which here flows along in a particularly romantic reach.

Nonceveux

Near the holiday village of Nonceveux, where the Amblève begins a great curve, the Ninglinspo tributary joins the river. By following this defile on foot we reach in a quarter of an hour the sandstone basin called "La Chaudière" from which flow two waterfalls.

After the bend in the river the road runs below the A6 motorway; on the left stands the Château Mon Jardin and soon we are in Sougné-Remou-champs. Here the visitor should see the grottos of Remouchamps, discovered in 1828 and open to the public since 1912. They were inhabited in the Stone Age by hunters. In the upper parts of the caves can be seen fantastic drip-stone and crystal formations. The lower part is watered by the Rubicon, a tributary of the Amblève. High points of the visit are the 100m/328ft-long and 40m/131ft-high "Cathedral" and the exit from the cave along the Rubicon. (Open: May–Aug. daily 9am–6pm; Sept.–Apr. until 7pm.)

*Grottes de Remouchamps

North of Sougné-Remouchamps lies the safari park of Deigné-Aywaille where large African animals live freely in 150ha/370 acres of grounds around which runs a tourist train.

Safari park

5km/3 miles south from Aywaille, beyond Sougné-Remouchamps lies Harzé with a 17th c. castle which has a very fine Renaissance façade and an impressive staircase. In the old mill in the castle park a milling museum has been established.

Harzé

Near Comblain-au-Pont (see Vallée de l'Ourthe) the Amblève finally joins the Ourthe.

Comblain-au-Pont

Temse

See Sint-Niklaas, Surroundings

Tienen · Tirlemont

F 5

Province: Brabant
Altitude: 35–89m/115–292ft
Population: 31,700
Intercity Station

Half way between Liège and Brussels, right on the linguistic border, lies the town of Tienen (French Tirlemont), centre of the fertile Hageland. The principal agricultural crop of the surroundings is sugar beet which is processed in Tienen, the town being the centre of the Belgian sugar industry.

Location

The former settlement on a Roman road, which in parts has been well maintained, was first mentioned in a charter of Charles the Bold in 872. As early as 1015 the counts of Leuven granted rights to the town, and a little later the first fortifications were erected. In the Middle Ages the skill of the cloth-makers assumed importance far beyond the town and helped it to gain prosperity and respect. The sugar industry developed in the 19th c. Towards the end of the war in 1944 the town suffered greatly from German bombing attacks.

History

Sights

The Stadhuis on the extensive Grote Markt was built in 1635 in Renaissance style; in 1836 it was partially demolished and afterwards provided with a Neo-Classical façade.

Stadhuis

The neighbouring Gothic Church of Our Lady was never finished; it has a choir and transepts completed in 1345, above which rises the mighty tower of 1660. 300 years before this Jean d'Oisy built the three excellent doorways with their fine figurative decoration. The Baroque choirstalls and the rich

Onze-Lieve-Vrouw-ten-Poelkerk

panelling are striking, as is the magnificent figure of the Madonna (1362) by Wouter Paus above the high altar. In the right side aisle can be seen a representation of St Anne by Verhaegen.

Stedelijk Museum Het Toreke
In the courtyard of the Palace of Justice, built as a cloth hall, is the 16th c. prison in which the municipal museum is now housed.

*Sint-Germanuskerk
With an elevated situation near the Veemarkt stands the Church of Sint-Germanuskerk founded in the 9th c. Its impressive western part, dating from the first half of the 13th c., is considered to be one of the most recent Mosan Romanesque architectural features. Extensions including the choir and the nave were carried out in the 14th and 15th c.; the Romanesque tower was rebuilt in 1550 and in the 18th c.

Tienen: Doorway to the Poelkerk

received a carillon of 54 bells which is played from July to August every Monday at about 8.30pm. Of particular merit in the church is a copy of a font of 1149, the original of which can be seen in the Musées Royaux d'Art et d'Histoire in Brussels (see entry).

Surroundings

Hakendover
3km/2 miles east on the far side of the Gete lies Hakendover, a well-known place of pilgrimage, where annually in January a procession in memory of the wondrous building of Sint-Salvatorskerk in 630 is held. The present church dates from the 13th c. and has a fine carved altar of 1430 and Baroque choirstalls from the abbey at Oplinter.

Hoegaarden
Barely 5km/3 miles south-west of Tienen we reach Hoegaarden which is famous for its white beer. An old beer cellar and a local museum can be visited.

Jodoigne
In the 12th c. church of Saint-Médard in Jodoigne, 12km/7½ miles to the south, the jaw of St Médardus is kept in a silver shrine.

Tongeren · Tongres   G 5

Province: Limburg
Altitude: 75–108m/246–354ft
Population: 29,600
Inter-regional Station

Location
The rural market town of Tongeren (French Tongres), which is also a local administrative centre, lies on the little river Jeker and is surrounded by the fertile fields of the Hesbaye (Hasbengouw). The town has considerable economic importance for the extensive region around it because of the number and variety of jobs available in many small industrial concerns. The sights of cultural and historical interest of the town mirror its long history and are attractions for the tourist.

History
Tongeren is proud of its claim to be the oldest town in Belgium. It has its origins in the Roman military camp of Atuatuca which Julius Ceasar mentions in the "Gallic War"; the Roman occupation was lifted by by Ambiorix,

Liège (Luik)

prince of the Eburon in 54 B.C. Under the Emperor Augustus, Germanic Tongerens settled here and there arose the Roman Civitas Atuatuca Tungrorum which became an important station on the road between Cologne and Bavay; in the 2nd c. A.D. it was provided with a great encircling wall. In the same period it is said that Saint Maturnus conducted a mission here. Tongeren was raised to be a bishopric around 315 but, however, soon this was removed to Maastricht and in the 8th c. to Liège. As a consequence the town became the property of the prince-bishop. Towards the end of the 4th c. the Salian Franks had destroyed Tongeren; the removal of the bishop's see brought a further decline, so that in the Middle Ages the town had a more modest position than in Roman times and this is clearly shown by smaller encircling fortifications. From now on Tongeren shared the fate of the estates of the prince-bishops and in 1677 was once again bombarded by the troops of Louis XIV. Industrialisation began about 1830 and, together with its function as a market and administrative centre for the surrounding district of rural Hesbaye, helped Tongeren to its present importance.

Concerts are given in the basilica every year during the Flemish festival.　　Church concerts

*Onze-Lieve-Vrouwbasiliek

Towering over the Grote Markt of Tongeren is the 64m/210ft high basilica of Onze-Lieve-Vrouw which is considered one of the most impressive Gothic church buildings in Belgium. The present church was begun in 1240 on the remains of several previous buildings and was the site where the first stone　　History of the building

church north of the Alps was erected in the 4th c. The choir, the transepts and the eastern part of the nave of the present church date from the 13th c., the apse was added a century later and the side aisles in the 15th c. Work was completed in 1541 with the tower, the top of which however has been damaged on several occasions.

The spacious and clearly articulated interior with its notable triforium is borne on tall round pillars. Tall windows from the Renaissance allow light to fall on to the choir in which the most valuable art treasures are the Gothic carved altar (first half 16th c.) from Antwerp with 23 detailed scenes from the life of Mary, two pascal candles of 1372 by the masters Jehan Josés of Dinant, and an eagle-lectern. The garlanded sculpture of Mary, the patron saint of the basilica, in the left side aisle, was carved in 1479 from walnut wood. From the right side aisle the visitor passes through a vestibule, in which hangs a huge 11th c. crucifix, into the cloisters.

Interior

The Romanesque cloisters are situated unusually on the east side of the church and not as normal on the south, because the Roman town wall allowed for no extension. The cloisters are the remains of a monastic complex of the 12th and 13th c. and are notable for their simplicity and for the side chapels, the most beautiful of which can be seen at the entrance. Around the cloisters more than 60 tombstones have been let into the walls.

*Cloisters

The treasury in the former chapter house is one of richest in Belgium and possesses more than 100 works of art from the Merovingian epoque up to the 18th c. Outstanding is the famous 11th c. Head of Christ a wooden sculpture of the greatest quality which seizes the moment of passing from life into death. Also notable is the Mosan metal work, including the reliquary of St Ursula made of silver-gilt with enamel inlay (about 1350). The oldest pieces include a Merovingian golden clasp of the 6th c. and an ivory diptych of St Paul which dates from about 500. The manuscripts include a specimen from the 10th/11th c. with ivory carvings on the cover and a 9th c. manuscript which was rebound in the 14th c. Every seven years (next in 1995) the crowning of the figure of Mary is the occasion for the most valuable relics to be carried in procession through the town.

**Treasury

Opening times
May–Sept.
daily 9am–noon
and 2–5pm

Other Sights

Opposite the church tower in the middle of the Grote Markt stands the monument to the Eburon prince Ambiorix who in 54 B.C. defeated the Roman legions of Sabinus and Cotta. The monument was created in 1866 by the sculptor Jules Bertin.

Ambiorix
Monument

On the ground floor of the City Hall, also in the Grote Markt, can be found the Civic Museum which exhibits documents and objects concerning the history of Tongeren (open: daily 10am–noon and 2–4.30pm).

Stedelijk Museum

The most interesting sight in Tongeren apart from the basilica is the Gallo-Roman Museum, provisionally closed until the middle of 1994 for comprehensive renovation. Its collections are among the most valuable of their kind in Belgium.

Provinciaal
Gallo-Romeins
Museum

Tongeren: Ambiorix Monument

◄ *The Basilica of Tongeren*

Tongerlo

Remains of the town walls	North-west of the centre a considerable part of the Roman town wall dating from the 2nd c., which was once 4½km/nearly 3 miles long, still remains. Near the south door of the basilica remains of a fortress tower of the second Roman wall, dating from the 4th c., were discovered. The third medieval town wall built from 1257–64 almost completely surrounds the town centre. Especially attractive is the section around Leopoldwal which ends at the Moerenpoort, the only one of the six town gates which has survived. It was built in 1379 and now contains a small museum of weapons (admission on enquiry at the tourist bureau). To the east by the wall of the béguinage stands the defensive tower Lakenmakerstoren.
Begijnhof (Béguinage)	Like almost all Belgian béguinages, that of Tongeren was founded in the 13th c., destroyed by iconoclasts and rebuilt again, until the French Revolution ended the Beguine communities here in Belgium. The 13th c. church is dedicated to St Catherine and has beautiful Baroque fittings and a crucifixion scene by Gaspar de Crayer. St Luitgard, the protective saint of Flanders, is said to have been born just outside the béguinage.
Kasteel Betho	Outside the town centre to the north-west near the Beukenberg, an earthwork constructed by the Romans, is the great castle of Betho built in the 17th c. and extended in the 18th. To the north in a park is the Pliniusbron, a spring rich in iron which was praised by Plinius the Elder.

Surroundings

*Kasteel van Alden-Blezen	11km/7 miles north-east of Tongeren lies the Kasteel van Alden-Blezen (1220) which was the headquarters of the German order of chivalry. The largest part of the recently restored building dates from the 18th c. and is now used as a cultural centre of the Flemish community. As well as the great moated castle, with four corner towers and a main tower, there are extensive gardens, stables, a hospital and a pilgrims' hostel in the complex. The chapel of 1638 contains among other items a picture by de Crayer.
Rutten	Every year on May 1st many spectators come to Rutten, 4km/2½ miles north of Tongeren, to see the graphic mystery play about the death of St Emervarus who was murdered by a certain Hacco as he returned from a pilgrimage to Santiago de Compostela in northern Spain.
Kasteel van Kolmont	On a hill 4km/2½ miles north-west of Tongeren stands the ruined castle of Kolmont. From the keep there is an extensive view into the Hesbaye.

Tongerlo (Abbey)

See Geel, Surroundings

Tournai · Doornik   B 6

Province: Hainaut
Altitude: 29–147m/95–482ft
Population: 67,700
Intercity Station

Location	Tournai (Flemish Doornik) lies on both banks of the Scheldt (French Escaut) near the Belgian/French border. As the administrative capital of an arrondissement, a seat of a bishop and of a Chamber of Industry and Trade and of a law court, Tournai is of more than administrative and cultural importance

Tournai
Doornik

Douai   St-Amand-les-Eaux

and possesses major industries. Several attractive but mostly reconstructed buildings testify to the prosperity of the old princely residence and
episcopal town. Most of the works of the celebrated medieval school of
painting were however destroyed by the iconoclasts in 1566. Cement
works, engineering, food processing and a traditional textile industry,
especially carpet weaving, form the basis of the town's economy. Tournai
has always been the most important market for the surrounding agricultural area.

Tournai is after Tongeren (see entry) the oldest town in the country. Its
origin was a settlement, Christianised by St Piat in the 3rd c., on the Roman
road between Cologne and Boulogne and by the 4th c. it was already a
considerable fortress. In the mid-15th c. Frankish Salians arrived and made
Tournai the capital of their kingdom. In 482 King Childerich, whose son
Chlodwig was born here in 465, died in Tournai. Chlodwig moved the royal
residence to Soissons, but elevated Tournai under St Eleutherius to the
status of a bishopric which soon fell to the county of Flanders and which
from 1188 was French. When the cathedral and several churches were built
in the 12th and 13th c. the prosperity of the town began to increase and it
became the centre of stonemasonry, drawing its material from nearby
quarries. In the Hundred Years' War Tournai remained the only large town
in Flanders on the side of France and withstood the siege in 1340 by the
English king Edward III. In the 15th c., thanks to its celebrated carpet
making, the town experienced a flowering and its school of painting (Robert Campin, Rogier van der Weyden) achieved international fame. In 1521
Charles V was the new ruler and he ceded Tournai to the Spanish Netherlands, the varied fate of which it shared from then on. Conquered by Louis

History

347

XIV in 1667 and subsequently fortified by Vauban, Tournai fell to the Austrian Netherlands in 1714. In 1750 a new period of considerable artistic achievement began with the manufacture of porcelain, but this ceased in 1891 with the closing of the factory. In 1794 Tournai belonged once more to France and in 1814 it became part of the United Netherlands until 1830 when it was finally Belgian. The First World War left the town virtually intact but on May 16th 1940 a violent bombing attack destroyed the greater part of the historic buildings but not the cathedral; however, much was capable of restoration.

Festivals

After a terrible epidemic of plague in 1092 Bishop Radbod inaugurated the great procession of Mary which henceforth has been held every year on the second Sunday in September. During the procession the shrine of St Eleutherius and other items from the church treasury are carried through the streets.

Fine secular festivals are the "Fête des Rois" on the Monday after the feast of the Epiphany with a procession and rabbit feasting, and the "Quatre Cortèges" on the second weekend in June, the climax of which is a gigantic procession of historical figures. A colourful flower market is held along the Scheldt on Good Friday.

**Cathédrale Notre-Dame

History of
the building

The five towers of the Cathédrale Notre-Dame are visible from afar above the roofs of Tournai. The cathedral is the jewel of the town, the most important ecclesiastical building in Belgium and one of the best examples of Romanesque in western Europe, the epitome of church architecture in the area of the Scheldt.

The present cathedral, a cruciform pillared basilica – the nave and choir are almost equal in length – has a ring of chapels and five towers. It occupies the site of Merovingian and Carolingian predecessors and was dedicated in 1171. At this time the Romanesque nave, the transepts and the 83m/272ft-high central tower resting on its pillars were finished. The remainder of the building, the four other towers, the conclusion of the transepts and especially the huge Gothic choir which dates from 1243–56, were added by 1325.

A narthex was built in front of the 14th main façade in the 16th c. also in Gothic style. Of the beautiful relief figures seen here the lower row (prophets, church teachers, Adam and Eve) date from the 14th c., and the upper row (processional scenes and the battle of Chilperich against his brother Sigbert) from the 16th and 17th c.; the central pillar bears the figure of Notre-Dame des Malades (14th c.). Considerably older is the figurative decoration on both side doors: on the north the Porte Manile has a representation of the Healing of Blind Mantilius by St Eleutherius (12th c.); on the south the sculpture on the Porte du Capitol is considerably damaged.

Interior

The three-aisled interior of the cathedral, 134m/340ft long, 66m/217ft wide and 22–23m/72–75ft high, shows most clearly the architectural development from Romanesque to Gothic. The dark, purely Romanesque nave rises in four distinct zones (arcades, balcony level, blind triforium and rose windows) on tall pillars finished with capitals showing human and floral motifs and is, except for the crucifixion scenes by Jordaens in the Chapel of Saint-Louis completed in 1299, relatively simply decorated. The adjoining transept (1140–60), which reaches a height of 48m/156ft at the crossing, shows in the finer detailed working and in the slender lines of the pillars the transition to Gothic. The transept ends unusually in semi-circular fashion as a kind of two additional choir ambulatories beneath the galleries. Remains of 12th c. frescoes show, on the right, the Heavenly Jerusalem, on the left the Martyrdom of St Margaret. The glass pictures (15th–16th c.) mostly by Arnold of Nijmegen draw their motifs from the history of the bishopric of Tournai. A magnificent marble Renaissance rood screen sep-

Nave

Transept

Rood screen

The towers of the Cathedral above the roofs of Tournai

arates the transepts and nave from the choir. It is one of the most important works of Cornelis Floris de Vriendt, made in the years 1570–73. Representation of biblical scenes is crowned by sculptures of the Virgin, St Eleutherius and St Piat. The three-aisled choir is pure Gothic with light falling on it from the high windows with 19th c. glass. The chapels of the choir ambulatory house valuable paintings of the Dutch-Flemish school;

Choir

Cathédrale Notre-Dame

© *Baedeker*

Place de l'Évêché

Nave

Choir Ambulatory

Choir

Chorumbang

Fausse Porte

Palais Episcopal

Cathedral Treasury

30m

1 Narthex
2 Porte du Capitole
3 Porte Mantile
   (Romanesque sculptures)
4 Chapelle de St-Louis
   ("Crucifixion" by Jordaens)

5 Renaissance rood screen
6 Frescoes
7 Remains of frescoes
8 Chapelle du St-Sacrement
   (Chapel of the Sacrament)
   "Purgatory" by Rubens

9 Chapelle du St-Esprit:
   Gobelin tapestry "Sts
   Piat and Eleutherius"
10 Chapter House
11 Maarten de Vos:
    "The Virgin"

the finest are a purgatory scene by Rubens in the Chapelle-du-Saint-Sacrement, the "Raising of Lazarus" by Pourbus the Elder in the chapel before the entrance to the treasury, and in the central chapel the "Virgin" by Maarten de Vos. Also of interest are a number of tombstones which were damaged by the iconoclasts but all are good examples of the school of sculpture of Tournai. Behind the high altar of 1727 a large marble memorial bears the names of all the bishops and canons of Tournai.

**Cathedral Treasury

Opening times
Daily 10–11.45am
and 2–4pm;
Apr.–Oct. to 5pm

The cathedral treasury, housed in rooms to the right of the choir ambulatory, contains a number of pieces of the first order, the finest of which are two Late-Romanesque reliquary shrines: the shrine of the Virgin (Châsse de Notre-Dame), worked by Nikolaus of Verdun in silver and copper in 1205 and restored in the 19th c., and the shrine of St Eleutherius (Châsse de Saint-Eleuthère) of 1247, a work by Hugo von Oignies created most beautifully with the figures of the apostles, the saint with a model of the cathedral in his hand, and a likeness of Christ in metal. Also very valuable is a Byzantine reliquary cross (6th/7th c.) and the manuscript of the Messe de Tournai (1247) the oldest multi-voiced mass of the west. Adjoining the Chapelle du Saint-Esprit is a magnificent pictorial tapestry from Arras (1402) which tells the legend of St Piat and St Eleutherius in fourteen scenes.

Grand'Place and Surroundings

The large triangular Grand'Place is lined by gabled houses most of which are restored. In the centre stands the bronze statue of Christine de Lalaing (Princess d'Espinoy) under whose leadership the town was defended during the siege of 1581. On the north-west side of the square is the Église Saint-Quentin, originally a Romanesque building of the 12th c., which was burnt down during the Second World War and has been restored. On the

View of the choir of Tournai Cathedral   *The Belfry*

south side of the square stands the former Hall aux Draps (cloth hall) which replaces a wooden predecessor blown away in 1601 in a storm. The hall was begun in 1610 but part of it fell down in 1881 and three years later it was rebuilt. It now serves as an exhibition and function centre.

On the west side of the square rises the 72m/236ft-high belfry, the oldest bell-tower in Belgium. The first four storeys were built in 1200 and completed in 1294 with the topmost storey and the spire. After a fire in 1391 the tower was rebuilt; the first carillon was mounted in 1392 of which two of the 43 bells of the present ring remain. (Open: daily except Tues. 10am–noon and 2–5.30pm.)

*Belfry

North of the market can be seen the slender tower of the Eglise Saint-Jacques which, after the cathedral, is the finest church in the town. It dates from the 12th c. and has a Romanesque tower, an early Gothic nave and transepts. The choir which was added in 1368 shows all the features of Scheldt-Gothic: the outer gallery, the triple windows, the side turrets and the triforium with alternate columns and pillars.

Saint-Jacques

Museums

All museums in Tournai can be reached easily on foot from the Grand-'Place. They are open daily except Tues. 10am–noon and 2–5.30pm.

Opening times

The Musée de Folklore is accommodated in a house with twin gables dating from 1673 (Maison Tournaissienne) not far from the cloth hall; it is devoted to customs and handicrafts of the town and its rural surroundings. Particularly charming are the many rooms reminiscent of the past with puppets and original features, such as a shoemaker's workshop, a wool-workers' workshop (so-called "baloitil"), a farm kitchen and a printing press. On the second floor there is a large model of Tournai in the year 1701.

Musée de Folklore

The most recent museum in the town, opened in 1990, can be found in the Place Reine Astrid; it is concerned with carpet weaving which has been carried on in Tournai since the 15th c. It not only tells the story of the craft and exhibits old examples, but visitors can also watch a carpet being made in the workshop.

Musée de la Tapisserie

From the belfry Rue Saint-Martin leads west and from it an archway opens into the courtyard of the Abbey of Saint-Martin (1642–1701), founded in the 11th c., the largest Benedictine abbey in Belgium before the French Revolution. In one wing is accommodated the Musée d'Histoire Naturelle (Natural History Museum) which is principally notable for a fine collection of birds; the palace of the abbots, a work of Dewez from 1743, is now the headquarters of the town administration.

Musée d'Histoire Naturelle in der Abbaye Saint-Martin

Opposite the town hall stands the star-shaped building of the Musée des Beaux Arts, built in 1928 according to plans by Victor Horta Its principal collection is that of the Tournai burgher Henry van Cutsem. Fine paintings of all epoques are displayed in fourteen rooms. Mention must be made of the pictures by the old masters: Roger van der Weyden ("Virgin with Child"), Jan Gossaert ("Saint-Donatien"), the Bruegel family who are represented with various works as are Jordaens and Rubens. A whole room is devoted to the Belgian romantic Louis Gallait and another to the Impressionists including Monet, Seurat, and Ensor, with two masterpieces by Manet: "Chez le Père Lathuille" and "Argenteuil". Also of interest are the drawings by van Gogh and Toulouse-Lautrec.

*Musée des Beaux Arts

North-west of the Grand'Place behind the Church of Saint-Quentin can be found the former pawnbroker's shop (Mont de Pitié) built by Coebergher in 1622. It now contains the historical museum which until 1940 was housed

Musée d'Histoire et d'Archéologie

in the cloth hall. It illustrates the history of the town with numerous exhibits from churches and other buildings which were saved from destruction in 1940. Of exceptional merit are a great collection of porcelain from the Tournai manufactory and fine pieces of local carpet weaving.

On the upper floor is the Musée de Paléontologie et de Préhistoire where prehistoric finds especially from the quarries round about Tournai can be seen.

On the right of the Scheldt

Saint-Brice

From the Grand'Place it is downhill and across the Scheldt straight along to the Church of Saint-Brice. Building of this church went on from the 12th c. into the 18th c. and in 1940 it was burned down. It was one of the first three-aisled hall churches in the west of the territory of present-day Belgium. In the Chapel of the Sacrament hangs a picture by de Crayer, and the crypt still remains of the original building. When excavations were being made for houses Nos.7 and 8 in Place Clovis, which lies around the church, the grave of the Frankish king Childerich was discovered and the burial gifts were taken to Paris.

* Maisons romanes

Obliquely opposite the main front of Saint-Brice stand two three-storeyed houses, the windows of which are divided by small central pillars. They were built about 1175 and are the oldest remaining Romanesque domestic houses in western Europe. A little way up the street can be seen another citizen's house, this time in Gothic style (14th c.).

Remains of the town fortifications

In the south-east of this part of the town can be found the best preserved parts of the medieval town wall (13th c.) with the towers called Tours Marvis and Tours Saint-Jean.

Tour Henri VIII

The north-west part of the town is also called the Quartier du Château (castle quarter) since in the Middle Ages the castle stood here. During the

Romanesque houses in Tournai

English occupation under Henry VIII (1513–18) the castle was constructed, of which only the Tour Henri VIII remains. It is a massive structure with two vaulted halls in which is housed a museum of weapons.

At the extreme north end of the old town centre the Pont des Trous spans the Scheldt; it is an impressive example of medieval defence architecture. The two towers (the one on the left dating from 1250/1281, the one on the right from 1304) were linked in 1329 by a three-arched bridge. When they were restored after the Second World War, both towers were raised by 2.4m/8ft in order allow the passage of ships.

*Pont des Trous

Surroundings

Agriculture is the principal occupation of the country around Tournai. There are many old farms and at the end of long drives and hidden behind hedges are fine country houses. Particularly in the east and south-east cement and building stone industries have arisen around numerous quarries.

In the castle in the little town of Antoing, 7km/4½ miles to the south, Philip IV of France and Edward III of England met in 1340 for peace talks. The castle was rebuilt in the 19th c. and only the great 15th c. keep remains from earlier times. The tombs of the Melun family in the chapel are fine examples of the skill of the stonemasons of Tournai.

Antoing

Just beyond the village of Hollain, 9km/5½ miles south, a narrow little road branches off to the right. By a road crossing stands the 4.5m/15ft-high menhir called "Pierre Brunehault" in the form of a trapezium. In the immediate vicinity there once ran the Roman road from Cologne to Bavai.

Pierre Brunehault

13km/8 miles to the east of Tournai we reach Leuze where the Church of Saint-Pierre (1745) stands on the site of a Romanesque predecessor. The exterior is uninteresting but the furnishing are far more worth while: wall panelling in the style of Louis XV with fine carving, a magnificent pulpit (1790), a 9th c. reliquary, and two brass desks in the choir (15th c.).

Leuze

Situated 6km/3¾ miles to the north, Mont Saint-Aubert, 147m/482ft high, is the only hill for miles; it is also called Mont Ste-Trinité because of the little church which was built on its summit. From the top there is a fine distant view of the plains of Flanders in the north, the French town of Roubaix in the west and back to Tournai in the south.

Mont Saint-Aubert

Turnhout   F 3

Province: Antwerpen
Altitude: 25m/82ft
Population: 37,600
Inter-regional Station (bicycle rental at station)

In the north of Kempenland near the Dutch border lies the little town of Turnhout, a centre of the Belgian paper industry since the early 19th c. when the production of playing cards was begun; these are now exported all over the world. Meanwhile metal, chemical and electronics factories have been established.

Location

Turnhout, part of Brabant from the 12th to the 16th c. was once popular with the Burgundian dukes, who found that hunting in the surrounding forest was very good, and they indulged principally in falconry. Charles V bequeathed the town to Maria of Hungary; after the Thirty Years War the princes of Orange-Nassau became the new overlords and they were followed in 1753 by the king of Prussia.
In 1789 history was made in Turnhout when the revolutionaries of Brabant defeated the Austrians and banished them at least until 1790.

History

Sights

Sint-Pieterskerk	Sint-Pieterskerk stands in the Grote Markt and its oldest parts date from the 13th c.; however from the 15th to the 18th c. it was rebuilt and enlarged on several occasions, especially around the remarkable ring of chapels surrounding the choir (1484). Notable in the interior are an "Ecce Homo" (early 15th c.), the confessionals, the high altar of 1740 by Walter Pompe and an artistic choir screen. The tower contains a carillon of 50 bells.
Kasteel	The former moated castle of the dukes of Brabant, not far from the Grote Markt and now used as a law court, once served as a hunting lodge. Maria of Hungary had the first building remodelled by Rombout Keldermans and Dominikus de Waghemakere in the first half of the 16th c. into a fine residence; there were other alterations in the 17th c.
Begijnhof	The béguinage, north of the castle was gifted in 1372 by Maria, Duchess of Brabant. Most of the houses of the present attractive complex were built after a fire in the 17th c.; the pretty Baroque Heilige-Kruiskerk (Church of the Holy Cross) dates from 1665. Begijnhof No. 56 is a museum illustrating life in the béguinage.
°Nationaal Museum van de Speelkaart	House No. 28 "Metten Toren" in the Begijnhof was built in 17th c. for a patrician. It now contains the Nationaal Museum van de Speelkaart (playing card museum). The first playing cards of Turnhout were printed in 1826 and in 1900 there were six factories producing them in the town; in 1971 they were combined to form the Carta Mundi playing card factory which is today the only one in the Benelux countries. The museum is devoted to the

The castle of the dukes of Brabant

history of playing cards from all over the world in documents which go back to 1100 B.C. and also exhibits a great number of original cards, of which the oldest date from the 16th c. (Open: Wed.–Fri. 2–5pm, Sun. 10am–noon and 2–5pm; in June also Tues. and Thur.; July and Aug. Tues.–Sun. at the above times.)

The Romans called Kempenland "Taxandria" a name which is also borne by the museum in Mermansstraat, south of the Grote Markt, which on the one hand exhibits archaeological finds including Merovingian shields, and on the other is concerned with the popular culture of the Kempenland. (Open: as the playing card museum except for Sunday mornings.)

Museum
Taxandria

This museum in house Gratakker 13 is devoted to the ornithology of the Kempenland.

Museum
"De Wielewal"

Surroundings

The countryside around Turnhout, the Kempenland (French Campine) was for a long time under the domination of the Romans until they were replaced by the Teutons. In A.D. 358 this area fell to the Salien Franks.

Kempenland

Oud Turnhout, 3km/2 miles to the east, was once the seat of the priory of Corsendonk whose comprehensive library was used by Erasmus of Rotterdam for his studies. In the numerous rooms of the restored 15th c. building the Albert van Dijck (1902–51) museum is now located. This painter, who came from Turnhout, was the leading representative in the 30s of the animists and often chose subjects for his paintings from the Kempenland.

Oud Turnhout

Passing through Oud Turnhout we reach Retie where the church contains furniture and objects d'art from the priory of Corsendonk. A little outside the village by the Witte Nete river stands a stone mill in which corn in still ground on Sundays. The "Prinsenpark" provincial estate nearby is ideal for walks. Originally this area was owned by the royal family but was inherited by the province of Antwerp in 1952. The estate is especially rich in bird- and wildlife and is a popular excursion and holiday destination.

Retie

There is good walking country also around Kasterlee, 9km/5½ miles south of Turnhout in the heath and moorland of the provincial estate of Hoge Mouw.

Kasterlee

The enclave of Baarle-Hertog, 14km/8½ miles north of Turnhout, is a curiosity as it is a Belgian enclave completely surrounded by Dutch territory. In the 12th c. the village was divided between the dukes of Brabant and the lords of Breda. Each part has a school, a town hall, a post office and a police station. The market, however, is in Holland, while the inn by the market stands on Belgian territory. Sometimes the frontier goes right through the houses; the nationality can be seen by the house numbers which are painted in national colours. The confusion is completed by the sister parish of Baarle-Nassau; this is a Dutch enclave surrounded by Belgian territory, and thus an enclave within an enclave.

Baarle-Hertog/
Baarle-Nassau

The parish of Moi, 23km/14 miles south-east of Turnhout, made headline news at the beginning of 1990 as here there was a recycling plant for nuclear fuel rods. The plant belongs to the Centre d'études de l'énergie nucléaire (centre for research into nuclear energy: CEN/SNK) which has headquarters in Brussels and runs the laboratories in Moi.

Moi

Vallée de la Meuse (Meuse Valley)   F/G 6–8

Province: Namur and Liège

Course

The Meuse (Flemish Maas) rises at an altitude of 456m/1497ft in the French plateau of Langres in Champagne. It has a course of 450km/280 miles in French territory and after crossing into Belgium near Givet – from here it is navigable – it flows for 192km/120 miles through Belgium until it reaches the Netherlands near Maastricht, where after a further 250km/155 miles it reaches the North Sea. Between Givet and Namur (see entry) the Meuse has cut a deep valley in the Ardennes plateau and flows northwards, sometimes between fine wooded slopes and sometimes between bare slopes. In the shadow of the steep ridges nestle pretty villages, with hotels and villa settlements in the valley of the river, which are popular summer resorts. The valley has always been of great attraction. As long ago as the Stone Age hunters and gatherers lived in caves along the river, and much later monks chose the lower reaches of the river to build their monasteries, while the secular lords erected imposing castles and fortresses on the heights. Some of these were rebuilt in the 17th and 18th c. and converted into fine châteaux. Thus the upper Meuse valley can claim to be one of the

**Cultural landscape

finest cultural landscapes in Europe. Yet from Namur where the river turns to the east, and finally beyond Huy (see entry) in the direction of Liège (see entry) the scene changes. The broad Meuse now flows through the heavily industrialised lower Meuse valley past numerous blast furnaces, engineering works and factories, and only isolated ruined castles and rocky sections give the scenery a certain charm. The Meuse became one of the European rivers most heavily polluted with chemicals and for this reason the neighbouring states are insisting on the construction of purification plants and the subsidising of more ecologically favourable technology.

River trips

From Namur and Dinant (see entries) trips up and down the Meuse are available. Those with sporting proclivities can undertake canoe trips on the lower course of the Lesse (see Dinant, Surroundings).

The Haimon children

The Meuse valley is one of the settings for the series of legends concerning the Haimon children which has as its subject the quarrels between Charles the Great and Renaut de Montauban, but historically is more concerned with the events about Charles Martell. Renaut was one of the four sons of Aymon (Haimon) of Dordogne and lived with his brothers Allard, Guiscard and Richard at the court of Charles the Great. When in a quarrel he killed Charles' nephew he fled with his brothers on the back of the mighty horse Bayard, which had been reared on an island in the Meuse, along the valley and into the Ardennes. From there they continued their flight to Gascony where Renaut founded the fortress of Montauban. Finally he was reconciled with Charles and undertook a pilgrimage to the Holy Land. He came back, settled in Cologne and worked as a mason on the cathedral. Jealous fellow workers murdered him and threw his body into the Rhine where, according to the legend, the fish brought his body again to the surface.

**Upper Meuse Valley: from Hastière to Namur

Grottes du Pont d'Arcole

A trip along the Meuse, which is also very pleasant by bicycle as there are few gradients, begins in the double parish of Hastière near the French border. A little further on is the part of the village called Hastière-Lavaux where are the grottos of Pont d'Arcole through which flows a subterranean spring.

Hastière-par-Delà

On the far side of the bridge over the Meuse lies Hastière-par-Delà where at the beginning of the 11th c. Irish monks founded a monastery. The purely Romanesque parish church with its massive tower remains from that time; the choir, however, was added in 1264. The choirstalls date from the same period and are some of the oldest in Belgium. In the crypt can be found two Merovingian sarcophagi.

Remaining on the left bank we come to Waulsourt on a bend in the river. The fine castle was originally the palace of the abbots of the convent founded in the 10th c. A little way downstream on the other bank rises the ruins of Château-Thierry, picturesquely situated on the Rocher du Chien (dog crag).

Waulsourt

Further on is Freÿr where the castle and its wonderful gardens should be visited. The castle was built between the 16th and 18th c. and unites the style of Mosan Renaissance with the Rococo of Louis XV. In 1675 Louis XIV used the castle as his headquarters during the siege of Dinant. The rooms which he used have been kept in their original condition as have the other salons, among which the dining room, with its Renaissance furniture and leather tapestry from Córdoba, as well as the vestibule with hunting scenes take a special place. A large balcony surrounded by an artistic wrought-iron balustrade looks out over the gardens.

*Château de Freÿr

Opening times
July and Aug.
Sat., Sun. and
public holidays
2–6pm

The gardens lie along the Meuse on three levels. They were laid out according to the principles of Le Nôtre from 1760 onwards under the jurisdiction of the dukes of Beaufort-Spontin. On the lowest level 33 orange trees in containers are set out and some of these are more than 300 years old. On the two levels above is a maze comprised of hedges, and to conclude the gardens there is a small hunting lodge.

*Gardens

The imposing background to the castle and park is formed on the right bank of the Meuse by the towering rock of Freÿr which the Belgian Alpine Club uses as a training ground.

**Rocher de Freÿr

The Meuse now describes another curve at the vertex of which lies Anseremme at the mouth of the Lesse (see Dinant, Surroundings).

Anseremme

Château de Freÿr

357

Vallée de la Meuse

Dinant

Now comes Dinant (see entry) the exceptionally picturesquely situated capital of the upper Meuse valley, and a little further on the suburb of Bouvignes with the Château of Crèvecœur (see Dinant, Surroundings).

Château de Poilvache

In Dinant our route crosses the Meuse and continues along the right bank of the river. High above the village of Houx are the overgrown ruins of the Tour de Géronsart and the Château de Poilvache, built, according to legend, by the Haimon children. Actually it dates from the 10th c. and was destroyed in 1430 by the soldiers of the Bishop of Liège. Its name "castle cowhide" refers to another legend, according to which the beleaguered inhabitants dressed themselves in cowhide in order to slip away. They were however discovered and the besiegers of Dinant donned the cowhide and were able to get into the castle which they quickly subdued.

Yvoir

A few kilometres past the castle we reach Yvoir, a popular holiday resort particularly for its island in the Meuse. Just south of the village lies the "Oasis nature" a 10ha/25 acre park. Signposted paths lead through botanical gardens, educational plantations, and past an old castle and a farm where visitors can study the flora and fauna of Belgium.

*Vallée de la Molignée

For the detour through the green valley of the Molignée it is necessary to cross the Meuse between Houx and Yvoir after reaching Anhée. Here the Molignée flows from the west into the Meuse. By following its course we

Château du Montaigle

reach in 9km/5½ miles the ruins of the Château du Montaigle on a crag; built in the 13th c., it was destroyed in 1554 by the French.

Falaën

Just beyond the castle a narrow road leads off to Falaën. Visitors to the 17th c. castle estate there can see a small historical exhibition and try the local specialities, bread and dark beer.

Abbaye de Maredsous

Back on the main road the Benedictine Abbey of Maredsous is soon reached. It was founded in 1872 by a Belgian monk from the monastery at Beuron who wanted to recreate the life style and architecture of the medieval abbeys. Building went on until the 1950s in Neo-Gothic style. The abbey has a small art collection, a library, a publishing house and a pedagogic centre.

Maredsous is also known for its Trappist cheese, its bread and its beer; The beer, however, is not brewed in the monastery but in the Duvel brewery in Breendonk.

Maredret

The Benedictines also built an abbey in 1893 in nearby Maredret. A little museum in the village shows varieties of timber, woodworking and rural life in the region between the Sambre and the Meuse.

Furnaux

Furnaux is the terminus of the excursion into the valley of the Molignée. Here the local church is worth visiting, for it has an extremely artistic font of black marble. This was created around 1135 and shows the Baptism of Christ on the basin which is borne by four lions.

*Château d'Annevoie

On the left bank of the Meuse lies the castle of Annevoie, the building of which was begun in 1627. In 1775 Charles Alexis de Montpellier had the brick building enlarged with a Rococo wing. The furnishings and equipment of the castle rooms date from this time; particularly fine are the music room and the chapel with stucco work by the Italian brothers Moretti.

**Gardens

However, the actual attraction of Annevoie is the gardens which were laid out at the same time as the castle was being extended. The principles of French horticultural layout are here integrated in the most harmonious manner – as can be seen in the geometric form and the many water features such as the cascade called "Buffet d'Eau" – with English and Italian garden layouts, the latter including statues of Carrara marble. The floral displays – in spring daffodils, hyacinths and tulips, in summer roses and begonias – are a first class attraction in the Meuse valley. (Open: castle tours mid Apr.–June and Sept., Sat, Sun. and public holidays 9.30am–1pm and 2–6.30pm; July and Aug. daily at the same times; gardens Apr.–Nov. 1st 9am–7pm.)

Godinne

Godinne on the right bank of the Meuse is linked to Annevoie by a bridge. It possesses a beautiful priory of the 16–17th c.

In the gardens of Annevoie

Remaining on the right bank we soon see the massive formations of the Rochers de Frênes which are pierced by grottos in which Stone Age men have left their traces. From the viewpoint on the top of the rock an extensive view over the Meuse can be enjoyed; on the opposite bank can be seen Profondeville, one of the most important holiday places in the valley.

Rochers de Frênes

Leaving the rock the Meuse is crossed for the last time; in Wépion, the centre of a large strawberry growing area, is a very original strawberry museum.

Wépion

The trip through the Upper Meuse Valley ends in Namur (see entry).

Namur

Lower Meuse Valley: from Namur to Huy

This trip leaves Namur on the right bank of the river following the N90. In a short distance the rock called Albert I (see Namur, Surroundings) can be seen on the far bank. The Meuse describes a broad loop to the south at the vertex of which the little river Samson joins the main stream. In its picturesque valley can be found the grottos of Goyet with impressive dripstone formations. In one part of the caves, which were inhabited by pre-historic men, there is a representation of their way of life. A little further upstream lies Faulx-les-Tombes with an 18th c. castle.

Vallée du Samson

Andenne, approximately halfway between Namur and Huy, lies on the border of the Condroz. The little town arose near a monastery which was founded about 700 by St Begga but of this nothing remains. Begga was the daughter of Pippin I, the sister of St Gertrude of Nivelles (see entry), and mother of Pippin II and therefore the progenitrix of the Carolingians. Her grandson Carl Martell is believed to have been born in Andenne; the bear fountain commemorates him and illustrates one of his first heroic deeds

Andenne

when, at the age of nine, he slew a wild bear with a hammer. For this reason a "bear carnival" is held annually in Andenne, at the climax of which little teddy bears are thrown from the town hall.

In 1273 the "battle of the cow" began in Andenne It was caused by a farmer who had stolen a cow from a citizen of Ciney but was recognised in Andenne market. However, he refused to return the cow and was immediately hanged in Ciney. His master the Count of Namur besieged Ciney with the help of the Luxemburgers. The owner of Ciney, the prince-archbishop of Liège hurried from Dinant with his supporters and there followed a two-year war at the end of which the Condroz was laid waste.

Collégiale
Sainte-Begge

The parish church of Sainte-Begge, dedicated to St Begga, was built between 1770 and 1775 on the site of seven monastic chapels (Encloîtres), the model of which can be seen in the church. Also in the church is the black marble tomb of St Begga and her reliquary shrine (16th c.). The Porte Sainte-Etienne (18th c.), the last remainder of the seven chapels, is preserved in the Place Sainte-Begge.

Musée de la
Céramique

In the 18th and 19th c. Andenne has a flourishing porcelain and ceramic industry which is commemorated in the Musée de la Céramique (open: May–Sept. Tues., Fri., Sat. and Sun. 2.30–5.30pm).

Huy

The trip ends at Huy (see entry) where the Meuse begins to widen out considerably and becomes more and more characterised by industrial complexes.

Vallée de l'Ourthe   G/H 6–8

Province: Luxembourg, Namur and Liège

Course and
*scenery

The Ourthe is a 130km/427 mile-long river in east Belgium. Its source is two streams in the Ardennes, the eastern Ourthe and the western Ourthe which unite near the village of Engreux. In a deeply cut winding valley the Ourthe flows in a north-west and later north direction through the plateau of the Ardennes and the districts of Famenne and Condroz, often called the pre-Ardennes region, and enters the Meuse near Liège. The breach valley of the Ourthe is one of the most charming and picturesque scenic regions of Belgium. On the banks of this river, which is rich in fish, are a series of holiday resorts which are ideal bases for walks in the forest and for trips in boats and canoes on the Ourthe and its tributaries. These resorts are provided with excellent hotels and restaurants. The long-distance footpath GR57 accompanies the valley of the Ourthe from Angleur in the vicinity of Liège as far as Houfflaize.

**Upper Ourthe Valley: from La Roche to Houffalize

In the upper valley of the Ourthe to the south of La Roche-en-Ardennes the river describes narrow bends through steep rock formations so that this section of the valley is the most wildly romantic. This region, as far as Bastogne (see entry) to the south, was one of the most violently disputed areas during the Ardennes offensive in December 1944 and January 1945, and there were many victims, especially among the civil population, caused by the atrocities of the SS and by bombardment; these events still remain vivid in the memory of the local people.

*La Roche-en-
Ardennes

La Roche-en-Ardennes, the "Pearl of the Ardennes", has an extremely picturesque situation surrounded by forests at the junction of several lateral valleys; with barely 4300 inhabitants it is the largest and most important tourist resort of the Ourthe Valley. There are many hotels, restaurants, facilities for renting boats, and more than 100km/62 miles of footpaths for the enjoyment of visitors. La Roche-en-Ardennes was almost completely destroyed in 1944 by an Allied bombing attack.

La Roche-en-Ardennes, chief town of the Ourthe valley

The little town is dominated by the ruins on a rocky spur. The castle was begun in the 10th c., rebuilt several times and destroyed in the 18th c., the material being used by the citizens of the town to build their own houses. In 1852 the remains were restored and can now be reached from the market place by a stepped path. In fine weather the ghost of the maiden Berthe appears (provided by the tourist office); according to legend she was killed by the devil although she was innocent. Just above the ruins stands the 16th c. Chapelle Ste-Marguerite which is linked to the castle by a sub-terranean passage constructed by the French in the 17th c. From here there is a good view of the town and the valleys. — *Castle ruins*

A speciality of local craft is the grey stoneware with cobalt blue salt glaze introduced in 1872. In the craft centre "Les Grès de La Roche" the production method is explained, an old kiln can be visited and, of course, stoneware can be purchased. — *"Les Grès de La Roche"*

Beyond the Chapelle Ste-Marguerite a path leads to the Deister plateau above the river bank where a 15ha/37-acre nature park with a little game park has been laid out. This can also be reached by the tourist train which leaves the "Pavillon des Deux Parcs" in the valley, one kilometre outside the town. — *Parc de Deister*

The route now follows the N384 and comes to Ortho on the plateau where a fortified Celto-Roman camp was found. — *Ortho*

To the east of Ortho near Nisramont the Ourthe is dammed to form a reservoir, the Barrage de l'Ourthe, which encloses 2.5 milliard cu.m of water. From the car park north of Misramont on the right of the road is a wonderful view over the lake into which flow the two source streams of the Ourthe, and across to the rock called "Le Hérou". — *Barrage de l'Ourthe* / **View*

Beyond Nisramont the road winds down into the valley, crosses the Ourthe and joins the N860 to Nadrin. From there there is a walk on a 2.2km/1½ — ***Belvédère des Six Ourthes* mile-long path to the fissured rock "Le Hérou" which is 1400m/4595ft long on two sides and falls steeply into the Ourthe; from the Belvédère des Six Ourthes viewpoint there is an extensive panorama embracing the six narrow loops which the river forms around the rock, the reservoir and the confluence of the two sources of the Ourthe. The last named can be reached from the observation point on the footpath which leads up through the forest on the right bank of the river.

Houffalize
A detour leads east from Nadrin for 12km/7½ miles to Houffalize on the east Ourthe, a pretty summer resort known as the "Heart of the Ardennes". In 1944 the little town was completely laid waste in ashes and rubble by Allied aircraft who stopped a German armoured advance here. In the Place Albert can be seen a memento of this event – a German Panther tank which was left behind. Houffalize possesses two museums: the town museum with a "Paul Verheggen" department concerned with the flora and fauna of the Ardennes and an archaeological section, and the museum of country life "Li Vi Forni". Shortly before reaching the village the road passes under the motorway viaduct over the Ourthe which is 65m/213ft high and 369m/1211ft long and is the largest in Belgium.

Petites Tailles
A diversion north from Houffalize reaches in 15km/9½ miles a marshy plateau the Petites Tailles, where the landscape anticipates that of the Hohe Venn which adjoins it to the north.

*Lower Ourthe Valley: from La Roche to Liège

The lower course of the Ourthe is quieter and flows along in broad curves only occasionally interrupted by narrows caused by the rocks. In several places underground watercourses have dug caves into the limestone; there are ruined castles, fortifications and old watermills to be seen.

Marcourt
From La Roche the road follows the river. In 7.5km/4¾ miles there can be seen on a hilltop on the left the little pilgrimage chapel of Saint-Thibaut, built in 1639. It belongs to the family resort of Marcourt once the seat of the counts of Montaigu whose castle (1050) ruins can still be seen.

Hotton
On the border between the Ardennes and the Famenne lies Hotton, a place which has long been inhabited, for in the vicinity were found relics of the Neolithic and Roman ages. From a steep cliff which dominates the village there is a fine view of the Ardennes and the Famenne: forested hillsides on one side and extensive meadows and pastures on the other.

Grottes de Hotton
The dripstone cave "Grotte des Mille et une Nuits" (grotto of the thousand-and-one nights) impresses especially because of its bizarre rock forms and play of light caused by crystal formations (open: Apr.–Oct. daily 9am–6pm).

Durbuy
Durbuy has an exceptionally charming townscape; although it has few more than 350 inhabitants it nevertheless has had the title of a town since 1331. It lies on both sides of the Ourthe and most of it is barred to traffic. The narrow streets and the old houses, as well as the remains of the town wall, give the impression that here time stands still. Not to be missed are the castle of the counts of Ursel, the old cloth hall, the law courts and the parish church (16th–18th c.).

Barvaux
Beyond Durbuy the road leaves the Ourthe Valley and meets it again near Barvaux, an important tourist resort with a large water-sports complex at the foot of the Rocher de Glawans. Easily reached from here are the villages of Tohogne in the north with its beautifully furnished Romanesque church, and Wéris in the east with the Church of Ste-Walburge (11th c.). In the vicinity of this village the great dolmen Nord and many smaller druidical stones have been discovered.

Bomal, Vallée de l'Aisne
Bomal which follows also earns its living from tourism. Here the Aisne coming from the south joins the Ourthe. The Aisne flows through a pretty

valley which is excellent for walking and where there is an imposing view of the rocky walls of the Roche à Frêne.

The Château de Logne is one of the finest castles in the Ourthe Valley. It was built in the 11th c. and in the 15th came into the possession of the quarrelsome de la Marck family who bore the scarcely flattering nickname of "Sangliers des Ardennes" (wild boar of the Ardennes). The castle, destroyed on the order of Charles V, was rebuilt in more recent times and can be visited. Finds from the castle on are show in nearby Vieuxville in the Ferme de la Bouverie.

*Château de Logne

The road now turns away from the river and returns to it in Hamoir. Here the celebrated sculptor Jean Delcour (1627–1707) and his son and painter Jean-Gilles (1632–95) were born; the latter carried out the painting on the high altar of the village church, whereas the father was responsible for the altar sculpture and part of the tabernacle in the Romanesque church of Saint-Pierre in nearby Xhignesse; this church is notable for the blind arcades in the apse.

Hamoir

In Hamoir the little river Néblon joins the Ourthe. This stream winds for 14km/8½ miles through wild vegetation to the pretty village of Ocquier, in the vicinity of which, near Vervoz, remains of Roman villas and 3rd c. graves have been found.

Vallée du Néblon

The next stage is to Comblain-au-Pont at the confluence of the Ourthe and the Amblève (see Stavelot, Vallée de l'Amblève) which is surrounded by impressive rocks such as the Rocher des Tartines, the name of which is due to its tart-like form.
Just outside the village a grotto with 20 chambers and a deep chasm was found in 1909.

Comblain-au-Pont

Between Comblain-au-Pont and Poulseur to the north the first nature park in Belgium was created on the bank of the Ourthe in 1946; this is the Parc naturelle des Roches-Noires, du Chession et du Vignoble.

Nature park

Near Esneux the Ourthe makes another large bend and forms a peninsula. Interesting rock formations, a few ruined castles in the surroundings and the Parc du Mary with its arboretum can here be explored.

Esneux

Tilff is the last rural village before reaching the industrial conurbation of Liège (see entry) and is therefore very popular for local excursions by the townsfolk. A very original museum is the Musée de l'Abeille which is concerned with the history and art of raising and keeping bees, illustrated by models, implements and a collection of beehives. Some of the beehives are active so that visitors can see the bees at work.

Tilff

Vallée de la Semois (Semois Valley)

F/G 9

Province: Luxembourg, Namur

The Semois rises in the extreme south-east corner of Belgium near Arlon (see entry), it flows first through the plain of Gaume in the Belgian part of Lorraine (Lorraine Belge) and at Tintigny enters the Ardennes. From here onwards it has cut a course deeply into the hills and forms broad curves around forested rocks which again and again offer charming views. Although the distance from its source to its joining the Meuse near the French town of Monthermé is only 80km/50 miles as the crow flies, the total length of the river is over 200km/124 miles.
The climate of the Semois valley is relatively mild, as its deep situation protects it from the predominantly westerly winds. Until a short time ago the most important agricultural product was tobacco grown along the

Course and *scenery

lower course of the river, but now this only thrives in the districts further to the south; however, the production of tobacco is becoming increasingly unprofitable.

The valley now lives by tourism and in its beautiful landscape it offers all kinds of attractions: canoe and boat trips, angling, numerous waymarked footpaths, camping sites, hotels and very good restaurants. There are not many cultural sites, the chief being the mighty castle of Bouillon (see entry) and the abbey of Orval (see entry) which is a little way off.

Sights

The steep flanks of the valley at times approach the river so closely that the roads are often high above the edge, therefore a trip through the Semois Valley is best done on foot or by boat if one is not to miss the finest parts of the landscape. Many of the larger villages are on the plateau of the Ardennes high above the windings of the river.

For those who are fit cycling through the valley offers fine views.

Jamoigne

A trip along the valley begins in Jamoigne which lies at the junction of the picturesque Vierre Valley and has an old castle (rebuilt in the 19th c.) and a notable church with a beautiful 12th c. font and pictures by Abraham of Orval.

Chiny
*Boat trip

From here the Semois winds to the north and flows around Chiny, once the seat of the lords of Chiny, and then becomes wildly romantic. A trip in a flat bottomed boat is recommended, by means of which it is possible to see picturesque rocks, such as the Rocher du Hât, or sail below the Rocher du Paradis (Apr.–Sept. daily 9am–6pm). The trip ends after 7km/4½ miles in Lacuisine from where the return to Chiny can be made on a fine footpath (¾ hour) or by bus.

View of the valley of the Semois

From a viewpoint about 2.8km/1¾ miles north of Lacuisine (the path has orange-white waymarks on the north of the road to Neufchâteau) there is an excellent view of the stretch which has just been completed by boat.

After Chiny the Semois again becomes quieter and there follows Florenville, a tourist centre on the upper course of the river. From the terrace behind the church there is an extensive view of the lovely scenery with its pastures and fields, and this is even more impressive when seen from the church tower. From Florenville a detour of 8km/5 miles to the abbey of Orval (see entry) lying to the south is recommended.

Florenville

From Florenville the Semois describes a broad curve and meets the through road again at Chassepierre, one of the prettiest villages on the Semois and a popular holiday resort. Slate-roofed houses surround the Church of Saint-Martin which has interesting choirstalls, probably from Orval. In the surroundings can be seen caves used by hunters in the Stone Age and prehistoric dolmens. About 1km beyond the village on the right of the road there is a look-out point with a good view of the village to the rear.

Chassepierre

The N384 in the direction of Herbeumont leads via Ste-Cécile through the Forest of Conques which belonged to the priory of the same name. This priory, founded in 1694 as a refuge for the monks of Orval, can be seen shortly before reaching Herbeumont on the left of the road; it is now a hotel. Herbeumont village is dominated by the ruins of the counts' castle dating from the 12th c. which was destroyed in 1658 by the French. From the top there is a wonderful view of a very narrow reach of the Semois around a rocky ridge which, because of its form, is called the "Tombeau du Chevalier" (knight's tomb). Around Herbeumont there are many footpaths.

Herbeumont

View

The route continues to Mortehan; from there it is possible to go on to Bouillon via the little tourist resort of Dohan, or to make a detour via Auby to the Saut des Sorcières, a series of waterfalls which fall into pools, and pass the viewpoint of the Mont de Zarton. On the latter stretch the road first passes through Cugnon, where St Remaclus is said to have lived in a grotto in the 7th c. Both detours finish in Noirefontaine, from where Bouillon is reached on the N89. But first visitors should continue from Noirefontaine to Botassart and look down on the bend of the river around the "Tombeau du Géant" (giant's grave).

Direction of Bouillon

View

After Bouillon the visitor should first take the N810 which is scenically very appealing and which passes the rock called "Hottée du Diable" (devil's basket) to Corbion, where in the 16th c. a certain Monsieur Pistole invented the pistol; and from there take a smaller road towards Poupehan, once an important place of tobacco processing. Shortly before reaching the village a path to the right leads to the viewpoint "Chaire à prêcher" (pulpit), a rock from which monks summoned people to the crusades to Jerusalem and Gottfried of Bouillon heeded their call.

Poupehan

At a great bend in the river the route reaches Rochehaut situated high up with its Church of Saint-Firmin adorned with frescoes from where there is yet another beautiful view, this time of the village of Frahan lying opposite and across to Alle where Joseph Pierret lived; he began tobacco planting in 1855 on the Semois and made Alle his centre.

Rochehaut

View

Vresse is almost the end of the trip. Here the Semois receives the Petit-Fays stream which rushes through a narrow valley which can be followed to the north on a minor road. Here can still be seen the bars on which tobacco was dried. Vresse itself has a museum which is primarily concerned with the tobacco world and with smoking.

Vresse

Before finally reaching the French frontier the Semois flows through the nature park of Bohan-Membre which is crossed by many footpaths, including one that leads to the viewpoint Jambon de la Semois and to the prehistoric megalithic Table des Fées.

Parc naturel de Bohan-Membre

Vallée de la Semois

Detour to France   Beyond the frontier the Semois winds its way towards the Meuse. This is the land of the legend of the four Haimon children who set out on the battle charger Bayard from Château Regnault on the banks of the Meuse on their adventures. Near the confluence of the Semois and the Meuse above Monthermé local tradition identifies four crags with the four riders and nearby their battle steed is chiselled in the rock.

Verviers

Province: Liège
Altitude: 200–240m/656–787ft
Population: 53,600
Intercity Station (bicycle rental at station)

Location   Where Limberg, the district of Herve and the foothills of the Ardennes meet extends the industrial town of Verviers, on the slopes of the valley of the Vesdre which flows through it, about half way between Liège and Aachen. Fine civic buildings testify to the prosperity of the town when the woollen industry was flourishing; even today Verviers still has a textile technical school. As well as the textile industry the production of leather goods, agriculture, paper and building materials are of importance. In addition tourism is playing an increasing role, for the town is the gateway to the scenically charming Herve region and to the Ardennes.

History   Verviers goes back to a Roman settlement called "Virovirus", but the settlement only acquired importance from 1651 when a charter was given to the town by the prince-bishop of Liège, and the increasing thriving of the woollen industry because of favourable conditions provided by water from the Vesdre and the proximity of sheep rearing areas in the Ardennes and the Eifel. The industrial revolution brought an unexpected impetus and the population rose from 20,000 in 1830 to 53,000 in 1900. Verviers was once the most important place in Europe for wool processing, but the world economic crisis in the 30s put a stop to its prosperity.

Sights

Hôtel de Ville   The traffic junction in the heart of Verviers on the left bank of the river is the Place Verte, from which the Crapaurue, the principal street, leads to the Hôtel de Ville in the Place du Marché which is flanked by beautiful Baroque and Rococo houses. This freestanding building in the Classical style dates from the 18th c. and is one of the most elegant of its kind in Belgium. In front of the Town Hall is a perron (raised platform) dating from 1732.

Musée d'Archéologie et du Folklore

° Lace

Further to the north in the Rue des Raines there are still a number of fine old burghers' houses dating from the 16th–18th c. which testify to the town's former prosperity. House No. 42, the Maison Cornet, contains the Musée d'Archéologie et du Folklore. Its greatest treasure is the wonderful collection of lace from all parts of Belgium; also of great interest are the rooms on the ground and first floors, as well as the Grand Salon in Dutch style and the Salon Louis XIII with three artistic secretaires. Commemorated in the Grand Salon is the violinist Henri Vieuxtemps (1820–81) who was born in Verviers. The second storey is devoted to archaeological finds from the surroundings. (Open: Mon.–Thur. and Sat. 9am–noon and 2–5pm, Sun. and public holidays 10am–1pm and 3–6pm.)

° Musée des Beaux-Arts et de la Céramique

In a former 17th c. hospice for elderly men in Rue Renier which branches off the Rue des Raines is the interesting Musée des Beaux-Arts et de la Céramique. On the ground floor is exhibited an excellent collection of faience and porcelain from the most important European factories and also china;

The Classical Town Hall of Verviers

in other rooms and on the first floor is a considerable collection of pictures including a fine portrait of a child with a lace hood by Cornelis de Vos and works by Pieter Pourbus, Guido Reni and Frans Snyders, as well as more modern paintings by René Magritte and Paul Delvaux; in the courtyard is a lapidarium and in the basement sculptures (open: as above).

Further to the west by the river stands the 18th c. Church of Notre-Dame which was the destination of a pilgrimage in honour of the Black Madonna sculpture of 1692. The tower has a fine carillon of 40 bells.

Notre-Dame

In the southern part of the town can be found the Musée de la Laine in the building of the textile technical school; it is concerned with the history of wool processing (Rue de Séroule; open: Mon.–Sat. 2–5pm).

Musée de la Laine

Surroundings

7km/4½ miles north-east of Verviers is the little town of Limbourg built on a hill. It was situated on the route between Bruges and Cologne and until the Battle of Worringen in 1268 was the chief town of the former Duchy of Limbourg but then it fell to Brabant. Because of its strategic importance it was subsequently fortified but suffered several sieges, especially heavy ones by Louis XIV and in 1703 by the Duke of Marlborough who destroyed the ducal castle which had been built about 1000 in the upper town.
The circular path along the old town walls leads around the upper town and offers fine views. Of interest is the Gothic Église Saint-Georges, of which the predecessor was the 12th c. castle chapel, and this in turn was built above a Romanesque crypt. The church received its present form in the 14th and 15th c.

Limbourg

Not far from Limbourg the Vesdre is spanned by the 20m/66ft-high viaduct of Dolhain which was completed in 1843.

Viaduc de Dolhain

Abbaye de Val-Dieu	Nestling picturesquely in the valley of the Berwinne is the Abbaye de Val-Dieu which is reached on a 15km/9½ mile drive via Thimister and Aubel north of Verviers. The abbey was founded around the year 1215 and was very prosperous. Of special interest in the present buildings, which are inhabited by Cistercians, are the refectory, the guesthouse of 1732 and the Renaissance choirstalls in the abbey church.
Barrage de la Gileppe	See Eupen, Surroundings

Veurne · Furnes   A 4

Province: West-Vlaanderen
Altitude: 0–30m/0–98ft
Population: 11,300
Inter-regional Station (bicycle rental at station)

Location

The little town of Veurne (French Furnes), not far from the North Sea coast and at the confluence of four canals, is the centre of a legal and administrative district and is worth visiting especially for its lovely marketplace. Its historic monuments dating from the Spanish period were damaged by bombardment during the First and Second World Wars but have been excellently restored. Ham from Veurne is a noted delicacy.

History

Veurne grew up around a castle erected by the Counts of Flanders in the 9th c. as protection against the Normans and it became the chief place of the counts' fortified estate of Veurne-Ambacht. It reached its zenith under the regentship of the Archduke Albert and Archduchess Isabella in the 17th c. when most of the stately buildings around the Grote Markt came into being. The French strengthened the fortifications which had been set up in the 14th c. and which, under the Austrians, were razed to the ground in 1783. In the First World War Veurne was the most important town of the small part of Belgium not occupied by German troops and in spite of artillery attack could not be taken. During the Battle of Ypres King Albert I chose the town hall as his headquarters. In the Second World War the town suffered more severe damage than between 1914 and 1918.

Penitential procession

The Penitential procession, which takes place annually on the last Sunday in July, dates back to the 12th c.; it was first held in 1644 and since 1656 has been celebrated every year. Members of the "Sodaliteit" brotherhood present scenes from the Passion of Christ in a procession, and they are followed by penitents in the garments of Capuchins dragging along heavy crosses. The Way of the Cross processions in Lent and at Easter are connected with Spanish traditions. The Way of the Cross begins at Sint-Walburgakerk and ends at the Sint-Niklaaskerk. During Lent it takes place every Friday at 8pm and during Easter week daily at the same time. On Maundy Thursday it is held at 8 and 9pm.

* Grote Markt

The impressive centre of the town is the Grote Markt, one of the finest market squares in Belgium. It is lined by several historic buildings in the characteristic west Flanders yellow brick. Interaction of the elements of architectural decoration of Flemish Renaissance and the sober Spanish influence becomes clear and it is for this that Veurne is often called the "Spanish town".

Stadhuis

The Stadhuis (town hall) in the north-west corner of the square built by Liéviun Lucas between 1596 and 1612 is, with its twin gabled façade and elegant loggia of bluish stone, is an excellent example of the style of the Flemish Renaissance. Above the roof rises the narrow stepped tower

Veurne: Old houses in the Grote Markt

erected in 1599. The rooms of the town hall have largely kept their form and furnishings of the 17th and 18th c.

The council chamber on the ground floor is particularly fine and impressive with its leather wall hangings from Mechelen as is the jury room with its linings of blue satin from Utrecht. On the upper floor can be seen the reception hall with leather wall hangings from Córdoba in Andalusia – here King Albert I had his office in 1914 – and the lawcourt with a painting by de Vriendt, as well as the marriage room, again with leather hangings from Mechelen and a still life by de Vos.

Opening times
Easter–Sept.
daily 10am–noon
and 2–5pm

In the right-hand corner of the square adjoining the town hall is the former Landhuis, built 1613–16 and now the palace of justice (viewing in conjunction with the town hall tour). It is dominated by its mighty Gothic belfry which, however, bears a Baroque spire. The tower, not finished until 1628, was set on fire by bombardment in 1940. Separated only by a narrow road, the Landhuis is adjoined by five very fine stepped gabled houses dating from the beginning of the 17th c.

Landhuis

Along the road mentioned above we come to Sint-Walburgakerk which was begun in 1250 on a magnificent scale but only the 27m/89ft-high sandstone choir (14th c.) with its ambulatory and chapels, the lower part of the tower and one arm of the crossing were completed in the Middle Ages. Also from this period date the remains of a pillar which can be seen in the park outside the church. The castle of the counts of Flanders is believed to have stood on this spot.

Sint-Walburga-kerk
* Choir

The transepts and other parts of the church were not added until 1901–04. In the choir which is supported by huge round pillars is some beautiful seating of 1596; also of interest are several paintings (17th and 18th c.), a Baroque pulpit and the reliquary of the cross which Count Robert II of Flanders is said to have brought from Jerusalem in the year 1100.

Noordstraat	In Noordstraat which leads from the market there are several beautiful Renaissance houses, including the house called "Die Nobele Roze" of 1572, one of the oldest hotels in Belgium now occupied by a bank. Opposite a monument commemorates the opening of the IJzer sluices in 1914 by means of which the German advance was stopped.
Spaans Paviljoen	The north-east side of the Grote Markt is taken up by the so-called Spaans Paviljoen. This was built between 1448 and 1452, extended in 1530 and until 1586 served as the town hall. In 1697 it was used to accommodate Spanish officers.
Vleeshuis	The Vleeshuis (meat hall) on the opposite side of the market place dates from 1615 and is a fine example of Late Renaissance architecture.
Hoge Wacht	On the south side of the market place facing the Appelmarkt is the Hoge Wacht, an arcaded building acquired by the town in 1636 for the guard.
Sint-Niklaaskerk	On the Appelmarkt rises the Gothic Sint-Niklaaskerk, the great tower of which dating from the 12–13th c. remained unfinished. It houses a carillon which includes the bell called "Bomtje" of 1379, one of the oldest Flemish bells. It is not known who was responsible for the triptych on the high altar; opinions vary between Jan van Aemstel and Bernard van Orley.
*Internationaal Bakkerijmuseum	To the south, away from the town centre, an 18th c. farmhouse houses the International Bakery Museum (Albert-I-Laan 2). It is divided into several sections: "Art in the Bakery", "Bread from all the world", an old bakery and a shop in which visitors can buy local delicacies such as "Kletskoppen" (biscuits), "Haantjes" (little chickens made from sandcake pastry, almond bread. (Open: Apr.–Sept. daily except Fri. 10am–noon and 2–6pm; July and Aug. also open Fri.; Oct.–Mar. Sun–Thur. 2–5pm.)

Surroundings

Kasteel van Beauvoorde	7km/4½ miles south of Veurne is the Kasteel van Beauvoorde, an attractive Renaissance château surrounded by a moat. It was constructed between 1591 and 1617 on the site of a destroyed castle by the master builder of Archduke Albrecht and Isabella and after a period when it became dilapidated it was bought by a private citizen Arthur Merghelynck and restored. He is responsible for the present interior furnishing (Renaissance furniture, paintings, objects d'art) which can be seen on a guided tour (open: Apr.–Sept. daily except Mon. 2–4pm).
Izenberge	In Izenberge, 10km/6 miles to the south, the museum "Bachten de Kupe" should be visited. It is devoted to local culture and divided into three sections: a dwelling house, a museum of popular art and an open-air museum with rural buildings including a smithy and a farmhouse.
Houtem	The village of Houtem, 10km/6 miles to the south-west was from the beginning of 1915 until the late summer of 1918 the headquarters of the Belgian army.
Lo	Lo is a pretty little town 15km/9½ miles south-east of Veurne. Its Gothic hall church is richly furnished with artistic features, especially valuable paintings including some by Mittendorf, Boeckhorst and Boucquet. Only a tower remains of the 14th c. fortifications.
De Panne	See entry
Koksijde	See entry

Virton   G 10

Province: Luxembourg. Altitude: 230m/755ft
Population: 10,500. Local Rail Station (bicycle rental at station)

The little town of Virton, at the extreme southern tip of Belgium right on the French border, is situated at the confluence of the rivers Vire and Ton. It is the chief place of the peaceful district of Gaume and the landscape is reminiscent of Lorraine; it is blessed with a mild climate so that in the extreme south viniculture is possible. Virton is to a large extent dependent on tourism and is an excellent base for excursions in the surroundings.

Location

*Landscape

Numerous finds testify that the area was settled in Neolithic, Roman and Merovingian times. Virton itself developed from the Roman foundation of Vertunum. From the 16th c. a thriving iron casting industry developed here.

History

*Musée gaumais

In buildings of a 17th c. monastery is the Musée gaumais which is concerned with the history and culture of the Gaume region. The various departments exhibit examples of iron casting, including more than 150 fireplace plates, the oldest of which date from the 16th c., firebacks and pothooks; finds from Gallo-Roman times, various items of household furniture and everyday articles typical of Gaume, a collection of Boch stoneware of the 18th c. as well as 16–18th c. woodcarving. Also on view are watercolours by Nestor Outer a friend of Toulouse-Lautrec, oil paintings by Camille Barthélemy, who painted views of Virton, and among other things the painting "Adam and Eve mourn for Abel" by Frère Abraham (18th c.) from the Abbey of Orval (see entry). Three other museums in the vicinity are associated with the Musée gaumais.

Opening times
Mar.–Oct.
daily except Tues.
9.30am–noon and
2–6pm

Surroundings

At the Ferme de Huombois, 9km/5½ miles from Virton on the road to Buzenol, it is possible to see kilns and pottery articles dating from the Gallo-Roman era (on enquiry at the Musée gaumais).

Huombois

Near Buzenol, 13km/8 miles north of Virton, there is a 340m/1116ft-high hill which was already fortified in Roman times. Remains of the fortification walls from this and later periods have been preserved and can be seen in the "Parc archéologique". In the adjoining museum there are fine Gallo-Roman reliefs including a representation of the Celtic reaper mentioned by Plinius the Elder. A number of old smithies and foundries have been preserved in the wooded valley.

Buzenol-
Montauban

4km/2½ miles south-east of Virton lies Montquintin. Here in an 18th c. farm the "Musée de la Vie paysanne" has been set up which, by means of furnishing and implements, brings the old rural existence to life. (Open: July and Aug. daily 2–6pm.)

Montquintin

Beyond Montquintin we reach Torgny, the most southern parish in Belgium. Around this pretty village vines are grown, the "Clos de la Zolette" which is a Riesling grape.

Torgny

Latour, 7km/4½ miles east of Virton, commemorates its past in the Musée Ballet-Latour. The history of the local castle is documented; the battle on the border on 22nd August 1914, as well as events in the First and Second World Wars are described. Several rooms contain everyday and folkloric articles devoted to the culture of the Gaume. (Open: Easter–Nov. Sun. 3–6pm; July and Aug. daily 3–6pm.)

Latour

Across the French border a detour leads to Montmédy (14km/8½ miles) where can be seen the very well preserved fortification complex of Vauban.

Montmédy

371

Visé

Province: Liège
Altitude: 60–85m/197–279ft
Population: 16,800
Intercity Station

Location	Close to the Belgian-Dutch border on the right bank of the Meuse the town of Visé is the most northerly city in Wallonia. It is popular in summer for the water sports centre in the "three countries corner".
History	Visé grew up around a wooden bridge over the Meuse and had its flowering between the 9th and the 13th c. In 1330 the town was fortified and subsequently had to defend itself in many sieges, including those against the troops of Charles the Bold in 1468 and Louis XIV in 1663. In the first days of the First World War Visé was set on fire by German troops and almost completely destroyed.
Festivals	Visé is rich in folklore. Here is celebrated the "Carnival of the Geese" commemorating the legend of 1334, when the geese of Visé on their search for food made it possible for the besiegers to enter the town: the geese simply chewed up the bolts of the gates. The three shooting guilds of the town are of great importance: the "Gilde des Anciens Arbalétriers" (Old Cross-bow Shooters Guild), founded in 1310, its successor the "Compagnie Royale des Anciens Arquebusiers" (Royal Company of Arquebusiers) dating from 1579 and the "Compagnie Royale des Francs Arquebusiers" (Royal Company of Free Arquebusiers) which came into being in 1909. Each of these guilds has a festival twice a year.

Sights

Collégiale Saints-Martin-et-Hadelin *Shrine of Saint Hadelinus	The collegiate church of Saints-Martin-et-Hadelin was founded by Berta the daughter of Charles the Great in 780. The church was destroyed by German troops and rebuilt from 1925; of the earlier work only the choir (1500) remains. However a visit to the church is well worth while because of its unique art treasures. The shrine of Saint Hadelinus, which contains the remains of the priest who preached by the Meuse in the 17th c., is the finest reliquary shrine in the Mosan area. Its gabled ends probably date from the 10th c.; one shows Christ crowning saints Remaclus and Hadelinus, the other an exceptionally rare representation of Christ as the vanquisher of death and the devil. On the sides, which date from 1150, are scenes from the life of Hadelinus and in their execution these are reminiscent of works by Renier de Huy. On the third Sunday in September the shrine is borne in procession through the town.
Hôtel de Ville	The present town hall is a reconstruction of the building which dated from the 17th c. in Mosan-Renaissance style. It has a notable onion-shaped tower. On the second floor is the Musée Regional d'Histoire et d'Archéologie (Regional Historical and Archaeological Museum) with a local history collection.
Gilden Museum	The three shooting guilds maintain their own museums which are sometimes open on Sunday mornings in summer and which exhibit weapons and documents about the history of their guilds. The museum of the Cross-bow Shooter's Guild is at No. 44 Rue Haute, that of the Old Arquebusiers at No. 11 and the museum of the Free Arquebusiers at No. 3 Rue Dodémont.

Surroundings

Eben-Emael	9km/5½ miles north-west of Visé lies Eben-Emael where the fort was completely destroyed by German troops in May 1940.

Walcourt

Province: Namur
Altitude: 150–238m/492–781ft
Population: 15,000
Local Rail Station (bicycle rental at station)

Walcourt is a little place of pilgrimage at the confluence of the Yvres and the Eau d'Heure in the extreme west of the province of Namur. Remains of defence works bear witness to its past as a fortified town.

Location

Every year on Trinity Sunday the "Grand Tour" takes place in Walcourt; this is a procession round the town in honour of the wonder-working statue of Mary. The procession is accompanied by soldiers in Napoleonic uniform together with pipes and drums.

Processions

Sights

The landscape of Walcourt is dominated by the Basilique Saint-Materne in the Grand-Place. The original church was built about the year 1000 in the Mosan-Romanesque style but in 1220 it burned down. When this happened it is said that the statue of Mary was swept out of the church into a birch tree where it was found by the Count of Rochefort, but he could only recover it after he had vowed to build a new church. This scene is the climax of the annual procession. The new church was built between the 13th and 15th c. in Mosan-Gothic style with five aisles. Only the west of the building and the lower part of the tower date from the time of its predecessor. The north doorway is adorned with a fine sculpture of the Virgin and Child (15th c.); the 63m/207ft high octagonal tower ends in a remarkable spire in a half-domed form dating from the 17th c.

**Basilique
Saint-Materne**

The furnishing of the interior is predominantly of 16th c. date; the rood screen (partly Late-Gothic and partly Early Renaissance) of 1533 has sculptures of white Avesnes stone and was a gift of Charles V. The relatively plain choir stalls (1510) are carved with intercession scenes and satirical motifs; the Late-Gothic tabernacle is also of exceptional beauty.

Interior

The wonder-working statue of Notre-Dame du Pélerinage (Notre-Dame du Walcourt) in the left transept was made in the 11th c. from wood and is covered with silverplate.

*Statue of Mary

Among the treasures of the exceptionally valuable church treasury are a reliquary cross of 1300, possibly by Hugo d'Oignies the silversmith born in Walcourt in the 12th c., a 14th c. silver Madonna and several monstrances and reliquary shrines (these can be seen only after enquiry in the basilica).

*Church Treasury

In the Musée de l'Uniforme (3 Rue de la Montagne) military uniforms from 1830 until the present day are on show (open: Easter–Nov. Sat., Sun. and public holidays 10am–noon and 2–6pm).

Musée de
l'Uniforme

Surroundings

Thy-le-Château, which lies 8km/5 miles north of Walcourt, had a flourishing iron industry in the 13th c. The fine restored castle (10–13th c.) is well worth a visit.

Thy-le-Château

About 4km/2½ miles south of Walcourt begins the lake district of the Barrages de l'Eau d'Heure; this was created by building dams to provide energy and as a reservoir for the Sambre and the canal from Charleroi to Brussels; it is the largest connected series of lakes in Belgium. At the same time the area has become popular for leisure activities and water sports including sailing, water-skiing, swimming and diving, and also paragliding. There are more than 100km/62 miles of footpaths for walkers, and short excursions can be made on the lakes in a little steamer.

*Barrages de
l'Eau d'Heure

The longest dam is the 790m/864yds-long Barrage de la Plate-Taille on the top of which an information centre with a 107m/351ft-high viewing tower has been built. The centre also contains a large aquarium and a relief model of the lake district. Technical details of the complex are provided by means of an audio-visual show (open: Easter–Sept. daily 9am–6pm).

Philippeville

13km/8 miles south-east of Walcourt Philippeville is the chief place of the region Entre-Meuse-et-Sambre. The town was constructed in 1555 at the behest of the emperor Charles V in order to counter the building of the French fortification of Mariembourg (see Chimay, Surroundings). The town owes its name to his son Charles V who later became the Spanish king Philip II. However, in spite of its heavy fortifications Philippeville was taken by the French in 1660; Louis XIV had it reinforced by his fortress builder Vauban. In 1860 the ramparts and walls were razed to the ground but even today it is possible to recognise the original layout as a fortification by the concentric roads leading to the Place d'Armes. Of the powerful fortifications only about 10km/6 miles of the subterranean passages and a former powder magazine dating from 1600 remain, the latter has been the Chapelle de Notre-Dame des Remparts since 1922. The passages and chapel can be seen on a guided tour (open: July and Aug. daily 1–6pm).

Roly

A well-maintained and almost unaltered fortified estate can be found 11km/7 miles to the south of Philippeville. It was built in 1554 around a large 13th c. keep. The argricultural buildings date from the 16th to the 19th c.

Romedenne
*Musée
Européenne
de la Bière

11km/7 miles east of Philippeville a road branches off to Romedenne which lies 2km/1¼ miles to the north. Here there is an attraction of a particular kind: the Musée Européenne de la Bière (European Beer Museum). In a country brewery dating from 1887 two enthusiastic connoisseurs of beer have collected together, in the space of 15 years, a considerable number of objects concerning beer mainly from Belgium, Northern France, Germany

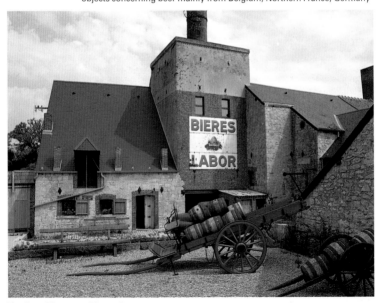

The Beer Museum of Romedenne

and England: glasses, bottles, more than 600 enamel signs, beer mats and a collection of clocks with advertisements. There is also an exhibition about the production of beer extending even to the printing of labels.

A guided tour through the old brewery takes in the drying kiln, the brewing room, the fermentation cellar and the bottling plant, all of which have original equipment,together with many other old implements. A peculiarity is the windlass system by which the machines are driven. At the conclusion of the visit visitors can taste the beer at the well-stocked bar and this is included in the admission fee. (Open: Apr.–Oct. 10am–noon and 2–6pm.)

Waterloo

E 6

Province: Brabant
Altitude: 90–130m/297–427ft
Population: 26,900
Local Rail Station

The little town of Waterloo in Brabant, 18km/11 miles south of Brussels, has become world famous through the historic battle of 18th June 1815. This decided not only the fate of France and its emperor Napoleon I but also the future of Europe, when the French army met the united armies of Britain, Hanover, the Netherlands and Prussia. While the British general Wellington spoke of the "Battle of Waterloo", to the Prussian field marshal it was the "Battle of Belle-Alliance" since both generals met after the successful victory at the farm of this name. Every year about 15th June the battles are re-enacted.

Location

A number of minor encounters had preceded the decisive engagement of the two armies. In order to confront the allies, who were advancing towards France, the French army made a forced march to the north where on 16th July 1815 they defeated the Prussians at Ligny and Marshal Ney did battle with the British. On the evening of 17th June Napoleon set up his headquarters in the Ferme du Caillou, while Wellington established his headquarters in Waterloo and bivouacked his troops in the Ferme Mont-Saint-Jean. The battle began on Sunday 11th June at about 11.30am with drawn-out fighting around the Ferme de Hougoumont which lasted until evening. After each side had made infantry and cavalry attacks – in the notorious "Chemin Creux" (sunken road) to Ohain, near the Ferme de la Haie Sainte and the Ferme de la Papelotte, which had no decisive result but where the British got into some difficulty – the first Prussians appeared at 4.30pm on the right wing of the French and provided some relief. About 6pm the Prussians made a massive attack on Plancenoit so that Napoleon was compelled to send the Imperial guard into the battle, but they could not stave off defeat. About 9 o'clock the battle was over and 49,000 dead men remained on the battlefield.

Course of the battle

* Battlefield

The battlefield is situated to the south of Waterloo mainly in the the parish of Braine-l'Alleud and now appears a peaceful scene of pastures and fields of cereals. In summer a tourist train runs from Waterloo station to the Butte de Lion, west of the trunk road to Charleroi.

Location

The Butte du Lion, lion hill, rises above the former battlefield and is visible from afar. It was constructed between 1823 and 1826 on the place where the Prince of Orange received his fatal wounds. The hill was built up with 32,000cu.m/42,000cu.yds of earth from the battlefield to a height of 40m/131ft and a circumference of 520m/1706ft on a supporting brick base. On the summit was placed the sculpture of a lion by Arthur-Louis van Geel which weights 28 tonnes and is more than 4m/13ft long. The lion stands with its right paw on a globe and looks to the south from where the French

* **Butte du Lion**

Panorama of Waterloo: Picture of the French cavalry attacking

came. From the platform beneath the monument (over 226 steps to climb) there is a panoramic view of the battlefield. Opening times: Nov.–Feb. daily 10am–3pm; Mar. and Apr., Sept. and Oct. daily 9.30am–5pm; May–Aug. daily 9am–6.30pm.

Visitors' centre

At the foot of Lion Hill lies the visitors' centre, where by means of diagrams and computer screens details of the historic events can be studied. From here there is an entrance to Lion Hill.

Battlefield of Waterloo/ Belle-Alliance (1815)

British

---- Sunken road

French   Prussians

1 Butte du Lion (Wellington's command post)
2 Ferme de la Haie Sainte
3 Ferme de la Papelotte
4 Cabaret de la Belle Alliance
5 Ferme de Hougoumont
6 Napoleon's command post
7 Ferme du Caillou

Near the visitors' centre stands a circular building which contains a 12m/39ft-high and 110m/310ft-long panorama of the battle. This is a work by the French military painter Louis Dumoulin and dates from 1913/1914 (open: Mon.–Sat. 9am–6pm, Sun. and public holidays until 6.30pm).

Panorama

On the opposite side of the road in a hotel which dates from 1818 is a waxworks museum, where not only the chief figures of the battle but also ordinary soldiers are exhibited in life size (open: Apr.–Oct. daily 9am–6.30pm; Nov.–Mar. Sat. and Sun. 10am–4.45pm).

Musée des Cires

On the extensive area of the former battlefield there are commemorative monuments of the bloody fighting including three around the crossing of the main road with the road to the Lion Hill. These are: a monument erected in 1914 for the fallen of Belgium in the form of a stone column with bronze standards bearing an inscription in French "To those Belgians who fell on 18th June 1815 in the battle for the defence of their standard and the honour of the armies"; a monument surrounded by a railing for the men of Hanover with the inscription "In memory of their brothers in arms who fell on 18th June 1815" and the monument for Lt. Col. Gordon, Wellington's adjutant, who was killed here. Both the last named monuments stand on the level of the former battlefield, the surrounding area was removed for the erection of the Lion Hill. A path to the Lion Hill which passes the monuments corresponds to the course of the sunken road of Ohain. Other interesting monuments can be found further to the south: in Plancenoit is one to the fallen Prussians, a work of Karl Friedrich Schinkel dating from 1819; still further south on the right of the main road the fallen French imperial eagle at the spot where the guard made its last stand and where the saying "the guard dies but does not yield" is reputed to have arisen.

Monuments

Further south on the left of the main road is the Ferme du Caillou in which Napoleon set up his headquarters. It is now furnished as a museum with

Musée du Caillou

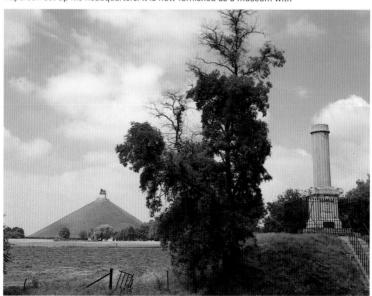

Waterloo: the Gordon memorial and the Butte du Lion

four rooms and includes among other things the emperor's tent. (Open: Apr.–Oct. daily 10.30am–6pm; Nov.–Mar. 1.30–5pm.)

Waterloo Town

Musée Wellington   In Waterloo itself a visit should be paid to the former headquarters of the Duke of Wellington on the main road to Brussels. Here there is more documentation about the battle and personal possessions of the British commander. (Open: Apr.–mid Nov. 9.30am–6.30pm; mid Nov.–Mar. daily 10.30am–5pm.)

Chapelle royale   Opposite the museum rises the domed building of the Chapelle royale, built in 1690 and originally dedicated to the Spanish king Charles II. In 1817 the chapel was declared a memorial for the battle and was provided with burial plaques of the Allied soldiers who had died. These can now be seen in the adjoining church of Saint-Joseph.

Ypres · Ieper   A 5

Province: West-Vlaanderen
Altitude: 17–45m/56–148ft
Population: 35,000
Inter-regional Station (bicycle rental at station)

Location   Ypres (Flemish Ieper) is situated in the plain of West Flanders on the River Ieper (Ieperlee), a tributary of the Iser. Ypres is the chief administrative town for the district and fulfills important trade and services functions. The principal industries are textiles, textile machinery and food processing. Tourism also plays a significant role in the town's economy. The name Ypres is closely associated with some of the most bitter battles of the First World War, at the end of which the town had been almost completely destroyed.

History   Founded in the 10th c., in the Middle Ages Ypres, together with Ghent and Bruges, was one of the three most important towns in Belgium because of its prosperous cloth-making, reaching the peak of its heyday in the 13th and 14th c. with a population of 40,000. The Cloth Hall, the largest and most beautiful building of its kind in Belgium, symbolises the wealth and power of that period. However, its decline began in 1316 when many of the town's citizens fell victim to a major epidemic. When the town took sides with the King of France against Ghent, which was allied to England during the Hundred Years' War, it was besieged in 1383. It withstood the siege but the massive destruction of the surrounding area and the suburbs forced many of the weavers to leave.
In the 16th c. it was devastated by the Iconoclasts and Duke of Alba's troops, conquered by the Geuzen and the troops of Alexander Farnese and finally, in the 17th c., was taken by the French following many sieges. Under the French Ypres was fortified by Vauban and taken over by the Habsburgs. Not until 1852 were the fortified walls razed and turned into walkways.
Despite all these volatile events Ypres retained most of its ancient buildings, evidence of its former splendour, until the First World War. The inferno broke out in November 1914 in the first Battle of Ypres. Ypres, lying at the junction of important roads, found itself in the middle of the Ypres Salient, the arc of the Allied front, which was bombarded by German and Austrian troops for four years and remained unbroken in the second battle of 1915, in the third of 1917 and during the Kemmel offensive of 1918 even though poison gas was used for the first time in history in April 1915 near Steenstraat to the north. The Allied counter-offensive of 1918 signalled the start of Belgium's liberation from German occupation. During the four years of fighting almost 500,000 soldiers on each side lost their lives; 170

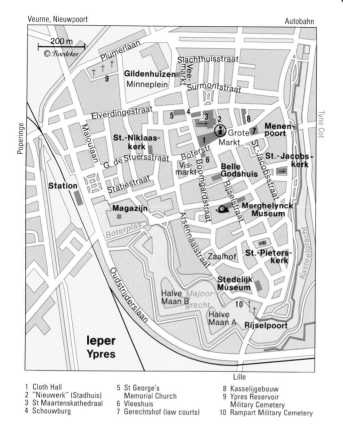

Veurne, Nieuwpoort

Autobahn

200 m

© Baedeker

Plumerlaan

Slachthuisstraat

Gildenhuizen
9
Minneplein

Veemarkt

Surmontstraat

Poperinge

Elverdingestraat

5
4
3
2
8

St.-Niklaas-
kerk

Grote
Markt

7

Menen-
poort

1

Boterstr.

6

G. de Stuersstraat

Vis-
markt

Belle
Godshuis

St.-Jacobs-
straat

St.-Jacobs-
kerk

Maloulaan

Boomgardstraat

Station

Statiestraat

Magazijn

Rijselstr.

Merghelynck
Museum

Boterplas

Arsenaalstraat

Zaalhof

St.-Pieters-
kerk

Oudstrijderslaan

Stedelijk
Museum

Majoor-
gracht

Halve
Maan B

10

Halve
Maan A

Rijselpoort

Kasteelgracht

Tyne Cot

Ieper
Ypres

Lille

1 Cloth Hall	5 St George's	8 Kasselijgebouw
2 "Nieuwerk" (Stadhuis)	Memorial Church	9 Ypres Reservoir
3 St Maartenskathedraal	6 Vleeshuis	Military Cemetery
4 Schouwburg	7 Gerechtshof (law courts)	10 Rampart Military Cemetery

military cemeteries at Ypres and in the surroundings commemorate this mass slaughter. Throughout this time the town stood in the line of fire and was subject to continuous bombardment by artillery so that by 1918 it was reduced to a heap of rubble. It has since been rebuilt according to the original plans, and the damage caused by the air raids in 1940 has been restored. The last building to be rebuilt was the town hall (Nieuwerck).

The Ypres Cat Festival which takes place on the second Sunday in May every other year is famous throughout the area. There is a large procession through the town with the giants Goliath, Robrecht the Friesan and Cieper the giant cat. It reaches a climax with stuffed toy cats being thrown down from the belfry.

Cat's festival

*Lakenhalle

In the Grote Markt stands the 132m/433ft-long Lakenhalle (cloth hall), rebuilt in 13th c. style. The original building was begun around 1260 and completed in 1304. It was completely destroyed in the First World War, but the new building is one of the finest and largest secular buildings in Europe.

The extent of the hall in which the cloth was stored, checked and sold, is indicative of the power wielded by the guilds within the town. Above the entrance door is the statue of the patron saint Onze-Lieve-Vrouw-van-Thuyne; in the niches statues of count Balduin and Mary of Constantinople together with King Albert I and Queen Elisabeth. The large hall on the first floor is open to visitors.

Belfry

The 70m/230ft-high square belfry which projects from the centre of the building is visible from the surrounding countryside. Its carillon of 49 bells is played from June to October at 9pm. From the tower there is a superb view over the plain of Flanders

Museum Ypres-Salient 14–18

This museum on the first floor chronicles the heavy fighting of the First World War. Exhibits include uniforms and equipment of all the armies, some architectural remains of the Lakenhalle and pictures of old Ypres (open: Apr.–mid Nov. daily 9.30am–noon and 1.30–5.30pm; mid Nov.–Mar. only for groups by previous arrangement).

Nieuwerck

On the east wing of the Cloth Hall a new building (Nieuwerck), a town hall, was added in 1619 in the style of the Spanish Renaissance, which has also been reconstructed. It bears the coat of arms of the Spanish King Philip II.

Other sights

Grote Markt

Opposite the Lakenhalle to the south on the corner of Boomgaardstraat stands the Nieuw Vleeshuis (meat hall), dating back to 1277, where meat was sold on Saturdays until 1947.
At the north end of the Grote Markt on the left is the Kasselrijgebouw (Old Town Hall) with the Seven Deadly Sins represented in the gables; on the east side is the Gerechtshof (County Court), a Renaissance reconstruction, on the site of the 12th c. Onze-Lieve-Vrouwgasthuis.

The rebuilt Cloth Hall in the Grote Markt

The Menin Gate, a memorial to British troops of the First World War

From the east end of the Grote Markt it is just a short distance to the Menin Gate, built by the architect Sir Reginald Blomfield on the site of the medieval town gate, through which the British soldiers marched to the front. The names of the 54,896 British soldiers who were killed or missing in action are inscribed under its arches. Every evening at 8pm since 1928 the Last Post is sounded.

Menin Gate
(Menenpoort)

Behind the Cloth Hall to the north stands Sint-Maartenskathedraal, rebuilt in 1922 (13th c. origin; 15th c. south entrance and tower). Its large-scale proportions are reminiscent of the monumental French cathedrals. The tower is over 100m/328ft high.
Inside are some art treasures which survived the war; a brass font (around 1600) and the picture of Onze-Lieve-Vrouw-van Thuyne, believed to have miraculous powers. Inside the church are buried Bishop Jansenius (founder of Jansenism), Georgius Chamberlain (died 1634; sixth bishop of Ypres) and Count Robrecht of Bethune.
The glass paintings are a present from Great Britain to commemorate the war losses.

Sint-Maartens-
kathedraal

North of the cathedral, opposite the theatre (Schouwburg) on the corner of Vandenpeerboomplein, the Anglican Church commissioned Sir Reginald Blomfield 1927–28 to build Saint George's Memorial Church to commemorate the soldiers of the British Commonwealth who were killed in battle in Flanders.
The entire interior of the church was funded by Great Britain and the Commonwealth, together with the statue of St George and the plaque with the famous poem "In Flanders Field". Nearby the Etonian Memorial School honours the 342 students of Eton College killed in action.

Saint-George's
Memorial Church

At the old fish market with the Fish Gate of 1714, south-west of the Grote Markt the small customs house (Minckhuisje) and two stalls have been reconstructed.

Oude Vismarkt

Belle Godshuis	In Rijselstraat south of the Grote Markt stands the Belle Godshuis, a hospital for the poor founded in 1276 and rebuilt in the 16th and 17th c. It is now a museum about the history of the hospital and has fine paintings, church artefacts and furniture from this period (open: weekdays on request).
*Museum Merghelynck	Not far south is the Merghelynck Museum, housed in the 1774 building of the Empress Maria Theresa's treasurer, Frans Merghelynck. Part of the splendid Louis XV and Louis XVI interior survived the First World War and was rehoused in the restored house (open: Mon.–Sat. 10am–noon and 2–5pm; closed second half of July).
Steenhuis	Diagonally opposite the Merghelynck Museum is the Steenhuis, now a post office, the only stone building left standing in Ypres (originally 13th c.).
Stedelijk Museum	At the south end of the Rijselstraat a narrow street leads off to the right to the Stedelijk Museum in a 13th c. poor hospital; it illustrates the town's history (open: Tues.–Fri. 2–6pm; Sept. also Sat. and Sun. 2–6pm).
*Rijselpoort and Majoorgracht	The Rijselstraat ends at the Rijselpoort (Lilletor), a massive fortified gate, from the Burgundian period. The British general staff had its headquarters in the casemates for a while. Near the gate ruins of the old ramparts can still be seen. A walk along the Majoorgracht with the "Halve Man" offers charming views. Boats can be hired from the "Eilandje". Not far from the gate inside the fortifications the "Houten Huis" has been restored, a 16th c. wooden house, one of about 90.
Bicycle museum	Part of a pub at 18 Vaartstraat has been converted into an unusual bicycle museum.

Surroundings

Safari park Bellevaerde	See Practical Information, Leisure Parks

Battlefields of the First World War

The area all around Ypres was, in the four years 1914–18, the scene of some of the bloodiest battles of the First World War. The dead are buried in 170 war cemeteries, their graves are still visited by relatives. The British cemeteries are scattered around close to Ypres, whereas the German soldiers' graves are concentrated in huge cemeteries (Langemark, Menen-Wald, Hooglede, Vladso-Praetbosch, see Practical Information, Military Cemeteries).

Route 14–18	From Ypres "Route 14–18" is signposted to the most important battle zones.
Round trip Zonnebeke	Another tour, unmarked, through the battlefields (63km/39 miles) begins at the Menin Gate. Take road N345 and N332 heading northeast through one of the most hotly contested areas, past several British cemeteries, for 9km/5 miles to the village of Zonnebeke. Once completely destroyed, it now has an attractive church with a freestanding belfry dating from 1921.
Tyne Cot Cemetery	In Broodseinde (2km/1 mile) turn left towards Passchendaele and 1km/½ mile further at the hamlet of Nieuwe-Molden turn left to the largest British war cemetery, Tyne Cot. It was laid out by Sir Reginald Blomfield with almost 12,000 war graves and a memorial to 35,000 missing soldiers after 16th August 1917. From here there is one of the best views of the former battlefields.
Canadian Monument	From the cemetery a narrow road leads to the N313. A short distance south of the junction, at the crossing with the road to Langemark, a memorial

commemorates the 2000 Canadians who died in the first German gas attack in 1915.

3km/2 miles further Langemark, a pretty village that was much contested in the war, has a huge German war cemetery (almost 45,000 graves). At Langemark in 1914 thousands of young, inexperienced recruits, mostly students and schoolboys, lost their lives; a fact which was exploited by the propoganda machine of the Third Reich and even today can be seen as being symbolic of the spontaneous willingness of youth to make sacrifices. From Langemark return towards Ypres, past the British cemetery of Cementhouse, to Boezinge with a view of the silhouette of Ypres. Langemark

A continuation of the tour leads south-west of Ypres on the N375 past Lake Dikkibus, created in 1320 to provide Ypres with water. The Vauban tower was built in 1648 to regulate the water supply. Dikkebus

At De Klijte (10km/6 miles) turn left to the village of Kemmel, once completely destroyed; 2km/1 mile south-west rises the much contested Kemmelberg (156m/511ft), the easternmost spur of an upland range in West Flanders. There is a panoramic view over Ypres and the plain of Flanders. A large French communal cemetery (about 5300 graves) with a memorial crowned by the Gallic cockerel is situated on its western slope. Kammelberg

In Mesen, 5km/3 miles further, there are several war cemeteries. The elevated ground north, between Mesen and Wijtschate, was taken by the British in 1917 by massive mineblasting. One of the largest mine craters of that battle, Lone Treé Crater, today a small lake, is preserved as a memorial (Pool of Peace). Lone Tree
Crater

The tour continues on N365 back north towards Ypres. 5km/3 miles beyond Wijtschate a small road turning off to the right leads to the village of Zillebeke and to Hill 60, 4km/2 miles south-east. It was an important artillery observation post and the centre of heavy fighting, now crowned by two British memorials. Hill 60

The main road continues past the above mentioned detour straight back to Ypres.

Zeebrugge B 3

Province: West-Vlaanderen
Altitude: Sea level
Population: 4400
Local Rail Station

Zeebrugge, at the western end of the Belgian coast, belongs to Bruges (see Brugge) and since 1907 has been linked to the latter by the Boudewijn-kanaal. It is the only Belgian seaport situated directly on the coast and is therefore of great importance both for freight and for passenger traffic. More recently the town has become increasingly popular as a resort, even if the beach is somewhat small, and Zeebrugge has no historic promenade such as Knokke-Heist (see entry) nor a nature reserve such as De Panne (see entry). Location
During the First World War Zeebrugge was the most important German U-boat base which was closed in 1918 in a spectacular action on St George's day. This event is commemorated by the St George Memorial at the landward end of the mole. Zeebrugge got into the headlines when on 6th March 1987 the British ferry "Herald of Free Enterprise" on leaving the harbour for Dover overturned about 800m/875yds from the quayside and 209 people were drowned. In the view of experts this happening was caused by the ferry having left harbour with the bow doors open.

Zeebrugge

1 Car Ferry Zeebrugge–Hull
2 Container Terminal

3 Car Ferry
Zeebrugge–Felixstowe

4 Fishing Harbour
5 Yacht Harbour

Port

The port of Zeebrugge was constructed between 1895 and 1907 and is protected from the sea by a 2.5km/1½ mile-long mole. In the port containers are loaded and unloaded; regular container traffic exists with Great Britain, North America, South Africa, Australia and New Zealand. By means of the Pierre-Vandamme lock, passable by ships up to 125,000 tons, the outer harbour basins are linked with the three inland basins and with the Boudewijnkanaal. For some years an extensive building programme has been in

Container terminal in the port of Zeebrugge

progress which will increase the area of the harbour considerably so that ships up to 250,000 tons can be handled in the port.

Ferries to the English ports of Felixstowe and Hull use the ferry harbour. Zeebrugge is the largest fishing port in Belgium. The departure and arrival of the colourful fishing boats attracts numerous sightseers. Every morning from 7am the catches of fresh fish are auctioned in the fish auction hall with a considerable amount of din; shrimps and prawns are sold from 9.30am. The yacht harbour of Zeebrugge has about 100 moorings.

Harbours

Surroundings

Lissewege, 6km/3¾ miles south of Zeebrugge, is an exceptionally romantic village of West Flanders with its low squat whitewashed brick houses. Worth a visit is the Early Gothic Onze-Lieve-Vrouwkerk (13/17th c.) from the mighty brick tower of which there is a magnificent view. The local museum near the church is also very interesting. Just to the south of the village, an extraordinary example of medieval secular architecture has been preserved: the great 13th c. barn of the Cistercian abbey of Ter Doest, of which the main gateway and the dovecote (17th c.) also remain.

*Lissewege

See entry

Blankenberge

See entry

Knokke-Heist

Zottegem

See Oudenaarde, Surroundings

Zoutleeuw · Léau

F 5

Province: Brabant
Altitude: 35m/115ft
Population: 7700

The present township of Zoutleeuw (French Léau), between Tienen and Sint-Truiden (see entries) in the extreme east of Brabant, came into being in the 11th c. under the name of Leeuw. It was linked by the little river Kleine Nete with Antwerp and in the 12th c. developed into an important trade centre and one of the principal towns of Brabant. At the same time Leeuw was of great importance for the dukes of Brabant as a frontier fortress, so that in the 12th and 13th c. (and later also in the 17th c.) it was provided with extensive fortifications. Finally Leeuw attracted notable artists as it was a cultural and religious centre with no fewer than eight monastic houses of various orders who left impressive testimony of their skill in St Leonard's Church (Sint-Leonarduskerk). French troops conquered the town in 1678 and destroyed the fortifications.

Location

**Sint-Leonarduskerk

St Leonard's Church in Zoutleeuw owes its national importance to the fact that it was one of the very few churches in Belgium which was spared both by the iconoclasts of the religious struggles in the 16th c. and by the French revolutionary troops. For this reason it enables the visitor to realise how richly the churches of the Spanish Netherlands must have been furnished before the mid 16th c.

St-Leonarduskerk
Zoutleeuw

© Baedeker

5 m

1 Triptych: "Glorification of the Cross" (16th c.)
2 Altar of St Anne (1565)
3 Triptych "Our Lady of Sorrows" (1575)
4 Romanesque Christ (11th c.)
5 Sacristy
6 St Leonard's Chapel with Treasury
7 Altar of St Leonard (1478)
8 Easter Candle (1483)
9 Tabernacle (1550–52)
10 Triptych: "Baptism of Christ"
11 Statue of the Virgin (1530)
12 "Seven friends of the Virgin" (1554)

The building began around 1230 with the west façade which is flanked by two asymmetrical towers; shortly afterwards the choir and the north transept followed, and in the 14th c. the south transept and the nave. The sacristy was added in the 15th c. to plans by Mattheus de Layens; the building was completed with the side chapels and the belfry above the crossing (today a reconstruction of 1926).

A walk round the interior of the church reveals the wealth of paintings, sculptures and other works of art of a religious character; only the more important can be mentioned here:
Interior

A multi-coloured painted wooden sculpture showing "Maria in the Rosary" surrounded by angels hangs from the roof of the nave; it was carved in 1530.
Marianum

In the right side-aisle the first feature of interest is the second chapel dedicated to St Anne. On the left is the St Anne altar of 1565 in the style of the Antwerp school with painted wings dating from the 17th c., and nearby a very fine little triptych with the Crucifixion scene in glass (1535). On the wall opposite there is a triptych of 1525 with a representation of the "Glorification of the Cross" by Spieken.
The adjoining chapel of St Hubertus contains a triptych of the "Sorrow of Our Lady" created by Pieter Aertsen in 1575.
Next comes the sacristy built in Flamboyant style, above the entrance to which is a Romanesque picture of Christ.
Right side-aisle

In the right transept we can first see the extraordinary St Leonard's altar which the Brussels' artist Arnold de Maeler made in 1478. The painted and gilded statue of the saint in the centre of the altar dates from the year 1300.
Right transept

The original chapel of St Leonard now contains the church treasury. It includes brass and copper work, processional crosses (13th and 14th c.), reliquaries, sculptures and liturgical vessels and vestments.
*Church treasury

In the niches of the ambulatory numerous sculptures have been set up including twelve of saints, dating from the 12th to the 16th c., and a polychromatic statue of Mary (15th c.). Also notable is a copper desk in the form of an eagle (Antwerp 1468).
The great six-branched pascal candlestick which weighs 950kg/2094lbs testifies to the fine artistic skill of its creator Reiner of Tienen. This candlestick, almost 6m/20ft tall, was cast in bronze in 1483.
Ambulatory

*Pascal candlestick

◄ *Zoutleeuw: the nave of Sint-Leonarduskerk*

A fifteenth-century pietà

Left transept	The left transept houses the finest artistic object of the church, the taber-
** Tabernacle	nacle created between 1550 and 1552 by Cornelis Floris de Vriendt out of Avesnes stone. The tabernacle is 18m/59ft high and on seven levels more than 200 figures, impressive in their authenticity, represent Old Testament scenes, Paradise, the Last Supper and other scenes of the New Testament, as well as saints, elders of the church and the Virgin Mary. Near the tabernacle are buried its creator, Marten van Wilre, and his wife Maria Pijlepeerts. The triptych opposite showing the baptism of Christ was created by Frans Floris de Vriendt, the brother of Cornelis.

Left side-aisle	The chapel in the left side-aisle is the Erasmus chapel. The triptych "The Seven Joys of Mary" (1554) is attributed to Pieter Aertsen. The wings portray the martyrdom of St Erasmus, St Blasius and St Laurentius.

Other Sights

Stadhuis	On the south side of the pretty market place stands the little Renaissance town hall with a stepped gable, a side tower and a balustrade on which the arms of Charles V, Brabant and Leeuw can be seen. The building was erected between 1530 and 1539 to the design of Rombout Keldermans.
Lakenhalle	Immediately adjoining the town hall is the former Lakenhalle (cloth hall), a fine building of brick and natural stone of 1314.

Spiegelhuis	Of the houses surrounding the market place the Spiegelhuis (1571) is worth mentioning. This house is also constructed of brick and white stone. A curiosity is the gable formed from four ionic pillars.

Brussels: the Rue des Bouchers, a paradise for gourmets ▶

Practical Information

Air Travel

International
services

Belgium is connected to the international network of routes by numerous international airline companies and by its own domestic service SABENA via the Brussels National Airport at Zaventem. There are few charter flights to Belgium.

Domestic
services

Belgium's small size means that there is little demand for domestic services.

Airline companies

SABENA

The Belgian national airline company SABENA WORLD AIRLINES offers connections to all important European cities and, mainly through tradition, to Africa.

In Belgium

Air Terminus, 35 Rue Cardinal Mercier
B–1000 Bruxelles; tel. (02) 5 11 90 30 (reservations) and
(02) 7 23 31 11 (administration)

De Keyserlei 74
B–2000 Antwerpen; tel. (03) 2 31 68 25

68 Boulevard de la Sauvenière
B–4000 Liège; tel. (041) 23 58 35 and 23 30 30

There are also offices in Charleroi, Ghent, Hasselt, Kortrijk, Mons, Namur and Ostend.

In the UK

Gemini House, 2nd floor, West Block, 10–18 Putney Hill
London SW15 6AA; tel. (081) 7 80 14 44 (reservations and administration)

In the USA

J. F. K. Airport
New York; tel. (800) 718 632 10

British Airways

Centre International Rogier, 9th floor
Bruxelles; tel. 2 17 61 11

TWA

5 Boulevard de l'Empereur
Bruxelles; tel. 5 13 79 16

Air Canada

66 Boulevard de l'Impératrice
Bruxelles; tel. 5 13 62 10

Airports

Information

Only Brussels National Airport is of importance for international air travel. The smaller airports at Antwerp, Liège and Ostend play little part in this traffic.

Brussels

Brussels National Airport is about 14km/9 miles north-east of the city centre at Zaventem, tel. (02) 7 23 31 11; SABENA reservations office, tel. (02) 5 11 90 30.

Transfer to and from Brussels: by bus 578–BZ (via Diegem) or 358 and 358b (via Woluwé) to and from Brussels North Station; by the airport express to and from South Station, Central Station and North Station every 30 minutes (daily 5.39am–11.46pm).

Banks

See Currency

Beaches

The Belgian North Sea coast extends for about 67km/42 miles from the Dutch to the French border. Fifteen seaside resorts are located in this area, a number of which are very popular in the summer such as the largest and most well-known resort of Ostend (long sandy promenade and wide beaches), the elegant Knokke-Heist with five varied beaches or Blankenberge with its 3km/2 mile long and, at low tide, 350m/1149ft wide beach, especially suitable for families with young children. The medium-sized De Panne boasts more than a third of all the dunes along the coast and beautiful national parks (see Nature Reserves, National Parks and Caves). The small, quiet resort of Wenduine has long been well-known as a holiday camp for children.
Information

The fine sandy beaches are gently sloping. Almost all parts of the beaches and dunes are open to the public without charge. The action of the tides has created a permanent beach area.
Composition

In each resort there are fenced-off areas of beach which are supervised throughout the day by members of the rescue service. On the boulevards immediately adjoining beaches members of the Red Cross offer first aid. Sun-loungers, windbreaks, etc. can be hired in many resorts. Changing cubicles can also be hired by the week or month.
Beach facilities

Red flag = bathing forbidden!
Yellow flag = bathing permitted;
   sailing and use of air beds forbidden!
Green flag = no danger
Beach regulations

Nudism on beaches is presently forbidden in Belgium. Going topless is only tolerated on or very close to the beach.
Dogs are generally banned from De Panne beach. This ban is also effective during the holiday period on the beaches at Blankenberge, De Haan, Knokke-Heist, Middelkerke, Ostend and Zeebrugge. Dogs may run freely on Koksijde and Oostduinkerke beaches; at Bredene and Nieuwpoort large dogs must be kept on a lead.

A coastal tram with numerous stops links the two resorts of De Panne (in the west) and Knokke-Heist (in the east) at the extremes of the Belgian North Sea coast.
Coastal tram

Beer

Beer is to the Belgians what wine is to the French. It is an everyday drink in cafés, as a refreshment, but it is also customary to serve one of the many special brands on festive occasions. No other country in the world has such a multitude of different beers as this country between the North Sea and the Ardennes; the taste of some of these takes time to acquire but, nevertheless, they should be sampled. More than 100 breweries now produce
Brewing tradition

over 500 fundamentally distinctive beers. Most Belgian beers are characterised by a top-fermentation process but in many cases fermentation is continued in corked champagne bottles. Many of the beers – such as the white and cherry beers – go back to the days when the use of hops as a flavouring was unknown. St Arnold of Oudenaarde was aware of the importance of beer when in the 11th c. a monastic brewery collapsed and he prayed to his god for an increase in beer. His wish was heard and from then on he was the patron saint of the brewers. Gambrinus, too, the king of beer, is a Belgian. According to legend it was the exceptionally thirsty Duke Jan I of Brabant, Leuven and Antwerp ("Jan Primus") whose name in the 13th c. was parodied to "Gambrinus".

Cafés

In Belgium most beer is drunk in cafés, but they have nothing in common with cafés in the normal sense of the word. The café is the normal daily meeting place; here the customers talk, play billiards and, of course, drink beer. Whoever orders a "beer" in a café either gets a normal Pils or he is asked what brand he would like, for every landlord worthy of the name has at least 20 to 30 different beers on offer; good cafés begin with 50 kinds, all of which, of course, are served in a special glass. The beer is accompanied by nibbles, simple sausage or cheese.
Worth a visit because of the beer are inter alia:
Antwerp: Kulminator, Vleminckxveld 32; Patersvaetje,
   Blauwmoezelstraat 1; 't Waagstuk, Stadswag 20.
Bruges: 't Brugge Beetje, Kemelstraat 5.
Brussels: De Ultime Hallucinatie, 316 Rue Royale; La Bécasse, Rue Tabora;
  *A la Mort Subite, Rue des Montagnes-aux-Herbes Potagères.
Ghent: De Hopduval, Rokererlstraat 10; *Het Waterhuis an de Bierkant,
  Groentenmarkt.
Leeuven: Domus, Tiensestraat; The Cambridge Arms, Ladeuzestraat.

Beer Museums

Belgian brewing can be studied in the beer museums of the country: in Brussels in the Museum of the Brewers' Guild and in the Gueuze Museum; in Leuven in the Brewery Museum; in the exhibition brewery in the Bokrijk open-air museum, and in the most attractive and technically informative way in the European Brewery Museum in Romedenne.

Bottom-fermented beers

The bottom-fermented beers are generally light and sweet and refreshing beers of the Pilsner kind. The most popular is Stella Artois brewed in the largest brewery of the country in Leuven; then come Cristal Alken, Jupiter and Maes Pils.

"Wild" beers

"Wild" beers are a unique speciality. They are produced in the Payotte region which is watered by the river Senne south-west of Brussels. It is here that a species of hops grows wild and the local brewers make use of this to produce Lambic. It consists of 30–40% of un-malted wheat and 60–70% of malted barley. The brew, produced according to the classic method, is exposed to the air of the Senne valley for one night in open wooden tubs and the hops are added; after this it is drawn off into wooden barrels and left to ferment. Each brewer takes great care to make no alterations in his fermenting cellar so that the combination of micro-organisms in the air and in the barrels are not disturbed. The Lambic is left to mature for between six months to two years in the barrels and then for a further period in bottles. It is generally golden in colour, bitter and with an alcohol content of between 4 and 5% and tastes something like apple juice. One version, sweetened with rock-candy, is Faro which like genuine Lambic is generally only obtainable in the little breweries of the Payotte region. However, the Brussels "A la Mort Subite" Brewery always has its own Faro on tap. Generally old and young Lambics are mixed with Gueuze which makes a pleasant sweet and sour refreshing drink in summer.

If cherries are added to Lambic and allowed to ferment with it the result is a Kriek, a very fruity sharp cherry-like beer, deep red in colour, the taste of which is sometimes reminiscent of Kir Royal. In the same way raspberry beer (Frambozen) is produced; other more exotic varieties are beers with strawberries, peaches and blackcurrants.

Large Lambic/Gueuze breweries are Belle-Vue in Brussels and St-Louis in Ingelmunster. From the Payotte region the varieties include Eylenbosch, De Neve, De Troch, Timmermans and Vanderlinden. Mort Subite in Brussels brews the best known bitter Lambic and also a Faro and an extremely individual Kriek.

Strickly speaking there is only one red beer today, Rodenbach from Flemish Roeselare. It is so sharp that nobody can be blamed for thinking it undrinkable and yet it is a Flemish classic. Its acidity is due to the hops used. Simple Rodenbach is brewed with 4.6% alcohol and Rodenback Grand Cru with 5.2%. If one first gets used to the taste Rodenbach is considered a very good thirst quencher.

Red beer

There are many brown or dark beers in Belgium, but pride of place must go to Liefmans from Oudenaarde, a beer similar to English ale. The simple version has about 4.6% alcohol; Liefmans Goudenband, especially popular at festivals, with bottles wrapped in tissue paper, is sweet and sparkling with 5.5% alcohol. A speciality is Liefmans Kriek, a soft cherry beer based on ale. Other good dark beers include Crombe from Zottengem and Van den Bossche from St-Lievens-Esse.

Brown beers

Belgian white beers are draught beers containing up to 45% malted wheat and a low alcohol content of about 3.5%. They are light, fruity and refresh-

White beers

Source: Hallweg Publishing Co.

Traditional beers

☐ Red beer
▨ Dark beer
☐ Top-fermented beer
▨ Bottom-fermented beer
☐ "Wild" beers
☐ White beers

⚇ Trappist breweries
🍃 Hop-growing areas
■ Brewery museum

© Baedeker

393

ing. The most popular and the best comes from Hoegaarden east of Leuven and its flavourings include coriander. Somewhat stronger is the Grand Cru from the same brewery. Other good white beers are the Dendergemse Wit and the Brugse Wit (Blanche de Bruges).

Trappist beers

The monastic breweries can look back on a long tradition. However, today Trappist monks in only five monasteries are still brewing beer, and only these five are allowed to sell their beers as "Trappist beers".

The best known Trappist brewery is that of Chimay which brews three beers: Chimay rouge (red Kapsel, 5.5%), Chimnay blanche (white Kapsel, 8%) and Chimay bleue (blue Kapsel, 9%). Similar beers are brewed by the monks of Rochefort. The Flemish monastery of Westvleteren is the smallest of these breweries but produces five different beers, the strongest of which is the heavy sweet Abbot with 10.6% alcohol. Also from Flanders comes the Trappist beer of Westmalle with a dark and rather tangy Dubbel (7%) and the light Triple (8%). Finally a quite exceptional beer is the orange coloured Orval from the extreme south-eastern corner of Belgium: very dry, rather acidic and bitter, with its 6% alcohol it is an acquired taste.

As well as these genuine Trappist beers other monastic beers are produced in normal breweries; these include Grimbergen, Leffe and Affigem.

Top-fermented specialities

As well as the brands already listed there are many generally top-fermented beers which often catch the eye by special bottles, labels and names such as "Lucifer" and "Verboden Vrucht" (forbidden fruit). Traditional is the production of light and dark ales such as De Koninck from Antwerp, the strong Gouden Carolus from Mechelen and the "Saisons" from the Hennegau between Charloi and Mons. A very light and sweet and therefore not to be despised strong beer is Duvel (8%) from the Moortgat Brewery from Breendonk.

Boat Excursions

Information

Excursions on ships or tourist boats on Belgium's lakes and canals, around the harbours of Antwerp and Zeebrugge, or canal tours count among the finest holiday experiences. Such excursions are offered in the following towns and villages described in Belgium from A to Z: harbour and tours on the Scheldt in Antwerp (see entry), canal trips in Bruges (see entry), canal trips from Bruges to Damme (see entry), Ghent (see entry) and Ostend (see entry), trips on the Meuse from Dinant (see entry) to Namur (see entry), excursions on the sloping lock (ship lift) of Ronquières near Ecaussinnes (see entry), towed barge or boat trips at the La Louvière and Strépy-Thieu ship hoists near Binche (see entry), trips on the Meuse departing from Liège (see entry), canal tours departing from Mechelen (see entry), excursions on board fishing boats and canal tours from Nieuwpoort (see entry), canal tours from Veurne (see entry) and harbour tours in Zeebrugge (see entry).

Boat hire

Various firms rent out cabin cruisers for trips on the network of Belgian waterways. Information can be obtained from tourist offices.

Camping and Caravanning

Information

At present there are more than 500 camp sites in Belgium. During the peak holiday period it is advisable to book pitches in advance, especially at sites located along the Belgian coast.

Classification

Most Belgian camp sites have been graded into categories and classified by a star system which indicates whether the site offers only minimum standards (*), or has simple (**), comfortable (***) or very good (****) facilities.

Unofficial camping is forbidden. One-off overnight stops in caravans or camper vans are permitted on picnic sites at motorway service stations.

A leaflet listing camp sites according to the province they are in is obtainable from tourist information offices (see Information).

Car Rental

The large car rental firms have offices or counters in all of Belgium's larger cities and at Brussels, Antwerp, Liège and Ostend airports. In addition many local car hire firms often charge more modest prices than the well-known firms.

Avis; tel. (02) 7 24 06 25
Europcar; tel. (02) 3 44 76 30
Hertz; tel. (02) 7 20 60 44
Sixt/Budget; tel. (02) 3 76 85 31

Avis: (081) 848 8733
Budget: (0800) 191 191
Europcar: (081) 950 5050
Hertz: (081) 679 1799

Castles, Monasteries, Béguinages

Most of the castles, monasteries and béguinages listed here are described in the Belgium from A to Z section.

1 Loppem (neo-Gothic)

2 Oidonk (13th c.)

3 s'Gravensteen (11th c.), moated castle in Ghent

4 Laarne (12th/17th c.)

5 Leeuwergem (18th c.)

6 Royal palace in Brussels (renovated in 1905)

7 Gaasbeek (13th/16th c.)

8 Beersel (14th c.)

9 Grand Bigard (14th/16th c.)

10 Rixensart (17th c.)

11 Horst (13th c.)

12 Alde Biezen (13th/18th c.)

13 Reinhardstein (medieval; renovated in the 17th c.)

14 Franchimont (12th c.)

15 Aigremont (18th c.) on the Meuse

16 Jehay (16th c.)

● Castles
● Abbeys and Monasteries
● Béguinages

17 Modave (17th c.)

18 Logne (ruins) on the Ourthe

19 Durbuy (16th c.) on the Ourthe

20 La Roche-en-Ardennes (11th c.; ruins) on the Ourthe

21 Bouillon (11th c.) on the Semois

22 Lavaux-Sainte-Anne (14th–18th c.)

23 Vêves (16th c.)

24 Freÿr (16th–18th c.) on the Meuse

25 Spontin (11th/12th c.)

26 Annevoie (16th c.) on the Meuse

27 Franc-Waret (18th c.)

28 Corroy-le-Château (13th c.)

29 Chimay (medieval)

30 Soire-sur-Sambre (13th c.)

31 Le Rœuix (15th/18th c.)

32 Lalaing (11th/15th c.)

33 Belœil (rebuilt in 1900)

34 Attre (18th c.)

35 Rumbeke (16th c.)

36 Beauvoorde (16th/17th c.)

37 Geraardsbergen (12th/18th c.)

38 Grimbergen (12th c.)

39 Postel (12th c.)

40 Tongerlo (19th c.)

41 Averbode (14th c.)

42 Maredsous (19th c.)

43 Chevetogne (19th c.)

44 Orval (11th c.)

45 Villers-la-Ville (12th and 16th/17th c.)

46 Bruges (13th c.)

47 Ghent (13th c.)

48 Dendermonde (13th/16th c.)

49 Antwerp (16th c.)

50 Lier (13th/17th c.)

51 Aarschot (13th c.)

52 Diest (13th/17th c.)

53 Leuven (13th/14th–18th c.)

54 Brussels (16th/17th c.)

55 Kortrijk (13th/17th c.)

56 Diksmuide (12th/17th c.)

Chemists

Belgian chemist's shops (Flemish apotheek; French pharmacie) have either a green cross or the symbol of Aesculapius outside.

Signs

The opening times of chemists are the same as those of retail shops (see Opening Times). There is an emergency service. Lists of addresses can be found in each chemists.

Opening times and emergency service

Currency

The unit of currency is the Belgian Franc (Bfr), which is made up of 100 centimes. There are banknotes for 100, 500, 1000, 5000 and 10,000 Bfr and coins in denominations of ½, 1, 5, 20 and 50 Bfr. Belgian currency is the same in value as the Luxembourgian Franc (Lfr/fLux) and is accepted in the Grand Duchy of Luxembourg.

Belgian coins and banknotes

Currency regulations	Import and export of local or foreign currency is not subject to any limitations.
Banks	Banks are usually open Mon.–Fri. 9am–4pm.
Eurocheques	Eurocheques can be drawn for amounts up to 7000 Bfr.
Changing money	Money can be changed in post offices, in banks, at Brussels National Airport or in official exchange offices (bureaux de change) in the large railway stations (higher rates of commission may be charged here).
Credit cards	Most international credit cards (American Express, Diners Club, Eurocard and Visa) are accepted by banks, larger hotels, higher-class restaurants and numerous shops. Loss of credit cards should be reported immediately to the police by contacting the credit card security office (tel. 539 15 02) and to the issuing authority.
Change machines	Change machines with instructions in four languages can be found in all larger towns. These machines will accept Eurocheque cards and many credit cards.

Customs Regulations

From 1st January 1993 new regulations came into operation. In theory there are no limits to the amounts of goods imported from one EC country to another, *provided they have been purchased tax paid in an EC country, are for personal use and are not intended for resale*. However, the customs authorities have issued a list of maximum amounts considered reasonable

for persons over 17 years of age of alcoholic drinks, tobacco goods, perfume, etc. These are:
Spirits or strong liqueurs over 22% volume – 10 litres; fortified wines (port, sherry, etc.) – 20 litres; table wine – 90 litres (of which not more than 60 litres may be sparkling wine); beer – 110 litres; cigarettes – 800 or cigarillos 400 or cigars 200 or pipe tobacco 1kg. Personal use includes gifts, but if a passenger is receiving any payment in return for buying alcohol and tobacco (such as help with travelling expenses) the transaction will be dutiable and the duty must be paid to the Customs authorities.

For those coming direct from a country outside the EC or who have arrived from another EC country without having passed through customs control with all their baggage, the allowances for goods obtained anywhere outside the EC are:
Spirits – 1 litre or fortified wine – 2 litres or table wine – 3 litres plus a further 2 litres of table wine. Perfume – 60cc; toilet water – 250cc. 200 cigarettes or 100 cigarillos or 50 cigars or 250gr. of tobacco. All other goods, including gifts, £36 worth.

"Duty-free" goods are still available at major airports, on aircraft and ferries; these are approximately 50% above the limits in paragraph two above and are controlled by the carriers concerned.

Diplomatic Representation

Embassy: Rue Joseph 28, Brussels; tel (217) 90 00 — United Kingdom

Embassy: Boulevard du Régent 27; tel. (513) 38 30 — United States

Embassy: Avenue du Tervuren 2; tel. (735) 60 40 — Canada

Electricity

Belgium is committed to the international voltage regulation IEC 38 (IEC standard voltages) intended to make 230/400 volts a standardised output for 50Hz low-voltage national grid distribution. The country will have converted its electricity supply to 230 volts by the target year of 2003. At present the Belgian electricity system runs on 220 volts AC at a frequency of 50Hz. — Voltage

An adapter is necessary for British and American-type plugs. — Plugs

Emergencies

Accident, fire, ambulance; tel. 100
Rijkswacht, police; tel. 101
Brussels poison antidote centre; tel. (02) 3 45 45 45 — National emergency numbers

Emergency telephones are stationed at intervals along the motorways. — Emergency telephones

See Chemists, Medical Assistance and Motoring

Events

The most important events are listed in Belgium from A to Z under the respective heading. — Information

Events

Calendar of
events

A calendar giving the exact dates of individual events is published annually by the tourist information offices listed under Information (see entry). It is available free of charge.

Selected events

January/February

Brussels	Antiques Fair
Aalst	Carnival

February

Binche	Gilles procession (Carnival Thursday)
Eupen	Old Woman's Shrovetide Carnival; carnival procession on the Monday before Ash Wednesday
Malmédy	Procession with Haguettes and Happechair (Sunday before Ash Wednesday)

Beginning of March

Ostend	Dead Rat's Ball (costume ball in the Kursaal casino)
Hasselt	International carnival procession
Stavelot	Carnival procession (including the Blancs Moussis)

March/April

Lessines	Penitential procession to St Peter's Church
Kruishoutem	Golden Egg Festival (egg parade, egg throwing from the church tower and much more)
Redu	Book Festival
Flanders	Flanders Festival (music and culture) – until the autumn

May

Mechelen	Hanswijk Procession (historic–religious)
Bruges	Holy Blood Procession (Ascension Day)
Ypres (Ieper)	Cats' Festival
Gerpinnes	St Rolende Hunting Procession (Whit Monday)
Brussels	Queen Elizabeth Competition (music competition)
Laeken	Opening of the Laeken Palace hothouse by the Belgian royal couple
Walcourt	Notre Dame March (Sunday after Whitsun)
Mons	Golden Carriage Procession and Battle of St George and the Dragon
Ronse	Fiertel Procession (procession with the relics of St Hermes)
Wallonia	Wallonia Festival (music and culture) – until November

June

Ligny	Napoleon Days
Oostduinkerke	Prawn Festival; procession with folklore groups, decorated coaches, etc.
Tournai	Hainaut Flower Show
Oudenaarde	Adriaan Brouwer Festival (beer festival)
Ostend	Blessing of the Sea (parade of ships; historical procession); Comic Festival in Duinbergen (until September)

July

Brussels	Ommegang (procession) – at the end of June–beginning of July
Vielsalm	Bilberry Festival and Witches' Sabbath
Aalst	Pikkeling (agricultural festival)
Libramont	Libramont Fair (Belgium's largest agricultural fair)
Veurne	Penitential procession
Ostend	Belgium Kite International (model kite festival)
Ghent	Ghent Festival (music and culture throughout the month)

August

Berlare	Flanders Water Festival
Rochehaut	Harvest Festival

Août folklorique en Outremeuse (summer and folk festival)	Outremeuse
Patershol Festival in the historic quarter of Het Patershol	Ghent
International Military Riding	Hasselt
Grape Festival	Overijse
Historical Golden Tree Procession to commemorate the wedding of Charles the Bold and Margaret of York	Bruges
Ath Public Festival (wedding of Goliath the Giant; procession)	Ath
Bokrijk Day and Rockrijk (various events in Bokrijk open air museum)	Genk
Flower Parade	Blankenberge
Giants' Procession	Dendermonde
International Firework Festival (every two days from the middle of the month)	Ostend

August/September

International Hunting and Nature Days	Saint-Hubert

September

Rozenberg Procession of Light (fairy lights; procession)	Mol
Festival of Peace	Sint-Niklaas
Flower Parade	Loenhout-Wuustwezel
Flower and Vegetable Parade; bell throwing	Mechelen
Grand Procession of Notre-Dame des Malades	Tournai
Wallonia Festivals (cultural and folklore events including processions and markets; fireworks and Chinese lantern balls in the evening)	Huy, Namur and Liège
St Gertrude's Tour (procession)	Nivelles
Giants' Festival	Ottignies/Louvain-la-Neuve
Europalia Mexico (cultural festival on a European theme)	Brussels

October

Genever Festival	Hasselt

November

International Antiques Fair	Bruges

December

Christmas fairs in Brussels and towns in the south of the country; in many places (Kempen/Antwerp, Manderfeld and Bullingen) so-called *Krippana* (exhibitions of Nativity scenes)	
Nut Market and Second World War remembrance services	Bastogne

Food and Drink

Belgium has always been the country of the gourmet and people enjoying a festive meal or relishing a picnic often figure in paintings of the Flemish Old Masters. The Belgian of today still seizes on any excuse to enjoy a good meal. The people of Flanders prize their food and drink very highly. — Information

Hotels usually serve a simple breakfast of bread, butter, jam and sometimes cheese. Expensive hotels offer a buffet breakfast. Ample lunches and dinners are optional according to individual requirements. Beer is mainly drunk with these meals, or wine in more modest measures. — Meals

Belgian dishes owe their reputation to the combination of French and Dutch influences. Basic dishes alternate with formal haute cuisine. In the Ardennes game and, of course, the famous Ardennes ham is enjoyed, while near the coast fish dominates the menu. A typical Flemish national dish is a large pan of cooked mussels shared by several people, served with — Dishes pommes frites, which are considered a Flemish invention. Belgium's most commonly-served vegetable is chicory, eaten with boiled ham and cheese sauce.

Gastronomic weekends

From the beginning of November until the end of April hotels and restaurants along the Belgian coast and, more recently, a number of inland pubs have staged "Gastronomic Weekends" (cheap weekend flat rates) for gourmets (details available from the Belgian Tourist Office in Brussels, see Information).

Specialities

Meat dishes

Flemish carbonnade, lean beef casseroled in beer; smoked ham from the Ardennes; "Heaven and Earth", potato and apple pureé with black pudding or liver sausage; veal kidneys à la liégeoise.

Game

Hare and rabbit à la flamande, marinated in Gueuze and braised with onions and prunes; pheasant à la brabançonne; fieldfare à la liégeoise.

Poultry

Brussels cockerel: particularly tender young birds reared near Brussels; Waterzooi: chunks of chicken stewed with a variety of vegetables and cream; roast goose à la visé: goose first boiled and then roasted.

Fish and shellfish

Green eel: boiled eel flavoured with green herbs; herring in cream; cod, pike, trout (particularly in the Ardennes), sole, mussels (especially Jacob mussels), oysters, lobster, crayfish, crab (served with a variety of sauces), Waterzooi with fish.

Vegetables

Hop vegetables (Poperinge); red cabbage à la flamande; asparagus de Maline; chicon (a Brussels endive); Brussels sprouts; Witlof: Brussels chicory with ham and cheese sauce.

Cheese

Belgian Gouda (St Bernard, Hertog van Brabant); Trappist cheese (Maredsous, Orval, Chimay); Remoudou; Cassette de Beaumont; Pavé de Bastogne (goat's milk cheese); cream cheese curd (fromage blanc) with onions, chives or cress and radishes; Herve à la liégeoise; Remoudou toasted on a slice of bread thinly covered with liégeoise syrup.

Pastries and desserts

Spekulatius (small short-crust pastry figures); Diester gingerbread and tartlets; cheesecake; creamed rice; sugar biscuits (e.g. from Namur); almond bread (e.g. from Veurne); Greek bread (a sugar biscuit); Brussels waffles served with sugar, butter, fresh cream and/or fruit; Liége waffles with caramel syrup; apple doughnuts; Kortrijk rusks; Bollen pastries. A well-known speciality from Dinant is Flamiche, a cheesecake. Favourite dainties from Ghent include Gent Mokken, little round cakes made from flour and syrup. Lierse Vlaaikens are typical pastries from Lier.

Sweets

Babulettes (caramel sweets); pralines; toffees.

Drinks

Beers

See entry

Wine

Wines are usually from the neighbouring countries of France or Luxembourg.

Spirits and liqueurs

Raisin rum and herbal liqueur are two popular drinks as are numerous types of Genever (gin).

Mineral water

Spa, Bru and Chaudfontaine are the best-known mineral waters.

The Belgian menu

General terms

English	**French**	**Dutch/Flemish**
breakfast	petit déjeuner	ontbijt
lunch	déjeuner	lunch

English	French	Dutch/Flemish	
dinner	díner, souper	diner	
the bill	addition	rekening	
menu	carte	spijskaart, menu	
wine list	carte des vins	wijnkaart	
soup	potage, soupe	soep	
clear soup	consommé	bouillon	
starter	hors-d'œuvre	voorgerecht	
carp	carpe	karper	Fish
cod	cabillaud	kabeljauw	(poisson; vis)
eel	anguille	aal, paling	
flounder	flet	bot	
herring	hareng	haring	
perch	perche	baars	
pike	brochet	snoek	
salmon	saumon	zalm	
sole	sole	zeetong	
trout	truite	forel	
crab	crevettes	garnalen	Shellfish
lobster	écrevisse	kreeft	(crustacés;
mussels	moules	mosselen	schelp-en-
oysters	huítres	oesters	schaaldieren)
grilled	grillé	gegrilt	Meat
roast	roti	gebraden, vlees	(viandes;
beef	bœuf	rund	vleesgerecht)
ham	jambon	ham	
kidney	rognons	nieren	
lamb	agneau	lam	
liver	foie	lever	
mutton	mouton	schaap	
pork	porc	varken	
pot-roast	bœuf en daube	gestoofd vlees	
sausage	saucisson, saucisse	worst	
veal	veau	kalf	
veal cutlet	escalope de veau	kalfsoester	
chicken	poule, poulet	kip	Poultry
duck	canard	eend	(volaille;
goose	oie	gans	gevogelte)
deer	chevreuil	ree	Game
rabbit	lapin	konijn	(gibier; wild)
wild boar	marcasson	wild zwijn	
beans	haricots	bonen	Vegetables
Brussels sprouts	chou de Bruxelles	spruitjes	(légume;
cabbage	chou	kool	groente)
cauliflower	chou-fleur	bloemkool	
chicory	chicorée	(Brussels)lof	
cucumber	concombre	komkommer	
peas	pois	(dop)erwten	
pickled cabbage	choucroute	zuurkool	
potatoes	pommes de terre	aardappelen	
red cabbage	chou rouge	rodekool	
salad	salade	sla, salade	
spinach	épinard	spinazie	
noodles	nouilles, pâtes	macaroni	
rice	riz	rijst	

	English	French	Dutch/Flemish
Desserts (dessert; nagerecht)	cheese	fromage	kaas
	custard tart	flan	pudding
	ice-cream	glace	ijs
	whipped cream	crème chantilly	slagroom
Fruit (fruits; fruit)	apple	pomme	appel
	cherry	cérise	kers
	grapes	raisins	druiven
	orange	orange	sinaasappel
	peach	pêche	perzik
	pear	poire	peer
	plum	prune	pruim
	strawberry	fraise	aardbei
Miscellaneous	bread	pain	brood
	white bread	pain blanc	wit brood
	roll	pistolet, petit pain	broodje
	cake	gâteau	koek
	flan	tarte	taart, gebak
	pastries	pâtisserie	gebak
	butter	beurre	boter
	jam	confiture	jam
	honey	miel	honing
	egg	œuf	ei
	hard	dur	hard gekookt
	soft	à la coque	zacht gekookt
	scrambled egg	œufs brouillés	roerei
	fried egg	œufs sur la plat	spiegelei (gebakken ei)
	salt	sel	zout
	pepper	poivre	peper
	sugar	sucre	suiker
	vinegar	vinaigre	azijn
	oil (salad)	huile alimentaire	(spijs)olie
Drinks (boissons; dranken)	beer	bière	bier
	coffee	café	koffie
	milk	lait	melk
	mineral water	eau minérale	mineraalwater
	cream	crème	room
	tea	thé	thee
	water	eau	water
	wine	vin	wijn
	white wine	vin blanc	witte wijn
	red wine	vin rouge	rode wijn

Getting to Belgium

By sea and road	Those travelling to Belgium from Britain by road can cross by ferry or jetfoil from Dover to Ostend, or from Hull or Felixstowe by ferry to Zeebrugge.
By rail	There is a direct rail and boat service between London and Brussels via Calais or Ostend. Brussels has three main railway stations: the Gare du Nord (North Station), Gare Centrale (Central Station) and Gare du Midi (South Station). There is also a fast jetfoil service between Dover-Ostend connecting with the London-Brussels trains.
By air	Brussels Airport at Zaventem is 14km/9 miles from Brussels city centre and has its own rail service in and out of the city (see Air Travel). There are numerous daily flights into Brussels from Gatwick and Heathrow, as well as frequent flights from Britain's other main airports. North Ameri-

can and Canadian travellers can fly direct to Brussels from New York and Atlanta (daily), as well as from Detroit, Chicago, Montreal, etc.

Help for the Disabled

Croix-Rouge (Red Cross), CEPIATH, Rue Joseph Stallaert 1–Bte 8
1060 Bruxelles/Brussels; tel. (02) 6 47 10 10, ext. 316
Has copies of the various access guides published in Belgium and can provide information from these to potential visitors.

Help in Belgium

Fonds National de Reclassement Social des Handicapés, Rue du Meiboom 14
1000 Bruxelles/Brussels; tel. (02) 2 18 30 80

Vlaamse Federatie voor Gehandicapten (VGF), 32–38 Rue St-Jean
1000 Bruxelles/Brussels; tel. (02) 5 15 02 60
Can provide information on holiday opportunities for disabled visitors to Belgium. Wheelchair rental is also available.

SOS-Jeunes, Bruxelles/Brussels; tel (02) 5 12 90 20
Help Lines (English spoken), Bruxelles/Brussels; tel. (02) 6 48 40 14

Inexpensive accommodation for the disabled can usually be found in the Social Tourism centres. These include a number of hotels and holiday homes, run by various organisations for social tourism, which include:

Social Tourism centres

Centrum voor Sociaal Toerisme, Spastraat 8
B–1040 Brussels/Bruxelles; tel. (02) 2 30 31 45

Broederlijheid, Charleroisteenweg 145
B–1060 Brussels/Bruxelles; tel (02) 5 38 83 00

A guide entitled "Holidays and Travel Abroad – a guide for disabled people" includes a section on Belgium and is available from
The Royal Association for Disability and Rehabilitation (RADAR)
25 Mortimer Street, London W1N 8AB
Price £3 plus p&p.

Help in the UK

Hotels

Hotels in Belgium's cities and holiday resorts are of the usual international comfort standards. Pleasant accommodation can also be found in the smaller towns. It is highly advisable to book in advance during the peak holiday season. Brussels, which offers a large choice of hotels, becomes very crowded in the spring and autumn when NATO and the EC are in session.

Information

Bookings can be made free of charge for hotels throughout Belgium from Belgium Tourist Reservations, B.P. 41 B
B–1000 Brussels/Bruxelles

Reservation

The Belgian Tourist Office in Brussels (see Information) publishes an annual list of hotels detailing prices and standards of comfort.

Hotel Categories

Hotels included in this selection are arranged according to prices given by the Belgian Tourist Office. The average prices of one night's accommoda-

Prices

Hotels

tion in a double room with bath or shower, and usually breakfast, fall into
the following categories.

Category A	over 5000 Bfr
Category B	4000–5000 Bfr
Category C	3000–4000 Bfr
Category D	2000–3000 Bfr
Category E	1000–2000 Bfr

Aalst

Graaf Van Vlaanderen, D, Stationsplein 37, 6r.; tel. (053) 78 98 51
Station Hotel, D, Albert Liénartstraat 14, 15r.; tel. (053) 77 58 20

Aarschot

Kasteel van Nieuwland, E, Nieuwland 6, 12r.; tel. (016) 56 58 46

Antwerp

Alfa de Keyser, A, De Keyserlei 66, 117r.; tel. (03) 2 34 01 35
* De Rosier, A, Rosier 23, 12r.; tel. (03) 2 25 01 40
Switel, A, Copernicuslaan 2, 310r.; tel. (03) 2 31 67 80
* Firean, B, Karel Oomsstraat 6, 12r.; tel. (03)2 37 03 60
Alfa Congress, B, Plantin en Moretuslei 136, 66r.; tel. (03) 2 35 30 00
Antwerp Tower, C, Van Ertbornstraat 10, 39r.; tel. (03) 2 34 01 20
Arcade, C, Meistraat 39, 150r.; tel. (03) 2 31 88 30
Colombus, D, Frankrijklei 4, 25r.; tel. (03) 2 33 03 90
Florida, D, De Keyserlei 59, 51r.; tel. (03) 2 33 08 35
Rubenshof, E, Amerikalei 115, 20r.; tel. (03) 2 37 07 89
Tourist Hotel, E, Pelikaanstraat 22, 148r.; tel. (03) 2 32 58 70

Arlon

Arlux, C, Rue de Lorraine, 78r.; tel. (063) 23 22 11
A l'Ecu de Bourgogne, D, 9 Pl. Léopold, 19r.; tel. (063) 22 02 22

Bastogne

Lebrun, D, 8 Rue du Marché, 20r.; tel. (061) 21 54 21

Blankenberge

Azaert, C, Molenstraat 31, 53r.; tel. (050) 41 15 99
Riant Séjour, C, Zeeddijk 188, 30r.; tel. (050) 41 10 14
Albatros, D, Consciencestraat 45, 20r.; tel. (050) 41 13 49
Ideal, D, Zeedijk 244, 44r.; tel. (050) 42 86 00
Petit Rouge, D, Zeedijk-Bakkerstraat 1, 60r.; tel. (050) 41 10 06

Bouillon

Gai Repos, D, 4 Rue-au-dessus-de-la-Ville, 6r.; tel. (061) 46 82 62
Poste, D, 1 Pl.St-Arnaud, 80r.; tel. (061) 46 65 06
* Moulin Hideux (in Noirefontaine), A, 1 Rte. de Dohan, 13r.;
  tel. (061) 46 70 15

Bruges

De Orangerie, A, Kartuizerinnenstraat 10, 18r.; tel. (050) 34 16 49
Pullman, A, Boeveriestraat 2, 155r.; tel. (050) 34 09 71
* De Tuilerieën, A, Dijver 7, 26r.; tel. (050) 34 36 91
* Die Swaene, B, Steenhouwersdijk 1, 24r.; tel. (050) 34 27 98
Adornes, C, St-Annarei 26, 20r.; tel. (050) 34 13 36
Azalea, C, Wulfhagestraat 43, 25r.; tel. (050) 33 14 78
Egmond, C, Minnewater 15, 9r.; tel. (050) 34 14 45
Parkhotel, C, Vrijdagmarkt 5, 56r.; tel. (050) 33 33 64
Jacobs, D, Baliestraat 1, 26r.; tel. (050) 33 98 31
't Putje, D, 't Zand 31, 11r.; tel. (050) 34 14 23
Ensor, E, Speelmansrei 10, 8r.; tel. (050) 34 25 89
Rembrandt-Rubens, E, Walplein 38, 13r.; tel. (050) 33 64 39

Brussels
Within the city

* Hilton International, A, 38 Blvd. de Waterloo, 450r.;
  tel. (02) 5 04 11 11
Jolly du Grand Sablon, A, 2 Rue Bodenbroek, 203r.; tel. (02) 5 12 88 00
* Métropole, A, 31 Pl. de Brouckère, 410r.; tel. (02) 2 17 23 00
* Pullman Astoria, A, 103 Rue Royale, 125r.; tel. (02) 2 17 62 90
* Royal Windsor, A, 5 Rue Duquesnoy, 275r.; tel. (02) 5 11 42 15
Ibis Centre, B, 100 Rue Marché-aux-Herbes, 170r.; tel. (02) 5 14 40 40

Sainte-Catherine, B, 2 Rue Joseph Plateau, 234r.; tel. (02) 5 13 7 20
Chambord, C, 82 Rue de Namur, 69r.; tel. (02) 5 13 41 19
Queen Anne, C, 110 Blvd. Emile Jacqmain, 60r.; tel. (02) 2 17 16 00
Vendôme, C, 98 Blvd. Adolphe Max, 92r.; tel. (02) 2 18 00 70
Elysée, D, 4 Rue de la Montagne, 18r.; tel. (02) 5 11 96 82
La Légende, D, 33 Rue de l'Etuve, 31r.; tel. (02) 5 12 82 90
La Madeleine, D, 22 Rue de la Montagne, 52r.; tel. (02) 5 13 73 92
Windsor, D, 13 Pl. Rouppe, 24r.; tel. (02) 5 11 20 14
Eperonniers, E, Rue des Eperroniers, 24r.; tel. (02) 5 13 53 66
George V, E, 23 Rue t'Kint, 17r.; tel. (02) 5 13 50 93
Mirabeau, E, 18 Pl. Fontainas, 29r.; tel. (02) 5 11 19 72
Sabina, E, 78 Rue du Nord, 24r.; tel. (02) 2 18 26 37

* New Siru, A, 1 Pl. Rogier, 101r.; tel. (02) 2 17 75 80   In the north
(each room has been individually decorated by a Belgian artist) of the city

* Stanhope, A, 9 Rue de la Commerce, 50r.; tel. (02) 5 06 91 11 In the east
                    of the city

* Mayfair, A, 381 Ave. Louise, 99r.; tel. (02) 6 49 98 00   In the south
                    of the city

Altea Socatel, B, 96 Boulevard Tirou, 65r.; tel. (071) 31 98 11 **Charleroi**
Le Mediterranée, D, 20 Avenue de l'Europe, 20r.; tel. (071) 31 74 24

* Host. du Gahy (Momignies), D, 2 Rue Gahy, 6r.; tel. (060) 51 10 93 **Chimay**

De Gulden Kogge, E, Damse Vaart Zuid 12, 6r.; tel. (050) 35 72 14 **Damme**

Jaloma, D, Steenweg van Aalst 122, 6r.; tel. (052) 22 37 38 **Dendermonde**

Prins van Oranje, D, Halensebaan 152, 16r.; tel. (013) 31 33 50 **Diest**

Polderbloem, D, Grote Markt 8, 9r.; tel. (051) 50 29 05   **Diksmuide**

Couronne, D, 1 Rue Sax, 21r.; tel. (082) 22 27 31   **Dinant**
Castel de Pont-à-Lesse, D, 36 Rte. de Walzin, 75r.; tel. (082) 22 28 44 In Anseremme

Ambassador, C, Haasstra-60-e 77, 30r.; tel. (087) 74 08 00 **Eupen**
Rathaus, D, Rathausplatz 13, 18r.; tel. (087) 74 28 12

Les 3 Cles, D, 17 Ch. de Namur, 45r.; tel. (081) 61 16 17   **Gembloux**

Kasteel Izegrim, D, Zonnebloemstraat 40, 8r.;tel. (054) 41 76 60 **Geraardsbergen**

Alfa Flanders, A, Koning Albertlaan 121, 45r.; tel. (091) 22 60 65 **Ghent**
* Gravensteen, A, Jan Breydelstraat 35, 17r.; tel. (091) 25 11 50
Novotel, B, Goudenmeeuwplein 5, 117r.; tel. (091) 24 22 30
Arcade, C, Nederkouter 24, 134r.; tel. (091) 25 07 07
Sint-Jorishof, C, Botermarkt 2, 28r.; tel. (091) 24 24 24
Carlton, D, Koningin Astridlaan 138, 24r.; tel. (091) 22 88 36
Europahotel, D, Gordunakaai 59, 39r.; tel. (091) 22 60 71
Himatel, D, Blankenbergestraat 2, 30r.; tel. (091) 20 15 15
Pension Maldegem, E, Antwerpsesteenweg 7, 10r.; tel. (091) 28 21 77

Les Eleveurs, C, Basiliekstraat 136, 13r.; tel. (02) 35 65 09 **Halle**

Ardennes, D, 2 Rue des Grottes, 26r.; tel. (084) 37 72 20 **Han-sur-Lesse**
Henri IV, E, 59 Rue Chasseurs Ardennais, 8r.; tel. (084) 37 72 21

Holiday Inn, A, Kattegatstraat 1, 107r.; tel. (011) 24 22 00 **Hasselt**
Hassotel, C, St-Josefstraat 10, 30r.; tel. (011) 22 64 92
Parkhotel, C, Genkersteenweg 350, 30r.; tel. (011) 21 16 52

Hotels

Huy	Aigle Noir, D, 8 Quai Dautrebande, 10r.; tel. (085) 21 23 41
	Du Fort, E, 6 Chaussée Napoléon, 34r.; tel. (085) 21 24 03
Knokke-Heist	Malibu, A, Kustlaan 43, 25r.; tel. (050) 61 18 03
In Knokke	Eden, D, Zandstraat 18, 19r.; tel. (050) 61 13 89
in Heist	Bristol, C, Zeedijk 291, 27r.; tel. (050) 51 12 20
	Square, E, De Kinkhoom 21, 31r.; tel. (050) 51 12 37
In Albertstrand	*La Réserve, A, Elisabetlaan 160, 110r.; tel. (050) 61 06 06
	Atlanta, C, Nellenslaan 162, 32r.; tel. (005) 60 55 00
	Lido, C, Zwaluwenlaan 18, 40r.; tel. (050) 60 19 25
	Parkhotel, C, Elisabetlaan 204, 12r.; tel. (050) 60 09 01
	Albert Plage, D, Meerminlaan 22, 16r.; tel. (050) 60 59 64
In Duinbergen	Bel Air, C, Patriottenstraat 24–26, 39r.; tel. (050) 51 13 00
	Monterey, C, Bocheldreef 4, 9r.; tel. (050) 51 58 65
	Les Pingouins, D, Duinendreef 52, 11r.; tel. (050) 51 33 40
in Westkapelle	Ter Zaele, D, Oostkerkestraat 40, 20r.; tel. (050) 60 12 37
in Zoute	Dorint Hotel, A, Kustlaan 84, 50r.; tel. (050) 61 01 28
	*Fairway, A, Tuinfluiterspad 9, 12r.; tel. (050) 61 14 67
	*Lugano, A, Villapad 14, 27r.; tel. (050) 61 04 71
	Duc de Bourgogne, B, Zoutelaan 175, 22r.; tel. (050) 61 16 14
	St. Pol, C, Bronlaan 23, 16r.; tel. (050) 60 15 21
	Les Arcades, E, Elisabetlaan 50, 11r.; tel. (050) 60 10 73
Koksijde	Apostroff, C, Lejeunelaan 38, 24r.; tel. (058) 52 06 09
	Le Régent, C, A. Bliecklaan 10, 10r.; tel. (058) 51 12 10
	Florian, D, A. Bliecklaan 32, 10r.; tel. (058) 51 69 82
	Rivella, E, Zouavenlaan 1, 28r.; tel. (058) 51 31 67
In St-Idesbald	Soll Cress, D, Koninklijke Baan 225, 25r.; tel. (058) 51 23 32
Kortrijk	*Broel, A, Broelkaal 8, 68r.; tel. (056) 21 83 51
	Parkhotel, C, Stationsplein 2, 72r.; tel. (056) 22 03 03
	Center Broel, D, Graanmarkt 6, 32r.; tel. (056) 21 97 21
Leuven	Begijnhof, B, Tervuursevest 70, 67r.; tel. (016) 29 10 10
	Garden Court, C, Tiensestraat 52, 100r.; tel. (016) 29 07 70
	La Royale, E, Martelarenplein 6, 27r.; tel. (016) 22 12 52
Liège	Holiday Inn, A, 2 Espl. de l'Europe, 219r.; tel. (041) 42 60 20
	Ramada, A, 100 Blvd. de la Sauvenière, 105r.; tel. (041) 22 49 10
	Le Cygne d'Argent, D, 49 Rue Beeckman, 22r.; tel. (041) 21 77 11
	Univers, D, 116 Rue des Guillemins, 49r.; tel. (041) 52 26 50
Maaseik	Kasteele Wurfeld, C, Kapelweg, 16r.; tel. (089) 56 81 36
Malmédy	Au St.-Esprit, E, 9 Pl. de Rome, 9r.; tel. (080) 33 03 14
In Bévercé	*Trôs Marets, A, 2 Rte. des Trôs Marets, 7r.; tel. (080) 33 79 17
Mechelen	Alfa Alba, A, Korenmarkt 24, 43r.; tel. (015) 42 03 03
	Egmont, D, Oude Brusselstraat 50, 19r.; tel. (015) 42 13 99
	Claes, E, O. L. Vrouwstraat 51, 15r.; tel. (015) 41 28 66
Mons	Résidence, E, 4 Rue A. Masquelier, 6r.; tel. (065) 31 14 03
	*Amigo (in Masnuy St-Jean), B, 3 Ch. de Brunehault, 52r.; tel. (065) 72 36 85
Namur	Château de Namur, C, Citadelle, 29r.; tel. (081) 74 26 30
	La Porte de Fer, D, 4 Ave. de la Gare, 14r.; tel. (081) 23 13 45
	Queen Victoria, D, 11 Ave. de la Gare, 21r.; tel. (081) 22 29 71
Nieuwpoort	Cosmopolite, D, Albert-I-laan 141, 32r.; tel. (058) 23 33 66
	Regina, D, Albert-I-laan 137, 20r.; tel. (058) 23 33 66
	Ysremonde, D, Victorlaan 1, 202r.; tel. (058) 23 65 44
	Parkhotel, E, Albert-I-laan 175, 20r.; tel. (058) 23 49 81

Nivelles-Sud, E, 22 Ch. de Mons, 115r.; tel. (067) 21 87 21   **Nivelles**

Andromeda, A, Albert-I-Promenade 60, 90r.; tel. (059) 80 66 11   **Ostend**
Thermae-Palace, A, Koningin Astridlaan 7, 96r.; tel. (059) 80 66 44
Imperial, C, Van Iseghemlaan 76, 60r.; tel. (059) 80 67 67
Oostendse Compagnie, C, Koningstraat 79, 13r.; tel. (059) 70 48 16
Danielle, D, IJzerstraat 5, 28r.; tel. (059) 70 63 49
Du Parc, D, Marie-Joséplein 3, 44r.; tel. (059) 70 16 80
Baudouin, E, Koningstraat 13, 24r.; tel. (059) 50 92 10
Pension Cardiff, E, Sint-Sebastiaanstraat 4, 14r.; tel. (059) 70 28 98

De Rantere, C, Jan Zonder Vreeslaan 8, 19r.; tel. (055) 31 89 88   **Oudenaarde**
Elnik, E, Deinzestraat 55, 14r.; tel. (055) 31 37 88

Sparrenhof, C, Koninginnelaan 26, 25r.; tel. (058) 41 13 28   **De Panne**
Royal, D, Zeelaan 180, 25r.; tel. (058) 41 11 16
Strand Motel, D, Nieuwpoortlaan 153, 43r.; tel. (058) 42 02 22
Terlinck, C, Zeelaan 175, 64r.; tel. (058) 42 01 08
Des Princes, E, Nieuwpoortlaan 46, 36r.; tel. (058) 41 10 91
Regina Maris, E, Botrierlaan 13, 69r.; tel. (058) 41 12 22

Amfora, E, Grote Markt 36, 7r.; tel. (057) 33 88 66   **Poperinge**

*Claire Fontaine, C, 64 Rte. de Hotton, 25r.; tel. (084) 41 12 96   **La Roche-**
*Host. Linchet, C, 11 Rte. de Houffalize, 11r.; tel. (084) 41 12 23   **en-Ardenne**
Pension du Midi, E, 6 Rue Beausaint, 9r.; tel. (084) 41 11 38

*La Malle Poste, D, 46 Rue de Behogne, 11r.; tel. (084) 21 09 87   **Rochefort**
La Vieux Logis, E, 71 Rue Jacquet, 10r.; tel. (084) 21 10 24

Borquin, E, 6 Pl. de l'Abbaye, 9r.; tel. (061) 61 14 56   **St-Hubert**
De l'Abbaye, D, 18 Pl. du Marché, 20r.; tel. (061) 61 10 23

Pip-Margraff, D, Hauptstra-60-e 7, 16r.; tel. (080) 22 86 63   **St-Vith**
Zur Post, E, Hauptstra-60-e 39, 8r.; tel. (080) 22 80 27

Flandres, C, Stationsplein 5, 20r.; tel. (03) 7 77 00 93   **St-Niklaas**
De Arend, E, O. L. Vrouwplein 8, 10r.; tel. (03) 7 77 11 73

Cicindria, D, Abdijstraat 6, 26r.; tel. (011) 68 13 44   **St-Truiden**

L'Auberge, B, 3 Pl. du Monument, 31r.; tel. (087) 77 44 10   **Spa**
*La Heid des Pairs, B, 132 Ave. Prof. Henrijean, 11r.;
tel. (087) 77 43 46
Le Relais, 22 Pl. du Monument, 9r.; tel. (087) 71 11 08

D'Orange, D, 8 Rue de Spa, 22r.; tel. (080) 86 20 05   **Stavelot**
Val d'Ambiève, D, 7 Rte. de Malmédy, 15r.; tel. (080) 86 23 53

Alpha, D, Leuvensestraat 95, 18r.; tel. (016) 82 28 00   **Tienen**

Ambiotel, C, Veemarkt 2, 22r.; tel. (012) 26 29 50   **Tongeren**
Chemin de Fer, E, Stationslaan 44, 14r.; tel. (012) 23 31 05

Condor, C, 9 Pl. St-Pierre, 38r.; tel. (069) 21 50 77   **Tournai**
Le Parc, D, 7 Pl. Reine Astrid, 13r.; tel. (069) 21 28 93

Ter Driezen, C, Herentalsstraat 18, 10r.; tel. (014) 41 87 57   **Turnhout**

Amigo, A, 1 Rue Herla, 56r.: tel. (087) 22 11 21   **Verviers**

't Belfort, D, Grote Markt 26, 8r.; tel. (058) 31 11 55   **Veurne**

Virton	Le Relais de la Venerie, D, Au-dessus de Rabais, 8r.; tel. (063) 57 7 84
Walcourt	Host. de l'Abbaye, 7 Rue de Jardinet, 10r.; tel. (071) 61 14 23
Ypres (Ieper)	Ariane, C, Slachthuisstraat 58, 36r.; tel. (057) 21 82 18 Regina, C, Grote Markt 45, 17r.; tel. (057) 21 88 88 Continental, E, Colaertplein 29, 18r.; tel. (057) 21 95 37
Zeebrugge	Monaco, C, Baron de Maereaan 26, 15r.; tel. (050) 54 44 37

Information

Information outside Belgium

In the UK	Belgian National Tourist Office Premier House, 2 Gayton Road, Harrow HA1 2XV; tel. (081) 8 61 33 00
In the USA	Belgian National Tourist Office 10151, 745 Fifth Avenue, New York; tel. (0101) 21 27 58 81 30

Information within Belgium

Main offices	Commissariaat-Generaal de Toerisme/Vlaamse Gemeenschap Office de Promotion du Tourisme/Communauté Française Grasmarkt 61/63 Rue Marché aux Herbes B–1000 Brussels/Bruxelles; tel. (02) 5 04 03 90
Ardennes	Ardenne et Meuse Tourisme, 15 Rue de l'Eglise B–6980 La Roche-en-Ardenne; tel. (084) 41 19 81 Information can also be obtained from the tourist offices in the provinces of Liège, Luxembourg and Namur.
Brabant province	Fedération du Tourisme de Brabant, 61 Rue Marché aux Herbes B–1000 Bruxelles; tel. (02) 5 04 04 00
Hainaut province	Fedération du Tourisme de la Province de Hainaut, 31 Rue des Clercs B–7000 Mons; tel. (065) 36 04 64
Liège province	Fedération du Tourisme de la Province de Liège, 77 Blvd. de la Sauvinière B–4000 Liège; tel. (041) 22 42 10
Limburg province	Provinciaale Dienst voor Toerisme, Domein Bokrijk B–3600 Genk; tel. (011) 22 29 58
Luxembourg province	Fedération Touristique du Luxembourg Belge, 9 Quai de l'Ourthe B–6980 La Roche-en-Ardenne; tel. (084) 41 10 11
Namur province	Fedération du Tourisme de la Province de Namur, 3 Rue Notre-Dame B–5000 Namur; tel. (081) 22 29 98
Ostkantone	Verkehrsamt der Ostkantone, Mühlenbachstr. 2 B–4780 St-Vith; tel. (080) 22 76 64
Vlaanderen	Vlaamse Commissariaat voor Toerisme, Grasmarkt 61 B–1000 Bruxelles; tel. (02) 5 13 19 90 Federatie voor Toerisme in Oost-Vlaanderen, Koningin Maria-Hendrikaplein 64 B–9000 Gent; tel. (091) 22 16 37

Westoerisme, Kasteel Tillegem
B–8200 Brugge 2; tel. (050) 38 02 96

Local tourist information offices

The tourist information offices within individual towns in Flanders are
called Vereniging voor Vreemdelingenverkeer (V.V.V.) or Dienst voor Toerisme and in Wallonia are called Syndicat d'Initiative or Office de Tourisme.

Grote Markt 3, B–9300 Aalst; tel. (053) 77 11 11	**Aalst**
Sint Rochustoren/Grote Markt, B–3200 Aarschot; tel. (016) 56 97 05	**Aarschot**
Grote Markt 15, B–2000 Antwerp; tel. (03) 2 32 01 03	**Antwerp**
Pavillon du Tourisme, Parc Léopold, B–6700 Arlon; tel. (063) 21 63 60	**Arlon**
Rue du Bouchain, B–7800 Ath; tel. (068) 28 01 41	**Ath**
24 Place McAuliffe, B–6650 Bastogne; tel. (062) 21 27 11	**Bastogne**
1 Rue sous les Cloches, B–6570 Beaumont; tel. (071) 58 86 84	**Beaumont**
Domaine de Belœil, B–7970 Belœil; tel. (069) 68 96 55	**Belœil**
Hôtel de Ville, Grand-Place, B–7130 Binche; tel. (064) 33 37 21	**Binche**
Leopold III-plein, B–8370 Blankenberge; tel. (050) 41 29 21	**Blankenberge**
Porte de France, B–6830 Bouillon; tel. (061) 45 51 55	**Bouillon**
Burg 11, B–8000 Bruges; tel. (050) 44 86 86	**Bruges**
Hôtel de Ville/Stadhuis, Grand'Place/Grote Markt B–1000 Bruxelles/Brussels; tel. (02) 5 13 89 40	**Brussels**
100 Av. Mascaux, B–6001 Charleroi-Marcinelle; tel. (071) 43 49 55	**Charleroi**
1 Grand-Place, B–6460 Chimay; tel. (060) 21 18 46	**Chimay**
Jacob van Maerlantstraat 3, B–8340 Damme; tel. (050) 35 33 19	**Damme**
Stadhuis, Grote Markt, B–9330 Dendermonde; tel. (052) 21 39 56	**Dandermonde**
Grote Markt 1, B–3290 Diest; tel. (013) 31 21 21	**Diest**
Grote Markt 14, B–8160 Diksmuide; tel. (051) 50 13 21	**Diksmuide**
37 Rue Grande, B–5500 Dinant; tel. (082) 22 28 70	**Dinant**
Fremdenverkehrsamt, Marktplatz, B–4700 Eupen; tel. (087) 55 34 50	**Eupen**
Gemeentehuis, Markt 1, B–2440 Geel; tel. (014) 57 09 55	**Geel**
Place de l'Hôtel de Ville, B–5800 Gembloux; tel. (081) 61 51 71	**Gembloux**
Stadhuis, Grote Markt 1, B–9500 Geraardsbergen; tel. (054) 41 41 21	**Geraardsbergen**
Parc Naturel Hautes Fagnes 131 Route de Botrange B–4898 Robertville; tel. (080) 44 57 81	**German-Belgian National Park**

Information

Ghent	Stadhuis, Botermarkt, B–9000 Gent; tel. (091) 24 15 55
Halle	Kardinal Cardijnstraat 7, B–1500 Halle; tel. (02) 3 56 41 74
Han-sur-Lesse	1 Rue des Sarrasins, B–5432 Han-sur-Lesse; tel. (084) 37 75 96
Hasselt	Lombaardstraat 3, B–3500 Hasselt; tel. (011) 22 95 40
Huy	1 Quayde Namur, B–5200 Huy; tel. (085) 21 29 15
Knokke-Heist	Lichttorenplein, Zeedijk 660, B–8300 Knokke-Heist; tel. (050) 60 15 16
Koksijde	Zeelaan 24, B–8670 Koksijde; tel. (058) 52 15 15
Kortrijk	Schouwburgplein, B–8500 Kortrijk; tel. (056) 20 25 00
Leuven	Naamsestraat 1 a, B–3000 Leuven; tel. (016) 21 15 39
Liège	92 Féronstrée, B–4000 Liège; tel. (041) 22 24 56
Lier	Stadhuis, Grote Markt 57, B–2500 Lier; tel. (03) 4 89 11 11
Maaseik	Markt 45, B–3630 Maaseik; tel. (089) 56 63 72
Malmédy	Maison Cavens, Place de Rome, B–4960 Malmédy; tel. (080) 33 02 50
Mechelen	Stadhuis, Grote Markt 57, B–2800 Mechelen; tel. (015) 29 76 52
Mons	20 Grand-Place, B–7000 Mons; tel. (065) 33 55 80
Namur	Square Léopold, B–5000 Namur; tel. (081) 22 28 70
Nivelles	Waux-Hall, Place Albert I., B–1400 Nivelles; tel. (067) 21 54 13
De Panne	Gemeentehuis, Zeelaan 21, B–8470 De Panne; tel. (058) 41 13 02
Ostend	Wapenplein, B–8400 Oostende; tel. (059) 70 11 99
Oudenaarde	Stadhuis, Markt, B–9700 Oudenaarde; tel. (055) 31 72 51
Poperinge	Stadhuis, B–8970 Poperinge; tel. (057) 33 40 81
La Roche-en-Ardenne	15 Place du Marché, B–6980, La Roche-en-Ardenne; tel. (084) 41 13 42
Rochefort	5 Rue de Behogne, B–5430 Rochefort; tel. (084) 21 25 37
Saint-Hubert	18 Rue de la Liberté, B–6900 Saint Hubert; tel. (061) 61 70 20
Sint-Niklaas	Grote Markt 45, B–2700 Sint-Niklaas; tel. (03) 7 77 26 81
Sint-Truiden	Stadhuis, B–3800 Sint Truiden; tel. (011) 68 68 72
Spa	41 Place Royale, B–4880 Spa; tel. (087) 77 25 10
Stavelot	Ancienne Abbaye, B–4970 Stavelot; tel. (080) 86 23 39
Tienen	Stadhuis, Grote Markt, B–3300 Tienen; tel. (016) 81 97 85
Tongeren	Stadhuisplein, B–3700 Tongeren; tel. (012) 23 29 61

14 Rue du Vieux Marché-aux-Poteries, B–7500 Tournai; tel. (069) 22 20 45

Tournai

Grote Markt, B–2300 Turnhout; tel. (014) 42 21 96

Turnhout

Grote Markt 29, B–8480 Veurne; tel. (058) 31 21 54

Veurne

Rue Croix-le-Maire, B–6760 Virton; tel. (063) 57 89 04

Virton

39 Alléedes Marguerites, B–4540 Visé

Visé

25 Grand-Place, B–6430 Walcourt; tel. (071) 62 25 26

Walcourt

Besucherzentrum, 252–254 Route du Lion B–1420 Braine-l'Alleud; tel. (02) 3 85 19 12

Waterloo

Stadhuis, Grote Markt, B–8900 Ieper; tel. (057) 20 26 26

Ypres (Ieper)

Zeedijk, B–8380 Zeebrugge; tel. (050) 54 50 42

Zeebrugge

Boogardenstraat 5, B–3440 Zoutleeuw; tel. (011) 78 02 53

Zoutleeuw

Insurance

Visitors are strongly advised to ensure that they have adequate holiday insurance, including loss or damage to luggage, loss of currency and jewellery.

General

British citizens, like nationals of other European Community countries, are entitled to obtain medical care under the Belgian health services regulations on the same basis as Belgians. Before leaving home visitors should apply to their local social security office for a form E111 which certifies their entitlement to insurance cover. If possible this should be presented to the local health office (Unità Sanitaria Locale) before seeking treatment. It is nevertheless advisable, even for EC nationals, to take out some form of short-term insurance cover (for example under the AA's 5-star service) providing full cover and possibly avoiding bureaucratic delays. Nationals of non-EC countries should certainly have insurance cover.

Health

Visitors travelling by car should ensure that their insurance is comprehensive and covers use of the vehicle in Belgium.

Vehicles

See also Travel Documents.

Language

Several languages are spoken in Belgium. The Flemings live in the river basin of the Scheldt and the Walloons in the basin of the Meuse. The language frontier between Flanders and Wallonia has hardly changed since the Middle Ages and runs more or less from Visé on the Meuse west across the Waremme, Halle and Ronse to Menin on the French border. North of this line the people speak Flemish, a dialect related to Dutch, south of the line they speak French. Brussels is officially bilingual, although the city centre is becoming a predominantly French-speaking island close to the southern border of the Flemish language area. In the eastern cantons, i.e. in the area around Eupen, Sankt Vith and Arlon, German is mainly spoken.
Like Dutch, Flemish is a branch of the Low German language group and in fact only differs from Dutch to the extent that Cockney differs from Geordie

Language areas

Language

in English language terms. Flemish ceased to be used as a written language after the Dutch War of Independence when all Flemish literature was burned by order of the Duke of Alba. It was only under the Dutch administration between 1814 and 1830 that Flemish ceased to be discriminated against. Soon afterwards Dutch was being spoken in the north of Belgium rather than Flemish. After bitter language disputes in the 19th century Dutch also displaced French which had been the official language of the Flemish area. In the forefront of the Flemish movement were several well-known 19th and 20th century writers, among them Felix Timmermans (1886–1947).

Walloon

Walloon, an ancient French dialect with some elements of Celtic and German, has practically died out. It never became important as a written language, French having tended to fulfil this function since the 12th c.

French

French developed from Vulgar Latin after the Roman Occupation of Celtic Gaul. Although it acquired a number of words of Celtic and later also of Germanic origin, it has kept its Romance character. For centuries it was the most important Romance language spoken by the educated élite and in diplomatic circles. The French polite forms are used when speaking to people, so that "Monsieur", "Madame" and "Mademoiselle" are added to the end of a phrase and "s'il vous plaît" (please) is often added when asking for something.

Numbers

English	French	Dutch/Flemish
0	zéro	nul
1	un, une	een
2	deux	twee
3	trois	drie
4	quatre	vier
5	cinq	vijf
6	six	zes
7	sept	zeven
8	huit	acht
9	neuf	negen
10	dix	tien
11	onze	elf
12	douze	twaalf
13	treize	dertien
14	quatorze	veertien
15	quinze	vijftien
16	seize	zestien
17	dix-sept	zeventien
18	dix-huit	achttien
19	dix-neuf	negentien
20	vingt	twintig
21	vingt et un	eenentwintig
22	vingt-deux	tweeëntwintig
30	trente	dertig
31	trente et un	eenendrtig
40	quarante	veertig
50	cinquante	vijftig
60	soixante	zestig
70	septante†	zeventig
80	quatre-vingt	tachtig
90	nonante†	negentig
91	nonante et un†	eenennegentig
100	cent	honderd
101	cent un	honderd een
200	deux cents	tweehonderd
1000	mille	duizend
2000	deux milles	tweeduizend

† numbers only used in Belgium; in France they are
70 = soixante-dix; 90 = quatre-vingt-dix; 91 = quatre-vingt-onze

English	French	Dutch/Flemish	
1st	premier (-ière)	eerste	Ordinal
2nd	deuxième	tweede	numbers
3rd	troisième	derde	
½	un demi	een half	Fractions
⅓	un tiers	een derde	
¼	un quart	een kwart, een vierde	
Do you speak . . .	Parlez-vous . . .	spreekt u . . .	Idioms
I do not understand	Je ne comprends pas	Ik versta niet; ik begrijp u niet	

Yes	oui	Ja
No	Non	Neen
Please!	S'il vous plaít!	Alstublieft!
Thank you!	Merci!	Dank u!
Thank you very much!	Merci beaucoup!	Dank u wel!
Excuse me!	Pardon!	Neemt u mij niet!
Sorry!	Excusez!	Kwalijk! Pardon!

Good morning!	Bonjour!	Goedemorgen!
Good day!	Bonjour!	Goedendag! (afternoons)
Good evening!	Bonsoir!	Goedenavond!
Good night!	Bonne nuit!	Goedenacht! Wel te rusten!
Goodbye!	Au revoir!	Tot ziens!
Mr	Monsieur	Mijnheer
Mrs	Madame	Mevrouw!
Miss	Mademoiselle	Juffrouw
Where is . . . ?	Où est . . . ?	Waar is . . . ?
. . . Street	La rue . . .	De . . . straat
. . . Square	La place . . .	De . . . plaats, het plein
A travel office	Un bureau de voyage	Een reisbureau
The church	L'eglise	De kerk
The museum	Le musée	Het museum
When?	Quand?	Wanneer?
When is . . . open?	A quelle heure . . . est ouvert(e)?	Wanneer is . . . open?
The town hall	L'hôtel de ville	Het stadhuis, het gemeentehuis

A bank	Une banque	Een bank
The railway station	La gare	Het station
A hotel	Un hôtel	Een hotel
I would like	Je voudrais	Heeft u
With one bed	A un lit	Met een bed
With two beds	A deux lits	Met twee bedden
With bathroom	Avec bain	Met bad
The key	Le clef	De sleutel
The toilet	La toilette, le cabinet	Het toilet
A doctor	Un médecin	De arts, de dokter
Right	A droite	Rechts
Left	A gauche	Links
Straight on	Tout droit	Rechtuit
Above	En haut	Boven
Below	En bas	Beneden, onder
Old	Ancien, ancienne, vieux, vieille	Oud

Language

	English	**French**	**Dutch/Flemish**
	New	Nouveau, nouvelle	Nieuw
	What does . . . cost?	Combien coûte . . . ?	Hoeveel kost . . . , wat kost . . . ?
	Expensive	Cher, chère	Duur
	Breakfast	Petit déjeuner	Ontbijt
	Lunch	Déjeuner, díner	Middagmaal
	Dinner	Souper	Avondeten
	Eat	Manger	Eten
	Drink	Boire	Drinken
	A lot	Beaucoup	Veel
	A little	Peu	Weinig
	Bill	Addition	Rekening
	Pay	Payer	Betalen
	Immediately	Tout de suite	Dadelijk
The Belgian menu	See Food and Drink		
Travelling	Departure	Départ	Vertrek
	Arrival	Arrivée	Aankomst
	Bus station	Gare routière	Autobusstation
	Railway station	Gare	Station
	Airport	Aéroport	Luchthaven
	Flight	Vol	Vlucht
	Platform	Voie	Spoor
	Stop	Arrêt	Halte
	Connection	Correspondance	Overstappen
	Train	Train	Trein
Traffic signs and warnings	Stop!	Halte! Stop!	Stop!
	Customs	Douane	Tol
	Attention!	Attention!	Pas op! Opgelet!
	Caution!	Prudence!	Waarschuwing!
	Drive slowly!	Au pas! Ralentir!	Langzaam rijden!
	Danger of death!	Danger de mort!	Levensgevaar!
	One-way street	Sens unique	Straat met eenrichtingsverkeer
	No entry!	Route barrée! Passage interdit!	Inrijden verboten, doodlopende straat!
	Roadworks!	Travaux!	Werk in uitvoering!
	Dangerous bend!	Virage dangereux!	Gevaarlijke bocht!
Geographical terms	Stream	Ruisseau	Beek
	Mountain	Mont	Berg
	Bridge	Pont	Brug
	Village	Village	Dorp
	Railway	Chemin de fer	Spoorlijn
	Ferry	Bac	Veer, Pont
	River	Fleuve	Rivier
	Rivulet	Ruissage	Beek
	Garden, Park	Jardin, Parc	Tuin, Park
	Summit	Sommet	Top
	Hill	Coline	Heuvel
	Island	Ile	Eiland
	Secondary road	Route	Landweg, Weg
	(Market)Place	Place	(Markt)Platz
	Moor	Tourbière	Veen
	Castle	Château	Slot, Kasteel
	Town	Ville	Stad
	Beach	Plage	Strand
	Road	Rue	Straat
	Bog	Marais	Moeras
	Valley	Vallée	Dal

English	French	Dutch/Flemish	
Tower	Tour	Toren	
Forest	Forêt	Bos, Woud	
Waterfall	Cascade	Waterval	
January	Janvier	Januari	Months
February	Février	Februari	
March	Mars	Maart	
April	Avril	April	
May	Mai	Mei	
June	Juin	Juni	
July	Juillet	Juli	
August	Août	Augustus	
September	Septembre	September	
October	Octobre	Oktober	
November	Novembre	November	
December	Decembre	December	
Monday	Lundi	Maandag	Days
Tuesday	Mardi	Dinsdag	
Wednesday	Mecredi	Woensdag	
Thursday	Jeudi	Donderdag	
Friday	Vendredi	Vrijdag	
Saturday	Samedi	Zaterdag	
Sunday	Dimanche	Zondag	
Holiday	Jour de Fête	Feestdag, vrije dag	
New Year	Nouvel An	Nieuwjaar	Special days
Easter	Pâques	Pasen	
Ascension	Ascension	Hemelsvaartsdag	
Whitsun	Pentecote	Pinksteren	
Corpus Christi	Fête-Dieux	Sacramentsdag	
Assumption	Assomption	Maria-Hemelvaart	
All Saints' Day	Toussaint	Allerheiligen	
Christmas	Noël	Kerstmis	
New Year's Eve	Le Saint-Sylvestre	Oudejaarsavond	
Post office	Bureau de poste	Postkantoor	At the post
Main post office	Bureau de poste centrale	Hoofpostkantoor	office
Stamp	Timbre-poste	Postzegel	
Letter	Lettre	Brief	
Postcard	Carte postale	Briefkaart	
Postman	Facteur	Postbode	
Recorded delivery	Recommandé	Aangetekend	
Express	Par exprès	Expres	
Airmail	Par avion	Luchtpost	
Telegram	Télégramme	Telegram	
Telephone	Téléphone	Telefoon	

A small pamphlet entitled "Bienvenue & Merci", which lists the most important idioms in both languages together with their English meaning, is available from the tourist information offices listed under Information (see entry).

Advice

Leisure Parks

Belgium has a large number of leisure parks offering a broad range of entertainment and opportunities for sports and games. The most attractive are listed here. An admission fee is charged in most parks.

Information

Leisure Parks

Adinkerke- De Panne	Meli-Park, De Pannelaan 68, with Europe's tallest waterchute. Opening times: end Mar.–mid Sept. daily 10am–6pm; mid–end Sept. weekends only, Oct. Sun. only.
Antwerp	Antwerpen-Miniatuurstaad, Scheldekai, Hangar 15 Model of Antwerp on a scale of 1:87 with scale models of ships, which sail along a miniature version of the Scheldt. Opening times: daily 10am–10pm.
Bruges	Boudewijnpark, A. de Baeckestraat 12 Reptile house and dolphinarium, roller-skating and go-karting rink. Opening times: beginning Apr.–end Sept. daily 10am–6pm.
Brussels/ Bruxelles	Bruparck, 20 Boulevard du Centenaire (near the Atomium) Opening times: Mar.–June and Sept.–Jan. daily 9am–6pm; July/Aug. Mon.–Fri. 9am–8pm, Sat. Sun. and public holidays until 9pm (Mini-Europe). Likewise Le Village and Parc Aquatique; Kinépolis (cinema city) remains open until later in the evenings. Mini-Europe: important European buildings on a scale of 1:25; Océadium: subtropical waterparadise; Le Village: various refreshment places, play area; Kinépolis (cinema city): the world's largest cinema complex.
Coo-Stavelot	Télécoo-Kayakcoo Bobsleigh run, cable railway, motorcycle track, kayak trips at the foot of Coo waterfall, zoo. Opening times: beginning Mar.–mid Nov. daily 9am–9pm, weekends in winter 10am–7.30pm.
Daadizele	Dadipark, Moorsledestraat 6 Suspension bridge, programme of animations. Opening times: end Apr.–June daily and weekends in Sept. 10am–7pm, July/Aug. daily 10am–7.30pm.
Ingelmunster	Aviflora, Bruggestraat 218 Thousands of animals (including waterfowl) in a natural setting, lakes, waterfalls; exhibition halls with exotic birds, plants and fish; monkey colony. Opening times: May–mid Sept. daily 10am–6pm.
Lichtaart	Bobbejaanland, Steenweg op Olen 45 Family park with numerous attractions such as the Mississippi Boat, fast-water course; trapeze tower; Indian museum. Opening times: Easter holidays, the first weekend of Apr., daily end Apr.–Sept.
Oud-Heverlee	Rekreatiepark Zoet Water, M. Noëstraat 15 Play village, open-air theatre, forest pavilion with large aquaria, terrarium. Opening times: end Mar.–Sept. Mon.–Sat. 10am–7pm, Sun. and public holidays until 8pm; Oct.–Mar. Sat. and Sun. 1–5pm.
Wavre	Walibi and Aqualibi Walibi: water adventure, Kangaroo Land, sea lion and parrot shows, puppet theatre. Aqualibi: water park with jet stream, breakers, tropical bar. Opening times: end Mar.–end Sept.: daily 10am–6pm for visitors to both establishments, for visitors to Aqualibi only 6–10pm.
Zillebekeleper	Bellewaerde, Meenseweg 497 Safari park, jungle boats, Cowboy village, Mexican village. Opening times: Beginning Apr.–Sept. daily and Sun. in Oct. 10am–6pm.
SunAqua parks/ Sun parks	Also of appeal are the SunAqua parks/Sun parks which can be found along the Belgian coast. They combine numerous sporting, games and leisure

facilities with luxurious holiday homes. Occupants of these homes have free entry to the relevant SunAqua park.

SunAquaPark De Haan, Wenduinsesteenweg 150
B–8420 de Haan; tel. (050) 42 95 96

SunAquaPark Groendyk, Polderstraat 158
B–8670 Oostduinkerke-Koksijde; tel. (058) 23 95 63

Those interested can find references to popular zoos, safari parks, aquaria and botanical gardens in the A to Z section. — Zoological and botanical gardens

Markets

In addition to strolling through the picturesque markets which take place once or more a week, a visit to the antiques, flea and flower markets can also prove a delight. — Information

Nearly every Flemish town stages a Kirmes: the largest event of this kind in Belgium is Kortrijk's Easter Kirmes (from Easter Saturday until the second Sunday after Easter). — Fairs

One of the most-visited pre-Christmas markets is that which takes place on the Grote Zavel in Brussels. Most Christmas markets are to be found in the south of the country. — Christmas markets

Selected markets

Antiques market on the Lijnwaardmarkt and art market on the Dageraard-plaats (Easter–Sept. Sat. 10am–6pm) — Antwerp

Flea markets on the Oud Arsenaalplaats, on the Oude Vaartplaats, on the Blauwtorenplein and on the Graanmarkt (Sun. 9am–1pm)

Junk market on the Vrijdagmarkt (Wed. and Fri. 9am–2pm)

Bird market on the Oude Vaartplaats (Sun. 8am–1pm)

Flea market on the Dijver (Apr.–Oct. Sat. 1–5pm, Sun. 10am–5pm) — Bruges

Zandfeesten am 't Zand (Flanders' largest antiques and flea market; each for one day at the beginning of July, mid Aug. and end Oct. 7am–1pm; see information at the local tourist information office)

Antiques market on the Place du Grand Sablon (Sat. 9am–6pm and Sun. 9am–2pm) — Brussels/Bruxelles

Flea market on the Place du Jeu de Balles (daily 7am–2pm)

Horse market on the Place de la Duchesse de Brabant (Fri. 5am–noon)

Bird and flower market on the Grand'Place/Grote Markt (Sun. 7am–2pm)

Dog market on the Place Charles II and in the Rue Vauban (Sunday mornings) — Charleroi

Flower market on the Kouter (daily 7am–1pm) — Ghent

Animal market (pets, poultry) on the Oude Beestenmarkt (Sun. 7am–1pm)

Flea market around St Jacob (Fri. and Sat. 7am–1pm, Sun. 9am–1pm)

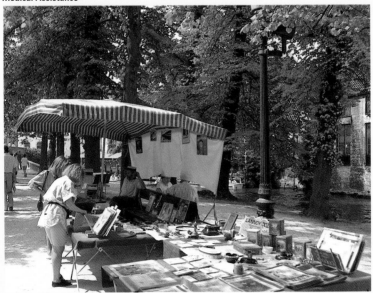

Flea-market by the Dijver in Bruges

	Bird market on the François-Laurentplein (Sun. 7am–1pm)
Hasselt	Art market (July and Aug. Sat. 2–6pm)
Liège	"La Batte" flea and grocery market, Quai Batte (Sun. 8am–1pm)
	Flea market on the Boulevard Kleyer (Sat. 9am–noon)
Lier	Flea market on the Tramweglei (every first Sat. in the month 1–6pm)
Mons	Junk market on the Place du Béguinage (Sunday morning)
Sint-Truiden	Antiques and flea market on the Veemarkt (Sat. 1–6pm)
Spa	Flea market in the Galérie Leopold II (Sun. 8am–2pm)
Tongeren	Antiques and flea market on the Oude Veemarkt (Sun. 5am–2pm)
Tournai	Antiques and flea market on the Quai des Salines (Sun. 10am–1pm)
	Grand Flower Market on Good Friday
Turnhout	Flea market in Warandestraat (Sun. 9am–noon)

Medical Assistance

Belgian medical services are excellent and the country is well supplied with doctors, many of them able to speak English.
British visitors to Belgium will find it helpful to obtain a free booklet from the Department of Health, "The Traveller's Guide to Health", which gives

information about health precautions and how to get urgent medical treatment when abroad.

See also Insurance.

Military Cemeteries

The following list of military cemeteries includes only the most important in Belgium. Further information can be obtained from the Commonwealth War Graves Commission, 2 Marlow Road, Maidenhead, Berks, SL6 7DX; tel. (0628) 3 42 21.

Advice

1 Poperinge-Lijssenthoek (WW1)
10,769 British and 213 German soldiers killed in action

2 Ypres-Memorial (WW1)
Menentor (Menin Gate) memorial with the names of 54,361 soldiers missing in action; every evening between 8pm and 9pm the traffic is stopped and "Last Post" is sounded

3 Tyne-Cot Memorial (WW1)
11,956 soldiers killed in action (including Germans) and the names of 34,855 soldiers missing in action

4 Menen (WW1)
47,864 soldiers killed in action
Largest German World War 1 military cemetery

5 Waregem Flanders Fiels (WW1)
368 soldiers killed in action

6 Poelkapelle (WW1)
7479 soldiers killed in action

General map of the principal Military Cemeteries

7 Langemark (WW1)

8 Houthulster Wald (WW1)

9 Hooglede (WW1)
8247 soldiers killed in action; arcaded hall constructed from material used for the German pavilion in the 1928 World Exhibition

10 Vladslo (WW1)
25,644 soldiers killed in action; sculpture entitled "Mourning Parents" by Käthe Kollwitz

11 Zeebrugge (WW1)
British and 173 German soldiers killed in action

12 Lommel (WW1, WW2)
541 soldiers killed in action in the First World War and 38,962 soldiers killed in action in the Second World War; also Polish soldiers killed in action in the Second World War

13 Leopoldsburg (WW1, WW2)

14 Bruxelles-Evere (WW1)
1147 German soldiers killed in action are buried in the local cemetery

15 Tarcienne (WW1)
178 German and 446 French soldiers killed in action

16 Maissin-National (WW1)
513 German and 3286 French soldiers killed in action

17 Anloy-Heide (WW1)
1384 German and 594 French soldiers killed in action

French Military cemetery on the Citadelle of Dinant

18 Bertrix-Heide (WW1)
254 German and 273 French soldiers killed in action

19 Neufchâteau- Malonne (WW1)
340 German and 288 French soldiers killed in action

20 Bellefontaine (WW1)
502 German and 518 French soldiers killed in action

21 Virton-Bellevue (WW1)
1288 German and 2445 French soldiers killed in action

22 Musson-Baranzy (WW1)
511 German and 454 French soldiers killed in action

23 Halanzy (WW1)
44 German and 22 French soldiers killed in action

24 Recogne (WW2)
6785 soldiers killed in action

25 St. Vith (WW1)
173 German soldiers killed in action are buried in the local cemetery

26 Eupen (WW1)
122 German soldiers killed in action are buried in the local cemetery

27 Ardennes Cemetery at Neuville-en-Condroz (WW2)
5310 soldiers killed in action

28 Herstal (WW1)
95 German soldiers killed in action are buried in the local cemetery

29 Liège-Robermont (WW1)
795 German soldiers killed in action are buried in the local cemetery

30 Henri-Chapelle (WW2)
7989 soldiers killed in action, mainly Americans

Motoring

Accidents

However careful a driver is, an accident can always happen. If one does, endeavour to remain calm and polite. Keep a clear head and take the following action.

Immediate action

1. Ensure that the site of the accident is safe, i.e. turn on hazard warning lights, position warning triangle and – if available – warning lights at a sufficient distance.

Precautions

2. Take care of anyone injured. First-aid advice can be found in a car first-aid kit. If necessary, call an ambulance.

Injured

3. Inform the police (tel. 101). They record every accident.

Police

4. Note the names and addresses of other people involved in the accident. Also note the registration number(s) and make(s) of any other car(s) involved and the names and telephone numbers of their insurers. The time and place of the accident are also important as well as the address of the police station alerted.

Notes

5. Secure evidence. Note the names and addresses of – if possible, impartial – witnesses; sketch the scene at the site of the accident or, better still,

Evidence

keep a small camera in the glove compartment to take photographs from various angles.

European Accident Report

If possible use the European Accident Report (available from insurance companies) and have it countersigned by the plaintiff for damages. Do not sign any admission of guilt and, above all, do not sign anything written in an unknown language.

Compensation

After an accident the handling of compensation claims should go as smoothly as possible. To achieve this follow this advice.

Claims against you

1. If a claim is made against you, report the damage to your own vehicle insurers. You can also contact the Belgian insurance company named on your Green Card.

Your claim

2. Make your own claim against the other party and his current insurers. The Green Card is of no help here! Legal costs insurance is useful in helping to pursue such claims.

Accident report

3. The police accident report is first sent only to the public prosecutor's office. This office will not issue a copy until the conclusion of the investigation.

Estimate

4. With the exception of minor damage, send an estimate by recorded delivery (with a specialist report if the damage is more severe) to the other party and his insurance company. Request that the insurance company obtains expert advice about the damages within a week. If no reply is forthcoming you are entitled to have the repairs carried out. The other party still has the right to dispute liability but his insurance company cannot refuse a repair bill if you have approved it.

Court

5. If you are summoned to appear in court inform your vehicle insurers immediately. Up to a certain level of damages, claims against the other driver can be made in the criminal court.

Lawyer

6. Is a lawyer required to pursue your compensation claim or to defend you in court? If so your legal costs insurers will issue names of Belgian laywers who speak English and whose fees are then paid by the insurers.

Compensation payments

7. In Belgium claims for loss of value are rarely proceeded with. The cost of a rented car is only refunded if it is for commercial use. Out of court costs for a lawyer are also not allowed. In the case of a write-off the appropriate customs authorities must also be notified.

Prompt action

Reporting damage promptly can accelerate any claim.

Breakdown Assistance

Automobile associations

Touring Club Royal de Belgique (T.C.B.)
44 Rue de la Loi
B–1040 Bruxelles/Brussels; tel. (02) 2 33 22 11

Royal Automobile Club de Belgique (R.A.C.B.)/Koninklijke Automobiel Club van België (K.A.C.B.)
53 Rue d'Arlon
B–1040 Bruxelles/Brussels; tel. (02) 2 30 08 10

Branches of these associations can be found in all larger towns.

Breakdown help

Antwerp; tel. (03) 3 53 88 88
Ardenne; tel. (062) 21 23 33
Bruges; tel. (050) 81 17 17
Brussels; tel. (02) 2 33 22 22
Charleroi; tel. (071) 50 38 38
Hainaut; tel. (064) 66 33 01
Leuven; tel. (016) 46 11 12
Liège; tel. (041) 68 79 91
Limburg; tel. (011) 42 05 45

Namur; tel. (081) 46 13 63
Oostvlaanderen; tel. (091) 62 65 65
Westvlaanderen; tel.(051) 77 81 40

Emergency telephones are stationed along all Belgian motorways.

Failure to observe motoring regulations leads to drivers, even visitors. being fined on the spot by police.

In Belgium vehicles travel on the right and overtake on the left.

A trial scheme, initially for a year, began in autumn 1992 making the use of lights compulsory during the day.
Fog lights must be used in fog, heavy rain, snow or visibility of less than 100m/110yds.
Children up to twelve must travel in the back of the car.
Yellow lines on the kerb mean that parking is forbidden.
Right of way must be given to police cars, fire engines or ambulances answering an emergency and vehicles on rails.

A warning triangle must be kept in the car. In the event of a breakdown on a secondary road it must be placed at least 30m/99ft from the vehicle. On a motorway it must be positioned at least 100m/328ft from the vehicle.

The maximum blood alcohol level is 80 grammes per litre.

The use of front seat belts is obligatory.
Motorcycle/moped riders must wear helmets.

Within most built-up areas 60kmph/37mph; on motorways and dual carriageways for vehicles up to 7.5t (including trailers) 120kmph/74mph, on secondary roads 90kmph/56mph; for vehicles over 7.5t (including trailers) 90kmph/56mph or 60kmph/37mph.
Maximum speed when towing is 25kmph/16mph; this also applies on motorways, where vehicles towing must leave at the first available exit.

Studded tyres are allowed in exceptional weather circumstances. Four rules must be obeyed; all four tyres must be studded, maximum speed on motorways and dual carriageways 90kmph/56mph, elsewhere 60kmph/37mph, this speed restriction must be shown on the rear of the car, maximum vehicle weight 3.5t.

Belgium is covered by a network of petrol stations supplying 4-star lead-free petrol (95 octane), some also sell 3-star lead-free petrol (90 octane). Leaded 3-star petrol is no longer available, only leaded 4-star (98 octane) and diesel fuel.

National Parks, Nature Reserves and Caves

National Parks and Nature Reserves

In general plants and animals should not be disturbed in their habitat but should be left in peace. Visitors should not stray from marked paths, bridleways and, if applicable, cross-country ski runs. Rubbish should not be thrown down but must be taken away; dogs must be kept on leads. Picking flowers, camping, radios, night-time walks and fires are banned. The ecologically very sensitive moorland area of Hohen Venn is particularly at risk of fire during summer.

1 Het Zwin (bird reserve)
Location: at Knokke-Heist. Area: 125ha/309 acres

National Parks, Nature Reserves and Caves

National Parks
Nature Reserves
● **Caves open to the Public**

2 Kalmthouder Heide
Location: north of Antwerp. Area: 1700ha/4201 acres

3 Molenheide (with zoo)
Location: at Helchteren north of Hasselt. Area: 100ha/247 acres

4 Bokrijk (with open air museum and arboretum)
Location: north-east of Hasselt. Area: 514ha/1270 acres

5 Maten (bird reserve)
Location: at Genk. Area: 300ha/741 acres

6 Mechelse Heide
Location: at Maasmechelen. Area: 400ha/988 acres

7 Bois de Soignes (Zonniënwoud)
Location: south-east of Brussels. Area: 4000ha/9884 acres

8 Furfooz (nature park)
Location: south-east of Dinant. Area: 819ha/2024 acres

9 Lesse et Lomme (national and game park)
Location: at Han-sur-Lesse. Area: 250ha/618 acres

10 Hohes Venn-Eifel (nature park)
Location: east of Malmédy. Area: 70,000ha/172,970 acres

11 Hohes Venn (nature reserve)
Location: east of Malmédy. Area: 4200ha/10,378 acres

The last two areas form parts of the German-Belgian National Park (see
A to Z).

Caves

In southern Belgium slate and limestone form the upper strata of the Ardennes; in the Condroz, Maas, Ourthe and Lesse in particular and in other rivers fissures have cut into the readily-soluble limestone layer in many places, with the result that water has gradually penetrated through them and formed stalactites. Many of the caves which arose in this way have an underground river flowing through them. The caves are accessible on guided tours.

Information

12 Grotte de Ramioul
Location: Ramet 14km/9 miles south-west of Liège
Pre-historic finds, cave museum

13 Grotte de Comblain-au-Pont
Location: Comblain-au-Pont, 18km/11 miles south of Liège
Sinter formations, find of bones

14 Grotte de Remouchamps
Location: Remouchamps, 13km/8 miles west of Spa
Sinter formations, underground river

15 Grotte des Milles et une Nuits
Location: Hotton, 23km/14 miles north-east of Rochefort
Sinter formations, dripstones, underground river

16 Grottes de Rochfort
Location: Rochefort
Crystal formations, underground river

17 Grottes de Han
Location: Han sur Lesse
Sinter formations, underground river, cave museum in Europe's largest cave complex

18 Grotte La Merveileuse
Location: Dinant
Sinter formations, cave lake

19 Grotte du Pont d'Arcole
Location: Hastière-Lavaux, 23km/14 miles south-west of Dinant
Sinter formations, dripstones, underground river

20 Grotte de Neptune
Location: Couvin 10km/6 miles east of Chimay
Pre-historic finds, cave museum

21 Grotte de Goyet
Location: Mozet-Goyet, 10km/6 miles east of Namur
Pre-historic finds, sinter formations

Newspapers and periodicals

The principal British and American newspapers are readily available in most parts of Belgium, often on the day of issue.

English language newspapers

Among the important Belgian daily newspapers are the Gazet van Antwerpen (catholic-conservative), Het Laatste Nieuws (Brussels, liberal), Het Volk (Brussels and Gent; catholic-conservative), Standaard (Brussels; catholic-conservative), La Wallonie (socialist), La Libre Belgique (Brussels; catholic-monarchist) and Le Soir (Brussels).

Belgian daily newspapers

Opening Times

Chemists	Chemists are open at the same times as retail shops.
Banks	Banks are usually open Mon.–Fri. 9am–4pm.
Shops	The law governing trading hours in Belgium is liberal and states that shops need only close for a mere 24 hours a week on the day of their choice. In general opening times are between 5am and 8pm; on Fridays late-night shopping is allowed until 9pm. Many shops close between noon and 2pm. Supermarkets are closed on Sundays. However, by contrast, many small shops (including bakers and greengrocers) open on this day, and close instead on Tuesday or Wednesday. In most North Sea coastal resorts shops have longer opening hours.

Post

Rates (correct at Dec.92)	Ordinary letters (up to 20 grams) and postcards for within Belgium and EC countries (except for Spain and Portugal) cost 14 Bfr; elsewhere abroad 25 Bfr. Stamps can be bought both in post offices and often in souvenir shops and kiosks.
Post boxes	Belgian post boxes are red and usually marked with a post-horn.
Post offices	In larger towns post offices are usually open Mon.–Fri. 9am–noon and 2–5pm. The Brussels X Post Office at the Gare du Midi (South Station), 48A Ave. Fonsny is open continuously.
Telephone	See entry

Public Holidays

Advice	If a public holiday falls on a Sunday the following Monday is usually taken as a public holiday.
Fixed public holidays	January 1st: New Year's Day May 1st: Labour Day July 11th: Festival of the Flemish Community (only in Flanders) July 21st: National Day August 15th: Assumption September 27th: Festival of the Wallonian Community (only in Wallonia) November 1st: All Saints November 11th: Armistice Day December 25th and 26th: Christmas
Movable holidays	Easter Monday, Ascension and Whit Monday.

Radio and Television

Information	To meet the needs of its multilingual population, Belgian radio and television transmit programmes in a variety of languages. Radio-Télévision Belge de la Communauté Française (R.T.B.F.) serves the French-speaking area, Belgische Radio en Televisie (BRT) caters for speakers of Flemish while for German speakers there is the Belgische Rundfunk-und Fernsehzentrum (BRF). There are also very many private stations.
Personal messages	In very urgent cases personal messages can be broadcast. Information is obtainable from the automobile associations and the police (see Motoring and Emergencies).

Within Europe Belgium has the largest number of premises linked to the cable network. Almost 95% of all Belgian households have a cable connection and are thus able to receive a wide selection of foreign programmes in addition to Belgian state and private broadcasts.

Cable
television

Railways

In 1835 the first railway line in continental Europe was constructed between Brussels and Mechelen. Since then Belgium has developed the world's densest railway network which makes rail travel highly recommendable. The operating authority is the Société Nationale des Chemins de Fer Belges (SNCB)/Nationaal Maatschappij van Belgische Spoorwegen (NMBS).

Information

Since the beginning of the railway age Brussels, with its present four stations, has been the country's most important railway junction. Connections with the French high-speed train TVG to Amsterdam, Paris and Cologne are planned. Together with Brussels, Liège is also of some importance.

Railway
junctions

Daily 6am–10.30pm:
tel. (02) 2 19 26 40 (in French)
tel. (02) 2 19 28 80 (in Dutch)

Central
information
In Brussels

Inter-city trains (IC) only stop at large stations, InterRegio trains (IR) also stop at some intermediate stations; both types of train are not subject to supplements. L trains are local trains which stop at almost every station. IC, IR and L trains run throughout the day, usually every hour.

Trains

There are both first and second class tickets which can be bought up to five days in advance. Buying a ticket on the train is considerably more expensive than buying it at the station. (Day) return tickets cost twice as much as single tickets; the return journey must be made on the same day.

Tickets

Information about cheap rail travel (including offers for senior citizens, families, groups, the disabled and students) can be obtained from Belgian railway stations.

**Reductions and
special rates**

Children up to the age of six travel free; there is a 50% reduction in price for children aged between six and twelve years.

Children

With a B–Tourrail ticket travel throughout the whole Belgian railway network is permitted for five days within a fixed period of seventeen days. This ticket is available for juniors (people aged under 26) and for those over 26.

B-Tourrail

The TTB ticket carries the same conditions as the B–Tourrail ticket but can also be used on all buses, trams and underground trains of the narrow gauge railway and the local town/city companies.

TTB ticket

To travel through all three Benelux countries the Benelux Tourrail ticket is particularly suitable. This is also valid for five days in any seventeen on all the railway networks of the Benelux countries.

Benelux
Tourrail

For weekend travel within Belgium (outward journey Fri. noon to Sun. noon; return journey Sat. noon to Mon. noon) there is a 40% reduction in the normal price for the first person and a 60% reduction for those accompanying him/her (2–6 people). The Benelux-Weekend ticket is valid for weekend travel to a particular place within the Benelux countries (outward journey Thur. 4pm to Sun. midnight; return journey Sat. 0.01am to Mon. midnight). The first person gains a reduction of 25% of the normal ticket price, for up to five people accompanying him/her there is a reduction of 50%.

Weekend
tickets

Reduced day tickets to the coast and to the Ardennes are only valid during carnival and Easter holidays, from mid June to mid September, during the week of All Saints' Day and the Christmas holidays. They enjoy the same reductions as weekend tickets (but not only at weekends).

Day trips to
the coast and
to the Ardennes

L
P } Local trains

every two hours

Interchange station

Streckennetz der
Belgischen
Eisenbahnen

Ⓑ dpt T 10.114

Restaurants

Half-price authorised tickets GO-PASS	The half-price authorised ticket is valid for a month and entitles the holder to a 50% reduction in the full price of a ticket for one or two people. The GO-PASS entitles young people (12–25 years) to travel inexpensively on nine journeys within Belgium.
Excursion tickets	The Belgian railway organises numerous day excursions by train with reductions both on the price of the ticket and on the admission fee to museums, castles, leisure parks, etc.
Train and bicycle	Cycles can be rented and returned at more than 60 railway stations in Belgium. These are listed in the A to Z section under the relevant town or village. The Belgian railway and the Flemish Central Youth Hostel (see Young Peoples' Accommodation) also offer two to three-day cycling excursions (it is advisable to reserve places a week beforehand). The price includes the return train journey, the rent of the bicycle and overnight accommodation with breakfast in a youth hostel.

Steam trains and museum trains

Within Belgium there are several opportunities to travel on steam trains and museum trains. The tourist trains which are to be found in many places are not real trains but street cars drawn by tractors.

Blégny	Museum train "Le Trimbleu". Nostalgic journey on a slow train from Blégny to Mortroux and back. Information: Freizeitbergwerk "Le Trimbleu" B–4670 Blégny; tel. (041) 87 44 33
Eupen/ Raeren	The Venn train travels on Sundays and public holidays in the summer from Eupen/Raeren via Monschau to Bullingen (an extension of the network is planned to Stolberg, Malmédy, Trois-Ponts and Losheim-Jünkerath). The Venn train is a historic diesel locomotive, which pulls carriages dating from 1930. The journey is made on both Belgian and German territory. Information: Vennbahn VOE, Bahnhof Raeren, Bahnhofstrasse B–4730 Raeren; tel. (087) 85 24 87
Han-sur-Lesse	Diesel-driven open train from the town centre to the entrance to the grottos (see A to Z, Han-sur-Lesse).
Maldegem	Journey on a museum train from the steam centre Maldegem to Eeklo or by narrow-guage railway to Donk. Information: Stoomcentrum, Stationsplein 8 B–9990 Maldegem; tel. (050) 71 68 52
Mariembourg	Steam train "Trois Vallées" Treignes–Mariembourg–Chimay–Momignies Information: 49/51 Chaussée de Givet B–5660 Mariembourg; tel. (081) 22 11 99 and (060) 31 24 40
Rebecq	"Kleiner Glückszug" Journey on a nostalgic steam train through the Vallée des Oiseaux along the Senne. Information: B–1430 Rebecq; tel. (067) 67 01 20
Vilvoorde	Museumstoomtrein der Twee Bruggen Museum steam train between Brussels and Willebroek Information: Museumstoomtrein der Twee Bruggen, Harensesteenweg 494. B–1800 Vilvoorde; tel. (02) 2 51 54 76 (2–6pm)

Restaurants

Infomation	Belgium is a gourmets' paradise. In no other country in Europe – in relation to population – are there so many excellent restaurants rewarded by

A vintage train in Han-sur-Lesse

restaurant guides with stars, chef's hats or cooking spoons as in the small kingdom lying between the Ardennes and the North Sea. In some of the streets behind the Grand'Place in Brussels there is a profusion of restaurants. The countryside inns located in small villages enjoy good to very good reputations. In addition, there are numerous pizzerias, snack bars (pommes frites!), sandwich bars and cafés serving light dishes.

A *café* is always an ordinary pub, where beer and lemonade are the most popular drinks, although coffee is also served. Those requiring coffee, tea, cake, etc. should visit a *salon de thé* or a *tearoom*.

Cafés
Salon de Thé

Bars are the most popular meeting places. Beer is predominantly drunk here and any landlord worth his salt has at least 20 to 30 varieties at his disposal – all, of course, authentically bottled. Sausages and sandwiches are available and billiards can be played in many bars.

Bars

Selection

Kelderman, Parklaan 4; tel. (053) 77 61 25

Aalst

* 't Fornuis, Reyndersstraat 24; tel. (03) 23 36 27 0
Den Gulden Greffoen, Hoogstraat 37; tel. (03) 23 15 04 6
De Matelote, Haarstraat 9; tel. (03) 23 13 20 7
* La Pérouse, Ponton Steen; tel. (03) 23 13 15 8
Petrus, Kelderstraat 1; tel. (03) 22 52 73 4
La Rade, Van Dijckkaai 8; tel. (03) 23 33 73 7
't Silveren Claverblat, Grote Pieter Potstraat 16; tel. (03) 23 13 38 8
* Sir Anthony van Dyck, Oude Koornmarkt 16; tel. (03) 23 16 17 1
De Zeste, Lange Dijkstraat 36; tel. (03) 23 34 54 9
* Lindenbos, Boomsesteenweg 139; tel. (03) 88 80 96 5

Antwerp

In Aartselaar

Peiffeschof, 253 Ch. du Peiffeschof; tel. (063) 22 44 15

Arlon

Restaurants

Delicacies in a Brussels restaurant

Ath	L'Hennepin, 23 Rue Brantignies; tel. (068) 28 11 71
Bastogne	Au Vivier, 183 Rue Sablon; tel. (062) 21 22 57
Beaumont	Le Grand Ryeu, 1 Rue Goëtte; tel. (071) 45 52 10
Binche	Bernard, 37 Rue de Bruxelles; tel. (064) 33 37 75
Blankenberge	Joinville, J. De Troozlaan 5; tel. (050) 41 22 69 De Wijngaard, Kerkstraat 196; tel. (050) 41 52 30
Bouillon	Auberge d'Alsace, 3 Faubourg de France; tel. (061) 46 65 88
Bruges	*'t Bourgoensche Cruyce, Wollestraat 41; tel. (050) 33 79 26 Den Gouden Harynck, Groeninge 25; tel. (050) 33 76 37 Huyze Die Maene, Markt 17; tel. (050) 33 39 59 *De Karmeliet, Langestraat 19; tel. (050) 33 82 59 't Pandreitje, Pandreitje 6; tel. (050) 33 11 90 *Patrick Provoost, Achiel van Ackerplein 2; tel. (050) 33 64 65 *De Snippe, Nieuwe Gentweg 53; tel. (050) 33 70 70 Spinola, Spinolarei 1; tel. (050) 34 17 85 Vasquez, Zilverstraat 38; tel. (050) 34 08 45 *Weinebrugge, Koning Albertlaan 242; tel. (050) 38 44 40 De Witte Poorte, Jan van Eyckplein 6; tel. (050) 33 08 83
Brussels In the centre	*La Belle Maraíchère, 11 Pl. Ste-Catherine; tel. (02) 5 12 97 59 Le Chablis, 6 Rue de Flandre; tel. (02) 5 12 46 31 *François, 2 Quai aux Briques; tel. (02) 5 11 60 89 't Kelderke, 15 Grand'Place; tel. (02) 5 13 73 44 *La Maison du Cygne, 9 Grand'Place; tel. (02) 5 11 82 44 La Marie Joseph, 47 Quai au Bois-à-Brûler; tel. (02) 2 18 05 96 De Ogenblik, 1 Galerie des Princes; tel. (02) 5 11 61 51

Taverne du Passage, 30 Galerie de la Reine; tel. (02) 5 12 37 31
Astrid "Chez Pierrot", Rue de la Presse;   East of the
tel. (02) 2 17 38 31   centre
Bernard, Rue de Namur; tel. (02) 5 12 88 21   South of the
*Au Beurre Blanc, 2A Rue du Faucon; tel. (02) 5 13 01 11   centre
*Comme Chez Soi, 23 Pl. Rouppe; tel. (02) 5 12 29 21
*L'Ecailler du Palais Royal, 18 Rue Bodenbroek; tel. (02) 5 12 87 51
*Trente Rue de la Paille, 30 Rue de la Paille; tel. (02) 5 12 07 15
*Les Brasseries Georges, 259 Ave. Churchill;   In the south
tel. (02) 3 47 21 00 (Uccle)   of the city
*L'Oasis, 9 Pl. Marie-José; tel. (02) 6 48 45 45 (Ixelles)
*L'Orangerie, 81 Ave. W. Churchill; tel. (02) 3 45 41 47 (Uccle)
*Villa d'Este, 142 Rue de l'Etoile; tel. (02) 3 74 31 63 (Uccle)
*Villa Lorraine, 75 Ave. Vivier-d'Oie;
tel. (02) 3 74 31 63 (B. de la Cambre)
*La Grignotière, 2041 Ch. de Wavre; tel. (02) 6 72 81 85 (Auderghem)   In the east
*Mon Manège à Toi, 1 R. Neerveld; tel. (02) 7 70 02 38 (Wol.-St-Lambart)   of the city
*Les Baguettes impériales, 70 Ave. Sobieski;   In the north
tel. (02) 4 79 67 32 (Atomium)   of the city
*Bruneau, 73 Ave. Broustin; tel. (02) 4 27 69 78 (Ganshoren)
*Dupont, 46 Ave. Vital-Riethuisen; tel. (02) 4 27 54 50 (Ganshoren)
*Eddie van Maele, 964 Ch. Romaine; tel. (02) 4 60 61 45 (Atomium)
*Le Sermon, 91 Ave. J. Sermon; tel. (02) 4 26 89 35 (Jette)
*Hostellerie Bellemolen, Stationstraat 11; (053) 66 62 38   In Essene
*Aloyse Kloos, 2 Ch. de la Hulpe; tel. (02) 6 57 37 37   In Groenendaal
*Romeyer, 109 Ch. de Groenendaal; tel. (02) 6 57 05 81
*De Bijgaarden, Van Beverenstraaet 20; tel. (02) 4 66 44 85   In Groot-
*Michel, Schepen Gossetlaan 31; tel. (02) 4 66 65 91   Bijgaarden
*Barbizon, Welriekendedreef 95; tel. (02) 6 57 04 62   In Jezus-Eik

La Mirabelle, 7 Rue de Marcinelle; tel. (071) 33 39 88   **Charleroi**
Le Clos de la Rochette, 16 Rue Anrys; tel. (071) 50 11 40   In Gerpinnes

Froissart, 8 Place Froissart; tel. (060) 21 26 19   **Chimay**

De Lieve, J. v. Maerlantstraat 10; tel. (050) 35 66 30   **Damme**
Drie Zilveren Kannen, Markt 9; tel. (050) 35 56 77
*Bruegel, Daamse Vaart Zuid 26; tel. (050) 50 03 46   In Oostkerke
                                        near Damme

*D'Hulhaege, Karel-Picquélaan 134; tel. (091) 86 56 16   **Deinze**

't Truffeltje, Bogaerdstraat 20; tel. (052) 22 45 90   **Dendermonde**

Empereur, Grote Markt 24; tel. (013) 31 14 65   **Diest**

Thermidor, 3 Rue de la Station; tel. (082) 22 31 35   **Dinant**
Le Freÿr, Point de vue de Freÿr; tel. (082) 22 25 75   In Anseremme
*Auberge de Bouvignes, 112 Rue Fétis; tel. (082) 61 16 00   In Bouvignes
Moulin de Lisogne, 60 Rue de la Lisonette; tel. (082) 22 63 80   In Lisogne

Le Pilori, 10 Rue de Pilori; tel. (067) 44 23 18   **Ecaussines-**
                                        Lalaing
Le Gourmet, Haasstr. 81; tel. (087) 74 08 00   **Eupen**

De Cuylhoeve, Hollandsebaan 7; tel. (014) 58 57 45   **Geel**

*Le Prince de Liège, 96b Ch. de Namur; tel. (081) 61 12 44   **Gembloux**

Deli's, Markt 12; tel. (054) 41 44 76   **Geraardsbergen**

*Apicius, M. Maeterlinckstraat 8; tel. (091) 22 46 00   **Ghent**
Jan van den Bon, Koning-Leopold-II-laan 43; tel. (091) 21 90 85
Het Cooremetershuys, Graslei 12; tel. (091) 23 4971

Restaurants

Patijntje, Gordunakaai 91; tel. (091) 22 32 73
St-Jorishof, Botermarkt 2; tel. (091) 24 24 24
Waterzooi, Sint-Veerleplein 2; tel. (091) 25 05 63

Habay-la-Neuve   *Les Forges du Pont d'Oye, 6 Rue du Pont d'Oye; tel. (063) 42 22 43

Halle   Les Eleveurs, Basiliekstraat 136; tel. (02) 3 56 53 09

Han-sur-Lesse   Belle-Vue, 2 Rue Joseph Lamotte; tel. (084) 37 72 27

Hasselt   Figaro, Mombeekdreef 38; tel. (011) 27 25 56
In Lummen   *Kasteel St-Paul, Lagendal 1; tel. (011) 52 18 09
In Stevoort   *Scholteshof, Kermtstraat 130; tel. (011) 25 02 02

Huy   L'Aigle Noir, 8 Quai Dautrebande; tel. (085) 21 23 41

Keerbergen   *Hostellerie Berkenhof, Valkeniersdreef 5; tel. (015) 73 01 01

Knokke-Heist   Panier d'Or, Zeedijk 659; tel. (050) 60 31 89
Le P'tit Bedon, Zeedijk 672; tel. (050) 60 06 64
In Albert-Strand   *Aquilon, Bayauxlaan 70; tel. (050) 60 12 74
In Heist   Old Fisher, Heldenplein 33; tel. (050) 51 11 14
In Westkapelle   Ter Dycken, Kalvekeetdijk 137; tel. (050) 60 12 37

Koksijde   Le Régent, Blieclaan 10; tel. (058) 51 21 10

Kortrijk   *Filip Bogaert, Min. Tacklaan 5; tel. (056) 20 30 34
Klokhof, Sint-Anna 2; tel. (056) 21 15 57
*Eddy Vandekerckhove, Sint-Anna 5; tel. (056) 22 47 56

Leuven   Belle Epoque, Bondgenotenlaan 94; tel. (016) 22 33 89
De Wandeling, Lei 6; tel. (016) 23 44 01
Zeester, Mechelsestraat 22; tel. (016) 23 62 21

Liège   As Ouhès, 21 Place Marché; tel. (041) 23 32 25
La Bécasse, 21 Rue de la Casquette; tel. (041) 23 15 20
Vieux Liège, 41 Quai Goffe; tel. (041) 23 77 48
In Neuville-   *Chêne Madame, 70 Ave. de la Chevauchée; tel. (041) 71 41 27
en-Condroz

Lier   't Cleyn Paradijs, Heilige Geeststraat 2; tel. (03) 4 80 78 57

Maaseik   Tiffany's, Markt 19; tel. (011) 56 40 89

Malmédy   Albert I, 40 Place Albert; tel. (080) 33 04 52
In Bévercé   Hostellerie de la Chapelle, 30 Bévercé-Village; tel. (080) 33 08 65

Mechelen   *D'Hoogh, Grote Markt 19; tel. (015) 21 75 53
Paul van der Heijden, Wollemarkt 22; tel. (015) 20 53 15

Middelkerke-Bad   *Bouquet, Zeedijk, Kursaal; tel. (059) 30 05 03

Mons   *Devos, 7 Rue de la Coupe; tel. (065) 35 13 35

Mouscron   *La Cuisine des Anges, 6 Rue Tombrouck; tel. (056) 33 39 22

Namur   Biétrumé Picar, 13 Rue Haute-Marcelle; tel. (081) 23 07 39
Le Colombier, 16 Place de l'Ilon; tel. (081) 22 74 50
In Lives-   *La Bergerie, 100 Rue Mosanville; tel. (081) 58 06 13
sur-Meuse

Nandrin   *Domaine du Château de Fraineux, 20 Rue Chapelle;
tel. (085) 51 14 37

Nassogne   *La Gourmandine, 2 Rue de Masbourg; tel. (084) 21 09 28

Ter Polder, Victorlaan 17; tel. (058) 23 56 66   **Nieuwpoort**

L'Haubergeon, 14 Rue Brasseurs; tel. (067) 21 29 14   **Nivelles**

Marina, Albert-I-Promenade 2; tel. (059) 70 35 85   **Ostend**
Lusitania, Visserskaai 35; tel. (059) 70 17 65
*Oostendse Compagnie, Koningstraat 79; tel. (059) 70 48 16
't Vistrapje, Visserskaai 37; tel. (059) 80 23 82

La Pomme d'Or, Grote Markt 62; tel. (055) 31 19 00   **Oudenarde**

*Le Fox, Walckiersstraat 2–4; tel. (058) 41 28 55   **De Panne**
Trio's, Nieuwpoortlaan75; tel. (058) 41 13 78
*La Souricière, Duinkerkekeiweg 28; tel. (058) 41 16 00   In Adinkerke

D'Hommelkeete, Hoge Noenweg 3; tel. (057) 33 43 65   **Poperinge**

Hostellerie Linchet, 11 Route de Houffalize; tel. (084) 41 12 23   **La Roche-en-Ardenne**

Auberge des Falizes, 90 Rue de France; tel. (084) 21 12 82   **Rochefort**
La Malle Poste, 46 Rue de Behogne; tel. (084) 21 09 87

*Shamrock, Ommegangstraat 148; tel. (055) 21 55 29   **Ronse**

Le Clos Saint-Michel, 46 Rue Saint-Michel; tel. (061) 61 25 59   **St-Hubert**
*Auberge du Sabotier, 21 Rue Grande; tel. (084) 36 65 23   In Awenne

*Zur Post, Hauptstr. 39; tel. (080) 22 80 27   **St-Vith**

't Mezennestje, De Meulenaerstraat 2; tel. (03) 7 76 38 44   **St-Niklaas**

De Fakkels, Stationsstraat 33 ; tel. (011) 68 76 34   **St-Truiden**

Manoir de Lebiolesin Creppe; tel. (087) 77 10 20   **Spa**

*Le Viviers d'Oies, 7 Rue d'Etat; tel. (083) 69 95 71   **Spontin**

Le Val d'Ambiève, 7 Route de Malmedy; tel. (080) 86 23 53   **Stavelot**

Vigiliae, Grote Markt 10; tel. (016) 81 77 03   **Tienen**

Biessenhuys, Hasseltsestraat 23; tel. (012) 23 47 09   **Tongeren**
*Clos St-Denis, Grimmertingenstraat 24; tel. (012) 23 60 96   In Vliermaal

Le Carillon, 64 Grand-Place; tel. (069) 21 18 48   **Tournai**
Charles Quint, 3 Grand-Place; tel. (069) 22 14 41

Ter Driezen, Herentalsstraat 18; tel. (014) 41 87 57   **Turnhout**

Maison Moulan, 37 Crapaurue; tel. (087) 31 22 50   **Verviers**

't Belfort, Grote Markt 26; tel. (058) 31 11 55   **Veurnes**
't Croonhof, Noordstraat 9; tel. (058) 31 31 28

Le Franc Gourmet, 13 Rue Roche; tel. (063) 57 01 36   **Virton**

Hostellerie de l'Abbaye, 7 Rue du Jardinet; tel. (071) 61 14   **Walcourt**

*'t Oud Konijntje, Bosstraat 53; tel. (056) 60 19 37   **Waregem**

La Maison du Seigneur, 389 Ch. de Tervuren; tel. (02) 3 54 07 50   **Waterloo**

't Molentje, Baron de Maerelaan 211; tel. (050) 54 61 64   **Zeebrugge**
* Maison Vandamme, Tijdokstraat 7; tel. (056) 54 58 61

Road Transport

Distances in kilometres using Motorways	Antwerpen	Arlon	Bastogne	Brugge	Bruxelles/Brussel	Charleroi	Dinant	Eupen	Gent	Huy	Ieper	Kortrijk	Leuven	Liège	Mechelen	Mons	Namur	Oostende	Tongeren	Tournai	Turnhout
Antwerpen	-	234	195	106	55	115	137	152	60	129	131	101	69	124	28	122	109	123	111	127	47
Arlon	234	-	39	287	188	167	120	142	244	122	300	271	187	131	206	197	127	301	151	242	276
Bastogne	195	39	-	248	149	128	81	102	205	83	261	231	148	92	167	158	88	262	112	203	237
Brugge	106	287	248	-	99	154	190	238	55	182	53	59	129	197	122	136	162	29	189	88	152
Bruxelles/Brussel	55	188	149	99	-	60	91	136	56	83	122	92	28	96	27	69	63	114	88	84	93
Charleroi	115	167	128	154	60	-	55	138	109	64	150	120	68	92	89	46	36	167	95	92	159
Dinant	137	120	81	190	91	55	-	111	147	62	189	159	90	90	109	85	28	205	93	131	175
Eupen	152	142	102	238	136	138	111	-	192	70	266	224	111	37	136	174	99	256	56	216	137
Gent	60	244	205	55	56	109	147	192	-	139	78	48	86	154	80	120	119	70	146	70	106
Huy	129	122	83	182	83	64	62	70	139	-	204	174	69	35	96	100	34	197	38	146	171
Ieper	131	300	261	53	122	150	189	266	78	204	-	29	159	232	145	106	176	56	219	58	177
Kortrijk	101	271	231	59	92	120	159	224	48	174	29	-	129	202	115	76	146	62	189	28	147
Leuven	69	187	148	129	28	68	90	111	86	69	159	129	-	80	24	87	62	144	72	133	111
Liège	124	131	92	197	96	92	90	37	154	35	232	202	80	-	107	128	62	212	25	174	105
Mechelen	28	206	167	122	27	89	109	136	80	96	145	115	24	107	-	90	81	137	90	114	53
Mons	122	197	158	136	69	46	85	174	120	100	106	76	87	128	90	-	72	139	131	48	160
Namur	109	127	88	162	63	36	28	99	119	34	176	146	62	62	81	72	-	177	69	120	147
Oostende	123	301	262	29	114	167	205	256	70	197	56	62	144	212	137	139	177	-	204	91	169
Tongeren	111	151	112	189	88	95	93	56	146	38	219	189	72	25	90	131	69	204	-	192	85
Tournai	127	242	203	88	84	92	131	216	70	146	58	28	133	174	114	48	120	91	192	-	173
Turnhout	47	276	237	152	93	159	175	137	106	171	177	147	111	105	53	160	147	169	85	173	-

Road Transport

Road network

Belgium is a densely populated and important transit country which has been served since the last century by an excellent road network.
All important cities and towns are linked by motorways (A) or through-routes in Europe (E). Motorways usually have three lanes and are illuminated at dusk; there are many petrol stations and services. The numbered main connecting roads (N) are equally as good.

Tourist routes

Attractive tourist routes, marked by hexagonal bright green signs with blue lettering, follow to one side of the connecting roads. The routes, which are between 50km/31 miles and 150km/93 miles long and which all have a distinctive name, cross the Belgian countryside. Informative coloured leaflets are obtainable from the offices listed under Information (see entry).

Shopping and Souvenirs

Information

Expensive souvenirs can be found in the high-class shops in the cities and larger towns. Some of Belgium's coastal resorts e.g. Knokke-Heist (Lippenslaan, Dumortierlaan and Kustlaan) also have shops such as jewellers and boutiques selling internationally-known products. The flea markets which take place throughout the country (see Markets) can prove real treasure-houses.

The covered shopping arcades in Brussels (e.g. Galeries Saint-Hubert, Agora, City 2, Louise, Passage 44, Ravenstein and Toison d'Or) do not attract custom only in bad weather. Statuettes of the Brussels *Manneken-Pis* are among the most popular souvenirs.

Brussels shopping arcades

Visitors to Brussels should not miss the opportunity of shopping in the Woluwé Shopping Center in Woluwé-Saint-Lambert or the Westland Shopping Center in Anderlecht.

Large shopping centres

As well as antique shops, the famous art and antiques markets and other markets (see Markets and Events) offer ample opportunities for shopping.

Art and antiques

From Kortrijk.

Batist linen

From Dinant (especially brassware, so-called *dinanderies*).

Ceramics, brassware

The world-famous crystal factory of Val-Saint-Lambert is located in Liège-Seraing. Glass-blowing, cutting and decorating can be observed and a valuable souvenir bought.

Crystal

e.g. from Antwerp, an international diamond centre of repute.

Diamonds

From Boom.

Glass

From Brussels and Kortrijk.

Jewellery

From Bruges (centre of the lace-making industry), Brussels and Mechelen. During the summer months it is possible to see the lace-makers of these towns at work.

Lace

Chocolates are a Belgian speciality

439

Pewter	From Huy.
Playing cards	From Turnhout (museum).
Puppets	From Liège.
Sweets	Belgian pralines are famous; the Brussels cake shops Neuhaus and Wittamer ("W"), whose beautiful displays offer very attractively packaged goods, are particularly well-known for their confectionery and gâteaux. Babelutten (caramels) from Veurne and Ypres, Kletskoppen (cakes), Mandelbrot, pancakes and waffles from Veurne are all popular sweets.
Tapestries	From Brussels, Ghent, Mechelen, Oudenaarde or Sint-Niklaas.
Wood carvings	From Spa.

Smoking

Smoking ban	Since 1st September 1987 Belgium has belonged to the group of countries with the strictest anti-smoking legislation. This bans smoking in all public buildings, hospitals, schools and universities, ministry departments, sports centres, theatres, railway station concourses and underground stations, telephone kiosks, police stations and anywhere where there is a "No Smoking" sign. Failure to observe the smoking ban can result in a heavy fine.

Spas and Resorts

Belgian North Sea resorts	Despite its relatively short coastline, Belgium possesses a number of well-known spas and resorts (in particular Knokke-Heist and Ostend), which are popular due to the invigorating effect of the North Sea waters and air.

Spas

Chaudfontaine	Complaints: rheumatism, gout in the initial stages, indigestion, neuritis, skin disorders. Treatments: thermal baths (the only radio-active springs in the country, 36.6°C/97°F), liquid remedies, therapeutic exercises.
Knokke-Heist	Complaints: arthritis, rheumatism, cellulite, oedema. Treatments: sea-water therapy in the Thalasso Therapy Centre.
Ostend	Complaints: rheumatism, bone and joint problems, rickets, calcium deficiency, neuritis, neuralgia, indigestion, circulation disorders, respiratory problems. Treatments: fango- and hydro-, helio- and electrotherapies (Thermal Institute), therapeutic exercises and massages, thermal baths and swimming pools with heated sea water (35°C/95°F).
Spa	Complaints: anaemia, gout, arthrosis, rheumatism, vascular diseases, respiratory problems, cellulite. Treatments: mud-baths, carbonated baths, inhalations, liquid cures, physiotherapy and massages.

Sport

Popular sports	So-called "popular" sports are played throughout Belgium and particularly in Flanders. These sports include *Gansrijden* (goose riding), *Pagschieten*

(club shooting), *Ringsteken* (a kind of quoits), *Struifvogelspel* (a wooden bird must be manœuvred into the goal) and *Vinkenzetten* (finch's game). *Kaatsen*, which is also played in public places; consists in shooting an arrow directed upwards at a bar lying horizontally across two poles. The favourite popular sport, however, is cycling and Belgium has some important cyclists, in particular Eddy Merckx.

Billiards should also not be forgotten – different variations of this game are played in many cafés. One of the greats at this game is the several-times world champion Raymond Ceulemans, whose son runs a billiard-café in the Hooverplein in Leuven.

Those interested in one of these sports should contact:
Vlaamse Volkssport Centrale, Tervuursevest 101
B–3001 Leuven (Heverlee); tel. (0 16) 22 54 38 or 23 72 72

Alpine climbing sports can be undertaken in Belgium on the cliff faces of the Meuse, Ourthe, Molignée and Samson valleys. Information can be obtained from:
Club Alpin Belge, 19 Rue de l'Aurore
B–1050 Bruxelles/Brussels; tel. (02) 6 48 86 11

Climbing

In Belgium a bicycle (French *bicyclette*, Flemish *fiets*) is used both for leisure and as a means of transport. The country's network of cycle lanes has been ideally developed, and cycling through the flat landscape of Flanders provides great pleasure for novices at this sport while the more ambitious can have a very good time in the Ardennes.

It is possible to rent a bicycle in many places. Apart from private rental, bicycles can be hired at many Belgian railway stations. These stations are listed under the relevant town heading in the A to Z section. The Belgian Railway (see Railways) also offers inexpensive two to three-day cycling holidays with accommodation on offer in youth hostels.

Cycling

Those wishing to fish must be in possession of an angling permit obtainable from any post office and valid for a year. This allows fishing in all state waters. Special permits (issued in post offices) are necessary for fishing in canals. Fishing at sea requires no special permission.

Fishing

The most popular spectator sport is football. Clubs such as RSC Anderlecht from Brussels, FC Antwerp, KV Mechelen and FC Brugge are among Europe's best.

Football

Information about golf courses is available from:
Fédération Royale du Golf, 19 Route de la Marché
B–1328 Ohain; tel. (02) 6 33 24 96

Golf

Riding stables are to be found in most of the resorts along the coast as well as in many other towns or villages. These offer riding lessons and horses for hire. For further information contact:
Fédération Belge des Sports Equestres, Hamoirlaan 38
B–1180 Bruxelles/Brussels; tel. (02) 3 75 08 84

Riding

A 2000km/1243 mile-long network of rivers and canals crosses Belgium, offering many opportunities for enjoyable holidays on water, e.g. on the Meuse, the Sambre, the Amblève, the Lesse, the Semois or the Ourthe in the Ardennes in private or rented boats. Information leaflets about canoes and kayaks are available from the Belgian tourist information offices (see Information). Motorised cruisers can be rented in many places.

River/canal holidays

Sailing clubs can be found along the coast and inland on the Meuse, the Scheldt and the Leie. Well-equipped yacht harbours with a large number of moorings are located at Blankenberge, Koksijde (St-Idesbald), Nieuwpoort (Euro Yacht Harbour with 2000 moorings), Ostend and Zeebrugge; there are also yacht harbours in Brussels, Antwerp and Maaseik. A unique feature of the Flemish coast is sand sailing in sailcarts (courses are available

Sailing

for beginners). A competition for beach-sailors takes place once a year in November in De Panne.

Walking
Throughout Belgium, and particularly in the Ardennes, there are many beautiful footpaths. A walk along the beach and through the dunes can also be delightful. European Long Distance Footpath 2 leads from the Netherlands through Diest, Liége and Malmédy southwards to Luxembourg. European Long Distance Footpath 3 takes walkers through the Eifel and the Ardennes and includes the Semois valley. Guidebooks and maps can be bought in shops.

Winter sports
Between December and March it usually snows sufficiently for six to eight weeks in the Ardennes to allow winter sports to take place. There are more than a dozen pistes for downhill skiing, around 80 cross-country ski runs and numerous toboggan runs and snow-scooter runs. Cross-country skiing through the beautiful wooded winter landscape can prove especially attractive. The most well-known ski areas are to be found in the Hohe Venn (French Hautes Fagnes; 650m/2133ft above sea level), around Bütgenbach, Eupen and Malmédy as well as at Spa-Francorchamps; further to the south at Vielsalm, on the plateau of the Baraque de Fraiture (Plateau des Tailles), on the Plateau de Bastogne, around Martelange–Anlier, in the Champion/Saint-Hubert district and above Gedinne on the Plateau de la Croix-Scaille. Information and a map entitled "Ski Ardennes" is available from the Belgian Tourist Office (see entry).

Telephone

Pay phones
Pay phones accept 5 and 20 Bfr coins. There are also public telephones which accept phone cards, known as Telecards. These magnetic cards cost 200 Bfr and can be bought in post offices, at railway station ticket counters and in some of the local tourist information offices. Callboxes suitable for long-distance telephone calls bear European flags.

International dialling codes
Code to Belgium from the UK 010 32
Code to the UK from Belgium 00 44

Charges
The normal tariff for international calls is 30 Bfr per minute (within the border area costs are lower). Between 6.30pm and 8am, at weekends and on public holidays rates are reduced.

Information
Inland and abroad; tel. 12 07 (Flemish) or 13 07 (French).

Time

In the winter Belgium observes Central European Time (one hour ahead of Greenwich Mean Time) then switches to summer time (two hours ahead of GMT) from the end of March to the end of September.

Tipping

Information
In hotels and restaurants a tip is included in the bill and in taxi fares. A suitable tip should be given for additional services and also to tour guides, maids, porters and cloakroom assistants.

Traffic Regulations

See Motoring

Travel Documents

A passport or identity card is needed to enter Belgium and for a stay of more than three months visitors from outside the EC require a visa.

Passport/identity card

Driving licence and car registration papers from EC countries are accepted. A Green Card is required for non-EC visitors. All foreign cars must display an approved national identity plate.

Driving licence/car registration papers

Boats over 5.5m/18ft long being brought into Belgium by road, etc. must have a triptych (customs certificate) or Carnet de Passage (customs certificate for several countries).

Boat documents

When to Go

While Brussels' rich choice of cultural and historical locations makes it suitable for a visit during any season, it is best to visit Belgium between May and September.

Information

North Sea bathers most enjoy their sport from June/July to the end of August. Many events (see entry) – in particular the magnificently colourful flower parades organised by the coastal resorts – are worth visiting.

Summer

Most rain falls in the coastal area during autumn and there is often a strong wind. However, even this season can be attractive; for example, for walks or cycle rides in the Ardennes; in addition many beer festivals take place throughout the country at this time of the year.

Autumn

Winters are relatively mild, although during the months from December to March (for between six and eight weeks) good snow conditions in the Ardennes allow the pursuit of a variety of winter sports (see Sport).

Winter

Throughout the country; tel. 17 02 (Flemish) or 17 03 (French).

Weather forecasts

See Facts and Figures, Climate.

Young People's Accommodation

Inexpensive accommodation for young people is offered by the numerous youth hostels in Belgium. Foreign youth hostellers must have an international youth hostel pass. It is advisable to book places in advance, especially for Easter and the months of July and August.

Youth hostels

Flanders:
Vlaamse Jeugdherbergcentrale, Van Stralenstraat 40
B–2008 Antwerpen; tel. (03) 2 32 72 18

Information

Wallonia:
Centrale Wallonne des Auberges de la Jeunesse, 52 Rue van Oost
B–1030 Bruxelles/Brussels; tel. (02) 2 15 31 00

Further youth accommodation is offered by the social holiday centres, whose addresses can be obtained from the tourist information offices listed under Information (see entry). Leaflets listing other inexpensive youth accommodation are also available from these offices.

Other youth accommodation

Index

Index

Sources of Illustrations

Anthony Verlag: p. 309.

Baedeker Archiv: pp. 58, 60, 62, 64, 65, 70, 72, 76, 82, 153(right), 182(2), 235, 243, 265, 267, 275(left).

Belgian Tourist Office: pp. 31, 54, 69, 85(2), 87, 120, 150, 206, 240(right), 252, 256, 273, 275(right), 287, 296, 305, 321,338, 357, 380, 381, 386, 388.

Bildagentur Lade: p. 169.

Bildagentur Schuster: p. 136

Herman Brinks: pp. 56, 100, 131, 133, 173(right), 180 199, 201, 211, 214, 240(left), 262, 264, 269, 281, 282, 314, 323, 330, 331, 340, 342, 354, 361, 367.

dpa: pp. 24, 250, 251, 336.

Rainer Eisenschmid: pp. 8, 11, 12, 13, 14, 16, 20, 28, 55(2), 63, 83, 94, 96, 103, 108, 111, 113, 115, 116, 124, 128, 130, 134(2), 138, 141, 143, 148, 149, 153(left), 154, 155, 156, 158, 170, 171, 173(left), 176, 184, 193, 194, 197, 204(2), 207, 208, 221, 226, 227, 229, 230, 232, 238, 247(2), 259, 261, 272, 276, 289, 292, 300, 301(2), 308(2), 310, 324, 326, 327, 344, 345, 349, 350(2), 352, 364, 374, 376, 377, 389, 398, 420, 422, 433, 434, 439.

Esterházy: p. 162.

Max Groenert: p. 359.

Hachette: p. 179.

Hallway Verlag: p. 392.

Historia Photo: pp. 37, 44(right), 46(middle).

IFA: p. 369.

Gabriele Maier: pp. 152, 195.

Mainbild: p. 384.

Messerschmitt: p. 172(left).

Musées Royaux d'Art et d'Histoire: p. 52.

Hans Naumann: pp. 217, 218(2).

Oudenaarde Tourist Office: p. 319.

Sperber: pp. 172(middle and right), 188.

Ullstein-Bilderdienst: pp. 39, 44(left and middle), 46(left and right), 48(3).